DÁN DO OIDE

Dán do Oide

C. R. Ó Cléirigh

DÁN DO OIDE

Essays in Memory
of
CONN R. Ó CLÉIRIGH

Edited
by
ANDERS AHLQVIST and VĚRA ČAPKOVÁ

Dublin
Institiúid Teangeolaíochta Éireann
1997

© 1997 Institiúid Teangeolaíochta Éireann

ISBN 0 946452 17 2

Dublin University Press Limited

Institiúid Teangeolaíochta Éireann
The Linguistics Institute of Ireland
31 Plás Mhic Liam,
Baile Átha Cliath 2

Table of Contents

Introduction

VĚRA ČAPKOVÁ & ANDERS AHLQVIST
University College, Dublin   University College, Galway

CONN R. Ó CLÉIRIGH left a unique and lasting mark on the development of language studies in Ireland. He was a superb teacher who brought up generations of students. Many of them later became eminent scholars in their chosen fields. It was he who led them through the maze of Old Irish structures, it was he who opened for them the exciting world of generative grammar. The clarity of his lectures became proverbial. He enjoyed participating in seminars, conferences and other fora for oral exchanges between scholars not only in linguistics, but in other areas of scholarly activity, as the wide range of articles in this collection demonstrates. His contributions to any discussion were always marked by his enormous learning and sharp and delightful wit.

Conn shared his constructive ideas and penetrating insights most generously. In the introduction to a very influential book, Wolfgang Meid[1] has paid a singular tribute to our honorand, by giving thanks to, 'last, not least, meinem Freund und ehemaligen Kollegen Conn R. Ó Cléirigh (Dublin), mit dem ich die Materie dieses Buches in zahlreichen Gesprächen an irischen Kaminfeuern immer durchdiskutieren konnte und der auf diese Weise manch wertvolle Bemerkung beigesteuert hat. Sein Anteil an diesem Buche soll—gerade weil er nicht sichtbar zum Ausdruck kommt—besonders betont werden'. It summarises and echoes very well what so many of Conn Ó Cléirigh's students and colleagues were happy to experience on countless occasions.

Conn Ó Cléirigh was born in Dublin on the 7th February 1927. In 1949, he was awarded the BA in Celtic Studies with first place and First Class Honours. He won the National University of Ireland Travelling Studentship, which enabled him to pursue postgraduate studies, first at Bangor, where he perfected his knowledge of Welsh, and later in Zurich, where he studied besides Celtic philology also Germanic, Indo-Iranian, Hittite, Indo-European and dialectology. His professors, whom he always remembered with great reverence, included among others Julius Pokorny, Manu Leumann and Eugen Dieth. In Zurich, Conn also became acquainted for the first time with European structuralism. This new interest in general linguistics was further strengthened after Conn's return to Dublin when he met Ernst Lewy who introduced him to the ideas of Wilhelm von

---

[1] *Die indogermanischen Grundlagen der altirischen absoluten und konjunkten Verbalflexion*, (Wiesbaden: Otto Harassowitz, 1963) p. vii.

Humboldt. During the fifties and early sixties, Conn worked in University College, Dublin, lecturing in the Welsh Department, and later in the Old and Medieval Irish Department.

When the first ever chair of linguistics in Ireland was established in UCD he was appointed professor. The academic year 1964–65, which he spent in the University of California at Los Angeles, proved to be most decisive for shaping his views on theoretical linguistics. His profound knowledge of Humboldt prepared him to accept and follow with enthusiasm the emerging theoretical paradigm of generative grammar. He became one of the rare scholars who are at home both in traditional philology and in the most recent developments in linguistics. Conn epitomised the well-known paraphrase of Terence's maxim: *Linguista sum: nihil linguistici a me alienum puto.*[2]

In 1972, the Irish government appointed Conn Ó Cléirigh chairman of Institiúid Teangeolaíochta Éireann. Under his wise, sensible and unobtrusive guidance the Institute grew steadily into an important national institution which devises and implements far-reaching language policies in Ireland.

Conn Ó Cléirigh's contribution to the history of linguistics in Ireland cannot be measured in terms of his scholarly publications. His importance is in a different but essential sphere of scholarly activity; it is in his inspiring teaching, selfless dedication to the transmission of knowledge and the profound influence he thus had on his numerous students, colleagues and friends. This volume of essays is therefore intended as an eloquent testimony of the high esteem in which Conn R. Ó Cléirigh was held in Ireland and many other parts of the world.

---

[2] Morris Halle, 'Foreword', in Roman Jakobson and Krystyna Pomorska, *Dialogues* (Cambridge: University Press, 1983) p. xii.

A Note on Pronominal Variable Binding and Linearity

PAOLO ACQUAVIVA
University of Venice

QUANTIFICATIONAL phrases like *every cat* or *who?* are standardly inter-preted as operators binding a variable in the appropriate position, as schematized in (1)–(2):

(1)   a. Every cat likes sleeping.
        b. For every x (such that x is a cat), x likes sleeping.

(2)   a. Who left?
        b. For what x (such that x is human), x left?

A pronoun can under certain conditions be interpreted as an additional variable:[1]

(3)   a. Every cat$_i$ despises its$_i$ owner.
        b. For every x (such that x is a cat), x despises x's owner.

(4)   a. Who$_i$ left his$_i$ hat on the counter?
        b. For what x (such that x is human), x left x's hat on the counter?

A considerable amount of research has been devoted to establishing the precise conditions constraining this interpretation, which appears to be systematically available to natural languages.[2] Any account is based on certain assumptions about phrase structure, in particular about the way quantificational expressions are represented in the syntax. In the tradition inaugurated by Chomsky 1976 and May 1977, it is generally assumed that these quantificational expressions are raised to an operator position in Logical Form (a *syntactic* level of representation), leaving behind a variable. The impossibility of pronominal variable interpretation in both (5a) and (5b) (standard cases of Weak Crossover) is thus directly derived from the parallel structures the two sentences receive in Logical Form, as illustrated in (6):

(5)   a. * Who$_i$ does his$_i$ mother like?
        b. * His$_i$ mother likes everyone$_i$.

---

[1] Coindexing represents coreference, or in this case co-valuation between the quantified expression and the pronoun. Throughout the text, grammaticality judgments refer to the intended interpretation.

[2] Among the extensive literature, see at least Reinhart 1976, 1983, Higginbotham 1980, 1988, Koopman and Sportiche 1982, Lasnik and Stowell 1991.

(6)   a. [who$_i$ does [his$_i$ mother like t$_i$]]
         b. [everyone$_i$ [his$_i$ mother likes t$_i$]]

As shown in (5)–(6), pronominal variable binding is blocked in the following structure:

(7)   quantifier$_i$ [...]   pronoun$_i$ [...]   variable$_i$

The analyses that have been proposed to derive the attested pattern have variously focussed on the reciprocal positioning either of the quantifier and the two argument positions (A-positions) to be interpreted as variables (the variable proper and the pronoun), or of the two A-positions themselves. An influential view, which goes back to Reinhart 1976, is represented by the following constraint, from Lasnik and Stowell 1991:

(8)   In a configuration where a pronoun P and a trace T are both A-bar bound by a category C, T must c-command P.[3]

The main thrust of this paper will be to show that this condition is unmotivated, and should be replaced by a linear approach along the lines of the Leftness Condition originally due to Chomsky 1976:

(9)   A variable cannot be the antecedent of a pronoun to its left.

A direct argument against the c-command condition (8) is presented in section 2. Section 3 considers 'backward' pronominal variable binding, which turns out to be problematic both for (8) and (9). Another general problem for any account of pronominal variable bindingis addressed in section 4: the status of subject negative quantifiers. These are problematic because most recent analyses locate the scope position for negative operators below the subject, in the projection normally labelled NegP. After a careful discussion of these issues, section 5 justifies the appeal to reconstruction (here loosely understood as the construal of a phrase in a structurally lower position in the phrase marker), and shows it to be independently necessary to account for the data considered. Section 6 turns the suggestion that reconstruction is at work into a definite proposal: topic preposed VP-level adjuncts are reconstructed into a topic position above

---

[3] X c-commands Y if and only if (i) X and Y do not dominate each other, and (ii) the first node dominating X also dominates Y. Lasnik and Stowell (1991) are not directly concerned with the proper structural requirement on pronominal variable binding, and do not argue for the validity of (8). On the basis of structures similar to those here exemplified in (10) they also mention an alternative analysis which, however, is still based on a hierachical relation between pronoun and variable (Lasnik and Stowell 1991, 691). This contrasts with the linear approach defended here, which is also more natural in that it does not require any reference to the argument / adjunct status of the XP containing the pronoun.

VP but below NegP. With this essential qualification, the Leftness Condition derives the full array of data.

2. Consider the following well-formed examples of pronominal variable binding:

(10)   a. We will sell no wine$_i$ before its$_i$ time (Higginbotham 1988, 124).
      b. We will sell no bottle$_i$ before it$_i$ is ready.
      c. I had to sell every bottle$_i$ before it$_i$ was ready.

In each example, the pronoun is straightforwardly interpreted as a variable bound by the coindexed quantifier. However, it is not to be taken for granted that *no wine*, *no bottle* and *every bottle* in (10) c-command the pronoun. Cinque (1990, 190, note 22), quoting several sources, points out that adjuncts of this type are in all probability right-attached to VP, in such a way that the object does not c-command them. Cinque mentions the absence of a binding-theoretic principle C violation in (11) (see Chomsky 1981 for a classic formulation of Binding Theory), and additional evidence is provided by the impossibility of split reciprocal and of licensing of a negative polarity item in (12) (note that *before* is itself a licenser for polarity items, so it has to be replaced by *after*):

(11)   Mary hit him$_i$ before John$_i$ had a chance to get up.

(12) a.   * Mary hit each man$_i$ before the other$_i$ could intervene.
     b.   * Mary hit no one after anyone could intervene.

The c-command requirement, therefore, does not seem to be met in (10); the availability of bound anaphora is the only reason to think otherwise.

These data strongly suggest that the pronoun construed as a bound variable does not need to be c-commanded by the position where the quantifier appears, in direct contrast to (8). Suppose now that the c-command requirement does not refer to the relation between the pronoun and the variable, but only to the relation between the pronoun and the operator which binds the variable. In the influential account of May 1985, all quantifiers can be adjoined at LF either to the VP or to the S (= IP) containing them, in both cases being interpreted as having scope over the whole clause. From the IP-adjoined operator position, a quantifier would then c-command both its variable and the coindexed pronoun, even in cases like (10) where the variable does not c-command the pronoun:

(13)   [$_{IP}$ Q$_i$ [$_{IP}$ ... [$_{VP}$ [$_{VP}$ ... var$_i$ ...] [$_{PP}$ ... pro$_i$ ...]]]]

The essential feature of this analysis, namely that the pronoun must be c-commanded by the operator, and not necessarily by the variable, is preserved under some alternative views that have been expressed on the LF representation of universal and negative quantifiers. Beghelli and Stowell (1993) have argued that distributive universal quantifers move at LF to a DistP projection above the subject; as for negative quantifiers, a consensus has emerged in a wealth of recent studies in identifying the scope position for them in an autonomous NegP projection, generally located inside the inflectional complex.[4] The NegP hypothesis, in any of its forms, poses a number of interesting questions, some of which will be taken up in the following section. However, these issues do not affect the present point: provided that the relevant operator position is above VP both for universal and negative quantifiers (and all analyses agree on this), c-command will hold between the operator and both its variable and the pronoun in (10). And, since (11)–(12) show that pronominal variable binding can obtain without c-command between the variable in VP and the pronoun in the VP-adjunct, (8) is incorrect.

A point should be clarified before proceeding any further. The examples of pronominal variable binding in (10) involve VP-adjuncts, but not all adverbial adjuncts are necessarily attached to VP. Rizzi (1990, 50) has argued, for instance, that reason adverbials are attached higher up, to TP (adopting a version of Pollock's (1989) split-Infl hypothesis). Following the NegP hypothesis, this means that NegP must be placed not only above VP, but also above TP; which is indeed a common assumption (not completely general: cf. Zanuttini 1991):

(14) $[_{AgrP} \ldots [_{NegP} Q_i \ldots [_{TP} [_{TP} \ldots var_i \ldots] [_{PP} \ldots pro_i \ldots]]]]$

This correctly predicts that pronominal variable binding is impossible if the clause-final adjunct is arguably attached in a higher position:[5]

(15) Mary would buy no book$_i$ * although / * when it$_i$'s been slated.

In conclusion, the data examined so far show that c-command between the variable and the pronoun is not a condition on the well-formedness of pronominal variable binding. C-command is, however, required between the A-bar position occupied by the operator at LF and the pronoun.

---

[4] See among others Pollock 1989, Belletti 1990, Laka 1990, Zanuttini 1991, Acquaviva 1992, 1993, 1994, Moritz and Valois 1994, Haegeman 1995.

[5] For independent evidence that the temporal clause is not below VP (which is not automatically excluded in the radical approach of Kayne 1995), cf. the lack of Principle C violation in (i): Mary would still defend John$_i$ although / when the idiot$_i$ had already confessed.

3. It is not so straightforward to conclude that a pronoun interpreted as a variable simply has to be A-bar bound. As is well known, 'backward' bound anaphora is possible with subject antecedents if the pronoun is embedded in certain fronted phrases, including clausal adverbials. The well-formed (16a–c) contrast with (16d), seemingly parallel to (16c), and with (16e–f), in which the pronoun is not in subject position:

(16) a. Near his$_i$ child's crib nobody$_i$ would keep matches.
b. In his$_i$ own home, everyone$_i$ feels safe.
c. ? If / when his$_i$ patients are careless, no doctor$_i$ is happy.
d. * After he$_i$ walked in, everyone$_i$ / no one$_i$ looked worried.
e. * In his$_i$ contribution, I forced everyone$_i$ / no one$_i$ to add a footnote.
f. * In his$_i$ paper, I told every / no student$_i$ that I had found a mistake.

In Reinhart's analysis (1983, 122), a quantifier licenses the bound variable interpretation for a pronoun in XP only if XP is in the c-domain of the quantifier. Her account of backward pronominal anaphora rests on two premises: the distinction between VP-level and sentence-level adverbials, and the assumption that a subject NP c-commands into a constituent left-attached to the sentence. On the basis of the first premiss, for which extensive empirical justification is offered (Reinhart 1983, chapter 3), fronted VP-level adverbials are argued to be left-attached to the sentence, while sentential ones are attached to a higher node. On the basis of the second premiss, a quantifier in subject position (and not in any lower position, as in (16e–f)) is correctly predicted to license backward pronominal anaphora only if the pronoun is embedded in a VP-level adjunct (as in (16a–c)), because only then does the subject c-command the pronoun. More recently, Cinque (1990, 90–94) has questioned the traditional analysis of adverb preposing, but in his account as well the sentence-initial constituents are either in the same position as Wh-phrases, or fill a higher Top position. In neither case would a subject NP c-command them, under current phrase-structural assumptions. Moreover, even a constituent adjoined to IP is not within the c-domain of the subject, according to the theory of adjunction proposed in May 1985, 56–58. It is not obvious how to reconcile Reinhart's theory with these standard assumptions.[6]

As for Reinhart's assumption that a pronoun interpreted as a variable must be c-commanded by the A-position where the quantifier appears (surface position for quantifiers that raise at LF, trace for Wh phrases), the

---

[6] Note also that (i-ii) would be incorrectly ruled in if the subject could c-command into the preposed adjunct: (i) *In any city, no one feels safe; (ii) *In the other's home, each man felt safe.

data reviewed in the previous section point to the opposite direction. However, the alternative view that the operator position should c-command the pronoun does not provide an immediate explanation for (16). To see why, consider the various possible LF representations for quantified sentences like (16). If the quantifiers adjoin to the outer sentential projection, following May 1985, the resulting schematic structure will look like (17):

(17)   [Q_i [... pro_i ... [var_i ...]]]

But this is a standard Weak Crossover configuration, under both approaches here considered: neither (8) nor (9) are respected. There is another possibility: the scope position for universal (distributive) quantifiers may be above the subject position (Beghelli and Stowell 1993), but below the 'adjunct':

(18)   [... pro_i ... [Q_i [var_i ...]]]

However, as is easy to see, both (8) and (9) still are violated by this structure. Sentences like (16) are still an open problem.

4. Apart from the issue of backward pronominal binding, the NegP hypothesis in its usual form (with NegP below the subject) poses for any theory of pronominal variable binding a more general problem, which to my knowledge has remained unnoticed so far. To see why, consider in detail a simple sentence like (19), where sentential negation is expressed by one negative quantifier:

(19)   a. John knows nothing.
          b. [$_{AgrP}$ John $_i$ Agr° [$_{NegP}$ OP Neg° [$_{TP}$ [$_{VP}$ t $_i$ knows nothing]]]]

No matter how the NegP hypothesis is implemented, the negative object *nothing* is related to its scope position in NegP by an operator-variable dependency. This dependency can be instantiated by actual raising of the object NP to Spec NegP, in which case its S-structure position is filled by a variable at LF (Zanuttini 1991, Haegeman and Zanuttini 1991, Moritz and Valois 1994). Alternatively, the negative NP is bound by an operator in Spec NegP (Acquaviva 1992, 1993, Haegeman 1995, Rowlett 1996). The necessary relation, in any case, must be expressed by coindexing. But simple sharing of referential indices will not do: firstly, in languages with Negative Concord there would be several referential indices on the unique OP binder; secondly, subjects would be a serious problem:

(20)   a. No one left.

b. $[_{AgrP}$ no one$_i$ $[_{NegP}$ OP $[_{TP}$ $[_{VP}$ t$_i$ left $]]]]$

If OP were coindexed with *no one*, it would also be coindexed with its trace in VP, thus counting as a local binder for the trace. This can be seen either as a violation of the locality constraints on chain links or an instance of improper movement, where an element moves through an A-bar position on its way to its A target. To solve these problems, the link between Spec NegP and the subject negative has to be expressed by non-referential coindexing, which is the only possible way to mark unselective binding (cf. Acquaviva 1993). OP is then non-referentially coindexed with the subject, but not with its trace:

(21)   no one$_i$ ^{k} [...] OP^k [...] t$_i$

Neither the trace nor the NP subject in (21) fall under any definition of (syntactic) variable—as is desirable. On the other hand, an object negative or indeed any NP which is locally bound by Spec NegP at LF will be syntactically a variable, under a definition like (22):[7]

(22) α is a variable if and only if α is in an A-position and it is locally A- bar bound.

To sum up to this point: assuming NegP, a negative preverbal subject is not a syntactic variable, although it is referentially dependent. The same status is arguably shared by indefinite expressions like *a person* or free-choice *anyone*.[8] When in embedded subject position, these NPs can at least marginally license a bound pronoun in the matrix clause:

(23)   a. ? In his$_i$ dreams at least, it's inevitable that anyone$_i$ should wish to be happy.
        b. In his$_i$ dreams at least, it's inevitable that a person$_i$ should wish to be happy.

However, with a negative NP in the same position the bound reading is just as unacceptable as with a universal quantifier, which is bound by a higher scope-position and therefore qualifies as a syntactic variable:

(24)   a. *? In his$_i$ dreams at least, it's inevitable that no one$_i$ should wish to be unhappy.
        b. *? In his$_i$ dreams at least, it's inevitable that everyone$_i$ should wish to be happy.

---

[7] Such a conclusion is necessary under any approach which treats indefinite expressions (including negatives) as semantic variables bound by a truly quantificational element. See, for example, Diesing 1992, 124–126. Progovac 1994 also makes use of non-selective indices to mark syntactic (as opposed to purely interpretive) dependencies.

[8] See among many others Heim 1982, Fodor and Sag 1982, Reuland and ter Meulen 1987, Beghelli and Stowell 1993; for the view that non-referential NPs like free-choice *anyone* differ from quantifiers, see in particular Hornstein 1984.

If NPs like *anyone*, used in a non-referential sense without being A-bar bound, behave differently from true quantifiers for the purposes of bound anaphora (and (23)–(24) suggest that they do), then a subject negative NP should be expected to pattern with *anyone*, rather than with *everyone*. This wrong prediction follows at once if a NegP is posited below the subject position: not being A-bar bound, a negative subject would then fail to instantate at LF the operator-variable dependency typical of quantifiers like *everyone*.

We have thus recognized two distinct problems for any account of pronominal variable binding: backward anaphora and, accepting the NegP hypothesis in its usual form, negative subjects. These problems are general; in addition, the facts reviewed in section 2 argue against a condition like the c-command requirement in (8) between variable and pronoun. We will now see that a unified solution is forthcoming once the role of reconstruction is taken into account, and that this solution is compatible with an approach in terms of the Leftness Condition in (9).

5. It should be noted that backward anaphora across a clausal boundary is not completely impossible, even when the antecedent is an A-bar bound syntactic quantifier like *everyone*. This is an additional piece of evidence against the c-command condition in (8): a theory that focuses entirely on the role of A-positions has nothing to say about contrasts like that in (25):

(25) a. ? If he$_i$'s really committed, I think every student$_i$ will pass.

b. * If he$_i$'s really committed, it's probable that every student$_i$ will pass.

For those speakers who accept (25a) in the relevant reading, some sort of lowering process must be posited, in order to allow the adverbial clause containing the pronoun to be within the scope of the quantifier.[9] Such an instance of adverbial reconstruction is not surprising with bridge verbs like *think* (cf. again Cinque 1990, 90–94). If one admits this possibility, however, the question immediately arises as to what prevents a similar lowering analysis for cases like (16d–f). Besides, reconstruction should not replace a fronted element in its original (or 'D-structure') position, witness the ungrammaticality of (26c) (from Reinhart 1983, 129):

---

[9] The construal of a left-attached *if*-clause below the scope of an epistemic verb to its right is known as 'protasis lifting'; see the brief mention in Fiengo and May 1994, 100, and references cited there. In the rich literature on reconstruction, see among others Barss 1988, Huang 1993, Chomsky 1993, Fiengo and May 1994, and Heycock 1995.

(26)   a. Near his$_i$ child's crib nobody$_i$ would keep matches.
      b. You should give nobody$_i$ matches near his$_i$ child's crib.
      c. * Near his$_i$ child's crib you should give nobody$_i$ matches.

Nevertheless, examples like (25a) suggest that some sort of reconstruction may play a role; if this can apply to (25a), then a properly constrained reconstruction process could be assumed *a fortiori* for cases where there is no clausal boundary. What is apparently called for is a reconstruction mechanism that represents the fronted adverbials not in an arbitrarily deeply embedded VP-internal position, but rather in the position appropriate for VP-modifiers: namely, immediately above VP:

(27)   XP$_i$ [$_{IP}$ NP Infl XP$_i$ VP]

The impossibility of (16e–f), (24) and (25b), where the fronted XP must be construed with a subordinate VP, shows that this hypothesized pre-VP 'reconstructed topicalization' is just like topicalization in being essentially restricted to root contexts. Marginal exceptions like (25a) turn out to be expected, since they are restricted to (a subset of) those predicates which are otherwise known to allow clause-bounded interpretive processes across the boundary of their complement clause (see Horn 1978 and the references cited in Cinque 1990, 58, respectively for Neg-Raising and Left Dislocation, and Culicover 1993 for embedded topicalization), and more generally to license root phenomena in their complement clause (see McCloskey 1992).

   These facts strongly suggest that backward bound anaphora can be handled by positing reconstruction (needed in any case to explain (25)) in a position between NegP (if present) and VP. We will now see that the topic reconstruction hypothesis in this form derives without further stipulations all the problematic facts considered so far.

6. The proposed LF structures for sentences with VP-level and sentence-level fronted constituents are shown, respectively, in (28) a. and b.:

(28)   a.   XP [$_{IP}$ NP$_1$ (Neg)   XP'   [$_{VP}$ V   NP$_2$ t]]
      b.   XP [$_{IP}$ NP$_1$ (Neg)   [$_{VP}$ V   NP$_2$]]

Suppose XP contains a pronoun. Only reconstruction of XP as XP' in (28a) allows this pronoun to be c-commanded by an operator: an operator in Spec NegP or, above the subject, an A-bar position hosting a universal quantifier. Because in (28b) no c-command holds between an operator and the pronoun, the latter cannot be interpreted as a bound variable. As we have seen, c-command between A-bar position and pronoun is independently required by cases like (15). Turning to (28a), suppose the operator (universal or negative) binds NP_2 inside VP—suppose, that is, that a negative or universal quantifier is in VP. Regardless of whether NP_2 actually raises at LF, it is syntactically a variable (cf. the discussion of (19): either because the raised NP_2 A-bar binds its own trace, or because a base-generated operator A-bar binds NP_2). The pronoun in the reconstructed XP' intervenes between the operator and its variable, and a standard Weak Crossover violation follows, as in *his$_i$ mother loves everyone$_i$.*

It is certainly possible to accept the reconstruction hypothesis while still thinking that pronominal variable binding requires an A-antecedent to c-command the pronoun at LF, as in (8). But this would leave unexplained the facts considered in section 2, which suggest that the pronoun only needs to be c-commanded by an A-bar operator, and not by its variable:

(29)   We will [$_{NegP}$ OP^k sell [no wine]^k_i [before its$_i$ time]]

The indicated operator in Spec NegP c-commands both the object NP and the adjunct. If *no wine* is A-bar bound by OP, it qualifies as a variable; if it raises to Spec NegP, its trace does. In neither case does the variable c-command the pronoun, contrary to the requirement in (8). We can derive the correct results for the whole set of facts by adopting the Leftness Condition of Chomsky 1976, here repeated:

(9)   A variable cannot be the antecedent of a pronoun to its left.

In (29) the object NP *no wine* qualifies as a variable (corresponding to NP_2 in (28a)), and the pronoun on its right can be coindexed with it. Consider now the sentences in (26), here repeated with the explicit indication of the reconstructed adverbial. The necessary linear order < variable-pronoun > obtains in (26a–b), but not in (26c):

(30)   a. [Near his$_i$ child's crib] nobody$_i$ would [near his$_i$ child's crib]
                                                                                        keep matches.
         b. You should give nobody$_i$ matches near his$_i$ child's crib.
         c. * [Near his$_i$ child's crib] you should [near his$_i$ child's crib]
                                                                                        give nobody$_i$ matches.

In (30c) *nobody* qualifies as a variable; the preposed PP is reconstructed below NegP, and the pronoun it contains is coindexed with the variable to its right. The resulting LF structure is parallel to that of Weak Crossover violations in double object constructions, like * *He gave his$_i$ nickname to each candidate$_i$.*

If the antecedent of the reconstructed pronoun is in subject position, however, no problem arises: the pronoun is on the right of the subject NP, whether the latter is a syntactic variable (if it is a universal quantifier) or not (if it is negative). In either case the pronoun is c-commanded by an operator. This requirement must be added, in order to rule out bound anaphora when the pronoun is higher than the operator. Apart from preposed sentence-level modifiers (as (16d) and (28b)), the c-command requirement is necessary to rule out (15), where the pronoun is above NegP but still to the right of the quantified NP, and sentences instantiating the abstract structure in (18):

(31)　　　　* His$_i$ soldiers believe that no general$_i$ is faultless.

Strictly speaking, the Leftness Condition does not even apply here, since a subject negative NP is not c-commanded by the operator in NegP and hence is not a syntactic variable.[10]

7. These considerations suggest three conclusions. Firstly, a c-command requirement does indeed constrain bound pronominal anaphora, but it concerns the relation of a pronoun to an A-bar operator position, not to the A-position of the variable bound by this operator. Secondly, the hypothesis that negatives are operator-bound by a scope position in NegP below the subject is not at odds with the facts of pronominal variable binding; the only apparent problem, represented by negative subjects, disappears once it is realized that such NPs are not syntactic variables. Thirdly, although no c-command requirement holds on the two A-positions involved in bound anaphora, a linear constraint to the effect of the Leftness Condition still seems to represent the correct generalization with respect to Weak Crossover. These results directly support the conclusions reached by Georgopoulos (1991), who convincingly argues in favour of the Leftness Condition on the basis of Palauan data. Besides, any account of Weak Crossover based on a linear condition supports the general approach to bound anaphora of Fiengo and May 1994, which clearly distinguishes the hierarchical structural relations relevant for Binding Theory from the linear relations relevant for Dependency Theory.

---

[10] The analysis of Palauan put forth by Georgopoulos (1991, 215–216) also complements the Leftness Condition with a precedence requirement between A-bar antecedent and pronoun.

REFERENCES

Acquaviva, Paolo 1992. 'The Representation of Negative 'Quantifiers'', *Rivista di linguistica*, 4, 319–381

— 1993. 'The Logical Form of Negation', PhD dissertation, Scuola Normale Superiore, Pisa

— 1994. 'The Representation of Operator-Variable Dependencies in Sentential Negation', *Studia Linguistica*, 48/2, 91–132

Barss, Andrew 1988. 'Paths, Connectivity, and Featureless Empty Categories', in *Constituent Structure*, ed. by Anna Cardinaletti, Guglielmo Cinque and Giuliana Giusti, Padova: Editoriale Programma, 9–34

Beghelli, Filippo and Stowell, Timothy 1993. 'The Direction of Quantifier Movement', ms., University of California, Los Angeles

Belletti, Adriana 1990. *Generalized Verb Movement*, Turin: Rosenberg and Sellier

—1994. 'Verb Positions: Evidence from Italian', in *Verb Movement*, ed. by Norbert Hornstein and David Lightfoot, Cambridge: University Press, 19–40

Chomsky, Noam 1976. 'Conditions on Rules of Grammar', *Linguistic Analysis*, 2, 303–351

—1981. *Lectures on Government and Binding*, Dordrecht: Foris

—1993. 'A Minimalist Program for Linguistic Theory', in *The View from Building 20*, ed. by Kenneth Hale and Samuel Jay Keyser', Cambridge, Mass.: MIT Press, 1–52

Cinque, Guglielmo 1990. *Types of A-bar Dependencies*, Cambridge, Mass.: MIT Press

Culicover, Peter 1993. 'Evidence against ECP-Accounts of the *That-t* Effect', *Linguistic Inquiry*, 24, 557–561

Diesing, Molly. 1992. *Indefinites*, Cambridge, Mass.: MIT Press

Fiengo, Robert and May, Robert 1994. *Indices and Identity*, Cambridge, Mass.: MIT Press

Fodor, Janet and Sag, Ivan 1982. 'Referential and Quantificational Indefinites', *Linguistics and Philosophy*, 5, 355–398

Georgopoulos, Carol 1991. *Syntactic Variables*, Dordrecht: Kluwer

Haegeman, Liliane 1995. *The Syntax of Negation*, Cambridge: University Press

Haegeman, Liliane and Zanuttini, Raffaella 1991. 'Negative Heads and the Neg Criterion', *The Linguistic Review*, 8, 233–251

Heim, Irene 1982. 'The Semantics of Definite and Indefinite Noun Phrases', PhD Dissertation, University of Massachusetts at Amherst

Heycock, Caroline 1995. 'Asymmetries in Reconstruction', *Linguistic Inquiry*, 26, 547–570

Higginbotham, James 1980. 'Pronouns and Bound Variables', *Linguistic Inquiry*, 11, 679–708

—1988. 'On the Varieties of Cross-Reference', in *Constituent Structure*, ed. by Anna Cardinaletti, Guglielmo Cinque and Giuliana Giusti, Padova: Editoriale Programma, 123–142

Horn, Laurence 1978. 'Remarks on Neg-Raising', in *Syntax and Semantics 9: Pragmatics*, ed. by Peter Cole, New York: Academic Press, 129–220

Hornstein, Norbert 1984. *Logic as Grammar*, Cambridge, Mass.: MIT Press

Huang, C.-T. James 1993. 'Reconstruction and the Structure of VP', *Linguistic Inquiry*, 24, 103–138

Kayne, Richard 1995. *The Antisymmetry of Syntax*, Cambridge, Mass.: MIT Press

Koopman, Hilda and Sportiche, Dominique 1982. 'Variables and the Bijection Principle', *The Linguistic Review*, 2, 139–160

Ladusaw, William 1980. *Polarity Sensitivity as Inherent Scope Relations*, New York: Garland

Laka, Itztiar 1990. 'Negation in Syntax', PhD dissertation, MIT

Lasnik, Howard and Stowell, Timothy 1991. 'Weakest Crossover', *Linguistic Inquiry*, 22, 687–720

McCloskey, James 1992. 'Adjunction, Selection and Embedded Verb-Second', MS, University of California at Santa Cruz

May, Robert 1977. 'The Grammar of Quantification', PhD dissertation, MIT

—1985. *Logical Form*, Cambridge, Mass.: MIT Press

Moritz, Luc 1989. 'Aperçu de la syntaxe de la négation en français et en anglais', Mémoire de licence, Université de Genève

Moritz, Luc, and Valois, Daniel 1994. 'Pied-Piping and Specifier-Head Agreement', *Linguistic Inquiry*, 25, 667–707

Pollock, Jean-Yves 1989. 'Verb Movement, Universal Grammar, and the Structure of IP', *Linguistic Inquiry*, 20, 365–424

Progovac, Ljiljana 1994. *Negative and Positive Polarity*, Cambridge: University Press

Reinhart, Tanya 1976. 'The Syntactic Domain of Anaphora', PhD dissertation, MIT

—1983. *Anaphora and Semantic Interpretation*, Chicago-London: The University of Chicago Press

Reuland, Eric and ter Meulen, Alice, eds. 1987. *The Representation of (In)definiteness*, Cambridge, Mass.: MIT Press

Rizzi, Luigi 1990. *Relativized Minimality*, Cambridge, Mass.: MIT Press

Rowlett, Paul 1996. 'Negative Configurations in French', PhD dissertation, University of York

Zanuttini, Raffaella 1991. 'Syntactic Properties of Sentential Negation', PhD dissertation, University of Pennsylvania

Anatomy of Sound Change

WIESŁAW AWEDYK

Adam Mickiewicz University, Poznań & Harstad College, Norway

MOST historical linguists will shrug off the question *What is sound change?* as self-evident and produce scores of examples like OE *he* 'he' [he:] → Mod.E [hi:]. Sound change may be then represented as a simple formula:

$$A \rightarrow B \qquad\qquad ([e:] \rightarrow [i:])$$

The analysis of the examples below will demonstrate that the formula is not simple indeed.

1.1 The *Longman Pronunciation Dictionary* (Wells 1992) gives an alternative pronunciation of *harass* ['hærəs] as [hə'ræs]:

> The traditional educated and RP form is ['hærəs]. The pronunciation [hə'ræs], which appeared first in the US, was seemingly first heard in Britain in the 1970's, and it has spread with the increased popularity of this formerly rather rare word: in time it may predominate. Meanwhile, it evokes strong negative feelings among those who use the traditional form. BrE poll panel preference: '-- 68%, -'- 32% (Wells 1992, 325).

Is then ['hærəs] → [hə'ræs] a change or merely an innovation? Milroy would, perhaps, treat it as a change: '[...] an innovation in a speaker's output is not a linguistic change until it has been agreed on and adopted by some community of speakers, *however small the community may be*' (Milroy 1992, 221 [emphasis W.A.]).

One could also split the RP speech community into the 'traditional' RP speech community and the 'advanced' RP speech community and maintain that the change has already taken place in the advanced RP speech community. I believe, however, that such acrobatics does not solve the problem and *fuzzy edges* should not be an excuse for theoretical and methodological inadequacies.

1.2. Over the past few decades the pronunciation of the vowel in words like *nut* has changed. According to Jones (1991 [1918], 86) the vowel [ʌ] was half-open and articulated with fore part of the back of the tongue, i.e., it was central-retracted. Gimson (1991 [1962], 109) gives the following description: '[...] the centre of the tongue (or a part slightly in advance of centre) is raised just above the fully open position, [...]'. The vowel may be then defined as open-raised and central-advanced; there has then been a shift in the pronunciation, i.e., [ʌ] → [ɐ].

One could further elaborate and maintain that the shift took place because of the danger of confusion with the vowel [ɒ] in words like *knot* or because of a natural tendency for vowels to disperse in the Universal Vowel Space (cf. Liljencrants and Lindblom 1972). Most linguists would, however, disagree that the shift in pronunciation in words like *nut* is a sound change since neither the RP vowel system has changed nor the RP speakers have noticed the shift.

1.3. In current RP the diphthong in words like *go* has a central starting point and this new diphthong has replaced, or ousted, the old diphthong with a back starting point, i.e. [ou] → [əu]

RP speakers are fully aware of the shift and believe it to be 'the ideal image of a "correct" or "beautiful" RP GOAT diphthong' (Wells 1982, 237). The shift has not *directly* affected the RP system as the number of diphthongs has remained unchanged. It has, however, affected the system in an *indirect* way, namely, there has been a change in the system of oppositions. Before the shift there was a binary opposition in the starting point between *front* /eɪ/, /aɪ/ and *back* /ou/, /ɔɪ/, /au/ (N.B. Careful speakers have [ɑ] as the starting point for /au/, cf.Gimson 1991 [1962], 137). With the rise of /əu/ a new element of the opposition has appeared and now there is a three-way opposition, namely, *front* /eɪ/, /aɪ/ : *central* /əu/ : *back* /ɔɪ/, /au/.

Followers of the teleological approach to sound change could also point out that the shift resulted in a more symmetrical system of diphthongs, namely, two diphthongs have a low front and low back staring point and three diphthongs have a mid staring point: front, central and back.

The shift of /ou/ to /əu/ *looks* more like a sound change and a number of linguists will perhaps agree that it is a real sound change.

1.4. The innovating diphthong [əu] as in *go* is not the only possible form in RP: 'Some forms of RP have a further advanced variant, [ëu]. Others retain some rounding, having a rounded mid central vocoid as the first element of the diphthong [ɵu]' (Wells 1982, 237).

Does the above data support the traditional view that sound change is phonetically gradual? Moreover, since the second element of the diphthong [əu] tends to be week, pairs of words like *goal* and *girl* or *own* and *earn* may be homophones. Is there then a case of 'drift' in the development of the old [ou], i.e. [ou] → [ɵu] → [əu] → [ëu] → [ɜ:] ?

Historical sociolinguists like Milroy would reject such an interpretation since 'phonetically gradual patterns that we are now able to observe are not sound changes in progress, but simply variation' (Milroy 1992, 162).

The interpretation may depend on how the RP speech community is defined: if the RP speech community is treated as a whole, then it is variation. If, on the other hand, one distinguishes between 'traditional', 'advanced', and 'progressive' speech communities within the RP speech community, the data demonstrates a phonetically gradual pattern of sound change.

1.5. How the above problems will be approached has serious implications for the theory of sound change and for the very *definition* of sound change as it cannot be reduced to a simple formula A → B. The resolution of this problem will, in turn, have implications for such fundamental issues in historical linguistics like whether sound change is phonetically abrupt or phonetically gradual. In this article I will examine the anatomy of sound change and look for the symptoms of gradualness and abruptness.

2.1. The starting point is Ohala's (1993) recent contribution to the theory of sound change. Although Ohala is primarily concerned with the pre-conditions for sound change, the reconstruction of the whole body of sound change is possible. If my inferences are correct, the following tiers may be distinguished:

(a)   preconditions for sound change that are mainly located in the physical phonetic character of the sound involved;

(b)   the listener's failure to correct the perturbations in the speech signal, which leads to variation;

(c)   the trigger that gives a *go-ahead* signal to variation and thus a sound change occurs. All pursuits to find the trigger have been fruitless;

(d)   the spread of the change in temporal, spatial, and social dimensions.

Ohala concentrates on (a) and (b), which will be briefly discussed below.

2.2. The physical phonetic character of sounds is mainly a precondition for sound change, for example, non-contextually nasalized vowels sound lower than corresponding (in terms of height) oral vowels. Thus the listener perceives a high nasalized vowel (the speaker's intention) as a mid vowel.

> [...] listeners *normalize* or *correct* the speech signal in order to arrive at the pronunciation intended by the speaker minus any contextual

> perturbations. [...] Such a perceptual correction of the speech signal by listeners serves to *prevent* sound change (Ohala 1993, 245 [emphasis original]).

Neither the speaker nor the listener wants to change pronunciation and the listener's efforts aim to reconstruct the speaker's intended pronunciation. Although the speaker is responsible for variation, the listener's correct deductions discount variation. Sound change *can* start when the listener *fails* to reconstruct the intended pronunciation. Sound change is then primarily located with the listener, i.e., sound change is 'essentially a parsing error on the part of the listener' (Ohala 1993, 264).

Thus it is the listener who is, first of all, held responsible for sound change:

> [...] change occurs not in message source (the speaker's brain) nor the message destination (the listener's brain) but in the transmission channel between them. This includes the speech production system and the listener's decoding system (Ohala 1993, 262).

It is this view that I will challenge in the paragraphs below.

3.1. First of all, the speaker is more than a deaf sender and the listener is more than a dumb receiver. The speaker hears his own speech through bone transmission, i.e., he is the speaker-listener, and the listener decodes sounds by referring to knowledge of how they are articulated ('motor theory of speech perception'), i.e., he is a listener-speaker:

> Wir sind, wenn wir hörend aufnahmen, mehr und ganz anderes als rein akustische Rezeptoren; und wenn wir selbst sprechen, sind wir mehr und anderes als taube Sender. Sondern wir nehmen das Gehörte innerlich mitkonstruirend (*oft förmlich nachsprechend*) auf und erzeugen die eigenen Sendungen unter der wirksamen Kontrolle unseres mithorenden Öhres (Bühler 1934, 268 [emphasis W.A.]).

Thus it is not only the listener's failure to correct the perturbations in the speech signal that is responsible for sound change, but also the speaker's failure to correct his own signal. If the perturbations are large enough for the speaker-listener and the listener-speaker to be detected and the mysterious trigger sends a go-ahead signal, then a sound change takes place.

3.2. In order for a sound change to be detected the shift from one pronunciation to another must be large enough (cf. Ohala 1993, 266). The shift from [ʌ] to [ɐ] was large enough since it consisted in both lowering and fronting. Yet it was not detected. On the other hand, the shift from [ou] to [əʊ] was detected, although it only involved fronting. The fronting was accompanied by the unrounding of the first element of the diphthong (the [o] in [ou] was slightly rounded) and that is perhaps why the shift was detected. The feature ROUND is then more 'conspicuous' than features involving tongue movements, at least for speakers of English. Moreover, the shift from [ʌ] to [ɐ] did not entail any change in the system of oppositions as both the vowels are central:

front /æ/ : central /ʌ/ or /ɐ/ : back /ɒ/.

Thus, the shift from one pronunciation to another, large or small, is not perceived as a change unless it involves certain features and/or entails changes in the system of oppositions.

3.3. Historical linguists are not unanimous in their account of cases of 'drift' like:

[ou] → [əʊ] → [əʊ] → [ɵ̈ʊ]

For some the data demonstrates that sound change is phonetically gradual while for others, who maintain that sound change is phonetically abrupt, it is simply variation. One possible solution was suggested in 1.4., namely, that each variant pronunciation is characteristic of a particular speech community ('traditional', 'advanced', 'progressive') within the RP speech community. Sound change will then be phonetically abrupt with an implication that both the traditional and the advanced variant are 'on the move' towards the progressive variant. This explanation is, however, methodologically suspect and I will propose another solution to the abrupt/gradual controversy.

3.4. It is commonplace knowledge that there is a lot of variability in speech events. There are measurable differences not only between the 'same' sound when pronounced by different speakers of one speech community, but also between the 'same' sound when pronounced by the same speaker on different occasions. Variation has certain limitations, otherwise communication will be hindered, for example, the speaker may use a number of raised variants of /e/ as in *pen* but the raising cannot be excessive, for the listener will perceive it as a variant of /ɪ/ as in *pin*. However, if the listener decodes [pɪn] as a variant pronunciation of *pen* and if he uses this variant as the speaker, i.e., if he fails to correct the perturbation, then—given a *go-ahead* signal by the trigger—a sound change takes place.

There may be an almost infinite number of different realizations of the raised /e/, but they will be decoded as variants of either /e/ or /ɪ/.

Thus sound change is gradual in the 'mouth' of the speaker and in the 'ears' of the listener, but it is abrupt in the brain of both the speaker and the listener.

Sound change, then, occurs in the speaker-listener's brain, and not in the transmission channel between the speaker and the listener although 'perturbation' is a prerequisite for a sound change to occur.

4.1. *Summing up*, sound change cannot be represented as a simple formula A → B but it must be supplemented by additional constraints concerning changes in the whole system and the native speakers' awareness. There remains, however, one problem to be solved, namely, how to define shifts in pronunciation like [ʌ] → [ɐ], as observed by linguists but not 'detected' by native speakers.

REFERENCES

Bühler, Karl 1934. *Sprachtheorie: Die Darstellungsfunktion der Sprache*, Jena: Fischer

Gimson, A.C. 1991 (1962). *An Introduction to the Pronunciation of English*, 4th ed. revised by Susan Ramsaran, London: Edward Arnold

Jones, Daniel 1991 (1918). *An Outline of English Phonetics*, 9th ed., Cambridge: University Press

Liljencrants, Johan and Lindblom, Björn 1972. 'Numerical simulation of vowel quality systems', *Language*, 48, 839–862

Milroy, James 1992. *Linguistic Variation and Change. On Historical Linguistics of English*, Oxford: Blackwell

Ohala, John J. 1993. 'The Phonetics of Sound Change', *Historical Linguistics: Problems and Perspectives*, ed. by Charles Jones, London/New York: Longman, 237–278

Wells, J.C. 1982. *Accents of English, 1. An Introduction*, Cambridge: University Press

—1992. *Longman Pronunciation Dictionary*, London: Longman

Foclóir Uí Bheaglaoich

TOMÁS DE BHALDRAITHE[*]
Acadamh Ríoga na hÉireann

I BPÁRAS sa bhliain 1732 a foilsíodh 'The English Irish Dictionary. An *Foclóir Béarla Gaoidheilge* ar na chur a neagar le Conchobhar Ó Beaglaoich mar aon le congnamh Aodh bhuidhe mac Cuirtin [...]'. Ba é an chéad iarracht é ar fhoclóir Béarla–Gaeilge a chur i gcló agus ba mhisniúil éachtach an iarracht í tráth a raibh lucht léinn na Gaeilge in ísle bhrí. Toisc gurb í gnáthGhaeilge na linne atá ann, ní hionann agus teanga liteartha na bhfilí nó teanga ársa na gcroiniceoirí, is fiú é a iniúchadh i dtaobh an stór focal, na bhfocal nár foilsíodh i bhfoclóirí roimhe sin, iasachtaí ón mBéarla, cúrsaí canúna, modhanna bisiúla cumadóireachta, i dtaobh fhorás mhodheolaíocht na foclóireachta, na deilbhíochta agus an litrithe, agus i dtaobh na hanála a bhí aige ar na foclóirí a tháinig ina dhiaidh. Déanfar iarracht ar chuid de na cúrsaí sin a phlé anseo ar chaoi a bhféadfadh an neamhshaineolaí chomh maith leis na saineolaí léargas agus blas éigin a fháil ar shaothar seo Uí Bheaglaoich, saothar ar fíorbheagán cóipeanna de atá ar marthain anois. Ní fios cén líon cóipeanna a foilsíodh. Bhí sé éirithe gann cheana féin sa mbliain 1820.[1]

1.2. Údar an fhoclóra. Is beag an t-eolas atá againn ar Ó Beaglaoich thar a bhfuil le baint as an dán a chuir Aodh Buidhe le réamhrá an fhoclóra ina a dtugann sé 'sagart sáir-riaghlach séimh' air agus ina ndeir sé gurbh é a sholáthraigh 'glanchlódh Gaoidheilge / Dathbheodh ar dteangan.[2] Níl a ainm ar na cáipéisí den tréimhse a cheadaigh stairithe ach meastar gurb ionann é agus an 'Thadée Begly', Dochtúir Diachta in Ollscoil Pháras, a bhí ag teagasc clainne an Chúnta Daniel O'Mathony sna blianta 1718–19, agus a bhí ag obair mar shagart i bparóiste St.Germain-L'Auxerrois faoi Lúnasa 1729.[3]

---

[*] Fuair údar an ailt seo bás go gairid tar eís dó a théacs a chur chuig na heagarthóirí; tá siadsan fíorbhuíoch den Dr Seán Ua Súilleabháin as ucht na bprofaí a cheartú.

[1] E. O'Reilly, 'A Chronological Account of nearly Four Hundred Irish Writers [...]'.in *Transactions of the Iberno-Celtic Society for 1820* (Baile Átha Cliath 1820) ccxxx.

[2] Mionchuntas ar an gcló sin in Dermot McGuinne, *Irish Type Design* (Baile Átha Cliath, 1992) 64–71.

[3] Féach Liam Swords, 'History of the Irish College, Paris 1578-1800' in *Archivum Hibernicum* xxxv (1980) 3.233, agus Richard Hayes, *Biographical dictionary of Irishmen in France* (1949) 12.

1.3. Bhí Aodh Buidhe á lua mar údar an fhoclóra ar a laghad ó lár an 19ú haois, mar shampla ag Mícheál Ó Raghallaigh,[4] scríobhaí, agus ag Peadar Ó Conaill,[5] foclóirí. Cé gur luaigh Eoghan Ó Comhraidhe 'Hugh McCurtin's English preface to his Dictionary'[6] d'athraigh sé a thuairim ar ball, agus scríobh sé 'altho his name [Aodh Buidhe] is introduced in the title page as an assistant to the compiler Conor O'Begly, yet it can be clearly seen by any good Irish scholar that a man of McCurtin's ability could not have had any hand in the construction of the very corrupt and silly text of that compilation'.[7] Ach leanadh de bheith ag cur an fhoclóra i leith Aodha Bhuidhe.[8]

1.4. Cé nach n-aontaím gur 'corrupt and silly compilation' an foclóir, measaim go raibh an ceart ag Ó Comhraidhe a rá nach bhfuil rian Aodha Bhuidhe air, is é sin nach í an teanga liteartha chrochta a chleachtadh leithéid Aodha Bhuidhe atá ann. Deir Ó Beaglaoich féin sa réamhrá go ndearna sé an foclóir chomh hiomlán agus ab fhéidir '[...] without swelling it with [...] antiquated words [...]' Fianaise eile a chuideodh lena mheas nach raibh lámh ar bith ag Aodh Buidhe ann is ea an litriú leasaithe, litriú ar chuir seisean go tréan ina choinne.[9] B'fhéidir gurbh amhlaidh a cheap Ó Beaglaoich gur mhó an meas a bheadh ar a shaothar ach ainm saoi cháiliúil a bheith leis is gur iarr sé ar Aodh Buidhe an dán brollaigh a chumadh agus gurbh shin ar thug seisean de chúnamh dó.

1.5. Ba iad cuspóirí an fhoclóra, de réir an réamhrá, meas ar an nGaeilge a mhúscailt i measc uaisle Éireann a bhí ag ligean faillí inti agus cur i

---

[4] '[...] do sgríobh sé [Aodh Buidhe] leabhar seanchus ar Éire, focalóir Sagsbhearla agus Gaoidhilge [...]' Mícheál Ó Raghallaigh, LS R69 (i), Coláiste Phádraig, Má Nuad.

[5] 'Hugh McCurtin's English Preface to his Dictionary', Seán Ó Conaill, LS 23.C.26 (a) 4, Acadamh Ríoga na hÉireann.

[6] 'Catalogue of Irish Manuscripts in the Royal Irish Academy ' LS iml.1 185.

[7] id. iml. 2 342.

[8] 'Begley [...] had a fount of Irish type cast [...] and invited Hugh MacCurtin [...] to come to Paris. Abbé Begley enabled him to publish there in 1732 his English-Irish Dictionary [...]' R. Hayes, op.cit.. 12. Ní luaitear ach Mac Cruitín sna na tagairtí don fhoclóir sa *Catalogue of Irish Manuscripts in the Royal Irish Academy. Index*, ii (1958) 895.

[9] '[...] to give my humble opinion of some objections which the industrious learned Mr. Lhoyd and others give against the Old Irish orthography and [...] that he believes a new method for the Irish orthography would be much better and more easy for strangers to come to the knowledge of the language [...] I answer, the dialect and idiom of the language necessarily require to keep close to its ancient orthography [...] great inconveniences that would unavoidably follow the omission of initials and other letters in Irish words'. Réamhrá in Hugh Mac Curtin, *The Elements of the Irish Language, Grammatically Explained in English* (Lobháin 1728).

gcoinne uaisle Shasana a bhíodh ag síorchaitheamh anuas uirthi agus ar lucht a labhartha.[10]

2.1. Bunús an Bhéarla. Thogh ÓBg 'Boyer and Bailey'[11] (sic), dhá fhoclóir a raibh cáil mhór orthu, mar fhoinse don Bhéarla. As Boyer is mó a bhain sé leas. Tá riar mhór ceannfhocal de chuid Boyer aige nach bhfuil ag Bailey[12] ach tá cuid de cheannfhocail Bailey aige freisin nach bhfuil ag Boyer.[13] Maidir le líon na gceannfhocal is na bhfrásaí ní furasta ÓBg a chur i gcomórtas le Boy, ach measaim nach bhfuil ag ÓBg ach tuairim is a hocht faoin gcéad de ábhar Boy, cé go bhfuil 672 leathanach 4to ann.

2.2. Ní léir cén tslat tomhais a bhí ag ÓBg agus é ag roghnú ceannfhocal nó frásaí. Más ait linn an líon mór focal ársa nach dtuigfí anois a roghnaigh sé, ní mór a mheabhrú gur cnuasaigh d'fhocail 'dheacra' a bhíodh sna foclóirí luatha aonteangacha Béarla agus go mbíodh aird ar leith fós ar a leithéid i bhfoclóir an 18ú haois. B'fhéidir nach raibh ÓBg sách oilte ar an mBéarla le go n-aithneodh sé an focal ársa deacair ón bhfocal coitianta. B'fhéidir eile gur bhreá leis a chuid eolais ar an gcruaBhéarla a thaispeáint. Tá na scórtha de na 'cruafhocail' sin aige, e.g. *bricken, brindice, bricken, brickoll, buss, caduke, calenture, camail, chowter, cincater, dizzard, dozel, dulcarnon.*[14]

2.3. Taobh le focail is le frásaí a bhaineann leis an seansaol, tá an-chuid leaganacha a d'oirfeadh i bhfoclóir nua-aoiseach, e.g. *hush-money, junket, shop-lifter, alimony, bill of divorce; a man well lined; to promote a book; to blow up a mine; insurance office; religion is on its last legs; they depend in all things on the lips of the clergy; money governs the world.* Ach is ait mar a fhágann sé ar lár riar mhór focal coitianta, e.g. *abbey, abyss, beech,*

---

[10] '[...] their language which, without being understood, has been hitherto cryed down and ridiculed by the English in general, and even by some gentlemen in particular, whose fine sense and good manners in other respects have deserv'd praise and imitation.[...] The Irish Gentry have therefore Opportunity enough, still left, for recovering and preserving their Mother-Language, and, consequently, are without the least Colour of Excuse if they shamefully continue to neglect it.' Réamhrá ÓBg,

[11] A. Boyer, *Le Dictionnaire François-Anglois et Anglois-François* (Londres 1699 etc.). (Foilsíodh cuid mhaith eagrán. Ag cur leis a bhítí. Eagrán 1753 a cheadaíos. Ní fios cé acu *An Universal Dictionary* (Londain 1721) nó *Dictionarium Britannicum* (Londain 1730) de chuid Nathan Bailey a d'oibrigh ÓBg. Tá cuid mhór den ábhar céanna iontu. Is é an ceann deiridh a cheadaíos.

[12] m.sh. *bittern, bog-trotter, bree, cattle, coat-cards, philistines.*

[13] m.sh. *acros, furole, Pan, Apollo.*

[14] Samplaí eile : *to ear, to ean, to fadge, fub, gare, geason, geir, glozer, gonch, hogoo, hulch, inlagary, laches, to lin, meacock, michés, merkin, mur, musrol, nizy, patache, pedee, pesage, to pome, pose* [=réama], *princock, to prog, pundle, rorid, quaviver, to quetch, sashoons, sasse, sarplar, snudge, tampoy, wittal.*

buttercup, hawthorn, poppy, violet, pear, plum, shin, pool, island, teacher, printer, adder, bat, hake, donkey, sock, stocking, cellar, stable.

2.4. Tharla gan litriú an Bhéarla a bheith caighdeánaithe faoin am sin b'fhéidir go gceapfaí focal a bheith ar iarraidh agus é ann faoi litriú eile, e.g. *ache s.v. ake, cemetry s.v. coemetry, celibate s.v. caelibate, choose s.v. chuse, suit s.v. sute, soap s.v. sope, ore s.v. oar, skein s.v. skain.*

2.5. Ar an taobh eile is minic an Ghaeilge a fhreagraíonn don cheannfhocal atá ar iarraidh le fáil i bhfrása faoi cheannfhocal eile, e.g. ankle (*rúitín* s.v. pastern), astrologer (*astroluíghe* s.v. weather), beam (*gaidh gréine* s.v. sun), butterfly (*féiliocán* s.v. flutter), cellar (*soiléar* s.v. stilling), mischance (*míothapa* s.v. sad), swallow (*fáinleog* s.v. summer), tapestry (*táipéis* s.v. imagery).

2.6. Is minic gur beag idir sainmhínithe Boy agus Bail nó gur mar a chéile go baileach iad agus nach fios mar sin cé acu a bhí mar fhoinse ag ÓBg, e.g.

> Boy agus Bail : Keel, a vessel for liquor(s) to stand and cool in.
> ÓBg : Keel, *soithioch ann a mbí deoch nuadh nó braithlis re fuara ann* .

2.7. Ba chuidiú ag ÓBg sainmhíniú i mBéarla nó i bhFraincis, nó uaireanta sa dá theanga, chomh maith le focal comhbhríoch go minic sa dá theanga, a bheith ag Boy. Uaireanta is é an sainmhíniú Fraincise a aistríonn sé, e.g.

> Boy : Dough : pate, farine détrempée dont on fait le pain.
> ÓBg : Dough, taos, min ar na dhéanadh na taos chum aráin.

Uaireanta eile is é an Béarla a aistríonn sé, e.g.

> Boy: Sceptics (philosophers contemplating things and leaving them in suspence professing they knew nothing). *Sceptiques, anciens philosophes qui doutoient de tout.*
>
> ÓBg: Scepticks, *sórt eagnuídheach do bhíodh ag léirsmuaineadh ar neithibh, agas dfágbhadh an tiomlán gan chríochnúghadh aga admháil nach ar thuigeadur éinídh.*

2.8. Téann ÓBg amú ar fad corruair agus é ag aistriú sainmhínithe, e.g. (i) de bharr gan 'wind-fall' a thuiscint agus an dá cheannfhocal 'by-blow (or a bastard)' agus 'a good by-blow (or wind-fall)' ag Boy a chur le chéile, rinne sé 'A by-blow bastard, *nó crann do leagfaoi le gaoith mhóir*', (ii) mheasc sé 'heron' le 'herring' agus rinne sé 'egret, *sórt scadáin* de' egret (a kind of heron)', (iii) scríobh sé 'boy' in áit 'bow' sa leagan 'his age has brought his body to the shape of a bow' s.v. 'bring', agus rinne sé '*thug a aos a cholann a riocht bhuachalla arí* de, (iv) d'aistrigh sé 'ham' *iosgad* agus 'ham' *baile margadh* go ceart ach *iosgaidín* a thug sé ar 'hamlet'.

3.1. Ní furasta anáil an Bhéarla agus nósanna lucht a labhartha a sheachaint i bhfoclóir Béarla–Gaeilge ós ar an teanga sin a chaitear é a bhunú, ach téann ÓBg chun áiféise nuair a mheasann gur gá a leithéid seo a aistriú: Free Bench is the Custom of the Manours of east and west Embourn and Chadleworth [...] that if a customary tenant die, the widow shall have her Dower [...] but if she commit incontinency she forfeits her estate; yet if she will come into the Court riding backwards on a black ram with his tail in her hand and say the words following, the steward is bound [...] to readmit her to her free bench: 'Here I am, riding upon a black ram, like a whore as I am; And for my crincum crancum, have lost my bincum bancum; And for my tails game have done this wordly shame; therefore I pray you Mr. Steward let me have my land again.' *Gnáthamh do bhí a Mainéaruibh an taoibh thoir agus thiar do Embourn .... Ag seo mise aniugh, ar Reithe mhór dhuibh, mur striapuigh do fuair guth, agus le mo thóinéis, do chaillios mo chóirléas agas tre mearbhull greadhalta do fuarus náire shaoghalta, ar an adhbhar soin, a Mhaighistir Stíobhard tabhair dhamh mh'innmhe tar ais.* [23 líne cló atá sa mBéarla, 26 san aistriú].

3.2. Anáil na Fraincise. Cé gur mhór an áis ag ÓBg foclóir Boy, bhí contúirt ann go leanfadh sé go ródhlúth de is nach ndéanfadh sé ach é a aistriú focal ar fhocal, rud a rinne sé uaireanta. Toradh amháin atá air sin is ea go mbíonn athrá sa Ghaeilge, (i) ag freastal ar fhoirm fhirinscneach agus bhaininscneach a d'oir a thabhairt sa Fhraincis, e.g. a jealous man (*un jaloux*), *fear éadmhar*; a jealous woman (*une jalouse*) *bean éadmhar*, (ii) focail éagsúla sa Fhraincis agus gan ach focal amháin sa Ghaeilge, e.g. a wild boar (*sanglier*), *collach fiadháin*; a young wild boar (*marcassin*), *collach óg fiadháin*. Sampla eile is ea an focal 'cruinniú' a bheith seacht n-uaire mar aistriú ar 'gather' i bhfrásaí ar leis na focail éagsúla Fraincise seo a léiriú a chuir Boy isteach iad: *moissonner* (arbhar), *vendanger* (grápaí), *amasser* (saibhreas), *cueiller* (bláthanna), *assembler* (arm), *se rouiller* (de mheirg), *se couvrir* (de dhusta). Níor mhór an tairbhe leagan Gaeilge a chur ar fhrásaí a bhain go dlúth le saol na Fraince mar iad seo: 'The Duke of Loraine was for cantling out some part of France which lay next to his territories 'nó 'St. Denis is the burying place for the the kings of France'.

3.3. Cé gur ag aistriú a bhíonn ÓBg go coitianta, tá neart leaganacha nádúrtha gaelacha aige, e.g. *teangaidh leam leat* double-tongued, *gan súghadh gan sútán* juiceless, *glúini geanalaigh agas craobhadh coimhneasa* pedigree, *sgéal ó bhéal go béal* hearsay, *lionán síth* incubus, *gan chuire gan iarra* without sending for, *ann a chulaith aonaigh agas oireachtuis*, in his pontificalibus, *spreallaire dona díomhaoin* lazy-bones. Ní bhíonn ceal focal air agus é ag cur síos ar dhaoine, e.g. weak, *lag, éiglídhe, amhneirt, gan bhrígh gan tapa, gan lúth gan luadur, gan spionnadh gan spracadh, fann.*

3.4. Ní i gcónaí a bhí ÓBg taobh le haistriúchán. Is minic leis aguisín uaidh féin a chur leis an sainmhíniú (cló iodálach ar an aguisín anseo), e.g. robin, spideog mhuire, *éinín beag ceannsa*; highlander, neach áitígheas ann áirdshléibhtibh *.i. albanach gaodhalach* ; onion, inniún, *sórt luibhe do bheir a thora ann a phréimh agas a shíol ann a bharr*; goat-wilker [recte m-], sgréachóg oídhche *.i.ean aga mbí radhrac*[sic] *san oídhche agus nach bhfaicionn énídh san ló.*

3.5. Bhí spéis ar leith ag Ó Beaglaoich, sagart, i gcúrsaí reiligiúin, eiriceachtaí, agus oird sagart, agus tá eolas breise ar na cúrsaí sin aige nach bhfuil ag Boy ná ag Bail, e.g. ainm bhunaitheoir na Norbertins, Norbert Easpog Madgeburg, is gur sa bliain 1120 a bunaíodh iad. Féach freisin Pelagians, Petrobusians, etc., etc.

3.6. Níorbh annamh tuairimí an údair sna seanfhoclóirí Béarla. Is corruair a ligeann ÓBg a dhearcadh féin linn, ach tar éis dó míniú Boy a aistriú s.v. cucking-stool, *stól túmthaigh .i. óirnís do hórduígheadh chum sgollóirídhe ban nó chum mná buaidheartha do smachtúghadh* [...], cuireann sé leis an t-aguisín *agus is tearc smachtuíghthear iad.*

De réir Boy ba ionann 'palmer' agus 'pilgrim', rud nár aontaigh OBg leis. Scríobh sé os cionn céad focal ag léiriú na ndifríochtaí eatarthu. Taispeánann sé an drochmheas a bhí aige, mar dhuine a raibh cleachtadh aige ar mheadarachtaí casta na Gaeilge, ar 'blank verse' a mhíníonn sé mar seo: *rann gan réim gan réasún gan uaighim gan aiste.*

Shílfeá gur racht feirge a bhuail é agus é ag sainmhíniú 'A Newgate bird' mar seo: *striapach fir nó mná, amhnaireach, uaillmhianach, earráideach, easonórach, bhréagach, bhuaidheartha, mhasluíghtheach, bhrúideamhuil, mhiostuama, bhradach, mhadramhuil, mhíonáireach.* B'fhéidir gur chomhrá le Aodh Buidhe, fear a chaith tréimhse i bpríosún Newgate i mBaile Átha Cliath, a spreag an sainmhíniú sin.

3.7. Uaireanta is ag cur le dea-chlú a thíre féin a bhíonn sé, e.g. microcosm, *domhan beag agas do bheir Ptolomy an tainm soin doiléan na héirionn ar mhéad a tora*; bug, *péisdeog bhréan mhillteach, chuireas buaidhreadh ar dhaoinibh ann a leabthaibh san oidhche a Saxaibh san bhfrainc, agas a mórán do thíribh oile, gidheadh ní faicthear iad a Néirinn;* house, *teagh, teaghas,* long, *bruíghean,* longport, *eachruis, cóisir, amhuil mur bhí a tteamhair na righ .i. an long laighneach teagh ann a mbídis uaisle laighean, an chóisir chonnachtach, teagh an a mbídís uaisle Connacht, an Eachrais ulaidh, teagh an a mbídís uaisle uladh, an bhruighean Muimh-neach, teagh an a mbídís uaisle Muimhneach.*[15]

3.8. Os a choinne sin ní luaitear Éire agus na focail 'kern' ná 'skein' ná na focail seo leanas á míniú: culdeys, *sórt daoine riaghalta do bhí a Nalbain a nallód*; druid, *draoigh, sagairt agas eagnuígheach ameasg na senbhrio-tainnioch, agas na bhfranncach*; bog-trotter, *ceithearnach coille, gaduighe* (mar a bhfuil 'coureur de marais, c'est ainsi qu'on appelle les voleurs d'Irlande [...]' ag Boy).

3.9. **Seanfhocail agus frásaí meafartha.** Is cuid suntais a mbíodh de sheanfhocail i bhfoclóirí dátheangacha tráth, agus ní taise do ÓBg é. Má bhíonn seanfhocal comhbhríoch dúchasach sa dara teanga ní bhíonn aon deacracht ann, e.g. to teach one's grandam to grope ducks, *uan do mhúnadh méilídhe dá mháthair.* Uaireanta aistríonn ÓBg an Béarla agus ansin tugann sé an seanfhocal dúchasach, e.g. you count your chickens before they are hatched, *áirmhidh tú d'éanacha súl fá léigthear amach iad, cró roimh na harcuibh.*

3.10. Oibríonn sé na bealaí eile seo freisin, (i) éirim an Bhéarla ach gan aon seanfhocal dúchasach a thabhairt, e.g. to take a hair of the same dog, *do dhul ag ól arís tar éis oídhche*; (ii) aistriú focal ar fhocal agus ansin a bhrí sin a mhíniú, e.g. to make ducks and drakes with one's money, *lachuin agas bárdail a dhéanadh d'airgiott dhuine .i. a chaithiomh go saob[h]-nósach*; (iii) aistriú ar an mBéarla agus ansin aistriú ar an sainmhíniú Fraincise, e.g. to pour water on a drowned mouse, *uisge do dhortadh ar luchóig bháighte .i. díbhfeirg do dhéanadh ar neach anbhfann ann nach bhfuil é féin do chosnamh* (= 'se venger lâchement d'une personne qui n'est en état de se défendre'); (iv) ré-aistriú ar an bhFraincis amháin, e.g. the devil rebukes sin (le renard prêche aux poules), *do ghnídh an sionnach searmóin dona geadheachaibh.*

4.1. **Forbairt an stór focal agus cumadóireacht.** Nuair a bhíonn údar foclóra dhátheangaigh gan aon fhocal a fhreagraíonn do fhocal iasachta ní bhíonn

---

[15] Cf. Seathrún Ceitinn, *Foras Feasa ar Éirinn* (Londain 1908) III, 543–52.

le déanamh aige ach (i) sainmhíniú a thabhairt, nó (ii) focal nuachumtha a oibriú. Oibríonn ÓBg an dá mhodh, e.g. (i) tea, *sórt gas do bhíos san India, nó na duilleogadh, deoch do ghníthear dana duilleoga céadna*; (ii) banker, *stórchúmhduíghtheoir*. Uaireanta déanann sé an dá rud faoin gceannfhocal amháin, e.g. geographer, *neach do sgríobhus nó do thuigeas tráchtadh na g[c]ríoch .i. críochstarthóir*.

4.2. Seo thíos na haicmí focal is mó a mbíonn cumadóireacht i gceist le freastal orthu :

(a)   aidiacht, e.g. *báisdeamhuil* pluvious, *collachamhuil* boarish, *flaithios-amhúil* heavenly; *cailíonta* girlish, *uachtaránta* imperious.

(b)   ainm teibí, e.g. *carraigeamhlacht* rockiness, *claonamhlacht* proclivity, *eagailseamhlacht* s.v. layty, *neamhdhuineatacht* inhumanity, *síothai-geantacht* placability.

(d)   ainm ceardaí nó gníomhaí, e.g. *árachóir* insurer, *brostuightheoir* instigator, *dlúthadóir* joyner, *péatróir* pewterer, *moghsantóir* inslaver, *tairgseanóir* bidder, *uaigheadóir*, grave-maker.

(e)   briathar, e.g. *amuidiughadh* befool, *cantúnadh* canton, *cásadh* cage, *colgadh* bristle, *searmóineadh* preach, *úrláradh* floor.

4.3. Le cois úsáid na n-iarmhíreanna dúchasacha atá sna samplaí thuas, oibríonn ÓBg na gnáthbhealaí eile seo le cur leis an stór focal, e.g.

(a) réimir, aidiacht nó ainmfhocal a chur le focal dúchasach, e.g. *aith-bhreathnúghadh* review, *deaghfhoghlumtha* well-read, *réamh-órdúghadh* predestination, *tuiléadach* apron ; *cianmhaoin* legacy, *diainghliocus* policy, *dileagra* address, *dlúthdhorchacht* opacity, *saor-aigeantacht* openness; *ceolchuirm* consort of music, *coirpbheirt* raiment, *coisliathróid* football, *cúilcheannach* bribe s.v.account.

(b) frásfhocal agus ainm sa ghinideach nó aidiacht mar dhara mír, e.g. *crann ualach* hod, *leabhar laetheamhuil* journal, *liathróid ionnalta* savonet, *roithleoir iomchair* wheel-barrow s.v. handle, *sgríbhneoir aithiseach* satiryst.

(c) gaelú ar iasacht, e.g. *bombarduígheacht* bombardment, *caimeiliún* camelion, *caimléatt*, camlet, *caitín* catkin s.v. gosling, *meisliún* meslin, *muislín* musselin.

(d) aistriú focal ar fhocal, e.g. *airgead tinnteáin* heart[h]money, *bogha báistíg[h]e* rainbow, *cathaoir uillionn* elbow chair, *lámhchlog* hand-bell, *sgian phinn* penknife.

4.4. Ní iontas ar bith é malairtí litrithe a bheith i leabhar de cuid an ochtú haois déag tráth nach raibh caighdeán docht ann. Is iomaí focal a bhfuil malairt litrithe ag ÓBg air, go fiú faoin gceannfhocal céanna, ní áirim ó ionad go chéile sa leabhar, e.g. *caithiomh, caithiodh, cathamh, cathadh* mar ainm briathartha s.v.cast. Is ábhar spéise í an mhalairt nó an giorrú a thugann leid dúinn i dtaobh na cainte nó na canúna. (Is minic an litriú ceart stairiúil ar na focail seo faoi cheannfhocail eile). Seo roinnt samplaí:

(a) Bá na gconsan *-dh, -gh*, caol agus leathan, sa siolla deiridh neamh-aiceanta, e.g. *geimhre* winter, *iarra* to request, *teagh samhra* summer-house, *do dhearbha sí* s.v. sacred; agus neamhbhrí na gconsan sin á léiriú ag na consain bhreise iontu seo: *drumagh* drum, *fear déantadh leannadh* s.v. furnace, *doimhnidh* depth s.v. sound, *brístigh* s.v. gantlope.

(b) Bá *bh, mh, dh, gh*, i lár focail, e.g. *dúllán* (dubhshlán) s.v. buff, *scrín* (scríbhinn) writ, *dathúil* brave, *braoine* (bruidhne) s.v. jangle, *bairíon* (bairghean) cake. Léiriú ar bhá *bh* idir gutaí is ea é a mhalartú le *gh*, e.g. bh > gh: *foghar* (= fabhar s.v. give, *rogha* (= rabhadh) harbinger; *tuibhe* (= tuighe) straw. Cf. *mh* in áit *dh* in *riamhánuíghe* (= riadh-) jockey.

(c) *thmh > thf* (= *f*), *thbh, mhth > f*, e.g. *maithfeach* s.v. allowance, *anchaithfeach* lavish, *tuaifill* (tuaithbhill gin.) s.v. eddy, *sgafadh* (scamhtha) codded.

(d) *dl, nl, ln > ll*, e.g. *colla* (codladh) asleep, *múllach* (múnlach) dirt, *cloch olladh* ([...] olna) stone of wool.

(e) Bá *th* ndiaidh *m*, e.g. *d'imigh mé* went, *timire* (timthire) usher.

(f) *ch* caol > *mhth* (= *f*) sa bhfocal *cluimhthidh* game.

(g) Nuair a thagann an consan céanna ag deireadh réimíre agus ag tosach an bhunfhocail aon chonsan amháin a scríobh, e.g. *drocháil* (droch-cháil) slander, *buídhearg* (buidhe-dhearg) brawney, *ruaghrua-gach* (ruadh-ghruagach) sandy, *caoilionn* (caoil-lionn) beer, *cómaith* (comh maith) good, *coimeinic* (comh meinic) oft, *neamothuigheach* (neamh-mothuigheach) s.v. stupify, *neimeasardha* (neimh-measartha) intemporate, *rúnochtadh* (rún-nochtadh), *diamharún* (diamhair-rún) mistery, *crosúilioch* (cros-súileach) blear-eyed, *glasúileach* (glas-súileach) gray-eyed.

(h) *r* tosaigh leathan, e.g. *racadóir* seller, *roimh rae* afore, *rae* moon, *ramhar* fat, *raobadh* rend, *raolt* star, *raomadh* flegm, *snaidhm ratha* slip-knot.

(i) an fhuaim *ae* a bheith ag *ao*, e.g. *hataor* haberdasher, *haitéar* hatter, *moirtéar* s.v. hod, *murtfhaor, murtaol* morter. Féach freisin *raobadh, raolt, raomadh* thuas.

(j) *a > u, ea > io* sa chéad siolla roimh *á* nó *ó* sa dara siolla, e.g.*cuisleán* s.v.turret, *cusóg* justacor, *fiodán* hicket, *fiorán* dove, *lionán* incubus, *niosgóid* beal, *priobán* s.v. mend, *siolánach* knave.

4.5. Bhí deis ag Ó Beaglaoich canúintí éagsúla a chloisteáil i gColáiste na nGael i bPáras, deis níos fearr ná a bheadh aige dá bhfanfadh sé in aon cheantar amháin in Éirinn. Is cinnte go mbíodh caint ar leaganacha éagsúla d'fhocail is ar fhocail éagsúla ar an gcoincheap chéanna i measc na nGaeilgeoirí ansin. Ní miste a mheabhrú gur sa choláiste céanna sin a scríobh Seán Ó Maoildhia leabhar gramadaí[16] a raibh sé liosta déag is fiche ann de leaganacha ag léiriú éagsúlachtaí canúna a bhí le cloisteáil aige ó na mic léinn ansin. [Sa bhliain 1867 a foilsíodh an leabhar, sula raibh an focal 'canúineolaíocht' ná 'dialectology' ar an saol].

4.6. Léiríonn Ó Beaglaoich a spéis sna canúintí in ailt den chineál seo: Dog s.v. *Madara, mada, maduigh, nó gadhar, do réir canumhna gach críche an éirinn.* Seo thíos riar samplaí d'fhoirmeacha éagsúla nó d'fhocail éagsúla a cuireadh isteach le ceannfhocal d'aon ghnó, ní hionann agus malairt litrithe a bheith de neamhaistear ó cheannfhocal go chéile nó i bhfrásaí, e.g. *aibhsiúghadh, taibhsiúghadh,* glorying; *ainrianta nó ainshrianta,* profligate; *blaosg nó plaosg,* shell; *bos nó bas,* buffet; *do dhéana cuiginne nó maistre,* churn; *cunnach nó caonnach,* moss; *deargnuit, dreangcuid,* flea; *faill nó aill,* cliff; *fathach nó athach* giant; *fiadhaile nó fiataoil,* weed; *feamuinn nó feamnach,* sea-wrack; *gabáiste nó cabáiste,* cabbage; *láighídhe, rábhann, cuibe* spade; *saimnéadh, saimléar,* chimney; *tolladh simléir, polladh simnéir,* funnel; *sinneán nó soighneán gaoithe,* puff; *smól nó spól,* shuttle; *téiglígheacht nó éiglígheacht,* weakness; *úirlis, óirnís,* implement.

[16] John H. Molloy, *A Grammar of the Irish Language* (1867).

4.7. Is minicí gur de neamhaistear le ceannfhocail éagsúla a bhíonn na foirmeacha éagsúla, e.g. *aimhrios* s.v. indeed, *amharus* doubt; *brúille* scrap, *blúiridh* pinch; *bugsadh* snuff-box, *busga* box; *doiséan* dozen, *duisín* s.v. gross; *fóirnís* stove, *fóirnéis* furnace; *lochtadh* loft, *lotadh* roost, *loftadh* garret; *ridire an ghairtéil* s.v. garter, r. *an ghairtéir* s.v. pall.

5.1. Cuid suntais a bhfuil d'fhocail ag ÓBg nach bhfuil sna foclóirí a foilsíodh roimhe, is iad sin ÓCl agus Ld, ná in DIL, ná Pl[17] nár foilsíodh fós. Seo thíos samplaí:

> (i) focail a bhfuil cuid acu i gcaint na Gaeltachta i gcónaí agus go bhfuil cuma na barántúlachta ar an gcuid eile acu. (A–C amháin): e.g. *achar* distance, *aibhseoir* braggard, fop, *áirdleog* toss, *aisge[adh]* to louse, *aisde gheirriaigh* form, *aisdeoir* jester, *aisdeoireacht* play, *aisdígheacht* stage play, *amarrán* nicampoop, *anshrán* ladle, *árachus* insurance, *beárnadh mhíl* hare-lip, *barrbéiseach* imperious, *bataireacht* club law, *beannaire* kill-cow, *cailín béirnéiseach* minx, *biotóg* gird (= jibe), (*do dhéanamh*) *borrachuis* to lord it, *brach* bear, *braimseánta, bramurrusach* s.v. huff, *breallsún* changeling, *breillicidh* lozel, *brillsgeánta* masty, *brinléan* choke of artichoke, *bruill-sgeántacht* impetuosity, *búibiollán* coxcomb, *cámálta* demure, *caonrus* tenderness, *caradrach* humane, *ceirtiochán* tatter-de-mallion, *cionnuaisgneach* mobile, *clamhdóir* shabb, *cloch rothnóis* mocking stock, *clodhaire* midwall, *coinnle braonáin* icicles, *cosdubh leathair* leather bottle, *cnámhnáireach* demure s.v. butter, *cnáimhín súgach* huckle bone, *crann dhealbhthaidh* warping loom, *creamaire* hawker, *créimioch* cripple, *crimse[á]il chainnte* grumble, *criothruas* lubricity, *crithéisioch* gamesome, *critiorluasach* (in a) huff, *cruinneán féir* hay cock .

> (ii) iasachtaí ón Nua-Bhéarla: e.g. *bailléad* pasquil, *béar* bear, *bíomadh* joyst, *boighteoir*, allurer, *bórdúir* s.v. indent, *buidséatsídhe* mustaches, *caidéal* pump, *cóta buiff* buff, *caimléatt* camlet, *caimeilliún* camelion, *caitín* gosling (= catkin), *cathfuire* caviller, *ciotal* kettle, *coimionóid* community, *cuitéal* cuttle, *cúirliún* curlew.

> (iii) focail a bhfuil blas na cumadóireachta orthu: e.g. *biaghchluain* kitchin, *brainfhíon* brandy, *bréigchiabhadóir* perwig-maker, *breiseoir* usurer, *buntasgóir* do-all, *cailbhínteacht* calvinism, *cíoradóir* comb-

[17] Tá mé faoi chomaoin ag an Dr. Seán Ua Súilleabháin, Scoil an Léinn Cheiltigh, Institiuid Ardléinn Bhaile Átha Cliath, a chuidigh liom leis an eolas i dtaobh an fhoclóra seo a chinntiú.

maker, *comhachtóir* commissioner, *comhghráidhtheóir* rival, *cosadh*
to kick, *crann ualach* hod, *críochsmacht* government, *críochstarthóir*
geographer, *crosaighneas* objections.

Fch. freisin 4,2, thuas.

6.1. D'fhág ÓBg a bheag nó a mhór de lorg ar na foclóirí a tháinig ina
dhiaidh. Ní luaitear sna liostaí thíos ach focail nach bhfuil in ÓCl, Pl· Ld,
ná *DIL*.

6.2. Ba é Bullet an chéad duine eile a d'fhoilsigh foclóir Gaeilge. Ceann é
ar ar éigean atá aon eolas air anois, toisc, is dóigh, nach luaitear é i
mbioblagraif an léinn ghaelaigh. Luaitear ÓBg mar fhoinse sa réamhrá[18]
agus is léir gur baineadh an-leas agus míleas as, ach is iomaí botún litrithe
atá ann.[19] Seo thíos samplaí d'fhocail a fuair Bull in ÓBg. (Má tá litriú
éagsúil ag Bull, seachas easpa síne fhada, cuirtear sin idir lúibíní leis an
míniú Fraincise anseo thíos):

> e.g. (i) *gé thiar* bum (fesses), *ládas* firmness (fermeté […]), *leithéis*
> derision (dé-), *mánta* demure (sérieux), *pullóg* pantry ([…] paneterie),
> *tilte* glib, learned (glissant […] savant […]), *tlochtán* hoarseness
> (*tlosan* voix enrouée), *tonnadóir* tunnel (*tonadoir* entonnoir).

> (ii) focail a bhfuil blas na cumadóireachta orthu: e.g. *biaghchluain*
> kitchin (cuisine), *breiseoir* usurer (usurier), *cianmhaoin* legacy (legs),
> *dileagra* address (adresse), *díolchuan* shop (boutique), *diolchúram*
> negotiation (*diolchuran* id.), *díolchomann* confederacy (*diolchoman*
> confédération), *gléachás* gallery (galerie), *tuilcheannach* hansel
> (étrennes), *tuiléadach* apron (*tuleadach* tablier), *tulaigne* aim (*tulaign*
> miré, visée).

6.3. Ní raibh ÓBg i bhfad ar fáil nuair a thosaigh ÓN ar fhoclóir Gaeilge–
Béarla a chur le chéile timpeall na bliana 1734, foclóir a chríochnaigh sé
faoi 1739, agus nár foilsíodh fós. Is léir gur bhain sé leas as ÓBg. Seo thíos
roinnt samplaí ar ionann iad sa dá fhoclóir ach neamhshuim a dhéanamh
den síne fada a bheith ar iarraidh ag ÓN. Ar thaobh na láimhe deise den
leathanach a fágadh bán le haghaidh ábhar breise atá na focail seo ag ÓN:

> e.g. *achar* distance, *búibiollán* coxcomb, *carraigeamhlacht* rockiness,
> *cathfuire* caviller, *cosdubh* leather bottle (a black jack or can of leather

---

[18] Luaitear é gan ainm údair mar seo: *Dictionaire Anglois-Irlandois imprimé a Paris 1732.* Cé nach
luaitear Ld mar fhoinse tá a lorg go follasach ar Bull.

[19] Cuid de na botúin níos measa ná a chéile, e.g. 'snaletipse, *aujourdhui, maintenant, dans le siécle ou
nous vivons* < now adays, *sna laethibhse.*

ÓN), *crannóg mhuilinn* mill hopper, *criothfhuar* coldish, *dianghrádh* darling, *dileagra(-dh* ÓN) address, *dísgín, leanbh do bhearthar do dhuine lánaosta* dilling (an old man's infant ÓN), *dlúthchara* adherent, *drilleán* drill, *fágóid* fagot, *fóiséatt (-éad* ÓN) faucet, *garrán* fortress, *óimle* homily, *sailéaracht* cellarage, *trudán ar a gcurthar páipéir,* (a file to file letters ÓN), *tuilcheannach* hansel, *tulaigne* design, aim.

6.4. Ní luaitear ÓBg ar liosta na bfoinsí in OBr, foclóir Gaeilge–Béarla a foilsíodh i bPáras sa bhliain 1768 agus níl aon fhianaise sa téacs féin a chinnteodh anáil ÓBg a bheith air.

6.5. Bhain foclóirithe an 19ú haois an-leas as ÓBg. Ar fhoclóir Béarla–Gaeilge is fusa lorg ÓBg a fheiceáil. Seo thíos samplaí as Conn (1814) atá ag freagairt go cruinn do ÓBg. Is rímhinic na sínte fada ar iarraidh in Conn. Cuirtear isteach anseo iad:

> e.g. cabinet *armaire,* canopy *léarfhalach,* chink *faosgladh,* client *bunaire,* elephant *trod,* fortress *garrán,* giddy *diúdánach,* gruff *graincéadanach, fícheachantach,* gudgeon *gúda,* handle *láimh-ghreidhm,* homily *óimle,* jockey *riamhánaíghe,* map *léarsgáil,* massacre *slaodmharbhadh,* padlock *glas fraincín,* pet *spuaic,* policy *diainghliocus,* tawney *téathbhuidhe,* wig *bréigchiabh.*

6.6. Is mór an riar focal ag OR atá ag freagairt go cruinn do ÓBg idir Ghaeilge agus mhíniú. Tharlódh gur ag Sh, foclóir ar bhain sé an-leas as, a fuair sé cuid acu. De bhreis ar mhórán focal atá ar an gcéad liosta thuas in 5.1. atá freisin aige, tá na samplaí thíos. Murab ionann go baileach leagan OR agus leagan ÓBg cuirtear idir lúibíní é, ach déantar neamhshuim den síne fada a bhíonn ar iarraidh go minic aige:

> e.g. (D–U) *díbheach* ant, *dileagra* address, *dínéadach* frock, *díol-bhoth* shop s.v. goldsmith, *díolchomann* confederacy (*diolcoman*), *díolchuan* shop, *diolchúram* negotiation (díolchuram), *diúdánach* giddy, *gúda* gudgeon, *lámhdóir* glover (*lámhdhóir*), *léarsgáil* map, *olcóir* offender, *pacadh* pack, *piollaire* pill, *puinteálta* precise, *ráigeamhuil* impetuous, *riamhánaíghe* jockey, *spuaic* a pet, *trod* elephant, *trudán ar a gcurthar páipéir* file, (a file for papers), *tuil-cheannach* hansel, *tuiléadach* apron, *téathbhuidhe* tawney.

6.7. Ba aon teanga amháin an Ghaeilge agus an Ghàidhlig ag foclóirithe an 18ú agus an 19ú haois. Mar sin ní miste lorg ÓBg ar Sh a thabhairt faoi deara go háirithe toisc gur bhain OR an-leas as Sh. Is mar a chéile idir

Bhéarla agus Ghaeilge cuid de na hiontrálacha seo thíos. Murab ionann baileach leagan Sh cuirtear idir lúibíní é. Ní bhíonn aon síneadh fada ag Sh:

> e.g. *achar* distance, *anshrán* ladle, *árachas* insurance, *armaire* cabinet (cupboard, closet), *bataireacht* club law (cudgelling [...]), *béar* bear, (*do dhéanadh*) *borrachuis* to hector (*borrachas* hectoring), *caidéal* pump, *caidiol* horologe (sun-dial), *ceolchuirm* concert, *cnámhnáireach* demure, *coisliathróid* football, *críochsmacht* government, *cúil-cheannach* (*cuilcheannag*) bribe, *cuirpeoir* brabbler (carper).

6.8. Rinne Peadar Ó Conaill foclóir Gaeilge–Béarla, c. 1826, foclóir nár foilsíodh riamh, ach ar bhain foclóirithe an-leas as. Scrúdaigh sé ÓBg. go mion agus bhain liosta fada focal as.[20] Bhí ardmheas ag a chomharsa Eoghan Ó Comhraidhe air is gan aon mheas aige ar ÓBg.[21] Ach is léir anáil ÓBg ar ÓCon. Seo thíos samplaí d'iontrálacha ar mar a chéile sa dá fhoclóir iad, seachas miondifríochtaí litrithe nó Béarla ag ÓCon atá idir lúibíní:

> e.g. *aisge* to louse (*aisceam*), *brach* a bear, *caidéal* pump (*-eal*), *caidiol* sun-dial (*-eal*), *cathfuire* caviller (*cafaire* prattler, babbler), *céilígheacht* copulation (*-idheacht*), *creamaire* hawker, *críochsmacht* government (territorial g.), *crithéisioch* gamesome (*-each*, fickle, giddy), *dor* door, *fágóid* fagot, *marbhán* margin, *ócumus* oakum (*ócamas*), *siobóitt* chibbot (*-óid*), *stuif* stuff (*stuf*)), *tuiléadach* apron.

6.9. Is é an foclóir Gaeilge–Béarla le Coneys an foclóir is cruinne leagan amach is ábhar a foilsíodh san 19ú haois. Toisc gurbh é an cuspóir cinnte a bhí aige cuidiú le lucht teagaisc chreidimh trí Ghaeilge ba ar an mBíobla is mó a bhunaigh sé a shaothar, ach tá corrfhocal aige a shíolraigh ó ÓBg, focail is dóigh a fuair sé ag OR:

> e.g. *ainchríostamhlacht*, infidelity, *boighte* allurement, *boighteoir* allurer, *ceolchuirm* concert, *cianmhaoin* legacy, *coisliathróid* football, *díolcomhán* (*diolcomhan* OR, *díolchomann* ÓBg) confederacy, *díolchúram* (*díol-* OR, *diol-* ÓBg) negotiation.

---

[20] 'Focail áirighthe as Fhoclóir Béarla–Gaoidheilge Aodha Bhuidhe Mhic Cruitín', LS 23 C 26 (a) 25, in Acadamh Ríoga na hÉireann; ag deireadh an liosta focal tá *'words proper to insert out of Hugh Mc Curtin's Dictionary'* id. 59.

[21] *'This dictionary is the best now known for the Irish language of the the last 150 years'*, signed: Eugene Curry, *Catalogue of Irish Manuscripts in the British Library*, 1 (1992) 162. *'Peter O'Connell* [...] *the best Irish scholar in the Ireland of a centuary ago'*, T.F. O'Rahilly, *The Irish Book Lover*, 8 (1917), 6.

6.10. Is é an Bíobla an fhoinse is mó a luann Foley ina fhoclóir Béarla–Gaeilge a foilsíodh sa bhliain 1855, ach is léir lorg ÓBg air cé gur dóigh gur ag OR a fuair sé na focail seo a fhreagraíonn do ÓBg go cruinn:

> e.g. *biadhchluain* kitchen, *cianmhaoin* legacy, *coisliathróid* football, *críochsmacht* government, *críochstarthóir* geographer, *dileagra* address, *diainghliocus* policy, *díolbhoth* shop, *diolchuram* (*díol-* Fol) negotiation, *gléachás* (*-as* Fol), *trod* elephant, *trudán* file, *tuiléadach* apron.

7.1. Maireann anáil ÓBg i bhfoclóirí na haoise seo agus dá bharr sin sa Ghaeilge choiteann. Seo samplaí d'fhocail a shíolraigh ó ÓBg, go díreach nó trí fhoclóirí eile, agus atá in ÓD nó in FGB (leagan ÓD nó FGB idir lúibíní más éagsúil):

> e.g. (a) (in ÓD amháin), *biotóg* gird, *bréigchiabh* wig, *cárnán c(h)aocháin* mole-hill, *díbheach* ant, *dileagradh* to address, *iasgloch* fishpond, *láimhghrei(dh)m* handle, *síothaigeantacht* placability, *tais-liochar* moistness (moisture), *tuiléadach* apron, *tuilcheannach* handsel

> e.g (b) (in ÓD agus FGB), *báisteamhail* pluvious, *bruachbhaile* suburb, *caidéal* pump, *caitín* catkin, *ceannuaiscneach* (*-uaisneach* ÓD) rash (-headed), *ceolchuirm* (*-choirm* FGB) concert, *dileagra* address, *díothdhaoineadh* (*dídhaoiniú*, FGB,*-iughadh* ÓD) depopulate, *giofóg* gipsy, *glas fraincín* padlock, *grianstad* solstice, *láimhleabhar* manual, *snáthadóir* needle-maker, *sporadóir* spur-maker, *tabharthóir* giver, donor; *tonnadóir* funnel, tunnel (tundish).

> e.g. (c) (in FGB amháin), *aibhseoir* fop, *bailléad* pasquil (*bailéad* ballad), *bombarduígheacht* bombardment, *caimléatt* (*caimleat*) camlet, *caimeilliún* camelion (*caimileon* chameleon), *gé b(h)eag* giblets, *miondíol* retail [s.v. by], *sgiathshúileach*, wall-eyed, *uisgrian* (*uiscerian*) aqueduct.

7.2. Is é ONL is mó a bhain solamar as ÓBg sa bhfichiú haois. Samplaí ar mar a chéile iad sa dá fhoclóir:

> e.g. *armaire* cabinet, *bréigchiabhadóir* wigmaker, *breiseoir* usurer, *cailín béirnéiseach* minx, *carraigeamhlacht* rockiness, *cianmhaoin* legacy, *coisliathróid* football, *comhghráidhtheoir* rival, *críochsmacht* government, *críochstarthóir* geographer, *diainghliocas* policy, *díbheach* ant, *dileagra* address, *díolchuan*, *díolbhrugh* shop, *dlúthadóir* joyner, *fuathadóir* abhorrer, (*amhail*) *gótach* gothic, *maide*

measg .i.topa maide bhíos ag aos óg *dá bhualadh timchioll* gig,
raeltiasg five-foot (=starfish) (*réiltiasg*), *raitín* ratteen, *roithleoir
iomchair* wheelbarrow [s.v.handle], *sgiathshúileach* wall-eyed, *snásán*
lick (=blow), *snáthadóir* needle-maker, *stóirbhriseadh* bankrupt,
tabharthóir giver s.v. precarious, *tairgseanóir* bidder, *trod* elephant,
trudán (ar a gcurthar páipéir) file, *uaigheadóir* grave-maker, *uisgrian*
aqueduct.

7.3. Le cois na bhfocal aonair bhain ONL go leor frásaí as ÓBg:

e.g. *trod a dhéanadh do chuil* .i. *morán cáis do dhéanadh do nídh shuarach*
ÓBg s.v.elephant, id. (ach […] dhéanamh) ONL; *do ghnídh Uirgil Aongus
n-a dheimhnightheoir dhána ar a shubháilcibh féin* ÓBg s.v. avoucher, id.
ONL; *sléibhtidh do dhéanadh do na carnánuibh caocháin, nó míolmhór do
dhéana do chuileog* s.v.mole hill ÓBg; *sléibhte do dhéanamh de
charnánaibh caochán nó míolmór do dhéanamh de mhíoltóig* ONL.

FOCAL SCOIR

Ní ceart an Beaglaíoch a lochtú ná a mheas de réir chaighdeán cheirde na
foclóireachta sna laetha seo. Ní miste na botúin iomadúla cló a mhaitheamh
dó, mar ba dhosheachanta a leithéid 'especially in a work under the Hands
of a Printer equally ignorant both of the English and the Irish' mar a deir sé
féin sa réamhrá, agus ina theannta sin gur ag plé le cló coimhthíoch a bhí
an printéir. Is ceart a mheabhrú freisin, ainneoin shaothar foclóireachta na
bProinsiasach go háirithe i Lobháin, nár éirigh leosan foclóir a fhoilsiú,
agus gur caitheadh os cionn ceithre scór bliain sular foilsíodh an chéad
fhoclóir Béarla–Gaeilge eile sa bhliain 1814. Tá súil gur leor na leideanna a
tugadh thuas ar ghnéithe áirithe de shaothar seo Uí Bheaglaoich lena
thaispeáint gurbh fhiú taighde mionchruinn a dhéanamh air mar fhoinse
thábhachtach eolais ar stair agus staid na teanga san 18ú haois, foinse ar
ligeadh faillí inti go dtí seo, b'fhéidir de thoradh an droch-cheann a chaith
Ó Comhraidhe leis.

NODA[22]

Bail	Nathan Bailey, *Dictionarium Britannicum*, Londain, 1730
Boy	A. Boyer, *Le Dictionnaire François-Anglais et Anglois-François*, Londain, 1753
Bull	M. Bullet, *Mémoires sur la Langue Celtique*, Besançon, 1753

[22] Baile Átha Cliath ionad an fhoilsithe mura luaitear a mhalairt.

Coneys	T. de Vere Coneys, *Focloir Gaoidhilge-sacs-Bearla or The Irish-English Dictionary*, 1849
Conn	T. Connellan, *An English–Irish Dictionary*, 1814
DIL	E.G. Quin ⅂ al., *Dictionary of the Irish Language*, Acadamh Ríoga na hÉireann, 1913–76
FGB	N. Ó Dónaill, *Foclóir Gaeilge-Béarla*, 1977
Fol	Daniel Foley, *An English-Irish Dictionary*, 1855
Ld	Edward Lhuyd, 'Foclóir Gaoidheilge-Shagsonach', in *Archaeologia Britannica*, Oxford, 1707
ÓBg	Conchobhar Ó Beaglaoich mar aon le congnamh Aodh bhuidhe mac Cuirtin, *The English Irish Dictionary. An Focloir Bearla Gaoidheilge*, Páras, 1732
OBr	John O'Brien, *Focalóir Gaoidhilge-Sax-Bhéarla*, Páras, 1768
ÓCl	Mícheál Ó Cléirigh, *Focloir no Sanasan Nua*, Lobháin, 1643
ÓCon	Peadar Ó Conaill, [*Foclóir Gaeilge–Béarla*] 1826, cóip in Acadamh Ríoga na hÉireann de LS Egerton 83, Leabharlann na Breataine
ÓD	Patrick S. Dinneen, *Foclóir Gaedhilge agus Béarla*, 1927
ÓN	Tadhg Ua Neachtain, [*Foclóir Gaedhilbhéarlach*], 1739 (Ls H.1.6 Coláiste na Tríonóide)
ONL	T. O'Neill Lane, *Larger English–Irish Dictionary*, 1916
OR	Edward O'Reilly, *An Irish–English Dictionary*, 1821
Pl	Risteard Pluincéad, [Vocabularium Latinum et Hibernum], 1662 (Ls Z.4.2.5 Leabharlann Marsh)
Sh	William Shaw, *A Galic and English Dictionary*, London 1780

On a Nominal Analysis of Welsh Verb-Nouns

ROBERT D. BORSLEY

University of Wales, Bangor

1. INTRODUCTION

LIKE all the Celtic languages, Welsh has what are traditionally known as verb-nouns (VNs) where English has a non-finite verb of some kind.[1] In Borsley (1993), I argue against the view, advanced in Willis (1988) and Fife (1990), that Welsh VNs are nouns and show that they have a variety of verbal properties. In his recent book on Welsh syntax, Rouveret (1994) develops an analysis of Welsh VNs in which they are verbs but verbs which like nouns are embedded in a DP. In this paper, I will take a critical look at Rouveret's analysis and argue that it faces serious problems. These problems suggest that the analysis is untenable and hence that Welsh VNs cannot be assimilated to nouns even in the limited way that Rouveret proposes.

2. ROUVERET'S ANALYSIS

As we have said, Rouveret claims that Welsh VNs are verbs embedded in a DP. More precisely, he proposes that they are embedded in a NomP (Nominalization Phrase), which is embedded in a DP, and that they move to the head of NomP to pick up their morphology. Thus, he assumes structures of the following form:

(1)

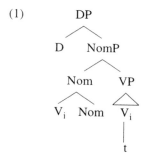

---

[1] The material in this paper was included in a paper presented at the Celtic Linguistics Conference, University College Dublin, June 22nd–23rd, 1995.

The main argument for this analysis seems to be that it allows proclitics with VNs, e.g. *ei* in (2), to be assimilated to proclitics with nouns, e.g. *ei* in (3): both are in D^0.

(2)　　Mae Mair yn gwybod [i Megan　ei　weld (o)]
　　　　is　Mair in　know　for Megan 3SGM see　he
　　　　'Mair knows that Megan saw him.'

(3)　　ei　　wraig (o)
　　　　3SGM wife　he
　　　　'his wife.'

One point that we should note immediately is that Rouveret does not assume that all proclitics are in D^0. He assumes that proclitics with *bod* 'be', e.g. *ei* in (4), are in C^0

(4)　　Dywedodd Emrys　ei　fod ef yn gweithio.
　　　　said　　Emrys 3SGM be he in work
　　　　'Emrys said he was working.'

Given this, it is not obvious that the motivation for assimilating proclitics with other VNs to proclitics with nouns is that strong.

Since Rouveret analyzes VNs as verbs, many of the verbal properties discussed in Borsley (1993) pose no problems for his analysis. For example, the fact that VNs are modified by adverbs and not adjectives, illustrated by the following, is unproblematic.

(5)　　Roedd Megan yn canu *(yn) hyfryd.
　　　　was　Megan in sing　in　pleasant
　　　　'Megan was singing pleasantly.'

Here, only the adverb *yn hyfryd* 'pleasantly' and not the adjective *hyfryd* 'pleasant' is possible. I will argue, however, that serious problems arise in connection with subjects.

Rouveret assumes with others, e.g. Manzini (1992), that there is no A-movement out of a DP. It follows that he must claim that subjects of VNs originate outside the DP that contains the VN. He is particularly concerned with clauses introduced by *i* such as the bracketed string in (6) and periphrastic constructions such as that in (7).

(6)　　Mae Mair yn gwybod [i Megan weld Emrys]
　　　　is　Mair in　know　for Megan see Emrys
　　　　'Mair knows that Megan saw Emrys.'

(7)   Mae Megan yn cysgu.
       is Megan in sleep
      'Megan is sleeping.'

He assumes that the VN subject *Megan* in (6) is in Spec TP but that it originates adjoined to the DP containing the VN. Thus, he assumes the following structure:

(8)   ... [$_{TP}$ Megan$_i$ T^0 [$_{DP}$ t$_i$ [$_{DP}$ weld Emrys]]]

Given fairly standard assumptions about adjunction, movement from the DP adjoined position to Spec TP does not count as extraction from DP. Rouveret assumes that aspectual particles such as *yn* are heads, either members of an Asp category or prepositions, and that they take a DP complement containing a VN. He assumes that the VN subject originates adjoined to the AspP or PP. Thus, he assumes something like the following structure:

(9)   [$_{AgrP}$ Mae$_i$ [$_{TP}$ Megan$_j$ T^0 [$_{VP}$ t$_i$ [$_{AspP}$ t$_j$ [$_{AspP}$ yn [$_{DP}$ cysgu]]]]]]

Mae here originates within VP but surfaces in Agr. I will argue on a number of grounds that VN subjects must originate within the minimal phrase containing the VN, henceforth VNP. If this is right and if A-movement is not possible out of a DP, the inevitable conclusion is that VNs are not embedded in a DP.

3. THE PROBLEMS

We can look first at simple cases involving the VN counterpart of a transitive verb. Rouveret suggests (1994, 272) that the subject of a VN is 'not thematically dependent' on the VN. Rather, it bears the 'subject of predication' role. He proposes (1994, 272–3) that Nom absorbs the single theta-role of an unergative or unaccusative verb and the most prominent theta role of a transitive verb. In short, he claims that one theta role disappears and another appears. There is quite strong evidence against this claim.

A consideration of a range of examples suggests rather strongly that the subject of a VN has the same theta-role as the subject of the related finite verb, and not some 'subject of predication' role. For example, *Mair* appears to have the same theta role in (10a) as in (10b), presumably agent.

(10)   a. Mae Mair wedi anfon neges   i Gwyn.
           is Mair after send message to Gwyn

'Mair has sent a message to Gwyn.'

   b. Anfonodd Mair neges   i Gwyn.
        sent   Mair message to Gwyn
    'Mair sent a message to Gwyn.'

Similarly, *Mair* seems to have the same theta role in (11a) as in (11b), something like recipient.

(11)   a. Mae Mair wedi cael   neges   gan Gwyn.
          is Mair after receive message from Gwyn
       'Mair has received a message from Gwyn

       b. Cafodd Mair neges gan Gwyn.
         received Mair message from Gwyn
        'Mair received a message from Gwyn.'

The following pairs are quite similar.

(12)   a. Mae Mair wedi benthyca llyfr i Gwyn.
          is Mair after lend   book to Gwyn
        'Mair has lent a book to Gwyn.'

       b. Benthycodd Mair lyfr i Gwyn.
         lent   Mair book to Gwyn
        'Mair lent a book to Gwyn.'

(13)   a. Mae Gwyn wedi benthyca llyfr gan Mair.
          is Gwyn after borrow book from Mair
        'Gwyn has borrowed a book from Mair.'

       b. Benthycodd Gwyn lyfr   gan Mair.
         borrowed Gwyn book from Mair
        'Gwyn borrowed a book from Mair.'

Notice also that the subject of a VN is an expletive if the subject of the related finite verb is an expletive. In other words, the subject of the VN has no theta role if the related finite verb has no theta role. The following pairs illustrate:

(14)   a. Mae hi wedi synnu pawb   fod Emyr yn hwyr.
          is she after surprise everyone be Emyr in late
        'It has surprised everyone that Emyr was late.'

       b. Synnodd bawb   fod Emyr yn hwyr.

surprised everyone be Emyr in late
'It surprised everyone that Emyr was late.'

(15)   a. Mae hi wedi bod yn hawdd i Emrys ganu.
          is it after   be in easy for Emrys sing
        'It has been easy for Emrys to sing.'

        b. Mae hi'n hawdd i Emrys ganu.
          is it in easy for Emrys sing
        'It is easy for Emrys to sing.'

Thus, we have quite strong evidence that the subject of a VN has the same theta role as the subject of the related verb.

In the light of this, it is natural to assume that the subject of the VN receives its theta role from the VN in the same way as the subject of a finite verb receives its theta role from the verb. In other words, it is natural to assume that they originate in the same position, presumably Spec VP. It seems, then, that we have some evidence here that the subject of a VN originates within the VNP, and hence some evidence against Rouveret's analysis.

Is there any way in which Rouveret's analysis could be maintained? As far as I can see, the only way to maintain it would be to claim that the subject of a VN receives its theta role through some theta role transmission mechanism. This would pass a theta role up from the VN to the sister of the subject, from which it could be assigned to the subject. Notice, however, that any such mechanism will have the properties of A-movement except that it is not blocked by a DP boundary. Thus, it will be little more than an ad hoc device for maintaining the assumption that VNs are embedded in a DP. I conclude, then, that we do have some real evidence here that the subject of a VN must originate within the VNP, and hence some real evidence against Rouveret's analysis.

Further evidence that the subject of a VN must originate within the VNP comes from the VN counterparts of raising verbs, henceforth raising VNs. The subject of a raising VN appears to derive a theta role from the complement in the same way as the subject of a raising verb. Thus, *Gwyn* in (16a) appears to derive its theta role from *darllen y llyfr*, just as it does in (16b).

(16)   a. Mae Gwyn wedi dechrau darllen y llyfr.
          is Gwyn after begin   read the book
        'Gwyn has read the book.'

        b. Dechreuodd Gwyn ddarllen y llyfr.

began   Gwyn read   the book
'Gwyn read the book.'

The obvious analysis for these examples is one in which the subject originates within the complement. This will give the following structures:

(17)   Dechreuodd$_i$ Gwyn$_j$ t$_i$ [$_{IP}$ t$_j$ ddarllen y llyfr]

(18)   Mae$_i$ Gwyn$_j$ t$_i$ wedi dechrau [$_{IP}$ t$_j$ ddarllen y llyfr]

In (18), the subject originates within the VNP. It looks, then, as if we have some more evidence that the subject of a VN must originate within the VNP and hence some more evidence against Rouveret's analysis.

A proponent of Rouveret's analysis must clearly reject the analysis in (18). However, if one rejects this analysis, one should on face of it also reject the analysis in (17) since it would be very odd for (16a) and (16b) to have quite different analyses. What could one propose instead of these analyses? The only possibility that I can see would be to assume the following structures and to propose that the subjects receive their theta roles from the complements through some theta role transmission mechanism.

(19)   Dechreuodd$_i$ Gwyn t$_i$ [$_{DP}$ ddarllen y llyfr]

(20)   Mae$_i$ Gwyn$_j$ t$_i$ [$_{PP}$ t$_j$ [$_{PP}$ wedi [$_{DP}$ dechrau [$_{DP}$ ddarllen y llyfr]]]]

The theta role transfer mechanism will be like A-movement except that it is not blocked by a DP boundary. Again, it seems to be just an ad hoc way of saving Rouveret's analysis. Again, then, I think we have real evidence that the subject of a VN must originate within the VNP and hence real evidence against Rouveret's analysis.

A final piece of evidence that the subject of a VN must originate within the VNP comes from passives. Given standard assumptions, there are two cases that should be distinguished, those where the passive subject corresponds to an object and those where it corresponds to the subject of a small clause complement. The following pairs illustrate the two cases:

(21)   a. Cafodd Gwyn ei weld.
              got   Gwyn 3SGM see
           'Gwyn was seen.'

         b. Gwelsan nhw Gwyn.
              saw-3PL they Gwyn
           'They saw Gwyn.'

(22) a. Cafodd Gwyn ei   alw yn ffwl.
    got   Gwyn 3SGM call in fool
    'Gwyn was called a fool.'

  b. Galwasan nhw Gwyn yn ffwl.
    called-3PL they Gwyn in fool
    'They called Gwyn a fool.'

In the first pair, the passive subject has the same theta role as the active object, and in the second pair, it has the same theta role as the subject of the active small clause complement. It is natural to account for these facts by assuming that Welsh passives involve the same A-movement as their English counterparts. In other words, it is natural to assume the following structures:

(23) Cafodd$_i$ Gwyn$_j$ t$_i$ ei weld t$_j$

(24) Cafodd$_i$ Gwyn$_j$ t$_i$ ei alw [t$_j$ yn ffwl]

Notice, however, that both structures involve subjects which originate within the VNP. Thus, we appear to have further evidence that the subject of a VN must originate within the VNP.

A proponent of Rouveret's analysis must obviously reject the structures in (23) and (24). Instead, one might assume something like the following structures and some theta role transfer mechanism:

(25) Cafodd$_i$ Gwyn t$_i$ [$_{DP}$ ei weld]

(26) Cafodd$_i$ Gwyn t$_i$ [$_{DP}$ ei alw [$_{XP}$ yn ffwl]]

(I label *yn ffwl* 'XP' because it is not clear what category it should be assigned to.) In fact, two rather different mechanisms would seem to be necessary given that it is an internal theta role that must be transferred in the first case but an external theta role in the second. We would also have two rather different active-passive relations. In one case, the passive sentence would lack an NP complement that the active verb takes while in the other case the passive verb would take a bare predicate complement where the active verb takes a small clause complement. Thus, this is not a very plausible alternative to the conventional movement analysis.

Once more, then, we have evidence that the subject of a VN must originate within the VNP and hence evidence that Rouveret's analysis is untenable.

4. CONCLUDING REMARKS

We have now seen that there is a variety of evidence that the subject of a VN must originate within the VNP. It seems that the only way to avoid this conclusion is to invoke certain theta role transfer mechanisms, but such mechanisms will have the properties of A-movement except that they are not blocked by a DP boundary. As such they are just an ad hoc way of maintaining the assumption that the subject of a VN originates outside the VNP. If this argument is sound, we must reject Rouveret's analysis of Welsh VNs. This obviously raises the question: how should Welsh VNs be analysed? A plausible alternative approach is sketched in Roberts and Shlonsky (1996). They propose that proclitics with VNs other than *bod* are in an AgrO (object agreement) category and that VNPs are VP complements of AgrO. Within this approach, the subordinate clause in (6) will involve something like the following structure:

(27)   ... $[_{TP}$ Megan$_i$ T^0 $[_{AgrOP}$ AgrO^0 $[_{VP}$ t$_i$ weld Emrys]]]

If we assume that aspectual particles are members of an Asp category, we can propose something like the following for (7)

(28) $[_{AgrP}$ Mae$_i$ $[_{TP}$ Megan$_j$ T^0 $[_{VP}$ t$_i$ $[_{AspP}$ yn $[_{AgrOP}$ AgrO^0 $[_{VP}$ t$_j$ cysgu]]]]]]

These structures involve the assumption that the subject of a VN originates within the VNP. This is unproblematic since there is no extraction from a DP. The one criticism that might be levelled against this analysis is that it does not assimilate proclitics with VNs to proclitics with nouns. However, as we noted at the outset, Rouveret only does this in part given his assumption that proclitics with *bod* are in C^0. Thus, it does not seem a very compelling criticism. I think, then, there are good reasons for preferring an analysis along these lines to Rouveret's analysis.

REFERENCES

Borsley, Robert 1993. 'On so-called Verb-Nouns in Welsh', *Journal of Celtic Linguistics*, 2, 35–64

Fife, James 1990. *The Semantics of the Welsh Verb: A Cognitive Approach*, Cardiff: University of Wales Press

Manzini, Rita 1992. *Locality: A Theory and Some of its Empirical Consequences*, Cambridge, Mass.: MIT Press

Roberts, Ian and Shlonsky, Ur 1996. 'Pronominal Enclisis in VSO Languages', in *The Syntax of the Celtic Languages*, ed. by Robert Borsley and Ian Roberts, Cambridge: University Press

Rouveret, Alain 1994. *Syntaxe du gallois: Principes généraux et typologie*, Paris: CNRS

Willis, Penny 1988. 'Is the Welsh Verbal Noun a Verb or a Noun?', *Word 39*, 201–224

On the Flexion of the *ā*-stems in Irish

LIAM BREATNACH
Trinity College, Dublin

THURNEYSEN, *GOI* § 289, gives four paradigms to illustrate the flexion of the *ā*-stems in Old Irish, namely *túath*, with palatal consonant before the *-e* of the genitive singular, *delb*, with non-palatal consonant, *deacht* with palatalisation lacking throughout the singular, and *buiden*, with syncope.[1]

In § 290, to illustrate vowel variation, he gives as examples *cíall* and *bríathar*, which have *é(i)* before a palatal consonant, and *gáu* and *náu*, which have the diphthong *-oí* in the accusative and dative singular and a short vowel in hiatus forms.

He also gives one example with *u* in the genitive and dative singular as opposed to *o* elsewhere, viz. *tol*, acc. *toil*, gen. *tuile*, dat. *tuil, toil*, nom. acc. pl. *tola*, and in his discussion of the accusative sg. in § 296 he refers to 'the fact, noted by Pedersen [...] that in Wb. the acc. of *tol* "will" is always written *toil*, but the dat. more often *tuil* than *toil*'.

1.1 The examples listed by Pedersen (*VKG*, I, 363) consist of eight instances of acc. sg. *toil*, viz. *na cuinged a thoil fessin* 'let him not seek his own desire', Wb. 11b18, *comalnatar toil dǽ* 'who fulfil God's will', 20d1, 20d2, *dogneith toil far coimded* 'that you should do your master's will', 27c9, *fri toil dé* 'against God's will', 4c23, *fri toil dée*, 11b17a, *ar thoil doine* 'for men's desire', 18c13, *fri toil* 'against (his) will', 28b1, one instance of gen. sg. *tuile*, viz. *sercc a tuile* 'love of their will', 30c11, seven instances of dat. sg. *tuil*, viz. *do thuil dée* 'to God's will', 5c18, *i tuil dée* 'in God's will', 5c20, 10a25, 11b17, *í tuil dée*, 9d27, *ho thuil mo chollno* 'from desire of my flesh', 3d1, *ho thuil* 'voluntary', 15d33, and three instances of dat. sg. *toil*, viz. *hó thoil cholno* 'as to the desire of the flesh',

[1] The abbreviations used are: *DIL = Dictionary of the Irish Language* and *Contributions to a Dictionary* [...] (Dublin: Royal Irish Academy, 1913–76), vii–xii, with the addition of: *CIH* = D.A. Binchy, (ed.) *Corpus Iuris Hibernici* (Dublin: Institute for Advanced Studies, 1978); *GOI* = Rudolf Thurneysen, *A Grammar of Old Irish* (Dublin: Institute for Advanced Studies, 1946); *IEW* = Julius Pokorny, *Indogermanisches etymologisches Wörterbuch* I (Berne: Francke, 1959); McCone, *Chronology* = Kim R. McCone, *Towards a Relative Chronology of Ancient and Medieval Celtic Sound Change* (Maynooth: Studies in Celtic Linguistics, I, 1996) Maynooth; *MV* = Rudolf Thurneysen, 'Mittelirische Verslehren', *Irische Texte*, III, 1. Heft (Leipzig: Hirzel, 1891) 1–182; *SnaG* = Kim McCone et al. (eds.) *Stair na Gaeilge in Ómós do Phádraig Ó Fiannachta* (Maynooth: Dept. of Old Irish, 1994); *VKG* = H. Pedersen, *Vergleichende Grammatik der keltischen Sprachen*, I–II (Göttingen: Vandenhoeck & Ruprecht. 1909-13).

19a17, *ho thoil* 'voluntary', 22d5, and in a compound, *iarsin chaíntoil* 'according to the good will', 20d19.

Other examples with *u* which he cites are: dative *ine chuis* 'in his foot', *Thes.* II, 245.36 (*Cambrai Homily*), Mid.Ir. *dia chuis* 'on foot', *LU*, 2994 (*Aided Echach meic Maireda*),[2] and genitive *rún inna cruche* 'the mystery of the Cross', Wb. 8a5, as against five examples of the accusative *croich* in Wb., viz. *tria chroich* 'by his cross', 8a14, *tre chroich crist* 'through Christ's cross', 20a11, *ar chroich crist* 'for the cross of Christ', 20c21, *fri croich* 'on the Cross', 20d13, *hi croich* 'on the Cross', 28b4.

Arguing that the opposition between *u* and *o* is clearly old, he states that it was neutralised in the course of time, citing the OIr. examples: *ticsath a chruich* 'let him take up his cross', *Thes.* II, 245.5 (*Cambrai Homily*), with *u* in the accusative,[3] and *airind loith domuin* 'for the deep mud', Ml. 60a6, *loithe* 'of the fen', Sg. 127a1 with *o* in the dative and genitive of *loth*. He also refers to Mid.Ir. *coiss*, acc. and dat. of *coss*, Mid.Ir. *cloich*, dative, and *cloiche*, genitive of *cloch*, and Mid.Ir. *croich*, dative, and *croiche*, genitive of *croch*, without examples.

1.2 Further examples can be adduced of the variation between *o* and *u* in OIr. The first is the genitive sg. *hi torrund cruisse* 'in the form of a cross', *Thes.* II, 254.19. In OIr. texts in later MSS I have found three rhyming examples in the case of the genitive singular: *dochum a scuile* (:*nduine*; *scoile*, MS) 'to his school', *ITS*, XLVII, 96 § 23 (*Irish Gospel of Thomas*), *hi timchuairt na scule-se* (:*guide-se*) 'around this school', *Thes.* II, 304.8 (*Colmán's Hymn*); *corp Chríst césta cruiche* (:*sruithe*) 'the body of Christ who suffered the cross', *Fél.* Epil. 270, and one in the case of the dative: *dom scuil* (:*muin*) 'to my school', *ITS*, XLVII, 98 § 30 (*Irish Gospel of Thomas*).

In *Éigse*, 18 (1981), 94, E.G. Quin argued convincingly that what Binchy, *Críth G*, 97, printed as *scaball cocúis* (= *scaball cocuis*, *CIH*, 778.28) 'a concave pot' should in fact be read *scaball co cuis* 'a pot with a handle'. Other non-rhyming examples in the dative and genitive are: *Íssu úas tuinn tuili* 'Jesus above the surface of the flood', *Fél.* Prol. 250, *ánbreo úas tuind trilis* 'a splendid flame over a sparkling wave', *Fél.* Apr. 23, *fuil chuise* 'a wound on a foot', *Ériu*, 12 (1938), 50 § 63 (*Bretha Crólige*), and *do thuinne* 'of your wave', *CIH*, 384.19 (*Cethairslicht Athgabálae*).

Examples with *o* in the accusative sg. are: *nad déni thoil ind ríg thuas* 'who does not do the will of the King above', *Thes.* II, 294.28, *cach oen*

---

[2] See below § 3.1.

[3] This text regularly has *cruche* in the genitive of croch, viz. *Thes.*, II, 244.29, 245.11, 246.25, 247.10.

dugní toil ind ríg 'everyone who does the will of the King', *Thes.* II, 294.30, while in an OIr. text in a later MS we find rhyming *carsa[i]t boith i nAlind aird* (:*Roith*) 'they loved to dwell in lofty Alenn', *Hail Brigit* 14 § 13d (cf. *ZCPh*, 8 (1912), 183).

1.3 Forms with *o* and *u* continue to co-exist in Middle Irish. Examples after prepositions, where the OIr. distinction between accusative and dative is not maintained (cf. *SnaG*, 240) are: *re crois* (:*fois*) 'against a cross', *Measgra Uí Chl.* 148 § 12, as against *for tuind* (:*Chuind*) 'with regard to the sea (wave)', *Ériu*, 7, 228 § 67 (*Secht O.F.N.*), '*gon chruich* (:*sruith*) 'beside the Cross', *Measgra Uí Chl.* 153 § 27, *cen luiṅg* (:*Chuind*) 'without ship', *MD*, IV, 98.2, *i tóeb chroisse* (:*Choisse*) 'beside the cross', *MD*, IV, 342.6.

2.1 Thurneysen strangely makes no mention of the interchange of *e* and *i* in feminine *ā*-stem nouns, although he does do so in the case of *o-/ā*-stem adjectives (*GOI* § 350). Pedersen (*VKG*, I, 366) had stated that originally such variation would have occurred in the same circumstances as that of *o* and *u*, and that this resulted in a non-regular alternation of *e* and *i* in a number of words in Old and Middle Irish, citing as examples various forms of the words *breth*, *feb*, *fled*, *sleg*, and also *med*, which however only has forms in *e* (cf. acc. sg. *i mmeid*, gl. *in pateram*, Ml. 79b4, dat. *hua meid* 'with a balance', Ml. 82a2, and see § 4.1 below).

Examples (including Pedersen's) from OIr. texts of *i* in the genitive sg. are, firstly from contemporaneous OIr. manuscripts: *fer brithe lésboiri* 'a man who carries a taper', Wb. 25d3, *á brithe do iudaib* 'of its reference to the Jews', Ml. 37a6b; and secondly from OIr. texts in later MSS: *is aircoillte brithe* 'who is debarred from being brought away', *Ériu*, 12 (1938), 14 § 17 (*Bretha Crólige*), *ar thrumme inna brithe* 'because of the difficulty of the birth', *Fraech* 107; *smacht peata chuirre ⁊ circe* 'the trespass-fine for a tame heron and a hen', *CIH*, 196.13 (*Bretha Comaithchesa*), *dīre circe* 'compensation for a hen', *CIH*, 982.22; *dílse mine* 'forfeiture of the flour', *Críth G*, 239 (nsg. *men*, Sg. 51b7); *co n-ev a slige* 'with the shaft of his spear', *RC*, 11 (1890), 446.61 (*Tochmarc Emire*); *slán slithi* 'non-liability for violating a woman', *ZCPh*, 15 (1925), 351 § 40 (*Gúbretha Caratniad*).

Examples in the dative sg. are firstly: *im mess fírían do brith for cach* 'to pass righteous judgement upon all', Ml. 103c15; *i noīnchis* 'in a single basket', *Thes.* I, 497.2;[4] *fib as deg ropriched* 'as it has been preached best',

---

[4] For the rest of this gloss see *ibid.* 725.

Wb. 23a3;[5] *hí flid crist* 'at Christ's feast', Wb. 9b14; *ón mlith* 'from the rubbing', Ml. 23a20, and secondly: *ar c[h]irc* 'for a hen' (or accusative?), *CIH*, 1979.22; *cin nī to chlith* 'without concealing anything', *CIH*, 597.24;[6] *do gin claidibh* 'by the blade of a sword', *Anecd.* i 2.4,[7] *día mblith* 'to scrub him', *Fraech*, 232; *for slig* 'on a spear' *RC*, 11 (1890), 444.27 (*Tochmarc Emire*); *for cach srith* (:*clith*) 'upon every battle-rank', *Fianaig.* 30.14;[8] *a tīr-so cona thrib* 'this land together with its dwelling-place', *CIH*, 913.30 (OIr. glosses on the *Senchas Már*), *la Día for-díastar tocud trib* '[punishment for] it will be inflicted by God on [moveable] goods and land-holding', *Bretha Nemed Toísech*.[9]

An example in the nominative dual is *óenflesc* [...] *dí flisc* 'one stroke [...] two strokes', Sg. 3b19.

2.2 The word *deug* 'drink', originally a *u*-stem (see Thurneysen, *GOI* § 308), is inflected in OIr. as an *ā*-stem, with *i* in the accusative, genitive and dative singular, e.g. nom. *deug*, Tur. 71, acc. *inna ndig* 'into their drink', Wb. 27a24, gen. *riathar inna dige* 'the torrent of drink', Ml. 56a13 (cf. Supplement to *Thes.*), dat. *ina dig* 'in one draught, *LU(M)*, 8794 (*Fled Bricrenn*), *ina óendig* 'in a single draught', *ibid.* 8826.

A few examples will suffice to illustrate the flexion of the commonly occurring word *cell* 'church': nsg. *cell mór*, *Thes.* II, 317.7; gsg. *clad cille*, *Ériu*, 17 (1955), 70 § 13 (*Coibnes Uisci Thairidne*); dsg. *hi Cill Dumi Gluinn*, *Thes.* II, 270.21, *cor maic do cill*, *CIH*, 1819.23 (*Córus Bésgnai*). The accusative singular is *cill* in OIr. texts in later MSS, e.g. *dul tar chill*, *CIH*, 239.15 (*Do Astud Chirt ocus Dligid*), and in the later language (see below §§ 2.6, 3.1), but the only instance I know of in an Old Irish MS does not show raising, viz. asg. *Con tubart Fland Feblæ a cheill dóo* 'and Fland Feblae gave his church to him', in the Additamenta in the Book of Armagh.[10]

---

[5] Contrast *feib*, Ml. 30c17, Sg. 144b3, 210b4, and cf. *GOI* § 911.

[6] *Bürgschaft*, 23 §65g. Note that *clith* is treated as separate from *cleth* in *DIL*.

[7] Binchy, *SCano*, 21 n. 20 points out that this belongs to *gen*, not *gin* 'mouth' as assumed by *DIL* s.v., although his emendation to *g[e]in* is not necessary.

[8] These rhyming words are emended by O Daly, *ITS*, L, 76.545–7 (*Scéla Moṡauluim*), to *sr[e]ith* and *chl[e]ith*. This is the only example I know of with *i* in this word, and the dative in *e* is well attested in Sg.; cf. *i ssreith*, 30a12, *hi sreith*, 95a2, *hí sreith*, 213a9.

[9] I have normalised the text here on the basis of *la dia fordiastar toicid treb*, *CIH*, 2228.29 (Nero A 7) and the citation in O'Davoren's Glossary, 850, [...] *la deo fordiastar tocud trib .i. digail fora tocad ⁊ a treab*, *CIH*, 1498.36; a more corrupt form is found in *la dia forniastar toc*ad(?) *trebaire* (?), *CIH*, 1989.8. The dative *trib*, found in *O'Dav.* alone, is clearly the *lectio difficilior*.

[10] Ludwig Bieler, *The Patrician Texts in the Book of Armagh* (Dublin: Institute for Advanced Studies, 1979) *Scriptores Latini Hiberniae*, X, 178.11. F.J. Byrne 'Varia III: 2. *cadessin*', *Ériu*, 33 (1982), 167–9: 169 proposes reading *a chēill* 'its sense' on the mistaken assumption that the asg. of *cell* must be *cill*.

2.3 In some words *i* would be historically regular in the accusative as well as the genitive and dative sg. (see § 4.1 below). Thus *breth* regularly has the accusative sg. with *i* in Wb.; cf. *ro-uiccius brith* 'I have passed judgement', 9b6, *berat brith fuiri* 'let them pass judgement on it', 13a11, and *berid cách brith for arele* 'each gives judgement on the other', 29b9.

The accusative in *i* is also found in the Milan Glosses, *ber brith étrunn* 'judge between us', 38c28, and in other OIr. texts in later MSS, e.g.: *co brith nó deroscc* 'until judgement or verdict', *CIH*, 462.21 (*Bretha im Fuillemu Gell*), *it hē berdai brith fuirri* 'it is they who give judgement on it, *CIH*, 899.9 (OIr. glosses on the *Senchas Már*); *fet* [...] *foceird fit* [...] *focerdat ind iascairi fit* 'a hissing sound [...] it makes a hissing sound [...] the fishermen make a hissing sound', *O'Mulc.* 527;[11] *dollēici in slig for Lugaid* 'he casts the spear at Lugaid', *Corm.* Y, 1084; while the forms with *e* and *i* appear side by side in *Dolléici a hathair sleig cóicrind* [...] *condo ragaib Fróech* [...] *in slig. Fosceird-side* [...] *in slig* 'her father casts a five-pointed spear [...] so that Fróech caught the spear [...] he throws the spear[...]', *Fraech* 211–14.[12]

2.4 Already in the OIr. period the original distribution of *e* and *i* is breaking down. As early as the Würzburg Glosses, we find the dative sg. of *breth* with *e* in *mo ainech-sa do breith less* 'that it should have my protection' 14a4.[13] The nominative sg. is *breth* in Wb. 10b1 and 12d38, while the nominative *brith* in Wb. 13d4, 23c11, Ml. 33c13, 36c20 (but *breth* 36c21), 37a10 is probably to be explained as the extension of the dative to the nominative common in other *ā*-stem verbal nouns.[14]

An OIr. (or early Mid.Ir.) rhyming example with *e* in the accusative is *ēbsa becān gabais gleith* (:*eich*) 'when he was small he began to graé, *MV* III § 6;[15] further examples in OIr. texts in later MSS are: *co bēr breith* 'how will I give judgement?' *CIH*, 2131.1 (*Findṡruth Fíthail*),[16] *fo-ruigellsad*

---

[11] Nominative sg. *ind fet* 'the whistling', Sg. 3a7; contrast accusative sg. *foceird feid* 'makes a whistling sound', *LU*, 1042 (= 9673), *ro lēg feid* 'whistled', *MV*, III § 167, dative sg. *co feit* 'with a whistling sound', *Celtica*, 11 (1976), 197.18.

[12] In a later edition (*Die Romanze von Froech und Findabair*, ed. by Wolfgang Meid (Innsbruck: Beiträge zur Kulturwissenschaft, 1970) 37.194–6) all the forms are emended to *sleig*; *slig* is neither registered in the *variae lectiones*, nor is there a note on it.

[13] See *DIL* E 131.26.

[14] Thurneysen, *GOI* § 294b includes this among 'verbal nouns whose original flexion is sometimes doubtful owing to the difficulty in deciding whether they are *i*-stems or *ā*-stems in which the dative form has replaced the nominative'. The genitive sg. in *-e* (*GOI* § 727) and all the plural forms, however, mean that they cannot have been *i*-stems.

[15] Read *Óbu* with *MV*, II, § 20, which has *glíth* in spite of the rhyme.

[16] This is a frequently occurring formula in this text and is usually found with *breith* abbreviated in the rest of the text (*CIH*, 2131.1–2143.40).

breith Amairgein meic Mīled 'they submitted to the judgement of Amairgein son of Míl', *CIH*, 2127.11, *fri breith* 'for judgement, *CIH*, 1125.33 (*Bretha Nemed Dédenach*); *sóerais cech fleid forcraid* 'freed every surfeiting banquet', *Fél.* Sept. 25; *i fleisc* 'for a rod', *Críth G*, 215; *ben ara-tūaisi a sleith* 'a woman who maintains silence as to her violation', *CIH*, 42.13 (*Sechtae*).

The genitive and dative in *e* is found in OIr. texts in later MSS, e.g.: *fri aithcomarc a breithi don breithemuin* 'to request the judge for his judgement', *CIH*, 410.8 (*Cethairślicht Athgabálae*), *cin mbreithe in chlaidib* 'the crime of bringing the sword', *Fraech*, 224, *mac sleithe* 'a son [conceived as a result] of violation', *CIH*, 1296.28, *do breith teneadh* 'to bring fire', *CIH*, 1118.41 (*Bretha Nemed Dédenach*).

2.5 Forms with *e* and *i* continue to co-exist in Middle Irish, however. Examples after prepositions are: *deichtreib do brith i ndoīre* 'the leading of the Ten Tribes into captivity', *Éigse*, 17 (1977), 34 § 23, *ara brith* 'for bringing it', *SR*, 2215, *can mo choscur do brith do Laignib* 'that I will not be defeated by the Leinstermen', *LL*, 38672 (*Bórama*); *cen chlith* 'without concealment', *Éigse*, 17 (1977), 37 § 38, *cen clith*, *SR*, 1313; *do-chōtar fo gin claideib* 'they perished by the blade of a sword', *SR*, 5068, *fo gin claidib*, *Trip.*2 1922; *dí-cain forsin slig* 'he chants over the spear', *ITS*, L, 84.676 (*Scéla Mośauluim*), as against *dia breith* 'to bring it', *SR*, 3455, *īar nach mbreith* 'after any judgement', *Éigse*, 17 (1977), 37 § 36; *cen chleith* (:*beich*) 'openly', Murphy *Lyrics*, 30 § 10, *cen cleith*, *SR*, 1073, *día cleith* (:*leith*) 'to hide them', Murphy *Lyrics*, 30 § 3; *fo gein cloidem ⁊ gæ* 'under the blade of swords and spears', *Anecd.* III, 68.1; *ar in mein*, *PH*, 5077.

Examples in the accusative as direct object of the verb are *coro thomliset a fleid* 'so they partook of their feast', *MD*, III, 78.17, and *sādis fïadna slūagaib sleig* (:*neim*) 'he lodged his spear, in the presence of the hosts', *MD*, II 36.16, as against *do-ratsaid dig dam* 'you gave me drink', *LU(H)*, 2326 (*Scéla Laí Brátha*), *dorigne dé min is lúaith* 'he was turned into dust and ashes', *SR*, 5411. The nominative sg. with *i* is also found in Middle Irish, e.g. *brith m'[f]eraind* 'to take my land', *ZCPh*, 8 (1912), 266 § 28, *ba lethach in min, .i. min bíd ⁊ min chorma* 'the meal was half and half, i.e. meal for food and meal for ale', Ó hAodha, *Bethu Brigte* (Dublin: Institute for Advanced Studies, 1978) 19.70 (Appendix). An example with *i* in the genitive sg. is *macsamla na crichi-se* 'the like of this plundering expedition', *ZCPh*, 3 (1901), 23.29.

2.6 *Cell* 'church', on the other hand, consistently has *i* in the acc., gen. and dat., e.g.: asg. *nīra cráid chill*, *LL*, 38643 (*Bórama*), *co Cill Culind, LL*,

38589 (*Bórama*), gsg. *i talmain cille* (*:linne*) 'to the church's soil' *MD* IV, 346.12, dsg. *in cach cill* (*:cinn*), *Celtica*, 14 (1981), 138 § 31.

3.1 These vowel variations survive in a limited number of words in Modern Irish. In a note in *Éigse*, 18 (1981), 285–7 on 'Vowel Changes in the Inflexion of *cos, cas*' Ó Cuív points out that genitive and dative forms in both *ui* and *oi* are recognised in *IGT*, II § 158 for *sgolb, bolg, lorg* and *mong*. We may also note that *IGT*, II § 165 includes some originally monosyllabic *ā*-stems amongst a number of words with a genitive[17] and dative sg. in *i*, namely, *ceall, cearc, deoch* and *mean* (a nom. sg. *min* is also recognised in *IGT*, II § 14.8).[18] On the other hand, forms with *i* are not recognised in *IGT*, II § 14 for *cleith, mleith, bleith, breith*.

With regard to the post-classical period, note that nominative *cearc* with genitive sg. *circe*, and nominative *deoch* with genitive *dighe/dí* are maintained down to the present day. On the other hand, *cill* and *min* have displaced *ceall* and *mean* respectively in the nominative sg., e.g., *cill*, *TSh*. 5808, *an mhin chomhchroitte*, *TSh*. 7753. The word *sned* 'nit' which is poorly attested in the early language,[19] varies according to dialect in Modern Irish; the older dative *snidh* is used as the nominative in Munster,[20] while Connacht[21] and Ulster[22] have reflexes of the nominative *sneadh*.

Ó Cuív (*op. cit.*) points out that the dative *cuis* survived in West Muskerry Irish in the idiom *im chuis*, *'na chuis* 'on foot' (with [u], as opposed to [o] otherwise), which corresponds to earlier *dia chuis*.[23] Similarly, the old dative *digh* survives in West Kerry Irish in the phrase *ina dhigh* 'in one draught'.

4.1 Although the examples surveyed above could doubtless be added to, they are sufficient to illustrate the variation between both *o* and *u* and *e* and *i* in the singular of the feminine *ā*-stems from Old Irish to Modern Irish. They also show clearly that a great amount of levelling has taken place. In

---

[17] As Damian McManus points out to me, the statement *acht dá tháoibhréim úathaidhe an dá chéd-ainm a n-eadhadh* 'except that the two genitive singulars of the first two nouns [viz. *días* and *sgían*] are in *e*' can be taken to imply that the others in the list have *i* in the genitive.

[18] Note also that genitive sg. *meine* (*:reime*) is condemned as faulty in *IGT*, II, ex. 1737; as Damian McManus points out to me this must be the implication of the comment *.l.* ⁊ *ní ón mhál* 'faulty, and not because of *mál*'.

[19] Cf. nsg. *sned*, Sg. 113b8, npl. *na snedha*, *MV*, III, §102.

[20] Cf. R.B. Breatnach, *Seana-Chaint na nDéise*, II (Dublin: Institute for Advanced Studies, 1961), and S. Mac Clúin, *Caint an Chláir* (Dublin: Stationery Office, 1940) s.v. Note that this is also the form used in Keating, *TSh*. 9792 (*an tsnidh*).

[21] Cf. Tomás S. Ó Máille, *Liosta Focal as Ros Muc* (Dublin: An Clóchomhar 1974) s.v. *sneá*.

[22] Cf. Heinrich Wagner, *Gaeilge Theilinn* (Dublin: Institute for Advanced Studies, 1959) § 117.

[23] Cf. also id., 'Ad *Éigse* xviii. 285–7', *Celtica*, 18 (1986), 123–4.

attempting to ascertain the state of affairs in OIr. we are hampered by the poor attestation of many of the relevant words in contemperaneous OIr. manuscripts. Although a number of early forms survive in OIr. texts in later manuscripts, it is likely that many have been altered by later scribes (as others have been by modern editors), especially in non-rhyming position, the example noted in footnote 9 above being a case in point.

On the other hand, there is a number of commonly occurring feminine ā-stems which always have *e*, such as *delb, selb, celg, selg, berg, ferg* (see *DIL* s.vv.), and the lack of forms in *i* is doubtless due to raising being prevented by these consonant-groups. It is remarkable, however, that whereas *cerc* regularly has oblique forms with *i*, the rhyming *serc* never does; cf. genitive *méit for serce lem-sa* 'the greatness of the love for you that I have', Wb. 14d16, *airde serce móre* 'a sign of great love', Wb. 24c2, *inna sercae* 'of love', Ml. 53c10, *du sercae-siu* 'of love for you', Ml. 92b1, accusative *ce seirc* glossing *quam caritatem*, Wb. 14d15, *ni taibrem seirc* 'we do not love', Wb. 15c9, and dative *attá di ṡeirc la laitnori inna ngrec co seichetar cid a comroircniu* 'the Latinists have such love for the Greeks that they follow even their errors', Sg. 1a2. Similarly *des*, 'right' (adj.); 'right hand' (feminine ā-stem) never shows raising, in contrast to *cis* dative sg. of *ces*. The solution to the problem of these contrasting treatments doubtless lies in the fact that historically we have to do with raising of *e* in the genitive and dative sg. in some words, and lowering of *i* in the nominative sg. and in all cases in the plural in others; for the preforms of the case-endings of the ā-stems see *SnaG*, 97-8. Thus, for example, we would have lowering of *i* to *e* in *ces* (< Lat. *cista*, McManus, *Ériu*, 34 (1983), 43), *fet* (see McCone, *Chronology*, 55, 63, 107), *fled* (< *ụlidā* < *ụldā*, *IEW*, 1137), *flesc* (< *ụliskā*, *IEW*, 1143), *sleg* (< *sligā* < *sḷgā*, *IEW*, 900), and *breth* (< *britā* < *bhṛtā*, *IEW*, 130). Raising of *e* to *i* is more restricted (cf. McCone, *Chronology*, 110–11, two certain examples being *treb* (< *trebā*, *IEW*, 1090) and *cell* (< Latin *cella*). It did not take place in other words with original *e*, such as *des* (*IEW*, 190) and *serc* (*IEW*, 1032), and the difference in treatment of the latter word[24] and *cerc* makes it virtually certain that we should reconstruct a preform **kirkā* for this word (cf. *IEW* 568).

4.2 On the basis of the foregoing, we can add two more paradigms to those of Thurneysen's, namely nsg. *cell*, asg. *ceill*, gsg. *cille*, dsg. *cill*, and nsg. *breth*, asg. *brith*, gsg. *brithe*, dsg. *brith*, the latter with the variations noted

---

[24] Note also the lack of palatalisation in the genitive sg. in Old Irish.

in § 2.4 above. Finally, I should add that my own treatment of the situation in Middle Irish (*SnaG*, 243) is entirely inaccurate.

When I began the study of Old Irish in University College, Dublin, in 1970, I was fortunate to have Conn Ó Cléirigh as my first guide through the complexities of the *Paradigms and Glosses* and *Thurneysen*. Conn had the gift. He was able to communicate clearly all the intricacies of the grammar of Old Irish. 'To try to regain at whatever cost our paradigms lost', as Myles said, this *felmac* offers a small contribution to the memory of a revered *aite*.

Criticism and the Irish Literary Revival
With Special Attention to John Eglinton

MARY E. BRYSON
Montana State University

I N 1919 an Irish critic wrote of one of those Dublin characters, who achieved a certain fame as 'a man [...] who, by way of reply to some disparaging remarks about Thomas Moore, had felled the critic to the ground'.[1] This little anecdote reported by critic-essayist John Eglinton (W.K. Magee) was intended to demonstrate, only half-jokingly, the difficulties of the critic in Revival Ireland. Although there is no record of such an incident in his own career, he did have his difficulties and, along with other Revival figures, generated much controversy. From 1894 to 1956, he wrote criticism for the national and international press—including *The Daily Express*, *The United Irishman*, *The Irish Review*, *The Irish Statesman*, and his own *Dana, A Magazine of Independent Thought*.[2] He published several collections of his essays, and was the biographer of AE (George Russell)[3] with whom he was colleague and friend, as he was to several other Revival leaders: George Moore, John Synge, and W.B. Yeats, who named him 'our most philosophic critic'.[4] In the twenties he was Irish correspondent for *The Dial Magazine*. Yet he is one of the most neglected figures of that circle. In this essay, I wish to reassess Eglinton's contribution as a critic to the development of the national literary tradition of Ireland.

He is known to most readers as a literary character, like Falstaff or Mr. Micawber. He is the 'Contrairy John' of Moore's *Hail and Farewell* and is a participant in the National Library colloquy in Joyce's *Ulysses*. Eglinton served as junior librarian under T.W. Lyster from 1895 to 1921. Son of a Presbyterian minister, he is classified by most historians as a Theosophist. While he was associated with that circle, he claimed he never became one.[5] Many of his writings suggest he was rather an Emersonian Unitarian, although at times he denied all traditional creeds. The narrator of *Hail and*

---

[1] 'Life and Letters', *The Irish Statesman*, July 5, 1919, p. 42.

[2] The name was changed in the second issue to *Dana, An Irish Magazine of Independent Thought*. Fred Ryan (journalist and editor and one-time playwright for the National Drama Company) was co-founder and editor with Eglinton. The entire run (1904–1905) was published by Lemma, New York, 1973. Further citations will be to this edition.

[3] *A Memoir of AE*, London: MacMillan and Co., 1931.

[4] W.B. Yeats, 'The Irish Dramatic Movement' *Plays and Controversies*, New York: MacMillan Co., 1924, p. 111. Originally published in 1904.

[5] *A Memoir of AE*, p. 21.

Farewell sees him as a complete skeptic, a 'Contrairy John' who 'believed in nothing'. Contrasted with AE, who stood for belief, 'Eglinton stood for unbelief—' at an opposite pole:

> On one side of me sits the Great Everything, and on the other the Great Nothing. [...] He [Eglinton] doubts everything [...] the future of Ireland, the value of literature, even the value of his own beautiful prose. [...] Contrairy John [...] [is] only happy when contrairy or contradicting [...].[6]

In the same passage AE agrees, noting Eglinton's magazine, *Dana*, should have been named 'The Heretic' (117). The same skepticism characterized his nationalism. He claimed his patriotism was that of Thoreau;[7] for Eglinton, the idea of 'nations' was outdated.

Literary historians are also familiar with Eglinton's retrospects of the Revival in his studies of its chief figures, collected in *Irish Literary Portraits*. The first international literary historian of the period, Ernest Boyd, named Eglinton as its only representative of serious criticism. He dismissed the criticism of Yeats and AE and deplored the 'consequent lack of intellectual discipline', which allowed 'the good and the mediocre to struggle on equal terms for recognition'.[8]

Boyd exaggerated. His claim can be countered with several examples, some from the second generation, true, but I would add Yeats.[9] All, of course, suffered from bias, as did Eglinton, and, it must be allowed, the tendency to over-enthusiasm produced some comically grandiose comparisons with the Greeks and Dante and Shakespeare: Yeats compared Synge to Aeschylus and Lady Gregory to Malory.[10] And surely a standard other than literary was operating when Thomas MacDonough named Alice Milligan 'The Best Irish Poet' because she was 'most Irish'.[11] But Boyd was apparently speaking mostly of normative criticism. The larger aesthetic questions were certainly addressed in these years, including: the

---

[6] George Moore, 'Salve', *Hail and Farewell*, Vol. 2, New York: D. Appleton and Co., 1925, pp. 116–117.

[7] 'Preface', *Irish Literary Portraits*, London, MacMillan and Co., 1935, pp 10–11.

[8] *Ireland's Literary Renaissance*, New York: John Lane and Co., 1916, 1922, p. 424. Further references to this edition are given in the text.

[9] See John Frayne, *The Uncollected Prose of W.B. Yeats*, New York; Columbia University Press, 1970, Vols. 1 and 2. Yeats' criticism from 1897 to 1939 makes an impressive body. Further references will be given in the text.

[10] E. Ruth Taylor, *Modern Irish Writers, Cross Currents in Criticism*, Lawrence, Kansas: University of Kansas Press, 1954, pp. 70–71.

[11] 'The Best Living Irish Poet', *Irish Review*, Sept., 1914, p. 287.

nature of literature, the role of the artist, the significance of myth and folklore and, most relevant, a canon for an Irish national literature. Indeed, some of these confusions of standards came from such quests after definition, as the MacDonough example demonstrates.

Some of these issues emerged in a rather famous literary controversy in the 1898 *Daily Express*. Later collected as *Literary Ideals in Ireland*,[12] the debate grew out of a seemingly irrelevant issue--that of subject matter. However, it developed into a serious consideration of some of the basics of aesthetic discourse, including one that has plagued critics since Plato: the relationship of the poet to his culture. Eglinton began it by questioning the suitability for drama of the great body of Irish legend and myth. A serial debate followed, mostly with Yeats, but with AE and William Larminie joining in. There is some evidence that the controversy was staged as a publicity stunt for the Irish National Theatre, but staged or not, the essays demonstrate Yeats' later description that it was a 'stirring row while it lasted and we were all very angry'. (Frayne, 128–129).

Certainly it had its caustic side, as when Yeats accused Eglinton of a 'petulance of rapid writing' (33). Contrary to some reports, Eglinton did not 'disapprove of Irish subjects', as Yeats later[13] put it, but of a 'determined preoccupation with ancient legends'. They were for Eglinton, 'a subject outside experience', whereas a 'national literature [...] is the expression of a strong interest in life [...] and its problems and a strong capacity for life among its people'. Furthermore, the treatment of myth in its literary redactions must go beyond 'literary archeology': He would 'welcome the reappearance of Finn and Cuchulain, but they must be expected to take on their shoulders some of the weariness and fret of our age' (24). Thus had Shakespeare succeeded in creating a Brutus and Cassius as 'rather reincarnations of Romans in the Elizabethan Age than as archeological Romans' (24).

This example did not impress Yeats, who had his own ideas about the process. He dismissed as 'external' Shakespeare, 'who had shattered the symmetry of verse and drama in order that he might fill them with things and their accidental relations' (73–74). His own examples of successful use of legend were Ibsen's *Peer Gynt* and Wagnerian opera, which he saw as the equivalent of Greek drama in the forging of a national literature (17). When Eglinton cuttingly questioned 'that Wagner was to his age what Sophocles and Shakespeare were to theirs' (24), Yeats offered another

---

[12] *Literary Ideals in Ireland*, first published Fisher Unwin, London, 1899; reprint New York: Lemma Publishing Corp., 1973, pp. 11–13. (There were nine articles.) Subsequent citations will be given in the text to this edition.

[13] *Plays and Controversies*, p. 111.

dimension to his standard: the comparison was valid because the German's work expressed the 'soul' of his nation (31). AE agreed and, as he put it, 'the province of a national literature' is to 'reveal Ireland in a clear and beautiful light' (83).

But for Eglinton they had got it backwards. It was not the function of the poet to reflect the 'soul' or ideals of his nation, he submitted, nations receive their ideals from their poets. 'In all ages', he declared, 'poets and thinkers have owed far less to their countries than their countries have owed to them' (13). Along the way, the arguments developed around such questions as the nature of literature itself: literature as a 'criticism of life', symbolism versus realism, the place of 'thought' or ideas in literature, art for art's sake, etc. Boyd called it 'history in the making [...] where the chief figures of the revival publicly formulated their standards and discussed their differences' (Boyd, 233–4). Indeed, some of these concerns continued to be important for the Revival. Was Synge's *Playboy* of *The Western World* an illumination of the 'soul' of Ireland? And was it obliged to be?

For Eglinton, at least two issues were to be of concern for the rest of his career: the relevance of the Celtic heritage to the development of a national literature; and the relationship of the poet to his culture. His argument about the latter was an earlier call to divest Irish literature of the burden of popular nationalism, in 1902, for 'The De-Davisisation of Irish Literature', or 'the getting rid of the notion that in Ireland, a writer is to think first and foremost of interpreting the nationality of his country'.[14] This, on the heels of the call for 'De-Anglicisation' by Douglas Hyde and Yeats, again sparked some controversy around Eglinton. But the idea, as well as the phrase itself, was to echo throughout later histories and criticism, sometimes unattributed. Sean O'Faolain notes only that the idea came from 'the first historian of the period' when he discusses the efforts to 'purify literature of this political impurity'.[15]

But Eglinton took the idea a step further to include an interpretation of the role of the poet as social critic. A year later in 'The Relationship of the Poet to his Country', he, himself, went to the Celtic sources to contrast the ancient satirists with what he saw as the pale moderns' evasions of unpopular issues. 'The indifference of modern Ireland to her poets', charged Eglinton, 'is the more marked when we remember that they have wholly discontinued their once terrible weapon of satire.' He called up that 'Erin where the counterparts of Yeats and AE had real power' and

---

[14] 'On the De-Davisisation of Irish Literature', *The United Irishman*, May 31, 1902, p. 3.

[15] *The Irish*, New York: The Devin-Adair Co., 1949, p. 159.

concluded with an amendment to his *Literary Ideals* argument—the poet's 'true relation to his country is one of admonition and reproof'.[16]

He took up the challenge on a larger scale the following year. Interpreting the controversy over Synge's *In the Shadow of the Glen*' as the first battle in the war to give Ireland freedom of thought,[17] he, with Fred Ryan, founded *Dana, A Magazine of Independent Thought*. Their self-stated aim was to foster a rebirth of critical discourse in Ireland—to add the dimension of a 'thought revival' to the movement.[18] *Dana* peeled a critical eye at all aspects of 1904 Irish society: nationality, language, religion. In this context, Eglinton offered Merriman's *Midnight Court*, a 'powerful piece of social criticism', as proof that there was no 'natural limitation on the Irish mind [...] for dealing boldly with substantial things' or for 'free speculation'.[19]

For many of the same reasons, Eglinton found in the Oisin dialogues 'the chief claim of Irish literature to be taken seriously'. Fascinated by the dramatic tension in this 'confrontation of pagan with Christian ideals', he found 'Nietzsche anticipated'. The conflict represented 'the primitive ideals of all the western nations [...] brought into dramatic contrast with the ideal of moral renunciation communicated to European civilisation from the East'.[20] The dialogues were not Irish only, they were cosmopolitan.

As a cosmopolitan, Eglinton became increasingly concerned about the more narrow view of the national culture—a view that seriously impinged on the establishment of a national canon. That canon, as now represented in *The Dictionary of National Biography*,[21] is enormous, occupying more than 700 pages. But during the Revival there was much dispute over such heretofore firmly canonized figures as Thomas Moore and Thomas Davis. As for Jonathan Swift or Oliver Goldsmith, and other eighteenth century Irish writers, most critics dismissed them as not 'informed by the spirit of the race' (Boyd p.10). Yeats' early rejection of these writers is well recorded (Frayne, 294). In 1902, Eglinton began a series of efforts to reclaim the Anglo-Irish tradition as a legitimate part of the Irish culture. He described the Anglo-Irishman as the 'bewildered offspring'—slightly schizoid—of a 'forced marriage', (the Union) a 'rough amour' his 'picturesque mother never ceases to deplore'. And while at times he 'would

---

[16] *The United Irishman*, Feb. 29, 1903.

[17] Francis J. Phelan, letter to writer, 1966.

[18] 'On the Possibility of a Thought Revival', *Dana*, p. 89.

[19] 'The Best Irish Poem', *Dana*, Feb., 1905, p. 298.

[20] 'St. Patrick on the Stage', *Shanachie*, 1907, see *Anglo-Irish Essays*, Dublin: The Talbot Press Ltd., 1917, p. 66.

[21] Edited by Robert Hogan, Dublin: Gill and MacMillan, paperback edition, 1985.

curse every drop of blood which comes to him from the paternal source',
when he 'has chosen to accept his own composite nature, he has shown the
capacity for doing great things'.[22] In 1916, he further explored the
significance of this 'composite race' in Ireland's history and culture, as the
Anglo-Irish became 'more Irish than the Irish themselves'.[23] From this
point he published a series of attempts to expand the canon to include Swift
and Goldsmith and other Irish writers in English of the eighteenth century,
where a 'wide no-man's land of literature' was 'waiting to be annexed'.[24]

His notion of a 'composite nationality' underlay his efforts to rescue
William Carleton for the canon. It seemed 'prophetic' to Eglinton that
Carleton had come out of Tyrone—'the locality in which the three
elements of modern Irish nationality were most naturally blended.' It was
the division of these elements, Eglinton worried, that 'threatened to spoil
Ireland's desire to have a literature'.[25] The general treatment of Carleton by
Revival critics reflected those divisions and offered a good example of how
nationalistic and religious attitudes split along these lines. Catholic critics
either ignored him or expelled him. As Thomas MacDonough put it, 'He
was not a patriot.'[26] Anglo-Irish critics gave him a firm approval. Yeats'
reintroduction of Carleton to the canon in his 'Best Lists' of Irish books
was attacked by nationalist extremists, one of whom insisted that the
'pervert' Carleton, because of his apostasy, should remain in the 'literary
pilory' (Frayne, 166-169).

Some of the same forces undoubtedly account for the neglect of Eglinton
by historians. First of all, he was unabashedly Anglo-Irish, which spelled
'west Briton' for many as well as suggesting a bias on his part. Furthermore, he generated much hostility in those early years in the withering way
he sometimes expressed his positions. He must have been extremely
offensive to language enthusiasts in his 1901 description of his attempt to
learn Irish, fetching up his 'g's from the back of his throat' and smashing
'up his r's' from his palate.[27]

As for the Celtic heritage, Eglinton was to return to it again and again,
particularly in regard to its use by modern writers. In 1919, he found a

[22] 'A Word for Anglo-Irish Literature', *The United Irishman*, March 22, 1902.

[23] 'The Modern Irishman and the Mere Irishman', *Living Age*, 1916, 425–426. Originally published in
The New Statesman. Edited version in *Anglo-Irish Essays*, Dublin: The Talbot Press Ltd., 1917, Donald
Torchiana suggests this essay influenced Yeats *Yeats and Georgian Ireland,* Evanston: Northwestern
University Press, 1966, p. 89 n.

[24] 'Life and Letters', *Irish Statesman*, (first series) April 17, 1920.

[25] 'Irish Books', *Living Age*, May 13, 1911, p. 400. First published in *The Irish Review*, 1911.

[26] *Literature in Ireland*, London: Kennikat Press, 1916, p. 33.

[27] 'The Grand Old Tongue', *Anglo-Irish Essays*, p. 30. Originally published in *The United Irishman*,
Dec. 21, 1901.

good example of a successful redaction in the emerging literature of James Stephens, as compared with the literary 'archeology' of Samuel Ferguson. Ferguson, the 'faithfulest interpreter', brings us 'great boulders from the past', where Stephens makes the imaginative leap to transform his reader into 'a salmon who has read Hamlet'. As Stephens' readers, we go

> [...] with our luncheon in our pocket to interrogate Druids and Patriarchs and with all that we have learned from Darwin and Ernest Seton-Thompson in our minds to become stags and wild boars, hawks and salmon. In such returns to the past we bring a good deal that was not there and find a good deal which for the first time acquires significance.[28]

The 1902 call for 'De-Davisisation' was also an argument for enlarging the concept of a national literature.

> For the questions which divide household and nation against themselves: religious, political, fundamental questions, these are the questions in respect to which the literary man must have a free hand. [...] Literature must be free as the elements. If that is to be cosmopolitan, it must be cosmopolitan.[29]

The elevation of the cosmopolitan over the parochial standard became more important to Eglinton by 1911 as he urged Irish writers to look to greater Europe for models. Nineteenth century prose writers had been misled by the unfortunate example of Scott, and but for his 'dazzling vogue', some Irish writer 'might have stumbled on the secret of Turgenev, and so made the literary fortune of his country'.[30] Moore produced *The Untilled Field* on this advice from Eglinton.[31] He yearned for an 'Irish Cervantes' and predicted the new genius of Irish literature would come from some unexpected quarter, in fact, that contemporary Catholic Ireland indicated the emergence of a comic genius.

> [...] a writer of the type of Cervantes rather than...an idealizing poet or romance writer. A hero as loveable as the great Knight of the Rueful Countenance. [...] We can imagine him issuing forth, fresh-hearted as

[28] 'Life and Letters', *The Irish Statesman*, Oct. 4, 1919, p. 362.

[29] 'The De-Davisisation of Irish Literature', *The United Irishman*, March 31, 1902.

[30] 'Irish Books', p. 410.

[31] 'Salve', p. 462.

a child at the age of fifty, and with glib and saffron-coloured kilt to realize and incidentally to expose the ideals of present-day Ireland.[32]

Thus, Eglinton seems a link between the Revival romantics and the post-Revival new wave of satirical or socially critical writers. Later he was to identify in Joyce's 'malign irony', in Moore's 'good humoured indecency', and Shaw's 'buoyant irreverence' traits he had earlier located in both Anglo-Irish and Celtic traditions.[33] Among these traits were the 'confidence in the elemental passions and a scorn for all the timidities of our hesitantly Christian civilization' that he had found in the Oisin dialogues in 1907.[34] An influence on Joyce is suggested. Certainly Eglinton's views about the relationship of the poet to his country are echoed in the remarks of Stephen Dedalus in *Ulysses*. If the Eglinton phrases about the 'Irish Cervantes' ring a bell for Joyce readers, it may be because Joyce heavily alludes to this passage in the library colloquy of *Ulysses*.[35] Eglinton's 1917 footnote to 'Irish Books' mentioned Joyce, Moore and Stephens as examples of this 'new wave', and suggested *Hail and Farewell* as 'partial fulfillment' of his Cervantes prophecy.[36] But does not Leopold Bloom, as well as *Ulysses* itself, 'expose the ideals' of Revival Ireland?

Whether directly influential or just prophetic, with all his biases and flaws, John Eglinton introduced ideas and argued positions later absorbed by both Revivalists and the new generation. That generation of Irish satirical, comic writers—Joyce, Sean O'Casey, Frank O'Connor—produced a literature of more international and lasting significance than many of those now forgotten or almost unread romantic Revival poets. Or, as a member of that new generation put it:

> All said and done, and though Eglinton himself would not for a moment admit it, any future writer concerning himself with Irish literature will find himself unable to neglect John Eglinton. [37]

---

[32] 'Irish Books', p. 403.

[33] 'Dublin Letter', *The Dial Magazine*, May, 1927, p. 410.

[34] 'St. Patrick on the Stage', *Anglo-Irish Essays*, p. 66.

[35] *Ulysses*, New York: Modern Library edition, 1934, p. 190.

[36] *Anglo-Irish Essays*, p. 89.

[37] 'John Eglinton, Irish Writer', (Obituary), *London Times*, May 17, 1961.

A Problem of Language Identity:
The Comparative Linguistics of Serbo-Croatian[1]

RANKO BUGARSKI
University of Belgrade

IN PRINCIPLE, any language has an assumed separate identity by virtue of being regarded as an idiom distinct from others. In practice, however, there are well-known difficulties with this notion, one result of which is the impossibility of counting up the languages of the world and determining with any precision their total number at any given time. According to one view (Katičić 1972; cf. also Bugarski 1993, Ch. 1), three aspects of the identity of a language can be analytically distinguished: the structural (what it is like), the genetic (how it originated) and the sociolinguistic (how it is evaluated). In many cases (e.g. French, Russian, Hungarian, Japanese) there is 'simple' identity in that the three aspects correlate, the language counting as a separate one under each of them. Yet there are also numerous instances of 'complex' identity, with the lack of such correlation, where a language (e.g. Norwegian, Serbo-Croatian, Hindi/Urdu, Chinese) may count as a single entity by only some but not all of the criteria.

At the 1990 meeting of the Societas Linguistica Europaea in Berne I presented a paper entitled 'Language identity and language conflict in Yugoslavia', in which I surveyed the sociolinguistic situation of the then Yugoslavia from the point of view of language identity. Having argued that this concept should be subjected to elaboration and refinement, particularly in view of 'complex' identity, I introduced the tentative idea that the identity of a language might under certain circumstances be described as relatively stronger or weaker, either internally (e.g. monocentric vs. polycentric standardization, or the extent and direction of variations within it) or externally (e.g. endonormative vs. exonormative standardization, or demarcation from neighbouring languages in linguistic or sociopolitical terms). Questions of language identity in this sense may, I argued further, lead to language conflict, understood as the linguistic reflection of social tensions.

---

[1] The sad news of the passsing of Conn Ó Cléirigh was imparted to me by our mutual friend Anders Ahlqvist during an otherwise enjoyable cocktail party in the yard of the Arsenaal Building of Leiden University, on the occasion of the 28th Annual Meeting of the Societas Linguistica Europaea, 31 August–2 September 1995. I dedicate the paper I read there to Conn's memory, in the belief that he—himself an active member of the Societas—would have appreciated learning of this unusual instance of linguistic decomposition in progress. The paper remains as written in July 1995, since the political events that have occurred in ex-Yugoslavia between that date and the appending of this note in March 1996 affect the case presented only in negligible external detail.

I then provisionally postulated three degrees of language identity ('strong', 'medium' and 'weak'), making the point that these highly metaphorical terms refer to the sociolinguistic descriptionof languages, rather than to any inherent features of language awareness among speakers, of subjective consciousness, or even of language attitudes per se—though these attitudes may over time lead to changes in the objective situation of languages. It is thus not claimed that speakers actually go about wondering 'Am I speaking Hindi or Urdu (Serbian or Croatian) or both at the same time?', nor is it suggested that you can only whisper in a 'weak' language but can shout in a 'strong' one—or anything of the sort!

Sociolinguistic description must then take account of such factors conditioning language identity as size of the language, concentration of its speakers, economic strength behind it, standardization, interference, sociopolitical status, prestige, language loyalty, etc. When matched against a matrix of such parameters, the languages of ex-Yugoslavia showed different degrees of strength of language identity. Serbo-Croatian, the sole topic of the remainder of my reflections in this paper, came out strong on external but weak on internal identity—and this is the take-off point for my present considerations.

The phrase 'comparative linguistics' in the latter half of my title is a somewhat tongue-in-cheek usage. While helping to accommodate my topic within the general theme of our conference, it also symbolically pinpoints the problem at issue. It seems highly idiosyncratic to pretend to talk about the comparative linguistics of what—according to its name at least—still looks like a single language, but this of course is the whole point: is it really? Let us see, then, how this question can be answered. I propose to examine it purely as a linguist, while suppressing any personal feelings or preferences I might have as a native speaker of the language. In particular, while dealing with this politically sensitive and emotionally charged subject I will refrain from grinding ideological axes or engaging in special pleading.

The identity of Serbo-Croatian has in some ways been a matter of controversy ever since the emergence of a standard language of that name (alternatively called Croatian or Serbian, Croato-Serbian) during the second half of the last century. The question of whether this label refers to a single, double or even multiple linguistic entity still admits of no simple answer, depending as it does on the level at which it is posed—strictly linguistic, sociolinguistic, social psychological, political, etc. To take these up in turn very briefly, a view which I found quite reasonable and myself expressed on various occasions prior to the disintegration of Yugoslavia might be summarized as follows. Linguistically, in the sense of historical, comparative and typological linguistics, Serbo-Croatian is a single language. Sociolinguistically, and focusing on the linguistic standard rather than on the underlying diasystem, it is a single standard language, but polycentric, having different standard variants in Serbia, Croatia, Bosnia-Herzegovina and Montenegro. The two relatively well-defined and mutually opposed variants, Serbian (Eastern) and Croatian (Western), function as standard languages in their own right. From the point of view of social psychology, largely concerning language attitudes and speaker identification, the issue becomes yet more complex, as some speakers (predominantly in the Eastern region) view the language as a single entity, though with variations within it, and tend to call it Serbo-Croatian, while others (mainly in the Western part) feel that two distinct though closely related langages are involved, Croatian and Serbian.

What is controversial, then, are not the linguistic differences themselves but the symbolic values attached to them in an ethnically, confessionally, socially and politically differentiated community of speakers administratively assembled in a shaky federation. Consequently, the identity of Serbo-Croatian is in large measure a matter of attitude and interpretation rather than of observable linguistic fact (cf. Bugarski 1990, 44–45).

In a complex situation like this, it was probably inevitable that, if a simple decision had to be made after all, it could only be brought about by political developments—and this is precisely what happened in the years immediately preceding armed conflict and the destruction of the Yugoslav federation. The country's disintegration duly led to the administrative demise of its largest language and major symbol of its precarious unity. The state and the language thus came to be buried side by side in the same tomb, to the tune of salvos which were by no means merely salutary (cf. Bugarski 1995, 161).

As a result, Serbo-Croatian no longer officially exists in any of the former Yugoslav republics, now independent states containing, in some cases, quasi-states within their recognized borders. On the administrative level it has dissolved into several distinct idioms. In Serbia, Montenegro and the Serb-dominated parts of Croatia and Bosnia-Herzegovina we now have Serbian; in Croatia and the Croat-dominated section of Bosnia-Herzegovina, Croatian; in Bosnia-Herzegovina the prevalent name is Bosnian, though the names Serbian and Croatian may also be officially used by the respective national populations of the part of the state controlled by the Bosnian government. (Whether or not there will be official recognition of a fourth offspring, Montenegrin, will depend on political developments within the present 'Yugoslav federation' of Serbia and Montenegro).

The idioms thus variously named play a major role as symbols of the national sovereignty of distinct states that have emerged on formerly Yugoslav territory. To the extent that language goes with state, then, they are separate languages administratively and politically. But the linguist may be pardoned if he or she wants to know how such formal pronouncements correlate with what appears to be linguistic reality—in other words, to what extent those idioms should be regarded as diferrent languages linguistically too. This is obviously a very different question, as languages do not have a way of simply decomposing and recomposing overnight. The short answer might be that Serbian, Croatian and Bosnian at present differ mostly in name, rather less in substance, and very little in structure. Given the very large common core of Serbo-Croatian, and the very short time that has elapsed since its formal dissolution, linguists will not need to be told that ordinary communication among people of average education from Belgrade, Zagreb, Sarajevo etc. goes on much as before. So if free, unhampered communication (disregarding possible artificially introduced obstacles) is the main linguistic criterion, Serbo-Croatian is still alive and well, and smells as sweet by any name.

Yes, but for how long? This is the next question the linguist is likely to ask. This, to be sure, is a matter of language policy and planning. In the case at hand, such activities are obviously aimed at further divergence on the whole, though differently in the individual instances. Croatian, and to a lesser extent Bosnian, are currently undergoing extensive linguistic engineering so as to diverge from each other, and especially from Serbian, as far and as quickly as possible. The Croatian aim to be different is understandable enough politically, even sociolinguistically; but what is surprising, and possibly unprecedented in the history of language planning campaigns, is the speed and thoroughness with which the state is attempting to overhaul its language practically beyond recognition. Croatian archaisms are reintroduced, neologisms are coined, terminologies in all fields are changed from traditional and international to new-fangled Croatian, a spelling reform is apparently under way, and so on. It is all very well to claim that official Newspeak is not to be confused with the everyday language of the man in the street. However, it will be instructive to see, if language-planning extremists have it their way, how long linguistic communication within Croatia itself can go on without serious failures, and what kinds of social divisions are to be imposed based on mastery or non-mastery of the new Croatian. (Communicating with Serbs or Moslems, hardly a current priority, may be disregarded here.)

As regards the newly proclaimed Bosnian, the war going on on its territory makes it difficult to engage in serious language planning activities, but there too new spelling rules and dictionaries are published, the chief purpose of which is emphasizing the Islamic (Arabic and Turkish) component in the native linguistic and cultural heritage. The language system has so far been little affected by this, and the changes one perceives are rather in speech patterns and linguistic behaviour (greetings, public announcements, religious service etc.).

Turning now to Serbian, we find a rather different situation in that, understandably enough from a political and psychological point of view, there is no general drive in Serbia or Montenegro to make the language different either from its own preceding phase or from Croatian or Bosnian. There have been a few extremist proposals for the 'Serbization' of spelling rules, the avoidance of Turkisms etc., but they have not attracted much public attention. Consequently, the language itself has not perceptibly changed over the last half-decade. The main changes, in fact, have occurred on the external or symbolic level: the Serbian name of the language, official priority for the Cyrillic alphabet over the Latin and, more controversially and less officially, for the Ekavian pronunciation over the Ijekavian—this last especially among the Serb leaders in Bosnia-Herzegovina and Croatia. Other largely symbolic initiatives are calls for the rewriting of the history of the standard language—as indeed of Serbian history generally—seen through the new 'nationally awakened' Serbian eyes, and the occasional changing of toponyms with Moslem or Croat associations. (A highly critical discussion of all these developments may now be found in Bugarski 1995.)

Even our necessarily superficial analysis should suffice to show how difficult it is to disentangle the linguistic and political issues underlying the unusual and fast-changing case of language identity that has been our concern in this paper. If anything, the identity question now seems even more complicated than a few years ago, as summarized above. To say resolutely that there exists today one single Serbo-Croatian language and leave it at that for all purposes is to speak plain nonsense. To claim with equal resolution that Serbian, Croatian and Bosnian are all fully legitimate and distinct languages, while there is simply no such thing as Serbo-Croatian on any level of fact or interpretation, is to make a political or emotional statement. This is fair enough as far as it goes, since political reality must be taken into account, while on the other hand people have a right to their collective or individual feelings, and their emotions are not to be argued about. The trouble is that such an argument does not go nearly far enough, as it completely bypasses the aspect of presumably greatest interest to linguists—that is, the linguistic aspect, or sociolinguistic if you will.

To take up a disciplinary vantage point first, it makes perfect sense to talk about both Serbo-Croatian (or Croato-Serbian) on the one hand, and about, say, Serbian and Croatian on the other. There are contexts—in dialectology and standardology, language history and synchrony, etc.— where it remains fully legitimate, indeed indispensable, to make parallel but discriminating use of all these labels, in view of evident differences in their semantic scope. For example, Croatian dialectology is obviously not coextensive with Serbo-Croatian dialectology, nor is the history of standard Serbian the same thing as the history of standard Serbo-Croatian. A dictionary of literary Serbo-Croatian must look rather different from dictionaries of literary Serbian or Croatian. And so on. To deny this would be to make scholarship subservient to ideology.

(Incidentally, awareness of such simple facts has not prevented the renaming of the relevant institutions in Serbia—from 'Serbo-Croatian' to 'Serbian'—when the new official name of the language was introduced, which has caused not a few practical problems along the lines just hinted at. I do not know if there is any such problem in Croatia).

These considerations also remind us that identity must by no means be equated with name, which is only one of its components. Languages, like people, may have more than one name, and again as in the case of people, the same name can be borne by more than one language.

We thus come—at least for the present—to the end of the strange life story of a language, in international scholarship still usually known as Serbo-Croatian, which has been broken up into several idioms by the ethnically, confessionally and politically different groups of its speakers in the belief that each might fare better that way. In a manner previously unknown, this was accomplished from within, with great zeal and efficiency, and without external pressure. (Recall that in my peacetime Berne analysis Serbo-Croatian rated strong identity externally but weak internally.) The future only can show to what extent this belief was justified, and how far it may have been a monumental collective error (cf. Bugarski 1995, 161).

Finally, as far as linguistics is concerned, it may stand to gain from an understanding of this rather confusing case of language identity. If nothing else, the fate of Serbo-Croatian exposes from a new angle an ambiguity inherent in the concept of 'a language', by demonstrating how it is possible for something to be both one language and several languages simultaneously, depending on the perspective one takes. To summarize my foregoing analysis, we seem to be dealing with a single overall linguistic system whose sociolinguistic subsystems function politically as distinct standard languages bearing different national names. In terms of the aspects of language identity noted at the beginning of this discussion, the first two, structural and genetic, essentially still spell out unity, but the third aspect of evaluation has recently speeded up diversity. In a nutshell, what remains one language linguistically has become several languages politically. An interesting point, which must await further theoretical and empirical clarification, is whether this sort of situation is merely transitional or perhaps capable of persisting over time, and what set of criteria might be found adequate to resolve the dilemma either way.

REFERENCES

Bugarski, Ranko 1990. 'The Social Basis of Language Conflict and Language Attitudes', in *Language Attitudes and Language Conflict*, ed. by Peter H. Nelde, Bonn: Dümmler, 41–47

—1993. *Jezici* ['Languages'], Novi Sad: Matica srpska

—1995. *Jezik od mira do rata* ['Language from Peace to War'], 2nd ed., Belgrade: XX vek/Slovograf

Katičić, Radoslav 1972. 'Identitet jezika' ['The Identity of a Language'], *Suvremena lingvistika*, 5–6, 5–14. (Reprinted in Radoslav Katičić, *Novi jezikoslovni ogledi*, Zagreb: Školska knjiga, 1986, 41–64)

The Acquisition and Properties of a Contact Vernacular Grammar

KAREN CORRIGAN

University of Newcastle-upon-Tyne

1 INTRODUCTION

THIS PAPER uses a real-time text-corpus[1] to examine the acquisition and syntactic properties of relative clause formation strategies in South Armagh English, a variety produced by recent language contact between speakers of conservative, non-standard English and speakers of Irish. Policansky (1982) gives a preliminary account of the Belfast English relative system from a sociolinguistic perspective and social, historical and syntactic aspects of Irish-English relativization have subsequently been examined by Ó Siadhail (1984), Filppula (1991) and, more recently, by Doherty (1993), Harris (1993) and Henry (1995). The account which is offered here differs from previous treatments since the entire system is reviewed and there is an attempt to assign particular strategies to substratal and/or superstratal sources.[2]

2 THE ACQUISITION OF A CONTACT VERNACULAR

2.1 Language Shift and Ethnolinguistic Vitality

According to Fishman (1989, 202), interaction between two ethnolinguistic communities generally results in one of the three resolutions given in Figure 1 below, where *A* represents the indigenous language and *B* the intrusive:

---

[1] I am indebted to Conn Ó Cléirigh for his suggestion that the archive of the Irish Folklore Department, UCD might provide this diachronic database of Irish-English vernacular.

[2] Cathal Doherty, 'The Syntax of Subject Contact Relatives'. MS. (University of California at Santa Cruz, 1993); Markku Filppula, 'Subordinating *And*' in Hiberno-English Syntax: Irish or English Origin?', in *Language Contact in the British Isles,* edited by P. Sture Ureland and George Broderick (Tübingen: Max Niemeyer, 1991), pp. 617–631; John Harris, 'The Grammar of Irish English', in *Real English,* ed. by James Milroy and Leslie Milroy (London: Longman, 1993), pp. 139–186; Alison Henry, *Belfast English and Standard English: Dialect Variation and Parameter Setting* (Oxford: Basil Blackwell, 1995); Mícheál Ó Siadhail, '*Agus (Is) /And*: a Shared Syntactic Feature', *Celtica,* 16 (1984), 125–37; Linda Policansky, 'Grammatical Variation in Belfast English', *Belfast Working Papers in Language and Linguistics,* 6 (1982), 37–62. Filppula (1991) and Ó Siadhail (1984) e.g. are restricted to a description of the so-called, 'Subordinating *And*' strategy and its probable origin, while both Doherty (1993) and Henry (1995) offer synchronic explanations for the Zero strategy which predominates in subject contact relative clauses.

Figure 1:

Resolution 1 : B → A = A

Resolution 2 : B → A = B

Resolution 3 : B → A = B + A

The general pattern seems to be that in language contact situations, groups with strong ethnolinguistic vitality[3] will desist learning a second language or, at the least, succumb to stable bilingualism and Fishman's Resolution 3. Thus, powerful groups maintain their first language and induce its loss in weaker ones. The underlying dynamics of Resolution 1, therefore, are most applicable to the case of migrants, for instance, and can be related to the econo-technical and cultural superiority associated with the *A* group which attracts those *B* speakers who are eager for advancement. Resolution 2 is that which is pertinent to the South Armagh case, since it schematises the shift in Ireland amongst the indigenous population to intrusive, non-standard English implying the breakdown of previously established societal allocation of language functions and the increasing restriction of Irish to vernacular rather than honorific domains. As Fishman (1989; 1991) would predict, the colonising dislocation associated with the Ulster plantation induced Resolution 2 for a variety of social, political and psychological reasons which will be ignored for present purposes. [4]

2.2 The Historiography of Southern County Armagh

According to the first language census of the area in 1851,[5] the planter population had exerted little influence on the peripheral south of the County primarily because of its mountainous terrain. Thus, most of its inhabitants are recorded as being predominantly Irish-speaking and a number of them

[3] For a discussion see the papers in *Language, Ethnicity and Intergroup Relations*, ed. by Howard Giles (London: Academic Press, 1977).

[4] Socio-political and psychological arguments for Resolutions 1, 2 and 3 in a range of speech communities are offered by Joshua A. Fishman, *Language and Ethnicity in Minority Social Perspective* (Clevedon: Multilingual Matters, 1989); Fishman, *Reversing Language Shift* (Clevedon: Multilingual Matters, 1991); Willem Fase and others, *Maintenance and Loss of Minority Languages* (Amsterdam: John Benjamins, 1992) and Rajend Mesthrie, *English in Language Shift* (Cambridge, 1992). For a detailed discussion of the Ulster Plantation and its effects, see Philip S. Robinson, *The Plantation of Ulster* (Dublin: Gill & Macmillan, 1984).

[5] Strictly-speaking, Pynnar's survey of 1659 was the first Census of Ireland to use linguistic criteria for returning population distributions, but it was not systematic and contains a number of inaccuracies (c.f. *A Census of Ireland, circa 1659*, ed. by Séamas Pender (Dublin: Coimisiún Láimhscríbhinní na hÉireann, 1939), xiii fn., xviii). For a discussion of the validity of the 1851 census, see G.B. Adams, 'The Validity of Language Census Figures in Ulster, 1851–1911', *Ulster Folklife*, 25 (1979), 113–122. Repr. in *The English Dialects of Ulster*, ed. by Michael V. Barry and Philip M. Tilling (Cultra, Co. Down: Ulster Folk and Transport Museum, 1986), pp. 125–134, who argues that despite its greater systematicity, the position of Irish at this time was considerably stronger than the returns suggest.

were returned as monoglots. Figures from the last language census conducted in Ulster before partition (1911) suggest that there remained over 2000 native speakers of South Armagh (SA) Irish.[6]

Their distribution, however, between the adult and younger generations (outlined in Figure 2 below) shows a marked decline in ability, a phenomenon which is generally held to be indicative of language shift towards Resolution 2.

PERCENTAGE OF IRISH SPEAKERS IN SOUTH COUNTY ARMAGH,
NORTHERN IRELAND, 1911

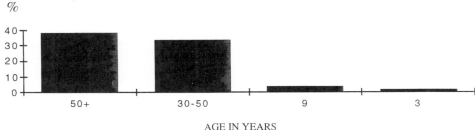

AGE IN YEARS
Figure 2 [After Adams (1964, 117)]

Although the Norwegian philologist Alf Sommerfelt wrote a grammar of SA Irish based on the intuitions of a native speaker in the late 1920s,[7] anecdotal and local historical evidence suggests that twenty years later there were fewer than ten speakers who had English as a second rather than a first language.[8]

2.3 Linguistic Consequences

This paper argues that the process of non-pathological language attrition i.e. the disintegration of the structure and function of SA Irish and the movement of its speakers through monoglot Irish, bilingual Irish-English

[6] G.B. Adams, 'The Last Language Census in Northern Ireland', in *Ulster Dialects: an Introductory Symposium*, ed. by G.B. Adams, Ulster Folk and Transport Museum (Cultra, Co. Down: Ulster Folk and Transport Museum, 1964), pp. 111–145 (p. 134).

[7] Aindrias Ó Marcaigh was Sommerfelt's subject and he is reported to have been born in Annagassan about 1845 and to have lived in a monolingual Irish-speaking community in the townland of Ballsmile, South Armagh until the age of 14: see Alf Sommerfelt, 'South Armagh Irish', *Norsk Tidsskrift for Sprogvidenskap*, 2, (1929), p. 107.

[8] For instance, in an article entitled 'Our Living Past' distributed in the pamphlet *Ard Macha* by the Gaelic League in June 1943, there is the comment: 'There are some thousands of native speakers in Ireland today—there are less than **ten** who know the historic Armagh dialect' (p. 16). I am grateful to my father, Oliver Corrigan, for locating a copy of the pamphlet.

and finally monoglot English phases has produced a number of interesting linguistic effects which can be demonstrated by close examination of the structure and development of SA English relativization processes.

According to Seliger and Vago (1991)[9] the path to attrition followed by communities in language shift is an incremental process alternating compound and coordinate bilingual stages such as those schematised in Figure 3 below :

STAGE 1	STAGE 2	STAGE 3
Compound I Bilingualism	Coordinate Bilingualism	Compound II Bilingualism
L1→L2	L1→L2	L2→L1
UG→L2	L2→L2	L2→L2
	UG→L2	L1→L2
		UG→L2?
		UG→L1

Figure 3 [After Seliger and Vago (1991, 5)]

In Southern County Armagh, the first phase of attrition began in the 1850's as SA Irish speakers (L1) began acquiring English as a second language (L2) from native speakers of regional non-standard English and from L2 English speakers whose first language was Irish. By using both their knowledge of L1 and innate universal grammatical principles (UG) they constructed for themselves an L2 English grammar which was marked by transfer effects from SA Irish.[10]

During the second stage, the L1 and L2 grammars gradually separated as the learners built up sets of English rules that were independent of Irish ones. Nevertheless, there is still evidence of both a role for transfer from Irish and from UG principles.

At stage three, early this century, increasing fluency in English begins to affect the domains of Irish and the direction of transfer becomes reversed. As far as UG is concerned, Seliger and Vago (1991, 6) point out that at this stage, it is not clear whether UG continues to impact upon L2 (UG→L2?) and may indeed impact on L1 as Figure 3 suggests.

---

[9] *First Language Attrition*, ed. by Herbert W. Seliger and Robert M. Vago (Cambridge: University Press, 1991).

[10] Sommerfelt's account of Ó Marcaigh's competence as 'his Irish was very largely unspoiled by his contact with English, and even his English reproduced the Irish phonetics almost exactly' (1929, 108), suggests that he was a compound bilingual at Stage 1. The general phenomenon of transfer between L1 and L2 in language contact situations is examined in considerable detail by Terence Odlin, *Language Transfer: Cross-Linguistic Influence in Language Learning* (Cambridge: University Press, 1989).

3 THE SOUTH ARMAGH TEXT-CORPUS

Labov (1970)[11] and others have argued that the nature and quality of the database partially determines the scope of linguistic inquiry, as such, there follows a brief outline of the corpus upon which this research is based and the method of data collection. It contains circa. 50,000 words which have been extrapolated from manuscript records of oral narratives on familiar, related topics collected in SA by the folklorist Michael J. Murphy between 1942 and 1974. These short texts were produced by male and female speakers who participated, along with the collector and his extended family, in a dense and multiplex, rural network. Murphy transcribed the material in shorthand and I have edited it to exclude doggerel verse and extraneous comments made by him on idiom, pronunciation and lexis.

4 SUPERSTRATE RELATIVE FORMATION STRATEGIES

Assuming the principle of 'colonial lag' first postulated by Marckwardt (1958; 1980) and later refined in Görlach (1991; 1994),[12] coupled with the fact that County Armagh was first colonised in the sixteenth century by groups of non-standard regional English speakers, we should expect the superstratal input to the dialect to resemble the relativization system of Early Modern English rather than that described e.g. in Quirk and others (1972, 13.14.15).[13] Section 4.1 below traces the development of relativization strategies in the history of English with a view to reconstructing what the Early Modern target for SA speakers might have been.

4.1 The Development of Standard Written English Relative Markers

Prior to the work of Romaine (1980; 1981; 1982 and 1984a)[14] on Middle Scots, accounts of relativization in the history of English were monolithic

---

[11] William Labov, 'The Study of Language in its Social Context', *Studium Generale*, 23 (1) (1970), 30–87.

[12] Albert H. Marckwardt, *American English* (New York: Oxford University Press, 1958), revised by Joey L. Dillard (Oxford: University Press, 1980); Manfred Görlach, 'Colonial Lag? The Alleged Conservative Character of American English and other 'Colonial' Varieties', in *Englishes: Studies in Varieties of English 1984–1988*, ed. by Görlach (Amsterdam: John Benjamins, 1991), pp. 90–107; Görlach, 'Innovation in New Englishes', *English World-Wide*, 15 (1) (1994), 101–126.

[13] Randolph Quirk, and others, *A Grammar of Contemporary English* (London: Longman, 1972).

[14] Suzanne Romaine, 'The Relative Clause Marker in Scots English: Diffusion, Complexity and Style as Dimensions of Syntactic Change', *Language in Society*, 9 (1980), pp. 221–49; 'Syntactic Complexity, Relativization and Stylistic Levels in Middle Scots', *Folia Linguistica Historica*, 2 (1981), pp. 56–77; *Socio-historical Linguistics: its Status and Methodology* (Cambridge, 1982); 'The English Language in

in that they assume, for example, monostylism between the periods (in written forms and between spoken and written discourse practices). Thus, in a standard treatment based on textual sources such as Mustanoja (1960)[15] (summarised in Table 1 below), the *WH*-relative pronouns, derived from Middle English interrogatives, are described as supplanting an earlier system in which *that* (from Middle English *þat*) was predominant.

RELATIVE MARKERS IN OLD, MIDDLE AND MODERN ENGLISH

MARKER TYPE	OE	ME	ModE
Demonstratives	se, sēo, þæt etc.	þat > þat	that
Indeclinable Relative Particle	þe	þe	
Interrogatives	hwā, hwilc, hwǣr etc.	who, which, where etc.	who, which, where etc.
Omission	∅	∅	∅ (non-subject relatives only)

TABLE 1 [After Mustanoja (1960, 190ff)]

Romaine has argued that these changes to the relativization strategies of speakers between the Middle Ages and the present-day are in some sense universally motivated and hence predictable since they correlate with the *Case Accessibility Hierarchy* proposed in research by Keenan (1972; 1975; 1985) and Keenan and Comrie (1977; 1979).[16] This *Hierarchy* makes four claims that are said to constrain relative clause formation:

1.)   Any language will relativize only the continuous subsequence given below :

Scotland', in *English as a World Language,* ed. by Charles-J. Bailey and Manfred Görlach (Cambridge: University Press, 1984a), pp. 56–83.

[15] Tauno Mustanoja, *A Middle English Syntax, Part I: Parts of Speech* (Helsinki: Mémoires de la Société Néophilologique, XXIII, 1960).

[16] Edward L. Keenan, 'Relative Clause Formation in Malagasy', in *The Chicago Which Hunt*, ed. by Paul Peranteau and others (Chicago: Dept. of Linguistics, 1972), pp. 169–90; Edward L. Keenan, 'Variation in Universal Grammar', in *Analyzing Variation in Language*, ed. by Ralph Fasold and Roger W. Shuy (Washington, DC, 1975), pp. 136–49; Keenan, 'Relative Clauses', in *Language Typology and Syntactic Description,* II, *Complex Constructions*, ed. by Timothy Shopen, (Cambridge: University Press, 1985), pp. 141–70; Keenan and Bernard Comrie, 'Noun Phrase Accessibility and Universal Grammar', *Linguistic Inquiry*, 8 (1977), pp. 63–99; Keenan and Comrie, 'Data on the Noun Phrase Accessibility Hierarchy', *Language*, 55 (1979), pp. 332–352.

The Case Accessibility Hierarchy

Subject > Direct Object > Indirect Object > Oblique > Genitive >
Object of comparison

Increasing Complexity →

Figure 4 [After Keenan (1972; 1975; 1985)/Keenan and Comrie (1977; 1979)]

2.)   Relativization of any category preceded by '>' will imply relativization of all categories above it.

3.)   If a language relativizes only one category, this will be subject.

4.)   The further down the *Case Hierarchy* you descend, relativization apparently becomes more 'complex' or 'difficult'.

In Romaine's discussion of the evolution of these relativization strategies (summarised in Table 2 below) she argues that the changes were incremental and that the ancestors of the modern *WH*-relatives occurred initially in the more complex positions. Thus, genitive *of which* and oblique object *to which* appear first and become established in the period 1400–1500. The pronouns *whom* and *whose* which distinguish animacy of the antecedent as well as object and genitive functions appear in the fifteenth century while the nominative *who* only becomes fully established in the sixteenth. Moreover, the adoption of the *WH*-strategy is sensitive to stylistic stratification in the sense of Labov (1966), i.e. it occurs first in more formal (particularly Latinate) styles and, again, the nominative type is restricted to formal usage for longer than the object or genitive types.[17]

Romaine's research has also taken into account the development of the so-called Zero relative strategy in which the antecedent is not marked by a co-referential pronoun or by *that* (indicated by the null symbol, in the last rows of Table 1 above and 2 below). The strategy occurred in Old English as in (1) but was rare.

(1) Ælfric [ø   wæs at Rēadingum   witena   ]
lit. *Ælfric (who) was at Reading   a counsellor*
'Ælfric who was a counsellor at Reading'

Zero relativization is believed to have originated in colloquial usage in Old English and to have continued into Middle English increasing in frequency

---

[17] William Labov, *The Social Stratification of English in New York City* (Washington D.C.: Center for Applied Linguistics, 1966). Roger Lass, *The Shape of English* (London: J.M. Dent, 1987), p. 191, makes a similar point.

and spreading from the upper to the lower end of the *Accessibility Hierarchy*. Gradually, subject relative omission became disfavoured to the extent that in the Modern standard *WH-* relative and *That* markers have become categorical in this function, though omission continues with objects in certain registers. Hence, Quirk (1972, 865) denotes (2) as ungrammatical, though it would be licensed in a number of non-standard dialects :

(2) *The table [ø stands in the corner has a broken leg]

THE EXPANSION OF RELATIVE MARKERS IN THE HISTORY OF ENGLISH: A RECONSTRUCTION

STRATEGY	c.1100	c.1400	c.1500	c.1600
'THAT'	þat	þat	that	that
'WH-'	þe	of which to which whose whom	of which to which which whose whom	of which to which which whose whom who
'ZERO'	ø	ø	ø	ø

TABLE 2 [After Romaine (1982, 53ff)]

4.2 Relative Formation Strategies in Regional and Non-Standard Varieties of English

The research available on relative formation strategies in contemporary spoken regional and non-standard English dialects (though principally on Scots)[18] suggests that the scenario presented in Table 1 cannot be generalised. In many of these varieties the typical ratio of relative pronouns lags behind the Modern English column given in Table 1 and they appear instead to be at various points along the reconstructed continuum of Table

---

[18] Jim Miller, '*That*: a Relative Pronoun? Sociolinguistics and Syntactic Analysis', in *Edinburgh Studies in the English Language*, ed. by John Anderson and Norman MacLeod (Edinburgh: John Donald, 1988), pp. 113–119; Miller, 'The Grammar of Scottish English, in *Real* English, ed. by James Milroy and Lesley Milroy (London: Longman, 1993), pp. 99–138; Suzanne Romaine, *The Language of Children and Adolescents: The Acquisition of Communicative Competence* (Oxford: Basil Blackwell, 1984b: Ch.3); S. Romaine, *Pidgin and Creole Languages* (London: Longman, 1988: ch.6). A more general list of possibilities within regional British Englishes is provided in Peter Trudgill, *Sociolinguistics* (London: Pelican, 1983), p. 41.

2.[19] This necessitates greater reliance by their speakers on Zero and *That* strategies in order to relativize heads at both the upper and lower positions of the *Accessibility Hierarchy*. Moreover, there is also evidence that contemporary, non-standard Englishes have recourse to other strategies, including 'Subordinating *And* ' (3, 4) and a Resumptive pronoun type (5, 6) which were extant, though residual in Early Modern English.[20]

(3)   [I] only found five$_i$ or six$_i$ in the said pond, [and those$_i$ very sick and lean]
    'I only found five or six in the said pond each of which was very sick and lean'
        (After Filppula (1991, 624) who located this in the Early Modern English section of the *Helsinki Corpus*)

(4)   She had a child$_i$ [and the child$_i$ died in the ship]
    'She had a child who died on the ship'
        (After Mesthrie 1992, 78)

(5)   the person$_i$ [that his$_i$ foot is touched]
    'the person whose foot is touched'
        (After Romaine (1988, 237))

(6)   the spikes$_i$ [that you stick in the ground and throw rings over them$_i$]
    'the spikes that you stick in the ground which you throw rings over'
        (After Miller (1993, 111–112))

On this basis, we can hypothesise that the relative pronoun ratio incorporated in the grammar of SA English will, likewise, not concur with that of written standard English and may contain gaps so that certain categories on the *Accessibility Hierarchy* become unrelativizeable without recourse to ancillary strategies.

---

[19] For instance, the archaic character of South African Indian English in this regard is noted by Mesthrie (1992, 71ff.).

[20] For details of the Early English types, see Filppula (1991); Otto Jespersen, *Essentials of English Grammar* (London: Holt & Company, 1983 [repr. 1933]); Franz H. Link, '*And* oder *With* + Partizipium', *Anglia*, 73 (1955), 322–327; Urban Ohlander, *Studies on Coordinate Expressions in Middle English* (Lund: C.W.K. Gleerup, 1936); Ó Siadhail (1984) and Fredericus Visser, *An Historical Syntax of the English Language*, 3 vols (Leiden: Brill, 1963), 1163ff. and 1278ff. See Miller (1988, 116) and (1993, 111–112) for examples of these strategies which persist in contemporary Scots.

5 SUBSTRATE RELATIVE FORMATION STRATEGIES

As Figure 3 (above) predicts, Mesthrie (1992, 75), for instance, found that South African Indian English ekes out its range of strategies by incorporating correlative, participial and 'prenominal external' strategies inherited from the Indic and Dravidian substrate languages. Since SA English is also a language shift variety which evolved from a period of transitional bilingualism it is feasible that its relative formation strategies will be marked by transfer effects from the Irish system in which three types of subordinating strategy can be identified:

   (i.)   Direct
   (ii.)   Indirect or Resumptive Pronoun
   (iii.)   'Subordinating *Agus*' [21]

A combination of these strategies permits relativization in accordance with the Keenan and Comrie *Hierarchy* of subjects, objects, obliques and genitives.

5.1 Direct Relatives in Irish

The direct relative strategy is accessible to relativized subject and object NP positions. It is signalled by the proclitic *a* which lenites[22] the following verb (*aL* is the conventional designation) and the antecedent subject or object is assumed to be co-indexed with an anaphoric gap at the extraction site ('t*i* ' in 7 and 8 below):

---

[21] See Paul Russell, *An Introduction to the Celtic Languages* (London: Longman, 1995), pp. 105–109 for a general discussion of types (i.) and (ii.) and see James McCloskey, 'The Modern Irish Double Relative and Syntactic binding', *Ériu*, 36 (1985), 45–84; 'Resumptive Pronouns, A' Binding and Levels of Representation in Irish', in *The Syntax of the Modern Celtic Languages*, vol. XXIII, *Syntax and Semantics*, ed. by Roberta Hendrick, (San Diego: Academic Press, 1990), pp. 199–248; 'Clause Structure, Ellipsis and Proper Government in Irish', *Lingua*, 85 (1991), 259–302. and Nigel Duffield, 'Particles and Projections' (unpublished Ph.D. dissertation, University of Southern California, 1991), ch. 3, for syntactic analyses of them. Type (iii.) in Irish is discussed in: Daniel Boyle 'Ach and Agus as Coordinate and Subordinate Conjunctions in Gaelic', in *You Take the High Node and I'll Take the Low Node: Papers from the Comparative Syntax Festival*, ed. by Claudia Corum, T. Cedric Smith-Stark and Ann Weiser (Chicago: Linguistic Society,1973), pp. 220–228 and Ó Siadhail (1984), pp. 125–130.

[22] C.f. Mícheál Ó Siadhail, *Modern Irish: Grammatical Structure and Dialectal Variation* (Cambridge: University Press, 1989, 6.2) and Duffield (1991: ch.2) for discussion of the initial consonant mutation processes found in Modern Irish and associated with both the Direct and Indirect relative formation strategies.

(7) SUBJECT

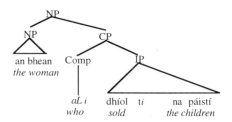

'The woman who sold the children'

(8) OBJECT

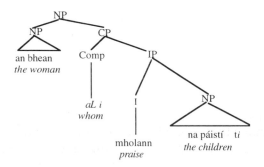

'The woman whom the children praise'

5.2 Indirect or Resumptive Pronoun Relatives in Irish

The Indirect strategy is ungrammatical in cases where the antecedent functions as subject and is the preferred option when the marking of oblique, indirect object (9) or genitive (10) case is required.[23] This type can be distinguished from (i.) by the fact that the proclitic *a*, in this case, triggers eclipsis of the following verb (*aN*) and because the extraction site, which in (7) and (8) contains a phonologically null anaphoric element, is filled by a resumptive pronoun.

---

[23] McCloskey (1985, 58–9) argues that this is because these structures are syntactic islands.

(9) INDIRECT OBJECT

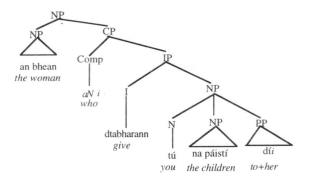

'The woman to whom you give the children' or
'The woman who you give the children to'

(10) GENITIVE

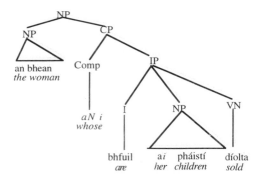

'The woman whose children have been sold'

5.3 'Subordinating *Agus*' Relatives in Irish

In this construction, the NP which is to be relativized is followed by an embedded small clause of the form :

The constituent 'XP' is an AP, PP or VP predicate and subordination is marked by the use of *agus*, a zero copula and, again, a resumptive pronoun.[24] As can be seen by the grammaticality of (11) and (12) there is no restriction on the accessibility of this type so that relativization can be achieved at both the upper and lower ends of the *Case Hierarchy*.

(11) SUBJECT

[CP Bhí [NP bean$_i$ ann] AGUS [SC [NP í$_i$ [VP ag coladh]]]]
lit. *was woman   there and   her   sleeping*
'There was a woman who was sleeping'

(12) GENITIVE

[NP Píosa de chlár$_i$ cearnógach péinne [CP bhí mar   mharc   aice]]
lit. *piece of board square   pine   was as (a) target   at-her*
AGUS [SC [NP fáinne beag   [PP ina$_i$ lár]]]]
lit. *and   ring   small   in-its   middle*
'Her target was a square piece of pine board in the middle of which was a small ring'

[Example from Ó Siadhail (1989, 11.1.8(i) 2 (197))]

6 STRATEGIES AVAILABLE IN SOUTH ARMAGH ENGLISH

6.1 Preliminary remarks on the analysis

As a product of language contact, we now turn to the question : 'to what degree and in what form have the available substrate and superstratal strategies outlined in Sections (4) and (5) been incorporated in SA English?'

In the ensuing discussion, I focus solely on the syntactic function of the relativized NP in restrictive and non-restrictive modification, ignoring the distinction between embeddedness and focus as well as the presence or absence of agreement features shared by the relative marker and its antecedent. Moreover, I assume Chomsky and Lasnik's (1977) proposal, that *WH-*, *That* and Zero relatives all contain a full CP projection and

---

[24] For the analysis of (11) and (12) as small clauses, c.f. Sandra Chung and James McCloskey. 'Government, Barriers and Small Clauses in Modern Irish', *Linguistic Inquiry* , 18 (1987), 173–237; McCloskey and Peter Sells, 'Control and A-chains in Modern Irish', *Natural Language and Linguistic Theory*, 6 (1988), 143–189 and McCloskey (1991). Compare the structure of (11) with that of (13) below where *agus* is used in a non-relative paratactic construction :

(13) [CP Bhí [NP bean$_i$ ann]] [conj. AGUS] [CP bhí [NP sí$_i$ ag codladh]]
lit. *was   woman there   and   was   she sleeping*
'There was a woman and she was sleeping'

involve operator movement, though the latter entails both a null operator and a null complementizer ('Op_i' and 'ø', respectively).[25]

It has been expedient, for present purposes, to treat existentials (14, 18), clefts (16) and the Resumptive pronoun (25–27) as well as the 'Subordinating *And*' (28–31) constructions as relative types, although they are thought to exhibit structural and functional differences from structures such as (15, 17, 19, 20 and 21).[26] I take this position on the basis that the semantic function of the embedded clause in each type is to restrict the set of entities that may be denoted by the modified NP.

6.2 Superstrate Strategies

Consider (14) to (21) which provide representative SA samples of the tripartite, superstrate relative system outlined in Section 4.

(1.) ZERO-RELATIVE

SUBJECT
(14) [NP the magistrate [CP Op_i [C' ø [IP t_i was to try him was an old soldier too]]]]

(Ms.1215/1946F/U1409/L2325–2328)

OBJECT
(15) Dominic Daly wanted to break [NP some lease [CP Op_i [C' ø [IP they had t_i on the bog]]]]

(Ms.976/1945F/U3072/L4394–4396)

OBLIQUE
(16) it was on [NP he's brother [...] [CP Op_i [C' ø [IP the priest put the curse t_i]]]]

(Ms.976/1945F/U2987/L4269–4270)

---

[25] For further discussion, see David Lightfoot, *Principles of Diachronic Syntax* (Cambridge: University Press, 1979), p. 314; Miller (1988); Romaine (1982, 58, 214ff); 'The Evolution of Complexity in a Creole Language: Acquisition of Relative Clauses in Tok Pisin', *Studies in Language*, 16 (1) (1992), 139–182 (p. 149) and Johan Van der Auwera, 'Relative *That*—a Centennial Dispute', *Journal of Linguistics*, 21 (1985), 149–179. On this analysis of the tripartite superstratal system, see Noam Chomsky and Howard Lasnik, 'Filters and control', *Linguistic Inquiry*, 8 (1977), 425–504 and see Doherty (1993) who argues that Zero relatives lack a CP projection and Henry (1995) for counter arguments regarding the latter.

[26] Policansky (1982) also assumes that these structures are (quasi-) relative types, however, Quirk and others (1972, 14.19 and 14.29) and James D. McCawley, *The Syntactic Phenomena of English*, II. (Chicago: University of Chicago Press, 1988), p. 451 offer general arguments against the treatment of them as relatives. Moreover, Henry (1995, ch. 6) proposes (contra Doherty (1993)) that existentials, clefts and copular structures in which the zero strategy is used to 'relativize' the subject are more appropriately analysed as root Topic phrases rather than true relatives.

(2.) *THAT*-RELATIVE

SUBJECT

(17) [NP Matha Locklin [CP *Op*i [C· that [IP t*i* lived under the roof with Padgy Bug]]]]

(Ms.976/1945F/U2976/L4255–4257)

OBJECT

(18) There wasn't [NP no house you'd see [CP *Op*i [C· that [IP t*i* wasn't like an apothecarie's shop with bottles]]]]

(Ms.976/1945F/U2860/L4104–4106)

OBLIQUE

(19)   [NP the part [CP *Op*i [C· that [IP he takes up t*i*]]]]

(Ms.1810/1973M/U123/L199–202)

(3.) *WH*-RELATIVE

SUBJECT

(20) [NP Dr McDonald [CP who*i* [C· ø [IP t*i* was the parish priest in Kilkenny]]]]

(Ms.1861/1974F/U6/L8–9)

OBJECT

(21) Coulter handed back [NP the bottle of water [CP which*i* [C· ø[IP Smyth placed t*i* on the shelf]]]]

(Ms.1807/1973M/U258/L402–404)

OBLIQUE

(22) [NP the shebeen [CP which*i* [C· ø [IP Hughes an' a fella named Coulter drank in t*i*]]]]

(Ms.1807/1973M/U256/L398–400)

6.3 Substrate and Ancillary Superstrate Strategies

Conventional GB syntactic analyses of NP relativization in both the Irish Direct strategy and the superstratal types postulate a process (23) which involves operator movement to the [Spec, CP] position leaving a phonologically null anaphoric element at the extraction site:[27]

---

[27] For instance, Liliane Haegeman, *Introduction to Government and Binding Theory* (Oxford: Basil Blackwell, 1991), pp. 370–376 and p 420–426 and McCloskey and Sells (1988, 157–158).

(23)

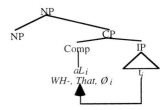

As (24) illustrates, since Irish Indirect and 'Subordinating *Agus*' relativization processes require the anaphoric gap to be filled by a resumptive pronoun (co-indexed with the relativized NP) they exhibit syntactic parallels with superstratal strategies extant in the Early Modern English target (3–6 above) in which the pronoun occupies its base-position and the relative marker is base-generated in [Spec, CP]:

(24)

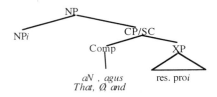

(25) to (27) illustrate the Indirect or Resumptive pronoun strategy and (28) to (31) exemplify the 'Subordinating *And*' type occurring in the corpus:

OBJECT
(25) You never saw [NP a basket_i [CP ø [XP it_i was made o' rods?]]]

(Ms.976/1945M/U2350/L3415–3416)

OBLIQUE
(26) He was married to [NP an old one_i [CP ø [XP she_i lived down here below the chapel]]]

(Ms.1785 /1971M/U425/L662–664)

GENITIVE
(27) God's curse the sight of a sowl I could see, only [NP this talk_i [CP ø [XP an' not a word of it_i could I make out]]]

(Ms.974/1942M/U3287/L4719–4721)

SUBJECT
(28) there was [NP an old lady_i] AN' [SC [NP she_i [XP a pair of tongs always beside her]]]

(Ms.1112/1945F/U1522/L2490–2493)

OBJECT

(29) you'll see [NP a wee clock in the window*i*] AN' [SC [NP it*i* [XP goin' yet]]]

(Ms.976/1945M/U1961/L3023–3024)

OBLIQUE

(30) we come on [NP the loveliest wee brick chimney*i* ever you seen built into the field] AN' [SC [NP a stone [XP across the top of it*i*]]]

(Ms.976/1945M/U2728/L3922–3925)

GENITIVE

(31) It was all [NP big black mud turf*i*] AN' [SC [NP every sod of it*i* [XP as hard as the hobs of hell]]]

(Ms.976/1945M/U2102/L3156–3157)

7 CONCLUSION

Frequency of Relative Strategies in the Corpus (1942–1974) Correlated with Syntactic Position

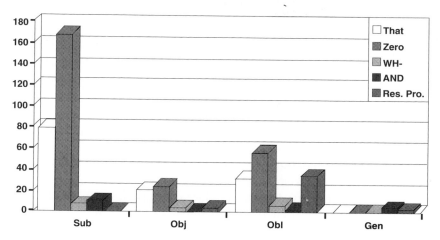

Figure 5

Figure 5 above summarises the frequency of the superstratal and substratal/ancillary strategies that occurred in the text-corpus for the period 1942–1974. The analysis suggests that an *Accessibility Hierarchy* exists in SA English with respect to the syntactic positions that are relativizeable which generally agrees with that proposed by Keenan and Comrie's universal scheme outlined in Figure 4. As it predicts, NP subjects were more frequently relativized in the corpus than NP genitives. This finding is similar to the Edinburgh data of Romaine (1984b) in which her informants used 94 subject relatives and only one genitive.

With regard to the strategies themselves, the superstratal *That* and Zero types are more prevalent than the substratal/ancillary superstratal strategies, while the *WH-* relative is the least preferred option for subjects, objects, obliques and genitives. Moreover, as we noted in 4.1, Romaine's reconstruction of the development of *WH*-markers in the history of Scots evidences their use in obliques as prior to that in either objects or subjects. Thus, the higher frequency of the *WH*-strategy in obliques than in subjects or objects in the SA corpus may imply a phylogenetic parallel.

Keenan and Comrie (1979) remark that, cross-linguistically, Resumptive pronoun and other, ancillary relativization strategies are normally reserved for relativizing NPs on the lower positions of the *Hierarchy*. Romaine (1988: 240) in her discussion of the acquisition of relative clauses by Scottish children also notes that: 'alternative strategies take up the slack in the system, particularly at the lower end of the hierarchy'. Likewise, Miller (1988, 114–117) includes these types in his discussion of adult Scottish norms and they are mentioned in Miller (1993, 111) as being typical strategies 'if the relative clause contains a long constituent or another clause'. In GB terms, Resumptive pronoun strategies are invoked by speakers when there is the possibility of violating subjacency requirements which is why in 5.2 we noted that in Irish they were confined to case-marking indirect objects, obliques and genitives.[28] If we assume this to be a universal principle, then the primary linguistic data offered by the Early Modern target and the substrate language would conspire to produce higher frequencies of the pronoun-retaining strategies at the lower end of the *Hierarchy* in SA English which is why they are avoided for relativizing NP subjects in the corpus, as Figure 5 shows.

Filppula (1988, 628), contrary to Ó Siadhail (1984), notes that the rarity of the 'Subordinating *And'* relativization strategy in the Early Modern English and contemporary British Dialectal English sections of the *Helsinki Corpus* suggests that the occurrence of the strategy in Irish-English is a transfer from the Irish substrate. The analysis presented here corroborates Filppula's finding in two respects: (i.) the frequency of its occurrence in the SA corpus and (ii.) the syntactic positions in which it is used. While this relative type is not frequent in the SA corpus (being

---

[28] See Ann Zribi-Hertz 'Orphan Prepositions in French and the Concept of Null Pronoun', *Recherches Linguistiques*, 12 (1984), pp. 46–91, on similar constructions in French.

roughly equivalent to the use of *WH-* markers), it occurred more frequently than the single usage which Filppula found in his database of Somerset/Devon, Cambridgeshire, and Yorkshire rural dialects which was more than twice as large. Moreover, 'Subordinating *And'* is used in SA English exactly as it is in Irish to relativize heads at both the upper and lower ends of the *Hierarchy* (c.f. 5.3).

In a discussion of Chomsky (1989), Trudgill and Chambers (1991) argue that: 'More grammatically sophisticated treatments of non-standard dialects are needed, and so is a more empirically based approach to grammatical theory.'[29] I hope that this paper presents evidence which supports their proposal, namely, the contribution which can be made to an account of relativization processes in Irish English that incorporates inter-disciplinary findings from GB syntax, sociolinguistics and language acquisition.

---

[29] Noam Chomsky (1989) 'Some Notes on the Economy of Derivation and Representation', in *MIT Working Papers in Linguistics 10: Functional Heads and Clause Structure*, ed. by Itziar Laka and Anoop Mahajan (Cambridge, Mass.: MIT Press, 1989), pp. 43–74, and *Dialects of English: Studies in Grammatical Variation*, ed. by Peter Trudgill and J.K. Chambers (London: Longman, 1991), p. 295.

VP-Clefting and the Internal Structure of VP[1]

M. SIOBHÁN COTTELL

Department of Linguistics, University of Wales, Bangor

IN THIS paper I argue that thematic considerations have direct consequences for the internal structure of Verb Phrases, and that the process of VP-clefting in Hiberno-English provides an insight into that structure. Furthermore, I suggest that the adoption of a layered VP in the sense of Larson (1988) allows a principled characterisation of the variation in the inventory of clefted elements between Hiberno-Englishand other dialects of English.

It is generally accepted in syntactic theory that the positions of arguments at Spell-out may differ from those in which they are generated. Work on topics such as passives (Jaeggli 1986) and unaccusative verbs (Burzio 1986) has shown this to be the case for internal arguments. More recently, however, research on external arguments has indicated that subjects too are base-generated lower than the IP-initial position which they occupy in languages such as English and French. It seems to me that there are two main strands to current research on the base position of subjects—first, in the purely syntactic domain there is the VP-Internal Subject Hypothesis of, for example, Koopman and Sportiche (1988, 1991), which has proved rather successful, not least in the analysis of VSO order in Celtic and Semitic.

(1)

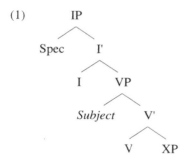

[1] This work was first presented as part of a séminaire de recherche on cleft constructions at the Université de Genève in March 1996 and has benefitted greatly from the comments of the audience there, especially Liliane Haegeman, Luigi Rizzi and Ur Shlonsky. I am also grateful to Bob Borsley, Cathal Doherty, Pam Macdonald, Ian Roberts and Anna Roussou for their help and criticism, and to Carol Craddock, Ailbhe Healy and Margaret Pilkington for help with judgements. None of these, of course, can be held responsible for what deficits persist.

Given the structure in (1), VSO order will be derived if the verb moves past the subject to check features of Tense and Agreement at the head of a functional projection which dominates VP.[2] In languages such as English and French, movement of the subject from within VP to the specifier of the highest functional projection within IP will derive SVO order.

Second, there is an approach which is driven by considerations of Argument Structure in the sense of Grimshaw (1990), where a thematic hierarchy is proposed:

(2)   (Agent (Experiencer (Goal/Source/Location (Theme))))

(Grimshaw 1990, 8)

Arguments are projected in a strict order, with the result that no verb can assign Agent to its complement and Experiencer to its subject. This order is mediated through a level of representation, A(rgument)-Structure, which maps onto, but remains distinct from, syntactic structure. If the VP-Internal Subject Hypothesis is accepted, and if there is only one specifier within VP, then the mapping from A-structure will have to be indirect. If, on the other hand, we admit the existence of VP-shells, following Larson (1988), so that VP may in a sense be recursive, a series of V-specifiers will be projected, and the possibility opens up that different types of subjects may be projected syntactically in different specifier positions.

Hiberno-English is more liberal than Standard British or American English in the range of elements which can be grammatically clefted. In addition to the NP and PP clefts described in Emonds (1976), predicates and VPs can appear in *it*-clefts:[3]

(3)   a. It was very ill that he looked.
       b. Is it stupid you are?
       c. It is looking for more land a lot of them are.
          ((a) and (b) from Trudgill and Hanna (1982), (c) from Harris (1991))

However, not all VPs can be clefted. If they could be, then the asymmetry in (4) would not be expected.

---

[2] But see McCloskey (1996) for arguments that adverb placement in Irish indicates that there are more functional heads above VP than the single I shown in (1).

[3] The fact that a wider range of elements than NP and PP can be clefted implies that *it*-clefts are derived, not by a combination of base-generation and operator-movement as in Chomsky (1977), but by actual movement, the position taken by Rochemont (1986). VP-clefting in Hiberno-English is particularly telling in this regard, since VPs normally resist operator strategies such as relative clause formation.

(4)　　a.　It was washing himself John was.

　　　　b.　It was drinking his pint he was.

　　　　c.　* It was admiring himself John was.

　　　　d.　* It was enjoying his pint he was.

Since VP-clefting is not grammatical in Standard British or American English, this contrast has not to my knowledge been noticed before. The generalisation is simply stated—if a verb assigns Agent to its subject, then its VP can be grammatically clefted; if the verb assigns Experiencer to its subject, then VP-clefting is ungrammatical. Indeed, many speakers of Standard varieties report that (4a) and (4b) sound odd, but that (4c) and (4d) sound very much worse. Furthermore, there is a construction in Standard English where precisely the same contrast emerges:

(5)　　a.　What John did was wash himself.

　　　　b.　What John did was drink his pint.

　　　　c.　* What John did was admire himself.

　　　　d.　* What John did was enjoy his pint.

Previous accounts of the pseudo-cleft contrast in (5) have attributed it to some feature of *do* in these constructions, but this cannot be maintained in the face of the data in (4), where no *do* appears. If all subjects are projected in a single position, this contrast remains a puzzling and impenetrable fact. On the other hand, if different thematic subjects are syntactically projected in different positions depending on their thematic relationship to the verb, then the contrast in (4) and (5) can be used to probe the internal structure of VP.

Given that we are concerned with the structural realisation of two types of subject, there are two logical possibilities. The first is that in Hiberno-English, Experiencer is projected in a higher specifier than Agent. I will not pursue this line of reasoning, since there is convincing evidence that Agents are cross-linguistically realised higher than Experiencers; this has been shown both in Grimshaw's (1990) work, and by Belletti and Rizzi (1988) with respect to Italian psych-verbs. I will, on the other hand, assume the internal structure of VP proposed by Chomsky (1995): verbs which assign Agent to their external argument do so in the Specifier of a VP shell headed by a light verb, but other verbs do not project a VP shell.[4] The VPs in (4) then have the structures shown in (6):

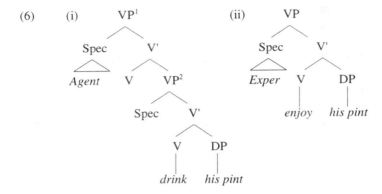

(6)   (i)   VP¹

The generalisation to be captured is that an Agent VP such as *drink his pint* can be clefted, while an Experiencer VP such as *enjoy his pint* cannot. Given the configurations in (6), there is a straightforward explanation: *drink his pint* is a maximal projection in (6i), but *enjoy his pint* in (6ii) is not. Since considerations of structure preservation allow only heads and maximal projections to be affected by movement processes (see Chomsky (1986) and Emonds (1976)), then we can account for the Agent-Experiencer asymmetry if VP-clefting may only affect the lower VP of a VP-shell.

It is instructive, then, to compare VP-clefting with another process which might be thought to involve movement of the same constituent. Huang (1993) shows that the reconstruction facts of predicates, such as VPs, do not pattern with those of wh-moved arguments. An anaphor contained within an argument can be interpreted as coreferent with either

---

[4] On a historical note, Ross (1972) prefigured the notion of VP-shells in proposing the remote structure of Agent clauses shown in (i), where the obligatory transformation Do-Gobbling raises the lower verb to replace *do* in the higher, followed by Equi-NP-Deletion of the lower subject:

(i)   Frogs produce croaks.

Do-Gobbling: X - [$_S$ *do* - NP - [$_S$ V - Y]] - Z   OBL

| 1 | 2 | 3 | 4 | 5 | 6 | → |
| 1 | 4 | 3 | 0 | 5 | 6 | |

the subject which c-commands the wh-trace or with any other subject which intervenes between the argument in Spec/CP and its trace.

(7)   a. Which pictures of himself$_{i/j}$ did John$_i$ think Bill$_j$ saw t ?
      b. Which friends of each other$_{i/j}$ did they$_i$ say that we$_j$ should talk to t ?

That is, ambiguous reconstruction effects are found where a wh-phrase has moved successive-cyclically, and that construal of an anaphor with a c-commanding subject can obtain at any Spec/CP transitted in the course of movement to the highest CP. On the other hand, in what is usually known as VP-movement, an anaphor in a fronted VP can only be interpreted as coreferent with the subject which most closely c-commands its trace:

(8)   a. Criticise himself$_{*i/j}$, John$_i$ thought Bill$_j$ would not t.
      b. Talk to friends of each other$_{*i/j}$, they$_i$ said we$_j$ should not t.

In order to account for this contrast, Huang suggests that the solution lies in adopting the VP-Internal Subject Hypothesis. Since the trace of the subject is contained inside VP, it always counts as a closer antecedent for the anaphor, protecting it from construal with any other subject. In wh-phrases, on the other hand, there is no subject within the moved constituent, and so the anaphor has a wider choice of antecedent. It is then possible to retain the notion of successive-cyclic movement in both cases. But given that the subject raises out of VP, the trace of the subject must be properly governed in order to satisfy the Empty Category Principle (ECP).

(9)   **ECP (Conjunctive formulation)**
      A non-pronominal empty category must be
      (i) properly head-governed (Formal Licensing)
      (ii) antecedent-governed or θ-governed (Identification)
      (Rizzi 1990, 33)

Huang proposes that the constituent which moves in (8) is not in fact VP, but Agr-oP, with the result that Agr-o suffices to head-govern the trace. As Rizzi (1990) shows, head-government is a condition on representations and must be satisfied after movement. Antecedent-government obtains since the VP-internal trace is γ-marked before movement in the sense of Lasnik and Saito (1984).

(10)   [$_{Agr-oP}$ Agr-o [$_{VP}$ t$_j$ criticize himself]]$_k$ John$_i$ thought Bill$_j$ would not t_k

In other words, the constituent which is moved in (8) is larger than that which is clefted in (4a) and (4b). This then predicts that there should be no observable Agent-Experiencer asymmetry in Agr-oP movement. This is borne out in (11).

(11) a. He said that he would drink his pint, and drink his pint he (damn
                                                                    well) did.

      b. He said that he would enjoy his pint, and enjoy his pint he (damn
                                                                    well) did.

Furthermore, the fact that the external argument is realised outside the constituent which clefts in (6i) implies that there will be no subject-trace in the moved constituent. The absence of a subject-trace thus means that VP-clefting should pattern with the arguments in (7) rather than with the predicates in (8). In other words, an anaphor contained inside the moved VP should be ambiguous in reference between the original closest subject and a higher one, and this prediction is fulfilled:

(12) a. It was talking to himself$_{i/j}$ John$_i$ thought Bill$_j$ was t .
      b. It was talking to each other$_{i/j}$ we$_i$ thought they$_j$ were t .

Additional evidence to show that Experiencer verbs do not occur in VP-shells is also forthcoming here. If a verb such as *admire* or *enjoy* appeared in a shell, nothing would prevent the lower VP from clefting. This would have two consequences. First, there should be no Agent-Experiencer asymmetry in clefts, contrary to fact; second, Experiencer VPs should be just as ambiguous in reconstruction as wh-phrases in (7) and Agent VPs in (12). But if there is only a single VP layer, then that layer must contain the trace of the subject, just as Agr-oP does in (10). If an anaphor contained within a clefted Experiencer VP can only be construed with the lowest subject, that is a strong indication that the only constituent available for clefting is in fact the unique VP in (6ii).

(13) a. (*)   It was admiring himself$_{*i/j}$ John$_i$ thought Bill$_j$ was t.
      b. (*)   It was enjoying each other$_{*i/j}$'s company we$_i$ thought they$_j$
                                                                    were t .

The data in (13) are admittedly awkward, but the binding facts are clear: only lowest construal is possible, indicating the presence of a subject trace clefted as part of the VP.

All this being said, however, there are two important questions which remain:

(14) A. Why can the highest VP in (6) not be clefted?
      B. Why is VP-clefting ungrammatical in dialects other than Hiberno-English?

The answer to (14A) lies with the ECP. The evidence in (11)–(13) shows that VP and not some larger constituent is clefted. After the subject raises out of VP to Spec/IP, its trace will be subject to the ECP in (9). Antecedent-government will hold as it does in VP-movement, by γ-marking in the original configuration. But in the clefted position, there is no head which can properly head-govern the trace within the clefted VP. Since the proper head-government clause of the ECP is a condition on representations, the trace will not be properly governed in the clefted position. The result is that only the constituent which contains no subject trace can be grammatically clefted: in other words, the lower VP in (6i).

The answer to (14B) must remain more tentative. Given that the grammar of a language is assumed to consist of a set of unvarying principles, together with a set of parameter settings unconsciously fixed by the child on exposure to the language, differences between dialects can be seen as reflecting a rather small number of differences in parameter settings. This assumption has underpinned much of the research which has been conducted into dialect syntax, mainly in Germanic and Romance, over the last decade. But given the abstract nature of parameters, we do not expect there to exist a particular parameter [± Cleft VP]. It is likely that dialect differences flow from more general properties, as Henry (1995) shows for Hiberno-English. There is one striking fact about the analysis of VP-clefting implicit in (6): with respect to the subject, the lower VP in (6i) is a predicate. Recall what was noted earlier with regard to the wider range of grammatical clefts in Hiberno-English: this dialect differs from the standard in permitting the clefting of predicates and the clefting of VPs. If these two facts derive from one deeper property of Hiberno-English, one which is absent from other dialects, then a tentative answer to (14A) may be attempted. Only the lower VP in (6i) can be clefted, since only that VP is a predicate; this in effect means that clefting can only affect Agent VPs. In other dialects, VP-clefting is ungrammatical as a consequence of the impossibility of clefting predicates.[5]

---

[5] Note, of course, that the relevant property of Hiberno-English cannot be the projection of VP-shells in Agent constructions, since we would then be at a loss to account for the existence of an identical asymmetry in the Standard English pseudo-cleft in (5); furthermore, layered VPs in the standard language have been argued for at length by Hale and Keyser (1993). Note also that Huang (1993) bases his argumentation on the assumption, attributed to Barss, that the relevant distinction between wh-movement and VP-movement slices neatly down between arguments and predicates. An anaphor in a moved argument is capable of ambiguous reference (cf. (8)). An anaphor in a predicate is capable only of construal with the lowest subject, whose trace it contains. The VP-clefting facts, however, show that this distinction is too coarse; the facts in (11)–(13) indicate that the relevant distinction lies in whether a moved constituent does or does not contain a subject. In Huang's terms the VP which moves in VP-clefting behaves like an argument, but is not an argument in any accepted sense of the term.

Of course, the question that immediately arises with respect to (14B) is precisely what property of the grammar allows predicates to be clefted in Hiberno-English but not in other varieties. Predicate is a functional, not a categorial, notion and so any statement to the effect that this dialect allows DPs, PPs and predicates to be clefted is unrevealing. The answer lies outside the scope of this paper, but is the subject of ongoing research by the author.

REFERENCES

Belletti, Adriana and Rizzi, Luigi 1988. 'Psych Verbs and θ-Theory', *Natural Language and Linguistic Theory*, 6.3, 291–352

Burzio, Luigi 1986. *Italian Syntax: A Government-Binding Approach*, Dordrecht: Kluwer

Chomsky, Noam 1977. 'On Wh-movement', in *Formal Syntax*, ed. by P. Culicover, T. Wasow and A. Akmajian, San Diego: Academic Press

—1995. *The Minimalist Program*, Cambridge, Mass.: MIT Press

Emonds, Joseph 1976. *A Transformational Approach to Syntax*, New York: Academic Press

Grimshaw, Jane 1990. *Argument Structure*, Cambridge, Mass.: MIT Press

Hale, Kenneth and Keyser, Samuel 1993. 'On Argument Structure and the Lexical Expression of Arguments', in *The View From Building 20*, ed. by S. Keyser and M. Halle, Cambridge, Mass.: MIT Press

Harris, John 1991. 'Conservatism versus Substratal Transfer in Hiberno-English', in *Dialects of English: Studies in Grammatical Variation*, ed. by Peter Trudgill and J.K. Chambers, London: Edward Arnold

Henry, Alison, 1995. *Dialect Variation and Parameter Setting: a Study of Belfast English and Standard English*, Oxford: University Press

Huang, Cheng Teh James 1993. 'Reconstruction and the Structure of VP: Some Theoretical Consequences', *Linguistic Inquiry*, 24·1, 103–138

Jaeggli, Osvaldo 1986. 'Passive', *Linguistic Inquiry*, 17.4, 587–633

Koopman, Hilda and Sportiche, Dominique 1988. 'Subjects', MS, UCLA

—1991. 'The Position of Subjects', *Lingua*, 85, 211–258

Larson, Richard K. 1988. 'On the Double Object Construction', *Linguistic Inquiry*, 19.3, 335–391

Lasnik, Howard and Saito, Mamoru 1984. 'On the Nature of Proper Government', *Linguistic Inquiry*, 15.2, 235–289

McCloskey, James 1996. 'Subjects and Subject Positions in Irish', in *The Syntax of the Celtic Languages*, ed. by R. Borsley and I. Roberts, Cambridge: University Press

Pollock, Jean-Yves 1989. 'Verb Movement, UG and the Structure of IP', *Linguistic Inquiry*, 20.3, 365–424

Rizzi, Luigi 1990. *Relativised Minimality*, Cambridge, Mass.: MIT Press

Rochemont, Michel 1986. *Focus in Generative Grammar*, Amsterdam: John Benjamins

Ross, John R 1972. 'Act', in *Semantics of Natural Language*, ed. by D. Davidson and G. Harman, Dordrecht: Reidel

Trudgill, Peter and Hanna, Jean 1982. *International English*, London: Edward Arnold

Zu einigen schweizerdeutschen Fischnamen

PETER DALCHER
Zug

CONN Ó CLÉIRIGH war mehrmals in der Schweiz. Die folgende Briefstelle vom 24. Januar 1966 nimmt Bezug auf ein Fischessen in einem Restaurant von Zug, einer mittleren Stadt 30 Kilometer südlich von Zürich, am Rande der Innerschweiz. 'I often think [schreibt er] of the wonderful meal we all had together in that restaurant beside the Zugersee. What was the name of the fish which looked like cod and tasted like trout?' Der in Frage stehende Fisch hiess oder heisst in meiner Mundart *Bale*, und *Bale* ist einer von 18 Fischnamen, die in Hans Bossards *Zuger Mundartbuch* (Bossard) aufgeführt sind. Von diesen Fischnamen soll im folgenden die Rede sein.

Bossards Buch ist gegliedert in „Grammatik" und „Wörterverzeichnisse". Letztere führen den ausgewählten Wortschatz in der Reihenfolge „Zugertüütsch—Schriftdeutsch" und „Schriftdeutsch—Zugertüütsch" auf. Das Ganze ist kein streng wissenschaftliches Werk, sondern populär gehalten und unter sprachpflegerischen Gesichtspunkten verfasst. Berücksichtigt sind demzufolge insbesondere vom Standarddeutschen abweichende Formen und Wörter. Unsere „Fischliste" kann so nicht Anspruch auf Vollständigkeit erheben (es fehlen z. B. die n Stich, S.wörter *Aesch / Aesche, Hasel, Hecht,* [...]); aber als ein in sich geschlossenes, „unabhängiges" kleines Corpus kann sie für unsere Zwecke durchaus dienen.

Die folgende Auflistung unserer Fischnamen ist gegenüber Bossard darstellerisch leicht modifiziert. Zusätzlich gebe ich zu jedem n Stich, S.wort die entsprechende Idiotikon-Stelle. Bossard schreibt nach dem sogenannten Dieth-System[1]. Wir belassen seine Schreibweise, verwenden aber je nach Quelle auch andere Systeme (z. B. zur Längenbezeichnung bei Vokalen).—Nun also die Aufreihung der Bezeichnungen:

> *Albeli* n. 'Art Weissfisch, kleiner Felchen' (*Id.*, 1, 185). *Bachbumbeli* 'Art Laube, Alburnus bip., Schneider' (*Id.*, 4, 1260). *Bachbutzeli* 'Elritze, auch Groppe' (*Id.*, 4, 2000 nur Grundwort). *Bambeli* = *Bachbumbeli* (*Id.*, 4, 1257). *Bale* f., auch *Balche* '(Blau-)Felchen'; dazu *Land-B.* 'grosser Felchen', *Schwääb-B.* (*Id.*, 4, 1191). *Bläuler*

---

[1] Eugen Dieth, *Schwyzertüschi Dialäktschrift. Leitfaden einer einheitlichen Schreibweise für alle Dialekte* (Zürich, 1938), 2. Auflage bearbeitet und hg. von Christian Schmid-Cadalbert (Aarau usw., 1986).

'Blaufelchen' (fehlt *Id.*). *Egli* n. 'Barsch' (*Id.*, 1, 144). *Fliengge* f.
'Blicke, Art Brachsme' (*Id.*, 5, 1249). *Forälle*, Dim. *Forändli*
'Forelle' (*Id.*, 1, 935). *Güngere* [!] 'kleine Art Hasel' (*Id.*, 2, 363).
Laugeli 1 Schweizerdeutsch, *Läugeli* 'Art Laube' (*Id.*, 3, 1172). *Ööl*
Sg. und Pl., auch *Ool* Sg. 'Aal' (*Id.*, 1, 167). *Röötel* 'Saibling, Rötel'
(*Id.*, 6, 1773). *Rottele* f. 'Rotfeder, Rotauge' (*Id.*, 6, 1785). *Schlye*
'Schleie' (*Id.*, 9, 3). *Schwaal* 'Rotauge, auch Hasel' (*Id.*, 9, 1805).
Trysche 'Trüsche, Quappe' (*Id.*, 14, 1358). *Winger* m. 'Art Laube' (im
Id. noch ausstehend).

Den Kommentar zu diesen Mundartnamen gliedere ich in vier Abschnitte.

1. ZU BILDUNGSWEISEN UND FORMEN

1.1 Auffällig ist die Häufigkeit der Diminutiva: *Albeli, Bambeli,
(-)Bumbeli, (-)Butzeli, Egli, Laugeli (-äu-)* stehen hier ohne ein
entsprechendes Grundwort, als Diminutiva tantum sozusagen, *Forändli* hat
Forälle neben sich. Als zugehörige mundartliche Grundwörter verzeichnet
das *Id.* immerhin *Albele* f., *Bambele* u.ä. (?), *Buuz* m., *Laugele* f., zu *Egli*
eine Rückbildung *Egel* m. Stilistisch[2] überinterpretieren darf man den
Befund auch deshalb nicht, weil es sich meist um ausgesprochen kleine
Fische handelt. Formal ist *-(e)li* der für unsere Gegend zu erwartende
Typus; vgl. *SDS*, 3, 149 ff.

1.2 Weitere konsonantische Suffixe weisen *Röötel* (m.), *Rottele* f. und
Forälle (f.) auf, sodann *Bläuler* (m.) und *Winger* m. *Güngere* (ohne
Geschlechtsangabe) ist unsicher, wohl fehlerhaft für *Günger* m. Teilweise
sekundäre Femininbildungen auf *-e* sind *Bal(ch)e, Fliengge, Schlye,
Trysche*. (Heute) endungslose Stammwörter sind nur *Ööl (Ool)* und
Schwaal.

1.3 Vokalische Besonderheiten. Die Verdumpfung von altlangem *â* zu *òò*
in *Òòl* entspricht Bossards stadtzugerischer Mundart. Unverdumpft ist
Schwaal; der Beleg mag aus einer andern Gegend des Kantons stammen
oder nach der Schriftsprache lauten. Vgl. *SDS*, 1, 61 (Fall 'Abend') mit *aa*
für (grosso modo) die Südhälfte des Schweizerdeutschen und, sekundär, für
Teile des Kantons Zürich[3], *oo* für die Nordhälfte, inklusive Teile des

---

[2] Vgl. den Abschnitt „Stilistische Beobachtungen an den Fischbenennungen des Unterseegebietes" in
Ribi S. 9–58.

[3] *aa* im Kanton Zürich scheint restituiert. Darauf deuten die Umlautformen *öö* im *aa*-Gebiet. Vgl. SDS.
1, 83 ff.; Albert Weber, *Zürichdeutsche Grammatik* (Zürich, 1948) S. 62, Anm. 4 sowie die Angabe: „A

Kantons Zug. In *Schlye* ist altlanges *î* im Hiatus erhalten; das weist die Form der Südhälfte des Schweizerdeutschen zu (vgl. *SDS*, 1, 148, Fall 'schneien'). Die lautgeographische Lage des Kantons und insbesondere der Stadt Zug wird durch diese Formen fast paradigmatisch festgehalten.—*Ööl* endlich für den Singular ist als Uebertragung der Pluralform auf den Singular zu verstehen; vgl. *Id.*, 1, 167.

1.4 Konsonantische Besonderheiten. Bossard verzeichnet *Bale* und *Balche*; letztere Form ist die ältere, nachweisbar seit dem Ende des 12. Jahrhunderts (s. *BSM*, 7, 51). Früheste zugerische Formen mit *ch*-Schwund erscheinen im 16. Jahrhundert (ebd. 53 mit Anm. 19). Zu den Parallelformen *mäle* = 'melken' und *Chile* = 'Chilche' (Kirche) s. *SDS*, 2, 109 f.; der Typus mit *ch*-Schwund ist mittel- (und nord-) schweizerdeutsch.—*Forändli* ist nicht „direktes" Diminutiv zu *Forälle*, sondern zur Vorstufe *Forene* o.ä.; vgl. *Id.*, 1, 935.

2. ZU HERKUNFT UND BENENNUNGSMOTIVEN

2.1 Als „durchsichtige" Namen, also Bezeichnungen, deren Etymologie auch dem linguistischen Laien sofort klar ist, kann ich aus unserer Liste nur *Bläuler* und *Röötel* auffassen; beide beziehen sich auf die Farbe der betreffenden Fische.

2.2 Mehr oder weniger gesicherte Etymologien bietet die Literatur für weitere sechs Bezeichnungen an.

Zu *Albeli* schrieb ich in *BSM*, 7, 43: „Mhd. *albel* wird meist als Lehnwort aus lat. *albula* angesehen". Die Reserve rühr(e) daher, dass lat. *albula* als Fischbezeichnung nur vereinzelt bezeugt ist (s. *BSM*, aaO.); Gr. *WB. Neub.*, 2, 236 formuliert (deshalb): „Mhd. *albel(e)*; zu mlat. *albulus* 'weiss', lat. *albulus* 'weisslich' [...]" Am Farbmotiv ist jedenfalls nicht zu zweifeln.

Rottele ist *Id.* 6, 1785 zur etymologischen Gruppe von *Rott* (auch einem Fischnamen) gestellt, und zu diesem wird (ebd.) als Ausgangspunkt „ahd. *roto, *rota [mit kurzem Stammvokal], im Ablaut zu *rôt* [mit langem Stammvokal]" vorausgesetzt. Zweifel an dieser Gleichung wird zwar Jud 310 f. erhoben; ich lasse aber den Bezug auf die Farbe einstweilen bestehen.

Unserem *Forälle* liegt, wie schon angedeutet, ahd. *for(a)hana* zugrunde; Kluge/Seebold setzt westgerm. *furhno f. voraus, „dieses zu idg. **pr̥k̑'-n-*

Einfach geschriben hatt seyn thon wie das Latinisch a allwägen: Das zwyfach aber (aa) ist ein teütscher thon zwüschend dem a vnnd dem o" bei Josua Maler, *Die Teütsch sprach*, (Tiguri [= Zürich]. 1561) S. 1a.

'gefleckt, gesprenkelt' [...] Die Forelle ist also nach ihrer gesprenkelten Zeichnung benannt".

Schlye 'Schleie', ahd *slîo*, „führt den Namen [...] möglicherweise von ihrer schleimigen Oberhautschicht, so dass *Schleim* [...] nächstverwandt wäre" (Kluge/Götze, mit gewisser Reserve auch Kluge/Seebold).

Das Grundwort unseres *Bachbutzeli* ist zweifellos *Buuz* 'kleines, unansehnliches Ding, von Personen, Tieren oder Sachen' (*Id.*, 4, 1999; ebd. 2000 i.S.v. 'eine Art kleiner Fische'). Ahd. *agabûz* 'Barsch' erörtert Lloyd/Springer 73 ff.: „Das Wort [-*bûz*] gehört zu einem im ganzen germ. Umkreis verbreiteten Adj. meist im Sinne von 'stumpf, kurz und dick, gedrungen' [...]" Zur Verwandtschaft mit nhd. *Butt* vgl. Kluge/Seebold unter diesem Wort.

Auf eine äussere Eigentümlichkeit geht endlich auch die Bezeichnung *Egli* zurück. Das Grundwort *ag* ist ahd./mhd. als Fischname belegt; vgl. *BSM*, 7, 20 und jetzt Lloyd/Springer 70 ff. Das Benennungsmotiv ist die spitzige Rückenflosse; die idg. Wurzel *ak- bedeutet 'scharf, spitzig' (Literatur bei Lloyd/Springer aaO.).

2.3 Eine weitere Serie möchte ich mit „unsichere Etymologien" überschreiben.

Zu *Bale/Balche* schrieb ich vor vierzig Jahren: „ Die Etymologie von *Balchen* [...] ist bis heute nicht restlos geklärt" (*BSM*, 7, 53), und noch deutlicher sagt Adolf Ribi: „Die Herkunft [von *Balche*] ist noch unerklärt" (*Thurgauer Jahrbuch* 1975, 38). Hingewiesen sei immerhin auf Juds ausführliche Diskussion der im angrenzenden französischen Patois gebräuchlichen Parallelform *palaye* u.ä.; er erwägt hier „une base d'origine préromane" (S. 299). Früh schon wurde versucht, *Balche* mit dem Vogelnamen *Belche* in Verbindung zu bringen (Gr. *WB.*, 1, 1439). Ahd. *belihha* ist zur adjektivischen Wurzel *bal* 'glänzend, leuchtend' gebildet (s. Lloyd/Springer 431); mit nicht Umlaut bewirkender Suffixvariante könnte unser Wort semantisch (als der silbrig schimmernde Fisch) durchaus hieher gehören.

Auch über den Fall *Bambeli* wurde schon verschiedentlich geschrieben. Gr. *WB.*, 1, 1095 wird (u.a.) Zusammenhang mit „*bammeln, bambeln* 'agitari'" erwogen, „wegen des fischleins rührigkeit"; ähnlich argumentiert *Id.*, 4, 1258. Sodann bemerkt *Gloss.*, 2, 222 zum Fischnamen *banbèla*: „se rattache à la famille de *bamb* français et allemand 'brandiller'" und verweist auf *FEW*, 1, 228, wo *bambella* neben schweizerdeutsch *Bambeli* gestellt wird mit der Bemerkung, dass es „kaum möglich [sei] zu sagen, auf welcher seite entlehnung vorliegt".

Bumbeli könnte allenfalls als ablautende Variante von *Bambeli* verstanden werden; ersteres ist im *Id.*, (4, 1260) seit dem 19., letzteres ebd.

(4, 1257) seit dem 16. Jahrhundert bezeugt, zuerst in Forers *Fischbuch* von 1563 (Weiteres s.o.). Zu vergleichen wäre *Günger* neben *Gänger* (dazu u.).

Kurz kann ich mich auch bei *Günger* fassen. *Id.*, 2, 363 heisst es „*Günger* m. = *Gänger* 7 [d.h. 'Hasel' u.ä.] [...] mit welchem es im Ablautverhältnis stehen könnte."

Unserem *Laugeli* n. entspricht am Bodensee die Regionalform *Logeli* n. bzw. *Logele* f. (*Id.*, 3, 1172; Ribi 15 f.). Nach Ribi geht *Logele*, „wie frz. *loche*, auf gall. *leuka* 'die Weisse' zurück" (S. 129). Die Beurteilung dieser These muss ich andern überlassen. Eine Hypo-These sei indessen noch beigefügt. *Id.*, 3, 1172 wird *Laugele(n)* (Dim. *Laugeli*) semantisch mit *Laubele(n)* (ebd. 962) gleichgesetzt. Damit ist etymologische Identität nicht postuliert, aber suggeriert. Zu (fachsprachlich verbreitetem) *Laube* vgl. weiter Gr. *WB.*, 6, 293; Fischer 4, 1024, zu *Laugele* noch Ochs *WB.*, 3, 397 (wo Weiteres). Eine Parallele für *g : b* -Wechsel könnte allenfalls in mhd. *dûge* : nhd. *Daube* gesehen werden; hier wird „Entlehnung aus einer Substratsprache" erwogen (Kluge/Seebold unter *Daube*; vgl. *Id.*, 13, 2240). Das könnte uns zurück in die Nähe von Ribi bringen.

Nach *Id.*, 9, 1805 ist *Schwaal* „höchst wahrscheinlich entlehnt aus dem lat. Fischnamen *squalus*". Zwar handelt es sich bei der lat. Bezeichnung um einen Meerfisch („an unidentified sea-fish" Glare S. 1812), und die Diskussion, ob und allenfalls wie lat. *squalus* und deutsch *Wal* (bzw. engl. *whale* usw.) in Verbindung zu bringen sind (vgl. Walde, 2, 581 f.; Kluge/Seebold unter *Wal*), macht unsern Fall auch nicht einfacher. *Id.* aaO. verweist indes auf Glossierungen von *squalus* durch deutsche Namen von Süsswasserfischen. Dazu kann ich noch stellen: „Von Fürn / Bliecken und Rotöglin [...] werdent zuo Zürch [!] gnent Squali schwalen [...]" aus Gregor Mangolts Fischbüchlein von 1557 (Ribi S. 94).

2.4 Unklare Fälle und blosse Vermutungen

Zu *Aal* (unserem *Ool* und *Ööl*) erwägt Kluge/Götze noch „Wurzelverwandtschaft mit *Ahle* [...] wegen der pfriemenförmigen Gestalt". Kluge/Seebold sagt kurzum „Herkunft unklar".

Unklar ist auch die Herleitung von *Fliengge*. *Id.*, 1, 1203 setzt *Fliengg(en) I* lediglich als Verweisung auf (später zu behandelndes) *Bliegg* an, bespricht den Namen dann aber unter *Pfliengg* (5, 1249), das, bei mehreren Bedeutungen, mit semantischen Gleichungen in die Nähe von *Blienggen* (5, 121) und *Blieggen* (5, 45) gerückt wird. Anlautvariation *Fl-* : *Bl-* : *Pfl-* ist nicht ausgeschlossen; so erscheint für 'weiche Masse' sowohl *Fluder* als auch *Bluder* und *Pfluder* (*Id.* 1, 1174; 5, 29; 5, 1219). Man könnte vielleicht auch hier von „assoziativer Variation" sprechen[4] und so über *Blienggen* (mit sekundärem *-n-*[5]) auf *Blieggen* (belegt seit dem 15. Jahrhundert) zurückgreifen. Weiteres sehe ich im Moment nicht deutlich.

Zu *Trysche* steht *Id.*, 14, 1360: „Das Wort ist offenbar vorgermanisch; verglichen werden (so Gr. *WB.*, 11, 1, 2, 386) italienisch *bottatrice* bzw. <ältermundartliche> Formen [...]" Abzulehnen ist die bei Hiersche unter *Aalquappe* wiederholte Herleitung aus germ. **threuskon*, „da die angenommene Form schweizerisch *Triesche* [mit Diphthong] mundartlich nicht nachweisbar ist" (*Id.* aaO., wo Näheres). Die Hintergründe bleiben noch zu erhellen.

Im Fall *Winger* ist bisher, soweit ich sehe, keine Lösung beigebracht worden. Das Problem ist aus verschiedenen Gründen schwierig. Einmal sind die Bedeutungsangaben verschieden: 'Alburnus lucidus' (Bossard sagt 'Art Lauben', Syn. ist sein *Laugeli*) ist im Material des *Id.* für den Zuger-, den benachbarten Aegerisee und (teilweise) für Luzern belegt; westschweizerdeutsch ist *Winger* Bezeichnung für 'Leuciscus rutilus', Bossards *Rottele*[6]. Sodann vermutet Jud 313, dass frz. *vangeron* (zuerst belegt 1380) mit *Winger* (belegt ab 1480. Aeschbacher 103) zusammenzubringen sei; *FEW*, 14, 478 setzt „**vingarius* (gall.?) rötel" an und bemerkt, es seien „keine romanischen belege des wortes aufzufinden". Auch die Redaktion des Mittellateinischen Wörterbuchs in München teilt mir brieflich mit (11. Januar 1996), dass ihre „Suche [nach Belegen für *vingarius*] erfolglos geblieben" sei. Eine ältere Luzerner Angabe definiert *Wingerle* als 'kleines Neunauge' und bemerkt: „Der Name dürfte herzuleiten sein von dem Schwänzeln des lebhaften Fischchens". Ob sich allenfalls *(sik) winge(r)n* 'sich krümmen' im Lüneburger Wörterbuch von Eduard Kück (3, 765) vergleichen und ob sich (mit Auslautvariation) *winken* beiziehen liesse, sei vorläufig offen gelassen.

2.5 Ich versuche die etymologischen „Resultate" zusammenzufassen.

2.5.1 Mit Bezug auf die sprachliche Zuweisung finden wir drei Gruppen: Deutsch (mit unterschiedlich weiten germanischen Verwandtschaften; vgl. 3.1) sind die Namen *Aal, Bläuler, Butzeli, Egli, Forelle, Rötel, Rottele* (wahrscheinlich), *Schleie.*—Lehnwörter aus dem Lateinischen sind *Albel*

---

[4] Vgl. dazu Verf. in *Proceedings of the Eighth International Congress of Onomastic Sciences*, hg. von D.P. Blok (Haag, Paris, 1966), S. 109.

[5] Zu *-n-*-Einschub „beim Uebergang von den Diphthongen *ie ue üe* zu labialem oder gutturalem Verschlusslaut" vgl. die Anmerkung zu *schiegge(n) Id.*, 8, 430.

[6] Für weitere Details muss ich auf den (noch ausstehenden) *Id.*-Artikel verweisen.

und vielleicht *Schwal.*—Für die Fälle *Balche (palaye)*[7], *Bambeli (bambella), Trüsche (bottatrice), Winger (vangeron)* bleibt es unsicher, ob ein deutsches, ein romanisches oder ein voraufliegendes Etymon anzunehmen sei.

2.5.2 Das Benennungsmotiv ist häufig die Farbe, so bei *Albel, Balche (?), Bläuler, Rötel, Rottele* (wahrscheinlich), die Zeichnung bei *Forelle.* Andere Merkmale der äussern Erscheinung waren namengebend bei *Butzeli, Egli, Schleie.* Die Bewegung ist ausschlaggebend bei den Bezeichnungen für *Bambeli* (und vielleicht *Bumbeli*) sowie für *Günger,* allenfalls (?) noch für *Winger.* Unklar ist das Motiv bei *Aal, Fliengge, Laugeli, Schwal, Trüsche.*

3. ZUR VERBREITUNG

Von einigem Interesse mag die geographische Reichweite unserer Namen sein. Ich führe die Benennungen, wie teilweise schon oben, in typisierter (nhd.) Form auf. Die Verbreitungsangaben sind mit einigem Vorbehalt zu lesen insofern, als die lexikographischen Voraussetzungen zur Lokalisierung ungleich sind. *Id.*-Verweisungen und dort verzeichnete Literaturangaben werden hier nicht wiederholt. Zum Ganzen vgl. die Arbeit von Tischler, der seine „Fischbenennungen" gruppiert nach idg., gemeingerm., westgerm. und südgerm. (bes. ahd.) Bezeichnungen.

3.1 Für *Forelle* und *Schleie* sind aussergermanische Entsprechungen nachgewiesen; s. Kluge/Seebold unter den entsprechenden Stichwörtern. *Aal* indessen ist „aussergermanisch (wie viele Fischnamen) nicht vergleichbar" (Kluge/Seebold), aber doch über das Deutsche hinaus in Entsprechungen vorhanden (engl. *eel* udgl.; vgl. ebd.).

3.2 Als oberdeutsche oder alemannische Bezeichnungen haben zu gelten *Albel(i)* (als Weissfisch; vgl. unter 3.3), *Bambeli* (Gr. *WB.,* 1, 1095; Ochs *WB.,* 1, 112; Jutz 1, 228), *Egli* (*BSM,* 7, 16 f.; Jutz 1, 667), *Laugeli* (Ochs *WB.,* 3, 397, wo Weiteres), *Rötel* (*BSM,* 7, 61), *Trüsche.* Die genauere geographische Verbreitung von *Schwal* kann ich nicht angeben; vgl. 4.3.

3.3 Nur schweizerisch (mit unterschiedlicher Reichweite und Dichte) sind zu belegen *Albeli* (als Felchenart; vgl. *BSM,* 7, 42), *Balchen* (*BSM,* 7, 50 ff.), *Bläuler* ? (*BSM,* 7, 49), *Bumbeli, Butzeli, Fliengge* (auch Aschw.-Clauss 159), *Günger, Rottele, Winger* (Gr. *WB.,* 14, 2, 337).

---

[7] *Id.,* 4, 1192 postuliert: „Aus unserm Wort [*Balchen*] stammt das Synonym *pallaye* am Murtner- und Neuenburger See".

4. ZUR SCHICHTUNG

Unsere Namenliste enthält schichtspezifisch unterschiedliche Typen, auch wenn alle (teilweise in besonderer Form, vgl. Abschnitt 1) mundartlich verwendet werden. Ich sehe vier Kategorien.

4.1 Der Mundarttypus ist auch standardsprachlich. Wahrig verzeichnet von unsern Namen *Aal, Forelle, Schleie, Trüsche;* als „schweizerisch" ist *Egli* aufgeführt (vgl. 4.2).

4.2 Als schweizerische Besonderheiten des Standarddeutschen nennt Meyer *Albeli* (Felchenarten), *Balchen, Egli, Rötel.*

4.3 Vom „Rest" empfinde ich als in Zug aufgewachsener Dialektsprecher (mit anders-dialektalen Eltern) als deutlich mundartlich *Fliengge, Laugeli, Rottele* und *Winger. Buzeli* überlebt zugerisch im Namen einer Fast-nachtszunft (*Letzibuzäli*, nach der Quartierbezeichnung *Letzi*). Bei *Bambeli* bin ich unsicher, *Bumbeli* und *Günger* sind mir nicht geläufig, *Bläuler* und *Schwal* scheinen mir eher fachsprachlich.

4.4 Man könnte versucht sein, die dem heutigen Durchschnitts-Mundartsprecher nicht bekannten Namen der Kategorie „(Sport-) Fischer-Sprache", also der Kategorie „Fachsprache", zuzuordnen. Dagegen spricht allerdings die Art unserer Quelle, ein „Mundartbuch für Schule und Haus". Bei Unkenntnis ist deshalb vielleicht eher mit Dialekt-Verlust zu rechnen[8].

* * *

Am Schluss möchte ich auf den Anfang zurückkommen und nochmals aus einem Brief Conns zitieren. Unser gemeinsamer Freund Georg Schoeck und ich hatten Conn die Festschrift für den Indogermanisten Manu Leumann, bei dem er in Zürich Vorlesungen besucht hatte, geschenkt, als Dank für in Dublin reichlich genossene Gastfreundschaft. Conn bemerkte dazu, dass er sich nicht revanchieren könne, 'because none of our professors deserve a Festschrift, and even if they did, nobody here would have the energy to compile one' (12. August 1963). Hier hat er sich, wie der vorliegende Band beweist, in einem Satz zweimal getäuscht und sich gleichzeitig mit lächelnder Selbstironie über das Tagesgeschäft gestellt. Ich bleibe ihm sehr verbunden.

---

[8] Eine genauere Standortbestimmung der Bossardschen Fischnamen innerhalb des heutigen „Zuger-deutschen" (bzw. seiner Varietäten) wäre eine Aufgabe für sich. *Bale* z.B. ist heute zugerisch weitgehend durch das standardsprachliche Marktwort *Felche* ersetzt, *Winger* (nach einer Umfrage von 1991) unter Schulkindern kaum mehr bekannt. *Günger* anderseits ist bei Fischern noch zu erfragen.

LITERATURVERZEICHNIS[9]

Aeschbacher = Paul Aeschbacher, *Die Geschichte der Fischerei im Bielersee*, Bern, 1923

Aschw.-Clauss = Felix Aschwanden [und] Walter Clauss, *Urner Mundartwörterbuch*, Altdorf, 1982

Bossard = Hans Bossard, *Zuger Mundartbuch. Grammatik und Wörterverzeichnisse*, Zürich, 1962

BSM, 7 = Peter Dalcher, *Die Fischereiterminologie im Urkundenbuch von Stadt und Amt Zug 1352–1528. Beiträge zur schweizerdeutschen Mundartforschung*, Band VII, Frauenfeld, 1957

FEW = Walther von Wartburg, *Französisches Etymologisches Wörterbuch*, Bonn, 1928–

Fischer = Hermann Fischer, *Schwäbisches Wörterbuch*, Tübingen, 1904–1936

Glare = P.G.W. Glare, *Oxford Latin Dictionary*, Oxford, 1982

Gloss. = Louis Gauchat [u.a.], *Glossaire des Patois de la Suisse romande*, Neuchâtel und Paris, 1924–

Gr. *WB.* = Jacob und Wilhelm Grimm [u.a.], *Deutsches Wörterbuch*, Leipzig, 1854–1960; *Neubearbeitung*, hg. von der Deutschen Akademie der Wissenschaften [...], Leipzig, 1965–

Hiersche = Rolf Hiersche, *Deutsches etymologisches Wörterbuch*, Heidelberg, 1986–

Id. = *Schweizerisches Idiotikon. Wörterbuch der schweizerdeutschen Sprache* [...]. Begonnen von Friedrich Staub und Ludwig Tobler [...] Band 1-, Frauenfeld, 1881–

Jud = Jakob Jud, *Les noms des poissons du Lac Léman*, 1912; zitiert nach J.J., *Romanische Sprachgeschichte und Sprachgeographie*, Zürich, 1973

Jutz = Leo Jutz, *Vorarlbergisches Wörterbuch mit Einschluss des Fürstentums Liechtenstein*, Wien, 1960, 1965

Kluge = Friedrich Kluge, *Etymologisches Wörterbuch der deutschen Sprache*, Strassburg 1883; 11.–14. Auflage bearbeitet von Alfred Götze, 1934–1948; 22. Auflage [...] neu bearbeitet von Elmar Seebold, Berlin, New York, 1989

Lloyd/Springer = Albert L. Lloyd und Otto Springer, *Etymologisches Wörterbuch des Althochdeutschen*, Band 1 (ff.), Göttingen, Zürich, 1988

Meyer = Kurt Meyer, *Wie sagt man in der Schweiz? Wörterbuch der schweizerischen Besonderheiten*, Mannheim [usw.], 1989

Ochs *WB.* = Ernst Ochs [u.a.], *Badisches Wörterbuch*, Lahr, 1925–

Pierrehumbert = W. Pierrehumbert, *Dictionnaire historique du parler neuchâtelois et suisse romand*, Neuchâtel, 1926

Ribi = Adolf Ribi, *Die Fischbenennungen des Unterseegebietes*, Rüschlikon, 1942

SDS = *Sprachatlas der deutschen Schweiz;* hg. von Rudolf Hotzenköcherle [...], Bern, 1962–

Tischler = J. Tischler, [Abschnitt] *Sprachliches* [des Kapitels] *Fische* in: *Reallexikon der Germanischen Altertumskunde*, begründet von Johannes Hoops. 2. Auflage, Band 9, Berlin, New York, 1995, 120–126

Wahrig = Gerhard Wahrig, *Deutsches Wörterbuch*, München, 1986

---

[9] Die folgende Liste führt die oben abgekürzt zitierten Titel in möglichst knapper Form auf.

Walde = A. Walde, *Lateinisches etymologisches Wörterbuch*, 3. Auflage, Heidelberg, 1938, 1954

VERWENDETE ABKÜRZUNGEN

aaO.: am angeführten Ort

ahd.: althochdeutsch

Anm.: Anmerkung

bes.: besonders

bzw.: beziehungsweise

Dim.: Diminutiv

ebd.: ebenda

engl.: englisch

f.: feminin

f(f).: folgend(e)

frz.: französisch

gall.: gallisch

germ.: germanisch

hg.: herausgegeben

idg.: indogermanisch

i.S.v.: im Sinne von

lat.: lateinisch

m.: maskulin

mhd.: mittelhochdeutsch

mlat.: mittellateinisch

n.: neutral

nhd.: neuhochdeutsch

o.: oben

o.ä.: oder ähnlich

Pl.: Plural

S.: Seite

s.: siehe

Sg.: Singular

Syn., syn.: Synomym, synonym

u.: unten

u.a.: unter anderem, und andere

u.ä.: und ähnlich

udgl.: und dergleichen

usw.: undsoweiter

Verf.: Verfasser

vgl.: vergleiche

z.B.: zum Beispiel

'Oh, it's I'm not pretty enough'
Expletive Structure and Relevance[*]

GERALD P. DELAHUNTY
English Department, Colorado State University

0. INTRODUCTION

THIS PAPER addresses a part of the general problem of how forms and their interpretations are related. It focusses on a sentence form which seems to be universal and interpreted in much the same way wherever it occurs. Because the interpretations vary with context, they must be assigned by universal principles of pragmatics. In the space available I can only sketch an account, based on Sperber and Wilson's (1986) Relevance Theory.

1. INFERENTIAL SENTENCES

In his autobiography, Oliver Gogarty describes the plight of his friend McLoren who, as a young British officer stationed in India, had 'ingress to' a sacred temple courtesan 'learned in the art and practice of the African Aphrodite and Diana of the Ephesians and Venus of the triple gate' (Gogarty 1968, 59). So:

(1)   'He groans when a really good-looking girl meets him. The prettier the worse it takes him. Sometimes he's damned rude.'
        'Perhaps it is that women in Ireland are not a form of prayer?'
        (Gogarty 1968, 58–9)

Sentences of the type highlighted in (1) and in the title (cited in Kies 1988) are the focus of this essay. In previous publications (Declerck 1992; Delahunty 1990, 1991, 1995), they are called 'inferentials' and I continue this practice here.

Inferentials consist of a tensed clause subordinate to a matrix containing at least an expletive subject and a form of copular *be*. These are defining characteristics, although they vary cross-linguistically. For example, pro-drop languages require a zero subject and some languages, such as Hungarian, allow a zero copula. Only languages that allow these characteristics manifest the inferential sentence form. The matrix may also

---

[*] To my colleague Jim Garvey I owe a debt of gratitude for his commentary and support on this and many other projects. Errors and infelicities that remain are mine alone.

contain any or all of the following: a modal verb, an adverb such as *just*, *simply*, or *only*, and the negator *not*, as the examples in the paper show.

I have examples from French, German, Italian, Spanish, Japanese, Modern Hebrew, Finnish, Hungarian, Chinese, and Korean, and Irish:

> (2)   'Sin deachomhartha nach bhfuil tada cearr le do choinsias!' a dúirt sé.
>   'Dar mo choinsias!' a dúirt mé.
>   '*Ní hé nach gcuireann sé isteach orm!*' a dúirt mé. 'Cé hé an té nach
>   gcuirfeadh?' (Breathnach 1996)

Because these are unrelated and non-contiguous languages we seem to be dealing with a true universal and not just a genetic or areal phenomenon.

2. THE INTERPRETATIONS OF INFERENTIAL SENTENCES

The inferential's interpretations fall into a range whose very narrowness requires an explanation, which I sketch below. In the following paragraphs I illustrate these interpretations with examples collected from a broad range of discourse genres.

2.1 EXPLANATIONS/ACCOUNTS

The most frequent use of the inferential is to suggest an explanation for whatever circumstances are under discussion. The inferential in (1) invites us to infer that McLoren's sexual problems may be explained by the assumption that Irish women are not a form of prayer.

That the inferential can convey an explanation is confirmed by the fact that when the sentence beginning 'The explanation was [...]' in (3a) is replaced by an inferential, as in (3b), the two versions of the text are well-formed and synonymous.

> (3)a   In England a new ruling element [...] had been content to divert to itself the labour and produce of the indigenous rural population. When the Normans had expanded into Wales, however, they had established new communities, which came to be known as 'Englishries', in the valley floors, while confining the Welsh inhabitants, by and large, to the uplands. *The explanation was, not that the Normans were more hostile towards the Welsh than towards the Anglo-Saxons, but rather that Welsh rural society, with its pastoral emphasis, was not geared to the satisfactory working of arable land.* (Frame 1981, 77)

> (3)b   It was not that the Normans were more hostile towards the Welsh than towards the Anglo-Saxons, [...].

In (3a) it is made explicit that the propositions in the highlighted subordinate clauses are to be interpreted as an explanation for the differences between the Norman colonizations of England and Wales. This interpretation is left implicit in the adapted version (3b).

The claim that the clause of an inferential may be interpreted as an explanation for some situation is also supported by Kuno's account of the Japanese *no desu* construction. (*Desu* is a copula and *no* is a nominalizing particle.) He claims that *no desu* can be 'roughly translated as "it is that"' (1973, 223). He glosses *no desu* sentences as 'the explanation is [...]' For example:

(4) Kaze o hikimasita. Ame ni hurarete   nureta *no desu.*
     cold   drew   rain by fallen-being got-wet
     'I have caught a cold. (Lit.) The explanation for
     my having caught a cold is that I was rained on
     and drenched.' (Kuno 1973, 224, no. 3a)

2.2 EVIDENCE

In a number of his examples Kuno adds 'or evidence' to his gloss. For example (Kuno 1973, 226, no. 6a):

(5) Byooki desu. Taizyuu ga zyuppondo hetta   *no desu.*
     sick   weight ten-pounds lessened
     'I am sick. The explanation (or evidence) for my
     being sick is that I have lost ten pounds.'

English inferentials do not seem to readily admit this interpretation, for reasons I do not yet understand.

2.3 REASONS

In (6), the clause proposes a reason for his cruelty.

(6) He had not been cruel to her, or if he was, *it was only that he seemed to know little of women's bodies and how to use them.* (Bradley 1982, 24)

2.4 CAUSES

Three potential causes of the delay in global warming are proposed in the three coordinated inferential clauses in (7).

(7)   If the observed temperature increase really is a greenhouse warming
       and not just 'noise'—a random fluctuation—one might account for the
       disparity in various ways. [...] Conceivably some other factor, not
       well accounted for in the models, is delaying or counteracting the
       warming. *It might be that the heat capacity of the oceans is larger
       than current models calculate, that the sun's output has declined
       slightly or that volcanoes have injected more dust into the
       stratosphere than is currently known, thereby reducing the solar
       energy reaching the ground.* (Schneider 1989)

2.5 CONCLUSIONS

In (8) the inferential rejects the inference that the conclusion to draw from
the counter-evidence is that the model is wrong.

(8)   Lichardus' model is a variant of a broader explanation of the cultural
       change seen throughout both Northern and Central Europe in the Late
       Neolithic. [Extensive discussion of the shortcomings of the model.] *It
       is not that the model is wrong*; there is just not enough evidence
       proposed to evaluate it. (Mallory 1989, 253)

2.6 RESULTS/CONSEQUENCES

In (9) the inferential rejects the inference that not believing in God results
in believing in nothing.

(9)   And someone else—was it Chesterton?—said that when men stop
       believing in God, *it isn't that they then believe in nothing*: they believe
       in everything. (Eco 1989, 620)

2.7 INTERPRETATIONS

These interpretations fall into two related groups. The first includes
explanations, accounts, evidence, reasons, and causes; the second includes
conclusions, results, and consequences. The members of the first group can
be viewed as representing the antecedent in an implication, with the
members of the second group representing the consequent. The inferential
form appears therefore to indicate that the proposition represented by its
clause is to be incorporated into an implication as either antecedent or
consequent. Just which is determined in context. For example, the
proposition 'women in Ireland are not a form of prayer' functions as the
antecedent in an implication such as 'If women in Ireland are not a form of
prayer then McLoren will be unhappy and rude'.

3. ANALYSIS

Before proceding, let's eliminate two potential analyses of the form. First, that it is an eliptical version of extrapositive sentences with predicates such as *true* or *the case*. This position is easily rebutted: the extrapositives cannot replace the inferential without change of meaning. We cannot replace the highlighted inferential in (10) with 'It is not true/the case that one fears treachery' without rendering the text contradictory:

(10)   On principle I usually avoid introducing my friends and acquaintances
        to each other. *It is not that one fears treachery, though of course one
        does.* (Murdoch 1975, 43)

Second, inferentials do not involve the replacement of the matrix subject with full NPs such as *the explanation* or *the reason* (see Declerck 1992). This is because the *it* subject is expletive rather than a true pronoun, and the recovery of just which NP *it* represents depends upon context and is therefore a pragmatic matter. Because pragmatic principles must be invoked in the analysis anyway, interposing such full NPs as well is clearly redundant.

3.1 RELEVANCE THEORY (RT)

RT's basic claim is that ostensive communication guarantees optimal relevance, i.e., adequate contextual implications for no gratuitous processing effort. These implications are derived by decoding the linguistic form, enriching the result in a manner consistent with the search for relevance, and then deriving further inferences. The first interpretation consistent with optimal relevance in a way that the speaker S could manifestly have foreseen is taken by the hearer H to be the one S intended.

It is in principle possible to imagine a very large range of potential interpretive relations between a pair of contiguous utterances, including cause, explanation, evidence, justification, motivation, implication, contrast, or irrelevance. Without more information H is left with no way of ranking their relevance. A relevance ranking can be derived from contextual assumptions, by the addition of various expressions such as *after all*, *so*, and the like, which according to Blakemore (1987) impose semantic constraints on relevance, or, by choosing a specialized syntactic form, such as the inferential, for the second utterance.

RT allows for a range of possible relations between form and meaning (see Wilson and Sperber 1993), several of which are potentially applicable to inferentials.

First it is conceivable that inferentials license pragmatic assignments to the explicature, like those described in Carston's (1988) analysis of *and*. However if this were so the matrix should contribute to the truth conditions of the overall proposition, which should then fall within the scope of logical operators. The non-contradictoriness of (10) shows that we are not dealing with aspects of the proposition expressed.

Alternatively inferential sentences might linguistically encode procedural, non-truth conditional, and non-conceptual constraints on relevance like those described in Blakemore's (1987) analysis of discourse particles. However these expressions seem to have quite determinate interpretations; *so*, for example, indicates that the expression it introduces is relevant as a conclusion. Such implications are 'stipulated in the grammar' (Wilson and Sperber 1993, 6). The inferential is relevant in much less determinate ways, so its implicatures appear not be be linguistically encoded.

What we seem to be dealing with is a processing constraint on relevance: the expletive matrix forces the hearer to do extra processing, which must, according to RT, communicate extra contextual effects (see Blass 1990; Moeschler 1993; Wilson and Sperber 1993).

The inferential constrains the way the proposition it expresses is to be related to its context. The expletive matrix appears to trigger the processing of the assumptions made manifest by the inferential so that they and assumptions derived from the local context are related as antecedent and consequent in an implication. Each set of assumptions can play either role. The following schema illustrates the idea.

(11)   P

          If P then Q (Constructed from the inferential)
          _____

          Q

In (11) either P or Q may be derived from the inferential and the other from the local context. The implication is constructed as an interpretation of the inferential form.

A negative inferential instructs the hearer to reject a particular implication (usually one likely in the context) as irrelevant, though not necessarily false--see (10).[1] After a negative inferential we often find a positive one:

---

[1] Alternatively (or perhaps additionally) the inferential, in comparison with its non-inferential congener, may prompt an implicature of unexpectedness. In this respect it is similar to the Sissala particle *ka* 'and', as analysed in Blass (1990). In reduced conjoined sentences, *ka*, a sentential conjunction,

(12)   When the movie was over I hurried Utch and the kids to the car. *It was not that I felt we had to avoid the Winters at that moment; it was just that it was raining.* (Irving 1973, 213–4)

But why should the expletive matrix prompt the construction of an implicational structure? First, implications seem to be very readily accessible and easily processed ways of connecting almost any assumption with its context. Second, implications underlie a range of the most important semantic relations: cause and effect, evidence and conclusion, and the like, so they guarantee rich contextual effects. Finally, implications guarantee the interaction of a currently-being-processed assumption and its context so as to allow new conclusions to be drawn, thus improving the processor's representation of the world. They are therefore very efficient and consequently very relevant.

Besides licensing the derivation of inferences, forms can communicate the stength of S's commitment to those inferences. The inferential, by requiring extra processing and directing the H to focus on the most accessible connection between the inferential and its context, strongly communicates S's commitment to this interpretation.

However, in spite of the apparent strength of this commitment, there remains a degree of interpretive vagueness. This derives from (at least) two sources: first the proposition made manifest by the inferential can play either an antecedent or a consequent role and second the hearer may choose (or not) among specific interpretations of the implicational relation: cause and effect, explanation, evidence, conclusion, and so on, which will also be selected so as to optimize relevance. Because the form merely prompts a particular line of processing, this is just as we should expect. More explicit communication of the intended interpretation can be accomplished by substituting expressions such as *the explanation* or *the point* and the like for the expletive matrix subject—see (3a–b).

4. CONCLUSION

In the space available I have been able only to sketch a RT account of the universal range of interpretations of the inferential form. Much work

---

communicates an implicature of 'unexpectedness' in comparison with the other Sissala word for 'and', *a*. a VP conjunction, by virtue of the extra processing it requires. The unexpectedness communicated by the inferential is apparent from (12). The narrator's wife, Utch, has been having an affair with Mr. Winter, so it would be natural for a reader to assume that the narrator, having become aware of the Winters' presence, would want to avoid them. Surprisingly, he claims that it is not because he wishes to avoid the Winters that he hurries his family to the car. Instead he claims that he is hurrying them away because of the rain. So negative inferentials unexpectedly deny the relevance of the most plausible assumption(s) in the context, and positive inferentials assert the relevance of less accessible ones.

remains to be done, especially in identifying the range of languages that manifest the form, in accounting for any cross-linguistic variation in its interpretations, and in more fully exploring the mutual implications of inferentials and relevance theory.

REFERENCES

Blakemore, Diane 1987. *Semantic Constraints on Relevance*, Oxford: Blackwell

Blass, Regina 1990. *Relevance Relations in Discourse*, Cambridge: University Press

Bradley, Marion Z. 1982. *The Mists of Avalon*, New York: Ballantine

Breathnach, Pádraic 1996. 'Dearcadh', *Anois*, 2-3 Márta, 16

Carston, Robyn 1988. 'Implicature, Explicature, and Truth Conditional Semantics', in *Mental Representations*, ed. by Ruth Kempson, Cambridge: University Press, 155–181

Declerck, Renaat 1992. 'The Inferential *it is that*-Construction and its Congeners', *Lingua*, 87, 203–230

Delahunty, Gerald P. 1990. 'Inferentials: The Story of a Forgotten Evidential', *Kansas Working Papers in Linguistics*, 15·1, 1–28

—1991. 'The Powerful Pleonasm: A Defense of Expletive *It Is*', *Written Communication*, 8, 2, 213–239

—1995. 'The Inferential Construction', *Pragmatics*, 5, 341–364

Eco, Umberto 1989. *Foucault's Pendulum*, translated by W. Weaver, San Diego: Harcourt Brace Jovanovich

Frame, Robin 1981. *Colonial Ireland 1169–1369*, Dublin: Helicon

Gogarty, Oliver St. J. 1968. *As I was Going Down Sackville Street*, London: Sphere Books

Irving, John 1973. *The 158 Pound Marriage*, New York: Pocket Books, 47–75

Kies, Daniel 1988. 'Marked Themes with and without Pronominal Reinforcement: Their Meaning and Distribution in Discourse', in *Pragmatics, Discourse and Text*, ed. by Erich H. Steiner and Robert Veltman, Norwood: Ablex

Kuno, Susumo. 1973. *The Structure of the Japanese Language*, Cambridge, Mass.: MIT Press

Mallory, J.P. 1989. *In Search of the Indo-Europeans*, London: Thames and Hudson

Moeschler, Jacques 1993. 'Relevance and Conversation', *Lingua*, 90, 149–171

Murdoch, Iris 1975. *The Black Prince*, New York: Penguin

Schneider, Stephen H. 1989. 'The Changing Climate', *Scientific American*, (September), 70–79

Sperber, Dan and Wilson, Deirdre 1986. *Relevance: Communication and Cognition*, Cambridge, Mass.: Harvard University Press

Wilson, Deirdre and Sperber, Dan 1986. 'Inference and Implicature', in *Meaning and Interpretation*, ed. by Charles Travis, Oxford: Blackwell, 4–75

—1993. 'Linguistic form and relevance', *Lingua*, 90, 1–25

Syntactic Innovation in Early Irish

DOROTHY DISTERHEFT

Linguistics Program, University of South Carolina, Columbia

S OME of my happiest memories of the year (1986–87) I spent at University College Dublin as Visiting Fulbright Professor are of talking about Old and Middle Irish syntax with Conn Ó Cleirigh in the Senior Common Room in the Arts Block. Conn was the chair of the Linguistics Department and my host, but he was really much more than that. He was my guide, helping me navigate the intricacies of Hiberno-English and a university system very different from my own. But best of all, he was my Old Irish informant, the nearest thing to a native speaker of the language of the glosses that one could hope to find. Thus I think it fitting to offer some reflections on syntactic change in early Irish as a tribute to his memory.

1. The manner in which syntactic innovations are introduced and spread in a grammar has been a topic of debate, most of which focuses on the gradual vs. abrupt issue. Some discussions have suggested that syntactic change is like phonological change, that it supports the lexical diffusionist position that change is phonetically abrupt but lexically gradual and that it follows an S-curve, starting off gradually, rapidly gaining momentum, then slowing down toward the end of its lifetime. While there is evidence that some syntactic change follows the same progression, I will present a different kind of innovation, one which introduces a new structure, rather than a change in an existing one, as many studies so far have done. I will examine a set of innovations in Pre-Old Irish which have occurred as the result of an innovation which introduced the infinitive as a distinct category and which resulted in the addition of a number of Raising structures. I will show that they all appear immediately as a result of the initial innovation, with no variation in their syntactic features. In the Irish case, there is no evidence of variation: Raising is not added gradually and all syntactic features (e.g. clause structure restrictions, case assignment) appear in their canonical form immediately.

2.0 INNOVATION: THE CASE OF THE IRISH INFINITIVE

The traditional designation for the infinitive (INF) in Irish is verbal noun; it is a form synchronically derived from a verbal nominalization, inflected like any other noun in the language, in all cases, both singular and plural. Aside from functioning like an ordinary NP, it also does duty as the predicate of non-tensed sentences. It is the standard infinitive, although its morphology continued to maintain its nominal association through late Middle Irish. Its object was possessive/genitive with its own case assigned by the matrix verb (in sentential objects, accusative; in sentential subjects, nominative). The fact that the infinitive carries the surface marking of a subject/object and that its own object uses possessive/genitive marking yields it highly indeterminate: in many passages from Old through the end of Middle Irish, it is impossible to assign it with certainty to either infinitival or to nominal status. Even though its case marking is assigned by the matrix verb, I will argue below that other syntactic properties exhibited by the nominative/accusative INF and its relationship to the newer prepositional INF indicate that they were both part of the same infinitival system.

In the earliest Irish sources, a series of embedded sentences with a new prepositional infinitive appear and by Middle Irish became central in subordination, competing successfully with the nominative/accusative type and ultimately becoming the dominant, least constrained type. Even though the old INF continued to appear, the prepositional one gained ground in the same positions (matrix subject and object). It is a member of the same verbal noun paradigm as the nominative/accusative type, but is dative and always preceded by *do* 'to, for'. Its importance lies in the fact that it becomes the dominant pattern during this period, eventually replacing the more nominal type in Modern Irish. Here I will examine the historical relationship of the two complement types and the manner in which the prepositional INF was introduced.

2.1 RAISING STRUCTURES

The surface structure of the prepositional INF clause is

(1)   V (NP(nom)) NP(acc) *do* INF

The nominative NP is subject of V and is either a lexical or a null subject.[1] The accusative NP is an argument of INF (either subject or object), but its case is assigned by V.

I have argued previously that a rule of Raising[2] has moved the accusative NP from its original position as subject or object of INF into the matrix

---

[1] I include both lexical subject and object positions in this schema, although both NPs rarely appear together in the same clause. Typically, lexical NPs appear as subjects with intransitive verbs, but as objects with verbs which have no overt subject (i.e. pro). It is for this reason that I parenthesize the subject NPs in the schemata.

where it is no longer a clause mate of INF, but rather of V. My argument rests mainly on its position and case marking.[3] INF only governs genitive NPs to its right or a proclitic possessive pronoun—never nominatives or accusatives to its left.

Raising applies widely in Middle Irish so that most nontensed clauses are formed by the prepositional INF with its argument in the matrix. In addition to occupying object position in the matrix, it can appear as subject of V. This occurs in copular sentences whose basic pattern is that of (2), where copula is followed by a predicate noun (2a) or adjective (2b) to form a VP, with NP_2 the subject.[4]

(2) $_{VP}$ [*be* NP_1/ADJ (nom)] NP_2(nom)

    a. is fer   Conall

        is man(nom) Conall(nom)
        'Conall is a man'

    b. is mór   in lebor

        is big(nom) the book(nom)
        'The book is big'

When the prepositional INF appears in such structures, its subject or object (NP_2) is in subject position, to the right of VP, but preceding INF:

(3) $_{VP}$ [*be* NP_1/ADJ(nom)] NP_2(nom) *do* INF

I claim that there is one rule which moves NP from the INF clause to the matrix:

(4)   NP-Raising: Move NP from S' to the first unfilled NP position in the matrix.

---

[2] This paper does not attempt to make any claim about current generative theory, but rather uses its terminology as a frame within which to present the data. McCloskey (1980) has analyzed these INF structures in Modern Irish differently, arguing that where arguments of INF appear to its left, it is INF that has undergone rightward movement. I see no fundamental discrepancy between our respective analyses of two different stages of the same language because the Modern Irish structures are so different from the early ones. The major innovation in the Modern period has been that INF may have two arguments and that they both appear to its left—a sequence which is impossible in Old and Middle Irish.

[3] See Disterheft 1982, 1984 for more detailed arguments about the application of this rule in Old Irish where I presented an account of Raising structures in Old Irish only, which was based on a limited corpus. In the present study, I have expanded the data to include most published manuscripts from the Old and Middle periods. Because of the increased data base, I have revised several opinions presented in Disterheft 1982, 1984.

[4] This is one of the few structures in Early Irish where one can argue for the presence of a VP, an unlikely constituent for a VSO language. See McCloskey (1983) for arguments that certain other structures in Modern Irish also have a VP.

Before presenting the material from all the Raising structures, it is necessary to state a constraint which governs INF clause structure:

(5)   Infinitive Structure Constraint: INF has at most one argument.

   a. The prepositional INF has one and only one argument, which must be a lexical NP;

   b. The nominative/accusative INF either has no argument (is intransitive), or one argument, which must be a pronoun.

2.1.1 Raising to Object: INF subject may be raised to object (SOR), in which case the following structure obtains. (Subscripts co-index the position INF subject has moved from (e) and the slot it fills at the surface.)

(6)   V (NP_1) NP_2 S· [do INF e_2]

   Focerd Eochaid i   ces   **a ben**   **do eludh**
   put(3sg) Eochaid into illness his wife(acc) to elope(INF)
   'It grieved Eochaid that his wife had eloped' (*Toch. Étáine*, 188.20)

In (6) NP_2 *a ben* is logical subject of INF, holds object position in the matrix, and is assigned accusative case by V.
   If there is a PP whose NP is not filled, INF subject may also be moved to that position:

(7)   V (NP_1) PP [PREP NP_2] S· [do INF e_2]

   cen   **ainim**   **do beth** ann
   without blemish(acc)   to be(INF) in-him
   'without a blemish being on him' (*Bretha Déin Chécht*, glosses 38.29,4)

Cen 'without' is the usual negator of INF. All INFs here are intransitive, following the Infinitive Structure Constraint.
   INF object is also raised to matrix object (OOR). If INF subject is PRO (i.e., has no surface manifestation due to coreference with an NP in the matrix; this is indicated by subscripts), INF must be transitive, following the Infinitive Structure Constraint:

(8)   V (NP_1) NP_2 S· [do INF PRO_1 e_2]

   ocus ni ro-gabsat uada   acht **a bréthir do comallad** friu
   and NEG took(3sg) from-him except his word(acc) to fulfill(INF) to-them
   'and they did not take (anything) from him except to fulfill his promise to them' (*PH* 907–8)

In (8) the object of INF, *a bréthir*, is located in the matrix and is assigned accusative case marking by V.

If a PP in the matrix has an unfilled NP, INF object is moved to that position, as in (9) where *nech* is logical object of INF:

(9)   V (NP$_1$) $_{PP}$[PREP NP$_2$] $_{S'}$[*do* INF PRO$_1$ e_2]

     lecid   uaib   mo muinnter **cen** **nech**   díb   **do ergabail**

     let(2pl imv) from-you my people   without someone from-them to seize(INF)

     'Let my people go without seizing any one of them' *(PH* 3109–10)

2.1.2 Raising to Subject takes place in copular sentences with configurations like (3). If INF has a lexical subject, it appears as NP$_2$ (*namad*), moved there from the INF clause:

(10) $_{VP}$[*be* NP$_1$/ADJ] NP$_2$ $_{S'}$[*do*   INF e_2]

     Is faisdine **namad**   a crichib   ciana comaigthecha **do thecht** a nErind

     is prophecy enemies(nom) from countries   far   distant   to come(INF) to Ireland

     'That enemies come from far distant countries to Ireland is prophecy'

     (First Moytura 18.21)

Where there is a PP in VP, NP$_2$ controls PRO, INF must be transitive (following the Infinitive Structure Constraint) and its object is raised to subject of *be* (NP$_3$):

(11) $_{VP}$[*be* NP$_1$/ADJ $_{PP}$[PREP NP$_2$]] NP$_3$ $_{S'}$[*do*   INF   PRO$_2$ e_3]

     nach   comartha   aithrige   dam **mo uli lebar do badud**?

     be-NEG-INTERROG sign(nom) repentance(gen) to-me my all books(nom) to drown(INF)

     'Is it not a sign of repentance for me to have drowned all my books?' *(PH* 2243)

2.2 Non-Raising Structures: in contrast to the Middle Irish patterns sketched in § 2.1, the central subordinating type in Old Irish was not the prepositional infinitive, but rather the nominative/accusative, whose case assignment was controlled by V. The accusative INF stood in object position, functioning as a verb complement, with the following surface order:

(12)   V   (NP$_1$) $_{NP_2}$[INF PRO$_1$]

     má frisáiletar **dul**   a n-angnáis na noém

     if   hope(3pl)   go(INF) into company the saints(gen)

     'if they should hope to go into the company of saints' *(Ríagul Pátraic* 219.9)

In (12) INF is intransitive and subject is PRO controlled by matrix subject. At most the accusative INF may have one argument; when it is the object, it must be a pronoun (PRON) in the possessive form, in this case *a*.

(13)   V (NP$_1$) $_{NP_2}$[PRON-INF PRO$_1$]

> Ocus ni-robe forsin tír   fer   ro-lamad   **a thabairt** dó
> and NEG-was upon-the land man(nom) dared(3sg rel) its bring(INF) to-him
> 'and there was not a man in the land who dared to bring it to him' *(TBFr 37.192)*

A lexical subject is also available for INF when it is intransitive; in such passages INF subject stands to its right and takes the form of PP (always with *do*, as in (14a)). If INF subject is pronominal, it must be part of a conjugated preposition (14b).

(14)   V (NP$_1$) $_{NP_2}$[INF] $_{PP}$[*do* NP$_3$/PRON]

> a. asrochoili inna chridiu **buid dond ingin** in ógi
>   determines in-his heart be(INF) to-the daughter in celibacy
>   'He determines in his heart that the daughter be in virginity' *(Wb 10^{b}20)*

> b. asindet som **tuidecht doib**   dochum a tire ...
>   says   EMPH come(INF) to-them towards their land
>   'he speaks of their return to their land [...]' *(Ml 104^{c}5)*

The configuration PRON + INF (acc) allows a great deal of indeterminacy throughout the history of Irish non-finite complementation, as in

(15)   [...] is samlid arrobertsom **ar nícc**   ni (*Wb* 29^{d}23)
>   is thus   said(3 sg) our save(INF/NP)EMPH(1pl)

where two readings are possible:

> a. active INF, PRO subject with pronominal direct object:
>   'It is thus he has determined to save us'

> b. possessive pronoun with NP direct object of V:
>   'It is thus he has designed our salvation'

Accusative INF may also be object of PREP and may appear with enclitic pronominal object:

(16) $_{PP}$[PREP   INF]

aine   re   forchetal fír **gan   a   iarraid**
period-of-fast from teaching   true   without   its   seek(INF)
'fasting from true teaching (and) not seeking it' (*Devotional Verse* 8.6)

Thus far we have seen matrix verb assigning case to INF in object position; INF may also be subject of V, where it occupies NP_2 position, as in (2) above.

(17) $_{VP}$ [V NP_1/ADJ] $_{NP_2}$ [PRON-INF]

ba   huisse **a imdídnad**
was(3 sg) fitting his protect(INF)
'to protect him was fitting' (*Blathmac* 8.22)

Alternatively, INF may have an object NP in the genitive:

(18)   ni   lour   dúnni **accubur   inna firinne**
not-is enough(nom) for-us desire(INF)   the justice(gen)
'for us to desire justice is not sufficient' (*Lambeth Commentary* 15.153)

3. HISTORY

The two patterns that we have seen in § 2.1 and § 2.2 illustrate very drama-tically two typologically different systems. Case selection of the nomin-ative/accusative one is controlled by matrix V, just like any NP; its argu-ments modify the INF just as adjectivals/possessives would the head noun. The combination of these two features naturally produces a high level of indeterminacy which is maintained as long as they are used. In fact, if it were not for the presence of the prepositional INF, one might claim that Early Irish had no INF.[5]

The prepositional INF, however, is clearly verbal in allowing Raising to move both subject and object from the embedded clause to matrix subject, object, or object of preposition. Furthermore, no indeterminacy is ever pro-duced in such structures.

---

[5] Until recently, Irish philologists have been divided on the noun vs. infinitive debate. Thurneysen 1946, 445 claimed that the nominative/accusative was nominal, the prepositional type infinitival. Fraser (1912) contended that the verbal noun was only infinitival, while Dillon (1955, 112 f.) and Lehmann and Lehmann (1975, 118) come down on the opposite side of the controversy. I myself have consistently maintained (since Disterheft 1980, 159) that in spite of its close nominal associations, the verbal noun was indeed an INF because of the syntactic properties displayed in §2.2. Likewise, McCloskey (1980, 1983) assumes that this form is infinitival in Modern Irish.

The side-by-side occurrence of these two INF types is striking. The implicit assumption for years until now has been that they co-occur freely, with little discrimination between the two. However, the close analysis of a large data base which resulted in the formulation of the Infinitive Structure Constraint has clearly revealed the opposite to be true. They are, in fact, in complementary distribution.

The first thing that comes to the mind of the historical linguist is the question: How were the Raising patterns introduced to the language and how did the neat pattern regulated by the constraint come about? The answer forms the remainder of this section.

I have found all Raising patterns in early Old Irish. They are indeed rare, but they do occur in the oldest strata, from the 6th (23) to mid-8th centuries (19)–(22):

(19) Subject-to-Object Raising:

> is cian do-rairngred in se, no   mbíthe   **int áugaire**
> is long prophesied(3 sg) this COMP struck-down(3sg) the shepherd(nom)
> ocus **essreud**   fiad doínib **do buith**
> and scattered(nom) before people to be(INF)
> 'Long has this been prophesied: that the shepherd be struck down and
> they [the sheep] dispersed before people' (*Blathmac* 44.127)

In (19), in fact, INF subject (*int áugaire*) has been promoted to subject of the main verb (*do-rairngred*) because the latter is passive.

(20)   Object-to-Object Raising:

> ciad cobrinn   **móidim**   **do dénum** ni bói adbar *híc*
> though desire(1sg subjn) boasting(acc)   to do(INF) NEG be cause
> 'though I would desire to boast, there would be no cause *híc* ' (*Wb* 17^{d}17)

(21)   Object-to-Object of PREP:

> **cen fert do dul**   inna lecht iar n-ebirt nád   n-eséracht
> without tumulus to go(INF) on-his grave after said(3sg) NEG-COMP arose(3sg)
> 'no tumulus should be put on his grave, having said that he had not arisen,'
> (*Blathmac*, 40.116)

(22)   Subject-to-Subject Raising:

> bid   soraid la cech n-ecnae **mac do buith** i mbrú oenduini
> be(3sg fut) easy with each wise son(nom) to be(INF) in womb single-person(gen)

'It will be very easy with each wise [man] [that] the son be in the womb of one person' (*Blathmac* 54.159)

(23)   Object-to-Subject Raising:

Mad i nadaid rig   ba   ecen   **tri lubai gall do cuingid** do
if-is in face king(gen) be(3sg subjn) necessity(nom) three herbs(nom) to seek(INF) for-him
'If it be [a wound] in the face of a king, it would be necessary to seek three herbs for him' (Bretha Dén Cécht 26.9)

Note that the only gap is with Subject to Object of PREP: I have not yet found an example in the early period. Although it is rare in Middle Irish, it may still exist in Archaic or early Old Irish and simply not yet have come to light.

Another striking fact is that there is no gradual transition from one type to another, e.g. the nominative/accusative type does not lend any of its features, like object case marking, to the prepositional one, so that (24) never occurs.

(24)   *V (NP$_1$) *do* INF PRO$_1$ NP(gen)

where the genitive object noun stands to the right of INF when its subject is PRO. Instead of seeing any variation at all, the major features of all Raisings are in place immediately. The only variation occurs in the rate of application of the Infinitive Structure Constraint. In Old Irish all aspects of the distribution are not yet set, thus producing the following violations by the accusative INF:

A. Nominative/accusative INF may govern a genitive NP object:

(25)   asrubartatar nad   coimnacuir dia   **tabairt uisci**   doib isin diserto
said(3pl) NEG-COMP was-able(3sg)God(nom)bring(INF) water(gen) to-them in-the wilderness
'for they had said that God had no power to give them water in the wilderness'
(*Ml* 97^{d}4)

This pattern is actually common in Old Irish, occurring in 29% (24 of 84) of the accusative verb complements with PRO subject. However, a dramatic drop occurs in Middle Irish, where only 10% (29 of 119) of such patterns have a nominal object. The nominative INF with genitive object also declines from 23% in Old Irish (28 of 108) to 15% (11 of 75) later.

B. Nominative/accusative INF may govern both subject and object NPs:
Type (14) with lexical subject is slightly less frequent (25 tokens) than its
prepositional counterpart (SOR, 37 tokens): it is generally intransitive, but
in three passages (12%) has a subject in PP and a genitive NP object, as in:

(26)   asanarbaram **do erscugud di neuch** dihilib   **a chenéuil** feissin

say(1pl)   to surpass(INF) to anything from-many its kind(gen)   own
'we say anything of many things surpasses its own kind' (*Sg* 40ª11)

In Middle Irish, such irregularities ceased altogether and the accusative INF
is invariantly intransitive. It also becomes moribund, falling to 19 attestations. The same irregularity is seen with the nominative INF in (27) with
pronominal subject (in postposed PP) and genitive object:

(27)   ar-ropad   maith limsa **labrad** **ilbelre**   **dúibsi**

for-be(3sg subjn) good(nom) with-me speak(INF) many-languages(gen) to-you
'for I should like you to speak many tongues' (*Wb* 12ᶜ29)

While the rate of violation here is likewise small in Old Irish (3%), it falls
to 1% in Middle Irish.

    The changes in frequencies seen in A and B are obviously the result of
the spread of Raising patterns, which are the domain of transitive INFs and
those with lexical subjects. During this same period, the prepositional INF
in OOR increases its frequency by 460% (from 24 in Old to 134 in Middle
Irish), and is clearly the reason for the move of NP objects away from the
accusative type. Similarly, SOR shows a 220% gain, increasing from 37
attestations in Old to 119 in Middle Irish.

    The historical relationship of these constructions is actually one of ad-
justing selectional restrictions on the older infinitive's structure. When the
new one is introduced, it shows up in all possible environments, with no
violation of the Infinitive Structure Constraint. The only change is a rise in
frequency over a 600-year period. It is difficult to ascertain exactly when
the prepositional INF was introduced to Irish, but to judge by its sparse
attestation in the 6th and 7th centuries, it could not have been long before
then. Of course, declaring the exact mechanism of its introduction is risky
business in the absence of a continuous and plentiful textual record from
the 4th century on, but the subsequent history of these structures holds the
key. The accusative INF structure (and to a lesser extent, the nominative) is
the continuation of an earlier syntactic pattern from late Proto-Indo-
European, whereas the prepositional type is an Irish innovation, which has
typological parallels in other languages which have lost inflectional
morphology of verb nominalizations and whose INFs have moved away
from the nominal system. I have elsewhere (Disterheft 1981) suggested

that the prepositional INF developed when the inherited verbal noun was reanalyzed as INF. The evidence from chronology and clause structure distribution indicate that Raising was an immediate characteristic of the new INF and that through the 12th century the existing system realigns to conform to the surface constraints established with the new category which could accommodate more NPs within its clause without any indeterminacy.

REFERENCES

Dillon, Myles 1955. 'On the Syntax of the Irish Verb', *TPhS*, 1955, 104–16

Disterheft, Dorothy 1980. *The Syntactic Development of the Infinitive in Indo–European*, Columbus: Slavica Publishers

—1981. 'Remarks on the History of the Indo-European Infinitive', *Folia Linguistica Historica*, 2, 3–34

—1982. 'Subject Raising in Old Irish', in *Papers from the 5th International Conference on Historical Linguistics*, ed. by Anders Ahlqvist, Amsterdam: John Benjamins, 44–53

—1984. 'Irish Complementation: A Case Study in Two Types of Syntactic Change', in *Historical Syntax*, ed. by Jacek Fisiak, 89–106, Berlin: Mouton

Fraser, James 1912. 'A Use of the Verbal Noun in Irish', in *Miscellany Presented to Kuno Meyer*, ed. by Osborn Bergin and Carl Marstrander, Halle: Niemeyer Verlag, 216–26

Lehmann, R. P. M. and Lehmann, W. P. 1975. *An Introduction to Old Irish*, New York: Modern Languages Association

McCloskey, James 1980. 'Is There Raising in Modern Irish?', *Ériu*, 31, 59–99

—1983. 'A VP in a VSO language?', in *Order, Concord, and Constituency*, ed. by Gerald Gazdar et al., Dordrecht: Foris, 9–55

Thurneysen, Rudolf 1946. *A Grammar of Old Irish*, Dublin: Institute for Advanced Studies

The Pronominal Augment in Irish Identificational Sentences[1]

CATHAL DOHERTY
University College Dublin

1. INTRODUCTION

IDENTIFICATIONAL sentences in Irish, e.g. (1) below, are distinguished from their predicational counterparts, (2), by the presence of an extra pronoun (termed the *pronominal augment*):[2]

(1)　　Is é　　　　Seán an dochtúir.
　　　　COP 3SG.ACC Seán the doctor
　　　　'Seán is the doctor.'

(2)　　Is　　dochtúir Máire.
　　　　COP doctor　Máire
　　　　'Máire is a doctor.'

The presence of this accusative pronoun is puzzling, given that identificational sentences contain only two nominal arguments, essentially by definition. One possible solution is that the augment is simply an agreement affix, indicating agreement between the copula and the following NP, analogous to subject-verb agreement. The agreement analysis has been maintained in varying forms in the literature (e.g. Carnie 1995, Doherty 1996) and is consistent with many of the syntactic and phonological properties of the augment.

This paper provides evidence, however, that the agreement analysis is empirically inadequate. On the contrary, it is proposed that the augment is a predicative expression which directly encodes the identification relation.

The structure of the paper is as follows. The arguments for and against the agreement analysis are respectively outlined in section 2 and 3 below. Section 4 then presents the details of the proposed analysis and finally section 5 concludes with some theoretical consequences.

---

[1] A previous version of this paper was presented at the Celtic Linguistics Conference at University College Dublin in June 1995. Thanks to participants of that conference, also to Bill Ladusaw and Kari Swingle for many helpful comments. All errors and omissions remain the responsibility of the author.

[2] Other terms include the *subpredicate* (Stenson 1981) or *temporary predicate* (O'Nolan 1940). In some dialects (e.g. Conamara, Ó Siadhail 1989), an accusative pronoun appears between the predicate and the subject of predicational sentences such as (2): i.e. *Is dochtúir í Máire*. However, I assume throughout this paper that such pronouns are not pronominal augments. Rather, they represent a pronominal copy of the postposed subject, as in the English equivalent *She's a doctor, Máire*.

2. THE AGREEMENT ANALYSIS

Traditional grammars (e.g. Ó Cadhlaigh 1938, 6; Ó Searcaigh 1939) observe that there is concord in gender and number between the pronominal augment and the immediately following nominal:[3]

(3)　　Is　　é　　　Brian　an Rí.
　　　　COP　3SG.M.ACC　Brian　the king
　　　　'Brian is the King.'

(4)　　An　　　í　　　an cailín sin　Máire?
　　　　Q.COP　3SG.F.ACC　the girl　that Máire
　　　　'Is that girl Máire?'

(5)　　Is　iad　　　lámha Esau　na lámha ach
　　　　COP　3PL.ACC　hands　Esau　the hands　but

　　　　is　é　　　glór　Iacob an glór.
　　　　COP　3SG.M.ACC voice　Iacob　the voice
　　　　'The hands are the hands of Esau but the voice is the voice of Jacob.'
　　　　(OC6)

Note that this is agreement with the leftmost nominal only, which becomes clear in sentences containing arguments differing in number features:

(6)　　a. Is　iad　　　na mic léinn　an trioblóid.
　　　　　COP 3PL.ACC　the students　　the trouble
　　　　　'The students are the trouble.'

　　　　b. *Is　é　　　na mic léinn　an trioblóid.
　　　　　COP 3SG.M.ACC　the students　the trouble
　　　　　'The students are the trouble.'

As pointed out above, identificational sentences contain exactly two arguments. Therefore, it seems unlikely that the pronominal augment is an argument. It also is unlikely to be an expletive, as there is strong evidence that copular sentences are not impersonal constructions.[4] Furthermore, expletives in other languages tend to be fixed forms which do not vary in person and/or number features. An analysis of the augment as an agreement affix (despite its orthographical representation) is an obvious means

---

[3] Abbreviations have the following interpretations: OC, Ó Cadhlaigh 1938; ON, O'Nolan 1920.

[4] See Doherty (1996, 13–14) for arguments that copular sentences are not impersonal.

of explaining its presence and is compatible with the major characteristics of the augment, as discussed below.

2.1 INTEGRITY OF COPULA AND AUGMENT

There is copious evidence that the copula and augment form an impenetrable complex word. First, note the phonological realizations of the various forms in (7):

(7) Is é   [ʃe:]
     Is í   [ʃi:]
     Is iad   [ʃi:d]

The phonological fusion of the copula and augment is entirely expected under the analysis of the augment as an agreement affix.

Second, ellipsis processes indicate that the copula and augment form a single word. Note that when the copula is elided in speech (as is often the case), the augment must also be omitted:

(8) a. Is   í   Éire mo thír dhúchais.
        COP 3SG.F.ACC   Ireland my country native
        'Ireland is my native country.'

     b. Éire mo thír dhúchais.

     c. *í Éire mo thír dhúchais.

The Irish equivalent of VP-ellipsis provides further evidence for this conclusion. This process typically applies in the response to a Yes/No question, among many other environments. Note that all the arguments of the verb delete, only the inflected verb remaining:[5]

(9) a. An ndéanfá   sin domh?
        Q do.COND.2SG that to.me
        'Would you do that for me?'

     b. Dhéanfainn.   / Ní   dhéanfainn.
        do.COND.1SG / NEG do.COND.1SG
        'Yes.'   /   'No.'

---

[5] See McCloskey 1991 for general discussion of this ellipsis process and Doherty (1996, 28–30) for discussion of ellipsis in copular sentences, in particular.

The behaviour of identificational copular sentences under ellipsis therefore provides a test for the status of the augment. If it is an agreement morpheme, then it should survive ellipsis. As the following examples show, this expectation is borne out:

(10)   a. An   é   Seán an dochtúir?
            Q.COP 3SG.M.ACC Seán the doctor
            'Is Seán the doctor?'

        b. Is   é.   /   Ní   hé.
            COP 3SG.M.ACC   /   NEG.COP 3SG.M.ACC
            'Yes.'   /   'No.'

On the other hand, if the pronominal augment were an argument, it would be expected to delete, as other arguments do.

In sum, there is strong evidence that the copula and augment form a complex syntactic and phonological word, a conclusion which is fully expected under the analysis of the augment as an agreement affix.

2.2 PREDICATIONAL SENTENCES

There is one puzzling fact which crucially requires an explanation if the agreement analysis is to be tenable: i.e. the absence of agreement from predicational sentences with nominal predicates, e.g. (2) above. If the copula agrees with the immediately following (definite) noun phrase in identificational sentences, it is unclear why there is no agreement with the following (indefinite) nominal in predicational sentences.

One possibility (explored in Doherty 1996) is that the definite/indefinite distinction in Irish can be re-interpreted in categorial terms as the distinction between DP and NP.[6] Assuming that agreement is triggered only by DP and not by NP, the absence of agreement in predicational sentences receives a plausible explanation. This proposal is supported by a variety of data. Those elements of nominal structure which are standardly assigned to the NP projection (common noun phrases and noun phrases with cardinal modifiers) fail to trigger the augment:

(11)   a. Is   duine deas é.
            COP person nice 3SG.M.ACC
            'He is a nice man.'

---

[6] See Abney 1987, Stowell 1989 for basic references on the NP/DP distinction.

b. Is   dhá rud éagsúla iad.
   COP two thing distinct 3PL.ACC
   'They are two distinct things.'

On the other hand, those items of nominal structure which are standardly assigned to the DP projection (determiners, genitive proclitics and quantifiers such as *gach* 'every') do trigger the augment:[7]

(12)   a. Is   iad   na gasúraí an trioblóid.
        COP 3PL.ACC the boys   the trouble
        'The boys are the trouble.'

        b. Is   í   mo dheirfiúr an cailín fionn.
           COP 3SG.F.ACC my sister   the girl   blonde
           'My sister is the blonde girl.'

        c. Ba   é   gach duine   ... an crann fíge.
          COP.PAST 3SG.M.ACC every person   the tree fig
          'Everyone ... was the fig tree.'

Assuming that agreement is triggered in Irish only by DP and not NP, the distributional facts largely follow.

2.3 SUMMARY

The agreement analysis, therefore, has much to recommend it. It is consistent with the phonological and syntactic properties of the copula and augment. Furthermore, following the above discussion, the absence of the augment from predicational sentences can be accounted for. Nonetheless, many problems remain with this approach and it will be argued below that it is ultimately untenable.

3. AGAINST THE AGREEMENT ANALYSIS

One immediate question is the morphological form of this alleged agreement affix. Specifically, it is unclear why the agreement affix associated with the copula takes the form of an accusative pronoun, while other agreement affixes in Irish are distinct from pronominals.[8] Furthermore, there are two serious analytical difficulties with the

---

[7] Example (12)c is adapted from Ó Cadhlaigh (1940, 161): the context is the explanation of a parable, in which the fig tree is a symbol.

[8] See McCloskey and Hale 1984 for general discussion of agreement phenomena in Irish.

agreement approach: (i) other productive agreement processes in Irish do not permit agreement with overt nominals; (ii) the distribution of the augment cannot be fully captured in terms of the NP/DP distinction.

3.1 AGREEMENT WITH OVERT NOMINALS

Agreement with overt nominals (pronominal or non-pronominal) is generally excluded in Modern Irish:

(13) a. Deirim.   a. *Deirim mé.
         say.1SG   *say.1SG 1SG*

       b. leo   b. *leo   na mná
         with.3PL   *with.3PL the women*

The alleged agreement process in identificational copular sentences is anomalous, therefore, in that it involves agreement with overt nominals.

Agreement with overt nominals is occasionally attested, however. As reported by McCloskey and Hale (1984, 528–31) some Munster dialects permit certain verbs inflected for the third plural to appear with overt subjects:

(14) Táid   na ba   ag innilt.
       be.PRES.3PL the cows grazing
       'The cows are grazing.'

(15) Táid   siad ag innilt.
       be.PRES.3PL they grazing
       'They are grazing.'

This phenomenon differs from the alleged agreement process in copular sentences in two major respects, however. First, it is a peripheral phenomenon which is dialectally restricted and is always entirely optional. This is not the case with the pronominal augment which is a feature of all geographical dialects and is obligatory when it appears. Second, this agreement process permits agreement with pronominal subjects, (15) above. Note, however, that pronominals never appear with the augment in identificational copular sentences:

(16) Is (*í)   ise   an dochtúir.
       COP 3SG.F.ACC 3SG.F.ACC.EMPH the doctor
       'She is the doctor.'

(17) Is (*mé) mise   Cathal.
      COP 1SG 1SG.EMPH Cathal
      'I am Cathal.'

It is not clear why this is the case, if the pronominal augment is simply an agreement affix.

3.2 DISTRIBUTION OF THE AUGMENT

A further problem for the agreement analysis is its distribution. The traditional generalization in terms of syntactic definiteness (re-interpreted in terms of the NP/DP distinction) is inaccurate. At least in some varieties, there are syntactically indefinite nominals which trigger the augment and, more seriously, syntactically definite nominals which fail to trigger it. It appears that it is the reference of the nominal following the copula, rather than its syntactic definiteness, which is the relevant factor.

First, note that some co-ordinate indefinites (e.g. mass nouns) may trigger the augment:

(18) Is   iad   bia agus uisce na rudaí   atá   de dhíth orthu.
      COP 3PL.ACC food and water the things that.are needed on.them
      'Food and water are the things they need.'

Furthermore, for some speakers, indefinite nominals induce the augment when they are made referentially heavy by a relative clause or other modifier:

(19) Is é   ainm a bhí air   ná Séadna. (ON20)
      COP 3SG.M.ACC name that was on.him prt Séadna
      'Séadna was his name.'

(20) Is   é   céad chrann tharla   dó   soileach mhór.
      COP 3SG.M.ACC first tree   happened to.him willow big
      'The first tree he met was a big willow.' (OC4)

On the other hand, some syntactically definite nominals fail to induce the augment. First, proper names, when used non-referentially, fail to trigger the augment:

(21) Dúirt sé gur   Dún Garbhán do bhí ar an mbaile sin riamh.
      said he that.COP.PAST Dún Garbhán prt was on the town   that ever
      'He said that Dún Garbhán was always the name of that town.' (ON42)

(22) An Séadna is ainm dó?
   Q.COP Séadna COP name to.him
   'Is Séadna his name?'

In all the above cases, however, the nominals in question are ambiguous between NP and DP. Following Longobardi 1994, it could be claimed that the indefinites which induce the augment are dominated by an (abstract) DP projection. Similarly, proper names, when used non-referentially, can be analyzed as NPs, rather than DPs. The analysis of Doherty 1996, therefore, could be maintained despite the above data.

Such an approach is not possible with the following data, however. Bare NP adverbs such as *an fhaid* 'the time' are unambiguously DPs, as they contain the definite article. Nonetheless, they fail to trigger the augment, for many speakers:

(23) Is dócha gur an fhaid a bhí an dealbhas air a dhein sé é.
   COP likely that.COP the time that was the destitution on.him that did he it
   'It's likely that he did it the time he was destitute.' (ON45)

The determining factor governing the appearance of the augment, therefore, is the reference of the following noun phrase, not its syntactic definiteness. The augment appears with referential nominals, in the pre-theoretical sense that they refer to individuals. The implications for the agreement analysis are serious, therefore, as it would be anomalous for the presence of agreement to depend on the reference of the following nominal.[9]

3.3 SUMMARY

In sum, although the agreement analysis of the pronominal augment is consistent with its phonological properties, this approach suffers from serious shortcomings. First, this alleged agreement process would be unique in the language: unlike other instances of agreement with overt nominals, the pronominal augment is a regular and obligatory pheno-menon, which is not dialectally restricted. Furthermore, it is unclear why agreement with overt pronominals is excluded while agreement with overt nominals is obligatory, unlike other instances of agreement in the language. Second, the distribution of the augment can be shown to depend

---

[9] This conclusion is consistent with the fact that the concord between the augment and the following nominal does not depend on grammatical gender or number, but on the referent of the nominal. For example, grammatically masculine nouns with feminine referents (e.g. *cailín* 'girl') appear with feminine pronouns, as in (4) above.

on the referent of the following nominal, an anomalous property for an agreement process. Therefore, the agreement analysis of the augment seems ultimately untenable.

4. AN ALTERNATIVE APPROACH

The use of a pronominal augment in identificational sentences is not restricted to Irish. For example, consider the following paradigms from Hebrew and Moroccan Arabic, which are strikingly reminiscent of the Irish facts:[10]

(24)   a. ani hu   ha-more.   (Hebrew)
       I 3SG.M the-teacher
       'I am the teacher.'

    b. ha-yalda hi   ha-more.
      the-girl 3SG.F the-teacher
      'The girl is the teacher.'

    c. david ve-Tali hem ha-morim.
      David and Tali 3PL the teachers
      'David and Tali are the teachers.'

(25)   a. ana huwa   l-mudir. (Moroccan Arabic)
       I 3SG.M the-principal
       'I am the principal.'

    b. Fatima hiyya l-mudira.
      Fatima 3SG.F the-principal
      'Fatima is the principal.'

    c. Fatima w̃-Malika   huma l-mudirat.
      Fatima and-Malika   3PL the-principals
      'Fatima and Malika are the principals.'

Therefore, the Irish facts are not as puzzling as might appear at first blush: the Irish pronominal augment simply reflects a deep, cross-linguistic

---

[10] These data are discussed in Déprez and Vinet (1992, 35-39) in comparison with copular sentences in Haitian Creole, which are less similar to Irish: a special particle (*se*) is used with all nominal predicates, not just referential ones. See Rapoport 1987 for extensive discussion of the Hebrew data and parallel facts from other languages (e.g. Russian). See also Watkins 1997 (this volume) for possible similarities with Old Welsh.

connection between pronominals and the expression of the identification relation.

The linear position of the pronominal is telling: in Hebrew (generally SVO), it appears in the medial position associated with the finite verb. Furthermore, in Irish (generally VSO) the augment appears in the clause-initial position associated with the finite verb.[11] Therefore, it is conceivable that the pronominal augment is a predicative expression which directly encodes the identification relation and which is structurally analogous to a finite verb.[12]

Under the standard assumption that VSO order in Irish is derived from an underlying SVO order via verb-raising (McCloskey 1991 and his earlier work), (26)a below, the structure of identificational sentences in Irish could be as schematised in (26)b (corresponding to example (1) above) in which the augment heads a PredicatePhrase containing the two arguments. The pronominal undergoes raising (head-movement) to clause-initial position, analogous to the finite verb:[13]

(26)   a. [$_{CP}$ [$_{IP}$ V$_i$ [$_{VP}$ Subject [$_{V'}$ t_i Object]]]]
       b. [$_{CP}$ [$_{IP}$ Is é $_i$ [$_{PredP}$ Seán [$_{Pred'}$ t_i [$_{DP}$ an dochtúir]]]]]

Under this approach, the pronominal augment is an 'unsaturator' morpheme which obligatorily combines with a complement referential nominal, permitting it to function as a predicate.

This analysis immediately restricts the augment to identificational sentences involving two referential nominals, accounting for the major distributional characteristics of the augment, in particular its absence from predicational sentences with nominal predicates.

Furthermore, the concord in number and gender between the augment and the following nominal also follows straightforwardly: the combination of the augment and a complement nominal forms a one-place predicate seeking a subject. Therefore, concord in number and gender between the pronominal and the subject noun phrase is entirely expected.

---

[11] The augment is preceded by the *is/ba* particle. However, I here follow Ahlqvist 1972 in assuming that these particles are not lexical verbs but functional elements, an amalgam of tense features and the complementizer head (Doherty 1996). The pronominal augment is, therefore, clause-initial: i.e. the first lexical element in the clause, the position normally occupied by a lexical verb.

[12] Rapoport 1987 makes a similar, though distinct claim for modern Hebrew. In particular, she claims that the pronominal is the realisation of agreement features on a (null) identificational copula.

[13] McCloskey 1996 provides strong evidence that the fronted verb in Irish does not move as high as C°, but only to the highest position within IP. Subsequent lowering of C° to this position derives the fact that complementizers and verbs in Irish form a complex word. These issues are of no direct concern here, however.

Finally, this approach is fully consistent with the phonological integrity of the augment and the copular particle, outlined in 2.1 above. Under this approach, the copula and augment form a complex head. Therefore it is entirely expected that they constitute a single phonological word.

4.1 REMAINING QUESTIONS

Many questions remain open, however. Recall from (16) and (17) above that the pronominal augment is obligatorily absent from sentences in which the nominal immediately following the copula is a pronoun. It is not immediately obvious how this fact follows from the above analysis.

One possibility, however, is that such sentences are predicational in structure: i.e. that the pronominal is a structural predicate:

(27)   *Is* [Predicate *pro*] [Subject DP]

Under the present analysis, pronominals are predicative expressions which are intricately connected with the expression of the identification relation.[14] Therefore, in a sense, it is unsurprising that the augment fails to appear in such cases: the pronominal predicate itself expresses the identification relation.

Furthermore, note that the pronouns which appear in this position are either first or second person (basic or emphatic grade), but if third person are obligatorily emphatic, never basic grade:

(28)   Is   (mé / mise)   Cathal.
         COP   1SG / 1SG.EMPH Cathal
         'I am Cathal.'

(29)   An   (tú / tusa   ) Cathal?
         Q.COP   2SG / 2SG.EMPH Cathal
         'Are you Cathal?'

(30)   Is   (eisean   / *é   )   Seán.
         COP   3SG.ACC.EMPH / 3SG.ACC Seán
         'He is Seán.'

It appears then that only *deictic* pronouns, which depend on the context of utterance for their interpretation, can appear in this position. Further

---

[14] See Ramchand 1995a,b for a similar proposal that pronouns are predicates in copular sentences such as (16) and (17).

investigation of this generalisation must be left for further research, however.

5. CONCLUSION

To sum up, it has been shown that the analysis of the pronominal augment in Irish copular sentences as an agreement affix is seriously problematic. An alternative approach is proposed which takes the augment to be a direct encoding of the identification relation. While many questions remain unresolved, this approach seems promising in that it provides a reasonable explanation for the major distributional characteristics of the augment. Furthermore, parallel facts from other languages such as Hebrew show clearly that the expression of the identification relation is intricately connected with pronominals. The investigation of the reasons behind this connection is material for further research.

REFERENCES

Ahlqvist, Anders 1972. 'Some Aspects of the Copula in Irish', *Éigse* 14, 269–274

Abney, Steven 1987. 'The English Noun Phrase in its Sentential Aspect', Ph.D. dissertation, MIT

Carnie, Andrew H. 1995. 'Non-verbal Predication and Head Movement', Ph.D. dissertation, MIT

Chomsky, Noam 1995. *The Minimalist Program*, Cambridge, Mass.: MIT Press

Déprez, Viviane and Vinet, Marie-Thérèse 1992. 'Une Structure prédicative sans copule', *Revue québecoise de linguistique*, 22, 11–44

Doherty, Cathal 1996. 'Clausal Structure and the Modern Irish Copula', *Natural Language and Linguistic Theory*, 14, 1–46

—forthc. 'Predicate-Initial Constructions in Irish', *Proceedings of the Fifteenth West Coast Conference on Formal Linguistics*, Stanford, California: CSLI Press

Kayne, Richard 1994. *The Antisymmetry of Syntax, Linguistic Inquiry Monograph*, XXV, Cambridge, Mass.: MIT Press.

Longobardi, Giuseppe 1994. 'Reference and Proper Names: A Theory of N-movement in Syntax and Logical Form', *Linguistic Inquiry*, 25, 609–65

McCloskey, James 1991. 'Clause Structure, Ellipsis and Proper Government in Irish', *Lingua*, 85, 259–302

—1996. 'On the Scope of Verb Movement in Irish', *Natural Language and Linguistic Theory* 14, 47–104

McCloskey, James and Hale, Kenneth 1984. 'On the Syntax of Person-Number Inflection in Modern Irish', *Natural Language and Linguistic Theory*, 1, 487–533

Ó Cadhlaigh, Cormac 1938. *Ceart na Gaedhilge*, Dublin: Mellifont Press

—1940. *Gnás na Gaedhilge*, Dublin: Oifig an tSólathair

O'Nolan, Gerald 1920. *Studies in Modern Irish*, I, Dublin: The Educational Company of Ireland

Ó Searcaigh, Séamus 1939. *Coimhréir Ghaedhilg an Tuaiscirt*, Dublin: Oifig an tSólathair

Ó Siadhail, Mícheál 1989. *Modern Irish: Grammatical Structure and Dialectal Variation*, Cambridge: University Press

Ramchand, Gillian 1995a. 'Non-finite Complementation in Scottish Gaelic', paper presented at the Celtic Linguistics Conference, University College, Dublin, June 1995

—1995b. 'Aspect and Predication: The Semantics of Argument Structure', MS, Oxford University

Rapoport, Tova 1987. 'Copular, Nominal and Small Clauses: A Study of Israeli Hebrew', Ph.D. dissertation, MIT

Stenson, Nancy 1981. *Studies in Irish Syntax, Ars Linguistica*, VIII, Tübingen: Gunter Narr Verlag

Stowell, Timothy 1989. 'Subjects, Specifiers and X-bar Theory', in *Alternative Conceptions of Phrase Structure*, ed. by Mark Baltin and Anthony Kroch, Chicago: University of Chicago Press, 182–218

Watkins, T. Arwyn 1997. 'The *sef*[...] Realization of the Welsh Identificatory Copular Sentence', *this volume*

Unbound Reflexives in Hiberno-English

MARKKU FILPPULA
University of Joensuu

1. INTRODUCTION

THE USE of reflexive pronouns in contexts in which they lack a coreferential antecedent is a well-known feature of the Irish dialects of English, commonly referred to by the term 'Hiberno-English' (henceforth HE). Reflexives can occur on their own, without reference to an antecedent in the same clause, for example, in subject position, in object position, or as prepositional complement in adverbial prepositional phrases. These are illustrated by examples (1)–(3), respectively. Unless otherwise indicated, all examples cited in this paper are taken from my own corpus of HE, which will be described in greater detail below (the provenance and speaker initials are given in brackets after each example).

(1)   And by God, he said, it would [...] he'd be the devil, if *himself* wouldn' make him laugh. (Kerry: M.C.)

(2)   And d'you hear me, you didn't know the minute they'd burn *yourself* an' the house. (Clare: J.N.)

(3)   [...] when Cromwell came over here..he was s'posed to say, he'd drive the Irish to hell or Connacht [...] The Irish used to say [...] the Irish went to Connacht and left hell *for himself*. (Dublin: W.H.)

According to Harris (1993, 147), the reference in these kinds of contexts remains 'implicit' and is based on 'the shared knowledge of the speaker and hearer'. Using the terminology of GB theory, we might say that the reflexive in HE is *not bound by an antecedent*, the domain of reflexive binding usually being of a *local* kind, i.e. a clause or a sentence (Haegeman 1991, 192 ff.).[1] In a more traditional perspective, it would seem appropriate to say that the HE reflexives can be used *non-anaphorically*. However, since there are cases in which reflexives used on their own do refer back to somebody mentioned in the earlier discourse (though not 'locally'), I prefer to speak of *unbound reflexives* (UBRs for short). The following example

---

[1] Neither 'clause' nor 'sentence' feature in Haegeman's definition of the binding domain (see Haegeman 1991, 209 for an exact formulation), but they should suffice for the purposes of this paper. I also ignore here the obvious problems associated with the applicability of these concepts to spoken language.

from my HE corpus illustrates the unbound, yet anaphoric, use of reflexives:

(4)   [...] and he thought he'd have a few wrastles with the bull before he'd
        go to bed. He went in the field, and *himself* and the bull were tuggin'
        and wrastlin'. (Clare: C.O'B.)

It is possible to attribute the HE UBRs to influence from the Irish substratum. Thus, Henry (1957, 120) points out that the Irish system of pronouns allows the same type of usage involving the emphatic pronoun *féin*. However, he implicitly notes the possibility of superstratal influence from earlier English by citing examples from Shakespeare's usage to show that reflexives could be used in earlier English in much the same way as in HE (Henry 1957, 120–121; see also Harris 1993, 147). On the other hand, Odlin (*forthcoming*) discusses the close parallelism in this respect between HE and another Celtic-influenced variety of English, viz. that spoken in the Hebrides, and, on the basis of the similarity of the substrate languages, defends the case for Celtic substratum influence on both HE and Hebridean English (HebE).

From the contact-linguistic point of view, UBRs seem to be yet another case in which it is hard to ascertain the origin of the HE feature because of parallels in *both* Irish *and* earlier English. Other similar features discussed in the literature include certain types of HE perfects (see, e.g. Harris 1984), word order arrangements such as topicalisation (see, e.g. Filppula 1990), and various other constructions.

My aim in this paper is to reconsider the issue of the origins of UBRs mainly in the light of evidence drawn from a corpus of present-day HE speech. This corpus has been collected from four broadly-defined dialect areas: Kerry and Clare in the (south-)west of Ireland, Wicklow and Dublin City in the east. The first two represent the most recent direct contact with Irish, whereas on the east coast Irish ceased to be spoken long ago. The eastern dialects can also be assumed to have been more open to influences from 'metropolitan' Englishes. The informants were elderly persons, 'born and reared' in their localities. They were interviewed in an informal fashion about topics ranging from the informant's personal background, local traditions and important events to the future prospects of the area (for further details of the informants and the nature of the material, see Filppula 1986). The regional set-up of the corpus has in some of my earlier research on HE helped to produce evidence for a *dialect continuum* with respect to several grammatical features, which include clefting, subordinating uses of *and*, and temporal uses of the preposition *with* (see, e.g. Filppula 1991, *forthcoming*). It will be interesting to see to what extent the same is true of the uses of UBRs.

2. THE REGIONAL AND SYNTACTIC DISTRIBUTION OF UNBOUND REFLEXIVES IN THE HE CORPUS

The table below shows the regional distribution of different syntactic types of UBRs in the four HE corpora. A distinction is here made between UBRs which function alone as subject (labelled as Subj/0 in the Table) and those which form part of a conjoined subject phrase ('reflexive conjoins' in the terminology of Odlin, forthcoming). Among the latter, a further distinction is drawn between those which have an UBR as their first member (CS/1) and those where it follows another constituent (CS/2). Furthermore, UBRs can occur as object (Obj) or as a part of a prepositional phrase, i.e. as 'prepositional complements' (PC) in the terminology of Quirk *et al.* (1985, 60). The category 'other' includes three tokens, two of which involve the focusing subjunct *only*, as in (5); the third one is an 'existential' sentence, given in (6):

(5)　　　[…]'twas in harvest time and the weather bad, and things going wrong and no helper, *only himself*, and there was no machinery that time there [...] (Clare: F.K.)

(6)　　　[...] I'll show you a photo here. Here's, here's *meself*. (Dublin: J.O'B.)

TABLE: THE SYNTACTIC DISTRIBUTION OF UNBOUND REFLEXIVES IN FOUR HE DIALECTS

Area	Subj/0	CS/1	CS/2	Obj	PC	Other	N	/1000
Clare	3	6	2	1	11	1	24	0.80
Kerry	3	4	—	—	2	—	9	0.20
Wickl	—	—	1	—	4	1	6	0.14
Dubl.	—	1	—	—	5	1	7	0.17
Total	6	11	3	1	22	3	46	0.29

The frequencies given in the Table make it clear that UBR subjects of all sorts are particularly favoured in the two western dialects, and especially in Clare speech, which also makes the most extensive use of prepositional complement UBRs.[2] In this respect, the results follow the pattern observed for some other syntactic features of HE and lend further support to the notion of a dialect continuum from the most Irish-influenced (south-)western dialects to the least-influenced eastern ones. Considering the HE corpus as a whole, object UBRs are rare; subjects of all sorts and adverbials are evenly distributed, although UBR subjects are very scarce in the Dublin and Wicklow corpora, as are UBRs in general. In fact, most of the UBRs functioning as prepositional complements in the Dublin corpus were of a type which could be considered possible even in standard English (cf. Quirk *et al.* 1985, 359–360), e.g.:

(7)   Now, there's at least four men up there in the same predicament *as meself*, heart trouble. (Dublin: M.L.)[3]

A striking feature of HE UBRs is the preferred order of constituents in conjoined subjects: the UBR comes first in most cases, a trend which is borne out by the figures for the two western varieties. This is also confirmed by Odlin (forthcoming). Another interesting characteristic has to do with the person distinction: in the Wicklow and Dublin corpora, the UBRs were almost exclusively first- or second-person pronouns, whereas third-person pronouns were just as often (and in the case of Clare, even more often) used in the corpora from the two western dialects. As will be seen below, these two features may be of some importance when we try to assess the possible role of the Irish substratum.

3. The Case for Substratum Influence Reconsidered

The observed regional stratification of the uses of UBRs provides one type of evidence which suggests influence from the Irish substratum. The substratum hypothesis can be further supported by some qualitative features of HE UBRs. Thus, Odlin (forthcoming) notes that reflexives can occur on their own in the focus position of clefts in the same way as their Irish counterparts. As an illustration, Odlin cites the following example from Henry (1957, 120):

---

[2] The difference between Clare and Kerry may be explained by the fact that the interviews in the Clare corpus contain more stories involving notable local personalities (musicians, dancing masters, landlords, etc.), hence the more frequent recourse to referring pronouns, including UBRs.

[3] Of course, the nonstandard form *meself* should be ignored here.

(8)   'Twas myself that remarked it.

Given that the same pattern is also found in Hebridean English, as Odlin points out, the likelihood of Celtic influence is high. He discusses the possible superstratal origins in Lowland Scots and Early Modern English, and more specifically, in Shakespeare's language, but concludes that substratum influence must be given first priority for two reasons. First, Odlin's study of all of Shakespeare's works yielded only two instances of this structure. Second, UBRs in both HebE and HE share some other qualitative features which evidently derive from the Celtic substrata, e.g. the order of conjoined subjects (for further discussion, see Odlin, forthcoming).

Although I agree with the general thrust of Odlin's argument, I must note that, at least on the basis of my HE corpora, clefts involving UBRs are rare in HE speech. In fact, there were no tokens in my corpora, which does not of course rule out the possibility of such structures appearing in a larger corpus or in even more conservative, and especially, earlier varieties of HE. It should be remembered that the mentioned study by P.L. Henry was made in the 1950s.

As regards the order of the constituents in conjoined subjects, which in HE and HebE is almost always reflexive-first, it is again easy to accept Odlin's explanation, which rests on the parallel feature of the Celtic substrate languages. Odlin notes the existence of a parallel in Shakespeare's usage, too, but the fact that the reflexive-first order in conjoined subjects is the minority option for Shakespeare, leads him to emphasise the substratum account.

Further evidence to the same effect can be found in the EModE part of the so-called Helsinki Corpus, which contains a wide variety of texts from the period 1500–1710, the length of this part of the Corpus being just over 550,000 words (for details of the Corpus, see Kytö 1991). To begin with, my investigation yielded no instances of UBRs in the focus position of clefts. As for conjoined subjects involving UBRs, I found only two tokens exhibiting reflexive-first order, as against nine in which the UBR came second (or third). Another factor which may be of importance is the predominance in EModE of first-person subject reflexives, whereas in both HE and HebE second- and third-person reflexives are quite common. What is more, conjoined subjects in the EModE part of the Helsinki Corpus always involved the first-person reflexive. The western dialects of HE, as was noted above, and HebE show no such restriction; consider, for instance, the Clare example cited in (4) above and the following examples from HebE recorded by Sabban (1982, 367):

(9)   *Yourself and Annie* could come and see me. (P&P, Skye)

(10)   But he didn't really see this and—*himself and one of the boys* got into
        a fight about it. (77.41)

Sabban's general conclusion concerning the origin of UBRs is that, in the
Hebridean setting, their use is modelled on that of Scots Gaelic rather than
earlier English (1982, 378). Besides the Gaelic parallels and the mentioned
restrictions on the earlier English constructions, she mentions that 'non-
emphatic' uses of reflexives (i.e. UBRs) in subject position were recorded
in Uist from very old speakers, whose English was not very good
('offensichtlich im E[nglischen] ungeübt'; Sabban 1982, 359–361).

4. CONCLUSION

From the contact-linguistic point of view, the challenge offered by the issue
of the origins of HE UBRs is a particularly interesting one. On the one
hand, there is sufficient evidence of the existence of UBRs in earlier
English. Although the relative frequencies of UBRs in the Helsinki Corpus
are clearly lower than those for especially the Clare and Kerry corpora,
there is little doubt that reflexives could be left unbound in earlier English
in ways which are not usable or acceptable in present-day standard English
and which resemble those attested in HE dialects. On the face of it, the
earlier English superstratum would appear to provide a sufficient
explanation for the HE uses of UBRs.

   On the other hand, I have in this chapter discussed various kinds of
evidence which suggest a very definite role for the Irish substratum as well.
To begin with, it was found that there are differences between HE dialects
in the frequencies of use of UBRs, and these seem to be conditioned by the
recentness of direct contact with the Irish language. Regional
differentiation was further confirmed by the preferred order of constituents
in conjoined subjects and by the frequencies of different person categories
appearing in UBRs. Both repeat the same west-east pattern which has
emerged with respect to a number of other grammatical features. The
substratum case is also backed by evidence drawn from Hebridean English,
another Celtic-influenced variety, which is strikingly similar to HE in
several other respects, too.

   Since it seems impossible in the light of the present evidence to rule out
either source, one has to conclude that HE UBRs reflect input from both
earlier English and the Irish substratum. The existence of UBRs in EModE
must have provided a basis for 'interlingual identifications' and thus made
it possible for 'positive transfer' to take place in the emerging contact
vernacular (cf. Odlin 1989, 36, 113–114). The input from Irish, then, is
clearly visible in certain aspects of UBRs such as the order of constituents

in conjoined subjects, their usability with different person categories and their general frequencies of use. In a sense, one could speak of 'overproduction' of a pattern and of 'negative transfer' (cf. Odlin 1989, 36), which continue to influence HE usage even today.

BIBLIOGRAPHY

Filppula, Markku 1986. *Some Aspects of Hiberno-English in a Functional Sentence Perspective*, Joensuu: University of Joensuu Publications in the Humanities, VII

—1990. 'Substratum, Superstratum, and Universals in the Genesis of Hiberno-English', *Irish University Review*, 20, 41–54

—1991. 'Urban and Rural varieties of Hiberno-English', in *English Around the World*: *Sociolinguistic Perspectives*, ed. by Jennifer Cheshire, Cambridge: University Press, 51–60

—*forthc.* 'The Influence of Irish on Perfect Marking in Hiberno-English: the Case of the 'extended-now' Perfect', to appear in *Focus on Ireland*, ed. by Jeffrey L. Kallen, Amsterdam: John Benjamins

Haegeman, Liliane 1991. *Introduction to Government and Binding Theory*, Oxford: Basil Blackwell

Harris, John 1984. 'Syntactic Variation and Dialect Divergence', *Journal of Linguistics* 20, 303–327

—1993. 'The Grammar of Irish English', in *Real English*: *The Grammar of English Dialects in the British Isles*, ed. by James Milroy and Leslie Milroy, London and New York: Longman, 139–186

Henry, Patrick Leo 1957. *An Anglo-Irish Dialect of North Roscommon*, Dublin: University College Dublin

Kytö, Merja 1991. *Manual to the Diachronic Part of The Helsinki Corpus of English Texts*, Helsinki: Department of English, University of Helsinki

Odlin, Terence 1989. *Language Transfer*: *Cross-linguistic Influence in Language Learning*, Cambridge: University Press

—forthc. 'Bilingualism and Substrate Influence: a Look at Clefts and Reflexives', to appear in *Focus on Ireland*, ed. by Jeffrey L. Kallen, Amsterdam: John Benjamins

Quirk, Randolph, Greenbaum, Sidney, Leech, Geoffrey, and Svartvik, Jan 1985. *A Comprehensive Grammar of the English Language*, London and New York: Longman

Sabban, Annette 1982. *Gälisch-Englischer Sprachkontakt*, Heidelberg: Julius Groos

Memento for a Lefto

JACEK FISIAK & CAMIEL HAMANS

UAM Poznań   *Breda*

1. INTRODUCTION

THERE are two types of morphological processes, regular and irregular ones. Traditionally clipping has been considered as one of the most irregular processes, however productive it may be.

According to Marchand (1960, 357) clipping is more a stylistic or sociolinguistic phenomenon than a morphological one. It does not even belong to the system of proper word formation:

> Clipping consists in the reduction of a word to one of its parts. It would, of course, be erroneous to think that the new word is nothing but a shorter form with no linguistic value of its own. It is true that the information received from a native speaker will probably be the one I have tentatively given: *mag* is short for *magazine*, *maths* is short for *mathematics*. The difference between the short and the long word is obviously not one of logical content. [...]
>
> What makes the difference between *mag* and *magazine*, *maths* and *mathematics*, is the way the long word and the short word are used in speech. They are not interchangeable in the same type of speech. *Magazine* is the standard term for what is called *mag* on the level of slang. The substitution of *Mex* for *Mexican* implies another shift in linguistic value in that it involves a change of emotional background, based on original slang character of the term. Moreover, the clipped part is not a morpheme in the linguistic system (nor is the clipped result, for that matter), but an arbitrary part of the word form. It can at all times be supplied by the speaker. The process of clipping, therefore, has no grammatical status that compounding, prefixing, suffixing, and zero-derivation have, and it is not relevant to the linguistic system (la langue) itself but to speech (la parole).

2. EXAMPLES

Clipping may be highly irregular and even not belong to the linguistic system, nevertheless it is very frequent and operates in many languages. Examples from English, French, German, Spanish, Polish, Dutch and Bahasa Indonesia will show how productive this kind of shortening is.

(1) English

ad	*pop*	*bike*	*obit*
vet	*pub*	*mike*	*prefab*
gas	*fan*	*coke*	*rehab*

(2) French

bac	*appart*	*ado*	*mégalo*	*sympa*	*ciné*
fac	*manif*	*promo*	*écolo*	*fana*	*télé*
pub	*coop*	*diapo*	*biblio*	*giga*	*pédé*

(3) German

Kino	*Uni*	*Alu*
Vopo	*Stasi*	
Demo(nstration)		

(4) Spanish

ape(tito)	*bici(cleta)*	*coca(ína)*	*choco(late)*
bibe(rón)	*combi(nación)*	*compa(ñero)*	*crono(metro)*
dire(ctor)	*pisci(na)*	*contra(revolucion)*	*saxo(fono)*

(5) Polish

dyr	(from *dyrektor*, 'head')	*kompu*	(from *computer*)
sor	(from *profesor*, 'professor')	*kalku*	(from *calculator*)
trak	(from *trakcja*, 'sawing machine')	*demo*	(from *democracy*)
fiza	(from *fizyka*, 'physics')		
plasta	(from *plastyka*, 'fine arts')		
muza	(from *muzyka*, 'music')		

(6) Dutch

Jap(anner)	*deo(dorant)*	*refo*	(from *gereformeerd*)
lab(oratorium)	*provo(cateur)*		
gym(nastiek)	*homo(sexueel)*		

(7) Bahasa Indonesia

kompi	(from *kompanyi*, 'military company')
letkol	(from *letnan-kolonel*, 'lieutenant-colonel')
Tim Tim	(from *Timur Timur*, 'Portugese Timor')

As may be clear from these examples clipping works in different ways. The most common type is back clipping, shortening from right to left, as in *ape(tito)*.

Fore clipping, from left to right, exists as well, as in the Polish word *sor*. Truncation from left to right is less frequent than back clipping, but *sor* is not the only example. In Scandinavian languages for instance the normal word for 'car' is not *auto*, but *bil* (from *automobil*). Other examples are English *(cara)van*, *(air)plane*, *(tele)phone* and *varsity* from *university*, or French *(Améri)cain* and *(Boulevard de Sébas)topol*.

Middle clipping may be found in this list too. The Dutch form *refo*, 'reformed' or 'extreme protestant', comes from *(ge)refo(rmeerd)*. Other examples are English *flu* from *influenza*, *tec* from *detective*, *fridge* from *refrigerator* and French *crim* from *brigade criminelle*.

The Bahasa word *letkol* as well as the German examples *Vopo* and *Stasi* are instances of the rare type of compound clipping. They originate from *letnan-kolonel* and *Volkspolizei* and *Staatssicherheitsdienst*.

The Polish examples *fiza*, *plasta* and *muza* seem to be of another type again. Most probably, these words are examples of the most frequent type, that of back clipping. In that case the words have preserved their original morphological endings.

From what has been shown above, Marchand seems to be right in stating that clipping is a very irregular process. There are different processes and truncation does not take place at a clear systematic boundary. However intriguing it may be to find the rule or rules behind clipping, we leave the question aside here. See Szpyra (1995, 25–89) for that.

3. PATTERNS

English may be said to have a preference for a VC-type of clipping, whereas French gives a priority to endings in *-o* (Kilani-Schoch, in press). The classical example *métro* versus *Met*, from *métropolitain* respectively *metropolitan*, gives an argument for this. As far as the past is concerned this difference in preference may be true.

There is another difference between English and French clippings. In English most of the clippings belong to a kind of slang or jargon or at least to a casual style, in French clipping is socially more accepted. Most of the examples under (2) are found in newspapers and magazines and not only in quotations.

This stylistic or sociolinguistic difference, together with the preference for *-o* endings, led to an extensive list of shortened technical terms, which were borrowed by other languages. The examples under (8) are originally French, but nowadays they belong to internationalese.

(8)			
mono	*meteo*	*auto*	*info*
stereo	*photo*	*radio*	*chromo*
expo	*micro*	*memo*	*moto*
repro	*polio*	*metro*	*zoo*

All these forms have a small part in common, the final -*o*. In terms of Zabrocki a 'confusivum'. Such a common segment gives the speakers of a language the impression that this rhyme has a linguistic status (cf. Zabrocki 1980, Awedyk & Hamans 1992 and Hamans, forthc.). Theoretically this final -*o* does not have any morphological or semantic status, but the intuitions of the language users do not work in a systematic way. At the moment the 'confusive' part becomes frequent, which it did, it starts working as a linguistic sign. So final -*o*, in this context, got the connotation 'short form'.

4. SUFFIX

English clippings tend to end in -VC. However, in American English the -*o*-type came up, under Hispanic and Italian, that is Latino, influence. See for instance the modern American English clippings under (9).

(9)	*mayo*	*disco*	*dipso*
	psycho	*homo*	*cosmo*
	typo	*demo*	*appro*
	nympho	*intro*	*biblio*

What has been said about the French/internationalese examples under (8), can be repeated here. Final -*o* in this context became a quasi-morpheme meaning 'short' and since clipped forms belong to a substandard variety of English, also of American English, a feature 'more or less vulgar' is part of the meaning of -*o* as well.

The next step in the development should be -*o* becoming a suffix. This happened. Jespersen (1942, 223) gives a small list of examples where a final -*o* has been suppleted.

(10)	*ammo*	from	*ammunition*
	commo		*commissary*
	clemo		*clemency*
	journo		*journalist*
	afto		*afternoon*
	heavo		*heavy*

In all these words truncation from left to right has worked, but the process of clipping did not stop there. After that 'a suffix -*o* of a slangy, often also hypocoristic, character which does not really change the sense of the root-word itself, has been added'.

This development is not restricted to American English only. French shows the same process.

(11) *hystér*-o   from   *hystérique*
      intell-o   *intellectuel*
      rédhib-o   *rédhibitoire*
      ex-o   *excercice*
      révis-o   *révisioniste*
      métall-o   *métallurgiste*
      prol-o   *prolétaire*
      propri-o   *propriétaire*
      péch-o   *péché*

Most of these French words have the meaning 'person who is a X or who has the quality Y'.

In Dutch, where there was a preference for -VC-clippings, as in English, the new suffix -*o* was taken over recently. Usually with the a slangy meaning, but also denoting a person.

(12) *alt*-o   from   *alternatief*
      lesb-o   *lesbisch*
      sad-o   *sadistisch*
      ruft-o   *rufter* ('a person who farts')
      maatj-o   *maatje* ('friend')
      broertj-o   *broertje* ('little brother')
      arb-o   *arbeider* ('labourer')
      Limb-o   *Limburger* ('person from Limburg')
      Brab-o   *Brabander* ('person from Brabant')

The process operates in German also.

(13) *Serv*-o   from   *Service*
      Anarch-o   *Anarchist*
      Real-o   *Realist*

5. PRODUCTIVITY

The development of this new suffix did not stop at this point. It even can be attached to non truncated forms. In English, French, Dutch and Polish.

(14) English
      lefto   *dumbo*
      creepo   *rapo*
      weirdo   *bravo*

(15) French

gaucho	*dingo*
chéro	*rapido*
follo	*blanco*

(16) Dutch

lullo	*saaio*	*diverso*	*positivo*
lijpo	*toeristo*	*lokalo*	*flexibo*
duffo	*deskundo*	*moderno*	*debilo*

(17) Polish

dyro	*stilo*	*stylo*

In all of these examples the suffix -*o* has a slang or jargon connotation. It combines with an adjective or a noun. The resulting form usually denotes a person, but not always. For instance the Polish forms *stilo* or *stylo* are the jargon words used by radio technicians for stil, tape. The recent Polish form *dyro* comes from the original clipping *dyr*, from *dyrektor*, 'head'. It belongs to schoolboys' slang. The suffix, which also might be a normal Polish morpholgical ending for masculine nouns, has been added to the lexicalised old clipped form.

The Dutch examples all have a negative meaning. They all stand for persons who are dull, lazy or quasi-experts. This word formation process became so productive in youngsters' Dutch that even a new quasi-suffix -*bo* came up in the same way.

(18)   *Limbo   Brabo*

These two words share a confusivum -*bo*, which became suffix-like along the same lines in the form *Zebo*, nickname for a person from Zeeland. Since the final vowel -*o* is known as an ending for masculine nouns in Italian and Spanish, it is not surprising to see that an alternative ending came up for typical female forms in Dutch.

(19)	*lesbo*	'lesbian'
	travo	'transvestite'
	macho	'macho'

(20)	*lesba*	'lesbian'
	trava	'transvestite'
	macha	'non-prototypical woman or girl'

6. CONCLUSION

According to Marchand (1960, 357), clipping is a very irregular process. However, it is so frequent that it caused a completely regular process of suffix-formation. Clipping does not belong to word formation, according to Marchand (l.c.). But on the basis of this non-systematic phenomenon a new systematic process arose. That is why Marchand's view has to be questioned.

Clipping, especially clipping on -o, is very frequent and appears in different languages. The ending -o has a specific morphological and semantic status. That is why at least this type of clipping should be considered as a normal kind of word formation. Frequency may not be equalised to productivity (cf. Kastovsky 1986), but there is no doubt that the ending or even the suffix -o is highly productive. That is one of the most important criteria for morphological processes.

BIBLIOGRAPHY

Awedyk, Wiesław and Hamans, Camiel 1992. 'The "Poznań School" of Structural Linguistics', in *Diversions of Galway, Papers on the History of Linguistics from ICHoLS V, Galway, Ireland, 1–6 September 1990*, ed. by Anders Ahlqvist, Amsterdam: John Benjamins, 213–225

Hamans, Camiel 1996. 'A Lingo of Abbrevs', *Lingua Posnaniensis*, 38, 1–10

Jespersen, Otto 1942. *A Modern English Grammar on Historical Principles*, Copenhagen: Ejnar Munksgaard

Kastovsky, Dieter 1986. 'The Problem of Productivity in Word Formation', *Linguistics*, 24, 585–600

Kilani-Schoch, Marianne in press. 'Syllable and Foot in French Clipping', in *Natural Phonology, The State of the Art*, ed. by B. Hurch and R. Rhodes, Berlin: Mouton de Gruyter

Marchand, Hans 1960. *The Categories and Types of Present-Day English Word-Formation*, Alabama: University Press

Szpyra, Yolanta 1995. *Three Tiers in Polish and English Phonology*, Lublin: Wydawnictwo Uniwersytetu Marii Curie Skłodowskiej

Zabrocki, Ludwik 1980. *U podstaw struktury i rozwoju języka*, ed. by Jerzy Bańczerowski, Warsaw: Państwowe Wydawnictwo Naukowe

On The Universality of Language

PATRICK GALLAGHER
University College, Dublin

IF LANGUAGE is an instinct, Universal Grammar is a fact, and no single language can be functionally peculiar, for it would then be inhuman. Chomsky's Martian would see this universality as he moved curiously about our planet, detecting in his progress the common denominator in all our languages: the same mechanism for ordering symbols. We would all be, for him, the same kind of alien.

Anthropologists and psychologists, since the 1920s, plus wayward Parisian Marxists and their disciples since the 1960s, have been telling us the opposite: that we are, in everything, culturally determined.[1] The exclusion of biology was essential to the maintenance of this politically correct account of the way we are. But cognitive scientists have recently exposed the absurdity of this position, effectively discrediting one of the most enduring and widely accepted pieties of the century: the Standard Social Science Model (SSSM). Yet so entrenched is this totalitarian nonsense, 'the secular ideology of our age', that to dislodge it could take more than what ought to be enough: the biological evidence. Steven Pinker's brilliant book is crushingly contemptuous of SSSM. What follows is a consideration of the universality of language in the light of his study.[2]

Pinker could not have written his book without questioning a dogma of the social sciences: 'Modern intellectual life is suffused with a relativism that denies that there is such a thing as a universal human nature, and the existence of a language instinct in any form challenges that denial.' (405) In rebutting relativism, he declares: 'Just as there is a universal design to the computations of grammar, there is a universal design to the rest of the human mind, [...] a discovery about the human species that is well motivated by evolutionary biology and genetics.' (410) A biology-excluding behavioural determinism cannot be valid because 'there is no learning without some innate mechanism that makes the learning happen.' (410)

---

[1] John B. Watson, *Behaviorism* (New York, 1925); Margaret Mead, *Sex and Temperament in Three Primitive Societies* (New York, 1935); in her classic *Coming of Age in Samoa*, Pinker tells us, Mead's account of Samoan free sex is all wrong because 'Among other things, her bored teenage informants enjoyed pulling her leg' (!) (412).

[2] Steven Pinker, *The Language Instinct: The New Science of Language and Mind* (New York, 1994). Page-references are to the Penguin edition (1995). For SSSM and 'secular ideology', see chapter 13, 'Mind Design', especially pp. 404–15.

The statement seems axiomatic, so that the wonder is how anthropologists and psychologists managed to delude anyone, apart from
themselves, into believing otherwise. That they have managed to delude
nearly everyone ('progressive' governments and their education policies,
universities, teachers generally, most other professions, society at large) is
disquieting proof of mass manipulability. As early as 1895, Le Bon had
argued that a crowd can be persuaded to acquiesce in or support ideas and
actions repugnant to the individuals that comprise it.[3] Such as killing
people that an orator declares its enemies. (Hitler's Germany was such a
crowd.) Believing in the SSSM is not quite the same thing as exterminating
people you've been told you don't like. However, it is in one respect
similar, for it goes against common sense and what we instinctively know
about ourselves.

It is common sense to suppose that babies cannot acquire language if
their brains lack the machinery to process the speech they hear. It is also
reasonable to suppose that when toddlers speak sentences they haven't
heard before, nobody is teaching them how to do it. And three-year-olds do
this all the time. They are not parroting, but creating. They are also
learning very fast from the speech of the people around them. But babies
would suffer unproductively this bombardment of utterance if they did not
have the discrete neural modules which, with sensory mediation, can
receive and transmit messages. And the modules must be universal: native
English speakers do not come into the world wired-up for English syntax.
They are born with a brain that can handle Kurdish or Quechua with
identical ease, because 'the same symbol-manipulating machinery, without
exception, underlies the world's languages'. (237)

The machinery is the human factor since, in this respect, though
biologically akin to very many animal species in hundreds of others, we are
unique. However, we are not unique in possessing a special and wonderful
ability: 'Some kinds of migratory birds navigate thousands of miles by
calibrating the positions of the constellations against the time of day and
year.' (19)

The birds' sophisticated scientific competence is inbuilt, and Pinker
exhorts readers to see language analogously: as 'a distinct piece of the
biological makeup of our brains'. (18) We speak; spiders spin.

> Spiders spin spider webs because they have spider brains, which give
> them the urge to spin and the competence to succeed. (18)

We spin words; they spin webs, and both skills are innate.

---

[3] Gustave Le Bon, *Psychologie des foules* (Paris, 1895).

WHERE PINKER 'GETS IT WRONG'

1. PINKER AND DARWIN

This, then, is language as instinct, but Pinker is sometimes less than exact in his use of these key-words. Language, for him, tends to mean just the biological faculty, not everything from innate mechanism to elaborate performance. He is much more interested in Universal Grammar than in baroque poetry, but exaggerates the sense in which the former makes us all equal by saying that 'language [...] is qualitatively the same in every individual'. The point about individuals is that they are not identical, but Pinker's egalitarianism is ideological, not scientific. He steers clear of things like baroque verse as 'language' because it is evident that we are not all equally good at composing it. But even if we take 'language' to mean unambiguously just that we are all wired-up for grammar, why should the wiring have to be equally good in every brain? Is there no such thing as a natural talent, and do different talents not vary in quality both within the individual and between individuals? Instincts are not qualitatively equal across a species. Have we not all observed that some people seem to possess more conspicuously than others some of the instincts all of us share, while there are also those of us who seem almost defective in, say, the instinct of self-preservation? We can't be 'qualitatively' the same, not even in our instincts, but the same only in having them, and that is a quantitative sameness.

Pinker works best with the real speech of people who have either healthy or damaged brains, showing by phrase-structure analysis that their sentences are never capriciously disordered but always regular products of their tacit possession of grammar. Without knowing it, they are as fastidious as the self-consciously 'correct' users of Standard American English. Yet they are reproved for 'bad grammar' by 'schoolmarms'— don't any men teach languages in North America?—and seem resigned to that humiliation. In fact, their speech is rule-bound: they cannot be ungrammatical, but only 'incorrect' with regard to a prescribed standard model which they have fallen short of mastering. A single innate mechanism accommodates all dialects of English and the world's other languages too, not identically, but with analogously and symmetrically equivalent manipulations.

This means that particular languages are templates placed over a general grid, or modulations on a base measure that is Universal Grammar. Pinker's diagrams show that English and Japanese order their sentences very differently, but not, however, discretely, since they are strict mirror-images of each other. (111) And thus it is in this structural sense that we possess language innately and universally: there is only one design for the human brain. But the rest of what is commonly meant by 'language' has to be learned.

Perhaps that is why Darwin, the hero Pinker cites for being so far ahead of his time in treating language as instinct, is careful not to adopt that unequivocal position.[4] Rather, he held that because every language has to be learned, language cannot be a true instinct but only 'an instinctive tendency to acquire an art'; hardly the same thing. (98) But Darwin was here thinking of language as articulation, not as a sort of cerebral blueprint:

> The sounds uttered by birds offer in many respects the nearest analogy to language, for all the members of the same species utter the same instinctive cries expressive of their emotions; and all the kinds which sing exert their power instinctively; but the actual song, and even the call-notes, are learned from their parents or foster-parents. (97)

It is a process of gradual acquisition:

> The young males continue practising, or as the bird-catchers say, 'recording', for ten or eleven months. Their first essays show hardly a rudiment of the future song; but as they grow older we can perceive what they are aiming at; and at last they are said 'to sing their song in the round'. (97)

The distinction is crucial: for Darwin, inarticulate cries are fully instinctive in human and other animals, but articulate language is not an instinct because we are not born with it and would never be able to develop it on our own. This is not to say that we don't acquire it spontaneously, but that, to do so, we need people around. It is from human society alone that the skill is developed. Without that, innate syntax would lie idle in our brains, eventually to atrophy like an unused limb. Language, as a faculty of the mind, cannot be a cultural invention, but the material it computes is not inbuilt: it is socially supplied and the child's brain is progressively furnished from infancy onwards. Pinker quotes a bit of Darwin but leaves out the songbirds because language as artistic performance presupposes instruction and prescription:

> The complexity of language, from the scientist's point of view, is part of our biological birthright; it is not something that parents teach their children or something that must be elaborated in school—as Oscar

---

[4] Charles Darwin, *The Descent of Man* (London, 1871). Page-references are to the second edition (1874).

> Wilde said, 'Education is an admirable thing, but it is well to remember from time to time that nothing that is worth knowing can be taught'. (19)

But the biological birthright cannot on its own generate speech, for it is wordless, so that Wilde's silly *boutade* does nothing to enhance Pinker's claim that 'language' is not taught or acquired. The language 'gene' has nothing to work on before the material is supplied. Parents or guardians provide the material. Granted the 'gene', language is still taught by parents / guardians and learned by children. And this is cultural activity, analogously illustrated by Darwin's observation that 'Nestlings which have learned the song of a distinct species, as with canary birds educated in the Tyrol, teach and transmit their new song to their offspring'. (97) And how apt here is the word 'educated'! The birds are led out of instinctive cries into song, noise is refined into music. A canary brought up with other songbirds learns their songs because that is what it is taught. This shows that the canary has the urge to sing, but cannot proceed without instruction, since otherwise it would spontaneously emit canary cries. Just as babies have the urge to talk but, without the company of older humans who can already do so, would never advance beyond a babble. It is the urge that is instinctive, and it is there because the mental mechanism is waiting to be activated. What triggers the activation is not instinct, but art.

2. PINKER AND THE SCHOOLMARMS

When Pinker mentions education he does so disparagingly, and with none of Darwin's etymological resonance. For example, by remarking that 'web-spinning does not depend on having had the right education', (18) he is sneering at genteel schoolteachers who correct children for 'bad grammar' but don't understand that children, like everyone else, are innately grammatical. This is hardly fair: there must be some schoolmarms who do understand—after all, everyone has heard of Chomsky—but what they are hired to teach is Standard American English, a subject expounded by prescription. In the pedagogical sense, 'ungrammatical' simply means dialect variations from an imposed norm. It is true that the norm has been imposed not just arbitrarily but in some ignorance of the way language really works. But it was imposed long before anyone knew how language really worked, and it survives because non-standard speakers want their children to learn standard in order to get a good job. This is a natural aspiration and teachers should not be indicted for trying to meet the demand.

But criticism of the way grammar, as distinct from 'correct' standard usage, is taught, is another matter, and Pinker is right to deplore the teaching of grammar which pays no attention to phrase structure and compounds with spurious rules its failure to analyse sentences properly. He could even be right in deriding such instruction as etiquette, a ticket to polite society. But pedagogical parsing, though a bit hit-and-miss in the light of contemporary linguistic science, is not always as invalid as Pinker apparently wants it to be. Consider the following argument:

> Because verbs have the power to dictate how a sentence conveys who did what to whom, one cannot sort out the roles in a sentence without looking up the verb. That is why your grammar teacher got it wrong when she [why 'she'?] told you that the subject of the sentence is the 'doer of the action'. The subject of the sentence is often the doer, but only when the verb says so; the verb can also assign it other roles:

The big bad wolf frightened the three little pigs.
   [The subject is doing the frightening.]
The three little pigs feared the big bad wolf.
   [The subject is being frightened.]
My true love gave me a partridge in a pear tree.
   [The subject is doing the giving.]
I received a partridge in a pear tree from my true love.
   [The subject is being given to.]
Dr. Nussbaum performed plastic surgery.
   [The subject is operating on someone.]
Cheryl underwent plastic surgery.
   [The subject is being operated on.] (114)

But 'she' did not get it wrong in any of these six sentences because the choice of active rather than passive voice in all of them points to the subject as the 'doer' in the mind of the speaker. In 'The three little pigs feared the big bad wolf', Pinker says that the pigs are being frightened, which is true, but they are doing the fearing, which is what the speaker wants to say, and has in fact said by composing the sentence in that form. In 'I received a partridge in a pear tree from my true love', I'm being given one by her but she is not the subject because it is I who am doing the receiving. In other words, though the sentence has two doers, syntax has seen to it that the first one gets the attention. Similarly, in 'Cheryl underwent plastic surgery', Cheryl does the undergoing, however passive a patient she might have been. Whereas in 'Cheryl was cut to pieces by a psychopath', for example, whoever the doer of the action is, it can't be Cheryl.

'John was hit on the head by a cricket ball' shows that the subject is not always the doer of the action, but none of Pinker's examples does. Perhaps he should take up cricket.

And it is Pinker again, not his 'schoolmarm', who 'gets it wrong' in analysing the joke: 'Call me a taxi.' 'OK, you're a taxi.' He says the ambiguity is caused by the verb, which has 'two distinct entries'. (114) But what causes it is the unmarked dative 'me', since as soon as you case-mark the sentence ('Call a taxi for me' = Ring for a taxi for me) the ambiguity and the joke disappear. The second meaning of 'call'—namecalling—comes into play only because the joker treats 'me', not 'taxi', as the direct object.

In fact, it is odd that a book so generally right and enlightening on phrase structure should even occasionally slip up on the logic of language. The African-American in the timberyard is usually the verb.[5] Somewhere between d- and s-structure sentences,[6] Pinker doesn't know how to handle them. For instance, 'He put the car in the garage' fulfils what Pinker says d-structure requires of 'put': that it have a subject, object and prepositional phrase. But 'put' is recalcitrant to these constraints and can lead a regular life in the following:

> The car was put in the garage.
> What did he put in the garage?
> Where did he put the car?

Pinker cites these to show how they deviate from d-structure requirements which comprise the norm. (121) In the first of the s-structure variants, he says that 'the car' would 'ordinarily' be the object, but is here showing up in subject position. But why should we listen to this Chomskyan twaddle? The car occupies subject position because the agent is unknown. It is the car that people are interested in, but nobody knows who put it in the garage. One of the functions of the passive voice is to cover for an unidentified agent: 'The body was found in the bathroom, nothing had been disturbed in the rest of the house and the car was put in the garage'. Anonymity can also be active: 'Somebody put the car in the garage.' But why should the *thing put* have to follow the verb to feel normal? 'The car was put in the garage' is not only a valid sentence, but just as ordinary as 'He put the car in the garage'.

---

[5] I am indebted to Stuart Daultrey, Department of Geography, University College, Dublin, for this example of politically correct metaphor, in his Analysis of the UCD *First Arts Examination Results (Summer, 1991)*, p. 47.

[6] Pinkerspeak for Chomsky's classification: deep structure / surface structure.

In the second sentence, people want to know what went into the garage that was put there by him, and that is why the *thing put* is in the subject position. In the third; it is about the location of the car that the speaker seeks information. Pinker comments that 'the "place" role shows up at the beginning, instead of after the object, where it ordinarily belongs'. (121) Once again, only adherence to d-structure theory can explain the conviction that it is more ordinary for the 'place' role to follow the object. 'Where did he put the car?' is the question to which the answer is 'He put the car in the garage'. The question, as phrased, is the most ordinary way of trying to find out where it was put.

Pinker next asks us to think of the difference between 'Beavers build dams' and 'Dams are built by beavers', and goes on to assure us that the active sentence is true but the passive is false, 'since some dams, like the Grand Coulee Dam, are not built by beavers.' (123) But the passive sentence is not false because it means that dam-building is one of the things that beavers do, not that they build all of them. 'Wine is drunk by alcoholics' doesn't mean they drink all of it, nor that they don't knock back other stuff too.

On English morphology, Pinker answers beautifully many of the big questions that puzzle amateurs. His analysis of stems, roots and affixes is one of the highlights of his work, yet, even here, he can be glaringly wrong, as when he says 'the suffix *-ness* converts any adjective into a noun, as in *crunchy–crunchiness*'. (134) Really? Well, not quite. You can have *friendliness*; *goodness*; *badness*; *foulness*; *thinness*; *stoutness*; *shortness*; *tallness*; *brightness*; *darkness*. But these are all Germanic words. Try tacking *-ness* on to the following: *amiable*; *hostile*; *significant*; *arrogant*; *obstinate*; *transparent*; *innocent*; *erudite*; *brilliant*; *independent*. It doesn't work because the adjectives are Latin and arrived in the English language with their own suffixes for noun-conversion. When Pinker thinks of an adjective, can he only think Anglo-Saxon?

Pinker hates what he calls 'style manuals' for getting things wrong in saying, for example, that any new form added to English must be regular. To refute this he says: 'if I coin new words like to *re-sing* or *to out-sing*, their pasts are *re-sang* and *out-sang*, not *re-singed* and *out-singed*.' (142) But these are not new words at all, just old strong verbs with a pre-positional prefix, a common enough arrangement.

3. PINKER AND CHOMSKY

Some of his larger claims are also questionable, particularly the one in which, parroting Chomsky's most famous 'fact' about language, he writes: 'virtually every sentence that a person utters or understands is a brand-new combination of words, appearing for the first time in the history of the universe.' (22) Would that it were so!

But has either of them ever listened to everyday speech? A vast amount of it is stock, cliché, jargon, formula. Language is more than a repertoire of responses, agreed, but people in their daily routines draw heavily on repertoire when they are not excited enough to be inventive; which, for most people, is most of the time.

In his eagerness to demolish the SSSM notion of language as a cultural invention, Pinker sometimes misses the mark. 'Language', he says, 'is not a manifestation of a general capacity to use symbols: a three-year-old [...] is a grammatical genius, but is quite incompetent at the visual arts, religious iconography, traffic signs and the other staples of the semiotics curriculum'. (19) But a toyless three-year-old girl can pretend a matchstick with a bit of fluff on top is a baby (I've seen it happen). Not knowing icons and traffic signs does not show that she is bereft of symbolic skills. Indeed, as Pinker himself repeatedly points out, the language instinct is a marvellously complex symbol-manipulating neural faculty. Society's conventional symbols, crude by comparison, have to be learned during education. The child's brain is more than adequately equipped to cope with them.

4. PINKER AND NONSENSE

It is dispiriting to record how obtuse brilliant scientific minds can sometimes be in analysing bits of language that they themselves have chosen, or even composed. Take Chomsky's celebrated sentence, 'Colourless green ideas sleep furiously' (which, not yet having read any of the great man's works, I was to hear for the first time—about 1972—from Conn himself). Pinker quotes it in a discussion of nonsense literature, straying uncharacteristically from the more pedestrian examples of language that he is happier examining. Chomsky composed the sentence, Pinker explains, to show that 'syntax and sense can be independent of each other' and immediately proceeds to belittle Chomsky's achievement by remarking that Edward Lear, 'the acknowledged master of nonsense', made the point last century. (88)

But is this example of grammatical nonsense (that is, nonsense couched in perfect syntax) really meaningless? Hearing the sentence for the first time all those years ago, I was struck as much by its beauty as by the rather different point it was designed to illustrate. The sentence seemed to have some poetic quality. It was too beautiful to be rubbish. Without knowing why, I got the feeling that there was something not quite right about the claim that the words meant nothing.

And certainly it is not hard to make up nonsense examples of the same syntax, for instance, 'Black pink dogs mourn hopefully', which sounds less beautiful and more meaningless than the Chomsky sentence. But it is not entirely lacking in semantic content. It could be interpreted as suggesting that pink dogs, swathed in black for mourning by some lunatic, were looking forward to being divested. Chomsky's example of nonsense could mean much more than that, something much more interesting, closer to a common human experience: 'When you have a dream that you remember afterwards as not being in colour but in black-and-white, it is the sort of dream in which your unconscious mind (green=submarine, the colour of the subconscious in surrealist art) chases abstract notions around all night, and you wake up exhausted.' The sort of dream to which Chomsky himself might be expected to be particularly prone! If he really wanted a meaningless sentence he ought not to have chosen that one.

But what could he have chosen instead? Is it even possible to compose an entirely insignificant grammatical sentence? Because Chomsky got the syntax right, his sentence means more than the same words scrambled:

> Green furiously sleep ideas colourless

Appearing like that on the page, grammarlessly, the words are not a sentence at all. But the unscrambled words, taken together, can be entertained by the imagination as some kind of idea or general truth, like a law of science, even if logic tells us it is nonsense.

The sustained nonsense of nonsense literature is, of course, not really nonsense but imaginative writing. As an example of nonsense, from the 'master' of the genre, Edward Lear, Pinker cites a couple of lines from a poem that children and adults once knew by heart:

> It's a fact the whole world knows,
> That Pobbles are happier without their toes.

But these lines do make sense, as well as being grammatical. Pobbles don't have to be real in order to be happier without their toes. Evolutionary psychologists might not understand. But children do.

The Jabberwock, which Pinker quotes next, (89) is grammatical too, and not nonsense. Everything is clear in Lewis Carroll's poem, except the neologisms. And not all of these are opaque: we can guess that 'whiffling' telescopes 'puffing' and 'whistling', and that 'galumphing' is 'galloping triumphantly'; 'beamish' in 'my beamish boy' is hardly a puzzle; it doesn't much matter what 'Callooh! Callay!' means, since we are told in the next line that it is a sort of joyous chortle; 'slithy' is another telescope ('slithery' and 'slidey') and 'toves' are fabulous creatures that 'slithe', 'gyre' (clear enough) and 'gimble' ('gamboll nimbly') in something called 'the wabe' which readers would not understand but might guess means the sea (waves). And if it doesn't, no great harm is done; on the contrary, the great charm of nonsense literature is not knowing precisely what every neologism means, yet having to make it mean something in order to appease the imagination: if it isn't in the waves, then the toves are having fun somewhere else, where they can slip and slide and slither, twist around and cavort.

With grammatical structures intact, a categorical or generic meaning can often be ascribed to words that the author has invented and we do not precisely understand. Not understanding, but wanting to, makes reading nonsense literature creative and enjoyable.

Real nonsense probably has to be grammar-free, a phraseless string of words. And this doesn't come naturally, for people, unless they are playing games, don't speak phraselessly in any language.

CONCLUSION

The language of the human brain is not itself the language of words. Of any words, in any language. Nobody's brain is 'wired-up' for English or Spanish syntax, just for Syntax. What this means is that we have a non-verbal machinery of concepts which needs a language of words for articulation. The machinery is there, ready to process any spoken language because it can already handle its own abstract symbols. Differences between languages are similar: structural options are analogous to one another in a single combinatory modular mechanism.

The language of abstract symbols, before it is clothed in words for the mind to hear or the speech organs to articulate, is what Pinker calls 'mentalese', a very apt term. He shows that it is real by citing ambiguous newspaper headlines (79). Each headline contains an ambiguous word, e.g., the fourth word in 'QUEEN MARY HAVING BOTTOM SCRAPED'. He argues that the writer knew what he meant, which thought he was thinking. But there are two. 'And if there can be two thoughts corresponding to one word, thoughts can't be words'.

And yet, it is those arbitrary things, the words of human languages, that we need, to break out of the mind's silent symbols and transmit to somebody else the thoughts that we have. And the 'somebody else' needs words for the same reason. But a brain can't speak directly to another brain, because it is not an organ of speech. In a beautiful sentence, Steven Pinker tells us what speech is: 'Speech is a river of breath, bent into hisses and hums by the soft flesh of the mouth and throat.' (163) And, talking earlier about how language works, he says, 'Grammar is a protocol that has to interconnect the ear, the mouth, and the mind, three very different kinds of machine. It cannot be tailored to any of them but must have an abstract logic of its own.' (125)

And it is to that abstract logic, in turn, that the grammars of all human languages are tailored.

Politically Correct Words, Bad Politics

TOM GARVIN
University College, Dublin

CONN Ó CLÉIRIGH was a marvellous conversationalist and wordsmith. He was also an impassioned political analyst, in a way that was strangely contradictory. He and I waged a genial, twenty-year and pretty bibulous war in the Common Room of University College, Dublin over the uses of words in political argument. Cohorts of concepts, legions of linguistic theories, fusillades of cheap shots, patrols of pints of stout, picquets of packets of cigarettes and all categories of intellectual soldiers were sent over the top into the hails of rhetorical bullets from our bar-room machine-guns. I know that he enjoyed these encounters with the young man that I then was as much as I did; I was the dog yapping at his heels, but, good democrat that he was, he took the yapping seriously. These encounters occurred every year, during our teaching for the old UCD Night Degree, at a meeting place for nocturnal democrats and compulsive arguers.

WORDS AND IDEAS

We had a fascination for the idea that if you fiddle around with words and language long enough, you can end up with a version of language that is somehow more correct, more polite, more democratic, fairer, even more virtuous. Perhaps unlike Conn, I did not believe that words have, or ought to have, that kind of intellectual dominance. Man does not live by phonemes alone. In this essay, I wish to look, in an amateur way, at the idea of words being able to crowd out and defeat ideas.

The obvious starting point is George Orwell's wonderful satirical appendix to his last novel, *Nineteen Eighty-Four*, a work banned at that time by some bunch of piotious jacks-in-office in The Republic of Ireland as being in general tendency indecent or obscene.[1] My first copy of this classic was smuggled in from that outpost of Saxon tyranny, Northern Ireland. As everyone knows, the rulers of the static and totalitarian state of Orwell's Oceania hated and feared the English language which they had inherited from the *ancien régime*. English was, they knew, a rich store-

---

[1] George Orwell, *Nineteen Eighty-four* (Oxford: Clarendon Press, 1984; first published 1949). A preliminary version of this argument was given at the Literary and Historical Society, University College, Dublin, in April, 1994. I wish to thank Maria Farrell and Tabitha Wood for their comments during and after that memorable debate.

house of pre-revolutionary ideas, references, cliches, proverbial wisdom, satire, sarcasm, slang, ironies, puns and systems of reference that were uncontrollable by anyone. English was, and is, anarchic and rulers are, by definition, archic. The evil rulers of Oceania were, of course, trying to replace the English language by a new language, a 'basic English' called Newspeak. The idea was to ensure that sentiments subversive of the regime became literally unspeakable. As Orwell put it:

> Newspeak was the official language of Oceania and had been devised to meet the ideological needs of Ingsoc, or English Socialism [...]. The leading articles of The Times were written in it, but this was a tour de force which could only be carried out by a specialist. It was expected that Newspeak would have finally superseded Oldspeak (or Standard English as we should call it) by about the year 2050 [...].
>
> The purpose of Newspeak was not only to provide a medium of expression for the world-view and mental habits proper to the devotees of Ingsoc, but to make all other modes of thought impossible.[2]

Oldspeak was to die out, and the thoughts expressible in it were to die with it. Newspeak was so constructed as to give perfect expression to political orthodoxy and eliminate all other meanings. This was done partly by inventing new words (Duckspeak, unbellyfeel, thoughtcrime, etc.) but mainly by 'eliminating undesirable words and by stripping such words as remained of unorthodox meanings [...]'.[3] The term *free*, for example could only be used in the sense of 'free from lice', and could not be used to denote the condition of political freedom. 'Newspeak was designed not to extend but to *diminish* the range of thought, and this purpose was indirectly assisted by cutting the choice of words down to a minimum.'

> Thus, the word *warm* was replaced by the term *uncold*, and any word could be negatived similarly by adding *un-*, or strengthened by adding *plus-*. The Times, in a leader, could solemnly announce that *Oldspeakers unbellyfeel Ingsoc* [i.e., speakers of Standard English educated under the *ancien régime* can have no true emotional appreciation of English Socialism]. Words denoting such ideas as *democracy, justice, honour, science* and *religion* ceased to exist. To love meant to approve of Big Brother.[4]

[2] Orwell, p. 417.

[3] Ibid.

[4] Ibid., pp. 418–422.

You could, in fact, *doubleplus uncoldly love* and *bellyfeel Big Brother* [i.e., warmly love and emotionally empathise with, Big Brother]. *Doublethink* was a much prized intellectual property, and meant the ability to entertain, quite happily, two mutually opposing opinions in one's head at the same time, while suppressing any awareness of any intellectual contradiction. Good doublethinkers were able to shift from an impassioned argument in favour of one intellectual or political position to an equally impassioned argument against the same position in mid-sentence with no awareness of what they had just done. Good doublethinkers were much prized by the regime's Ministry of Truth (Minitrue, or Ministry of Propaganda). Irish civil servants, lawyers and student debaters are commonly personally familiar with a relatively benign version of this mental condition. Again, someone who is an impassioned Irish republican, for example, will commonly assert and deny at the same time the authenticity and legitimacy of Ulster Unionism. Equally impasssionedly, Ulster Unionists will assert and deny the legitimacy of the political aspirations of Irish nationalists in Northern Ireland, while being only too aware of its reality.

WORD REFORM AND POLITICAL CORRECTNESS

All of this is familiar, and Orwell's great satire has gone into the English language that we all speak, a language that remains a version of Oldspeak, despite the best efforts of some teachers and journalists over the past generation. Orwell's satiric nightmare has come to be seen as such, but the impulses which he recognised presciently as lurking behind attempts to reform the English language still persist. The urge to sanitise our language and to ensure that certain thoughts become unspeakable, or rather, unsayable, still exists. That urge has little to do with true concern with creating a more civilised and just society, and much to do with power-seeking.

The English language, in its spoken and written versions, has survived many linguistic revolutions. The meanings of words, for example, commonly change over time. A good and recent example of this process is the word disinterested, which meant 'uninterested' three centuries ago, but later acquired the quite distinct, and very useful, significance of 'detached', neutral and capable of fair-minded judgement in, for instance, a dispute. Lately it is showing signs of reverting to its original function of being a synonym for 'uninterested', which is rather a pity. However, no power-seeking force lies behind the change, which seems to be due to ignorance and honest semantic muddle, and a real need for a noun that signifies the opposite of interest, one which the language does not readily supply: 'uninterest' is not an English noun—yet.

Confusion is sometimes behind these shifts. For example, some Irish journalists and one American historian of my acquaintance seem to be in a conspiracy to turn the words reluctant and reticent into synonyms of each other. Similarly, some Irish newspapers, some of them with fantastic intellectual pretensions, seem hellbent on equating refute, rebut, contradict and deny. The Ministry of Truth of Airstrip One would be proud of their efforts, and would abolish all four words in favour of some neologism on the lines of *untruefind* (verb), *untruefound* (adjective), *untruefinder* (noun), etc.

Most linguistic change such as the refute-rebut confusion occurs innocently and unconsciously, as words lose one meaning and gain another. Commonly, words fall out of use because they are not needed any more, or they are transferred to a new use; the terms *gender* and *gay* spring to mind as, in my opinion arguable, but perhaps necessary, recent examples. We are no longer very clear what a postillion is and are not sure whether or not a cataphract has something to do with rivers. We do not automatically assume that a mouse is a small rodent. A *hanger* is no longer a short sword, as it was in *Gulliver's Travels*, and an instrument of government sounds rather sinister now; it meant 'written constitution' in Oliver Cromwell's time. The old thug incidentally despised the idea of such a constitution. Again, a *plane* once shaved wood, but now may also fly to Australia, *internet* has nothing to do with fishermen getting tangled up in their tackle and tapes may be used not only for strapping something up but also for eavesdropping on someone. This adaptation of traditional language to new purposes is sensible, inevitable and usually desirable.

However, because of the increasing control of education by state agencies, our language is being changed as much because of the ideological prejudices of certain powerful or at least noisy people as it is being adapted for practical and everyday considerations. Attempts are being made to make certain sentiments unsayable. We (and by that I mean 'we English-speakers') are beset by a new variety of cultural bully: the person who is 'politically correct' (PC) and insists on making everyone else share his condition.

A PC individual objects to the traditional, often racy, irreverent, racialist, comic and obscene ways in which people express themselves and h/she (sic) wishes to prevent certain attitudes, opinions and imageries being expressed at all. To achieve these ends the PC person is willing to try to butcher the English language and make large parts of it unavailable to the next generation. The handiest, if somewhat melodramatic, label for this attitude in its extreme form is linguistic totalitarianism.

Totalitarian doctrines can arise in leftist, rightist, religious, anti-religious and secularist forms. All forms of totalitarianism hold that some opinions are true, others are untrue, and error hath no rights. The holding of an unorthodox opinion is resented, and the holder of such opinions is regarded as an enemy. Counter Reformation Catholicism, Soviet Communism, Maoism, Nazism and fundamentalist Islam had at least this in common: all feared free speech and all held that the truth was known and was the monopoly of a chosen group. They shared a common hatred for freedom of expression and for mental independence. Also, interestingly, these people commonly had a less than total grasp of the local language; certainly, that was true of both the German Nazis and the Soviet Russians.

Soviets and Nazis alike were addicts of their own versions of linguistic political correctness, much like our contemporary PC censors. In power, both attempted to deprave the Russian and German languages by inventing new, orthodox words and prohibiting the use of other, often emotive, non-orthodox and traditional words.[5] Alternatively, they turned traditional descriptive words into 'technical' ideological terms which were essentially words of praise or abuse. The socialists and the Soviets managed to make the harmless term bourgeois, which originally meant 'citizen' or 'inhabitant of a city', into a murderous term of abuse; millions of people were dispossessed and murdered because of the ideology lying behind the redefined version of this word. Similarly, the Nazis managed to convert the innocent term 'Jew' and the meaningless word 'non-Aryan' into terms that would be used as legitimation for the murder of millions of people.

Orwell saw it coming in the thirties and forties of this terrible century. He spoke out against the 'smelly little orthodoxies' of his own time and country and warned, most crucially, that any attack on language immediately presaged an attack on free speech and free thought. Without a language that could be used freely for good and evil purposes, we would become less than human, and we would be unable to reason morally. Of course, Nineteen Eighty-four satirised the monstrous cultural pretensions of the Soviet commissars of the period, and the equally monstrous claims of their western supporters, who energetically represented Joseph Stalin as a hero and the hope of the future instead of what he actually was: a genocide who gave Hitler serious competition for the title of Murderer of the Century. It is only since the extinction of the Soviet Union that Lenin's status as a prematurely extinguished mass murderer has been fully recognised, at least by those who have eyes to see.[6]

---

[5] Ernst Cassirer, *The Myth of the State* (New Haven and London: Yale University Press, 1946), pp. 282–284.

[6] Dmitri Volkogonov, *Lenin: Life and Legacy* (London: Harper/Collins, 1994) is a fascinating and damning original-sources analysis of Lenin and his murderous 'Stalinist' legacy, written by a penitent ex-Stalinist Colonel-General of the Soviet Army. He confirms the arguments of western scholars such as

The Fall of the Wall finally silenced the communists and their fellow-travellers, but it seems that the impulse toward self-righteous bullying has to find its way out somehow. In this post-modern and post-communist world, PC is a useful multi-purpose means of engaging in cultural policing. It is far better, for example, than Ecologism; the study of the ecology of the planet is fundamentally a scientific matter, and not just a matter of political prejudice; scientists can refute or confirm the arguments of the Greens. Arguments about language are more difficult to rebut, partly because arguments about truth-telling can become entangled in arguments about common politeness and the wish not to give offence. PC ideologues take ruthless advantage of people's wish to be polite; cripples become differently abled and dwarves become, according to Tom Sharpe's prophetic satire of two decades ago, PORGs (Persons of Restricted Growth).

A case in point is the PC use of the term 'gender'. *Gender* is, or was until very recently, a grammatical term, and signifies traditional ways in which Indo-European languages are organised. In English, for example, there exist, notionally at least, masculine, feminine, common and neuter genders. *Man* is a masculine word, *woman* is a feminine word, *human* is common and *television* is neuter. *Man* can also be in effect, like *human* or *person*, common in gender when used to denote humanity as a whole or when used as an abstraction. The term *Man* originally included what are now termed *women*. The arguably sexist (why not genderist?) term *woman* was coined by a barbaric and sexist hierarchical society a millennium ago. The battle over this new, illiterate use of the term 'gender', as in Centres for Gender Studies which teach no grammar, seems to have been lost. We may now have to devise a new set of terms for the grammarians.

To emphasise the obvious, gender is common to most Indo-European languages, and often, unlike in English, bears only a very tenuous relationship to biological sex or even to grammatical gender in the English-language sense. In French, houses are feminine, but not female, and children are masculine but either male or female. In German, girls are neuter, but surely female. Stones are, happily I suspect, sexless and non-female in France, but clearly feminine. Their big brothers, rocks, are masculine but equally sexless. Motor-cars can be either masculine or feminine in the wonderful world of the French language, but, *pace* Stephen King, neither French nor American cars have sexes. There is simply no necessary connection between gender and sex, and this is obvious to anyone who has any primitive grasp of some Indo-European languages.

Robert Conquest, long denounced as bourgeois apologists and cold warriors by western leftist intellectuals, PC to a man (stet) in their day and way.

The reason the PC people got away with this exercise in word-stealing is the close correspondence that happens to exist between gender and sex in the English language. Admittedly, even in English the correlation is not perfect; ships are still feminine, as are, sometimes, much-loved old cars. Hurricanes were feminine until the PC people got at the weathermen, and Coleridge's famous Storm-Blast (from *The Rime of the Ancient Mariner*) was definitely masculine, if not male. Men may be windy, but winds are not male. Great powers and other nations are sometimes spoken of as being feminine, but noone with any sanity ever thought of them as being female.

A revealing characteristic of much PC vocabulary is its essential ugliness. This ugliness is derived in large part from its Newspeak-like clumsiness; in the long run, this clumsiness will be its downfall. For example, *Humankind* for either *Mankind* or *Humanity* is not only superfluous, it is inelegant. It also shows disregard for, and ignorance of, one of the central features of the English language: its two-tier Germanic/Romance vocabulary, which offers an unrivalled set of shades of meaning. Personhole, Chairperson, h/she, and female actor, together with a myriad other elephantine devices to avoid an imagined linguistic sexism are commnly hideous. Some feminists have actually tried to establish the term *herstory* for the history of women. Logically, history would then have to delete women and hand them over to the Department of Herstory: no more Cleopatra, Good Queen Bess, Gráinne Ní Mháille, Jane Austen, Marie Curie, Margaret Thatcher or Indira Ghandi. Actually, the term 'history' has nothing to do with the possessive case of the English language masculine pronoun, but is derived from a Greek word, ἰστορεῖν, 'to enquire'.

The ugly and intellectually inappropriate character of much PC Newspeak (*Correctspeak?*) can be easily exemplified. A good example is provided by the US term *Afro-American*, offered to us as a non-racialist alternative to the term *Black [American]*. If *black* is racialist, so are the commonly used descriptive terms *white, brown, yellow* and *red*. These are the conventional divisions, biologically meaningless but accepted as a shorthand, by which ordinary people sort other ordinary people by appearance and possible cultural provenance. There is nothing necessarily racialist about their use, any more than the way into which we sort people into male, female, tall, small, left-handed, right-handed, smokers, non-smokers, Urdu-speaking, French, German, etc.

The logic of the term is eminently questionable, not to say quite barmy. Not all Americans of African descent are black, for starters. Are Egyptian-Americans Afro-Americans? I have a friend, Jan Reif, who is Afro-American. He was born in Atlanta, his father is Afrikaner and his mother is Irish South African. He is six feet tall, blond, blue-eyed and athletic. He is a very nice fellow, buys his round and all; he is not a black, but he is definitely Afro-American. Maybe we could call him a WAFRAM (White Afro-American)? The PC term is less accurate, less efficient, less honest, and longer. Similarly, the PC term *Native American* elides the important distinction between Indian and Eskimo, while gratuitously insulting hundreds of millions of white, black, brown and yellow native Americans. The allegedly racialist and certainly non-PC term *Red Indian* echoes an innocent historical error of five centuries ago; there is no implied insult in the term. To suggest that there is is to suggest there is something wrong with being Indian. It is rather like objecting to the term *Welsh*, on the grounds that it means 'foreign' in archaic English. The term *Gael*, incidentally, means something rude in early Welsh. Scotland should find a new name; the name means Ireland, and was pinched from us by our Caledonian cousins centuries ago.

To give a local analogy: if I were to be rather insistently labelled a *native Irishman* by some PC bore in view of the fact that I am descended from the mainly Catholic and Irish-speaking earlier settlers on this island, I would immediately wonder whether someone was trying to drive some kind of ideological and psychological wedge between people of my background and those of other religious, ethnic or racial ancestries who are my fellow citizens.

I admit immediately that many of the restrictions that PC attempts to impose on the rest of us derive from a genuine impulse to avoid terms that are, or might be deemed to be by somebody, hurtful. I would, however, also argue that PC exploits the wish of decent people to be polite and not offend. PC people can be fantastically rude in their attempts to hold to the moral high ground and to tick off the rest of us. A civilised impulse is being exploited, and is mobilised for a deeply uncivilised purpose: the silencing of unwelcome opinion. Some PC terms are possibly improvements, the term *gay* being, on balance, one of them. But: what on earth is wrong with the *-ess* termination, as in words like *actress*, *poetess*, *Jewess*, or the word *heroine*? In German, if you have a friend who happens to be female and also feminine, she is your *Freundin*. Why object to the parallel formation in English? Is *schoolteacher* about to replace the far more informative *schoolmaster/mistress* pair of words? Why not abolish the much-loved words *boyfriend* and *girlfriend* on the grounds that they are demeaning to adults? I suggest as substitutes the terms *female significant friend* and *male significant friend* or *FESIF* and *MASIF* for short. What an improvement! he crowed proudly. It is interesting to note that the PC people have not proposed *woman seamster* for *seamstress*, or *woman monarch* (WOMARCH) for *Queen*. Maybe they'll get around to it.

Presumably, French, German and Spanish, with their strong gender structures, are inherently more sexist than English, with its weak gender structure, thus making English a superior and more correct language. Alternatively, is there something inherently wrong with PC? I believe that PC is a symptom of an organised and deeply philistine illiteracy, and is gradually being found out; the ancient weapon of ridicule will eventually do it in. Behind the undoubted good intentions of many PC advocates lies a dangerous possibility: the empoverishment of English, a great and flexible language, which expresses man's noble and evil purposes with an unrivalled richness of vocabulary. Such an empoverishment could conceivably be brought about by ill-informed or even mischievous monkeying by a group of energetic and well-organised ideologues who appear to know little about language or who, perhaps, do know about it and do not care.

Oldthinkers and newthinkers undifferently doubleplusunbellyfeel Correctthink. Correctthinkers duckspeak well. Correctspeak is doubleplusgood Duckspeak. It is little else.

The Verbal Noun in Irish Nonfinite Clauses[*]

EITHNE GUILFOYLE
University of Calgary

0. INTRODUCTION

IN THIS paper we examine the structure of nonfinite clauses in Modern Irish and show that they provide evidence for two recent claims pertaining to the structure of VP. First, that the VP is a bipartite structure where the lower maximal projection is headed by a verbal noun (Travis 1991), second that the VP contains a functional category AspP (Travis 1991, Ramchand 1993). We use these two assumptions to explain the word order of Irish nonfinite clauses, and a number of other puzzling facts of Irish syntax. We also claim that Southern Irish dialects lack the upper VP position, and consequently place certain restrictions on the appearance of lexical subjects in nonfinite clauses.

In section 1, we discuss the word order of Irish finite and nonfinite clauses focusing our attention on the two major dialects, Northern and Southern Irish.[1] We note the word order differences in the dialects, and the restriction on lexical subjects in Southern Irish. In section 2 we present an analysis of the clause structure of Irish, and argue that the major difference between Northern and Southern Irish is the lack of an upper VP, and hence an external argument position in Southern Irish. In section 3 we use morphological evidence to support our claim that nonfinite clauses are headed by a VN, and show that our analysis sheds new light on three well known properties of Irish syntax: the lack of complementary distribution of PRO and lexical NP, the impossibility of pronominal object postposing in nonfinite clauses, and the lack of 'double subject' constructions in Southern dialects. A summary of our conclusions is given in section 4.

[*] The research for this paper was supported by the Social Sciences and Humanities Research Council of Canada (grant # 410-95-0382), and by a Fellowship from The Calgary Institute For the Humanities. Earlier versions of the paper were presented at *NELS 24* at the University of Massachusetts (Guilfoyle 1994), and at *The Parasession on the Generative Grammar of Irish,* University of Ulster at Jordanstown, 1994.

[1] Northern Irish refers to the variety of Irish spoken in Ulster, Southern Irish refers to the dialect spoken in Munster. Preliminary investigations suggest that nonfinite clauses in the third major dialect, Connaught Irish, appear to pattern with those of Northern Irish, however further research needs to be done to verify this.

1.0 WORD ORDER IN IRISH FINITE AND NONFINITE CLAUSES

Most recent treatments of Irish within generative grammar assume that the underlying word order is SVO (McCloskey 1983), (Guilfoyle 1990), and that the surface VSO order is derived by movement of the verb to clause-initial position. Under this view, we expect that when the verb fails to move (for whatever reason) we should get a surface SVO order. Many VSO languages do in fact allow SVO order, although they vary widely in the extent to which this possibility is allowed.

All dialects of Irish show VSO order in tensed clauses as shown in (1) and (2) below:

(1)   D'fhan   Seán sa bhaile inniu

        stay-PAST Seán at home today 'Sean stayed at home today'

(2)   Chuaigh Siobhán ar scoil

        go-PAST Siobhan on school 'Siobhan went to school'

Under standard assumptions the verb raises to Infl from within the VP to assign nominative case to the subject. We would expect then, that in nontensed clauses the verb should remain within the VP and SVO order should surface. As we shall see below, SVO order is possible only in Southern Irish dialects, and then only in formal registers.

Following Fukui and Speas (1986) and Koopman and Sportiche (1991) we shall assume that subjects are generated in Spec of VP, and may remain there in VSO languages. The verb raises to the head of a functional projection external to VP; we will assume this is IP. This is shown in (3) below:

(3)

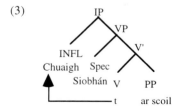

When the clause is non-tensed the verb remains within the VP. The VP is headed by a nonfinite verb form which is referred to in traditional grammars as a verbal noun (VN). The VN may be preceded by preverbal particle *a* under conditions which vary from one dialect to another as will be seen below. For the purposes of later discussion, we note that Irish, unlike English, has a productive rule of accusative case-assignment to the subject of a nonfinite clause, and that case-assignment takes place independent of any outside governor (Chung and McCloskey 1987). Thus the response to the question in (4) is fully grammatical in all dialects of Irish:

(4)   Q: Caidé a   chuir sin in do   cheann?
         what COMP put   that in your head
         'What put that in your head?'

      A: Tú a bheith 'do luí
         you be-VN lying down
         'The fact that you were lying down' (literally 'You to be lying there')

Turning now to dialect differences, the language divides into two major dialect groups, Northern and Southern Irish. There are significant differences between the dialects at the phonological, morphological and syntactic levels; we concentrate here on the syntactic properties of nonfinite clauses in the dialects starting with the Northern group.

1.1 Northern Irish

In Northern dialects nonfinite clauses show SOV order, as can be seen in (5) to (7) below. In (5) we have an intransitive clause, in (6) a control structure, and in (7) a transitive clause. Note that in (5) and (7) the subject is lexical and bears accusative case in spite of the absence of a governing case assigner.

(5)   B'fhearr   liom [tú fanacht   sa bhaile inniu]
      COP -better with-me you remain-VN home   today
      'I would rather you remain at home today'

(6)   Ba mhaith liom [PRO an doras a phéinteáil]
      COP good with-me   the door ptc paint-VN
      'I would like to paint the door'

(7)   Ba mhaith   liom [sibh   an doras a phéinteáil]
      COP good with-me you-pl   the door ptc paint-VN
      'I would like you to paint the door'

These data are problematic for the assumption that VSO languages are underlyingly SVO. Because V-movement has not applied, we expect that we should find SVO order, yet as can be seen in (6) and (7) the object precedes the VN. These examples also raise another issue. What is the status of the particle *a* which appears before the VN in the two transitive examples (6) and (7)? Why is it absent in the intransitive example in (5)? Because this particle is associated with the appearance of an object, it seems reasonable to analyze it as an accusative case assigner, and this solution has been proposed by Chung and McCloskey (1987). They propose that VNs are noun-like in that they cannot assign accusative case. Consequently, a case assigning particle *a* adjoins to the VN, and the object adjoins to the V' projection to receive accusative case. This is shown in (8):

(8)

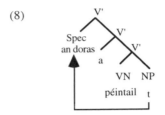

Note that this solution explains why *a* only appears when the verb is transitive, and allows us to maintain that the underlying order of the language is SVO. However there are two significant problems with the adjunction analysis. First, it involves A-bar movement of the object for case-assignment, unlike the usual A-movement for case (i.e. passive and raising). Second, it involves adjunction to an X' position, rather than the expected XP or X°. Finally, it cannot account for the word order and case-assignment facts of nonfinite clauses in Southern Dialects as we shall see below.

1.2 Southern Irish Dialects

In Southern dialects also, the subject and the object normally precede the VN in nonfinite clauses (Ó Siadhail 1989). However there are several differences between the word order patterns of Northern and Southern dialects. The first concerns the particle *a* which, in Southern dialects, is found whenever a lexical NP, either subject or object, precedes the VN. Thus it intervenes between the subject and the intransitive VN in (9), between the object and the transitive VN in (10), but does not appear in the control structure in (11) which has no lexical NP.

(9)   B'fhearr   liom [tú **a** fanacht   sa bhaile inniu]
        COP-better with-me you **ptc** remain-VN home   today
        'I would rather you remain at home today'

(10)   Ba mhaith   liom [PRO an doras **a** phéinteáil]
        COP good with-me   the door **ptc** paint-VN
        'I would like to paint the door'

(11)   B'fhearr   liom [PRO fanacht   sa bhaile inniu]
        COP -better with-me   remain-VN home   today
        'I would rather remain at home today'

In addition, Southern dialects restrict the appearance of lexical NPs
preceding the VN to *at most* one. As a result sentences like that in (12), a
transitive clause with a lexical subject, are ungrammatical in Southern
dialects, although they are grammatical in the North:

(12)   *Ba mhaith liom   [sibh   an doras **a** phéinteáil]
        COP good with-me you-pl the door **ptc** paint-VN
        'I would like you to paint the door'

Instead of (12) Southern Irish speakers would tend to use an embedded
tensed clause such as the one in (13):

(13)   Ba mhaith   liom [go   bpéinteáilfeadh sibh an doras]
        COP good with-me that   paint-cond you-pl the door
        'I would like that you paint the door'

Alternatively, in formal registers, the genitive marked object may follow
the VN as in (14):

(14)   Ba mhaith   liom [sibh   **a**   phéinteáil   an dorais]
        COP good with-me you-pl **ptc** paint-VN   the door-GEN
        'I would like you to paint the door'

To summarise, in Southern nonfinite clauses:

    (a) The particle *a* appears whenever a lexical NP precedes the VN

    (b) Only one lexical NP may precede the VN

Note that it is not always clear whether the NP which precedes the VN is a
subject or an object, leading to ambiguities such as that in (15):

(15)   Ba mhaith   liom [tú   **a** phósadh]
        COP good with-me you **ptc** marry
        'I would like you to marry/ I would like to marry you'

                                        (based on Ó Siadhail 1989, 258 (36))

These data present a challenge to the GB theory of clause structure because
in this theory subjects and objects occupy distinct positions at D-structure.
How can we state a restriction limiting the lexical realization of NPs to one
at most, given that two positions are available for theta-marking? How can
we account for the role of *a* which is only associated with lexical NPs?
Finally, how can we account for the facts of nonfinite clauses in Northern
and Southern Irish in such a way as to capture the differences between the
dialects and yet produce the same word order in finite clauses in both
dialects? We note that the object adjunction analysis proposed by Chung
and McCloskey (1987), does not adequately account for Southern Irish, as
the particle *a* is present with both lexical subjects and objects. This casts
doubt on the claim that *a* is exclusively associated with accusative case-
marking for objects. Furthermore, the object adjunction operation would
have to be sensitive to the presence or absence of a subject, given the data
in (14), again suggesting that the adjunction analysis is not on the right
track. In Section 2 below we will suggest that we can solve these three
problems if we assume that the VN is a noun which has an external
argument position in Northern dialects, but not in Southern dialects.

2. NEW APPROACHES TO VP STRUCTURE

A number of recent proposals on the internal structure of VP will be
relevant to our discussion. Most important will be the proposals of Travis
(1991). Drawing on work by Larson (1988), she proposes that the VP
consists of two segments each of which discharges an argument within its
own projection. Following Hale and Keyser (1990) she assumes that the
lower VP is headed by a VN. She further proposes that a functional
projection AspP intervenes between the two segments of the VP. Under
certain circumstances objects move to the Spec of AspP to receive
accusative case. Thus the internal structure of VP would be as in (16)
below:

(16)

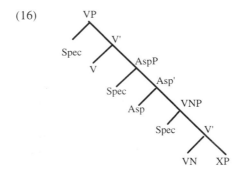

While the VP structure in (16) was not proposed with Irish in mind, in fact the data just discussed presents strong supporting evidence for this type of analysis. We first look at the Northern dialects and see how these proposals can handle the SOV word order and the assignment of accusative case to objects. We will then consider the Southern dialects within this framework.

2.1   The Structure of Irish Finite and Nonfinite VPs

2.1.1 Nonfinite clauses in Northern Dialects

In all dialects the word order is VSO in tensed clauses, and we assume that the VN moves through the head of AspP, into V and on to Infl. In nontensed clauses the VN fails to move. As the VN is a noun and cannot assign accusative case, the object is forced to move to Spec AspP to receive case from *a* in the head of AspP. This is shown in (17) below:

(17)

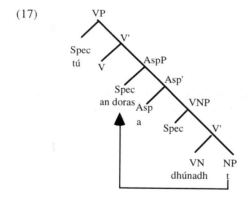

Under this analysis then the VN becomes a true verb only when it incorporates with the higher V in tensed clauses. The failure of V-movement in nonfinite clauses reveals the underlying structure of the VP. This analysis provides us with a means of explaining the intermediate status of the VN as somewhat noun-like but having the argument structure of a verb.

2.1.2 Nonfinite Clauses in Southern Dialects

In Southern dialects we assume that tensed clauses have a similar analysis to those in the North, so that the VN moves out of the VP through Asp and V by a series of head-movements. In nontensed clauses, however the situation is different. As in Northern dialects, the VN remains in its D-structure position. However while -Tense subcategorizes for VP in

Northern Irish, it subcategorizes for AspP in Southern Irish. The result is that Southern nonfinite clauses do not contain the higher VP projection, and thus have no position for a true external argument. We assume that this constitutes the major difference between nonfinite clauses in the two dialects. The structure of a nonfinite intransitive clause is shown in (18):

(18)

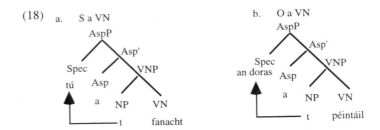

In (18a) we have a nonfinite intransitive clause with a lexical subject, and in (18b) we have a transitive control clause. In each of these structures, *a* is a case-assigner generated in the head of AspP. It can assign accusative case to either the subject or the object of the VN. Note that the VN takes a single internal argument in each instance, to which it assigns a theta-role but no case.

This analysis is consistent with the claim that nouns unlike verbs do not have external arguments (Grimshaw 1990). As pointed out by Travis (1991), the reason for the higher V is to discharge the external argument of the VNP. Under the analysis here, the absence of the higher VP results in a restriction on lexical NPs in these clause types; there is only one syntactic position to which an argument may be assigned, Spec of VNP. Note that this also gives us insight into the ambiguity of sentence (15) where the pronoun *tú* 'you' can be interpreted as either an agent or a theme. This ambiguity is similar to that which arises in English nominals such as (19a), where *the enemy* can be interpreted as an agent as in (19b), or as a theme as in (19c).[2]

(19)   a. The enemy's destruction
         b. The enemy's destruction of the city
         c. The enemy's destruction by the army

A final issue to be addressed for Southern dialects is the status of the controlled argument in structures such as the example in (10). We will

---

[2] It has been pointed out to me that a theme interpretation is the most natural in these instances, I am not sure if that is also the case for the Irish example in (15).

consider this further when we discuss the status of PRO in these dialects in section 3.3 below.

3. ADDITIONAL EVIDENCE

In a sense, it is not difficult to make a case for treating VNPs as nouns rather than verbs. Traditional grammarians have always done so, and even those who assume that they are verbs rather than nouns assume that they retain nounlike qualities (e.g. genitive case assigning properties) in certain instances. In this section, I look at some of the morphological evidence for treating the VNP as a noun and show that our analysis goes part way to explain three longstanding puzzles of Irish syntax.

3.1 Morphological Evidence: VNP as a 'Real Noun'

The verbal noun can appear in a variety of different constuction types aside from the nonfinite clauses discussed above. Within these structures the nominal characteristics of the VN become evident in the morphology. In various constructions the VN can bear genitive case, assign genitive case, and appear with nominal emphatic and reflexive affixes. Each of these properties is discussed below.

   The VN bears genitive case when it appears with a head noun in structures such as those shown in (20) below:

(20)   a. fonn troda
            desire fight-VN-GEN
            'a desire to fight' (lit. 'fight's desire')

         b. lá breithe
            day birth-VN-GEN
            'birthday'

The VN can also assign genitive in progressive structures. These are formed by combining the VNP with the verb *a bheith* 'be'. The VNP is preceded by the progressive particle *ag*. In some dialects and registers the NP object (which follows the VN) bears genitive case. In all dialects however, pronominal objects appear as genitive pronouns. This is shown in (21a. and b.) below:

(21)   a. Tá   sé **ag** baint   an fhéir
            be-PRES he **ptc** cut-VN the grass-GEN
            'He is cutting the grass'
                                      (The Christian Brothers 1980)

> b. Tá   siad mo mharú
> be-PRES they my kill-VN
> 'They are killing me'

In progressive structures the VNP may be associated with the same emphatic and reflexive morphology as ordinary nouns as can be seen by comparing the progressive structures in (22) with the NPs in (23):

(22)   a. Tá mé   mo mharú féin   **ag** obair
           be-PRES my kill-VN REFLEX **ptc** work-VN
           'I am killing myself working'

        b. An   bhfuil   tú á dhéanamh sin   le   fada?
           Q   be-PRES you its do-VN EMPH with long
           'Have you been doing that for a long time?'
                          (McCloskey 1983)

(23)   a. mo theach féin 'my own house'
           my house REFLEX

        b. a theach sin 'that one's house'
           his house DEMON
                          (McCloskey and Hale 1984)

The morphological evidence just discussed here suggests that the VN behaves as a true nominal in progressive structures in that it takes affixes that are normally associated with nouns (see (Guilfoyle 1990) for further discussion). The same VN form heads both nominal and progressive clauses, and the fact that in formal registers the object may bear genitive case suggests that we may treat the VN as a noun in each instance.[3]

3.2 Object Pronoun Postposing

All dialects of Irish have an optional rule of object pronoun postposing to a clause-final position, which can apply in **tensed** clauses only. Pronominal objects of nonfinite clauses may not be postposed. This can be seen in (24) and (25) below.

---

[3] Borsley (1993) suggests that Welsh VNs are verbal rather than nominal forms; for a discussion of his analysis, see Guilfoyle (1996).

(24)   a. Thug   mé é do Chiarán i nDoire inniu
           give (PAST) I **it** to Ciarán in Derry today
           'I gave it to Ciarán in Derry today'

        b. Thug   mé do Chiarán i nDoire inniu **é**
           give (PAST) I   to Ciarán in Derry today **it**
           'I gave it to Ciaran in Derry today'
                                            (Chung and McCloskey 1987)

(25)   a. Níor mhaith liom Ciarán **iad** a   fhostú
           I-would-not-like Ciarán **them** ptc hire-VN
           'I would not like Ciarán to hire them'

        b. *Níor mhaith liom Ciarán t$_i$ a fhostú **iad**$_i$
           I-would-not-like Ciarán ptc hire-VN them
           'I would not like Ciarán to hire them'

In (24) the pronominal object may appear immediately after the subject as in (24a), or following the object as in (24b). In the nonfinite examples in (25) however, only the example where the pronominal object precedes the VN is acceptable. Under the analysis developed here this contrast is attributable to the ECP, in that the extraction site is not the same in finite and nonfinite clauses. In finite clauses the verb properly governs its object, however, in nonfinite clauses the object occupies the Spec of AspP. AspP is not a proper governor, and thus the pronominal object cannot be extracted.

3.3 The Status of PRO in Modern Irish

Under standard assumptions, we expect that PRO and lexical NPs should be in complementary distribution. This is because lexical NPs must be governed by some case-assigning head, while PRO must not appear in a governed position. As pointed out by Chung & McCloskey (1987), this generalization breaks down in Irish. As we saw in the example in (4), the subject position of Irish nonfinite clauses has a clause-internal mechanism for case-assignment, and yet PRO can also appear there. Under the analysis proposed here, Southern dialects do not have PRO in nonfinite transitive clauses, as there is no syntactic position to which it could be assigned. Rather these control stuctures should be treated as control of an implicit argument such as has been proposed for English nominals in Williams (1985). Assuming that this kind of analysis could be generalized to intransitive clauses, we claim that PRO does not appear in Southern Irish at all, so the problem of the lack of complementary distribution between PRO and lexical NPs in Irish disappears, at least for Southern dialects.[4]

3.4 Northern Double Subject Constructions

Irish has a number of psychological predicates which are formed by combining *a bheith* 'be' with a noun expressing a psychological state as in (26) below:

(26)   Tá eagla   ort
        is fear on-you
        'you are afraid'

These predicates have a number of interesting properties which are discussed in some detail in McCloskey and Sells (1988). Of interest to us here, is the fact that the experiencer argument appears within a PP. When it appears in a nonfinite clause, this experiencer argument can be controlled by a verb in a higher clause as shown in (27):

(27)   Níor cheart duit$_i$ eagla a bheith ort$_i$
        you$_i$ shouldn't   fear ptc be-VN on-you$_i$
        'You shouldn't be afraid'

Under the analysis proposed by McCloskey and Sells the structure of (27) is as in (28), where the higher verb controls a PRO in subject position of the nonfinite clause, which is in turn co-indexed with the experiencer PP.

(28)   Níor cheart duit$_i$ [PRO$_i$ eagla a bheith ort$_i$]

In a sense, we could say that the experiencer theta-role is split between the subject position, and the PP position. Note that this analysis gains support from examples such as that in (29), where the subject position is occupied by a lexical NP instead of PRO, and the same coindexation occurs:

(29)   Níor cheart duit$_i$ [tusa$_i$ eagla   a bheith ort$_i$]
        you$_i$ shouldn't   you fear ptc be-VN at-you$_i$
        'You shouldn't be afraid'

Structures such as (29), where the nonfinite subject position is occupied by a lexical NP, are referred to as Double Subject constructions by McCloskey

---

[4] It would also be possible to extend this kind of analysis to Northern dialects, but questions of space prevent us from discussing that here.

& Sells. They point out that while they are fully grammatical in Northern dialects, in Southern dialects they are not. In Southern Irish only the examples where the subject is not lexically realized are grammatical.

Note that this dialect difference is expected under the analysis proposed here. The Northern dialects have an upper VP and thus external argument position to which a lexical NP can be assigned. The Southern dialects lack this position, so the experiencer argument may be controlled, but not lexically realized as a subject argument.

4. CONCLUSION

In this paper, we have argued on the basis of evidence from nonfinite clauses in Modern Irish, that the VP is a bipartite structure where the lower maximal projection is headed by a verbal noun, and that the VP contains a functional category AspP. We used these two assumptions to explain the word order of Irish nonfinite clauses, and the differences between the admissibility of subjects in nonfinite clauses in Northern and Southern dialects of Irish.

REFERENCES

Bobaljik, Jonathan and Carnie, Andrew 1996. 'A Minimalist Approach to some Problems of Irish Word Order', in *The Syntax of the Celtic Languages*, ed. by Robert Borsley and Ian Roberts, Cambridge: University Press, 223–240

Borsley, Robert 1993. 'On so-called Verb-Nouns in Welsh', *Journal of Celtic Linguistics*, 2, 35–64

The Christian Brothers 1980. *New Irish Grammar*, Dublin: C. J. Fallon

Chung, Sandra and McCloskey, James 1987. 'Government, Barriers and Small Clauses in Modern Irish', *Linguistic Inquiry*, 18.2, 173–238

Duffield, Nigel 1995. *Particles and Projections.* Dordrecht: Kluwer

Emonds, James 1980. 'Word Order in Generative Grammar', *Journal of Linguistic Research*, 11, 1–10

Fukui, Naoki and Speas, Margaret 1986. 'Specifiers and Projections'. *MIT Working Papers in Linguistics*, 8, 128–172

Grimshaw, Jane 1990. *Argument Structure*, Cambridge, Mass.: MIT Press

Guilfoyle, Eithne 1990. *Functional Categories and Phrase Structure Parameters*, unpublished doctoral thesis, McGill University

—1994. 'VNPs, Finiteness and External Arguments', *Proceedings of the 24th Annual Meeting of the North Eastern Linguistic Society*, Amherst, Mass.: University of Massachusetts, 141–155

—1996. 'Subjects and Initiators in Modern Irish', unpublished MS, University of Calgary

Hale, Kenneth and Keyser, S. Jay 1990. 'The Syntactic Character of Thematic Structure', unpublished MS, MIT

Koopman, Hilda and Sportiche, Dominique 1991. 'The Position of Subjects', *Lingua*, 85, 211–258

Larson, Richard 1988. 'On the Double Object Construction', *Linguistic Inquiry,* 19, 335–393

McCloskey, James 1983. 'A VP in a VSO Language', in *Order Concord and Constiutency*, ed. by Gerald Gazdar, Ewan Klein and Geoffrey Pullum, Dordrecht: Foris, 9–55

McCloskey, James and Hale, Kenneth 1984. 'On the Syntax of Person-Number Inflection in Modern Irish', *Natural Language and Linguistic Theory*, 14, 487–535

McCloskey, James and Sells, Peter 1988. 'Control and A-Chains in Modern Irish', *Natural Language and Linguistic Theory*, 6, 143–190

Ó Siadhail, Micheál 1989. *Modern Irish: Grammatical Structure and Dialectal Variation*, Cambridge: University Press

Sproat, Richard 1985. 'Welsh Syntax and VSO Structure', *Natural Language and Linguistic Theory*, 3, 173–216

Ramchand, Gillian 1992. 'Aspect Phrase in Modern Scottish Gaelic', *Proceedings of the North Eastern Linguistic Society*, 23, 415–429

Travis, Lisa 1991. 'Inner Aspect and the Structure of VP', paper presented at the *Twenty-Second Meeting of the North Eastern Linguistic Society*, Ottawa, Ontario

Williams, Edwin 1985. 'PRO and the Subject of NP', *Natural Language and Linguistic Theory,* 33, 297–316

Polish Palatalisations Return to the Fold

EDMUND GUSSMANN

Department of Celtic, Catholic University of Lublin

PALATALISATIONS occupy a central position in all generative studies of Polish phonology. The recognition of palatalisation rules as phonological phenomena in the contemporary language was one of many innovations introduced by the generative approach. As is well-known, the classical structural tradition, going back in the case of Polish palatalisations to the early work of Baudouin de Courtenay and Kruszewski, did not regard this as an issue. Quite simply, as palatalised and non-palatalised consonants contrast freely, their members were assigned phonemic status in much the same way as voiced and voiceless consonants were. The alternations between the classes were interpreted to some extent as cases of the neutralisation of the opposition, but for the most part they were viewed as constituting the subject matter for morphophonemics. Against this background the different phonological palatalisations identified within the generative approach could hardly have formed a more drastic departure from the structural tradition.

Before proceeding further it is necessary to clarify some terminological ambiguities, as the term *palatal* and its various derivatives tend to be applied loosely to different phenomena. Specifically, it is necessary to discriminate clearly between the phonetic and phonological (or functional) usage of the terms *palatalised* and *palatal*. Phonetically a consonant is palatalised when it involves the articulatory gesture of bunching up the front part of the tongue towards the hard palate or advancing a back constriction to the front; in such cases palatalisation is sometimes called secondary articulation and is marked by a diacritic, e.g. [p´, s´, k´]. Palatal consonants are those whose primary articulator involves the palato-alveolar region, e.g. [š, č].[1] (In Polish the palatal consonants are palatalised only in exceptional cases such as foreign words, e.g.: *Chile* [č´ile] 'Chile', *dżinsy* [dž´insy] 'jeans'.) The palatalised consonants are informally referred to as *soft* while palatal and non-palatalised ones are called *hard*. This very rough characterisation produces a division of Polish consonants into a soft and a hard group. In addition, some of the consonants appear in hard-soft pairs, whereas others have no corresponding congeners:

---

[1] A word should be added about the system of transciption adopted in ths paper. Following the Slavic tradition we transcribe the Polish palatalised dentals with a prime placed over the consonantal symbol, e.g. [ć] and all remaining palatalised consonants with a prime following the consonant, e.g. [m´].

(1)   p´ b´ m´ f´ v´ ń ś ź ć dź k´g´ χ´
        p b m f v n s z t d k g χ

        c dz š ž č dž j l w

The above classification is grossly oversimplified and bypasses various
details, for example, the fact that the affricates [ć, dź] are treated as the
palatalised counterparts of the plosives [t, d] rather than of the hard
affricates [c, dz]. These doubts need not occupy us too much since the
above phonetic classification must be contrasted with—or perhaps replaced
by—the functional one. In the latter classification, a consonant is assigned
either to the hard group (also called basic) or to the softened one (also
called derived). The division is based on the function a given consonant
plays within morphologically conditioned alternations. To illustrate this
with an example: the stem final non-palatalised consonant is invariably
replaced by its palatalised congener before the vowel -e of the locative
singular. In derivational terms this has been taken to mean that the vowel
evokes palatalisation of the preceding hard consonant. Alternations like
those in (2) illustrate this phenomenon:

(2)   ła[p]a   ła[p´]e 'paw'
        ry[b]a   ry[b´]e 'fish'
        ra[m]a   ra[m´]e 'frame'
        so[v]a   so[v´]e 'owl'
        ra[f]a   ra[f´]e 'reef'
        wo[d]a   wo[dź]e 'water'
        świa[t]   świe[ć]e 'world'
        ska[z]a   ska[ź]e 'blemish'
        no[s]   no[ś]e 'nose'
        sta[n]   sta[ń]e 'state'

In the examples above a phonetically hard consonant is replaced by a
phonetically soft one before the front vowel. However, in the same context
the liquids [ł, r][2] and the velar consonants [k, g, χ] are replaced by the
phonetically hard liquid [l] and the palatals [ž, c, dz, š], as shown below:

---

[2] In point of fact what we call the lateral liquid appears phonetically as the labial glide [w] in most
pronunciations. It has been extensively argued in the literature that this is a mere phonetic effect and that
the relevant consonant is phonologically a lateral.

(3) ska[ł]a   ska[l]e 'rock'
     ka[r]a   ka[ž]e 'punishment'
     rę[k]a   rę[c]e 'hand'
     no[g]a   no[dz]e 'leg'
     mu[χ]a   mu[š]e 'fly'

Because the hard consonants appear in a context predominantly reserved for soft consonants, they are taken to be *functionally* soft. Similar observations lead to a division of consonants into two groups which is partly different from the phonetically based classification. Consider Szober's (1923, 48) functional pairing of consonants:

(4) basic   b p m v f d t z s n ł r g k χ
     (hard)   g´ k´

     derived b´ p´ m´ v´ f´ dź ć ź ś ń l ž ž č š
     (soft)   dz c ž š   dz c ś

The examples in (3) illustrate alternations in a palatalising environment. We now consider cases involving three- or four-way alternations between hard dental or velar obstruents and their functionally soft congeners, which may or may not be phonetically palatalised. Here are some examples of morphologically related forms:

(5) wi[d]ać   wi[dź]eć   wi[dz]ę
     'to be seen'   'to see'   'I see'
     kobie[t]a   kobie[ć]ina   kobie[c]y
     'woman'   'id. express.' 'female'
     wo[z]u   wo[ź]ić   wo[ž]ę
     'cart, gen. sg.'   'to carry'   'I carry'
     pa[s]łem   pa[ś]e   pa[š]a
     'I grazed'   'he grazes'   'fodder'
     wa[g]a   wa[g´]i   wa[ž]yć   wa[dz]e
     'scales' 'gen. sg.' 'weigh',   'loc. sg.'
     proro[k] proro[k´]ini proro[č]y   proro[c]ki
     'prophet' 'id. fem.' 'prophetic'   'of the prophet'
     Wło[χ]   Wło[ś]li   Wło[š]ka
     'an Italian'   'nom. pl.'   'nom. sg. fem.'

The derived class contains not only phonetically palatalised but also phonetically hard consonants because these hard consonants pattern like palatalised ones. What is far more striking, however, is that the phonetically palatalised velars [k´] and [g´] are classed together with the hard consonants, a point that Szober comments on. The reasons for this are not difficult to see: the -*e* ending of the nominative plural of non-masculine adjectives requires the preceding consonant to belong to the hard set, e.g.: *dob*[r]*e* 'good', *bo*[s]*e* 'bare-footed', *ład*[n]*e* 'pretty', but the two velar plosives are palatalised in this context, e.g.: *płas*[k´]*e* 'flat', *dro*[g´]*e* 'dear'. This means that the palatalisation of velar plosives does not make them functionally palatalised. As Szober states elsewhere (p. 45), the palatalisation of velars is a phonetic change (i.e. conditioned by the phonetic context) while the functionally soft or derived consonants are conditioned by grammatical factors. These notions can be straightforwardly translated into subphonemic and phonemic alternations in the structural tradition.

There are several issues that structural linguists disagreed about in the Polish system, for example the status of palatalised labials, or the palatalised velar spirant (not included in Szober's list above) and other such cases. However, nobody disputed the phonemic distinctiveness of the soft congeners of the basic hard consonants. Minimal or near minimal pairs like [sat] *sad* 'orchard'—[śat] *siadł* 'he sat down'—[šat] *szat* 'garment, gen. pl.' can be found for practically all of the alternating segments. For this reason we can conclude that the structural interpretation amounted to a reformulation of the traditional insights in the more rigorous terms of the phonemic and morphophonemic analysis.

As is well-known, the generative analysis took morphophonemic alternations as evidence for existing *phonological* regularities. With reference to Polish, this meant that, ideally, all of the alternations between hard and soft(ened) consonants in (4) above should be derivable by means of phonological rules. This ambitious objective was attempted only once: in 1963 Theodore Lightner published his *Preliminary Remarks on the Morphophonemic Component of Polish*. Although the term *morphophonemic* is still adhered to in this work, it is understood as equivalent to *systematic phonemic*, as obviously there is no intermediate level of classical phonemes between that and the phonetic representation. The express objective of this study is to eliminate as much allomorphy as possible:

> We suggest that sharping of consonants and nasalization of vowels in Polish is always predictable (and hence nonphonemic). Moreover, the occurrence of the palatals *cz ż sz* and of the glides *j w* is shown to be predictable. Furthermore, we want to indicate that at least some of the rather complex consonant and vowel alternations that occur in Polish inflection may be accounted for by a simple set of rules, all of which are of general application (Lightner 1963, 220).

Lightner's analysis displays all the advantages and disadvantages of generative phonology: it all but eliminates underlying (lexical) allomorphy by reducing the underlying inventory of phonological units; on the other hand it operates with highly abstract structures, which at times require an intricate interplay of phonological rules to derive the systematic phonetic representations of words. Lightner's Polish system comprises just nine obstruents /p, b, t, d, s, z, k, g, χ/, four sonorants /l, r, m, n/, and eight vowels: lax and tense variants of /u, i, e, o/. Thus, the analysis derived not only all the phonetically palatalised consonants of (4) above but also all the palatals and the dental affricates.

The underlying system posited for Polish recaptures the history of the language. As admitted by Lightner (p. 233): 'It seems reasonable to assume from the work presented thus far that the Polish phonemic forms are essentially identical with the phonemic forms that historical linguists postulate for Proto-Slavic'.[3] It is hardly surprising, then, that most of Lightner's phonological rules are little more than restatements of changes studied by historians of the language; rule no. 1 in his phonological component of Polish is the progressive palatalisation of velars, familiar from Slavic historical phonology as the Baudouin de Courtenay palatalisation (see Lunt 1981; Carlton 1990, 130 ff). As an example, let us look at the word *chłopiec* [xłop′ec] 'boy', which Lightner derives from underlying /xolp+ik+os/; disregarding the liquid metathesis consider the final two morphemes /ik+os/, where /ik/ is a kind of diminutive suffix (cf. *chłop* 'man, peasant') while /os/ is taken to be an inflectional ending realised as phonetic zero. The vowel of the inflectional ending is required to create the necessary context for the progressive palatalisation of the preceding velar, it is subsequently raised to a yer and finally deleted. The consonant /s/ is justified as it creates the necessary context for the raising of the preceding vowel; it is subsequently deleted by a general rule deleting all word-final obstruents. An analysis along these lines allows us to account for the alternation in *chłopie*[c] 'nom. sg.'—*chłop*[č]*e* 'voc. sg.' as the underlying representation /xolp+ik+e/ fails to evince the progressive palatalisation. In such cases the regressive front vowel palatalisation derives the surface [č].

There can be no argument **in principle** against phonological rules recapitulating historical changes, as obviously whatever exists synchronically must have arisen at some stage in the past. One wonders, however, why Lightner stopped at the Proto-Slavic forms rather than delving even

---

[3] He adds *Such an assumption is confirmed by the results of our work on Russian.* Lightner's study of Russian, published as Lightner (1972) applies the same methodology to Modern Russian (and partly also to Modern Turkish).

deeper into history. He could have suggested, say, that vowel tenseness be eliminated in favour combinations of lax vowels with laryngeals. Appropriate rules could clearly have been worked out and the system simplified even further.

Lightner's study would not merit much attention today were it not for the fact that it established the standard principles which all phonological descriptions of (parts of) Polish tried to meet or to challenge for the next thirty years. These include, among others, Paulsson (1974), Laskowski (1975), Gussmann (1978, 1980), Rubach (1984), and Bethin (1992). All the numerous published and unpublished accounts, no matter how concrete or abstract they otherwise may be, agree that at least some alternations involving palatals and palatalised consonants should be captured by means of rules. They thus view palatalisation as part of phonology and they differ in the extent to which palatalisation is held to be productive in Modern Polish: the general tendency is to restrict some of the phonological operations to morphological contexts, and to recognise more and more cases of underlying palatals and palatalised consonants. This is the position taken by Gussmann (1992); it is also represented by what is probably the most recent generative foray into Polish phonology, if not actually its swan song, i.e. Szpyra (1995). In the latter work a claim is made that palatalisation as a phonological process is restricted to the context of a following front vowel or palatal glide, while elsewhere the regularity is morphologised (p. 203). In this way, thirty years after Lightner's paper the investigation of Polish palatalisations has come a full circle, as it has virtually returned to its structural starting point: of the alternations in (4) only a tiny portion are ascribed to the phonology. A research project currently in progress (Cyran, Gussmann and Kaye, in prep.) which is based on the nonderivational Principles and Parametres approach,[4] takes the final step and argues that *none* of the alternations between hard and soft consonants in (4) are phonologically governed. In this way we return to the position of the early structuralists like Baudouin de Courtenay and Kruszewski and their 20th century followers. We may also note, with a sigh of relief, that the phonological system of Modern Polish is not the same as that of Proto-Slavic.

---

[4] The most important published accounts of the framework include Kaye, Lowenstamm and Vergnaud (1990), Charette (1991), Harris (1994), Brockhaus (1995); additional references can be found in these works.

PALATALISATION ALTERNATIONS AND THEIR STATUS

Linguists working within the generative tradition who tried to constrain the scope of phonological palatalisations did so for a variety of reasons. The most important of these was undoubtedly the difficulty of justifying certain abstract structures which are required in a number of cases. Note that reflexes of alleged instances of palatalisation can occur relatively freely within morphemes and words. Thus they are found not only before front vowels but also before back ones (6a), or before no vowel in particular (6b); in the latter case the palatalised consonant remains intact throughout the morphological paradigm even if it is followed by some other vowel (here -*e* represents the inflectional ending of the nominative singular).

(6)   a.   bu[t] 'shoe'   bu[ć]ik 'id. dimin.'   bu[ć]or 'id. express.'
          mło[d]y 'young'   mło[dź]eniec 'young man'   mło[dź]an 'id.'
          ban[d]a 'gang'   ban[dź]e 'dat. sg.'   ban[dź]or 'gangster'
          lo[d]y 'ice-cream'   lo[dź]arz 'ice-cream vendor'
          upar[t]y 'stubborn'   upar[ć]uch 'id. n. express.'
          zło[t]y 'golden'   zło[ć]utki 'id. dimin. express.'
          nu[d]a 'boredom'   nu[dź]arz 'a bore'
          tłu[st]y 'fat'   tłu[ść]och 'a fatty'

      b.   sło[v]o 'word'   przysło[v′]e 'proverb'
          gło[v]a 'head'   pogło[v′]e 'head of cattle'
          kło[s] 'ear of corn'   pokło[ś]e 'aftermath'
          lu[d]u 'people, gen. sg.'   odlu[dź]e 'seclusion'
          wo[z]u 'cart, gen. sg.'   podwo[ź]e 'chassis'
          ry[b]a 'fish'   bezry[b′]e 'absence of fish'

Examples can easily be multiplied (see Gussmann 1992, 23 ff.). Some strategy can be devised to accommodate palatalisation as a phonological process: one could say, for example, that the back vowel is preceded phonologically by a front one which is deleted after causing palatalisation. Alternatively one could say just as well that the palatalised consonant is not conditioned by the nature of the following vowel but rather is triggered by a specific set of suffixes, a solution which merely disguises the non-phonological nature of the alleged palatalisation. Finally, one could, quite simply, view the appearance of palatalised reflexes in some forms as a matter for the lexicon which is of no phonological consequence. This is the traditional solution, a solution which regards reflexes of palatalisation as something distinct from phonology.

Additional arguments for the traditional view are both phonological and morphological in nature. Let us review some of them.

Palatalised reflexes appear not only before back vowels as in (6), but also word-finally and before consonants.

(7) pła[k]ać 'to cry'   pła[č] 'crying, n.'
     jabł[k]o 'apple'   jabłe[č]nik 'apple-pie'
     ko[st]ka 'bone, dim.'   ko[śċ] 'id.'
     gło[s] 'voice'   gło[ś]ny 'loud'
     niedźwia[d]ek 'bear, dimin.' niedźwie[dź] 'id.'
     chę[t]ny 'willing'   chę[ċ] 'willingness'
     ko[n]ny 'equestrian'   ko[ń] 'horse'
     Londy[n] 'London'   londy[ń]ski 'id. adj.'
     cia[ł]o 'body'   cie[l]sko 'id. express.'

Another point worth mentioning here is the fact that at times the same suffix seems to appear after both a palatal(ised) and a non-palatal(ised) consonant. Consider the contrast in (8):

(8)   kwa[s] 'accid'   kwa[ś]ny 'sour'
         wyra[z]y 'words'   wyra[ź]ny 'clear'
     vs. mię[s]o 'meat'   mię[s]ny 'meaty'
         żela[z]o 'iron'   żela[z]ny 'id. adj.'

If the suffix -ny is to be marked as palatalising or if it is to contain a palatalising vowel, the lexicon will have to be invoked to decide whether a given derivative contains the palatalising or the non-palatalising suffix. In other words, -ny adjectives have to be entered in the lexicon. This is further confirmed by the non-compositional semantics of a great many of the -ny derivatives (as in our examples kwaśny, wyraźny). If the forms have to be listed in the lexicon, there is nothing surprising about the unpredictability of their phonological shape, i.e. the presence of soft or hard consonants.

The importance of the preceding example cannot be overemphasised: it is *not* the case that a specific suffix or set of suffixes causes palatalisation or fails to do so (cf. the English suffix -ity. This softens the preceding velar in words like domestic—domesticity, but there is no softening in kitty, where no suffix can be identified). The point about -ny is that it 'palatalises' the preceding consonant in some morphemes but not in others; it might be more appropriately said that the suffix -ny can be appended to both palatalised and non-palatalised bases, which is another way of saying that no palatalisation takes place. Obviously one can invent gimmicky solutions of the type that there are two -ny suffixes, one palatalising and one non-palatalising, or one containing a 'palataliser' in the form of a front vowel and another one without this element. Unless independent evidence can be produced to support the existence of two separate affixes, such a solution can hardly be seriously entertained. It should be noted further that there are quite a few suffixes which display this sort of Janus-like behaviour. The agentive suffix -*arz* can serve as another illustration.

As shown by Grzegorczykowa and Puzynina (1979, 286), the attachment of this suffix is regularly accompanied by the appearance of stem-final soft consonants in certain cases; in others hard consonants or both hard and soft consonants appear, depending upon the particular lexical item. There are individual derivatives where both soft and hard variants can appear, although usually one is more marked than the other (archaic, specialised etc.). Thus, /v´, f´, p´, ź, l/ appear invariably before -*arz*, which results in paradigmatic alternations:

(9)　　łyż[v]a 'skate'　　　　　　　łyż[v´]arz 'skater'
　　　　har[f]a 'harp'　　　　　　　har[f´]arz 'harpist'
　　　　knaj[p]a 'dive, low joint'　　knaj[p´]arz 'restaurant owner'
　　　　kob[z]a 'bag-pipes'　　　　　kob[ź]arz 'bag-piper'
　　　　myd[ł]o 'soap'　　　　　　　myd[l]arz 'soap-maker'

The velars /g/ and /χ/ always appear in their unmodified form before the suffix, which is also the predominant pattern with /k/ (10a). There are, however, eight derivatives where /č/ precedes the suffix (10b) and one with /c /(10c):

(10)　　a. sklepi[k] 'shop, dim.'　　sklepi[k]arz 'shop-owner'
　　　　　　pił[k]a 'ball'　　　　　　pił[k]arz 'ball-player'
　　　　　　dru[k] 'print'　　　　　　dru[k]arz 'printer'
　　　　b. mle[k]o 'milk'　　　　　　mle[č]arz 'milkman'
　　　　c. garne[k] 'pot'　　　　　　garn[c]arz 'potter'

Likewise, the remaining consonants can be either soft or hard before the suffix, e.g.: *karcz*[m]*a* 'inn'—*karcz*[m]*arz* 'inn-keeper' vs *rekla*[m]*a* 'advertisement'—*rekla*[m´]*arz* 'advertiser'; *gospo*[d]*a* 'inn'—*gospo*[d]*arz* 'inn-keeper' vs *lo*[d]*y* 'ice-cream'—*lo*[dź]*arz* 'ice-cream vendor'; *mo*[c] 'power'—*mo*[c]*arz* 'ruler' vs *ow*[c]*a* 'sheep'—*ow*[č]*arz* 'sheep-herd' etc. Note also the co-existence of unmarked *legen*[dź]*arz* 'legend collector' with the less frequent but completely well-formed *legen*[d]*arz*. These examples show that there is nothing either in the base or in the suffix which requires the presence or absence of palatalisation on the base final consonant—in other words, palatalisation is an accidental property of the consonant, in much the same way as voicing or plosiveness is. Thus the softness or hardness of the consonant is part of the lexical characterisation of a given base. Rather than looking for ways of patching up the cracks, we take examples like these as evidence that palatal and palatalised consonants are independent of the phonological context, i.e. their presence does not depend on the nature of the following vowel.

Yet another argument comes from the way we represent vowels alternating with zero, or the reflexes of the historical yers. As argued at length in Gussmann and Kaye (1993) and elsewhere, such vowels are best interepreted within a non-derivational framework as empty nuclei. Being empty they cannot contain features that would palatalise the preceding onset in some cases but not in others. The examples below show nouns containing such vowels alternating with zero. In some cases, (11a), the consonant preceding the alternating vowel would have to be a reflex of palatalisation, whereas in others (11b), no palatalisation would be involved:

(11) a. [če]ść 'honour'   [č]ci 'gen. sg.'
          [le]w 'lion'   [l]wa 'gen. sg.'
          [će]m 'moth, gen. pl.'   [ć]ma 'nom. sg.'

      b. [se]n 'sleep'   [s]ny 'nom. pl.'
          [łe]z 'tear, gen. pl.'   [ł]za 'nom. sg.'
          wę[ze]ł 'knot'   wę[z]ła 'gen. sg.'

Clearly the presence or absence of palatalisation on a given consonant is an individual property of that consonant alone rather than a result of its interaction with a following nucleus. Thus, we no longer regard the derivation of, say, /č/ or /c/ from /k/ or /ć/ from /t/ as a phonological phenomenon. Such alternations are a matter for the lexicon or morphology and have no place in phonology.

The case of Polish palatalisations seems representative of a large body of data that has occupied the attention of phonologists for the past three decades. The fact that at the end of that period we are forced to consider the approach fundamentally misguided is somewhat disheartening. On the negative side, the conclusion reached is fairly unimpressive and to many people pathetically obvious, namely, that grammatically conditioned sound alternations are not part of phonology. The same explicitness and analytic rigour that have become associated with generative linguistics can sometimes be used to promote artificial concepts and misleading directives. It remains to be seen whether the generative enterprise has just been a pointless detour, a phonological wild goose chase, or whether some of its results are there to stay. This is a question which requires a balanced account of the recent history of phonology and calls for a lengthy and impartial study.

REFERENCES

Bethin, Christina Y. 1992. *Polish Syllables. The Role of Prosody in Phonology and Morphology*, Slavica: Columbus, Ohio

Brockhaus, Wiebke 1995. *Final Devoicing in the Phonology of German*, Niemeyer: Tübingen

Carlton, Terence R. 1990. *Introduction to the Phonological History of the Slavic Languages*, Slavica: Columbus, Ohio

Charette, Monik 1991. *Conditions on Phonological Government*, Cambridge: University Press

Cyran, Eugeniusz, Gussmann, Edmund and Kaye, Jonathan in prep. *Polish Phonology: Principles and Parameters*

Grzegorczykowa, Renata and Puzynina, Jadwiga 1979. *Słowotwórstwo współczesnego języka polskiego. Rzeczowniki sufiksalne rodzime*, Warsaw: Państwowe Wydawnictwo Naukowe

Gussmann, Edmund 1978. *Contrastive Polish-English Consonantal Phonology*, Warsaw: Państwowe Wydawnictwo Naukowe

—1980. *Studies in Abstract Phonology*, Cambridge, Mass.: MIT Press

—1992. 'Back to Front: Non-linear Palatalisations and Vowels in Polish', in *Phonological Investigations*, ed. by Jacek Fisiak and Stanisław Puppel, Amsterdam: Benjamins, 5–66

Gussmann, Edmund and Kaye, Jonathan 1993. 'Polish Notes from a Dubrovnik Café. I: Yers', *SOAS Working Papers in Phonetics and Linguistics*, 3, 427–462

Harris, John 1994. *English Sound Structure*, Oxford: Blackwell

Kaye, Jonathan, Lowenstamm, Jean and Vergnaud, Jean-Roger 1990. 'Constituent Structure and Government in Phonology', *Phonology*, 7, 193–231

Laskowski, Roman 1975. *Studia nad morfonologią współczesnego języka polskiego*, Wrocław: Ossolineum

Lightner, Theodore, M. 1963. 'Preliminary Remarks on the Morphophonemic Component of Polish', *MIT Quarterly Progress Report*, 71, 220–23.

Lightner, Theodore, M. 1972. *Problems in the Theory of Phonology, I: Russian Phonology and Turkish Phonology*, Edmonton: Linguistic Research

Lunt, Horace G. 1981. *The Progressive Palatalization of Common Slavic*, Skopje: Macedonian Academy of Sciences and Arts

Paulsson, Olaf 1974. *Aspects of Polish Verb Morphology and Phonology*, Gothenburg: The University

Rubach, Jerzy 1984. *Cyclic and Lexical Phonology: The Structure of Polish*, Dordrecht: Foris

Szober, Stanisław 1923. *Gramatyka języka polskiego*, Lwów: Książnica Polska

Szpyra, Jolanta 1995. *Three Tiers in Polish and English Phonology*, Lublin: Wydawnictwo Uniwersytetu Marii Curie Skłodowskiej

Perlocutionary Cause and Effect

PHILIPPE HAMEL

University College, Dublin

IN THE research on Speech Acts, Perlocution has always attracted far less attention than Illocution. This imbalance may be due on the one hand to the fact that perlocutionary effects are felt to be infinite in number, unpredictable in quality, and on the other hand to a long linguistic tradition of investigation of isolated utterances produced by a single speaker. Seldom are the connections considered between the utterances of two speakers. Although the hearer is never absent from Speech Acts investigation, his role is never reversed: he never becomes a speaker. The purpose of this article is to consider the notions of perlocutionary intent, cause and effect to try and dispel some of the misconceptions concerning the unpredictability of perlocutionary effects.

Austin (1962) defines Perlocutionary Acts as the bringing about of effects on the hearer(s) by means of uttering a sentence: these effects being special to the circumstances in which the utterance is made. Perlocutionary effects can be:

—the mere understanding of what has been said with no further reaction,
—a wordless action of the hearer obeying the speaker's request,
—a refusal to pursue the conversation,
—an objection to the validity of the original speech act, etc.

Although all the above perlocutionary effects deserve proper investigation, the scope of this article will be limited to cooperative utterances, ie linguistically expressed responses made by the original hearer-turned-speaker. Such responses may exhibit discrepancies between the speaker's communicative intent and the perception of this intent by the hearer-turned-speaker. The explanation of these discrepancies will provide an account for the apparant unpredictability of perlocutionary effects.

Although bets, for example, require an uptake from the speaker to be validated, most illocutionary acts do not require specific responses to become felicitous. An order remains an order provided all its felicity conditions are fulfilled at the moment of utterance, even though the hearer never obeys it or does not even acknowledge it. A question does not need an answer to be a question. However each speech act has a point which is its speaker's communicative intention: he wishes by his utterance to elicit a desired response from the hearer, to create a specific perlocutionary effect. Thus obedience should ideally follow an order, an answer should follow a question, the recommended action should follow an advice, etc. Such ideal responses rarely occur in conversation because the hearer and the speaker do not necessarily share the same knowledge of the overall context or the same interest in the conversation.

Knowledge of context is the awareness of a certain set of extra-linguistic conditions, represented as propositions. that impinge on the overall meaning of the utterance and give it its illocutionary and perlocutionary forces. However, given a certain context and two individuals observing it and involved in conversation about it, it is not possible to maintain that these locutors possess two absolutely identical sets of conditions. Each may be aware of a number of conditions that the other does not know; each may grant certain conditions a degree of prominence not granted to them by the other; each may bring into the conversation outside information from his own store of personal knowledge. Although the two locutors trade on each other's knowledge to elaborate their conversation, it cannot be expected that they always operate in unison on the same quality and quantity of information. The ideal response to a question is an answer. But consider:

A1: Are you going to the party Saturday night ?
B1: May I bring a friend along ?

In this partial dialogue, a question follows another where an answer is expected. Yet the two locutors are still involved in the same conversation, discussing the same topic. They are still cooperating in Grice's sense of the term. B1 is not a refusal to provide an answer to A1, but a request for information to enable the speaker to provide an adequate response. The original question stays valid as long as B is unable to respond properly as demonstrated in the complete dialogue.

A2: Who do you have in mind ?
B2: Do you know Mary Smith ?
A3: You mean the tall girl with the long blond hair ?
B3: That's right.
A4: Bring her along.
B4: Fine, then I'll come to the party.

A2 to B4 are adjustments to achieve total match in contextual knowledge and assure that B responds adequately to A's initial perlocutionary intent. Refusal to obey a valid order is another case in point: conversationally, this is rarely done with a flat 'no'. The hearer-turned-speaker frequently offers some form of explanation, even though this explanation may be as insignificant as 'I won't' or 'I can't': these provide a new direction for the conversation, whereas a flat 'no' is often followed by a demand for justification or reiteration of the original order. A speaker issueing a greeting, to take a last example, ideally expects to be greeted in return or at least to receive some other form of acknowledgement; he objects and feels offended if he obtains no reaction. A hearer who correctly interprets the speaker's perlocutionary intent tends to respond to this intent: even in cases where an immediate response is not possible, the hearer-turned-speaker seeks means to preserve the relationship of cause and effect. It can be said that on the whole a speaker does receive the perlocutionary response that he strives to arouse: it is this faculty that makes language such a powerful tool to give orders, issue warnings, make threats, give advice, make promises, etc. Yet it happens that the speaker does not to achieve his perlocutionary intent.

Austin (1962, 147) insists that 'the total speech act in the total speech situation is the only actual phenomenon which, in the last resort, we are engaged in elucidating'. Consider the following hypothetical situation of an adventurous hiker looking for a short-cut and making ready to jump over a gate and into a field where a bull is grazing; the angry farmer intends to threaten the hiker into not crossing the field. To achieve his perlocutionary effect, the farmer has the choice among a vast range of sentences: he can explicitly warn the hiker of the danger, order or advise him not to cross the field, remind him that the bull is there, point out to him that the bull is ready to charge, promise him a good goring, etc. Yet the farmer chooses to say only this:

My bull is in this field.

With this utterance, the farmer literally commits himself to the truth of the proposition $\exists x \ \exists y \ ((B \ x + F \ y) \rightarrow I \ xy)$ in which 'B' stands for 'my bull', 'F' stands for 'this field' and 'I' stands for the two place predicate 'in' (The finer points of deixis can be neglected). On the basis of Grice's Cooperative Principle and the exploitation of the maxims of Quantity: 'Make your contribution as informative as is required for the current purposes of the exchange' and 'Do not make your contribution more informative than is required', the threat is implicated rather than directly uttered. The farmer is satisfied that he has said enough for the hiker to understand what he means. One should remember however that the speaker has no guarantee whatsoever that the hearer understands the same message as has been implicated: the speaker has no control over the implication he creates in the hearer's mind. The implicated meaning in our example could be expressed literally as: 'If you cross my field, my bull—for whose behaviour I am responsible—will attack you'. The farmer cannot possibly utter his threat as a direct speech act because there exist no grammatical IFIDs for a threat:

* I threaten you that if you cross my field my bull will attack you.

Along with such verbs as 'insult', 'frighten', 'persuade', 'amuse'and 'offend', 'threaten' is not an illocutionary verb, but a perlocutionary verb as demonstrated by applying Steven Davis's (1980, 49) test to it:

(i)   By Σ-ing X, S ß-s H Y.
(ii)   S's Σ-ing X, ß-s H Y.
(iii) H was ß-ed by S 's Σ-ing X.
       (where S stands for the speaker, H stands for the hearer, Σ ranges over illocutionary or propositional act verbs, and ß ranges over perlocutionary verbs).

(i)   By mentioning his bull, the farmer threatened the hiker.
(ii)   The farmer's mentioning his bull threatened the hiker.
(iii) The hiker was threatened by the farmer's mentioning his bull.

Any actual threat is thus veiled as a warning, an advice, a recommendation or a simple reminder. Indeed the strongest threat that the farmer can issue in this situation has the surface form of a warning:

—I warn you that if you cross my field, my bull will attack you.

Using the nomenclature provided by J.R. Searle (1969), a threat can be defined as follows:

Propositional content:	If a future action AH of H then a future action AS of S.
Preparatory conditions:	1: S believes H will do AH and S believes he can do AS.
	2: S believes AS will be detrimental to H.
Sincerity condition:	S does not want H to do AH.
Essential condition:	Counts as an attempt to stop H doing AH.

By AH read: 'The hiker crosses the field', and by AS read: 'The farmer— responsible for his bull's behaviour—will hurt the hiker'. All conditions pertaining to a threat are found in the conversational implicature created by 'My bull is in this field'.

In the same manner as the farmer could choose among a vast array of utterances to make his threat, so can the hiker select his reply among a large range of sentences, not only to signify that he is responding to a threat, but possibly to a multitude of other speech acts which it was never the farmer's intention to perform:

(1)   Don't you threaten me!
(2)   Thanks for the warning.

(3)   Thanks for the advice.
(4)   Nobody orders me about!
(5)   Congratulations!
(6)   Promises, promises! etc.

Whether the hiker responds facetiously to a correctly interpreted threat or genuinely to any other wrongly interpreted type of speech act, any one of these responses is an acceptable perlocutionary effect of the farmer's utterance: none creates a feeling of non-sequitur in the exchange.

(1) is only a token-response indicating that the hearer has understood the threat in spite of its being only implicated, not literally expressed. The hearer has perceived all the felicity conditions that constitute the threat and, whether he chooses to respect or ignore it, his perception of the speaker's perlocutionary intent is correct. The two sets of felicity conditions brought into consideration for the encoding and the interpretation of the speech act are identical.

By uttering (2) the hearer indicates that he is reacting not to a threat but to a warning. Searle (1969, 67) lists the conditions that go into making a warning as:

Propositional content: Future event or state, etc, E.
Preparatory conditions: 1: S has reason to believe E will occur and is not in H's best interes
                             2: It is not obvious to both s and H that E will occur.
Sincerity condition: S believes E is not in H's best interest.
Essential condition: Counts as an undertaking to the effect that E is not in H's best
                             interest.

In his comments Searle writes that a warning is not necessarily an attempt to get H to take evasive action. He also mention that a warning may be hypothetical: If you do (or do not do) X, then Y will (or will not) happen. A warning and a threat share a number of conditions:

—S informs H of the impending occurence of E (our AS),
—E will be detrimental to H,
—S does not want H to be hurt by E.

They also differ in one important respect: S's involvement in and responsibility for E. A threat is a warning with speaker's involvement in and responsibility for the impending event. By thanking the farmer for his warning, the hiker fails to (or pretends not to) notice these two conditions and to include them in his interpretation of the utterance.

By saying (3) the hiker clearly indicates that he is responding to an advice whose conditions are listed by Searle (1969, 67) as:

Propositional content:	Future act A of H.
Preparatory conditions:	1: S has reason to believe that A will benefit H.
	2: It is not obvious to both S and H that H will do A in the normal course of events.
Sincerity condition:	S believes A will benefit H.
Essential condition:	Counts as an undertaking to the effect that A is in H's best interest.

In his comments Searle mentions that 'advising is more like telling what is good for you'. Instead of insisting on the detrimental aspect of some future event E, an advice emphasizes the beneficial aspect of another event E'. If E is detrimental, it appears logical that non-E is beneficial to the hearer.

A threat, a warning and an advice are all announcements of impending events with consequences relevant to H; these events are not obvious to H but they are to S who presumably has H's best interest at heart. In each of these speech acts it is in H's best interest to heed S's announcement. On the other hand, these acts differ through S's degree of involvement and responsibility, and the harmfulness of E to H.

By saying (4), the hiker shows that he is reacting to an order which Searle (1969, 67) describes as a type of request:

Propositional content:	Future act A of H
Preparatory conditions:	1: H is able to do A. S believes H is able to do A.
	2: It is not obvious to both S and H that H will do A in the normal course of events of his own accord.
	3: S must be in a position of authority over H.
Sincerity condition:	S wants H to do A.
Essential condition:	Counts as an attempt to get H to do A.

Unlike threats, orders are not subjected to any preconditions: there is no need for H to behave in a certain manner for the order to apply. H has to submit to S's authority whose quality influences the nature of the order. In the case of a malevolent authority, an order may be felt as a threat: if the order is not heeded, retribution is meted out by S.

In responding to an intended threat as if it were a warning, an advice or an order, the hearer fails to include in his interpretation of the original speech act one or several of the felicity conditions that bunch together to define the threat. It may even happen that in this process of erosion the hearer rejects all these conditions and responds solely to the propositional content.

By replying (5) the hiker reacts to a propositional act of the farmer: a simple declaration whose truth is immediately verifiable and which—as far as the hiker is concerned—carries no conversational implicature. The hiker bypasses the implicated threat and indicates that he is responding with pleasure to some happy occurence concerning the farmer and reported by him: i.e. part of the propositional content of the speech act (the fact that the farmer owns a bull). None of the conditions constituting the threat have been perceived: the utterance is interpreted literally.

In addition to disregarding one or several felicity conditions in his interpretation of S's speech act, H may also introduce conditions which only he is aware of and which alter the nature of the act. In replying (6) the hiker introduces a distortion in the make-up of the implicated threat: he refuses to consider the future AS as detrimental to himself and on the contrary declares that AS would be desirable. He may be an amateur bull-fighter, have a death-wish or any other reason to enjoy E, but he is in possession of an extra element of which the farmer is unaware. Promises are defined as (Searle 1979, 44):

Preparatory condition:	S is able to perform A.
	H wants S to perform A.
Sincerity contition:	S intends to do A.
Propositional content:	S predicates a future act A of S.
Essential condition:	Counts as an undertaking by S of an obligation to do A.

The difference between a threat and a promise lies in the quality of the speaker's future action: if AS is harmful to H, the utterance is recognized as a threat; if AS is desirable to H, the utterance is interpreted as a promise. The evelution of the desirability of AS for H differs from one speaker to another, so changing the force of the original utterance and the nature of its intended perlocutionay intent.

The speaker who wishes to produce a certain perlocutionary effect on the hearer and elicit a specific reaction has no guarantee that the same felicity conditions which are present at the moment of encoding and utterance will be evident to the hearer at the moment of decoding. Any speech act—even preceded by an IFID that would literally name its illocutionary force—is subject to misinterpretation that can give rise to unexpected reaction. S and H can only concur about the literal meaning of S's speech act, but the context upon which they can base a common opinion regarding its accompanying felicity conditions is often a shifting ground. H may disregard some felicity conditions, he may even add a few of his own, but he can only respond to the act that he has perceived, not necessarily to the act that it was S's intention to perform. Perlocutionary cause and perlocutionary effect are separated by the distance between two minds at variance with each other.

BIBLIOGRAPHY

Austin, John 1962. *How to Do Things with Words*, Cambridge, Mass.: Harvard
University Press

Davis, Steven 1980. 'Perlocution', in *Speech Act Theory and Pragmatics*, ed. by J.
Searle, F. Kiefer and M. Bierwisch, Dordrecht: D. Reidel, 37–55

Grice, Paul 1975. 'Logic and Conversation', in *Speech Acts* (*Syntax and Semantics*, III),
ed. by P. Cole and J. Morgan, New York: Academic Press, 41–58

Levinson, Stephen 1983. *Pragmatics*, Cambridge: University Press

Schiffrin, Deborah 1994. *Approaches to Discourse*, Oxford: Blackwell

Searle, John 1969. *Speech Acts*, Cambridge: University Press

—1979. *Expression and Meaning*, Cambridge: University Press

Wardhaugh, Ronald 1985. *How Conversation Works*, Oxford: Basil Blackwell

Speech and Silence in the Irish-Language Class

JOHN HARRIS & LELIA MURTAGH

Institiúid Teangeolaíochta Éireann

1. INTRODUCTION

TEACHERS have always been concerned with the extent to which pupils involve themselves in the lesson in progress: how frequently different individuals volunteer answers or comments, how closely they attend to ongoing activities, and the quality and accuracy of their contributions. In second and foreign language classes, the contributions of pupils have had an even more important role, in so far as pupil speech is seen as providing both the evidence of, and the mechanism for, language learning. More recently, teacher and pupil language-use has caught the attention of researchers in a new way as the emphasis in classroom second-language learning research shifted from the study of teaching methods to a concern with the relationship between different kinds of classroom discourse and successful language learning (Chaudron, 1988; Ellis, 1994; Allen & Carroll, 1988; Allen, Swain & Harley, 1988).

Despite the perceived importance of pupil talk in the second-language classroom, research indicates that, as in the case of *first* language classrooms, it is teachers who tend to do most of the talking. About two thirds of classroom speech can be attributed to the teacher, mostly as soliciting and reacting moves, with students uttering most of the responding moves (Bialystok, Frohlich & Howard, 1978; Ramirez, Yuen, Ramey & Merino, 1986). Furthermore, pedagogic discourse appears to be more restricted than naturalistic discourse (Ellis, 1994; Kasper, 1986; Pica & Long, 1986). In particular, the proportion of unpredictable and sustained speech in the L2 classroom seems to be very small (Allen & Carroll, 1988). The nature and length of pupil discourse, of course, will be determined in many instances by the kinds of questions asked. Studies have found that 'display' questions are more common than 'referential' questions in second language classrooms, in comparison with out-of-class interactions between native and non-native speakers (Long & Sato, 1983; White & Lightbown, 1984; Early, 1985; Ramirez et al, 1986; and Johnston, 1990). Display questions are those to which the answer is already known by the teacher. They are characteristic of language practice or form-focused activities and typically elicit short predictable answers from pupils. Referential questions, in contrast, are associated with real communication and with tasks involving meaning negotiation and they tend to elicit more complex output from pupils (Ellis, 1994).

Another traditional concern of language teachers which has attracted the attention of researchers in recent years is the nature and extent of pupil participation in classroom discourse and its relationship to eventual achievement in the target language. The evidence in the international literature relating to this question, however, is conflicting. Studies by Seliger (1977), Naiman, Frohlich, Stern & Todesco (1978) and Strong (1983; 1984) report positive correlations between various measures of learner participation/output (e.g. actual speech, amount of verbal interaction, hand-raising) and second language proficiency. Other researchers (Day, 1984 and Ely, 1986), however, have found no such relationship. Even where positive correlations have been established, however, the question of whether increased second-language proficiency results from more production, or vice versa, remains unanswered. Another aspect to the relationship between pupil ability in the target language and pupil participation in class relates to the frequency with which teachers use questions to elicit responses from different pupils. Mizon (1981) and Early (1985), for example, found that teachers used more questions with students who are not native speakers than with students who are native speakers. One possible explanation for this is that questions may facilitate interactions involving less proficient students by clearly establishing both the topic and who is expected to speak next (Chaudron, 1988).

A third aspect of classroom discourse which has attracted attention in recent years is the extent to which the learner is exposed to *comprehensible input* (Krashen, 1985). According to Krashen's model, humans acquire language by understanding messages rather than by consciously focusing on form. The model also posits a mental screen between the learner and the environment, a screen which is activated by affective factors (e.g. anxiety, self confidence) and which controls the amount of input a pupil converts into intake. In order for comprehensible input to result in successful language acquisition, therefore, the learner must be 'open' to the input or have a 'low affective filter'. To be maximally effective, the input must also contain a new aspect of the language which the learner has not yet acquired but is ready to acquire (Krashen, 1991). Thus, the quality of pupil attention and interest, as well as appropriateness of language content and context, may be important predictors of success in second language acquisition.

The present paper examines some of these issues of classroom language use and pupil participation in the context of the teaching and learning of Irish at sixth grade in primary school. It reports on a direct classroom observation study of language use by pupils during the regular Irish lesson. In particular, we concentrate on (a) pupil speech and silence (b) the communicative features of pupil utterances and (c) variations in language use and attentiveness in pupils with different levels of ability in Irish. The study is part of a larger investigation into the teaching and learning of Irish in twenty primary schools nationally. While the number of classes involved is not large, they do represent the full range of social and educational circumstances under which Irish is taught at present. They also represent all levels of achievement in spoken Irish and, as a group, the classes depart relatively little from the national average in terms of achievement in spoken Irish, general academic ability and social class (Harris & Murtagh, 1996).

2. METHOD

2.1 Subjects

Sixth-grade classes in each of twenty schools nationally were involved in the study. Full details may be found in Harris & Murtagh (1996). Within each class, one pupil of high ability in Irish, one of middle ability in Irish and one of low ability in Irish was randomly selected. In this way, pupils of different ability levels in Irish and from different types of classes contributed to the picture of pupil language use which finally emerged. The initial categorisation of pupils as high, middle and low ability in Irish was done by the class teacher. An observer then randomly selected one pupil from each of the three ability groups to be the focus of study. The observers were all primary school inspectors of the Department of Education. In each class, two inspectors worked side by side, one using the *Pupil Communicative Behaviour Record* (see below), which provides the data for the present paper, and the other using a different instrument which provided a record of language-teaching activities. Teachers participated in the study on an entirely voluntary basis.

2.2 Procedure

The inspector observed the selected pupils, one at a time in succession, and recorded various aspects of the behaviour of each pupil. This record was made by placing ticks in the appropriate columns of an A3 size coding sheet which listed the behavioural categories and sub-categories of the *Pupil Communicative Behaviour Record (PCBR)*. The *PCBR* is based in part on the *COLT (Communicative Orientation of Language Teaching)* system (Allen & Carroll, 1988). A full description of the categories of the *PCBR*, as well as directions for carrying out the observation work, were given in a manual which had been previously studied by the observers and which could also be referred to during the observation work itself (see Harris & Murtagh, 1996). The observers had earlier been involved in a training session during which the coding schedules and method of categorising and recording behaviours were explained in detail.

The observation work proceeded in 5 minute sequences, with the first three minutes being given over to observing the target pupil, and the last two minutes being used to record more fully his/her behaviour on the coding sheet. Two full lessons were observed. The lessons ran for varying lengths of time in different schools and covered all aspects of Irish—listening, speaking, reading and writing. The same three pupils were observed in Lesson 1 and Lesson 2.

Within any one three-minute observation period, it was possible that more than one type of pupil behaviour would occur. For example, a pupil might be engaged in a question-and-answer type spoken interaction with the teacher in the first minute of the observation period, after which there might be a whole-class choral response, followed by yet another exchange between the same pupil and his/her teacher in the last minute of the observation period. In such a case, three different pupil behaviours would be coded for that observation period. The observer would code each new behaviour by drawing a line within the row for that unit on the *PCBR* record sheet and placing ticks in the relevant categories for each new behaviour. Thus, the number of pupil behaviours recorded for each lesson is substantially greater than the number of observation units.

2.3 Instrument

The *PCBR* defined behaviour under three main headings: *(1) Pupil speaks individually, (2) Pupil is silent* and *(3) Other pupil behaviour*. Behaviours under each main heading could be coded in relation to a range of descriptive categories:

(1) Pupil speaks individually
Language used: 'Irish' was ticked if the utterance was in Irish or mostly in Irish, and 'English' if the utterance was in English or mostly in English.
Question: This category was relevant if the pupil asked a question. There were two options—'Pseudo' and 'Genuine'. 'Pseudo' would be the appropriate option where the question was only posed as part of a drill or some other practice (and the answer to it was, therefore, highly constrained and predictable). The 'genuine' question option might be ticked when the pupil, for example, having been reading, decides on his/her own initiative to ask the teacher for an explanation of some word he/she did not understand.
Answer: This category was ticked if the pupil answered a question, and was coded as 'predictable' or 'unpredictable'.

Length of utterance: The sub-categories here were 'one word', 'clause', 'sentence', and 'sustained' and were intended to measure the extent to which the pupils engaged in extended or restricted discourse.

Takes turn: This category was intended to capture the situation where the pupil took the initiative in some fundamental way, departing from the formal agenda of the lesson to some extent (asking questions or making comments unprompted by the teacher). These could consist either of (a) question-forms or phrases which might be used routinely in class communication but which in the specific instance observed were not related to the ongoing lesson or (b) 'new' or original contributions.

Interaction type: Each pupil's spoken contribution was coded in relation to one of two sub-categories, 'pupil-pupil' or 'pupil-teacher'.

(2) If the pupil is silent (or engaged in non-task related pupil-pupil exchange)

This main heading was relevant if the pupil was silent during a particular activity e.g. listening more or less attentively. Being silent does not include engagement in any 'Other' behaviour such as silent reading or writing (see below). This heading was also relevant if the pupil was not actually engaged in any formal language activity or task but was chatting to neighbouring pupil(s) (i.e. non-task-related exchanges). There were two categories to be ticked in the case of 'Silent' behaviours: 'Attending' (High/ Moderate/ Low) and 'Disruptive' (High/ Moderate/ Low). In the case, for example, where a pupil was not engaged at all in the task, but was chatting loudly to his/her neighbours, the rating might consist of ticking 'Low' for 'Attending' and Moderate' or 'High' for 'Disruptive'.

(3) Other pupil behaviour

There were four categories under this heading: 'Choral speech', 'Reading silently', 'Reading aloud', and 'Writing'. Only one of these four would be ticked for a particular pupil behaviour. We will not be considering behaviours in these four categories in the present paper.

3. RESULTS

In general, we analysed the observers' record of pupil behaviour using *PCBR* as it was presented to us, resorting to interpretation only in the relatively small number of cases where coding appeared to be inconsistent or ambiguous. Details of the types of problems encountered and how they were dealt with may be found in Harris & Murtagh (1996). It should be noted that no specific guidance was given about the simultaneous use of the major headings 'Pupil speaks individually' and 'Other' pupil behaviour. In the event, the observers opted to represent some 'Complex' pupil behaviours by placing ticks in categories under both these main headings.

For example, in one case a target pupil who was part of a group engaged in a discussion had also been assigned to make written notes on what was happening. Thus, the observer recorded a series of ticks under the major headings of both 'Other' pupil behaviour and 'Pupil speaks individually'.

3.1 The Analysis

The main data presented here consist of the relative frequency of occurrence of different categories of pupil behaviour (aggregated over classes and pupils). We use Chi square to test for differences in the distribution of these frequencies. Frequency of behaviours rather than of observation units is used as the dependent variable, because using units involves some loss of information in cases where more than one behaviour occurs during the observation period. Chi-square statistics are quoted here primarily as a means of distinguishing between more important and less important trends in the data for these particular pupils and classes. Reporting these statistics should not be seen as implying any claims about the population of schools and classes generally.

3.1.1 Frequency Of The Main Categories Of Behaviour

Table 1 shows the distribution of pupil behaviours according to the main language/communication categories of the *PCBR*.

TABLE 1

DISTRIBUTION OF PUPIL BEHAVIOURS ACCORDING TO LANGUAGE/COMMUNICATION
BEHAVIOURAL CATEGORY.

BEHAVIOURAL CATEGORY	NUMBER OF BEHAVIOURS (N)	PERCENTAGE OF BEHAVIOURS
1. *Individual only* (Pupil speaks individually)	324	41.6
2. *Complex* (Pupil speaks individually and also reads or writes.)	64	8.2
3. *Other only* (Pupil is engaged in choral speech, reading or writing but excluding 1 & 2 above).	233	29.9
4. *Silent* (Pupil is silent)	157	20.2
Total	778	100%

About one fifth of the behaviours (20.2%) consist of the pupil being 'Silent', presumably listening/looking. About half the behaviours involve the pupil speaking individually (i.e. composed of 41.6% of cases where the pupil simply speaks individually and another 8.2% of 'Complex' behaviours where the pupil speaks while also being involved in 'Other' activities such as writing). A little less than a third of behaviours (29.9%) are classified as 'Other only' (i.e. choral speech, reading or writing apart from 'Complex' behaviours).

These results indicate a high level of overt, definite pupil participation in class. While pupils remain silent, without being involved in any other behaviour, for one fifth of the units, data presented below indicate that they were most often listening with a moderate or high level of attention during these periods. For the rest of the time, they were switching in and out of different forms of participation—speaking individually or chorally, reading, or writing. In particular, there is a high level of individual spoken contributions by pupils.

3.1.2 Individual Pupil Speech

Tables 2–5 provide a more detailed analysis of various characteristics of pupils' individual spoken contributions—the general communicative function of their utterances and to whom they spoke (to other pupils or to the teacher). We also examine the manner in which these utterance characteristics vary with ability in Irish.

3.1.2.1 Pupil ability in Irish: Table 2 shows the distribution of instances of the pupil speaking individually according to his or her ability in Irish. It can be seen that while 61.6% of all behaviours recorded for 'higher ability-in-Irish' pupils involve the pupil speaking individually, only 36.3% of the behaviours of pupils with a lower level of ability in Irish involve individual speech. A Chi-square analysis confirms that the frequency of the pupil speaking individually is distributed significantly differently over the three ability levels in Irish (Chi square = 34.4; df=2; p<.001).

Table 2 also shows that more behaviours of all kinds are recorded for 'higher ability in Irish' (40.9%) compared to 'middle' (31.9%) and 'lower ability-in-Irish' (27.2%) pupils. This unequal distribution of behaviours is due to the fact that in each lesson the 'higher ability-in-Irish' pupil was always observed first in each lesson. The unequal distribution does not affect the validity of our conclusions, however, since it is taken into account in comparing the proportion of behaviours in different categories associated with pupils of different ability levels in Irish.

TABLE 2

PERCENTAGE DISTRIBUTION OF INSTANCES OF PUPIL SPEAKS INDIVIDUALLY *
ACCORDING TO PUPIL'S ABILITY IN IRISH (N = 60 PUPILS)

PUPIL ABILITY IN IRISH (as rated by teacher)	*Pupil speaks individually* n=388	*Pupil does* **not** *speak individually* n=390	*Total* (n = 778)
Higher	61.6	38.4	40.9
Middle	46.4	53.6	31.9
Lower	36.3	63.7	27.2
Total	49.9	50.1	100%

PERCENTAGE OF BEHAVIOURS

* Almost always in Irish. Includes *Complex* behaviours.

3.1.2.2 Length of utterance in Irish: Table 3 shows the distribution of instances of the pupil speaking individually according to (a) length of utterance (word, clause, sentence, sustained) and (b) pupil ability in Irish.

TABLE 3

PERCENTAGE DISTRIBUTION OF INSTANCES OF PUPIL SPEAKS INDIVIDUALLY
ACCORDING TO LENGTH OF UTTERANCE AND PUPIL ABILITY IN IRISH.

PERCENTAGE OF BEHAVIOURS

PUPIL ABILITY IN IRISH	*Length of utterance*				
	One word n=70	*Clause* n=56	*Sentence* n=198	*Sustained* n=50	*Total** (n=374)
Higher	20.3	15.1	48.4	16.1	51.3
Middle	16.7	16.7	56.5	10.2	28.9
Lower	17.6	12.2	59.5	10.8	19.8
Total	18.7	15.0	52.9	13.4	100%

*'Length of utterance' was not recorded for a further 14 instances of 'Pupil speaks individually'.

It can be seen (last row, Table 3) that only 13.4% of all spoken utterances are longer than a single sentence (i.e. 'sustained'). Most utterances (52.9%) are one sentence long, while just under one fifth (18.7%) consist of no more than one-word. Regarding pupil ability in Irish, a Chi-square analysis confirms what is already clear from an inspection of Table 3—that there is no significant relationship between the pupil's proficiency in Irish and the length of his/her spoken contributions (Chi square=5.03; df=6; NS). In other words, while pupils with higher ability in Irish are more likely to speak individually in class, as we have just shown, they are no more likely than less able pupils to speak at greater length on each occasion. One possible interpretation of this is that the kind of exchanges which are possible or expected are so constrained by the lesson format itself—by the form of the teacher's language or by precedent within the class—that being of higher ability in Irish, being capable for example of more sustained contributions, is irrelevant.

3.1.2.3 Interaction type

Table 4 presents further data on individual spoken contributions, this time focused on the participants and on the language chosen.

TABLE 4

LANGUAGE USED IN PUPIL-PUPIL AND PUPIL-TEACHER INTERACTIONS.

| | PERCENTAGE OF BEHAVIOURS | | | |
| | Interaction type | | | |
LANGUAGE	Pupil-pupil (n=50)	Pupil-teacher (n=316)	Interaction type not recorded (n=22)	Total (n=388)*
Irish	70.0	94.0	95.5	91.0
English	12.0	5.7	4.5	6.4
Half & half	6.0	0.3	-	1.0
Language not recorded	12.0	-	-	1.5
Total	12.9	81.4	5.7	100%

*Includes *Complex* behaviours.

The table consists of a crosstabulation of 'Interaction type' ('pupil-pupil' or 'pupil-teacher') and the amount of Irish used ('Irish', 'English, or 'half-Irish and half-English'). The first thing to be noted is that Irish (or mostly Irish) is the predominant language choice in all interactions (91% of interactions are in Irish). While 18% of 'pupil-pupil' lesson-related interactions are in English (or 'half-and-half), however, only 6% of 'pupil-teacher' interactions are in English. We exclude from the analysis of 'Language used' informal non-task-related chatting/gossiping among pupils—coded as 'Silent' behaviour in the present study—which is almost certainly conducted in English. In the case of a further 12% of 'pupil-pupil' interactions, the language used was not recorded—presumably because the observer could not hear the dialogue in question.

The Chi-square analysis carried out involves combining the 'English' and 'half and half' language categories in order to obtain satisfactory cell frequencies. The result confirms that the language used is distributed differently in pupil-pupil and pupil-teacher interactions (Chi square=9.31; df=1; p<.01). Pupils more often use some English when talking to each other in a *lesson* context than when they are talking to the teacher— although as we have just pointed out, use of Irish is quite high overall (over 90%) in lesson-related interaction.

A Chi-square analysis, not shown here, showed no evidence that the likelihood of 'pupil-pupil' interactions as opposed to 'pupil-teacher' interactions occurring was affected by the pupils' ability in Irish (Chi square = .02; df = 2; NS).

3.1.2.4 Type of utterance

Table 5 shows the distribution of instances of the pupil speaking individually according to the kind of utterance involved—(a) questions (b) answers or (c) as instances of the pupil taking the initiative in a more fundamental way (i.e. 'takes turn').

The most frequent type of pupil utterances were answers. It may be seen that roughly two thirds (65.2%) of utterances involve the pupil making a 'predictable answer' (mostly, presumably, to teacher questions). A further 17.5% of utterances were rated as 'unpredictable answers'. Thus, 82.7% of all exchanges consisted of the pupil answering. Less than 4% of utterances were coded as pupil questions, a little less than half of these (1.8%) being considered 'genuine' (as opposed to 'pseudo' questions which are posed as part of language practice or formal exercises of some kind).

In an apparent misunderstanding of our definition of 'Takes turn', observers sometimes placed ticks in this category as well as one or other of the adjacent 'Asks a question' and 'Answers' category. Filtering out those behaviours which were included in more than one category, we found that only 3.1% of utterances could be unambiguously interpreted as evidence of the pupil taking the conversational initiative (i.e. 'Takes turn'). Because of this ambiguity, we will not be basing any of our conclusions on the 'Takes turn' data.

Due to the small number of pupil behaviours in the 'Question' sub-category, it was not feasible to examine differences in the distribution of pupil behaviours in the 'Answer' and 'Question' categories according to pupil ability.

Finally in this respect, looking at the last row of Table 5, it can be seen that just under a tenth (9.5%) of all individual pupil utterances were not assigned to any of the three main categories ('Question', 'Answer' or 'Takes turn').

TABLE 5

DISTRIBUTION OF INSTANCES OF 'PUPIL-SPEAKS-INDIVIDUALLY' ACCORDING TO THE TYPE OF PUPIL CONTRIBUTION.

| TYPE OF UTTERANCE | PUPIL SPEAKS INDIVIDUALLY | | |
	n	Percentage of behaviours	Total %
Pupil 'Answer'			
'predictable'	253	65.2	
'unpredictable'	68	17.5	82.7
Pupil 'Question'			
'pseudo'	8	2.1	
'genuine'	7	1.8	3.9
Both 'Answer' & 'Question'	3	0.8	0.8
Pupil 'Takes turn'*			
'routine'	5	1.3	
'new'	7	1.8	3.1
None of the above	37	9.5	9.5
Total	(388)	100%	100%

* Other than those behaviours already coded under 'Answer' and 'Question' above.

3.1.3 Silence

3.1.3.1 Ability in Irish and silent behaviours

Table 6 shows that pupils who are of 'lower' ability in Irish are more than twice as likely (31.6%) to be silent as pupils who are of 'higher' ability in Irish (12.6%). A Chi-square analysis confirms that the tendency to remain silent is distributed significantly differently across ability levels in Irish (Chi square=28.58; df=2; p< .01).

In cases where pupils remained silent for the whole observation unit (not shown here in tabular form) we again found that the tendency to remain silent varied significantly with ability in Irish—pupils who were of lower ability in Irish stayed silent for the whole unit in 23.6% of cases whereas pupils who were of higher ability in Irish stayed silent for the whole unit in only 8.2% of cases (Chi square = 24.2, df=2, p<.01).

TABLE 6

PERCENTAGE DISTRIBUTION OF INSTANCES OF 'PUPIL IS SILENT' ACCORDING TO TEACHER'S RATING OF PUPIL ABILITY IN IRISH.

| PUPIL ABILITY IN IRISH | PERCENTAGE OF PUPIL BEHAVIOURS | | Total |
	Pupil is 'Silent' (n=157)	'Rest' of pupil behaviours (n=621)	(n=778)
Higher	12.6	87.4	40.9
Middle	20.2	79.8	31.9
Lower	31.6	68.4	27.2
Total	20.2	79.8	100%

3.1.3.2 Ability in Irish and attentiveness

Table 7 shows that low levels of attentiveness to the lesson are relatively uncommon, occurring in just 15.4% of all behaviours where pupils are silent.

TABLE 7

LEVELS OF ATTENTIVENESS ASSOCIATED WITH *SILENT* BEHAVIOUR AS A FUNCTION OF PUPIL ABILITY IN IRISH.

| PUPIL ABILITY IN IRISH | PERCENTAGE OF BEHAVIOURS | | | Total |
	High attention n=62	Moderate attention n=70	Low attention n=24	n=156
Higher	62.5	27.5	10.0	25.6
Middle	40.0	48.0	12.0	32.1
Lower	25.8	53.0	21.2	42.3
Total	39.7	44.9	15.4	100%

It also shows the distribution of different levels of attentiveness during silent periods according to pupil ability in Irish. It can be seen that in more than three-fifths of those cases (62.5%) where 'high-ability-in-Irish' pupils are silent, a high level of attention to the Irish lesson is exhibited. During similar silent periods involving 'low-ability-in-Irish' pupils, however, a high level of attentiveness is exhibited in only a quarter of the cases (25.8%). A chi-square analysis based on all silent behaviours confirms that there is a significant difference in the distribution of attention levels across levels of ability in Irish (Chi square=14.8; df=4; p<.01).

When we limited our analysis to instances where pupils were silent for the whole observation unit the same pattern emerges i.e. higher attention levels among the 'higher ability in Irish' pupils (Chi square 6.75; df=2; p <.05). In other words, whether we look at all silent behaviours, or just those silent behaviours which last for the whole 3 minute observation unit, higher levels of attention to the lesson are characteristic of pupils with higher levels of ability in Irish.

4. DISCUSSION

One of the more important findings of the study is that about half of all behaviours recorded during the three minute observation period consisted of the pupil speaking individually—and in Irish in 91% of the cases. This finding is of interest in the light both of the focus in the primary school curriculum on developing competence in speaking the language, and the fact that the Irish class in ordinary schools is the main, and sometimes the only situation where we can be absolutely sure that the majority of pupils actually use the language. This is not to disregard the fact either that Irish is often used to a limited extent for routine communication in ordinary schools (Harris, 1984; Irish National Teachers Organisation, 1985) or that a small minority of parents use Irish at home. The finding is also important to the extent that many teachers and parents would probably consider a high rate of individual spoken contributions by pupils as evidence of the general vitality and success of the Irish lesson.

Any satisfaction we might feel at the fact that pupils speak individually so frequently during the Irish lesson must be tempered, however, by three other findings of the study (1) that pupil speech is not produced very often in the context of real communication or of meaning negotiation (2) that the frequency of individual speech is not at all evenly distributed over different kinds of pupils in the classroom and (3) that those with lower levels of ability in Irish who remain silent are less attentive to the lesson than those with higher levels of ability in Irish who remain silent. We will now look at each of these issues in more detail.

Regarding the first point, it may be noted that individual pupil speech most frequently took the form of answers (82.7% of all utterances) and these were in general short, predictable responses to 'display' questions from the teacher, something which is characteristic of language practice rather than real communication or meaning negotiation. The fact that a substantial proportion of the utterances were so short, however, raises doubts about their effectiveness, even as language practice. Only 13.4% of pupil utterances were sustained beyond the single-sentence level and 18.7% consisted of just single words. While the remaining 67.9% of utterances consisted of clauses or whole sentences, even this may give a somewhat misleading impression of the linguistic sophistication of pupils' responses. This is because of the pedagogic practice in Irish language classrooms, as in classrooms generally, of requiring pupils to incorporate part of the teacher's question or prompt into their answers in order to make a complete sentence. On the positive side, it must be acknowledged that the proportion of sustained utterances which were recorded in this study probably does not represent a particularly low proportion for a non-immersion classroom—it certainly compares very favourably with a study of French *immersion* classrooms where less than 15% of student turns were coded as sustained (Allen, Swain & Harley, 1988). Answers consisting of sustained pupil utterances in the present study, incidentally, were much more likely to be coded as 'unpredictable' (i.e. occurring in the context of meaning-negotiation) than were shorter answers consisting of a single word, a clause or a sentence.

The second aspect of the high frequency of individual pupil speech in Irish which is undesirable is that its occurrence actually varies substantially and to a statistically significant degree according to the ability of the individual pupil in Irish. For example, only 36.3% of the behaviours of pupils who have lower levels of ability in Irish involve individual speech, compared to 61.6% of the behaviours of pupils with higher ability in Irish. If frequent individual speech really is conducive to an improvement in the pupil's command of Irish, then it seems as if those most in need, pupils with lower levels of ability in the language, are the ones least likely to be engaged in it.

What are pupils with lower ability in the language doing while those with a better command of Irish are engaging in individual speech interactions? There are two indications, one indirect, the other direct, that they are listening/looking rather than engaging in some other language-learning task more in tune with their particular level of ability in Irish. First, we know from other kinds of observation data collected in the course of this study (Harris & Murtagh, 1996) that the most common form of classroom organisation during the Irish lesson is 'whole class' and that the most common teacher mode of involvement with the class is 'interacting'. Thus, on the basis of this information alone, it is unlikely that pupils with lower levels of ability in Irish will be engaged in different individual tasks (involving silent reading or writing, for example) or working in pairs or groups on language or communication tasks. In fact, regarding this last point, it may be noted that only 12.9% of individual pupil speech behaviours, and only 6.4% of all pupil behaviours, involve pupil-pupil exchanges. The second kind of evidence that those with lower levels of ability are listening/looking while the more able pupils make individual spoken contributions is the finding that pupils who are of lower ability in Irish are more than twice as likely to be silent as pupils who are of higher ability in Irish, and this difference is statistically significant.

This brings us to a third difficulty—that the silence of 'lower-ability-in-Irish' pupils is not the same as the silence of 'higher-ability-in-Irish' pupils. Pupils with higher levels of ability-in-Irish are much more likely than pupils with lower levels of ability in Irish to be rated as 'highly attentive' during these periods of silence. Likewise, low levels of attention are more common in pupils with lower levels of ability in Irish.

Before considering possible ways to change this situation, assuming that change is feasible, it may be useful to consider briefly some of the factors which may lie behind the emphasis on individual speech in the Irish lesson and the uneven participation by pupils. This exploration is necessarily speculative since we have no information from teachers about the strategies they may have been pursuing, or even whether they were aware of the variation in participation which we discovered. Nevertheless, we hope that our observations may at least serve as working hypotheses which might be tested in future studies.

Listening to the tape recordings of the lessons made by the observers and examining the transcripts of these (Harris & Murtagh, 1996), the impression is compelling that an important secondary goal of teachers in so frequently soliciting individual spoken contributions from pupils may simply be to maintain attention to the lesson more generally. In other words, the actual language practice provided by these exchanges is only part of the desired result—equally important is producing a high level of expectation among individual pupils that they will be nominated to speak. The brevity of the exchanges which are typical of the Irish lesson means that individual pupils can be required to speak at just about any time. In this situation, it may not matter too much that the content of display questions do not engender a high level of interest per se among pupils, since their attention is guaranteed by the high likelihood of having to 'perform'.

The problem for pupils who are weaker at Irish is that, for whatever reason, they seem to have a much lower probability of either being asked to perform or of volunteering to perform. Without the same motivating force of imminent public performance as the more able pupils have, lower ability pupils are probably more dependent on the intrinsic interest of the lesson material to keep them engaged—an interest which may not be high when 'display' type questions predominate. Admittedly, there is a possibility that some instances of 'silence' on the pupil's part may actually consist of an inability to respond (orally) to a question or prompt from the teacher, rather than from non-involvement, disinterest or actual resistance. Since we only observed and recorded the pupil's behaviour and speech, and not the teacher's, we have no way of identifying which instances of silence consist of a failure to respond. The evidence we have presented that lower-ability-in-Irish pupils are not as attentive as higher-ability pupils during periods of silence, however, seems to undermine the notion that inability could be sufficient general explanation for the observed differences in speech and silence.

Another perplexing issue is who ultimately determines how often pupils speak: the teacher or the pupil? Are teachers the more important in this respect, in that it is they who nominate the pupils to speak? Or is it the pupils themselves who play the larger part in determining their own selection by volunteering to answer? As mentioned earlier, the evidence in the international literature concerning the relationship between pupil participation and second language development is conflicting (Seliger 1977; Naiman, Frohlich, Stern & Todesco, 1978; Strong, 1983, 1984; Day, 1984 and Ely, 1986). Ellis (1994), reviewing these studies alongside others relating to the effect of quantity of practice on specific grammatical structures believes that, on balance, the interpretation that 'proficiency causes participation' is more plausible.

Even if Ellis is correct—and the correlational evidence is ambiguous—this does not mean either that teachers of Irish routinely leave it up to weaker pupils themselves to decide on their own level of participation in class, or that lower levels of participation by weaker pupils can be attributed to any oversight or lack of effort on the teacher's part. It is plausible to think that in making decisions about which pupil to nominate to speak, teachers are trying to achieve an optimum balance between a range of concerns—e.g. not slowing the class down too much; ensuring that there is a high proportion of successful (correct) public exchanges in Irish in order to provide a good language model for pupils in general, and so on. Teachers may also be trying to take account, for example, of the discomfort for weaker pupils of being nominated to speak in situations where their is a high probability that their answer, or failure to answer, will expose them to embarrassment. Teachers may feel that certain weaker pupils will do better at Irish in such circumstances by listening to the (linguistically correct) public exchanges involving the more able pupils. Again, it must be borne in mind that these are only speculations and that much more wide-ranging research would be needed to establish the connections between pupil behaviour and teachers' strategies.

While acknowledging this kind of complexity in classroom processes and teachers' decisions, are there any suggestions which could be made for changing some of the negative outcomes we have documented in this study? For example, taking the typical existing Irish lesson as given for a moment (i.e. a lesson which is highly teacher-focused, has a 'whole-class' form of classroom organisation, and is primarily concerned with language practice) can the problem of differential participation and attentiveness be tackled? Findings from studies in other countries may be of some help here, particularly in those cases where silence arises from inability or difficulty in answering rather than from disengagement and disinterest. A number of researchers claim that in cases where a spoken response is called for, a greater 'wait-time' will result in longer pupil utterances as well as an increase in the participation of less able pupils (Holley & King, 1971; White and Lightbown, 1984; Long, Brock, Crookes, Deicke, Potter & Zhang, 1984). Holley & King propose at least a five-second wait and report that that teachers in third-level German classes who waited that long obtained an increase in responses following initial hesitations. Long et al (1984) suggest that additional wait-time should allow second-language students a better opportunity to construct their response. White & Lightbown (1984) point out that teachers in their study rarely gave enough time for students to formulate answers before repeating, rephrasing or redirecting the question to another student. The shorter the wait time, however, the fewer and the shorter the student responses. They found three secondary ESL (English as a second language) teachers asking up to four questions per minute with overall about 40% of the questions receiving no response and up to 64% being repetitions of previous questions, with as many as nine repetitions of the same question. They claim that the success rate of students responding to subsequent repetitions of questions was quite low, lower often than rate of response to questions asked only once. Of course, this may simply mean that easy questions are answered quickly, without being redirected, while the redirected difficult questions continue to pose problems for students.

In any case, there are probably limits to the extent to which the participation of pupils with lower levels of ability in Irish can be improved without relaxing some of the other constraints imposed by existing lesson structures. Even if increasing wait time does help less able pupils, it may pose new problems of lesson dynamics in a situation where the engagement of pupils is primarily maintained by the fast pace of the ('display') question-and-answer exchanges, rather than by the inherent challenge or interest offered by the lesson material itself. Thus, a more basic change in direction seems to be needed, most plausibly towards the so-called 'communicative approach'. This refers to the general view that understanding and communicating messages in the target language is more important than linguistic form, and to a constellation of proposals that have evolved from research and practice over the last 20 years. These proposals include a greater emphasis on real communication, the use of authentic texts, communicative tasks involving meaning negotiation, situations and contexts of language use which reflect pupils' real-life experience and interests, and learning and interacting in smaller groups.

Since we cannot discuss all these issues in any detail here, let us simply take 'small-group' or 'pair' work as an example of what communicative language teaching might entail. Increasing the proportion of class time devoted to small-group work should increase the amount of individual pupil speech occurring in more one-to-one communicative activities, thereby reducing the need for such a high rate of individual pupil speech in a whole-class context. This more private and negotiable context of language use should also reduce some of the social risk for less able pupils who wish to make use of whatever Irish they have. Long & Porter (1985) summarize the main pedagogic arguments in favour of group work—it increases language practice opportunities, it improves the quality of student talk, it helps to individualise instruction, it promotes a positive affective climate and it motivates learners to learn. There is also evidence that small-group work provides more opportunities for meaning negotiation if the tasks are of the required 'information-exchange' type (Pica & Doughty, 1985; Ellis, 1994). Long, Adams, McLean & Castanos (1976) also found that small groups provided more opportunities for language production and a greater variety of language use in initiating discussion, asking for clarification, interrupting, competing for the floor and joking. The quality of interaction appears to be enhanced if the learners comprising the pair/group are heterogeneous with regard to sex and proficiency level. It is also interesting to note that the results of a study by Porter (1986) show very little evidence that learners pick up each others linguistic errors. Some caution in relation to group work, however, is suggested by Wong-Fillmore's (1982) longitudinal study using qualitative research methods.

Adopting a more communicative approach to teaching Irish may be desirable not just for the sake of those pupils who have difficulty with Irish at present. In all probability, existing classroom learning conditions also have limitations—albeit of a different kind—for pupils with higher levels of ability in Irish. Some results of the present study, for example, suggest that pupils' contributions in class may be so strongly governed by the form of the teacher's questions or prompts, that the higher level of ability in Irish possessed by many of them is not reflected in the content of utterances. For example, despite the strong association between ability and frequency of individual pupil speech found in this study, no association was found between ability and length of utterance. While acknowledging that it is always problematical to try to assign a 'positive' interpretation to the acceptance of the null hypothesis, a strong expectation of a difference does seem reasonable in this case i.e. other things being equal, more able pupils should produce more sustained utterances than less able ones. If what we are suggesting is actually true, it means that not only are existing lesson structures producing a certain kind of frustration in more able pupils, but the more extended and enriched linguistic input which such pupils might otherwise be expected to produce is denied to all pupils.

Recently, ITÉ carried out a project in association with the Irish Curriculum Committee of the National Council for Curriculum and Assessment which tried to chart the kind of change in direction which might be needed (Harris, Uí Dhufaigh, Ó Néill and Ó Súilleabháin, 1996). The project involved applied linguists working side by side with teachers to produce sample teaching materials which it is hoped represent a better balance between language practice and communicative activities than exists in the present courses. In devising these materials, considerable use was made of the results of the larger research study on which the present paper is based. Initial reaction to the new materials among teachers appears to be positive. Quite aside from the merits or otherwise of these particular materials, however, there is some evidence that language practice and communicative activities are complementary and that they provide essential support for each other in the language classroom (Allen, Swain & Harley, 1988).

What we are proposing here, then, is not a revolution, not a wholesale replacement of existing practices, but simply the beginning of a change in direction. It would be foolish, in particular, to undervalue what has been achieved and is being achieved with existing approaches (Harris, 1993). We have already documented some of the positive outcomes of Irish language teaching in primary schools, particularly the fact that most pupils have an opportunity to speak Irish of some kind quite often. And anyone who is familiar with Irish language classrooms will have been impressed by the energy, fluency and pace of the typical Irish lesson at present. Thus, the advantages and disadvantages of change will have to be carefully weighed. Ultimately, it is teachers themselves who will decide how far it is desirable to go in this new direction, and indeed there is no reason why there should not be considerable variation from teacher to teacher in the extent to which the communicative emphasis is incorporated into a new approach.

ACKNOWLEDGEMENTS

We are greatly indebted to the teachers and pupils who participated in this study and to the Primary School Inspectors of the Department of Education who carried out the observation work.

REFERENCES

Allen, Patrick and Carroll, Suzanne 1988. 'Analytic and Experiential Dimensions in Core French Classrooms', *The Canadian Modern Language Review,* 45, 43–64

Allen, Patrick, Swain, Merrill, and Harley, Birgit 1988. 'Analytic and Experiential Aspects of Core French and Immersion Classroom', *Bulletin of the CAAL,* 10 (2), 59–68

Bialystok, Ellen, Frohlich, Maria and Howard, J. 1978. 'Variables of Classroom Achievement in Second Language Learning', *Modern Language Journal,* 62, 327–335

Chaudron, Craig 1988. *Second Language Classrooms: Research on Teaching and Learning,* Cambridge: University Press

Day, Richard 1984. 'Student Participation in the ESL Classroom or some Imperfections of Practice', *Language Learning,* 34, 69–102

Early, M. 1985. 'Input and Interaction in Content Classrooms: Foreigner Talk and Teacher Talk in Classroom Discourse', Ph.D. dissertation, University of California at Los Angeles

Ellis, Rod 1994. *The Study of Second Language Acquisition,* Oxford: University Press

Ely, Christopher 1986. 'An Analysis of Discomfort, Risktaking, Sociability, and Motivation in the L2 classroom', *Language Learning,* 36, 1–25

Harris, John 1984. *Spoken Irish in Primary Schools,* Dublin: Institiúid Teangeolaíochta Éireann

—1993. 'An Ghaeilge Labhartha sa Ghnáthscoil: Fadhbanna is Féidearachtaí sa Ré Nua', *Teangeolas,* 33, 50–59

Harris, John and Murtagh, Lelia 1996. *An In-Depth Study of the Teaching and Learning of Irish at Sixth Grade in Twenty Schools Nationally* (provisional title)

Harris, John, Uí Dhufaigh, Máire, Ó Néill, Pádraig and Ó Súilleabháin, Eoghan 1996. *Cúrsaí Nua Gaeilge na Bunscoile. Imleabhar* I 7 *Imleabhar* II, Dublin: Institiúid Teangeolaíochta Éireann

Holley, Freda M. and King, Janet K. 1971. 'Imitation and Correction in Foreign Language Learning', *Modern Language Journal,* 55, 494–498

Irish National Teachers' Organisation 1985. *The Irish Language in Primary Schools: Summary of the Main Findings of a Survey of Public Attitudes by the Market Research Bureau of Ireland.* Dublin: INTO

Johnston, M. 1990. 'Teacher Questions in the Academic Language-Content Classroom', unpublished paper, Tokyo: Temple University

Kasper, Gabriele, ed. 1986. *Learning, Teaching and Communication in the Foreign Language Classroom,* Aarhus: University Press

Krashen, Stephen 1985. *The Input Hypothesis: Issues and Implications,* London: Longman

—1991. 'The Input Hypothesis: An Update', in *Georgetown University Round Table on Languages and Linguistics 1991,* ed. by James E. Alatis, Washington, DC: Georgetown University Press, 409–31

Long, Michael and Porter, Patricia 1985. 'Group Work, Interlanguage Talk, and Second Language Acquisition', *TESOL Quarterly,* 19 (2), 207–28

Long, Michael and Sato, Charelene 1983. 'Classroom Foreigner Talk Discourse: Forms and Functions of Teachers' Questions', in *Classroom-oriented Research in Second*

Language Acquisition, ed. by Herbert Seliger and Michael Long, Rowley, Mass.: Newbury House, 268–86

Long, Michael, Brock, Cindy A., Crookes, Graham, Deicke, Carla, Potter, Lynn and Zhang, Shu-qiang 1984. *The Effect of Teachers' Questioning Patterns and Wait-Time on Pupil Participation in Public High School Classes in Hawaii for Students of Limited English Proficiency*, Technical Report No 1, Honolulu: Centre for Second Language Classroom Research, Social Science Research Institute, University of Hawaii at Manoa

Long, Michael, Adams, Leslie, McLean, Marilyn, and Castanos, Fernando 1976. 'Doing Things with Words: Verbal Interaction in Lockstep and Small Group Classroom Situations', in *On TESOL '76*, ed. by John Fanselow and Ruth Crymes, Washington DC: TESOL, 137–53

Mizon, S. 1981. 'Teacher Talk: A Case Study from the Bangalore/Madras Communicational ELT Project', M.A. Thesis, University of Lancaster, England

Naiman, N., Fröhlich, M., Stern, H., and Todesco, A. 1978. *The Good Language Learner. Research in Education Series No 7*, Toronto: The Ontario Institute for Studies in Education

Pica, Teresa and Doughty, Catherine 1985. 'The Role of Group Work In Classroom Second Language Acquisition', *Studies in Second Language Acquisition Research*, 7, 233–48

Pica, Teresa and Long, Michael 1986. 'The Linguistic and Conversational Performance of Experienced and Inexperienced Teachers', in *Talking to Learn: Conversation in Second Language Acquisition*, ed. by R. Day, Rowley, Mass.: Newbury House, 85–98

Porter, Patricia 1986. 'How Learners Talk to Each Other: Input and Interaction in Task-Centred Discussion', in *Talking to Learn: Conversation in Second Language Acquisition*, ed. by R. Day, Rowley, Mass.: Newbury House, 200–22

Ramirez, J.D., Yuen, S.D., Ramey, D.R., and Merino, B. 1986. *First Year Report: Longitudinal Study of Immersion Programs for Language Minority Children*, Arlington, Va.: SRA Technologies

Seliger, Herbert 1977. 'Does Practice Make Perfect? A Study of the Interaction Patterns and L2 Competence', *Language Learning*, 27, 263–78

Strong, Michael 1983. 'Social Styles and Second Language Acquisition of Spanish-Speaking Kindergarteners', *TESOL Quarterly*, 17 (2), 241–58

—1984. 'Integrative Motivation: Cause or Result of Successful Second Language Acquisition?', *Language Learning*, 34, 1–14

White, Joanna and Lightbown, Patsy 1984. 'Asking and Answering in ESL Classes', *Canadian Modern Language Review*, 40 (2), 228–44

Wong-Fillmore, Lily 1982. 'Instructional Language as Linguistic Input: Second Language Learning in Classrooms', in *Communicating in the Classroom*, ed. by Louise Wilkinson, New York: Academic Press, 283–96

Variation in Early Irish Linguistic Terminology

PATRICIA KELLY
University College, Dublin

THE OLD IRISH glosses on the St Gall manuscript of Priscian's *Institutiones Grammaticae* constitute a substantial body of evidence for the creation of a Latin-based linguistic terminology in Irish in early medieval times. According to Professor Ó Cuív's analysis (1966, 155), the technical terms in the glosses have a threefold classification. In the first place, an Irish gloss can be macaronic, incorporating Latin words in an otherwise Irish frame. Secondly, Latin terms can be adapted as phonetic borrowings. The third and final category is that of native Irish words which are presssed into service to accommodate new technical meanings. This classification could be understood as reflecting degrees of assimilation to Irish.

The three categories are not mutually exclusive, as the same Latin term can be treated in more than one way. For example, the Latin word can appear in both uncompromisingly 'foreign' and partially 'native' guise. Thus Latin *pronomen* 'pronoun' falls into the first of Ó Cuív's three categories in *huare nengraicigetar pronomina anman cach folaid* 'because pronouns take the place of nouns of every substance' (Sg. 200 b 5), but is inflected like an Irish noun in the next gloss: *robo opronoibneib foilsigdde phersin frecṅdairc* 'either by pronouns which demonstrate a present person' (Sg. 200 b 6). Further, while some phonetic borrowings are fully assimilated to the native declensional system, Thurneysen (1946, 191) notes that others remain uninflected in the singular. Nevertheless, loan-words in general 'were adapted as far as possible to the Irish language' (Thurneysen 1946, 573). This study will examine how a number of the basic Latin terms required for linguistic analysis are adapted to the model of Irish words, and propose that the existence of variants gives an insight into the process of 'vernacularization'.

Latin *grammatica*, for example, occurs in two forms. The Carlsruhe glosses on Augustine[1] have *dán inna grammatic* 'the art of grammar' (Acr. 13 b 1), which Thurneysen (1946, 192) interprets as an uninflected *i*-stem. The standard manuscript orthography of Early Irish suggests that the last two consonants have the phonetic values /d/ and /g/. The voicing of the Latin stops reflects the influence of British Latin (cf. Welsh *gramadeg*). Modern Irish *gramadach* confirms the quality of the medial dental but differs with respect to the final. Precursors of the modern form, in which

---

[1] The bulk of these are considered to date to the ninth century (Stokes and Strachan 1903, ix).

the ending has been assimilated to the native adjectival ending in -*ach*, can be seen in *grammataig* (acc. sg. of a feminine *ā*-stem) in the *Eulogy of Colum Cille* (Best and Bergin 1929, 39.1148)[2] and *gramatach* in the commentary to the early linguistic treatise *Auraicept na n-Éces*[3] (Calder 1917, 173.2342).[4]

A comparison with the treatment of a morphologically similar Latin borrowing may be instructive. Latin *dialectica* appears as *dialectic* (Wb. 30 b 11), which matches *grammatic* exactly in the representation of Latin -*ica*. A gloss in a different collection features a geminated final consonant in *dudialecticc* 'to dialectic' (Acr. 13 b 3), which may indicate that the guttural stop is unvoiced. Here it is likely that we have a late learned borrowing, so that the -*cc* of the Irish has the same phonetic value as in Classical Latin -*ica*. A more obviously nativized form is also recorded in Middle Irish, in the commentary to the *Auraicept*, where it is coupled with the similarly inflected *grammatica*: *eter gramadaigh ⁊ dileachtaigh* (Calder 1917, 6.51) 'both grammar and dialectic'. These two examples point to at least two phases of vernacularization, whereby phonetic borrowings underwent more than one stage of adaptation to native models. In the case of *grammatica*, however, the more assimilated form is already attested in a very old text.[5]

It is well-known that a recurring item in many of the early Latin grammars, including that of Priscian, was the analysis of the letters of the alphabet into vowels and consonants, semi-vowels, liquids and mutes. Many of the Old Irish equivalents for the Latin terms are recorded in the St Gall glosses, with some variation.[6] 'Vowel' for example is expressed by two different loan-translations on Latin (*littera*) *vocalis*, both being derivatives of the native word for 'voice'. These are (1) *guttae* < *guth* + adjectival ending -*dae*, and (2) *guthaigthe*, a participial formation of a non-attested verb *guthaigidir* (Ó Cuív 1966, 156). This variation is reflected in the word for 'semi-vowel' also, for which the St Gall glosses have both *lethguttae* and *lethguthaigthe*. The Old Irish stratum of the *Auraicept* has only *guttae*, though the later commentary features *guthaige* (< *guth-*

---

[2] As this text is generally considered to have been written not long after the death of Colum Cille in 597, Ó Cuív (1966, 158) considers that this may be the 'oldest recorded instance of a borrowed linguistic term' in Irish.

[3] The oldest stratum in this text has been ascribed to a 'fairly early stage of the Old Irish period' (Ahlqvist 1983, 36). The extensive commentary is in Middle Irish.

[4] A variant reading *gramadach* (Calder 1917, 6.54) has the modern representation for the intervocalic voiced dental.

[5] See further McManus 1984, 140–141.

[6] These glosses do not form a homogeneous collection, but are drawn from various sources of different age (Stokes and Strachan 1903, xxiii).

aig(th)e) and also another adjectival formation *guthach* (Calder 1917, 28.365).

A comparison between the St Gall glosses and the *Auraicept* reveals another instance of variation in this lexical field, in the Irish word for (*littera*) *muta* 'mute'. This is consistently *mút* in St Gall, a feminine *ā*-stem. In the *Auraicept*, however, it is an *i*-stem (Ahlqvist 1983, 58), and the spelling *mu(i)tti* for the nominative plural (Calder 1917, 34.446, 451), if it is old, could suggest a voiceless dental.

In default of the evidence of metrical examples or modern pronunciation to enable us interpret the spelling, there remains the final recourse to later texts. Three late tracts on the alphabet have survived. Two have been published: Meyer 1918 (M) and Ahlqvist 1987 (A). The third has been identified in the Trinity College Dublin manuscript No. 1337, H.3.18, p. 414 (Ahlqvist 1983, 16) (H), the greater part of which is also found in the Royal Irish Academy Stowe manuscript C i 2, f. 39a (C). All agree with the *Auraicept* against St Gall in treating the Irish for 'mute' as an *i*-stem, but the agreement does not extend to the phonology. Where M has *t* (*muit* and *muiti*), A has *d* throughout (*muid, muidi, muidibh*). The two versions of the third tract diverge also: H has consistently *t*, while C has *d*. These spellings may either reflect a mixture of the old and new orthography in the representation of intervocalic and final stops, or they could also indicate varying pronunciations, and thus perhaps different borrowings.

For (*littera*) *liquida* 'liquid' A uses the term *leaghtach* or *leachtach*.[7] These are reflexes of the earlier *lechdach* in the St Gall glosses,[8] and *legtachaib*[9] in the commentary to the *Auraicept*. This borrowing belongs to the third of Ó Cuív's categories, as it is an adjectival formation based on the verbal noun *legad* of Old Irish *legaid* 'melts': the starting point can be seen in the St Gall gloss *dliged lechtha ·n· post ·m* 'the law of the liquidation of *n* after *m*' (11 b 2). In the third tract (H/C), C breaks off before this point, so there is only the evidence of H. Here we find a marked divergence from A in that the term used is one which is not otherwise attested: the forms are sg. *licit* and *licid*, pl. *liciti*.[10] This appears to represent a phonetic borrowing of Latin *liquida*.[11] The lack of vowel affection from the Latin -*a* suggests that it is a learned form. Given that this type of analysis of the

---

[7] There is no treatment of the liquids in M.

[8] The variation recalls that in OIr. *machthad, magthad, machdad,* MIr. *machtad* 'object of wonder' (Thurneysen 1946, 89)

[9] Sic leg. (*DIL* L 69.79).

[10] The manuscript reading is *lethciti*: I am assuming that this is a mistake, under the influence of the preceding *lethguta*.

[11] The Vulgar Latin pronunciation would have been /likida/ (McManus 1983, 36).

letters of the alphabet is not a central interest in the Early Modern Irish grammatical tracts, and that there are other indications[12] that this is a modernization of an older text, it is unlikely that *licit/licid* is a new formation. I suggest that we have here Early and Early Modern Irish spellings respectively of an Early Irish learned phonetic borrowing *liccit*, with final voiced dental stop. In *liccit* and *lechdach* 'liquida' we may therefore have another pair which reflect different solutions to the problem of the creation of an Early Irish linguistic terminology.

BIBLIOGRAPHY

Ahlqvist, Anders 1983. *The Early Irish Linguist*, Helsinki: Societas Scientiarum Fennica

—1987. 'An Irish Text on the Letters of the Alphabet', in *Studies in Honour of René DEROLEZ*, edited by A.M. Simon-Vandenbergen (Ghent: Dept. of English and Old Germanic Philology) 3–16

Best, Richard Irvine and Bergin, Osborn, eds. 1929. *Lebor na hUidre*, Dublin: Royal Irish Academy

Calder, George, ed. 1917. *Auraicept na n-Éces*, Edinburgh: John Grant

McManus, Damian 1983. 'A Chronology of the Latin Loan-Words in Early Irish', *Ériu*, 34, 21–69

—1984. 'On Final Syllables in The Latin Loan-Words in Early Irish', *Ériu*, 35, 137–162.

Meyer, Kuno 1918. 'Vom Buchstaben', *Zeitschrift für celtische Philologie*, 12, 294–5

Ó Cuív, Brian 1966. 'Linguistic Terminology in the Mediaeval Irish Bardic Tracts', *Transactions of the Philological Society*, 1965, 141–164

— 1980. 'Irish Words for "Alphabet"', *Ériu*, 31, 100–110

Stokes, Whitley and Strachan, John 1901–1903. *Thesaurus Palaeohibernicus*, I–II, Cambridge: University Press

Thurneysen, Rudolf 1946. *A Grammar of Old Irish*, Dublin: Institute for Advanced Studies

[12] I hope to deal with these in an edition of this text, which contains some very interesting Latin material, already noted in Ahlqvist 1983, 16.

Notes de celtibère

PIERRE-YVES LAMBERT

C.N.R.S., E.P.H.E.

1. CELTIBÈRE *osCuez*

LA THÉORIE de Francisco Villar sur la valeur de -*z* final est maintenant confortée par de véritables preuves : comme il l'a écrit dans son dernier livre[1], le deuxième bronze celtibère de Botorrita (BB III) apporte la preuve qu'il faut traiter différemment la désinence -*as*, génitif singulier de thème en -*ā*, réservée sur BB III à des noms de personnes, et rencontrée à la place du patronyme au génitif dans les dénominations personnelles, et la désinence en -*az*, réservée à des noms de ville sur BB III, fréquente sur les monnaies à la fin d'un nom de ville, et vraisemblablement issue d'un ablatif singulier -*ād*.

Dans son livre, F. Villar étend largement cette explication de -*z* final issu de -*d*, aux dépens d'une autre explication qu'il admettait auparavant dans un plus grand nombre de cas, un -*z* final issu d'un ancien -*s*- intervocalique, mais qui serait devenu final par chute de la voyelle finale. Les formes en -*uz* sont donc des ablatifs thématiques (anciennement -*ōd*)—sauf dans *rusimuz*, BB I, les formes en -*ez* sont des ablatifs de thèmes consonantiques, sauf quelques cas comme *oscuez* ou mieux *osCuez*.

Je crois nécessaire de souligner l'importance de cette double découverte : d'une part Francisco Villar apporte une solution élégante au problème des deux sifflantes, et d'autre part il introduit une hypothèse tout à fait inattendue pour les langues celtiques, en supposant l'existence d'un ablatif en celtibère, ablatif constitué de façon parallèle à celui du latin. Je ne suis pas sûr cependant que nous devions accepter les exceptions relevées par Francisco Villar au principe que tout -*z* final soit issu d'un -*d* final. Il me semble que *osCuez* lui aussi admet une explication par un -*d* final.

Bien sûr, F. Villar a envisagé cette solution, mais il considérait une telle forme avec -*d* uniquement comme un cas de pronom neutre nom.-acc. sg. Or ce pronom neutre aurait plutôt un autre vocalisme, soit *k^wid, soit *k^wod, et il serait d'après lui trop hypothétique de supposer en plus un changement de *k^wid en *k^wed : c'est, d'après lui, une explication ad hoc. Il ne manque pas cependant d'argumenter en faveur de cette explication, avant de l'abandonner : l'existence d'ablatifs en -*iz* tirés de thèmes en -*i*-

---

[1] Villar 1995.

bref comme *orosiz* n'est pas une objection si l'on admet un allongement du -*i*- dans cette désinence d'ablatif, -*īd*, comme c'est le cas en latin.

De fait, la raison principale pour laquelle F. Villar renonce à l'explication par -*d* final est syntactique : il lui paraît nécessaire d'avoir à cet endroit du texte un pronom au nominatif singulier masculin, et non pas neutre. Il préfère donc supposer un ancien *os-kʷesi. Les reconstitutions proposées auparavant par Joseph Eska et Wolfgang Meid sont tout à fait comparables.

En fait, en traduisant *osCuez* par 'quiconque', les précédents commentateurs ont tous accepté l'idée qu'il fallait ici la présence d'un relatif indéfini, équivalent du lat. *quicumque*. Il s'agit vraisemblablement de prescriptions, que l'on a isolées avec au début *uTa osCuez* (répété) = ut quicumque, et avec un verbe à la fin, *uerzoniTi*, *amPiTiseTi*. On peut citer comme exemples les trois traductions les plus récentes, Eska 1989, Eichner 1989, Meid 1993 :

> *uTa osCuez sTena uerzoniTi,*
> 'and whoever carries out these things' Eska 1989, 20
> 'und wer immer in irgendeiner Weise dagegen verstösst (oder : wer [...] benützt)', Eichner 1989, 53
> 'wer immer aber diese (Verbote) übertritt', bzw. 'wer immer aber derartige (Tätigkeiten) durchführen möchte', Meid 1993, 46.

> *uTa osCuez PousTom-ue Coruinom-ue maCasi(a)m-ue ailam-ue amPiTiseTi,*
> 'and let him rebuild the cow stable or (animal) enclosure or wall (of an enclosure) or (outer ?) wall, (i.e. whatever it should be)' Eska 1989, 21.
> (Zweite Sanktionsformel, wegen Errichtung landwirtschaftlicher Baulichkeiten) Eichner 1989, 53.
> 'wer immer aber einen Rinderstall oder eine (Pferde)koppe oder eine Umwallung oder einen Understand errichten möchte', Meid 1993, 50.

Pour cette dernière phrase nous souscrivons volontiers à l'interprétation commune à Eichner, Meid et plusieurs autres : le sens doit être que quiconque construit un bâtiment doit aussi ouvrir un chemin d'accès. Deux détails appellent une remarque : *MaCasi(a)m* est très certainement un dérivé de *magos, gén. *magesos 'champ' ; je pense qu'il s'agit du correspondant exact de v.irl. *macha*, *magesiā, 'enclos pour le bétail', cf. le dérivé *machaire*. *AmPiTiseTi* doit donc être plutôt un verbe signifiant 'enclore'.

Il est proposé ici de retrouver dans le celtibère *os-Cuez*, deux particules *os et *kʷed, qu'il est possible d'isoler en celtique insulaire. Seul le vieil-irlandais conserve la première, comme coordonnant, et il présente aussi la seconde dans l'adverbe *ced* 'même'. Il peut lui aussi combiner ces deux éléments, mais dans l'ordre inverse, *cid-os* (+ pronom personnel), ex. *cid-os-ní* 'nous-mêmes, nous aussi'.

1) *os* est un coordonnant archaïque attesté dans deux emplois principaux :

a) coordonnant de phrase devant une conjonction temporelle ou conditionnelle (*os mani* ..., Lois);

b) coordonnant introduisant une proposition sans verbe ('phrase nominale') avec sujet pronominal ; l'ordre est toujours : coordonnant *os* + pron. personnel 'sujet' + nom ou adjectif prédicat, ou autre complément prédicativé.

Ced 'même', a une variante fréquente *cid* ; il semble plus ou moins confondu avec *cid* (*k^wid) forme neutre de l'interrogatif *cia*, avec lequel il est parfois difficile de le distinguer.

Ce *k^wed pourrait être présent dans l'expression du relatif indéfini :

1) en brittonique, on utilise le pronom interrogatif suivi d'un mot invariable, gall. *bynnag*, bret. *bennag* ; *k^wed expliquerait bien la formation de brittonique *pynnag*, *k^wed-na-k^we avec fermeture ultérieure du *-e-* intérieur en *-i-* devant le groupe *-dn-*, comme dans *$sento$- > gall. *hynt* 'chemin'. (*$na-k^we$ à comparer probablement au thème indéfini *$ne-k^wos$, 'quiconque').

2) pour l'expression du relatif indéfini en irlandais ancien, on a le choix entre diverses combinaisons du pronom interrogatif avec le subjonctif du verbe être[2] :

> *cía bé a mmét* 'quelle que soit sa quantité' Ml. 61 b 28
> *cip cruth* 'de toute façon' Wb., *cip cenél* 'quelle que soit la nation'
> Wb. 3 b 20.

cía bé et *cip* se sont confondus en *cipé*, souvent analysé comme s'il contenait le pronom masculin (= *ci-p-é*), ce qui est probablement erroné.

Vieil-irlandais *cip* s'explique certainement par une combinaison de *cid* et de *-b* copule au présent du subjonctif, 3 sg. Doit-on voir dans ce *cid* le neutre de l'interrogatif ou un élément adverbial identique à *ced* 'même'? J'opterais pour la deuxième solution. Il n'y a pas de doute dans l'emploi particulier suivant:

---

[2] Nous laisserons de côté les expressions consistant dans le pronom *k^wo-/*k^wei- ou *so-* suffixés par -k^we, + une particule relative (*cecha-*, *sechi-*, Thurneysen 1946, 289–290). La valeur généralisante de -k^we est exactement celle que l'on retrouve dans lat. *quisque, quicumque* (ombr. *pisipumpe*).

> *ced molad ced tatháir beraid-si domsa is beicc limsa a brig*, Wb.
> 8d21, 'que ce soit louange ou blâme que vous me donniez, j'y attache
> peu d'importance'.

Je pense que *osCuez*, lui aussi répété a exactement la même valeur : 'et si
c'est [...] et si c'est' (*os* coordonnant, *k^wed* particule de sens conditionnel).

   Cid, *ced* peut venir de *k^wed*, instrumental du thème relatif, avec sens
indéfini (de quelque façon que ce soit, *quācumque*). Mais ce pourrait être
aussi bien deux particules associées, *k^we* et *de*. Ces deux éléments sont
peut-être ceux qui apparaissent dans l'adverbe lat. *quidem* 'justement'.
L'origine de la particule *os* du vieil-irlandais est tout à fait obscure. Il est
sûr en tout cas qu'il ne s'agit pas d'une abréviation du coordonnant
habituel *ocus*.

   On peut regretter qu'il n'y ait plus aucun élément fléchi dans la séquence
osCuez : (équivalent donc au lat. *etsi*) mais le vieil-irlandais n'a pas de
pronom relatif et une telle situation devait être commune aux langues
celtiques depuis très longtemps.

2. CELTIBÈRE *TuaTe[r]es, TuaTeros* (BB III)

Francisco Villar propose d'identifier, dans *TuaTeres* (nomin. pl.) et
TuaTeros (gén. sg.), le nom indo-européen de la 'fille', *dhughH-ter-*. Cela
n'est pas irrationnel : le mot est associé à celui du fils dans le contexte,
Centisum TuaTerosCue 'des fils (gén.pl.) et de *TuaTer*' (BB III, III–24).

   Mais cette forme est bien curieuse : pourquoi le -g- intervocalique serait
disparu dans cette seule forme, alors qu'il est parfaitement conservé dans
des mots celtiques bien connus comme *Segobriges* (*seCoPiriCes*), et tous
les composés à second terme -*genos* (*ReTuCenos*, *MezuCenos* BB III etc.)?

   D'autre part, puisque le gaulois livre une forme nom. sg. *duxtir*, n'est-il
pas probable que le celtique entier, avec le germanique, conservait du mot
indo-européen une forme abrégée *dugter-*, sans aucune trace de la
laryngale? Ce même mot est attendu en celtibère sous la forme *duxtir*,
duxteros, (écrit *TuTir* ou *TuCuTir* ?). On ne s'explique pas comment le -*x*-
se serait vocalisé en -*a*-.

   Sans aucune certitude, je proposerais la comparaison d'un mot
brittonique, v.bret. *tenterion* gl. procos, m.corn. *tanter* gl. procus
'prétendant'. Fleuriot et Campanile tiraient ce terme du th. verb. *ten-*
'tendre'[3]. Si la comparaison avec le celtibère est correcte, il faudrait poser
twanter-, nom d'agent dérivé du thème verbal *tew-* 'enfler' suffixé en
-*en*- (cf. Pokorny 1979, 1082–3). J'ai proposé de comparer le vieil-irl. *tét*

---

[3] Fleuriot 1964, 312b ; Campanile 1974, 98.

'luxurieux'[4]. On notera que le celtique aligne plusieurs synonymes de formes comparables:

> *swanto-*, 'désir' (gall. *chwant*, bret. *hoant*, > irl. anc. *sant*)
> *twan-to-* adj. 'plein de désir'
> *twan-ter-* nom d'agent, 'prétendant'.

Le sens exact dans l'inscription de Botorrita pourrait éventuellement être 'gendre' (ce que le 'prétendant' aspire à devenir). On notera que *Cenis* dans certains cas admettrait un sens étymologique de 'famille' (c'est un mot en rapport avec celt. *kene-tlo-* 'descendance, tribu' ou bien lat. *gens, gentis* : *ken-* ou *gen-*, Pokorny 1979, 363 et 573), cf. Villar 1995, 101 n. ; dans ce cas *TuaTeres* désignerait les alliés, beaux-frères, belles-soeurs etc.

3. CELTIBÈRE *CorTiCa*

Le nom de la tessère d'hospitalité, *Caruo CorTiCa*, a été isolé par A. Tovar et M. Lejeune, avec des analyses différentes[5]. Dans cette expression, qui revient fréquemment sur les tessères d'hospitalité (avec le premier mot parfois abrégé, ou omis), et qui est attestée au complet sur le Bronze de Luzaga[6], l'adj. en *-ko-* doit certainement être le correspondant de *hospitālis*, comme l'a proposé M. Lejeune. Mais les étymologies proposées (**ger-* gr. ἀγείρω, **gher-* lat. *cohors*) ne paraissent pas s'imposer. On trouvera dans l'excellente synthèse de Javier de Hoz sur le celtibère[7] l'état actuel des connaissances sur la série des tessères d'hospitalité avec inscription celtibère. Or il y a un mot v.irl. *gart* signifiant la générosité, l'hospitalité (gén. sg. *garta*). Le mot est glosé *féile* 'générosité', Corm.[2] 691. Exemples :

> *ní frith gáes ná gart ná genus conom thicse* 'il n'a pas été trouvé d'intelligence, de générosité ni de (pudeur?) jusqu'à ce que tu me rejoignes' (*LU*, 8327)

> *cia do-rigni gart ar tús? Seth ... do-rat fleid dia brathrib ... ocus tuc crod da cach brathair dib* 'Qui montra ('fit') l'hospitalité en premier? Seth ... qui offrit un banquet à ses frères, et il donna un bijou à chacun de ses frères' (*ZCPh*, 13, 132 § 10).

---

[4] Lambert 1986, 127. Cf. Murphy 1956, 317.
[5] A. Tovar, 1949, 50–51, 168, 170, 179–180 et Lejeune 1955, 60–61.
[6] Texte: *Caro Cenei CorTiCa luTiaCei* 'Tessère d'hostitalité de la famille de Luzaga'.
[7] De Hoz 1986, 66–77.

La flexion de *gart* n'est pas claire. On a *garta* au génitif (*co lín garta* 'avec abondance de générosité', *LU*, 3544). Les dérivés sont *gartach* (adj.) et *gartaid* (agent) 'généreux'. *Gart*, dans un exemple, semble se rapporter à un contrat : *fial-sum fial-si cotagaiu comrair garta diblioniuu* (lire *cotagaib, díb línib*) 'il est généreux, elle est généreuse, un coffret d'hospitalité les contient tous les deux' (*Anecd.* II, 69.14 : Airec Menman Uraird Maic Coisse § 27). Quel que soit l'objet exact désigné ici par *comrair* ('écrin', 'reliquaire', 'cassette', tardivement 'cercueil'), on doit retenir l'idée d'un récipient destiné à entreposer et protéger un objet précieux et fragile ; on le trouve souvent dans un sens symbolique, pour désigner des êtres humains, 'reposoir de sagesse' (*comhrair* […] *eccna*, Quatre Maîtres), 'dépositaire de secret' (*bá-sa chomrar cacha rūni* 'j'ai été le dépositaire de chaque secret' *LU*, 9335). Comme *comrair* s'applique en particulier à une boîte d'archive (*a cur a comhraigh leis féin* 'le mettre dans une boîte chez lui' O'Grady, *Cat. of the Irish Mss. in the British Museum*), *comrair garta* pourrait bien se référer au même champ sémantique. En somme, il est tentant de le comparer à la tessère d'hospitalité.

Pour le substantif qui accompagne *CorTiCa*, c.à d. *Caruo*, il est difficile de ne pas penser au groupe du grec γράφω 'j'écris' : néanmoins, l'emprunt reste obscur à la fois dans sa source (de quel mot grec est-on parti, et de quel dialecte?) et dans son cheminement (pourquoi -w- à la place de /f/ ?).

BIBLIOGRAPHIE

Campanile, Enrico 1974. *Profilo etimologico del cornico antico*, Pise : Pacini, 1974 (Biblioteca dell'Italia Dialettale e di Studi e Saggi Linguistici, 7)

Eichner, Heiner 1989. 'Damals und heute: Probleme der Erschliessung des Altkeltischen zu Zeussens Zeit und in der Gegenwart', in *Erlanger Gedenkfeier für Johann Kaspar Zeuss*, éd. par Bernhard Forssman, = *Erlanger Forschungen*, Reihe A, Geisteswissenschaften Bd. 49, 1989, 9–56 (Botorrita : 23–56)

Eska, Joseph F. 1989. *Towards an interpretation of the Hispano-Celtic inscription of Botorrita*, Toronto : Thèse doctorale (*Innsbrucker Beiträge zur Sprachwissenschaft*, 59)

Fleuriot, Léon 1964. *Dictionnaire des gloses en vieux-breton*, Paris : Klincksieck

De Hoz, Javier 1987. 'La epigrafía celtibérica', *Reunion sobre Epigrafía Hispanica de Epoca Romano-Republicana*, éd. par Guillermo Fatás, Saragosse : Fundación «Institución Fernando el Catolico», 43–102

Lambert, Pierre-Yves 1986. 'Les gloses celtiques aux commentaires à Virgile', *Études celtiques*, 23, 81–128

Lejeune, Michel 1955. *Celtiberica*, Acta Salmanticensia, Filosofía y Letras, VII, 4, Salamanque : Ediciones Universidad Salamanca

Meid, Wolfgang 1993. *Die erste Botorrita-Inschrift, Interpretation eines keltiberischen Sprachdenkmals*, Innsbruck : Innsbrucker Beiträge zur Sprachwissenschaft, XLVI

Murphy, Gerard 1956. 'Té, Tét, Téith', *Celtica*, 3 (Zeuss Memorial Volume), 317–319

Pokorny, Julius 1979. *Indogermanisches etymologisches Wörterbuch*, Berne : Francke

Thurneysen, Rudolf, 1946. *A Grammar of Old-Irish*, Dublin : Institute for Advanced Studies

Tovar, Antonio 1949. *Estudios sobre las primitivas lenguas hispanicas*, Buenos-Aires : Casa editora «Coni»

Vendryes, Joseph 1905. 'Mélanges italo-celtiques (7. Sur quelques formes interrogatives du vieil-irlandais)', *Mémoires de la Société de Linguistique de Paris*, 13, 384–408 (396–405)

—1906. 'L'évolution de l'adverbe *cid* en vieil-irlandais', *Mélanges H. d'Arbois de Jubainville*, Paris : A. Fontemoing, 279–287

Villar, Francisco 1993. 'Las silbantes en Celtibérico', *Lengua y Cultura en la Hispania Prerromana, Actas del V Coloquio sobre lenguas y Culturas Prerromanas de la Península Ibérica, Acta Salmanticensia, Estudios Filologicos*, 251 (Colonia 1989), éd. par Jürgen Untermann, Salamanque : Ediciones Universidad Salamanca, 773–811

—1995. *Estudios de Celtibérico y de toponimia prerromana, Acta Salmanticensia, Estudios Filológicos*, 260, Salamanque : Ediciones Universidad Salamanca

Aspectual Properties of Passive Auxiliaries in Old English

CLODAGH LYNAM
University College, Dublin

1. INTRODUCTION

IN GRAMMARS of German a distinction is often drawn between the Vorgangspassiv or actional passive, which appears with the auxiliary *werden* 'become' and the Zustandpassiv or stative passive, which appears with the auxiliary *sein* 'be' (cf. eg. Jude 1975). The Vorgangspassiv is said to have a verbal participle, while the participle in the Zustandpassiv is adjectival (cf. eg. den Besten 1981). There are also two passive auxiliaries in Dutch, *worden* 'become' and *zijn* 'be' which seem to pattern in a similar way to their German cognates. Old English (OE) also has two passive auxiliaries which are cognate with the German and Dutch auxiliaries. This paper is an examination of the aspectual or event properties of the two OE passive auxiliaries and an attempt to answer the question of whether the OE auxiliaries share semantic and syntactic characteristics with their Dutch and German cognates. The content of this paper arises from research which I have been carrying out for a PhD thesis on passives in Old English and Modern English within the framework of Noam Chomsky's theory of Universal Grammar, originally under the supervision of Professor Conn Ó Cléirigh. My primary data base is MS A of the *Anglo-Saxon Chronicle* (known as the Parker Chronicle), a section of Ælfric's *Lives of the Saints* and Alfred's version of the *Soliloquies*. I have also made use of data collected by other scholars, especially Kilpiö (1989), Mitchell (1985) and Visser (1963–73).

2. PASSIVE AND EVENT STRUCTURE

Although Modern English (MnE) has only one passive auxiliary, it has been argued that there are two types of passive in MnE also, one with a verbal participle which has an eventive or actional reading and one with an adjectival participle which has a stative reading (cf. eg. Wasow 1977, Chomsky 1981). In fact, it is widely assumed among generative grammarians at least, that the correlation of eventive reading with verbal participle and stative reading with adjectival participle holds for all languages which have a periphrastic passive similar to that in MnE. However, this two-way distinction is rather too simplistic. For example, verbal passives may be derived from stative verbs and the resultant passive has a stative reading (see 1).[1]

1   a) The employees feared the manager
        b) The manager was feared by all the employees

It would seem that verbal passives have the same aspectual properties as the verbs from which they are derived. Adjectival passives, on the other hand, have either a stative or eventive-perfective reading (see 2, below), but never a simple eventive reading, even when derived from eventive verbs. It is not clear why adjectival passives should never have an eventive interpretation. However, if one accepts Grimshaw's (1990) theory of the linking of thematic and argument structure hierarchies, it might be argued that the external argument is always linked with the most prominent sub-event in the event structure of a predicate. Where the event structure of a predicate includes an action, that will always be the most prominent sub-event. The external argument of a verb is always lost in the formation of adjectival passives, unlike verbal passives, which are generally considered to have an implicit external argument.[2]

The verb *load* is clearly an eventive verb. A verbal passive such as (2a) has an eventive interpretation. The adjectival passive participle in (2b) is stative. However, the adverb *recently* in (2c) refers to the recent event of loading and not to a recent loaded state. The reading of the phrase in (2c) as a whole is resultative or eventive-perfective, rather than stative.

2   a) The truck was loaded by the workers
        b) The loaded truck
        c) The recently loaded truck

Thus we can say that where a passive has a simple eventive reading it must be verbal. Stative or eventive-perfective interpretation can only be taken as an indication that a passive is adjectival if the participle is derived from an eventive verb. Where a participle is derived from a stative or perfective verb, we must look to syntactic evidence to decide whether it is verbal or adjectival.[3]

---

[1] See Grimshaw (1990) on the aspectual properties, or, in her terms, event structure of psych-predicates like *fear*.

[2] Jaeggli (1986), Guilfoyle (1991), Baker et al (1989) all argue that the external argument is syntactically present. Grimshaw argues for a semantically present but syntactically unrealised argument in verbal passives.

[3] Cf. eg. Wasow (1977).

3. THE PERIPHRASTIC PASSIVE IN OE

Traditional grammars of Old English distinguish up to three different constructions which might be classified as passive; (1) a synthetic passive or, more properly perhaps, a middle voice construction (*Se munuc hatte Abbo* 'the monk was called Abbo' *ÆLS*, 32.3), (2) an active construction with indefinite 3sg subject (*Her Þeodorius mon hadode to ercebiscepe* 'In this year, Theodorius was ordained archbishop' *ASC(A) An.* 668) and (3) a periphrastic passive with an auxiliary verb and a participle. The focus of this paper is the aspectual properties of the auxiliary verbs of the periphrastic passive.

Just as in Modern English (MnE), the periphrastic passive in OE is formed with an auxiliary verb and a passive participle. Unlike MnE, however, in OE there are two possible auxiliaries for the passive; *wesan/beon*, 'be' (see 3a,b), and *weorÞan*, 'become' (see 3c), both of which can also function as main verbs.

3   a) Her Bregowine **wæs** to ercebiscepe gehadod to Ste Michaeles tide.
        'In this year, Bregowine was ordained archbishop at Michaelmas'.

                        ASC(A) An. 759

       b) [...] Þu **bist** on heofonum gebroht
        '[…] you will be brought to heaven' *ÆLS*, 2.411

       c) Þær **wearÞ** monig mon ofslægen & adruncen on gehwæÞere hand
        'Many men were slain & drowned there, on both sides'. *ASC(A) An.* 853

The two forms of 'be', *wesan* and *beon*, are usually treated as one auxiliary (although see Kilpiö 1989 passim, Mitchell 1985, §§ 652–664 and see below). The most obvious differences between the verbs *wesan* and *beon* are, first, that *beon* does not appear in a past tense form, and, second, *beon* is usually used to indicate futurity.[4]

4. ASPECTUAL PROPERTIES OF THE OE PASSIVE AUXILIARIES

It has been claimed that there are only adjectival passives in OE and that the verbal passive entered the language during the Middle English (ME) period (cf. eg. Mustanoja 1960, Lightfoot 1979, Mitchell 1985). However, I have argued elsewhere (Lynam 1996) that there is syntactic evidence to indicate that there are also verbal passives in OE. Given the premises laid out in section 2, above, if there are verbal and adjectival passives in OE

---

[4] *Beon* is the OE reflex of the Indo-European root **bheu-/bh(e)wi-* 'become'.

then we would expect to find both passives with stative readings and passives with eventive readings. It would not be surprising to find that OE passive auxiliaries have the same syntactic and semantic properties as their German and Dutch cognates. I argue, however, that *wesan/beon* is commonly used in both verbal and adjectival passives.

It has been claimed by scholars of OE that eventive or actional readings are associated with the auxiliary *weorþan*, while stative readings are associated with the auxiliary *wesan*.

> These forms are very vague in meaning, and the distinction between the two auxiliaries is not clearly marked, but *wesan* appears to indicate a state, *weorþan* an action. (Sweet 1905 § 93)

> [...] *wearþ*, which by its nature expresses a change brought about by an action, serves to denote a significant event, a step forward in the narrative, something 'new': *wæs* denotes a state, without regard for how it came into being. (Klaeber 1923, 188)

> *Weorþan* is a word of change or becoming, while *wesan* expresses the idea of state or fact, of being or existing. Hence *weorþan* is found frequently in moments of action; *wesan* in moments of rest. (Frary 1966, 15)

Those who see a distinction differ as to whether they regard it as a consistent grammatical rule, or just a tendency; a stylistic rather than grammatical difference. However, Bruce Mitchell (1985 §§ 786–801) is adamant that there is no clear or consistent distinction between the two auxiliaries.

> First, the subsequent disappearance of *weorþan* would lead us to expect that if the distinction ever existed, it would already have been blurred in OE. Second, I do not believe that the distinction ever did exist as something consistently applied or understood in either the conscious or subconscious mind of the generality of speakers, hearers or writers. Mitchell (1985 § 787)

It is hardly surprising that scholars do not agree on the matter of whether passives in OE have stative and eventive readings and on whether or not there is a clear cut distinction between the auxiliaries, since in many cases there is little or no concrete morphological or syntactic evidence to decide the matter. But most are agreed that there are a number of cases in which the only plausible reading is a stative one and others which are unambiguously eventive. There will of course be quite a number of instances where the matter remains unresolved. Nevertheless, some conclusions may be drawn from the evidence as it stands.

4.1 *WESAN/BEON*

Despite the remarks of Sweet, Klaeber and Frary as cited above, there is evidence to support Mitchell's assertion (1985 § 787) that the two auxiliaries in OE were interchangeable. Mitchell (1985 § 790) cites a number of examples of passives with *wesan* which are clearly eventive rather than stative.

4   a) [...] swa him byð betyned heofona rices duru ongean on domes dæge
'[...] so shall the door of heaven be closed against him on the day of judgement'
WHom, 37.239.1

b) Seo burg wæs getimbred an fildum lande
'The city was built on level ground' *Or*, 74.11

I have also found a large number of eventive passives with *wesan* or *beon* in my research for the PhD.

5   a) Þa foresædan gedwolmen wæron gefullode on gode.
'The afore-mentioned heretics were baptised into God.' *ÆLS*, 3.353

b) [...] on þæm xlii geare his rices Crist wæs acenned
'[...] in the 42nd year of his reign Christ was born' *ASC(A) An.* 1

Visser (1973) argues that there had once been a clear distinction between the two auxiliaries, but that by the time of attested OE, *weorþan* was probably already passing out of the language and its eventive or dynamic function was gradually being taken over by *wesan*.

> This replacement of the static connotation by the dynamic connotation of the construction consisting of *be* + past participle was naturally a very slow process and not complete until after a period of vacillation and wavering, which may have begun in OE. (Visser 1973 § 1909)

Visser later states that there was 'a good deal of free variation' in the usage of the two auxiliaries (§ 1916), citing parallel clauses from two versions (MSS C and H) of Wærferth's translation of Pope Gregory's *Dialogues*. These are clauses in which MS C has a passive with *wesan*, but the corresponding clause in MS H has a passive with the auxiliary *weorþan*. The scribe copying from the original saw no significant difference, evidently, between the two auxiliaries, at least in those contexts.

6) [...] þær **wæron** eac oþre VII brodru be naman gecigde (MS C)
[...] þer **wurdon** eac odre seofon brodru be hyra naman gecigede (MS H)
'[...] there each of the brothers was summoned by name'.

Dialogues, 52, 26

Kilpiö (p.83) cites similar discrepancies between MSS B and T of *Bede*.

7 a) [...] 7 ealle ætgædere gehruran 7 ofslagene **wurdon**(B)/**wæron**(T)
mid heora campwerode.
'[...] and all together they fell and were killed with their soldiers'.

Bede II, 675

b) [...] 7 micel dæl þære ceastre **weard**(B)/**wæs**(T) fornumen.
'[...] and much of the city was destroyed'. *Bede* II, 751

I have also found 10 parallel entries in different MSS of the Anglo-Saxon
Chronicle, where at least one MS has a passive with *weorþan* and at least
one other has *wesan*. I cite two instances of such parallel clauses in (8).

8 a) [...] þær **wæs**(A C D E)/**wearþ**(B) ungemetlic wæl geslægen
Norþumbra
'[...] there was immeasurable saughter (slain) of the Northumbrians
there'. *ASC An.* 867

b) Her Cenwalh adrifen **wæs** fram Pendan cyninge (MS A)
Her Kenwealh king **wearþ** ut adrifen fram Pendan cinge (MSS B C)
'In this year, Cenwalh was driven out by King Penda'. *ASC An.* 644

In all of the examples cited by Visser and Kilpiö and in all of the examples
which I found in the *ASC* where the two auxiliaries seem to be interchangeable, the passives in question clearly have an eventive reading. Such
evidence points to a conclusion that *wesan/beon* is associated with both
eventive and stative passives, but it does not suggest that *weorþan* passives
could ever be stative.

In his (1983) analysis of the use of the auxiliaries in passives in the *Cura
Pastoralis* and *Bede*, Kilpiö states (section 2.3.4.) that *wesan* is often used
in eventive as well as in stative passives (sometimes with a perfective
reading). However, in the present tense, *wesan* passives, he says, are 'predominantly statal' (p. 38). He continues: 'There are instances in which the
IS passive can be best interpreted as actional, but they are not numerous. In
the preterite the situation is different: WÆS + past participle frequently
expresses action as well as state'. In the past tense, 50% of all *wesan*

passives in *Bede* and *CP* fall into his category (i); 'Actional, Single Action, No Pluperfect Implication' (p. 84).[5] Incidentally, actional/eventive passives in the present tense are rare in MnE, except in certain types of narrative or news reporting, presumably for pragmatic reasons. Thus we would expect most present tense passives in OE to have a stative reading, for pragmatic rather than syntactic reasons.

The auxiliary *beon* is treated together with *wesan* in most studies of the passive in OE, but there are some slight statistical differences between the two auxiliaries with regard to stative and eventive readings. Aside from the fact that *beon* passives usually have a future reference or refer to unchanging truths, Kilpiö finds that 'the BIÐ passive is actional in the majority of instances [...]' (p. 57). The percentage of 'actional' as against non-actional *beon* passives in the translated texts which are the subject of his study he estimates as between 72% and 91% (with some variation between the different texts).

In any case, it seems clear from the evidence presented by Mitchell (1985), Visser (1973), Kilpiö (1983) and my own findings that both *wesan* and *beon* were used as auxiliaries in both verbal and adjectival passives.

4.2 WEORÞAN

Kilpiö's (1983) analysis supports a hypothesis that there was, at the very least, a strong tendency to use *weorþan* for eventive passives. Kilpiö finds that *weorþan* passives in the translated texts which are the subject of his study are always 'actional' in both present tense and past tense, 'often implying a sudden change' (p. 85. See also p. 63). However, Mitchell (1985, as quoted above) asserts not just that *wesan/beon* passives could be eventive, hence verbal, but that the two auxiliaries, *wesan/beon* and *weorþan* are freely interchangeable. He cites some a number of clauses with *weorþan* both as wa main verb and as an auxiliary where, he claims, *weorþan* expresses a state (Mitchell 1985, § 798). Denison (1993, p.418) remarks that '[Mitchell] does not produce *many* convincing counter-examples [...]' (my emphasis) to the theory that *weorþan* passives were always eventive. He cites two of Mitchell's stative *weorþan* passives which he says are the most convincing. To my mind, these two passives are unambiguously stative. I have asked the opinion of other OE scholars and their judgement is in agreement with mine.

---

[5] The others are (ii) Actional, Pluperfect Implication, 23%; (iii) Actional, Iterative Implication 3%; (iv) Actional, Durative Implication, 12%; (v) Statal, 12%.

9   a) Þæt cweartern **weard afylled** mid fulum adelan and butan ælcum leohte atelice stincende
'The prison was filled with foul mud and without any light horribly stinking'. *ÆLS* II, 35.244

b) [...] hi **wurdon** ða utan **ymbsette** mid Romaniscum here swa lange þæt [...]
'[...] they were/ then besieged by Roman army so long that [...]'
ÆCH I, 28.402.33

Despite the fact that the sentence in (9b) is clearly stative, it is not necessarily an adjectival passive. The OE verb *ymbsettan* 'surround' is stative, at least in some uses, therefore we would expect a verbal passive derived from *ymbsettan* to be stative also.[6]

However, (9a) constitutes a clear counter-example to the hypothesis that *weorþan* is only used as an auxiliary in the verbal passive. The verb *afyllan* 'fill up' is unambiguously eventive, but the participle *afylled* in (9a) can only have a stative interpretation, and so must be adjectival.

I can offer no explanation for the existence of (9a). The question arises as to what significance if any we should attach to one example of a particular type of passive. This one use of *weorþan* in a stative adjectival passive could be attributed to scribal error, perhaps. On the other hand, much of the evidence is ambiguous anyway; the existence of one clear example could be taken as an indication that there are many more.

5. CONCLUDING REMARKS

The event characteristics of the two (or three) passive auxiliaries in OE are the subject of continuing research for my PhD thesis and perhaps beyond. In my thesis I compare the OE passive auxiliaries with those in Italian and Spanish, both of which also have two passive auxiliaries. Italian *venire* 'come' is only used in verbal passives, while *essere* is used in both verbal and adjectival passives. Spanish has two forms of the verb 'be'; one of which *ser*, is used in verbal/eventive passives, while *estar* is used in adjectival/stative passives. Comparisons can also be made between the OE *weorþan* passive and the MnE *get* passive; both of these verbs indicate a change of state. In any case, it seems clear that the verb 'be' in OE, in both its forms *wesan* and *beon*, was used freely in both adjectival passive and verbal passives, whereas *weorþan* seems to have been used most often, but

---

[6] According to Máire Noonan, German native speaker, it is quite possible to translate this sentence into German with the auxiliary *werden*, which is the auxiliary normally associated with the verbal passive.

perhaps not exclusively, in verbal passives. A fruitful area for further study would be the use of *weorþan* as a main verb, especially with adjectival complements, and a comparison with German *werden* and Dutch *worden* as main verbs with predicative adjectival complements.

PRIMARY TEXTUAL SOURCES CITED

ÆCH: *The Homilies of the Anglo-Saxon Church*, ed. by Benjamin Thorpe (London: the Ælfric Society, 1844–6)

ÆLS: *Ælfric's Lives of the Saints*, ed. by Walter W. Skeat (London: Early English Texts Society, 1881)

ASC: *The Anglo-Saxon Chronicle*, ed. by Benjamin Thorpe (London: Longmans, 1861)

ASC(A): *The Anglo-Saxon Chronicle, MS A*, ed. by Janet Bately (Cambridge: Brewer, 1986)

Bede: *König Alfreds Übersetzung von Bedas Kirchengeschichte*, ed. by J. Schipper (Leipzig: Bibliothek der Angelsächsischen Prosa, 1899)

CP: *King Alfred's West-Saxon Version of Gregory's Pastoral Care*, ed. by Henry Sweet (London: Early English Texts Society, 1958)

Dialogues: *Bischof Wærferths von Worcester Übersetzung der Dialoge Gregors des Grossen* (Leipzig & Hamburg: Bibliothek der Angelsächsischen Prosa, 1900–7)

Or: *King Alfred's Orosius*, ed. by Henry Sweet (London: Early English Texts Society, 1883)

WHom: *The Homilies of Wulfstan*, ed. by Dorothy Bethurum (Oxford: Clarendon Press, 1957)

REFERENCES

Besten, Hans den 1981. 'A Case Filter for Passives', in *Theory of Markedness in Generative Grammar*, ed. by A. Belletti, L. Brandi and L. Rizzi, Pisa: Scuola Normale Superiore, 65–122

Chomsky, Noam 1981. *Lectures on Government & Binding*, Dordrecht: Foris

Denison, David 1993. *English Historical Syntax*, New York: Longman

Frary, Louise G. 1929/66. *Studies in the Syntax of the OE Passive*, New York: Kraus Reprint Corporation

Grimshaw, Jane 1990. *Argument Structure*, Cambridge, Mass.: MIT Press

Jude, Wilhelm K. 1975. *Deutsche Grammatik*, Braunschweig: Westermann

Kilpiö, Matti 1989. *Passive Constructions in OE Translations from Latin*, Helsinki: *Mémoires de la Société Néophilologique de Helsinki*, XLIX

Klaeber, Fr. 1923. 'Eine Bemerkung zum Altenglischen Passivum', *Englische Studien*, 57, 187–95

Lightfoot, David 1979. 'Rule Classes and Syntactic Change', *Linguistic Inquiry*, 10, 83–108.

Lynam, Clodagh 1996. 'Lexical and Syntactic Passives in Old English', to appear in *Pages*, 3

Mitchell, Bruce 1985. *Old English Syntax*, Oxford: University Press

Mustanoja, Tauno F. 1960. *A Middle English Syntax*, Helsinki: Société Philologique

Sweet, Henry and Davis, Norman 1882/1953. *Sweet's Anglo-Saxon Primer*, Oxford: University Press

Visser, F.Th. 1963–73. *An Historical Syntax of the English Language*, 3 vols, Leiden: Brill

Wasow, Thomas 1977. 'Transformations and the Lexicon', in *Formal Syntax*, ed. by A. Akmajian, P. Culicover and T. Wasow, New York: Academic Press

Gnéithe den Chéasta sa Nua-Ghaeilge

PROINSIAS MAC CANA ⅂ DÓNALL P. Ó BAOILL
Scoil an Léinn Cheiltigh   *An Institiúid Teangeolaíochta*

1. RÉAMHRÁ

B A MHAITH linn cur síos a dhéanamh anseo ar roinnt gnéithe suntasacha a bhaineann le húsáid chéasta na Gaeilge. Beimid ag díriú go láidir ar na foirmeacha comhréire a úsáidtear agus go háirithe ar an chiall a ritheann leo. Ar mhaithe leis an méid atá le rá againn a shuíomh i gcomhthéacs níos ginearálta, déanfaimid iarracht chomh fada agus is féidir sin leaganacha céasta na Gaeilge a cheangal le húsáidí den chéasta mar atá siad ar fáil i dteangacha eile. Déanfar iarracht fosta na rólanna éagsúla atá ag na foirmeacha ar leith den chéasta a bhfuilimid ag díriú orthu a ríomh taobh istigh de chóras na Gaeilge féin.

2. AN FHOIRM CHÉASTA AGUS A TRÉITHE

Is í an chéad cheist is ceart a chur is dócha cad é go díreach an leagan amach a bhíonn ar an chomhréir dhromchlach a bhíonn ar chlásal céasta a idirdhealaíonn é ó bhunchlásal atá gníomhach? De réir an taighde a bhaineann le hábhar, is é an chuma atá ar an scéal gurb í an phríomh-dhifríocht a bhíonn idir abairt ghníomhach agus abairt chéasta go mbíonn foirm ar leith ar na frásaí briathartha a fhaightear sa dá shórt abairte.

Maíonn Keenan (1985) ina alt ar aicmeolaíocht teanga gurb í an bhunabairt chéasta is coitianta i measc theangacha an domhain an cineál atá léirithe in (1) thíos:

(1)   *Buaileadh Dónall.*

Tá dhá ní a idirdhealaíonn abairt den chineál sin ó abairtí céasta eile, mar atá: (a) ní luaitear an gníomhaí agus (b) is briathar aistreach an bun-bhriathar. Tugtar an neamhphearsanta go minic ar abairtí dá leithéid i nGaeilge de bhrí go mbíonn an gníomhaí intuigthe iontu.

Nuair nach mbíonn ach aon chineál amháin céasta i dteanga is cosúil gurb é an cineál bunúsach sin atá luaite againn a fhaightear de ghnáth. Ach d'fhéadfadh teanga cineálacha eile céasta a bheith inti a bhféadfaí céastaí bunúsacha a thabhairt orthu fosta. Feicfimid níos faide ar aghaidh go mb'fhéidir go bhfuil a leithéid sa Nua-Ghaeilge.

Déantar idirdhealú go leitheadach idir dhá mhórchineál céasta ó thaobh an struchtúir a bhaineann leo i dteangacha. Baintear úsáid as deilbhíocht le ceann acu a chumadh agus tabharfar *céasta na deilbhíochta* air anseo feasta. Is i bhfoirm frása briathartha a chuirtear an dara bunchineál in iúl agus tabharfaimid *an céasta timchainteach* air seo. Is gnách gur bunbhriathra a úsáidtear sa chéad chineál agus go mbíonn briathra cúnta in úsáid sa dara sórt. Baineann an dara cineál seo le húsáid na haidiachta briathartha (nó na rangabhála caite) in éineacht leis an bhriathar shubstainteach, mar atá sa sampla seo a leanas:

(2)   *Tá Dónall buailte aici.*

Is ceart dúinn fosta a bheith ar ár n-aire faoin chéasta timchainteach mar gur minic débhríochas nó éiginnteacht áirithe ag baint leis. Braitheann an débhríochas ar cé acu ciall staide a shíltear a bheith leis an abairt a bhíonn i gceist nó an meastar dynamaic éigin a bheith ag baint leis an bhrí atáthar a léiriú. Déanfaimid plé ar chuid den débhríochas seo níos faide ar aghaidh.

3. ÚSÁID NEAMHGHNÁCH DEN NEAMHPHEARSANTA

Tá roinnt úsáidí den chéasta le fáil sa Nua-Ghaeilge ar díol suime iad de thairbhe go mbaineann na tréithe seo a leanas leo: (a) cuirtear foirm chéasta na deilbhíochta (an briathar saor i gcás na Gaeilge) ar an bhriathar chúnta iontu, (b) bíonn foirm an ainm bhriathartha nó na hinfinide ar an phríomhbhriathar agus (c) ní bhíonn gníomhaí i gceist. Is léir go bhfuil ciall chéasta leo ón chomhthéacs ina n-úsáidtear iad. Seo a leanas roinnt samplaí as foinsí scríofa den úsáid atá i gceist againn:

(3)   *Chuaidh Eoghainín Eoghain ar a' tsnámh, acht tháinig cearthaidh ar Thuathal agus **bhíthear a' bháthadh** ('Máire' 1942, 164).*

(4)   *Bhéarfaidh sé a sháith, lá ar bith, do bheirt fhear duine **atáthar a bháthadh** a thógáil isteach i mbád (ibid., 165)*

(5)   *Sé rud **a bhítear á slugadh** 'In fact it ('cliobóg') was being swallowed up' (ibid., 91)*

(6)   *'Ní rachainn-se amach ar an fhairrge i ndiaidh fir ar bith, gan fhios **nach mo bháthadh a dhéanfaidhe**,' arsa Róise, [...] ('Máire' 1968, 105)*

(7)   *Bhí garbhánach leis ar an chéad iarraidh. Ní dhearn' sé mórán bogadaighe ar an tslait, ach **bhíthear ag baint na h-anála de** nuair a fágadh síos ar urlár an bháid é (Ó Domhnaill 1934, 20)*

(8)   *Bhí Ruth ag gol.* **Bhíthear ag baint** *'ach'n chnead as Rachel* (ibid., 137)

(9)   *Is beag* [...] *nár chualaidh trácht* [...] *ar shaghart na nGrásta—sin an saghart a thig as na Flaithis le freastal ar dhaoine* **a bidhthear a bháitheadh** *nó a bíos ag fághail bháis ar dhóigh ar bith eile* (Uí Bheirn (eag.) 1989, 163)

(10)   *Bhithear ag deánamh 'ach uile ghléas iasgaireachta* **a rabhthar a fhliuchadh** *anseo sa bhaile* (ibid., 106)

(11)   [...] *ach chaitheadh an bhearna san do dhúnadh, mar nuair a thagadh anfadh an gheimhridh bhíodh an iomarca reatha isteach innte, agus* **bhítí ag briseadh na mbád** '[...] and the boats were getting broken' (Ó Cionnfhaolaidh (eag.) 1956, 135)

(12)   [...] *do n-a gcuid bád, agus nuair a thagadh garbhshíon an gheimhridh* **go mbítí á mbriseadh ortha** '[...] that they would be getting broken on them' (ibid., 134)

(13)   **Bhíthear ag baint na súl asainn** *leis an lóchán* (Seán Ó Baoill, *Mín an Chladaigh*, Gaoth Dobhair)

Is léir sna samplaí sin ar fad gur brí chéasta atáthar a chur in iúl. Tabhair faoi deara chomh maith sa mhórchuid de na samplaí go bhfuil béim nó fócas ar leith ar an ghníomh de réir mar a bhíonn sé ag tarlú, rud a dhéantar trí úsáid a bhaint as foirm den ainm bhriathartha.

4. AN BRIATHAR *BÍ* + RANGABHÁIL CHAITE

Ba mhaith linn anois díriú isteach ar chuid de na húsáidí ar leith a bhaineann le habairtí ina mbíonn an rangabháil chaite agus spíonadh beag a dhéanamh orthu. Is léir ó na samplaí gur brí an chéasta atáthar a chur in iúl cé nach bhfuil aon rian de fhoirm an chéasta deilbhíochta le feiceáil ar na habairtí. D'fhéadfaí a agairt chomh maith go bhfuil an cainteoir ag díriú isteach ar an tráth ina mbeidh an gníomh tugtha i gcrích agus go dtugtar an gníomh agus an toradh chun solais trí úsáid a bhaint as an rangabháil. Maítear in amanna gur treise an sórt seo abairte i nGaeilge na Mumhan, ach mar a fheictear ó na heiseamláirí, tá a leithéidí sna canúintí ar fad.

Chonacthas dúinn gur cheart na samplaí go léir atá sa rannóg seo againn a scaradh ó chéile agus fo-aicmí a dhéanamh astu ar bhonn céille. Sa chéad fho-aicme atá againn tá an t-expreisiúnachas agus an drámatúlacht le feiceáil go láidir. Tá cuma ar an scéal go mbítear ag iarraidh drámatúlacht an scéil a choinneáil os comhair an éisteora agus gur bealach amháin le seo a dhéanamh úsaid a bhaint as an rangabháil chaite. Tabhair faoi deara gur minic nach luaitear an gníomhaí. Tugann an chomhréir seo radharc láithreach don éisteoir ar an aicsean atá le mothú san insint agus ar chomh gasta agus a d'fhéadfadh rudaí titim amach. Dírítear sna habairtí seo fosta ar chríochnúlacht nó ar fhoirfeacht an ghnímh atá faoi chaibidil. Tá seans go bhfuil ceist stíle nó réime i gceist chomh maith. Seo a leanas roint samplaí arbh as téacsanna foilsithe an mhórchuid acu:

(14)   *'Ar son Dé', ar sise, 'rith nó **beidh tú báidhte'*** (Sayers 1939, 226)

(15)   [...] *mar, an t-am díreach go bhfeaca sí ag rinnce iad, **bhíodar báidhte**, slán mar a n-innstear é!* (ibid., 26)

(16)   *Ach is minic ina dhiaidh sin a deireadh sé liomsa gur ar mhaithe leis an muirear óg a bhí ag brath air féin ná raibh aon choinbhlíocht iontu a thug a pardún di, mar 'bhí a fhios agam go maith **go mbeinn féin crochta** gan rómhoill', ar seisean* (Ua Maoileoin (eag.) 1973, 74)

(17)   *Agus níl aon fháil ag aon ghaiscíoch dá fheabhas dár leag cos ar bhóthar ná dár rug ar chlaimhe, dhul thairsti [an ollphéist] **gan é bheith slogtha marbh aici*** (Ó Nualláin (eag.) 1982, 78)

(18)   *Níl agat ach baoite de sin a chur amach [...] agus **tá sé slogtha síos ina corp aige*** (Uí Bheirn (eag.) 1989, 73)

Tá neamhréir éigin le feiceáil i sampla (18) mar go mbeadh duine ag súil le séimhiú ar *corp* le bheith ag réiteach leis an fhorainm réamhfhoclach *aige*. Ach is sampla dleathach é mar sin féin den úsáid atá faoi chaibidil againn.

Anuas ar an expreisiúnachas a chuireann na samplaí atá sa chéad fho-aicme thuas in iúl, thig tuilleadh treise agus práinne a chur leis an teachtaireacht trí úsáid a bhaint as an chaite mhódúil (den bhriathar shubstainteach), foirm a chuireann treise agus drámatúlacht in iúl aisti féin. Samplaí den chineál seo atá sa dara fo-aicme againn:

(19)   *Sin é an t-ainm a bhí ar an bhfathach, Ceann an Ascaill, mar is é an t-údar a bhí leis ní dheachaigh sé a chodladh ariamh ach ina shuí sa suíochán agus a chloigeann a chur faoina ascaill, agus osna a ligfeá **bhí an fathach dúisithe*** (Ó Nualláin (eag.) 1982, 98)

(20)   *'Seachtain ón lá sin bhí Micheál bocht i dtigh na cúirte aici, agus dhearbhaigh sí seo agus siúd air, agus **bhí sé crochta aici** mura mbeadh ar labhair ina pháirt,' ar seisean* (Ua Maoileoin (eag.),1973, 75)

Sa dá shampla seo a leanas is léir gurb é an chiall atá le baint as a bhfuil ráite go mbeadh an gníomh a luaitear curtha i gcrích cheana féin mura gcomhlíonfaí cibé ar bith coinníoll a thugtar sa chéad chuid den abairt:

(21)   *agus mura mbeadh an cíos aca Lá Bealthaine agus Lá Samhna chô math **bhíodar caite amach** ar an gcnoc nú cois a' chluí ag an máistir* (Ó Duilearga (eag.) 1948, xxx–xxxi)

(22)   *mur mbeadh airgead an chíosa leat i do lámh **bhí tú caite amach** ar an doras aige féin nó ag an bháillí* (Aodh Ó Dubhchon, Mín an Chladaigh, Gaoth Dobhair)

Tá na húsáidí seo an-chosúil leis an chaite mhódúil a fhaightear in abairtí mar iad seo a leanas: *mura dtógfaí an leanbh as an chosán bhí sé marbh* '[...] he would have been killed'; *dá rachfá thusa thart an bealach mór bhí tú sa bhaile fada ó shin* '[...] you would have been home long ago'. Cé go bhféadfaí an neamhphearsanta a úsáid in (21) agus (22), ní thabharfadh sé leis an bhrí nó an fórsa atá i gceist le húsáid na rangabhála. Tá iarracht sna habairtí an t-éisteoir a thabhairt ar láthair an 'chaite amach' lom díreach le taispeáint dó é chomh gasta agus a dhéanfaí an gníomh.

Ní bhíonn an drámatúlacht agus an t-expreisiúnachas chomh láidir i gcónaí le húsáid na rangabhála caite. Sa tríú fo-aicme atá déanta againn is comhthéacs cineál 'neodrach' atá le mothú ar an insint a thugtar agus ní bhíonn lorg ar bith den phráinn ná den déine atá le fáil i samplaí 19-22 le brath ar eiseamláirí de chuid an fho-aicme seo. Tugann muid anois samplaí da bhfuil i gceist:

(23)   *acht níl aon mhaith i gclaoidheamhaibh an domhain anaghaidh an fhathaigh sin, [...] agus **níl sé le bheith claoidhte** acht leis an aon rud amháin* (de híde (eag.) 1933, 152)

(24)   *Cuirim faoi gheasaibh troma draoidheachta thú [...] **do cheann agus do chosa agus do chaoi bheatha a bheith bainte dhíot*** (ibid., 203, 204, 205)

Maidir le samplaí (23)–(24), d'fhéadfaí an bhrí chéanna a chur in iúl ach úsáid a bhaint as leaganacha mar seo in áit na gcodanna a bhfuil cló dubh orthu thuas [...] *agus níl sé le cloí acht* [...] *agus* [...] *do cheann agus do chosa agus do chaoi bheatha a bhaint dhíot.*

(25)   *Fiafraigh de cén áit ar mhaith leis **an chúirt sin a bheith déanta*** (Ní Dhíoraí (eag.) 1985, 109)

(26)   *gheall ar innse duit an rud a shaoilim is cóir* **a bheith déanta** (Ó
        Domhnaill 1934, 358)

(27)   *Agus goidé níos fear[r] atá Dia de dhuine 'na* [sic] *de dhuine eile, le
        duine a chruthughadh fa choinne* **bheith slánuighthe** *agus duine eile
        fa choinne* **bheith damnuighthe?** ('Máire', *Castar na Daoine ar a
        chéile*, srl., caib. 2)

(28)   *Nach iomaidh fiche* **crochta orainn** *ó tháinic an oidhche* 'Isn't it
        many's a time we have been stopped from passing twenty in the
        course of the night' (Uí Bheirn (eag.) 1989, 68)

Ó tharla gur as Tír Chonaill samplaí (25)–(28), measadh nár mhiste tagairt
do na canúintí eile. Seo dhá shampla a taifeadadh ó chainteoirí as Contae
na Gaillimhe:

(29)   **Tá siad íocaí** *lena aghaidh sin* (Máire Uí Dhufaigh, Inis Oírr)

(30)   *Tá iarratas anseo agam* **a bhí iarrta** *i rith na seachtaine* (Máirtín Tom
        Sheáinín, Raidió na Gaeltachta)

Is le céasta na deilbhíochta a bheadh duine ag súil sna samplaí seo de réir
gnáis ach is cosúil gurb ar an bhealach seo is fearr le mórán cainteoirí
tuiscint an chéasta a chur in iúl. Cheal samplaí eile, ní léir an mbaineann an
gnás seo le briathra ar leith nó an bhfaightear é i measc briathra i gcoitinne.
Baineann an rud céanna le cuid d'úsáidí an bhriathair *tóg* 'raise, rear', mar
atá sna samplaí seo a leanas as Tír Chonaill. Sa chás ar leith seo tá
cosúlacht bhrí an chéasta go han-soiléir ar habairtí (31)–(32):

(31)   *Duine ar bith* **nach bhfuil tógtha** *leis an fharraige* [...] (Seán Ó Baoill,
        Mín an Chladaigh, Gaoth Dobhair)

(32)   *Caithfidh tú* **a bheith tógtha** *aníos leis* (id.)

5. ÚSÁIDÍ EILE DEN RANGABHÁIL

5.1 Gnéithe Stíle

Is minic fosta a bhaintear feidm as an rangabháil chaite in éineacht leis an
bhriathar *bí* le faobhar a chur ar stíl inste scéil. Seo a leanas roinnt samplaí
a léiríonn an úsáid seo:

(33)   *Agus ghuigh sé Dia [...] an bheirt* **a bheith adhlactha** *sa leacht
        céanna i ndeireadh ama* (Ó Cnáimhsí (eag.) 1989, 34)

(34)   *agus chomh maith le céad* [*agus*] *míle gaiscíoch eile ag breathnú orthu, agus iad ag ceapadh i gcónaí **go mbeadh Mac Rí in Éirinn leagtha agus an ceann bainte dhe** le crochadh ar an spiacán* (Ó Nualláin (eag.) 1982, 84)

I gcás (33) is léir nach gníomh céasta ach staid atáthar a mhaíomh. I dtaca le (34), is soiléir gur cúrsaí stíle atá sa treis mar go bhféadfaí an bhrí chéanna a thabhairt amach agus a rá mar seo: [...] *agus iad ag ceapadh i gcónaí go bhfeicfeadh siad Mac Rí in Éirinn leagtha agus an ceann bainte dhe* [...].[1]

5.2 Briathra Comhtháisc

Tá abairtí le fáil i nGaeilge Thír Chonaill ina mbaintear úsáid as briathra a bhaineann le gníomhaíocht na hintinne agus na cainte agus a bhfuil cosúlacht acu le húsáid an chéasta. Briathra comhtháisc a thabharfar mar ainm orthu anseo agus feasta má dhéantar tagairt dóibh. Ar ndóigh, ní céasta simplí atá anseo ach iarracht a chur in iúl go mbítí ag insint nó ag caint ar an ábhar atá i gceist i measc an phobail le tamall roimhe sin. Tabhair faoi deara mar sin nach ainmní uatha a bhíonn sna habairtí seo ach aicme nó iolra éiginnte éigin. Seo a leanas traidhfil samplaí:

---

[1] Ní dheachaigh muid ar thóir samplaí den bhriathar *bí* + rangabháil chaite le brí an chéasta i bhfoinsí níos faide siar ná an fichiú haois, cé go mb'fhéidir gurbh fhiú sin a dhéanamh amach anseo. Níor mhiste áfach tagairt d'abairt shuimiúil amháin atá sa chéad leagan den *Táin* (O'Rahilly 1976, 18.580, 141). Nuair a rinne an chú a bhí ag Culann ionsaí ar Chú Chulainn agus geata an dúin dúnta roimhe, shíl Conchobhar agus an mhuintir eile a bhí istigh go raibh deireadh leis an ghasúr: *Indar leó ní faircbítis i mbethaidh ara cind cid ersloicthe in less,* abairt a aistríonn an t-eagarthóir go Béarla mar seo: 'They thought they would not reach him alive though the fort was open'. Ach ó dúradh linn cheana féin gur dúnadh an longphort nuair a rinne siad dearmad de Chú Chulainn agus gur scaoil siad an chú, ag déanamh go raibh gach aon duine istigh, is deacair a thuiscint cad é an chiall a bheadh lena rá gur shíl siad nach bhfaigheadh siad beo é 'fiú dá mbeadh an dún ar oscailt' (nó 'nuair a bheadh an dún ar oscailt). Aimsir phointeáilte a chuireann an briathar *faircbítis* in iúl agus bheadh súil le briathar pointeáilte eile ina dhiaidh: i bhfocail eile, shíl siad nach bhfaigheadh siad beo é nuair a d'osclófaí an dún. Ach más ea, ní hí an fhoirm chéasta fhinideach den bhriathar a gheibh muid sa téacs ach an chopail agus an rangabháil chaite den bhriathar mar fhaisnéis, agus, ar ndóigh, de réir gnáis ní gníomh ná tarlúint a chuireann sé sin in iúl ach staid. Ar ndóigh ní tréad caora, agus go dtí go bhfaighthí samplaí eile dá mhacasamhail 'idir eatarthu' ó na téacsanna luatha, ní féidir an iomarca tábhacht a chur leis an abairt aonair seo. Tá sé suimiúil mar sin féin a thabhairt dar n-aire an difríocht atá idir an chéad agus an dara leagan den *Táin* i dtaca leis an mhír seo. I leagan LL níl caint ar bith ar dhúnadh an longphoirt agus is é an rud atá ag freagairt ann don abairt a thug muid thuas an méid seo: *Ciarbo óebéla oslaicthi dorus na cathrach, dochúaidh cách 'na irchomair dar sondaib in dúnaid immach,* is é sin, in aistriúchán Cecile O'Rahilly: 'though the gateway of the dwelling was wide open, they all went to meet him out over the palisades of the stronghold' (O'Rahilly 1970, 25.889, 162). D'fhéadfaí a cheapadh mar sin gur fearr a oireann *ciarbo óebéla oslaicthi doras na cathrach* don chomhthéacs seo ná mar a oireann *cid ersloicthe in less* do chomhthéacs *LU*. An féidir gur seo an chúis, nó cuid den chúis, ar athraíodh an comhthéacs sa téacs níos déanaí?

(35)   *Tá sé canta* ariamh ag na seanmhná gur [...] (Uí Bheirn (eag.) 1989, 68)

(36)   *Tá sé ráite* ariamh **ag daoine** gur sin an deireadh a bheadh air (Bríd Bean Mhic Íomhair, Mín an Chladaigh, Gaoth Dobhair)

(37)   *Bhí scéal greannmhar inste* faoin fhear chéanna (Mac Grianna 1976, 1)

(38)   *Bhí scéal inste* faoi sin dá bhféadfainn smaoiteamh air (Gaoth Dobhair)

(39)   *Chuala mé ráite* ariamh é gur mar sin a bhí (Gaoth Dobhair)

In eiseamláirí (40)–(42), tugann muid roinnt samplaí eile d'úsáid bhriathra comhtháisc áit nach 'rá' is ciall don bhriathar iontu. Mheasadh duine b'fhéidir gur príomhaimsir seachas aimsir leanúnach a ba chóir a úsáid ina leithéid de chásanna; is é sin shílfeadh duine gur *creideann sé go diongbhálta é, níor chreid sí sin* agus *níor thuig sé sin,* faoi seach, ab fhearr ann. Ach is léir nach ea agus go bhfuil brí éigin eile ar iompar leis na frásaí atá i gceist. Is fusa b'fhéidir an bhrí atá i gceist a fheiceáil sna habairtí diúltacha a thugann le fios nár creideadh nó nár tuigeadh cibé rud atá i gceist go fóill, go fiú ag am na tuairisce nó na cainte:

(40)   *Tá sé creidthe* go diongbhálta **aige** ('Máire' 1966, 5).

(41)   *Agus má dubhairt féin mar* **ní raibh sin creidthe aicí** ('Máire' 1961, 13)

(42)   *Bhí sé diúlta aici má diúltadh aon fhear ariamh. Ach do réir chosúlachta* **ní raibh sin tuigthe aige** ('Máire' 1962, 13)

5.3 Úsáidí Eile

Tá úsáidí eile ann ina mbíonn ciall leanúnach seachas brí staide le húsáid na rangabhála caite le briathra áirithe. Is léir ón chiall bhunaidh a bhíonn leis na briathra, arbh í foirm na rangabhála di a úsáidtear in abairtí dá leithéid seo, gurb ionann an bhrí a chuirtear in iúl agus an bhrí a bhíonn le '*being* + past participle' an Bhéarla nó le '*á* + infinid' na Gaeilge. Seo roinnt samplaí a bhaineann le hábhar:

(43)   *Char mhothaigh mé* an t-amhrán **ceolta** riamh (Raidió naGaeltachta, Doirí Beaga)

(44)   *Chan fhaca mé* an damhsa sin **déanta** aroimhe (Gaoth Dobhair)

D'fhéadfadh duine ciall na n-abairtí sin a thabhairt leis ach úsáid a bhaint as an infinid in áit na rangabhála. I gcás (43), mar shampla, d'fhéadfadh duine *char mhothaigh mé an t-amhrán á cheol riamh* a rá lán chomh maith.

Tá roinnt úsáidí eile ann nach furasta a thabhairt faoi riail. Baineann an chéad cheann acu sin le cur síos ar phróisis leanúnacha a chuirtear i bhfeidhm agus é mar aidhm acu sprioc ar leith a bhaint amach. Cuirtear an sprioc féin in iúl trí úsáid na rangabhála ach is léir nach rud a tharla i dtoibinne an gníomh. Tá sampla maith den úsáid seo san abairt seo a leanas.

(45)   ***Cuireadh ólta í*** (Uí Bheirn 1989, 73)

Is doiligh a rá cén sórt aistriúchán Béarla a chuirfeadh duine ar a leithéid d'abairt cé go bhfuil a brí breá soiléir i nGaeilge. Gach uile sheans gur ar bhealach éigin mar seo a leanas a chaithfí a theacht thart air leis an teachtaireacht a chur in iúl: *'They' got her drunk*. Cib bith scéal é, is úsáid shuimiúil í seo ina nasctar an neamhphearsanta agus an rangabháil le chéile le ciall ar leith a nochtadh. Díreach mar a bheadh súil ag duine leis, thig úsáid a bhaint as *faigh + rangabháil* leis an bhrí atá le (45) a thabhairt. Is léir go bhfóireann an úsáid dheiridh seo de *faigh* don chomhthéacs mar go bhfuil 'réamhphleanáil' i gceist agus go dtugann bunbhrí an bhriathair *faigh* an chiall léi ina cosa, mar a déarfá:

(46)   ***Fuarthas í a chur ólta*** 'They succeeded in getting her drunk' (Gaoth Dobhair)

Tá cineál eile abairte ann i nGaeilge Chúige Uladh ina mbaintear úsáid as an bhriathar shubstainteach + rangabháil chaite le ciall chéasta a chur in iúl:

(47)   ***Cha raibh*** sé maith ***déanta agaibh!*** (Cit Bhán Nic Giolla Chóill, Mín an Chladaigh, Gaoth Dobhair)

Cha doiligh bunchiall na habairte a léiriú ach is deacra ná sin a rá cad chuige a bhfuil an struchtúr uirthi atá. Cuireann an abairt féin in iúl go ndearnadh gníomh éigin agus gur gníomh gránna é agus nach maith an rud go ndearnadh a leithéid. Déarfaí abairtí mar seo i gcomhthéacs mar é seo a leanas. Abair go raibh daoine óga ag bobaireacht ar sheanduine éigin ach go ndeachthas rófhada le cuid den eachtraíocht agus gur fágadh mairg nó bris éigin nach raibh súil leis ar an tseanduine. D'fhéadfadh sé fosta gur cuireadh an seanduine dá threoir agus gur tharraing sin buaireamh air agus mar sin de. Seo sampla de théacs a foilsíodh cúpla bliain ó shin:

(48)   *De réir mar a bhí leagtha síos ag [John Stoupe] Charley **ní raibh sé***
          ***ceart déanta ag duine** teach nó cónaí de chineál ar bith a chur suas*
          gan cad an tiarna a bheith aige roimh ré. (Ó Cnáimhsí 1988, 90)

5.4 Staid nó Céasta

Tá mórán gnáthabairtí ann a bhfaightear an rangabháil chaite iontu agus
nach furasta a rá in amanna cé acu abairtí staide nó céasta iad. Ní bheidh
mórán plé againn ar an tsórt seo abairte anseo, ach ó tharla díospóireacht
áirithe i litríocht na teangeolaíochta fúithi, mheas muid nár mhiste tagairt di
anseo. Tá sampla den chineál abairte atá i gceist i (49) thíos:

(49)   *Tá an teach tógtha ag Seán*

Braitheann réiteach na ceiste ar an dearcadh a ghlacann duine chuige féin
agus é i mbun anailíse ar abairtí dá leithéid. Níl na scoláirí go léir ar aon
tuairim faoin cheist. I gcur síos réasúnta cuimsitheach déanann Ó Sé (1992,
42) argóint in éadan glacadh leis an leagan seo mar chéasta. Deir sé:

> The view held by Dillon and others will be upheld, therefore, as
> against that of Greene and the transformationalists.

Ba é an 'view' a bhí ag Dillon agus ag daoine eile gur 'periphrastic perfects' a bhí in abairtí mar *Tá teach tógtha agam*, ina nglactar leis gur frása
seilbhe ar nós *Tá teach agam* an bhunfhoirm agus go gcuirtear an aidiacht
bhriathartha *tógtha* isteach inti. Agus níos faide ar aghaidh san alt chéanna
deir Ó Sé (1992, 52) arís:

> An exception is DIL (s.v. *oc* 'at') which states that 'in Mod. Ir. *ag* is
> commonly used to denote the agent after a part[iciple] in periphrasis
> for perf[ect] tense: *atá an litir scríobhtha agam*'. However, the
> description of *ag* as an agent marker is more typical of
> transformational grammarians, such as Stenson (1981, 148-150) and Ó
> Siadhail (1989, 299). They would regard both *tá sé déanta* and *tá sé*
> *déanta agam* as passive, the latter with agent indicated'.

Déantar cás arís eile (McCloskey 1996), gur abairtí céasta iad leithéidí *tá*
sé déanta agam, ó thaobh na coimhréire ar chuma ar bith. Ar ndóigh tá siad
ó thaobh leagan amach de díreach cosúil le habairtí céasta i dteangacha eile
san Eoraip. Cé nach ionann go díreach na húsáidí a bhaintear as abairtí
céasta an Bhéarla agus an céasta foirfe seo (mar thugtar air) i nGaeilge, tá
cosúlachtaí móra céille eatarthu i gcomhthéacsanna ar leith. Tá na hargóintí
seo agus tuilleadh le fáil sna hailt atá luaite againn agus ní bheidh níos mó
trácht againn anseo ar an chinéal seo abairte.

5.5 *i ndiaidh/tar éis* + Rangabháil Chaite + *ag*

Arís eile faightear abairtí ina mbíonn an rangabháil chaite minic go leor ar thóir na bhfrásaí ama *i ndiaidh* agus *tar éis*. Tá brí an chéasta le brath orthu ainneoin gan deilbhíocht an chéasta a bheith le feiceáil orthu in aon áit. Ní i gcónaí a luaitear an gníomhaí in abairtí mar seo, ach nuair a dhéantar, baintear úsáid as an réamhfhocal *ag*. Seo traidhfil samplaí as foinsí scríofa:

(50)   [...] *ceist a chuireas ar Mhicil, a bhí tar éis **a thrucail a bheith tabhartha** ó na tránna **aige*** (Ua Maoileoin (eag.) 1977, 262)

(51)   [...] *tar éis mo dhóthain a chodladh agus mo bhricfeast **a bheith caite agam*** (ibid., 202)

(52)   *iad tar éis bia **a bheith caite acu*** (Ua Maoileoin (eag.) 1973, 43)

(53)   *D'fhágamar an com ar maidin Dé Luain **tar éis bleaist mhaith a bheith ite againn*** (Í Chearnaigh 1974, 26)

(54)   *Bhí seanbhád ochtar **tar éis a bheith ceannaithe acu** (de Bhaldraithe* (eag.) 1977, 145)

(55)   *fear [...] a raibh teach nua ceann slinne **tar éis a bheith déanta aige*** (ibid., 175)

(56)   *Ní raibh sé ach **tar éis a bheith insithe** dó cén chaoi a ndéarfadh sé I mBéarla é* (ibid., 43–4)

(57)   ***I ndiaidh an béile bheith caite** shuidh siad [...]* ('Muirghin' 1934, 67)

(58)   *D'fhág sé na Gardaí **i ndiaidh an leabhair seo a bheith foilsithe*** (Ua Maoileoin 1978, 56)

Mar atá ráite thuas againn ní hí seo an chomhréir a mbeifí ag súil léi in abairtí den chineál atá in (49–57) de thairbhe stair na teanga de. Cluintear an leagan 'traidisiúnta' de réir ghnás na teanga ina mbíonn an t-ainm briathartha taobh le taobh leis na leaganacha sin thuas. D'fhéadfadh duine a agairt go bhfuil rian an Bhéarla ar chuid de na leaganacha ar scor ar bith ach arís eile tá siad chomh fairsing sin agus le fáil ar fud na nGaeltachtaí ar fad gur doiligh géilleadh go hiomlán dó sin. Caithfear mar sin an cheist a chur, más áil linn glacadh le leaganacha den chineál sin mar chuid d'inneach na teanga, cad é go díreach an bhrí atá leo agus cén difríocht atá idir péirí abairtí mar iad seo thíos:

(59)   (a) *tar éis mo bhricfeasta* ***a chaitheamh***

        (b) *tar éis mo bhricfeasta **a bheith caite agam***

(60)   (a) *Bhí siad tar éis seanbhád ochtar **a cheannach***

        (b) *Bhí seanbhád ochtar tar éis **a bheith ceannaithe acu***

(61)   (a) *Bhí sé i ndiaidh móin **a bhaint** ann le dhá bhliain*

        (b) *Bhí móin i ndiaidh **a bheith bainte aige** ann le dhá bhliain*

Tá cosúlacht ar an scéal gurb ionann an difríocht idir an dá chineál abairte seo agus an difríocht bhunúsach a dhéantar idir *aimsir* agus *gné* i ngnáth-abairtí. Is é sin le rá má úsáidtear an t-ainm briathartha go bhfuiltear ag díriú isteach ar leanúnachas an ghnímh ina iomláine gan róthagairt d'aon chuid de. Ach nuair a bhaintear úsáid as an rangabháil chaite go bhfuiltear ag díriú aird an éisteora ní hamháin ar leanúnachas an ghnímh ach ar fhoirfeacht nó ar chríochnúlacht an ghnímh.

6 *Faigh* + an Rangabháil Chaite

Tá leaganacha eile sa teanga a bhféadfaí a rá gur foirmeacha céasta iad ach ar beag tagairt a dhéantar dóibh i gcáipéisí foilsithe. Sna leaganacha seo baintear úsáid as leagan den bhriathar *faigh* leis an rangabháil chaite. Bíonn na habairtí seo débhríoch ar uairibh agus is cosúil go bhfuil éagsúlachtaí ann ó chanúint go chéile. Amharcaimis ar abairt (61), mar shampla:

(62)   ***Fuair** mé an claí **tógtha***

Tá dhá chiall leis an abairt seo ag brath ar cé acu an t-ainmní féin nó duine éigin eile an gníomhaí. Is é sin le rá *thóg mé féin an claí*, sin nó *thóg duine éigin eile an claí domh*, an chiall atá leis an abairt. Ar chuma ar bith tá an obair críochnaithe anois. Tá cosúlachtaí ag an struchtúr seo leis an rud ar a dtugtar an *'got passive'* air i mBéarla in abairtí mar *'John got his hair cut'*. Cé go mbeadh fonn ar dhuine a rá go mb'fhéidir gur iasacht ón Bhéarla an struchtúr seo i nGaeilge, caithfear a bheith cúramach lena leithéid de ráiteas mar ní hionann dáiliú d'úsáidí an Bhéarla agus na Gaeilge gan an forainm athfhillteacha a bheith in úsáid. Féach (70). Ní fhaightear aon mhacalla d'abairtí mar *'John got arrested/fired'* i nGaeilge. Go deimhin féin bíonn an tríú ciall leis an abairt, is é sin nuair a tháinig mé ar an láthair go bhfaca mé an claí agus é tógtha. Ní bheidh ár n-aird ar an tríú brí sin anseo.

Bíonn dhá ní a mbíonn fócas orthu sna habairtí seo; go n-éiríonn leis an té a luaitear mar ainmní toradh éigin a bhaint amach agus go dtugtar an toradh sin chun críche. Déantar idirdhealuithe caolchúiseacha in amanna idir úsáid na hinfinide agus na rangabhála caite le *faigh*. Tabhair faoi deara an difríocht a d'fhéadfadh a bheith idir an dá shampla seo thíos:

(63)   ***Chan fhuair*** *Séamas na soithigh* **a ní** *ó mhaidin*

(64)   ***Chan fhuair*** *Séamas na soithigh* **nite** *ó mhaidin*

D'fhéadfaí a rá ar bhonn praiticiúil nach bhfuil difríocht ar bith ó thaobh céille idir an dá abairt seo. Ach tá. Nuair a úsáidtear an infinid (62) tugtar le fios nár thosaigh Séamas ar ní na soitheach ar chor ar bith ach tá sé le tuiscint ar (63) gur thosaigh sé ar an níochán cúpla uair ach nár éirigh leis go fóill an jab a chríochnú.

Ar ndóigh, thig an fhoirm chéasta den bhriathar *faigh* a úsáid fosta nuair nach luaitear gníomhaí. Seo a leanas beagán eiseamláirí as foinsí scríofa ina bhfaightear foirm neamhphearsanta an bhriathair *faigh* agus ceann den dá bhrí tosaigh a luaigh muid thuas leis:

(65)   *ach go bé gur [...]* **ní bhfuighfí** *an snáth* **gearrtha** *go deo* (Uí Bheirn 1989, 197)

(66)   *Tá ór na gCríostíní thíos ansin [ar thóin na farraige]* **nach bhfághthaí caite** *go brách* (ibid., 67)

(67)   *Scalltar feoirthíní do eallach a bhéas i bhfad* **gan a bhfághail durtha** (ibid., 104)

In abairtí ina mbíonn *faigh* + rangabháil chaite, is féidir gníomhaí na rangabhála a thaispeáint trí úsáid a bhaint as an réamhfhocal *ag*. Is láidre cuma an chéasta orthu fiú ná na heiseamláirí leis an bhriathar shubstainteach a pléadh níos luaithe (amharc 17, 18). Seo roinnt samplaí:

(68)   *Fuair mé an chulaith déanta ag an táilliúr*

(69)   *Gheobhaidh tú na bróga cóirithe ag an ghréasaí*

Is spéisiúil fosta go dtig forainmneacha athfhillteacha a úsáid sa chineál seo abairte nuair is é an t-ainmní an gníomhaí:

(70)   ***Gheobhaidh*** *Seán é féin* **goite** *leis an amaidí atá air* 'John will get himself arrested because of his carry-on'

Seo a leanas sampla as téachs foilsithe áit nach é gníomhaí na habairte a dhéanfar a ghabháil.

(71)   *'Bhail, gheobhaidh mise gaibhte é', arsa fear an tsiopa.* (Ó Searcaigh
       (eag.) 1983, 68)

Is ábhar staidéir ann féin é úsaid an bhriathair seo. B'fhéidir amach anseo
go mbeadh am ann tabhairt faoi scrúdú níos cuimsithí a dhéanamh air, rud
ab fhiú a dhéanamh. Measaimid mar sin féin gurbh fhiú dúinn beagán a rá
faoi anseo ó tharla gaol chomh gearr sin a bheith aige do théama na haiste
seo againn.

7. Úsáidí Eisceachtacha

Tháinig muid ar abairt amháin a bhfacthas dúinn comhréir cineál
eisceachtúil a bheith uirthi agus síleann muid nár mhiste í a lua anseo mar ó
thaobh na céille de go mbaineann sí leis an ábhar ata faoi chaibidil againn:

(72)   *Thoisigh an bia dá dhéanamh réidh ansin* [...][2] (Ní Dhíoraí (eag.) 1985, 103)

Ní léir dúinn faoi láthair an mbaintear úsáid níos coitianta as an chineál seo
abairte mar nach bhfuil againn ach an sampla seo. Mheasfadh duine gurb é
an briathar saor (e.g *toisíodh*) ab fhearr dá mba rud é gurb í brí an chéasta a
bhí le cur in iúl. Ach ní sin an rud atá againn. Tá cuma ar an scéal go
mb'fhéidir gur analach le habairtí ina bhfaightear an briathar substainteach
ar nós *bhí an bia dá dhéanamh réidh (acu) ansin* is cúis le leagan amach na
habairte. Caithfear ar ndóigh tuilleadh samplaí a fháil sular féidir aon rud
cinnte a rá faoin tsórt seo abairte. Tá cosúlachtaí áirithe idir abairt (70) agus
an ceann seo a leanas:

(73)   *Bhí daoine dá gcastáil dóbhtha ar gach aon bhaile dá raibh ar a*
       mbealach ('Máire' 1966, 106)

Tá de dhifríocht eatarthu mar sin féin gurb é an briathar céasta a bheadh in
úsáid le *cas* murach foirm leanúnach an bhriathair a bheith roghnaithe ag
an údar. Is léir measann muid go bhfuiltear ag déanamh idirdhealaithe san
abairt dheiridh seo idir aimsir phointeáilte agus gnéithe leanúnacha den
ghníomh. Dá scríobhadh an t-údar *casadh daoine dóbhtha* [...] ní bheadh an
chiall chéanna leis an abairt mar go bhfuiltear ag iarraidh a thaispeáint go
raibh daoine ag bualadh leo go leanúnach fad a bhealaigh (aistear shé mhíle
dhéag).

---

[2] Rinne muid an abairt seo a sheiceáil sa bhunlámhscríbhinn agus tá sí díreach mar atá anseo ach
amháin gur *Thosaigh* seachas *Thoisigh* a bhí curtha sios ag Sean Ó hEochaidh. Bá í an seanchaí clúiteach
Anna Nic An Luain as na Cruacha an cainteoir.

8. CONCLÚID

Níl san alt seo ach sceirdeadh gasta ar líon áirithe d'úsáidí céasta na Nua-Ghaeilge ar fiú do dhuine sonrú a chur iontu. B'fhéidir go bhféachfaimis am éigin eile a ghabháil isteach níos doimhne sna réimsí céille a bhaineann leo. Is léir go bhfuil cuid mhaith de na húsáidí seo le fáil ó cheann ceann na tíre agus chomh maith leis sin go bhfuil foráis éagsúla ar siúl i gceantair éagsúla le fada an lá. Tá creatlach éigin mar sin féin ag coinneáil smacht agus srian ar na forbairtí ar leith ionas gur cuid dhílis d'athruithe inmheánacha sa teanga féin iad. Bíonn ceist i gcónaí faoi thionchar an Bhéarla agus is mithid dá bhrí sin foirmeacha mar atá pléite anseo againn a chruinniú agus a thiomsú faoi ord agus faoi eagar, ionas go mbeidh a fhios againn cén cineál athruithe atá ag teacht ar an teanga agus cén stair a bhaineann leis na hathruithe sin.

TAGAIRTÍ

Boyle, Daniel P. 1973. 'The Passive in Irish', *University of Michigan Papers in Linguistics*, 1, 1–10

Comrie, Bernard 1976. *Aspect*, Cambridge: University Press

De Bhaldraithe, Tomás, eag. 1977. *Seanchas Thomáis Laighléis*, Baile Átha Cliath: An Clóchomhar

De hÍde, Dubhghlas, eag. 1933. *An Sgeuluidhe Gaedhealach*, Baile Átha Cliath: Institiúid Béaloideasa Éireann

Dillon, Myles 1941. 'Modern Irish *atá sé déanta agam* "I have done it"', *Language*, 17, 49–50

Greene, David 1979. 'Perfects and Perfectives in Modern Irish', *Ériu*, 30, 122–41

Harris, John 1985. 'The Hiberno-English "I've it eaten" Construction: What is it and where does it Come from', in *Papers on Irish English,* in eagar ag Dónall P. Ó Baoill, Baile Átha Cliath: Irish Association for Applied Linguistics, 36–52

Í Chearnaigh, Seán Sheáin 1974. *An tOileán a Tréigeadh*, Baile Átha Cliath: Sáirséal agus Dill

Keenan, Edward L. 1985. 'Passive in the World's Languages', in *Language Typology and Syntactic Description*, in eagar ag Timothy Shopen, I, Cambridge: University Press, 243–81

Mac Grianna, Seán Bán 1976. *Ceoltaí agus Seanchas*, Rann na Feirste: Coiste Choláiste Bríde

Mac Meanman, Seán Bán 1989. *Cnuasach Céad Conlach*, in eagar ag Séamas Ó Cnáimhsí, Baile Átha Cliath: Coiscéim

'Máire' = Ó Grianna, Séamas 1942. *Rann na Feirste*, Baile Átha Cliath: An Preas Náisiúnta

—1962. *Úna Bhán*, Baile Átha Cliath: Oifig an tSoláthair

—1966. *Bean Ruadh de Dhálach*, Baile Átha Cliath: Oifig an tSoláthair

—1968. *An Sean-Teach*, Baile Átha Cliath: Oifig an tSoláthair

—1961. *Ó Mhuir go Sliabh*, Baile Átha Cliath:

—*Castar na Daoine ar a Chéile srl.* (úrscéal nár foilsíodh)

McCloskey, James 1996. 'Subjects and Subject Positions in Irish', in *The Syntax of the Celtic Languages,* in eagar ag Robert Borsley agus Ian Roberts, Cambridge: University Press, 241–283

'Muirghin' = Ó Gallchóir, Pádraig 1934. *Cáitheamh na dTonn*, Baile Átha Cliath: Oifig Díolta Foilseacháin an Rialtais

Ní Dhíoraí, Áine, eag. 1985. *Na Cruacha: Scéalta agus Seanchas*, Baile Átha Cliath: An Clóchomhar

Ó Baoill, Dónall P. 1985. *Papers on Irish English*, Baile Átha Cliath: Irish Association for Applied Linguistics

Ó Cionnfhaolaidh, Micheul, eag. 1956. *Beatha Mhichíl Turraoin*, Baile Átha Cliath: Oifig an tSoláthair

Ó Cnáimhsí, Pádraig 1988. *Róise Rua*, Baile Átha Cliath: Sáirséal agus Dill

Ó Criomhthain, Tomás 1973. *An tOileánach*, in eagar ag Pádraig Ua Maoileoin, Baile Átha Cliath: Cló Talbot

—1977. *Allagar na hInise.* Baile Átha Cliath: Oifig an tSoláthair

Ó Domhnaill, Niall 1934. *Muintir Chois Locha*, aistr. ar *The Loughsiders* le Shan F. Bullock, Baile Átha Cliath: Oifig Díolta Foilseacháin an Rialtais

Ó Duilearga, Séamas, eag. 1948. *Leabhar Sheáin Uí Chonaill.* Baile Átha Cliath: An Cumann le Béaloideas Éireann

Ó Nualláin, Caoimhín, eag. 1982. *Eochair, Mac Rí in Éirinn.* Baile Átha Cliath: Comhairle Bhéaloideas Éireann

O'Rahilly, Cecile, eag., 1970. *Táin Bó Cúalnge from the Book of Leinster*, Baile Átha Cliath: Scoil an Léinn Cheiltigh

—1976. *Táin Bó Cúailnge, Recension 1*, Baile Átha Cliath: Scoil an Léinn Cheiltigh

Ó Sé, Diarmuid 1992. 'The Perfect in Modern Irish', *Ériu*, 43, 39–67

Ó Searcaigh, Lorcán, eag. 1983. Micí Sheáin Néill Ó Baoill, Lá de na Laethaibh, Muineachán: Cló Oirghealla

Ó Siadhail, Mícheál 1989. *Modern Irish: Grammatical Structure and Dialectal Variation*, Cambridge: University Press

Sayers, Peig 1939. *Peig .i. a Scéal Féin*, in eagar ag Máire Ní Chinnéide, Baile Átha Cliath: Clólucht an Talbóidigh

Stenson, Nancy 1981. *Studies in Irish Syntax*, Tübingen: Gunter Narr

Ua Maoileoin, Pádraig 1978. *Ár Leithéidí Arís*, Baile Átha Cliath: Clódhanna

Uí Bheirn, Úna 1989. *Cnuasach Focal as Teileann*, Baile Átha Cliath: Acadamh Ríoga na hÉireann

Progress in Irish?

JAMES McCLOSKEY

University of California, Santa Cruz

PREFACE

THERE has been in recent years a small explosion of work on the linguistics of Irish from within the theoretical paradigm of generative grammar. I believe that this work has yielded in very recent times (within the past five years or so) some real progress in our understanding of the syntactic system of the language. To say that a breakthrough has been made would be an overstatement, but the sense is palpable that certain things have fallen into place in surprising and somewhat unexpected ways. My purpose here is to review some of these developments and to argue (in a way that attempts to rise above the level of the technical) that perhaps some serious progress has been made. The vast majority of those who have contributed to this increasingly exciting line of work were introduced to the disciplines of generative grammar by Conn Ó Cléirigh. Had he not been the inspiring teacher that he was, this body of work would not exist.

The fundamental thesis of generative grammar is that underlying the apparently limitless heterogeneity of human linguistic systems, there lies a deep commonality—a shared structural bedrock invariant across the species. The best work in generative syntax has always sought to understand that commonality by constructing detailed models of syntactic subsystems within particular languages—in the hope of catching a glimpse of the underlying patterns in the workings of those subsystems. When the work goes well, two things happen simultaneously—first, a language or construction which had previously seemed exotic or isolated will suddenly be seen to reflect a well-known or well-understood pattern; second, properties of the language or construction which had seemed quirky, idiosyncratic and unrelated fall into place as aspects of a larger pattern. If the same analytical move which brings the language within the reach of theoretical understanding reveals something about its internal detail, then some optimism is justified.

It is always possible, of course, if one is determined enough or ignorant enough, to bludgeon a language into submission, so to speak, to force it into a pre-formed mould which conforms to theoretical expectation. The fundamental challenge that the generative paradigm asks us to meet, however, is to reconcile two imperatives often apparently at odds with one another—the need to do full justice to the particularity and internal spirit of the language one works on, and the need to respect what is known, or half-known, or plausibly speculated, about general principles of language design. One must try to make these two concerns meet in such a way that each informs and illumines the other.

I have been optimistic in a small way in recent years because I believe that something like this has been achieved for Irish. Certain core aspects of its syntax which seemed exotic can now be understood in a general framework which places them rather precisely within a known syntactic typology. The moves which make this integration possible, furthermore, shed light on some of the curious details of its clausal structure, uncovering a unifying pattern not previously visible.

IRISH CLAUSES

Theoretical puzzles emerge as soon as we look at the simplest sentence of Irish. The transitive finite clause in (1) is an instance of the informal syntactic schema given in (2):

(1)   Cheannaigh siad teach i mBaile Átha Cliath anuraidh.

(2)   [Verb Subject Object Adverbial Phrases]

This structure is odd because the subject intervenes between the (finite) verb and its object. A substantial minority of the world's languages (the VSO languages) show this peculiar property.

The property in question, of course, is peculiar only given some assumptions. To get a sense of what those assumptions are, consider the English equivalent of (1):

(3)   They [bought a house in Dublin last year].

The sequence *bought a house in Dublin last year* is set off by brackets because it is a syntactic constituent—a phrase consisting of a verb, complements of the verb, and certain optional modifying elements. It does not, though, include the subject Noun Phrase. Viewing the matter in terms of the dynamics of structure-building, we can say that an important difference between subjects and complements is that, as larger structures are gradually built up, complements are combined with the verb earlier, subjects later. Subjects and complements differ in many ways (having to do with the special semantic properties of subjects, the positioning and interpretation of certain adverbs, the distribution of referentially dependent elements such as reflexive and reciprocal pronouns and so on). Most of these differences are now thought to follow from the more fundamental difference in order of composition. The facts here are very general and

certainly hold of Irish. But if the theories which derive these general properties are on the right track, then Irish too must have a constituent like the
bracketed one in (3)—one within which the verb has combined with its
complements but not yet with the subject. The Irish clause in (1), however,
evidently contains no such thing. Since the subject intervenes between the
verb and its complements, there can be no surface constituent of the
language which includes the verb and its complements but excludes the
subject. This conclusion seems obvious to the point of triviality, but it is
incompatible with a large body of otherwise successful theorizing.

One possible response to this apparent dilemma, of course, is to say that
the theoretical claims with which Irish seems to be in conflict are hope-
lessly stupid and should be abandoned immediately, if for no other reason
than that the facts of Irish plainly show them to be wrong. This is probably
the response that most specialists in Celtic studies have been inclined to
give, to the extent that the question has been of interest.

However, the puzzles which led to the development of these theories are
real and pressing, and those who have been inclined to reject their
consequences for particular languages have not had much in the way of
alternative proposals to offer. It behoves us then to probe the Irish facts a
little more closely. We can approach a resolution of the dilemma from
what might seem initially to be an unpromising or at least an unlikely direction.

SMALL CLAUSES

Consider the italicized phrases in the English examples of (4):

(4)   a. What I really can't stand is *children disobeying their parents.*
       b. What I really can't stand is *students flirting with each other.*
       c. What I really can't stand is *people making rude noises in class.*

The italicized phrases in (4) are each built from two major
subconstituents—a Noun Phrase (*children* in (4a)), and a phrase which
consists of a verb combined with its complements (*disobeying their parents*
in (4a)). The second is predicated of the first. The resulting phrase
([*children* [*disobeying their parents*]]) defines an event-type or situation-
type, but does not anchor that description by providing a specification of
tense or modality. Nor does it express a proposition—the italicized phrases
of (4) define situation-types but make no claim that such situation-types
actually hold or fail to hold. Otto Jespersen coined the term 'bare
predicational nexus' for a phrase with these properties. In the literature of
generative grammar, they have usually been called 'small clauses'. Both

terms suggest that the italicized phrases of (4) have at least one of the core properties of full clauses (a predication relation) but lack certain others.

Let us begin by trying to understand something of the syntax of such expressions. Their internal structure presupposes the existence of two combinatorial principles. First we need one which combines a verb with its complements to make a larger phrase. Let us call this larger phrase a V^1. Second, we need a combinatorial principle which combines a V^1 with a Noun Phrase (NP) to form the small clause or predicational nexus itself. Let us call this second, larger, phrase a Verb Phrase (VP). This much granted, we can represent the structure of the italicized phrases in (4) schematically as in (5):

(5) $[_{VP}$ NP $[_{V^1}$ V Complement(s) $]]$

We call a phrase such as [*children* [*disobeying their parents*]] a VP, rather than a 'small clause' or a 'bare predicational nexus' because it turns out that there are a number of different types of small clause which need to be distinguished, in that their distributions are not identical. Consider the examples in (6)

(6)   a. What I really can't stand is *pets in the kitchen*.
         b. What I really can't stand is *cartons on the table*.
         c. What I really can't stand is *lit matches between my toes*.
         d. I want *that dirty laundry off the floor*.

The italicized phrases of (6) are also 'small clauses' in exactly the sense in which the phrases under examination in (4) are. The difference is that the predicative expressions of (6) (*in the kitchen* in (6a) for instance) are built out of prepositions and their complements rather than verbs and their complements. This difference aside, the schematic structure of these small clauses can be described in exactly the same terms as the earlier ones, namely as in (7):

(7) $[_{PP}$ NP $[_{P^1}$ P Complement(s) $]]$

So far, then, we have VP small clauses and PP small clauses. But clearly there are also adjectival small clauses—the italicized phrases of (8), for example:

(8)   a. What I really can't stand is *Adam Clayton nude on an album-cover*.
         b. What I really can't stand is *children scared of their parents*.
         c. What I really can't stand is *people drunk early in the morning*.

Extending the analysis already developed, we can understand the internal structure of adjectival small clauses as indicated schematically in (9):

(9)   [$_{AP}$ NP [$_{A^1}$ A Complement(s)]]

In fact, there are also small clauses whose predicative expressions are nominal. However, that type involves certain extra complexities which we should probably avoid here.

Summarizing to this point, we can see that we have here a structure of some generality—small clauses can be built from any of the major lexical categories (verb, preposition, adjective or noun); each involves the building of a predicative expression consisting of a lexical head (verb, preposition, adjective or noun) in combination with its complements, if any. The predicative expression is in turn combined with a Noun Phrase with which it stands in a relation of predication. The phrase-type so constructed can in turn fulfill a variety of grammatical functions—complement to a verb such as *hate* or *see*, for instance. Some of the syntactic contexts which permit the appearance of small clauses in English are illustrated in (10):

(10)   a. There is/are [...]
        b. I noticed [...]
        c. [...] is a terrible thing.
        d. [With [...]], it was impossible to proceed.

We can encapsulate our discussion so far by assuming that the general theory of grammar includes two principles of structure-building—the Head Complement Principle and the Maximal Phrase Principle.

The Head Complement Principle: Combine a V, P, or A with its complements. Label the resulting phrase V^1, P^1, or A^1, as appropriate.

The Maximal Phrase Principle: Combine an X^1 (that is, any of V^1, P^1, or A^1) with a NP. Label the resulting phrase VP, PP, or AP, as appropriate.

A maximal phrase so constructed is conventionally referred to as a small clause (or in Jespersen's term 'a bare predicational nexus'). We will occasionally refer to the NP which combines with X^1 as the 'specifier' of X^1, or the specifier of X. Finally, it is sometimes convenient to represent the internal structure of a small clause in the form of a tree-diagram:

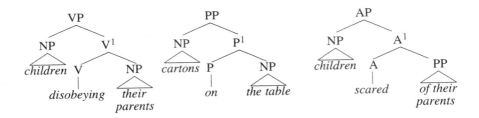

SMALL CLAUSES IN IRISH AND IN GENERAL

It turns out that small clauses are structures which are very widely attested indeed in languages of the world and whose internal makeup does not seem to vary much, if at all, from language to language. Consider Irish, for instance. (11) illustrates the case of verbal small clauses.

(11)   a. Ba mhinic [iad a' léamh leabharthaí].
        b. Níor thúisce [an teach leagtha] ná ...

(12) illustrates the case of prepositional small clauses:

(12)   a. Is minic [an Eaglais faoi ionsaí].
        b. Níor thúisce [an sagart sa teach], ná ...

Finally, (13) illustrates the case of adjectival small clauses:

(13)   Ba mhinic [mo mháthair marbh tuirseach ag deireadh an lae].

The most striking thing we notice here is that, despite the typological differences between the two languages, the internal structure of small clauses in Irish is identical to the internal structure of small clauses in English. The Irish structures can be described in exactly the same terms as those we used to describe the English constructions, and the order of elements in the two languages is the same. This would be an astonishing coincidence, if it were not true that the two languages conformed to the same fundamental design principles (the principles of Universal Grammar).

But there is also an important difference between Irish and English in this area. Although the internal structure of small clauses is identical in the two languages, their distribution is interestingly different. Small clauses occur in a much broader range of syntactic environments in Irish than they do in English (or in any other language that I know of).

They occur as complements to both nouns and adjectives:

(14)   a. Is mór an trua [fear croí mhóir i mbaile mór gan airgead].
       b. Is beag an iúnadh [airgead ag Séadna].
       c. Ba annamh [mo dheartháir as baile].

Neither of these possibilities exists in English, where, as in most languages for which the question has been investigated, small clauses may occur as complements to verbs and prepositions only:

(15)   a. *It's a pity [you so tired].
       b. *It's unlikely [them at home].
       c. She hates [pets in the kitchen].
       d. [With [the president out of the way]], the coup could proceed.

Most dramatically, small clauses in Irish may stand alone in texts and in discourse, again an impossibility in English:

(16)   a. Ghaibh criú naomhóige isteach. Iad righin ar a gcois, fad
          thruslógach, ag guailleáil rompu tríd an bpobal. (Pádraig Ua
          Maoileoin, *Bríd Bhán*, 19)

       b. Bhí láir aige … Coirce lom á theannadh aige léi. (*ibid.*, 25)

Small clauses may even occur in constituent questions:

(17)   Cén t-achar [Bríd agus Eoghan pósta anois]?

and in relative clauses:

(18)   Níorbh é seo [an chéad uair [na rudaí céanna ráite aige]].

There is a large and interesting set of puzzles locked up in these observations (see McCloskey 1985, McCloskey and Sells 1988, and especially Chung and McCloskey 1987 for extended discussion), a set of puzzles which extends to the syntax of nonfinite clauses (which show a similarly broad and unusual distributional pattern). In most languages, the distribution of small clauses is limited because they are extremely sensitive to the context in which they occur (more precisely, their subjects are very sensitive to the contexts in which the small clause occurs). In Irish no such sensitivity to context is evident, and small clauses occur freely, as discourse and semantic factors make appropriate.

What is general, then, are the principles which govern the internal structure of small clauses; what is particular to Irish is a parameter which has the effect of licensing or legitimizing small clauses independent of context:

Small Clause Parameter for Irish: Irish has a way of legitimizing small clauses independently of context. Most languages do not.

The interplay between the general and the language-particular seen here is very typical.

SMALL CLAUSES AND FULL CLAUSES

To this point, then, we have identified a syntactic structure of some generality. It is general in the sense that it is uniform across categories and uniform across languages. Schematically, it is of the form in (19):

(19)

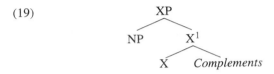

Two structure-building principles define this schematic structure as well-formed—the *Head Complement Principle* and the *Maximal Phrase Principle*. The syntactic relation between X^1 and the NP in specifier position corresponds to the semantic relation of predication. These principles of structure-building and of interpretation belong to the general theory of grammar. Irish in addition possesses a parochial property (a 'parameter') which has the effect that phrases of the form in (19) have a much broader distribution than in other languages.

These, obviously, are rather large conclusions to draw on the basis of the very limited body of data we have examined so far. They are not unreasonable, though, and there exists a large body of detailed analysis from a wide variety of languages and language-types to support them (see the papers in Cardinaletti and Giusti 1995, for instance, for extended discussion). One important caveat is in order, though—I have taken the liberty of introducing certain simplifications here for expository purposes. However, nothing crucial, I believe, is lost to the present discussion because of that simplification.

If we push our examination a stage further, an obvious question now arises: what is the relation between small clauses and full clauses ('real clauses' or inflected clauses)? Consider the pairs of examples in (20) and (21), the bracketed constituents especially.

(20)   a. I hate [people smoking in my office].

           b. [People have been smoking in my office].

(21)   a. Ní minic [scoláirí eile ag taobhú liom sa chonspóid seo].

b. [Thaobhaigh scoláirí eile liom sa chonspóid seo].

Clearly there is a systematic relation between the small clauses of (20a) and (21a) and the full clauses of (20b) and (21b). There are both systematic similarities and systematic differences. (20a) and (20b) both involve a relation of predication between a NP (the subject) and another phrase. The other phrase in both (20a) and (20b) is built from a lexical head combined with its complements (and optional modifiers). The order of elements within this predicative constituent is the same in the small clause and in the full clause

The differences are both syntactic and semantic. The full clause contains inflectional morphology of a familiar sort (inflection for tense, agreement, modality, aspect) and allows the expression of negation. If a small clause defines an event-type or situation-type, then a full clause situates an instance of that event-type or situation-type in time (tense) and in a possible world (modality). Further it involves an existential claim of a particular sort. Many of the most influential among recent approaches to semantics would hold that an English sentence like (20b) means that a certain event took place—one token of the type described by the small clause in (20a). The corresponding negative clause involves the negative existential claim that no such event took place. (For an extended discussion and defence of this approach to sentential semantics, see, among many others, Parsons (1990, 1995).) Putting these observations together, we see that the structure (syntactic and semantic) of the full clause subsumes the structure (syntactic and semantic) of the small clause (as is suggested by the informal terminology). We need, then, a theoretical account of this relation. The most economical such account we could give would seem to be to maintain that a full clause simply consists of a small clause in combination with an extra element (or perhaps set of elements). This element must specify the inflectional information that makes a clause a clause—information about tense, agreement, modality, aspect and so on. Let us use the abbreviation Infl(ection) for the complex element (or set of elements) within which this information is encoded. On the semantic side, it is the presence of this element which triggers the interpretation of the clause as an existential claim about events. What we minimally need, then, to understand the internal structure of a full clause, is a structure-building principle which will combine the inflectional complex (Infl) with a small clause. Schematically:

(22)   Clause $\overset{def}{=}$ Infl + Small Clause

This crude formula captures in an informal way the systematicity of the relation we have been discussing—the relation between small clauses and full clauses. It remains to make some theoretical sense of it, however. (22) is a principle of structure building and we have seen two such principles already—the *Head Complement Principle* and the *Maximal Phrase Principle*. Jointly these two principles provide for schematic structures like that in (19) above. Considerations of symmetry and economy would lead us to hope that the same principles would govern all instances of structure-building. If that is the case, then we would expect that the structure built by combining the inflectional complex (Infl) with a small clause would also be an instance of the general pattern seen in (19). That is, we would expect that the Head Complement Principle would combine Infl with its small clause complement, and that the Maximal Phrase Principle would in turn provide a NP-specifier position for the resultant structure. For the case where the small clause is verbal, this would provide for structures like (23):

(23)

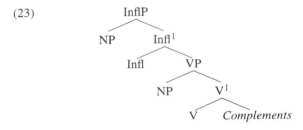

The burden of the rest of this paper is to argue that the view of clausal architecture schematized in (23) is largely correct. More specifically, even though we have been brought to this view by considerations of theoretical economy and symmetry alone, it is a view which lets us understand Irish clausal structure in a way which simultaneously reveals its kinship with other languages and explains some of its apparent eccentricities. I should point out before proceeding that I will deal here only with the case in which the complement of Infl is a verbal small clause (a VP). This seems to be the only possibility which English allows. Languages which allow the complement of Infl to be a PP, AP, or NP are those languages (such as Irish, Hebrew or Russian) which have finite non-verbal clauses (so-called 'copula clauses' in Irish, in which the copula is plausibly a realization of Infl). See Ahlqvist (1972) for relevant discussion, and see Doherty (1996) for an extension of the approach described here to such clauses. Let us put these difficult and interesting issues aside here, though, and concentrate on the case where the complement of Infl is VP.

TWO LANGUAGE-TYPES

We have been led to the hypothesis represented in (23) by a fairly abstract line of reasoning (mostly by a faith in theoretical symmetry). (23) incorporates a certain idea about the way in which clauses in natural language are organized. It holds that a clause consists of two 'layers'—an inflectional layer (which specifies its tense, its modality, whether it is affirmative or negative and so on), and a lexical layer, which defines its core content—the kind of event or situation it specifies and the kind of participants which are involved in that event-type or situation-type. This kind of information is supplied by the verb, its subject and its complements. The lexical layer (VP), according to (23), is embedded within the inflectional layer. It follows from this conception that the verbal head of the clause is initially separated from Infl—the complex of inflectional information. But of course in many languages, and certainly in Irish, the inflectional information is in fact realized as verbal morphology. It follows in turn that for a structure like (23) to be realizable on the surface in a language like Irish, V and Infl must combine. One way for this to be achieved is for V to raise to combine with Infl, the syntactic complex so created being ultimately realized as an inflected verb. Schematically (where *t*, mnemonic for 'trace', marks the original position of the verb):

(24) $[_{\text{InflP}} \text{INFL}+\text{V} [_{\text{VP}} \text{NP } t \text{ Complements }]]$

This derivation yields the surface order of elements (25):

(25)   Inflected-Verb Subject Complements

which is, of course, the normal order of elements in a finite clause in Irish. If this general view is correct, then the (initially puzzling) VSO order of Irish reflects the interaction of two sets of principles—on the one hand, the fundamental structure-building principles that give rise to (23), and on the other the 'need' to combine the verb with the inflectional material in the course of the syntactic derivation—ultimately to permit morphological realization.

We will explore some of the detailed empirical ramifications of these proposals shortly. For the moment, let us note that they lead us to expect that when the verb is uninflected, it should appear in its 'original' position (the position defined by the principles of structure-building, unobscured by movement operations) and that that position is one in which the verb follows the subject and precedes complements. We have seen one case of this already—small clauses. Another is the case of infinitival clauses (so-called 'verbal noun constructions'). Such clauses resemble small clauses in lacking most inflectional specification (they are formally un-marked for tense, mood and subject agreement). If the general framework of assumptions developed so far is roughly on the right track, then verb movement (at least of the kind found in finite clauses) should be inapplicable in nonfinite clauses. Many complexities and difficulties arise in working through this idea (having to do, in particular, with the position of the object in the various dialects), but the fundamental expectation is clearly correct, I believe, as seen for instance in the Donegal examples in (26):

(26) a. Níor mhaith liom [iad breith orm].
      b. B'fhearr leat gan [mé creidbheáil sa rud].

For extended discussion of these issues, see McCloskey (1980, 1984, 1985), Chung and McCloskey (1987), McCloskey and Sells (1988), McCloskey (1991), Guilfoyle (1990, 1993), Duffield (1995), Bobaljik and Carnie (1996), Watanabe (1996).

Where, though, will an SVO language like English fit into this theoretical scheme? The position of the inflectional complex in English is indicated most surely by the meaningless auxiliary *do* whose only purpose seems to be to bear the crucial information (present or past tense, and the minimal agreement that present-day English exhibits):

(27) She doesn't always agree with me.

It is also in this position that the various modalities are expressed in English, as well as negation:

(28) a. She might not agree with me.
      b. She must agree with me.

If the position of *doesn't, might not*, and *must* in (27) and (28) marks the position of Infl in these examples, then the subject must appear to its left. Given the assumptions about structure-building that we have been guided by, we must conclude that the subject in English occupies the specifier-position associated with Infl. That is, we have a structure like (29):

(29)

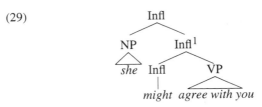

This seems right for English, but how is it consistent with the view that English and Irish share a basic structure—that in (23)? The answer that has emerged from recent work is that (23) is indeed the underlying structure for both Irish and English (and more broadly), but that English (unlike Irish) has a rule which raises the subject NP from its original position within VP to the specifier position of Infl. That is, a more detailed theory of English clause structure would be the derivational scheme below, in which *t* marks the underlying position of the subject:

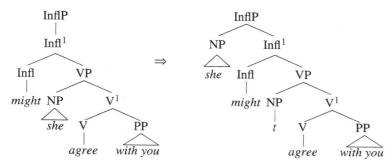

What this hypothesis amounts to is the claim that the NP conventionally called the 'subject' serves two distinct functions (at least) in a sentence. One function is to specify one of the participants (typically the agent-participant if there is one) in the event-type to which the verb refers. To fulfill this function it must be in a local syntactic relation with the verb. Its other function (or functions) has to do with the inflectional complex and to fulfill that function the subject must be in a local syntactic relation with Infl. Hence the movement from inside VP to the specifier-position of Infl—to allow the NP to occupy two distinct positions in the structure and thereby to fulfill two different functions (at distinct points in the syntactic derivation).

Why should we believe that subjects in English originate inside VP? One piece of evidence has to do with quantified expressions like those in (30):

(30)   a. I saw *them all.*
        b. We hired *them both.*

These are complex NP consisting of a NP (pronominal in the case of (30)) and a universal quantifier of a particular type—either *all* or *both.* The crucial property of such Noun Phrases is that they consist of one Noun Phrase contained within another:

(31)   [NP [NP them] all]

Consider now what happens when such complex noun phrases are subjects. There are two possible realizations, as seen in (32)–(34):

(32)   a. *They* might *all* go to the pictures.
        b. *They all* might go to the pictures.

(33)   a. *They* can *both* apply for the job.
        b. *They both* can apply for the job.

(34)   a. *You* have *all* seen this film?
        b. *You all* have seen this film?

Note that the 'stranded' quantifiers in the (a)-examples occur in just the position in which we have hypothesized that the subject originates. We can account for the availability of both options by assuming that either the inner or the outer NP of (31) may raise from the VP-internal position to the specifier-position of Infl. When the inner NP raises, the quantifier is stranded in its base position, which thus provides a visible mark, so to speak, of the position occupied by the subject at an earlier point in the derivation (Sportiche (1988, 1995), Shlonsky (1991), Merchant (1996), McCloskey (1996c), McCloskey (to appear)).

Since its general adoption in the mid eighties, the view of clausal organization schematized in (23) has formed the basis for a great deal of research and it has made available a subtle typological framework within which many well-studied languages can be placed rather precisely. Two parameters define this typology—whether or not the subject raises from VP into the specifier-position associated with Infl—yes for English and French; no for Irish, and whether or not V raises to combine with Infl—yes for Irish, French and most of the other Romance languages; no for English and the mainland Scandinavian languages (but yes for Icelandic and Faroese). It would be impossible to survey the results of this work in the space available here, but its general implications are clear. The picture of syntactic variation which emerges is one in which the basic structure-building operations (and associated semantic operations) are identical for languages of great superficial diversity. Differences emerge in the course of syntactic derivations and are possibly linked ultimately to morphological properties of languages (that is, to the way in which a language negotiates the gap between the syntactic and morphological aspects of inflectional information).

The hypothesis represented by (23) provides the basis for this typology and it also resolves the theoretical anomalies considered in the opening paragraphs of this paper. There it was pointed out that certain very general properties of subjects were to be accounted for by maintaining that subjects are folded into syntactic structure in a different way than complements (that is, by what we have called the *Maximal Phrase Principle* rather than by the *Head Complement Principle*). Irish, as we saw, presented an important prima facie difficulty for this scheme of explanation, given the VSO order of its finite clauses. But given (23), that difficulty dissolves and the same explanatory paradigm can be applied to Irish as can be applied to other, superficially different, languages.

It is reasonable to maintain, then, that the approach to clausal organization represented by (23) and associated assumptions provides some substantial theoretical benefits. But what of the other question raised in the opening paragraphs? In making these analytical moves, are we discovering something about Irish, or are we merely forcing it into a mould originally formed for other languages, notably the imperially successful languages like English? My own view is that a genuine deepening of understanding has been attained. In the final two sections I want to try to show that given (23), certain otherwise puzzling features of Irish yield to understanding.

WHERE THE CLAUSE DIVIDES

According to the analysis developed here, an Irish finite clause has the outline structure in (35):

(35)

InflP
|
Infl¹
Infl   VP
d' V   NP   V¹
ólfadh Eoghan V   NP
            t pionta

A striking feature of (35) is that it defines a major constituency-break between the finite verb and the rest of the clause. The sequence of subject, followed by complements followed by optional modifiers, if any, is defined as a VP and should therefore function (i) like a syntactic constituent and (ii) more specifically, like a VP. Surprisingly, both of these expectations are realized. We know that this material must be a syntactic constituent because it can be coordinated (for more detailed discussion and defence of this position, see McCloskey 1991):

(36)   cha raibh madadh ar bith againn nó muid ábalta madadh a cheannach
         (Micí Mac Gabhann, *Rotha Mór an tSaoil*, 159)

(37)   Ní raibh aoinne marbh nó aon chnámh briste (An tAth. Peadar Ua
         Laoghaire, *Eisirt*, 95)

(38)   ní rabh uchtách agam nó eagla orm (*Imeachtaí Fhear Dheireadh
         Teaghlaigh*, transl. by Seosamh Mac Grianna, 13)

(39)   nuair nach dtáinig siad ar ais ná scéala ar bith uatha (Séamas Ó
         Searcaigh, *Laochas*, 134)

The possibility represented by (36)–(39) is straightforwardly expected
given (35); it is mysterious given other imaginable assumptions.

The possibility of so-called 'Right Node Raising' suggests the same
conclusion. Right Node Raising is a much-studied construction in which a
single constituent, which appears rightmost in a clause and set off by a
strong intonational break, is shared between two coordinated fragments
earlier in the sentence:

(40)   The secretary draughted, and the treasurer reviewed, *a brief summary
         of the current financial situation.*

Examples of the same type, but involving the sequence consisting of
subject and complements, occur freely in Irish, suggesting once again that
this sequence of items in a finite clause is a syntactic constituent:

(41)   Níor thug, nó is beag má thug, an pobal aon aird ar an bhean bhocht.
         (Raidió na Gaeltachta, Casla)

         Bhí agus tá fós ard-mheas agam ar an bhfoinse seo. (Pádraig Ua
         Maoileoin, *Iomairí Críche*, 20)

So far so good. These initially very surprising properties of Irish finite
clauses fall into place right away given the analysis proposed. We can go a
step further, though. What are we to make of the very odd claim that the
sequence of subject followed by complements is in fact a Verb Phrase
(VP)? What is so peculiar about this claim is that this sequence of elements
does not seem to contain a verb at all, but does contain a subject. The
analysis developed here, though, commits us to the view that it must indeed
be a Verb Phrase, as inspection of (35) quickly reveals—a VP out of which
the verb has been raised and out of which the subject has not been raised,
but a VP nonetheless. How might we tell if this claim was right or not?

A number of languages (including at least English, Hebrew and a
number of Bantu languages, perhaps also Japanese, Chinese and Korean)
have an ellipsis process which has the effect of deleting a VP under identity
with a VP which occurs elsewhere in the sentence or in the discourse:

(42) a. They said they'd buy a house and they did [_VP ...].
      b. Will you sit for a minute? I will [_VP ...].

In terms of the conception of clausal structure we are dealing with here, what happens in such cases is that the complement of Infl is elided, and the inflectional element itself *did* in (42a), *will* in (42b) is, as a consequence, stranded.

If Irish possessed such an ellipsis process, and if the general conception of clausal organization that we have developed is on the right track, what should we expect? The operation (VP-ellipsis) consists of the elision of VP and the consequent stranding of Infl. But in Irish, we have argued, the subject remains within VP. Therefore the subject should disappear, since it is a subpart of VP. But we have also argued that the verb raises out of VP and combines with the sentence-initial inflectional complex. This means in turn that when VP-ellipsis applies, the finite verb should survive the ellipsis process (having fled the doomed constituent, so to speak, before its destruction) and should appear amalgamated with Infl in the usual way (this is indeed what happens in Hebrew and in Bantu). Putting these two expectations together, what we expect for Irish is that there should exist structures like (43):

(43) a. Dúirt siad go gceannódh siad teach agus cheannaigh.
      b. An n-ólfá bolgam tae? D'ólfainn.

It turns out that when one examines the properties of this Irish ellipsis process closely, they mirror the properties (syntactic and semantic) of VP-ellipsis in English down to the smallest details (McCloskey 1991, Fiengo and May 1994, 161).

This result is, I believe, a remarkable vindication of the general approach described here. The same analytical move which brings Irish into the range of theoretical understanding provides an account of many details of its syntactic system (the coordination facts, the right node raising facts and the ellipsis facts just considered) and (in the case of the ellipsis facts in particular) reveals an Irish construction to be, not an isolate as it first appears to be, but rather a hidden instance of a broadly recognized grammatical process.

HARDER PROBLEMS

I want to end with some more speculative remarks about problems which are much more difficult and obscure than those we have so far been dealing with. We can begin with the following question. What is the difference between, say, English and Irish, such that raising of the subject from VP into the specifier-position of Infl is obligatory in English but impossible in Irish?

It is clearly a property of English (and in fact of many languages) that every clause must have a subject. In a range of cases, this requirement is met by the presence of a semantically contentful NP in subject-position (the specifier-position of Infl in our scheme of things):

(44)   a. *She* won a bronze medal.

   b. *They* were promoted last year.

   c. *Many people* are afraid.

This is not, however, the only way in which the requirement may be met. Under certain conditions, the specifier-position of Infl ('subject position') may be filled by a semantically empty element such as the pronoun *there* (distinct in this use from the locative pronoun *there*):

(45)   a. There were many people on the street.

   b. I arranged [for [$_{InflP}$ *there* to be wine on the table]].

   c. *There* will come a time when all will be forgiven.

   d. *There* exists no solution to this problem.

Such contentless pronouns are known as 'expletive pronouns' (sometimes 'pleonastic' or more informally 'dummy' pronouns). The principal or only function of expletive pronouns seems to be to fill the specifier-position associated with Infl. When an expletive pronoun occupies this position, no NP can or may raise from within VP to occupy it. In general, though, the two options (insertion of an expletive and raising of the highest NP within VP) exist side by side. Beside (45) we have (46) in English:

(46)   a. *Many people* were on the street.

   b. I arranged [for [$_{InflP}$ *wine* to be on the table]].

   c. *A time* will come when all will be forgiven.

   d. *No solution* exists to this problem.

In these cases, the requirement that the specifier-position of InflP be filled is met not by insertion of an expletive pronoun, but rather by raising of a NP (the most accessible in a technical sense) to fill that position. Many languages have this strange requirement (most European languages certainly), and the general theory of grammar seems to provide these two means of satisfying it—insertion of an expletive element, or NP-raising from VP. The option of inserting an expletive is severely restricted in English (it is possible only in some intransitive clauses), but is much more widely available in other languages. French, for instance, uses *il* in this function and allows it also in passive clauses (47b):

(47)   a. *Il* n'existe aucune solution à ce problème.
       b. *Il* a été tué trois hommes à Paris hier.

Some of the Scandinavian languages (as well as Dutch) allow the expletive option even in transitive clauses. In Icelandic, for instance, we have intransitive examples (48) and also transitives (49):

(48)   Það dansaði maður í garðinum.
       there danced *a-man in garden-the*
       'There danced a man in the garden.'

(49)   Það grefur kona gröf í garðinum.
       there digs a-woman a-grave in garden-the
       'There digs a woman a grave in the garden.'

In (colloquial) Finnish also (Holmberg and Nikanne 1995), expletive constructions are much more productive than in English, as shown for instance in (1} (here the expletive pronoun is *sitä*, formally a partitive):

(50)   Sitä eivät nämä lapset olisi ikinä oppineet kävelemään.
       EXP NEG–P3 *these children* AUX *ever learned walk* [–FIN]
       'These children would never have learned to walk.'

Summarizing, we see that many (or perhaps most) languages impose a requirement that the highest specifier position in the inflectional layer must be filled. We see further that the general theory of grammar provides two mechanisms by way of which this requirement may be met—raising of an accessible NP from inside VP, or insertion of an expletive pronoun. The first option seems always to be available; languages differ in the degree to which they dispose of the second.

This, then, is what drives raising of the subject from VP in English. In the absence of an expletive, raising of the subject out of VP will be obligatory.

One of the most striking properties of Irish is that it seems to entirely lack this 'obligatory subject' requirement. This can be seen in the wide variety of impersonal constructions that the language enjoys, particularly in its southern dialects—the intransitive constructions illustrated in (51), for example, and the perfective (passive) constructions illustrated in (52):

(51)   a. Laghdaigh ar a neart.
       b. Bhreisigh ar an ghluaiseacht.

    c. Tiocfaidh as na brístí sin.

    d. Thoisigh eatarthu.

(52)   a. Tá labhartha aige le cúpla duine cheana.

    b. ... go bhfuil díolta go ró-dhaor againn astu

    c. sula raibh ite agus ólta acu

    d. ní fada a bhí siúlaithe aige

    e. nuair a bhí tráite síos uaidh

There are numerous semi-lexicalized expressions which make the same point:

(53)   a. Beidh daor ort.

    b. Bhí ina chogadh dhearg eatarthu.

    c. Ná fuil ort fós?

    d. Bhí linn!

    e. Tharla duit mar tharla dom féin.

The task of demonstrating fully that Irish lacks the 'obligatory subject' property is beyond the scope of the present paper (see McCloskey 1996a, 1996b for a full discussion and full citation of relevant examples) but it does seem to be a true property of the language. If this is the case, then we have an account of what the difference is that separates Irish from an SVO language of the English type—raising of an NP from inside VP is not motivated (because Irish lacks the obligatory subject property) and is therefore impossible. When V raises to Infl in finite clauses, SVO order is the ultimate outcome.

CONCLUSION

If these speculations are on the right track, we place the Irish syntactic system within a known typology and we also establish a systematic connectedness among certain internal properties of the language: VSO order in finite clauses, subject-initial order in small clauses and infinitival clauses, certain patterns of coordination, certain patterns of Right Node Raising, certain patterns of ellipsis, the absence of expletive constructions, and the absence of the obligatory subject property. We do this, furthermore, within the terms of a theory which has some claim to general applicability and which reveals (one might claim) the regularity hidden beneath superficial heterogeneity.

    As always, new questions arise and the deeper mysteries remain untouched. We have no understanding, for instance, of what the real nature of the 'obligatory subject' property is. Why should some or most languages have this deeply strange requirement? And the most puzzling question of all remains far beyond the reach of understanding—why should the syntactic systems of natural languages be organized in this preposterous way?

REFERENCES

Ahlqvist, Anders 1972. 'Some Aspects of the Copula in Irish', *Éigse*, 14, 269–274

Bobaljik, Jonathan and Andrew Carney 1996. 'A Minimalist Approach to Some Problems of Irish Word Order', in Borsley and Roberts 1996, 223–240

Borsley, Robert and Roberts, Ian, eds 1996. *The Syntax of the Celtic Languages, a Comparative Perspective*, Cambridge: University Press

Cardinaletti, Anna and Guasti, Maria Teresa 1995. *Small Clauses, Syntax and Semantics*, XXVIII, San Diego and New York: Academic Press

Doherty, Cathal 1996. 'Clausal Structure and the Modern Irish Copula', *Natural Language and Linguistic Theory*, 14, 1–46

Duffield, Nigel 1995. *Particles and Projections in Irish Syntax, Studies in Natural Language and Linguistic Theory*, Dordrecht, Boston and London: Kluwer Academic Publishers

Fiengo, Robert and May, Robert 1994. *Indices and Identity, Linguistic Inquiry Monograph*, 24, Cambridge, Mass.: MIT Press

Guilfoyle, Eithne 1990. *Functional Categories and Phrase Structure Parameters*, unpublished doctoral dissertation, McGill University

—1993. 'Nonfinite Clauses in Modern Irish and Old English', *Proceedings of the Twenty-Ninth Regional Meeting of the Chicago Linguistic Society*, Chicago, Illinois

Holmberg, Anders and Nikanne, Urpo 1994. 'Expletives and Subject Positions in Finnish', *Proceedings of the Twenty-Fourth Annual Meeting of the Northeastern Linguistics Society, NELS*, 24, 173–187

McCloskey, James 1980. 'Is there Raising in Modern Irish?', *Ériu*, 31, 59–99

—1984. 'Raising, Subcategorization and Selection in Modern Irish', *Natural Language and Linguistic Theory*, 1, 441–485

—1985. 'Case, Movement and Raising in Modern Irish', in *Proceedings of the Fourth West Coast Conference on Formal Linguistics, WCCFL*, 4, ed. by J. Goldberg, S. MacKaye and M. Wescoat, Stanford Linguistics Association, 190–205

—1991. 'Clause Structure, Ellipsis and Proper Government in Irish', *Lingua*, 85, 259–302

—1996a. 'Subjects and Subject-Positions in Irish', in Borsley and Roberts 1996, 241–283

—1996b. 'On the Scope of Verb Movement in Irish', *Natural Language and Linguistic Theory*, 14, 47–104

—1996c. 'Quantifier Float and WH-Movement in an Irish English', paper presented to the Twenty-Sixth Annual Meeting of the Northeastern Linguistics Society, Harvard and MIT, November 1995

—to appear. 'Subjecthood and Subject Positions', in *A Handbook of Formal Syntax*, ed. by Liliane Haegeman, Dordrecht, Boston and London: Kluwer Academic Publishers

McCloskey, James and Chung, Sandra 1987. 'Government, Barriers and Small Clauses in Modern Irish', *Linguistic Inquiry*, 18, 173–237

McCloskey, James and Sells, Peter 1988. 'Control and A-Chains in Modern Irish', *Natural Language and Linguistic Theory*, 6, 143–189

Merchant, Jason 1996. 'Scrambling and Quantifier Float in German', *Proceedings of the Twenty-Sixth Annual Meeting of the Northeastern Linguistics Society, NELS*, 26, 179–183

Parsons, Terence 1990. *Events in the Semantics of English*, Cambridge, Mass.: MIT Press

Parsons, Terence 1995. 'Thematic Relations and Arguments', *Linguistic Inquiry*, 26, 635–662

Shlonsky, Ur 1991. 'Quantifiers as Functional Heads: a Study of Quantifier Float in Hebrew', *Lingua*, 84, 159–180

Sportiche, Dominique 1988. 'A Theory of Floating Quantifiers and its Corollaries for Constituent Structure', *Linguistic Inquiry*, 19, 425–449

—1995. 'French Predicate Clitics and Clause Structure', in Cardinaletti and Guasti 1995, 287–324

Watanabe, Akira 1996. *Case Absorption: Studies in Natural Language and Linguistic Theory*, Dordrecht, Boston and London: Kluwer Academic Publishers

A Note on Palatalisation and the Present Inflection of Weak *i*-Verbs

KIM McCONE

Department of Old Irish, St. Patrick's College, Maynooth

HAVING often heard a distinguished former student of his wax lyrical about our late lamented honorand's rare ability to teach Old Irish 'in all its complexity' and yet with utter clarity, I offer this short study to the memory of Conn the Old Irish linguist and take as my starting point a classic article on the growth of palatalisation in Irish by his friend and fellow savant the late David Greene (1973). Taking full account of subsequent refinements by André Martinet (1955, 199–211) and Warren Cowgill (1969) to the somewhat unsatisfactory treatments in the standard grammars by Holger Pedersen (1909, 336–56) and Rudolf Thurneysen (1946, 96–104), Greene's article presented a masterly synthesis and further elaboration of the relevant rules that for the first time accounted for the vast majority of actually attested Old Irish forms straightforwardly.

Greene made a basic distinction between an invariably palatalising schwa (*ĭ*) that arose from short (including shortened) *i, e* or *ü* (allophone of *u* before a front vowel) in unstressed syllables subsequently liable to apocope or syncope on the one hand and retained unweakened front vowels with appreciably less indiscriminate palatalising effects on the other. To begin with, only single consonants or groups of nasal plus voiced stop (*Nd* etc.) were affected by palatalisation in the second category, whence alternations such as that between *erbaid* 'entrusts' < **erbiθ'ĭ* < **erbiθ'i* and *eirbthi* 'entrusts himself, trusts' < **er'b'ĭθ'i* < **erbiθ'i-e(n)* with non-palatal and palatal *rb* respectively. Thereafter the palatalising potency of retained front vowels rose from invariably non-palatalising low *ü* (e.g. nom. *Luguid* < **luγüθ'e(h)* versus gen. *Luigthech* < **luγ'iθ'ex* < **luγüθ'exa(h)*) through mid *e(:)* to high *i(:)*. The major limitation on *e(:)* was that it only palatalised a preceding consonant if this was in turn preceded by a front vowel, whence *beirid* 'bears' < **ber'eθ'ĭ* or *lingid* 'leaps' < **lin'g'eθ'ĭ* with palatal *r/ng* but *carae* 'friend' < **kare:(h)* or *canaid* 'sings' < **kaneθ'ĭ*, prot. *-tabair* 'gives' < **taver'ĭ* < **tover'eh* with non-palatal *r/n/b* (but conj. *-cain* < **kan'ĭ* < **kane(h)*, 3pl. *-taibret* < **-tav'ĭrod* < **-toveront*). In addition to palatalising a consonant preceded by a front vowel (e.g. *léicid* 'leaves' < **le:g'iθ'ĭ*), *i(:)* was also capable of palatalising a consonant preceded by a back vowel under rather complicated conditions that are the main concern of this investigation.

According to Greene, *i(:)* palatalised a consonant preceded by short *a* (e.g. *gaibid* 'takes' < **gav'iθ'i*, *cainnenn* 'leek' < **kaN'ina*) but, when *u* (including from *o* by raising), *o:* or *a:* were involved, palatalisation only occurred if the intervening consonant was neither guttural nor labial. Hence contrasts such as those between *buiden* 'company' < **buð'ina* (< **buði:na:*, MW *bydin*) and *cucann* 'kitchen' < **kugina* (< Lat. *coquina*, MW *kegin*), *do·sluindi* 'denies' < **-sLuN'd'i:* < **-sLoNdi:h* and *do·lugai* 'forgives' < **-Luγi:* < **-Luγi:h* (both old *o*-grade causatives), *uile* 'all' < **ul'iya(h)* < **oliyah* and *umae* 'bronze' < **uµiya(n)* < **oµiyan*, *ráithe* 'quarter (of year)' < **Ra:θ'iya* (< **-a:*) and gen. *lámae* 'hand's' < **La:µiya:(h)*, gen. *túaithe* 'kingdom's' < **to:θ'iya:(h)* and *ógae* 'wholeness' < **o:γiya* (< **-a:*).

As has been pointed out elsewhere (McCone, 1994, 281–2), Greene's assumption of an originally stem-final palatal consonant throughout the paradigm of the weak *i*-verbs *ráidid* 'says' and *sáidid* 'places' (< **Ra:ði:θ i*, **sa:ði:θ i*) is at odds with Old Irish examples like pres. 2pl. -*rádam* (Ml. 93ª5), -*rádat* (Wb. 1ᵈ7, Ml. 31ª18), 3sg. rel. *rádas* (Ml. 42ᶜ4&10), 1sg. -*sádu* rhyming with *dánu* in *Félire Óengusso* (Jan. 23), subj. 3sg. -*ráda* (Wb. 23ᵇ24). Since weak *i*-verbs of this type (W2a) normally had palatal final throughout (e.g. -*léicet*, *léices*, -*léiciu*, -*léicea*), it seems inconceivable that the non-palatal *d* so clearly seen in these forms was due to analogy. As with Old Irish inherited *do:lugai* versus analogical *do:luigi* 'forgives', the obvious approach is to start from a paradigm which basically had a non-palatal stem-final consonant, whence 3sg. -*rádai* < **ra:ði:(h)*, 3pl. -*rádat* and so on, and generate the palatal variant from those forms in which the front vowel underwent weakening to invariably palatalising *i* prior to syncope, as in OIr. passive -*ráter* 'is said' < **Ra:ð'θor* < **Ra:ð'îθor* < **Ra:ði:θor*. This suggested the need to emend Greene's rule to one stating that, unlike *a* or *o/o:*, *a:* impeded palatalisation of any following consonant by *i/i:*, whence *rádaid* 'says' < **Ra:ðiθî* < **Ra:ði:θi*, *cnámai* 'bones' < **knaµi:h*, *máthair* 'mother' < **ma:θir* < **ma:ti:r*. Weak *i*-verbs like *erbaid* 'entrusts', *sádaid* and *rádaid* with an inherited opposition between syncopated forms with palatal and unsyncopated forms with non-palatal stem-final consonant were then liable to experience spread of the palatal consonance from syncopated to unsyncopated forms in line with the majority type (*léicid* etc.) with palatal final throughout, the upshot being *sáidid*, -*ráidi* etc. Significantly, unsyncopated forms of the verbal nouns *sádud* and *im(b)rádud* < **sa:ðiθuh*, **-ra:ðiθuh* regularly exhibit non-palatal *d*.

This modified rule was subsequently (McCone, 1996, 117) restated along with a further suggestion that forms like *ráithe* above and *áithœ* 'sharpness' (Sg. 108ª4) < **a:θ'iya* < **a:tiya:* might indicate that, unlike its voiced counterpart, a voiceless dental fricative was palatalised between *a:* and *iy* as opposed to *a:* and *i(:)*. The basic argument to be advanced below

is firstly that this tentative differentiation between the palatalising effects of
iy and *i(:)* in one restricted context only does not go far enough and
secondly that *o:* behaved in the same way as *a:* with regard to impeding
palatalisation of any consonant between it and *i(:)* unaccompanied by *y*.

To begin with, the lack of evidence for a difference in the effect of short
o and *u* upon a following consonant plus *i(:)* or *(i)y* is hardly surprising in
the likely enough event that the palatalisation in question occurred after
raising, which would normally have changed *o* to *u* in this environment. Be
that as it may, palatalisation would seem to have affected any single
consonant or group of nasal plus stop between a short unrounded back
vowel (namely *a*) and *i(:)* or *(i)y*, whereas a labial or guttural was clearly
resistant to palatalisation between a short rounded back vowel (in effect, *u*)
and *i(:)* or *(i)y*. That being so, in the absence of evidence to the contrary
pairs such as *áithe/lámae* or *túaithe/ógae* above are best taken to exemplify
a similar immunity to palatalisation between a long back vowel (*a:, o:* and
presumably *u:*) and *(i)y* specifically on the part of labials or gutturals as
opposed to other catgories of consonant.

It would follow from this that the effects of *i(:)* and *(i)y* upon a
consonant preceded by the low back long vowel *a:* were different, the
former generally failing to palatalise whereas the latter did palatalise unless
the intervening consonant was labial or guttural. To judge from OIr.
súilech 'having eyes' < **su:lixa(h)* < **su:li-ko-* from an *i*-stem base *súil*
'eye' < **su:li(h)* (similarly *dúilech, dúil*), *i(:)* like *(i)y* would seem to have
palatalised a non-labial and non-guttural consonant preceded by the high
back long vowel *u:*. That leaves the question of what effect, if any, *i(:)* had
upon a consonant preceded by a mid back long *o:*, which brings us to the
notorious problem of *búadach* 'victorious'.

For Thurneysen (1946, 221–2) *-ach* < **-a:ko/a:-* was the basic form of
the suffix in Irish, *-ech* arising secondarily after a palatal consonant in the
normal way. While this doubtless accounts for plenty of examples such as
creitmech 'believing' < **kred´ïμax* < **kredi:μa:-ko-* (base *cretem* 'belief'
< **kred´ïμa* < **kredi:μa:*) or *guidech* 'praying' < **guð´ax* < **gʷið´iyaxa-* <
*gʷeð´iya:-ko- (base *guide* 'prayer' < **gʷeð´iya:*), its applicability to an *i*-
stem base where **-i-ko-* might be expected is less obvious. Nevertheless, in
Thurneysen's rather tentative opinion 'in derivatives of *i*-stems both *-ach*
and *-ech* are found, e.g. *búadach* 'victorious' from *búaid* (probably the
older formation) beside *súilech* 'having eyes' from *súil*' (1946, 222). This
implies a derivation of OIr. *buadach* from **bo:ða:ko-* with generalised **-
a:ko-* despite its neuter *i*-stem base *búaid* < **bo:ði*. If this can be
swallowed, *súilech* and *dúilech* could presumably be later formations
retaining the palatal consonance of their bases *súil* and *dúil*.

James Carney took the bold further step of arguing from the derivative
for an old *a*-stem base *bód* that he claimed to have found in one or two
early sources. 'It would appear that in archaic O.I. the word for 'victory'
was *bód*. Hence the adj. *búadach* (never *búaidech*) [...]. Cf. *Caīn srū,
Esrū, boad ban*, O'Brien *Corpus Gen.*, p. 7, l. 3; *Eochu Buaid* (leg. *Buad*)
= *Eochu Buadach*, rhyming with *sluaig* (leg. *sluag*), *ibid.*, p. 6, l. 6.
Thurneysen says (*Gramm.* p. 191): "It is doubtful if *búade* is occasionally
gen. sg., not gen. pl., of *búaid* neut. 'victory'; see Wb. 24ᵃ17, Fél." *búade* is
possibly gen. sg. of an old *a*-stem; if *bód* was a fem. *ā*-stem the *m* of
mBreg would be secondary' (1971, 50). His case, however, dissolves on
closer inspection. As Carney's admirable analysis of the metrical structure
of the poem in question makes clear, this is based upon stanzas of eight
two-stressed lines with rhyme between the finals of the fourth and the
eighth. Although rhyme sometimes occurs between the finals of the second
and third or sixth and seventh lines, plenty of exceptions show that this was
no more than an optional ornament. That being so, in the first half of the
tenth stanza of poem II (Carney, 1971, 42) it seems quite unjustified to
emend the manuscript's *má búaid* in line three to otherwise unattested *má
bód* in order to obtain an unnecessary rhyme with *for-beir óg* (MS *foirbrig
ogh*) in line two, especially when a preceding neuter is strongly indicated
by a nasalisation in line four's *mbr[eg mbras?]* that cannot plausibly be
emended away. Of the two forms Carney cites from a Leinster genealogical
poem preserved in the twelfth-century Rawlinson B 502 *boad* can be
emended to normal *búaid* without the slightest metrical difficulty, while
búaid rhymes with presumably gen. sg. *slúaig* in a quatrain too obscure to
warrant the rather violent emendation of both to *búad* and nom. sg. or gen.
pl. *slúag* (or even *bód* and *slóg*). As for gen. *búade*, a couple of the
attestations in *Félire Óengusso* are undoubtedly plural belonging to *i*-stem
búaid and Thurneysen is quite right to observe that none of the Old Irish
attestations need be taken as the singular of what would then be an *a*-stem
with no remotely reliable attestation elsewhere.

Paul Russell has since elevated Carney's suggestion to a certainty
without troubling to scrutinise the evidence, or rather the lack of it, upon
which it is based. 'Further confusion between palatalizing and non-
palatalizing suffix was also caused by shifts in the form of the base, notably
in derivatives where there was an alternation between forms with and
without a palatal final consonant. Here the confusion is compounded by the
editors of *DIL*, who sometimes quoted misleading forms as the base of
derivatives. This results in a large number of apparently puzzling
examples, where the base shows a final palatal consonant but the derivative
is -*ach*. The phenomenon is particularly common with *ā*-stem nouns, where
in Old and Middle Irish there is a considerable confusion between the *i*-

stem and *ā*-stem declensions. A good example is *búadach*, which is derived from *búaid* in *DIL*, where in fact the base was the form attested as *bód* in archaic Old Irish; similarly we may note *osrach*: *osair* (*osar*), *forbasach*: *forbais* (*forbas*), *forcradach*: *forcraid* (*forcrad*), *trotach*: *troit* (*trot*), *congbálach*: *congbáil* (*congbál*) [...]. The above groups, then, are cases where the derivative often preserves an older form of the base than the current independent form in the language, or at least a form older than that quoted by *DIL* as its base' (1990, 100–101).

It is difficult to see the point of Russell's criticism of *DIL*'s base for *búadach*, since the dictionary cautiously describes *búaid* itself as 'i, n., perh. earlier ā, f.', and it is still harder to see the relevance of examples of the *congbálach*: *congbáil* type above to *búadach* versus *búaid*. It is quite understandable that alternations of this kind should have resulted from the well-known tendency, incipient in Old Irish and a good deal more widespread in Middle Irish, to develop a feminine *a*-stem inflection with palatal consonance throughout the singular (nom./acc./dat. -C´, gen. -C´e; whence nom. *congbáil* for old *congbál* etc.) and that this pattern of derivation should have become productive in the case of some feminine *i*-stems assimilated to this -C´/-C´e type in Middle Irish and later by replacing an inherited gen. sg. such as *súla* with *súile* (McCone, 1992, 196). A probable case in point is Russell's *trotach*: *troit* 'pugnacious: fight', where it is clear from the examples in *DIL* that the Middle Irish *i*-stem gen. sg. *trota* is older than Early Modern Irish *troide* (plus innovatory nom. sg. *trod* beside *troid*) alongside *troda*. That being so, in the absence of a good Old Irish attestation the Middle Irish form *troitech* 'pugnacious' at *TBC* 4136 (O'Rahilly, 1976, 124), although ignored by Russell, has a good chance of being older than *trotach*. Similarly the variant *forcrad* cited by Russell from *Togail Bruidne Da Derga* (l. 553 of Knott, 1936) is from the fourteenth-century YBL, the editor rightly advising 'read *forcraid* with DU' (Knott, 1936, 82; U being the twelfth-century LU), given that Wb. *forcrith* 'excess' proves an Old Irish *i*-stem. Moreover, *DIL*'s sole example of the word from the so-called 'A' version of *Audacht Morainn* (Thurneysen, 1916, 84) is no guarantee that *forcradach* 'excessive' existed in Old Irish.

In short, Russell's chronologically undifferentiated collection has no demonstrable relevance to Old as opposed to Middle or Modern Irish developments. That being so, it casts no light upon the relationship between the neuter *i*-stem *búaid* 'victory' amply attested in the Old Irish Glosses (including early 'prima manus' *boid* for *bóid*, later *búaid*, at Wb. 24[a]16) and its derivative *búadach* 'victorious', which is the only attested Old or Middle Irish form and occurs several times in the Glosses and *Félire* to boot. The evidence for an earlier feminine *a*-stem **bód* has already been seen to be chimerical and one might add that, since neuter (as opposed to masculine or feminine) *i*-stems are quite a rarity in Old Irish, it is surely inconceivable that a perfectly normal feminine *a*-stem could somehow have been replaced by such a non-productive formation, as Carney and Russell seem to imply. Any lingering doubts about the antiquity of the neuter *i*-stem are anyway dispelled by Gaulish *boudi* (McCone, 1996b, 110 & 113–4). Quite simply, a Proto-Celtic neuter *i*-stem **boudi* is the only preform capable of generating Gaulish *boudi*, Old Irish *búaid* (neut.) and British forms such as Old Breton or Middle Welsh *bud* straightforwardly.

As Russell (1990, 97–103) points out, assimilation of consonant quality after syncope and loss of distinctions between most non-final unstressed vowels through weakening conspire to make it difficult to distinguish **-i(:)ko-* from **-a:ko-* in Old Irish as opposed to Welsh. Nevertheless, *pace* Russell (1990, 102; see McCone, forthcoming, 7.8), Thurneysen (1946, 223) was quite right, since OIr. **airchennach* would have resulted from **arekʷenn-a:ko-*, to state that OIr. *airchinnech* 'chief, leader' must be derived from **arekʷenn-i(:)ko-* and so cognate with Middle Welsh *arbennic* 'supreme, excellent'. In the likely event that Russell (1990, 68–76) is justified in arguing that the **-i:ko-* underlying MW *-ic* is largely due to a secondary lengthening of **-iko-* in British only, the Insular Celtic form will have been **arekʷenn-iko-*.

Boudica etc. on Gallo-Latin inscriptions and the name of the celebrated first-century rebel British queen *Boudicca* (Ellis Evans, 1967, 157) provide good evidence for a straightforward adjectival **-ko/a:-* extension of **boudi* in Celtic. Allowing for lengthening of the adjectival suffix, this **boudiko-* obviously underlies OBret. and MW *budic* 'victorious, prosperous' via Insular Celtic **bo:ðiko-* (McCone, 1996, 81–7 & 103). If Old Irish *búadach* could also be derived from the same **bo:ðiko-*, it would stand in precisely the same relationship to MW *budic* as OIr. *airchinnech* to MW *arbennic* and clinch the reconstruction of a Proto-Celtic adjective **boudiko-* evincing a perfectly straightforward morphological relationship with its base **boudi*. The serious problems that troubled Carney and Russell would then disappear at a stroke.

The morphological advantages of such a derivation are such that only clear evidence to the contrary should dissuade us from postulating that, like *a:*, long *o:* impeded the palatalisation of any following consonant (and not just a labial or guttural) by an *i(:)* unaccompanied by *y*. Acceptance of this rule, of course, makes *búadach* the utterly regular Old Irish outcome of **bo:ði(:)ko-*.

A factor that seems not to have figured in the discussion so far is the incontrovertible and apparently uncontradicted evidence for non-palatal *d* in the genitive and dative plural of *búaid* in Old Irish provided by the rhymes *búadae/Rúamae, búad(a)e/úag(a)e* and *mbúadaib/n-úagaib* in *Félire Óengusso* (Mar. 12, May 3, Jan. 27 respectively). Since Greene's rules would predict *búaide < *bo:ðiyan (< *boudeyom)* and *búaidib < *bo: ðivih,* the existence of these forms with non-palatal *d* within the plural paradigm of *i*-stem *búaid* itself constitutes a further potential objection to Carney's and Russell's view of the same alleged anomaly in *búadach* as a matter of derivation only. The majority of Old Irish *i*-stems show historically regular palatal consonance throughout the plural, as in fem. *súili* 'eyes' < **su:l´i:(h)* etc. (cf. *súilech* above) or neut. *muire* 'seas' < **mur´iya < *moriya:* (sg. *muir < *mori*), but a small minority including *cnámai* 'bones' (dat. *cnámaib*) and *drummai* 'backs' display non-palatal consonance in accordance with the generally acknowledged resistance of a labial or guttural to palatalisation between most back vowels and *i(y)*. The spread of the second type in Middle Irish (e.g. *mara* for *muire* in line with gen. sg. *mara* for OIr. *moro/a*) was probably triggered in the genitive plural in the first instance on the analogy of the *u*-stem pattern (nom./acc. sg. *cruth* 'shape') gen. sg. *crotho/a* versus gen. pl. *croth(a)e*, whence *i*-stem (nom./acc. sg. *flaith*) gen. sg. *flatho/a* versus gen. pl. *flathae* (rhyming with *Machae*) as early as *Félire* Prol. 166 and Nov. 27 instead of historically regular *flaithe* (cf. gen, pl. *dúile* at Wb. 5ᶜ16). That being so, an analogical gen. pl. *búadae* for **búaide < *bo:ð´iyan* seems to be a distinct possibilty in Old Irish but the further step of replacing dat. pl. **búaidib* with *búadaib* created from the new gen. pl. on the model of *u*-stem *crothae* versus *crothaib* would be rather surprising at such a date. However, this difficulty ceases to exist if *búadach < *bo:ðiko-* is accepted on the strength of the proposed rule that *o:* as well as *a:* blocked palatalisation of any following consonant by *i(:)*, since *búadaib* would then simply be the regular Old Irish reflex of **bo:ðivih.*

In view of Greene's (1971) convincing comparison with Middle Welsh *odit < *au-ti:tos*, the non-palatal *th* of Old Irish *úathad < *o:θiθa(h) < *auti:tos* is best taken as further instance of our rule. As Bergin rightly pointed out, '*úaithed* Wb. 25ᵃ38 is remarkable. Elsewhere the *th* is non-palatal, *huathad* Wb. 4ᵈ4, *ōthad* Sg. 198ᵃ22 &c., cf. the syncopated forms *huaiti* Ml. 90ᶜ12, *úatiu* Fél.' (1907, 74). The normal form in Old Irish, including Würzburg, was thus undoubtedly *úathad* and the nonce byeform *úaithed* is, as Bergin implies, easily enough to explain as due to the influence of the palatal consonance of the syncopated nom./acc. pl. *uaitti < *o:θ´θ- < *o:θïθ- < *o:θiθ- < *o:θi:θ- < *auti:t-.* Strict application of Greene's rule would by contrast make *úaithed* the inherited form already largely replaced by *uathad* for no obvious reason by the early eighth century, a scenario which must be regarded as most unlikely.

If the rule about non-palatalisation of *o:Ci(:)* is valid, an Old Irish weak *i*-verb containing *ó* or its development *úa* might be expected to behave like *-rádi* or *-sádi* and provide at least some instances of a non-palatal stem-final consonant. This prediction receives striking substantiation from the forms of *imm:lúadi* 'sets in motion, discusses' cited by *DIL* from the Glosses, since these comprise two clear examples of non-palatal consonance in 3sg. imperfect *im·luadad* (Ml. $33^{b}25$) and 1pl. subjunctive *im·luadam-ni* (Ml. $93^{d}13$), the only unambiguous example of palatal consonance being the syncopated 3sg. passive (rel.) *imme·luaiter* (Ml. $135^{b}9$) where it is, of course, historically regular.

These weak *i*-verbs are *-e-ye/o-* denominatives in origin. Whereas there is reason to suppose that *-eye-* had become *-i:-* as early as Proto-Celtic (McCone, 1996, 49), *-ey-* is usually assumed to have become *-iy-* before a back vowel (Pedersen, 1909, 66; if so, hardly before Proto-Irish according to McCone, 1995, 128). The upshot should have been a present indicative paradigm of the type conj. 1sg. *-iyu:*, 2sg. *-i:h* < *-i:s(i)*, 3sg. *-i:h* < *-i:t(i)*, 1pl. *-iyoµah* < *-iyomos(i)*, 2pl. *-i:θih* < *-i:tes(i)*, 3pl. *-iyod* < *-iyont(i)*. According to the basic rule proposed here that a non-labial and non-guttural consonant preceded by *o:* or *a:* was palatalised by a following *(i)y* but not by *i(:)* non-palatalisation would then have been confined to those unsyncopated forms (2sg., 3sg.; 2pl. conj.) with *i:*, palatalisation prevailing in the rest of the paradigm and throughout the subjunctive (with *-iya:-*). However, this prediction is flatly contradicted by OIr. forms such as pres. 1sg. *-sádu*, 1pl. *-lúadam*, 3pl. *-rádat*, subj. 3sg. *-ráda*, 1pl. *-rádam*, and it is hard to see why an indicative paradigm with non-palatal and palatal forms in rough equilibrium should have generalised the former on the model of the rare *erbaid* type with two consonants rather than the latter in conformity with the normal single-consonant *léicid* type.

It is well known that the Latin second conjugation, which like its weak *i*-counterpart in Old Irish (McCone, 1994b, 139–40) contains a few primary verbs but mostly thematic denominatives and *o*-grade causatives as well as athematic statives (Ernout, 1953, 143–7), displays 1sg. *-eo:* (< them. *-eyo:*), 2sg. *-e:-s*, 3sg. *-e-t,* 2pl. *-e:-tis* (< them.*-eye-* and/or athem. *-e:-* < *-e-h₁-*), 1pl. *-e:-mus*, 3pl. *-e-nt* (< athem. *-e:-* < *-e-h₁-*). In this case, apart from unsurprising preference for productive *-o:* over athematic *-m* in the 1sg., the regular emergence of *-e:-* in the 2/3 sg. and 2pl. seems to have triggered homogenisation in favour of originally stative *-e:-* and at the expense of originally denominative *-e(y)o-* in the 1/3pl. Although it is true that clear reflexes of *e:*-statives (on which see Watkins, 1971) are a great deal more numerous in Italic than in Celtic, it nevertheless seems quite possible that a similar generalisation of *-i:-* (< *-e:-*) in the 1 and 3 pl. occured in the latter at an early stage when statives may have been significantly commoner. Alternatively, this may simply have happened because, however rare, the stative variant with 1/3pl. as well as 2/3sg. and 2pl. *-i:- seemed more straightforward and in tune with the *-a:- through-out the paradigm of weak a-verbs than the originally causative and denominative alternation between 2/3sg./2pl. *-i:- and 1/3pl. *-iyo-. Be that as it may, evidence that *-i:- was indeed spread in this way in Celtic seems to be provided by the Insular Celtic *-sagi:- denominatives (see Joseph, 1987). These had *-i:- in the 1 and 3pl. on the evidence of the Old Welsh 3pl. *scamn-hegint* 'lighten' and the syncope pattern of Old Irish deponent 1pl. *dechrigmir* (Ml. 117ᵇ9), rel. *cosmiligmmer* (Sg. 211ᵃ14) probably reflecting (after analogical delenition of μ) *-haγἶμor < *-haγἶ:μor. If this is granted, non-palatal consonance will have been regular in all unsyncopated forms of the present indicative except the 1sg. and its further spread to this and the a-subjunctive from so substantial a base is easy enough to motivate with the help of the pattern seen in pres. 1sg. *-erbu*, 3sg. *-erbai*, subj. *-erba* etc.

The foregoing argument that a single non-labial, non-guttural consonant or *Nd* preceded by a: or o: was palatalised by (i)y but not by i(:) obviously raises the question of whether the difference between an i followed by a glide y and one not so followed is likely to have been sufficient to account for this divergence. There can be no question that the neatest way of accounting for the behaviour of final syllables containing post-consonantal -y- in Primitive Irish is Greene's doctrine that in Irish, unlike British, -Ciy- and -Cy- had fallen together as a result of an anaptyxis that changed the latter to -Ciy- also (Cullen, 1972). A derivation such as OIr. *aile* 'other' < *al´eyah < *al´iyah < Ins. Celt. *alyos (> MW *eil*) necessitates placing this anaptyxis before lowering (McCone, 1996, 109) but there seems to be no firm criterion for locating it before or after palatalisation and/or raising of stressed o or e, given that y is at least as likely a candidate as iy for causing either. However, if anaptyxis did occur prior to palatalisation, it seems necessary to resort to the rather forced postulate of a significantly higher and more fronted pronunciation of i before y than elsewhere in order to account for its stronger palatalising effect in the former context.

Jürgen Uhlich (1993) has recently made a morphologically attractive case for the failure of anaptyxis to apply in some cases in Irish too, a particularly persuasive instance being OIr. *bóchaill* (Sg. 58ᵇ6) 'cowherd'. Direct comparison of this with MW *bugeil* 'herdsman' < *bo:-kolyo-s (PIE *gʷow-kʷolo-s underlying Greek βούκολος) not only makes better morphological sense than a preform *bo:-koli-s (cf. McCone, 1995b, 4–6) but would also explain the otherwise difficult strong L on the assumption that -ly- here first underwent palatalisation to -l´y- and then assimilation (cf. Greek ἄλλος < *alyos) to the -l´l´- responsible for Old Irish -L´. It has further been suggested (McCone, 1995, 130–1) that the 3sg. rel. of the proclitic copula (as < *esa < *esya < *es(s)i-ya) and some other -s relatives in Old Irish are best accounted for by positing reduction of *-siy(-) > *-sy(-) > *-s(-) between an unstressed vowel and a back vowel, this time before palatalisation. These considerations raise the possibility that unstressed -CiyV(-) regularly became -CyV(-) in Goedelic and that anaptyxis had not yet taken place when palatalisation first occurred in Primitive Irish. If so, it would be no surprise if y had a more powerful palatalising effect than i(:), whence áithe 'sharpness' < *a:θ'ya: but máthair 'mother' < *ma:θi(:)r'. We may then suppose that between palatalization and lowering -C(')yV(-) regularly underwent anaptyxis to -C(')iyV(-). This development could not, of course, take place in a minority of cases where y had already been absorbed by a preceding sibilant (apparently before palatalisation) or liquid (and perhaps nasal, apparently after palatalisation). The precise details remain to be established but position after an unstressed vowel may have been maximally conducive to loss of post-consonantal y.

BIBLIOGRAPHY

Bergin, Osborn 1907. 'Palatalization', Ériu, 3, 50–91

Carney, James 1971. 'Three Old Irish Accentual Poems', Ériu 22, 23–80

Cowgill, Warren 1969. 'A Note on Palatalization in Old Irish', in Festschrift für Konstantin Reichardt, ed. by Christian Gellinek and Herwig Zauchenberger, Berne/Munich: Francke, 30–37

Cullen, John 1972. 'Primitive Irish Vowels', Ériu, 23, 227–9

Ellis Evans, D. 1967. Gaulish Personal Names: A Study of some Continental Celtic Formations. Oxford: University Press

Ernout, A. 1953. Morphologie historique du latin, Paris: Klincksieck

Greene, David 1971. 'Ir. úathad, óthad: W. odid', Ériu, 22, 178–80

——1973. 'The Growth of Palatalization in Irish', TPhS, 1973, 127–36

Knott, Eleanor 1936. Togail Bruidne Da Derga. Dublin: Stationery Office

Joseph, Lionel 1987. 'The Origin of the Celtic Denominatives in *-sag-', in Studies in Memory of Warren Cowgill (1929–1985), ed. by Calvert Watkins, Berlin/New York: de Gruyter Mouton, 113–59

Martinet, André 1955. Économie des changements phonétiques, Berne: Francke

McCone, Kim 1992. 'The Etymology of Old Irish déis "Clients"', Ériu, 43, 193–6

——1994. 'Zum Ablaut der keltischen r-Stämme', in In Honorem Holger Pedersen, Kolloquium der Indogermanischen Gesellschaft vom 26. bis 28. März 1993 in Kopenhagen, ed. by Jens E. Rasmussen, Wiesbaden: Ludwig Reichert, 275–84

——1994b. 'An tSean-Ghaeilge agus a Réamhstair', in Stair na Gaeilge in Ómós do Phádraig Ó Fiannachta, ed. by Kim McCone, Damian McManus, Cathal Ó Háinle, Nicholas Williams and Liam Breatnach, Maynooth: Dept. of Old Irish, 61–219

—1995. 'Der Präsens Indikativ der Kopula und die Relativendung -s im Altirischen', in *Verba et Structurae, Festschrift für Klaus Strunk zum 65. Geburtstag*, ed. by Heinrich Hettrich and others, Innsbruck: Beiträge zur Sprachwissenschaft, 123–33

—1995b. 'OIr. *senchae, senchaid* and Preliminaries on Agent Noun Formation in Celtic', *Ériu*, 46, 1–10

—1996. *Towards a Relative Chronology of Ancient and Medieval Celtic Sound Change*, Maynooth: Studies in Celtic Linguistics, I

—1996b. 'Der Teller von Lezoux', in *Die grösseren altkeltischen Sprachdenkmäler, Akten des Kolloquiums Innsbruck, 29. April–3. Mai 1993*, ed. by Wolfgang Meid and Peter Anreiter, Innsbruck: Beiträge zur Sprachwissenschaft, 107–16

—forthc. 'Prehistoric, Old and Middle Irish', in *Progress in Medieval Irish Studies*, ed. by Kim McCone and Katharine Simms, Maynooth: Studies in Celtic Linguistics

O'Rahilly, Cecile 1976. *Táin Bó Cúailnge, Recension I*, Dublin: Institute for Advanced Studies

Pedersen, Holger 1909. *Vergleichende Grammatik der keltischen Sprachen*, I, Göttingen: Vandenhoeck & Ruprecht

Russell, Paul 1990. *Celtic Word-Formation: the Velar Suffixes*. Dublin: Institute for Advanced Studies

Thurneysen, Rudolf 1916. 'Morands Fürstenspiegel', *ZCPh*, 11, 56–106

—1946. *A Grammar of Old Irish*. Dublin: Institute for Advanced Studies

Uhlich, Jürgen 1993. 'Die Reflexe der keltischen Suffixvarianten *-yo-* vs. *-iyo-* im Altirischen', in *Akten des ersten Symposiums deutschsprachiger Keltologen*, ed. by Martin Rockel and Stefan Zimmer, Tübingen: Niemeyer, 353–70

Watkins, Calvert 1971. 'Hittite and Indo-European Studies: the Denominative Statives in *-e-*', *TPhS*, 1971, 51–93

Atógáil na Tíre ón Taobh Istigh: Conradh na Gaeilge mar Fhoras Oideachais Aosaigh agus Forbartha Pobail

RISTEARD MAC GABHANN
Ollscoil Uladh, Doire

IS EOL do gach duine a bhfuil breaceolas féin aige ar stair an chéid seo in Éirinn an Conradh na Gaeilge a bhí mar fhoinse inspioráide ag na gluaiseachtaí náisiúnta eile—gluaiseachtaí polaitiúla agus gluaiseachtaí liteartha a tháinig chun cinn i mblianta tosaigh an chéid. Níl de locht ar an phictiúr seo den Chonradh ach nach dtugann sé a ceart iomlán don eagraíocht mar nach rianaíonn sé an pictiúr iomlán. Is cuid thábhachtach den phictiúr gan dabht an tionchar a bhí ag an Chonradh ar eagraíochtaí agus ar imeachtaí suntasacha eile sa tír, agus tá cuimhní cinn na tréimhse seo breac ballach le tagairtí don pháirt a bhí ag an Chonradh i múnlú mheon na glúine sin: mar a scríobh Daniel Corkery (1931, 50): 'the institution that most significantly manifested the pressure of the time was, of course, the Gaelic League'.

Ach cuid eile den phictiúr nach miste a thabhairt sa chuntas is ea an chuid sin a léiríonn an Conradh mar fhórsa tábhachtach ina cháilíocht féin, agus a thaispeánann dúinn eagraíocht a raibh aici cuspóirí a bhí lán chomh dúshlánach le cuspóirí gluaiseachtaí eile, is é sin atógáil agus uaireanta athbheachtú thraidisiún cultúrtha na tíre, agus a chuir foras oideachais ar bun chun na cuspóirí sin a thabhairt i gcrích. Is ar an chuid sin den phictiúr, an foras oideachais, a bheidh an t-alt seo dírithe.

Ar bhealach amháin, is féidir a rá go raibh fréamhacha doimhne ag an chuid seo d'obair an Chonartha. Is furasta, cuir i gcás, réamhshamplaí a aimsiú sa stair sa tír seo agus thar lear de go leor de chomharthaí sóirt an réimse seo d'obair na heagraíochta.

Tá an múinteoir taistil, mar shampla, ina chomharba ar an scoláirte scairte sa mhéid is go raibh siad beirt peiripitéiteach (féach Dowling, 1935, 150[1]). Ar dhóigh eile is mó ba chosúla é le múinteoirí *ysgolion cylchynol* (scoileanna taistil) na Breataine Bige nó scoileanna carthanachta na hAlban san 18ú Céad (féach Kelly, 1970 agus Mason, 1954) sa mhéid is go raibh cúraimí eile ar an mhúinteoir taistil chomh maith le teagasc ranganna teanga: eolas ar an Chreideamh Críostaí a scaipeadh ba mhian le lucht reáchtála na *ysgolion cylchynol* agus na scoileanna carthanachta chomh maith leis na gnáthábhair scoile; craobhscaoileadh theachtaireacht na hathbheochana cultúrtha ba chúram do mhúinteoirí taistil an Chonartha.

---

[1] Tá cuntas ag Dowling ar Pheadar Ó Gealagáin, máistir scoile agus scríobhaí, mar shampla, a mhúin scoil i 16 áit idir Meitheamh 1814 agus Aibreán 1825.

I gcaitheamh an 19ú Céad bhí obair Ghrundtvig ag fréamhú agus ag bláthú sa Danmhairg agus is léir go raibh mórán den inspioráid chéanna i gceist i *folkelighed* na daonscolaíochta i gCríoch Lochlann agus bhí taobh thiar d'obair an Chonartha in Éirinn.[2]

Ní hionadh é go ndeachaigh an Conradh i dtreo an oideachais, nuair a chuimhnítear gur oideasóirí an bheirt is mó atá luaite le bunú an Chonartha an chéad lá, mar tá Dubhglas de h-Íde agus Eoin Mac Néill. Is fiú cuimhneamh fosta gur mar dhuine fásta a thosaigh Eoin Mac Néill ar an Ghaeilge a fhoghlaim ar dtús, rud, ní foláir, a thug dó tuiscint ar leith agus bá leis an fhoghlaimeoir aosach.

Maidir le de h-Íde, cé go raibh sé níos óige ná sin—bhí sé sna déaga nuair a thosaigh sé ag cur spéise sa teanga—is ar a chonlán féin gan taca ó aon mhúinteoir aige a thug sé faoin teanga a thabhairt leis. Ní haon dóichín teanga a fhoghlaim ar do chonlán féin am ar bith, ach san am atá faoi thrácht anseo, na seachtóidí den Naoú Céad Déag, caithfidh go raibh sé an-deacair ar fad. Is suimiúil an rud é amharc ar na hiarrachtaí Gaeilge a bhreac sé síos ina dhialann san am (féach Daly, 1974), rud a thugann le fios nach gan dua a bhí an Ghaeilge ag teacht leis. Ach choinnigh sé leis agus i ndeireadh na dála, cúig bliana déag níos moille, bhí sé in ann a fhógairt don saol in óráid a thug sé in Nua-Eabhrac:

> Tá mé faoi gheasa agus faoi mhóid gan aon fhocal Béarla a labhairt a choíche ná go deo ach amháin an uair nach dtuigfear mé i nGaeilge […] deirimse libhse agus deirim arís é nach bhfuil aon rud eile leis an teanga a choinneáil beo ach amháin í do labhairt eadraibh féin. (de h-Íde, 1971)

Bhí cuid den daingne agus den ghlinne radhairc chéanna ag baint le hEoin Mac Néill fosta. In alt in *Irisleabhar na Gaeilge* a d'fhoilsigh sé[3] in 1893 ar ar thug sé *Toghairm agus Gléas Oibre chun Gluaiseacht na Gaeilge do chur ar aghaidh in Éirinn*, leag sé os comhair an phobail go lom neamhbhalbh a phlean oibre do ghluaiseacht na Gaeilge agus liostáil sé roinnt prionsabal ar a raibh an plean bunaithe:

---

[2] Téarma é *folkelighed* ar deacair a mhíniú i mbeagán focal ach a bhaineann, de réir Thaning (1972, 100–107), le coincheapa ar nós meanma, comhar agus féinmhuinín pobail. Féach fosta Peers (1958, 250–251) a deir: 'The People's High School […] was inspired by a need to awaken a peasant community to a new sense of responsible nationalism, and there is no doubt that the People's High Schools have played a leading part in raising this sturdy people to the high position in the world, which they occupy today'.

[3] Níl aon údar luaite leis an alt seo ach tá sé beagnach cinnte gurb é Mac Néill a scríobh é—féach F.X. Martin agus F.J. Byrne, *The Scholar Revolutionary* (BaileÁtha Cliath: Irish University Press, 1973).

—Teanga ar bith níor mhair beo riamh, nár mhair cois teallach na tuaithe (i.e. an pobal);

—Cé tábhachtach an ní an Ghaeilge do mhúineadh, ní hé an ní is mó tábhacht é;

—Is í céadobair is indéanta dúinne an Ghaeilge do choinneáil beo cois na dteallach;

—Ar chaoi go mb'amhlaidh éireos linn, is éigean dúinn an toghairm dhíreach do dhéanamh chun na tuaithe. (Mac Néill, 1893)

D'aithin Mac Néill fosta má bhí rath le bheith ar obair na gluaiseachta, go caithfí teagmháil dhíreach a dhéanamh leis an phobal. 'Na leabhair agus na máistrí níor choinníodarsan teanga ar bith beo riamh', ar seisean. Chomh maith leis sin d'aithin sé mar laige ar ghluaiseacht na teanga, mar a chonaic seisean í ag an am, nach raibh páirteach ann ach *coterie* meánaicmeach: 'Níor chorraigh gluaiseacht na Gaeilge fós ach lucht léinn agus muintir na mbailte móra', a dúirt sé.

Cúpla mí i ndiaidh don toghairm seo theacht amach, tionóladh cruinniú tionscnaimh an Chonartha i mBaile Átha Cliath ar an 31 Iúil, 1893.

Ainneoin an díspeagaidh atá le tuiscint as an abairt thuas faoi na leabhair agus na máistrí, níl aon dabht gur cuid an-tábhachtach d'obair an Chonartha ón chéad lá an rang teagaisc. Agus bhí sé le rá fosta faoi Chonradh na Gaeilge go raibh úire agus fuinneamh agus flosc ag baint lena chuid ranganna, a chuaigh i bhfeidhm go mór ar an phobal agus a mheall daoine chucu ina sluaite. Seo cuntas ó Earnán de Blaghd, mar shampla, ar an rang a bhíodh ag Sinéad Ní Fhlanagáin, an cailín a bheadh ina bean chéile ag Éamon de Valera níos faide anonn, a thugann blas éigin den atmasféar a bhíodh sna ranganna san am:

Bhíodh a rang sise plódaithe i gcónaí le scoláirí a bhí ó sé bliana déag go dtí seachtó bliain d'aois agus ba mhinic idir dhosaen agus fiche duine nach mbíodh slí sna suíocháin dóibh ina seasamh thart timpeall leis na ballaí. I measc na ndaoine a d'fhág an rang chomh hil-ghnéitheach sin is cuimhin liom a leithéidí seo: Nóra Ní Chuinneagáin, a bhí an uair sin ina bean ceannais in ospidéal Sir Patrick Dun; sean-tailliúir darbh ainm Mac Giolla Mhártáin, a bhí ar a laghad seachtó bliain d'aois; Gearaltach, a bhí gairid do bheith meánaosta agus a throid i gcoinne na Spáinneach i gCúba; innealltóir as stáisiún aibhléise an Bhardais; bean uasal mheánaosta dar sloinneadh Wilson a bhí an-staidiúil agus tuin Gallda ar a cuid cainte; óganach de mhuintir Cheallaigh, a bhí tar éis an-chuid duaiseanna rince a bhuachaint. Ach ba státseirbhísigh óga nó ceardaithe nó cúntóirí siopa nó lucht oifige furmhór na scoláirí agus gan aon rud suntasach ag baint leo. (de Blaghd, 1957, 95)

Cad é mheall slua chomh hilghnéitheach sin isteach sa Chonradh? Spiorad na haoise ba chúis le cuid mhaith de gan dabht, ach is cinnte gur bhain daoine taitneamh as atmasféar agus modh oibre an ranga féin, go háirithe na daoine sin nach raibh de thaithí acu ar an oideachas ach an méid a fuair siad sa scoil náisiúnta. Ba eispeireas nua acu siúd áit foghlama inar glacadh leat mar dhuine fásta agus inar cuireadh fáilte roimh aon tuairimí ná taithí a bhí agat le roinnt leis an chuid eile den rang. Bhí an méid seo le rá faoi ranganna an Chonartha ag an Athair John Ryan in aiste cuimhneacháin ar Eoin Mac Néill a scríobh sé in 1945:

> [...] an hour of class followed by an hour of conversation or discussion in Irish. Those who knew a little taught those who knew less; those who could speak, however haltingly, spoke. (Ryan, 1945)

Ach ní ar an chaint agus ar an díospóireacht amháin a bhí obair na ranganna beo. D'fhéach an Conradh chuige go mbeadh riar a gcáis de leabhair agus d'ábhar taca ag na ranganna seo agus is doiligh sampla níos oirirce a fháil d'fhoilseachán a chuaigh i bhfeidhm ar an phobal ná *Ceachtanna Simplidhe* an Athar Eoghan Ó Gramhnaigh. Ní minic a fhaigheann aon leabhar an greim ar shamhlaíocht an phobail a fuair leabhar Uí Ghramhnaigh—rithfeadh Leabhar Beag Dearg na Síneach leis an duine a bheadh ag iarraidh sampla eile a aimsiú. Bhí sé á cheannach agus á staidéar ag achan chineál duine idir uasal agus íseal, sa bhaile agus thar lear. Is mar seo, mar shampla, a chuireann Tarlach Ó hUíd, fear a tógadh i Londain agus a chuir eolas ar an Ghaeilge den chéad uair ansin:

> Níor luaithe a d'oscail mé an chéad leabhar de chuid Uí Ghramhnaigh ná d'aithin mé gur teanga bheo mar gach teanga a bhí inti, agus nach fuíoll teanga mairbhe, agus go bhféadfaí í a fhoghlaim. [...] Bhí draíocht ag baint le Leabhar a hAon, draíocht nach dtuigfeadh an té a d'fhás aníos in Éirinn. [...] Má deirim gur oscail sé geata dom, níl ann ach an fhírinne lom. Ba é Leabhar a hAon Uí Ghramhnaigh an eochair, agus in éagmais na heochrach sin is doiligh liom a chreidiúint go dtabharfainn an chéim thar an tairseach. (Ó Ceallaigh 1968, 109)

Agus bhí díol as cuimse ar na leabhair seo. I mbliain amháin 1899, mar shampla, díoladh os cionn 20,000 cóip den chéad chuid den chúrsa.

Ainneoin go raibh díol mór ar *Na Ceachtanna Simplidhe*, ní raibh sé gan locht mar chúrsa. *Learn Irish without a Master* an gealltanas a bhí le léamh ar an chlúdach; tuigimid anois go dteastaíonn níos mó ná bhí le fáil sna *Ceachtanna Simplidhe* le áis féinteagaisc a dhéanamh de chúrsa. Chomh maith leis sin dúradh go raibh róshimplíocht ag baint leis na ceachtanna agus gur chuir siad an teanga as a riocht ar bhealach le cuid de chastachtaí gramadaí na teanga a sheachaint sna ceachtanna tosaigh. Cuireadh ina leith fosta gur bhain ábhar an chúrsa barraíocht le saol na tuaithe—agus le leagan maol róshimplí den saol sin, san am a bhí an chuid is mó de na foghlaimeoirí ina gcónaí sna bailte móra. Ar ndóigh, cá mhéad uair a chualathas an locht sin á chur ar ábhar foghlama Gaeilge ó shin?

Fuair Eoghan Ó Gramhnaigh bás sula raibh sraith iomlán na *gCeachtanna Simplidhe* críochnaithe aige agus is é Eoin Mac Néill a d'ullmhaigh Cuid 4 agus Cuid 5. Rinne sé seo mar ghníomh ómóis don sagart a bhris a shláinte ag obair ar son na Gaeilge agus fosta ar an ábhar go raibh bearna á líonadh ag na *Ceachtanna Simplidhe* nach raibh á líonadh ag cúrsa ar bith eile.

Ach cheana féin bhí an tóir ar rud éigin níos fearr a chuirfeadh le héifeacht na ranganna, agus shín an tóir amach thar chríocha na tíre seo agus isteach sa Mhór-Roinn, áit a raibh modh nua teagaisc teangacha á thionscnamh ag François Gouin, scoláire Beilgeach, a d'fhéach i measc rudaí eile le béim a chur ar an chaint sa rang teagaisc agus a dhearbhaigh gur rud gníomhach é foghlaim teanga.

Níl aon rud i modh oibre Ghouin a chuirfeadh iontas ar mhúinteoirí teanga an lae inniu, ach nuair a chuimhnítear go raibh na smaointe seo á gcur chun tosaigh aige nuair ba mhinice rialacha gramadaí agus liostaí focal le cur de ghlanmheabhair ba chúram don rang teanga, is féidir a rá nach áibhéil ar bith é modh réabhlóideach a thabhairt ar an saothar seo. Léiríonn an sampla seo chomh maith gné eile de phearsantacht an Chonartha san am a bhí tábhachtach: an spéis sa tionscnamh nua a chuirfeadh le héifeacht a chuid oibre agus an oscailteacht aigne sin a d'fháiltigh roimh smaointe nua cibé aird as ar tháinig siad.

Ach, mar dúirt Eoin Mac Néill, níor choinnigh leabhair ná máistrí teanga ar bith beo riamh, agus b'fhíor dó, ar ndóigh. Bhí an Conradh ag borradh agus ag bláthú i rith an ama agus níorbh é feabhas a chuid leabhar ná ábaltacht a chuid múinteoirí ba chúis iomlán leis. Sa bhliain 1898 bhí caoga craobh cláraithe leis an Chonradh; sé bliana níos moille in 1904 bhí 750 craobh cláraithe. Cad é ba chúis leis an fhás iontach sin?

Ní féidir neamhiontas a dhéanamh den spiorad a bhí ag borradh gach áit ar fud na tíre san am, ach thar gach rud eile is iad na timirí agus na múinteoirí taistil ba chúis leis, misinéirí seo na gluaiseachta, a thaisteal gach bealach mór agus bóithrín sa tír le teachtaireacht na hathbheochana a chraobhscaoileadh i measc an phobail.

Is scéal ciúin éachtach scéal na ndaoine seo, a chuaigh amach i dteagmháil leis an phobal, mar a mhol Eoin Mac Néill, a d'eagraigh ranganna agus cruinnithe agus imeachtaí den sórt, a mheall daoine eile chun imeachtaí eile a eagrú, a chaith tamall ag tláithínteacht leis an sagart áitiúil ag iarraidh cead uaidh halla a úsáid fá choinne céilí nó rang nó le feirmeoir éigin ar lorg páirce uaidh fá choinne aeraíochta—fiche cúram mór agus mion agus ansin ar a rothar agus chun bóthair leis arís go dtí an chéad bhaile eile. Agus ba mhaslach an obair é, ag taisteal de lá agus d'oíche samhradh agus geimhreadh, agus ní hiontas é ina thrúig bháis luaith do chuid de na timirí seo.[4]

Cé go raibh eagraíochtaí ann roimh an Chonradh ar nós *SPIL, the Society for the Preservation of the Irish Language*, a bhí ag plé leis an Ghaeilge, bhí difríochtaí bunúsacha idir iad agus an Conradh. Sa chéad dul síos ba mhó a bhí na cumainn luatha seo ag freastal ar scoláirí agus literati ná ar an ghnáthdhuine. I gcomparáid leo siúd, ba eagraíocht radacach é an Conradh a bhí i ndlúthcheangal leis an phobal idir íseal agus uasal, idir muintir na mbailte móra agus pobal na tuaithe. Ba eagraíocht é fosta a thuig an gaol idir leas spioradálta pobail agus a leas saolta. Is réidh a thuigimidne inniu an ceangal sin idir ardmheanma agus rath saolta, an pobal nach bhfuil meas air féin, gur minic nach mbeidh an spionnadh ann is gá le dul chun cinn a dhéanamh sa saol praiticiúil.

Ní raibh an fhírinne sin tuigthe ag mórán daoine i dtosach an chéid. Níor thuig Horace Plunkett, aspal an chomharchumannachais in Éirinn, ar dtús fiú amháin, gurbh ionann i ndeireadh na dála a theachtaireacht siúd do phobal na tíre agus teachtaireacht an Chonartha—gurb é a bhí ag teastáil atógáil na hÉireann ón taobh istigh. Seo an rud a dúirt an Pluincéadach féin ón mhéid a bhí feicthe aige d'obair an Chonartha ar fud na tíre:

> Of this movement I am myself but an outside observer, having been forced to devote nearly all my time and energies to a variety of attempts, which aim at the doing in the industrial sphere of very much the same work as that which the Gaelic movement attempts in the intellectual sphere—the rehabilitation of Ireland from within. But in the course of my work I naturally came across this new intellectual force and found that when it began to take effect, so far from diverting the minds of the peasantry from the practical affairs of life, it made them distinctly more amenable to the teaching of the dry economic doctrine of which I was an apostle. (Plunkett 1904, 148)

---

[4] Níor mhair Proinsias Mac Uinseannáin, an chéad mhúinteoir taistil in OirDheisceart Uladh a ghairm i bhfad, mar shampla. Fuair sé bás dhá bhliain i ndiaidh dó dul i mbun an phoist agus d'fhág cúram mór clainne ina dhiaidh. Tá fonóta suimiúil le cur leis an scéal sin mar nuair a d'éag Proinsias, b'éigean dá iníon a bhí ag súil le bheith ina múinteoir go dtí sin, an plean sin a chaitheamh uaithi agus aghaidh a thabhairt ar an aonach fostaithe in Iúr Cinn Trá. Fuair sí fostaíocht ó fheirmeoir i gContae Aontrama mar chailín aimsire, agus is uaithi a d'fhoghlaim mac an tí, Earnán de Blaghd, a chéad cheachtanna Gaeilge.

I dtéarmaíocht an lae inniu is dócha gur mar fhoras oideachais forbartha pobail is fearr smaoineamh ar an Chonradh mar a bhí sé san am seo. Buanú agus leathnú na Gaeilge ba phríomhchúram don eagraíocht sa chéad áit, ach tuigeadh fosta gur ghá leas na teanga bheith ceangailte go dlúth le leas an phobail i gcoitinne. Ní ar an arán amháin a mhaireann an duine gan dabht, ach ní ar na briathra amháin a mhaireann sé ach oiread.

Más mar fhoras oideachais le haghaidh forbairt pobail is cruinne amharc ar an Chonradh i dtús a ré, ní miste a fhiafraí cad é mar chruthaigh an eagraíocht i mbun na hoibre seo de réir chritéir an lae inniu. Ar ndóigh, ní raibh an machnamh déanta ar theoiric na forbartha pobail a rinneadh ó shin, agus dá réir sin is ón Chonradh féin agus as a stuaim féin a d'eascair cuid mhór de na modhanna oibre a d'fheidhmigh sé.

Is fiú, mar sin, obair an Chonartha a mheas de réir na modhanna oibre a chleachtann lucht forbartha pobail na linne seo. Seo a leanas, mar shampla, achoimriú ar na buntuiscintí de réir Hamilton (1992, 2), a thugann treoir don scéim forbartha pobail, a bhfuil rath i ndán di:

1. tá éifeacht pobail i mbun scéim forbartha dó ag brath go mór ar an eolas agus ar na scileanna atá faoina réir;

2. tá dílse pobail d'aon tionscnamh gníomhaíochta ag brath ar mhéid a rannpháirtíochta i mbeachtú agus i stiúrú an tionscnaimh sin;

3. dá mhéid atá tionscnamh pobail dírithe ar fhuascailt fadhbanna agus ar fhreagairt riachtanas, mar a thuigtear don phobal sin iad, is amhlaidh is fearr a éireoidh leis comhoibriú an phobail sin a fháil;

4. is mó an éifeacht a bhíonn leis an oibrí proifisiúnta agus é/í ag plé le pobal áitiúil má amharctar air/uirthi mar éascaitheoir agus ní mar threoraí;

5. is fearr go hiondúil an toradh atá ar an tionscnamh áitiúil ná an ceann a thagann ón taobh amuigh;

6. cuidíonn foghlaim i ngrúpaí le naisc ceangail a chruthú i measc pobail, rud a thacóidh ina dhiaidh sin le tionscadail ar ghá daoine bheith ag obair i gcomhar a chéile orthu;

7. bíonn réimse talann, scileanna agus cumais ar fáil in aon phobal, agus is fearr a éiríonn leis an phobal na talanna etc sin a earcú chun a leasa féin, má bhíonn sé eagraithe;

8. is éifeachtaí agus is buaine go hiondúil an fhorbairt a thosaíonn ón bhun aníos.

Sealbhú eolais, rannpháirtíocht, áitiúlacht, comhar, eagar agus forbairt ón bhun aníos: cár sheas an Conradh i leith na gcritéar seo?

Is luath a d'aithin an Conradh an tábhacht a bhí lena chuid ball bheith oilte eolach chun a gcuid oibre a dhéanamh le héifeacht agus níorbh fhada i ndiaidh a bhunaithe, mar shampla, gur tosaíodh ar córas a chur ar bun chun oiliúint a sholáthar dá chuid múinteoirí. Is iad na coláistí Gaeilge an córas a roghnaíodh, agus osclaíodh an chéad cheann díobh, Coláiste na Mumhan, in 1904.

Ainneoin go raibh ceannairí láidre cumasacha i mbun na heagraíochta, rud a d'fhéadfadh olagarcacht a dhéanamh di, is amhlaidh a cuireadh bonn maith daonlathach fuithi ón chéad lá, agus chuidigh sin agus na craobhacha ar fud na tíre—964 acu cláraithe in 1906 de réir Uí Ghlaisne (1991)—agus an iliomad scéimeanna agus imeachtaí idir aeraíochtaí, feiseanna, ranganna, feachtais poiblíochta agus forbartha srl, lena dhearbhú do na baill gur leo féin an Conradh agus gur orthu a bhí an eagraíocht ag brath.

Is beag cearn den tír dá iargúlta é nach raibh an Conradh i dteagmháil leis ar bhealach amháin nó ar bhealach eile. Is ó na teagmhálacha iomadúla seo le pobal na tíre a fuair an eagraíocht cuid mhór dá fuinneamh, agus d'oibrigh an próiseas seo sa treo eile chomh maith sa mhéid gur mhóide féinmhuinín an phobail áitiúil é bheith páirteach in imeachtaí mórghluaiseachta náisiúnta a raibh aird agus meas na tíre uirthi.

D'aithin Horace Plunkett, mar tá luaite thuas, go raibh an aigne agus an spiorad céanna taobh thiar d'imeachtaí an Chonartha agus a bhí mar bhonn tuisceana dá chuid oibre féin—pobail a dhéanann comhar le chéile, déanann siad leas a chéile. Is ar an tuiscint sin a bhíodh conraitheoirí saite go domhain i bhfeachtais den uile chineál a bhain le forbairt agus atógáil na tíre—scéimeanna nua tionscail, tionscnaimh nua talmhaíochta, plean ar bith a thug leas an phobail céim éigin eile chun tosaigh. Ba é an Conradh, mar shampla, a chuir tús leis an chéad fheachtas *Ceannaigh Earraí Éireannacha*, agus seo sampla eile d'fheachtas a eagraíodh in 1905 agus atá ina léiriú suimiúiil den aisling a bhí taobh thiar den ghníomh agus den nithiúlacht a bhí taobh thiar den aisling in obair an Chonartha. *Seachtain na gCrann* a tugadh ar an fheachtas agus is é ba chuspóir dó an pobal a spreagadh chun crainn a chur. Is mar seo a scríobhadh faoi in *An Claidheamh Soluis*:

> Má chuirtear na crainn, beidh slacht ar an tír agus obair ag na daoine. Triomófar an talamh íseal agus clúdófar na cnoic le coillte glasa a dhéanfas créafóg nuair a chríonfas a nduilliúr. I gcionn tamaill beidh na monga a's na cnoic sin in ann daoine agus beithigh a chothú in áit nach bhfuil siad in ann coinín a bheathú anois.
>
> Cuirtear na crainn agus faoi cheann leathchéad bliain is iomaí taobh tíre, atá anois chomh huaigneach le reilig an mheánoíche, a bheas faoi

bhláth agus fá shlacht, na céadta duine ina gcónaí iontu, tithe agus bailte agus beithigh, fir agus mná agus páistí go líonmhar iontu.

Agus ba eagraíocht é agus ní gluaiseacht amháin: rinneadh comhrá, mar mhol Mac Néill (1893) le 'drongaibh beaga [...] ins gach paróiste fá leith' agus dá réir sin ba í an chraobh áitiúil bunaonad na heagraíochta agus ba as ballraíocht na gcraobhacha sin a d'aimsigh an Conradh na múinteoirí dá chuid ranganna, na coistí reáchtála do na feiseanna agus na haeraíochtaí a d'eagraigh sé agus na tionscnóirí dá chuid scéimeanna forbartha.

Más ón bhun aníos a bhí an eagraíocht á beathú féin, ní hionadh é agus a raibh de dhaoine díograiseacha cumasacha ar fáil sna craobhacha áitiúla.[5] Ní hionadh ach oiread go meallfadh an Conradh, a raibh féith radacach ann agus blas na réabhlóide sóisialta ar a chuid oibre (Mac Aodha 1972) daoine radacacha chuige féin; is minic a tharraingíonn eagraíochtaí, a bhíonn ag plé le ceisteanna bunúsacha ar nós athbhreithniú agus athbheachtú traidisiúin chultúrtha, daoine den chineál sin chucu.

I ndiaidh 1922, nuair a ghlac an rialtas i mBaile Átha Cliath air féin cúram an chórais náisiúnta oideachais agus nuair a tuigeadh don Chonradh gur cuid de chúram an stáit feasta athshlánú na teanga, thosaigh spiorad an radacachais ag meath san eagraíocht. Inniu má mhaireann sé in aon áit ar bhealach a thabharfadh fiú faonléargas ar éifeacht an Chonartha nuair a bhí sé ina neart, b'fhéidir gurb é an tuaisceart an áit sin. Má mhair an aigne neamhspleách sin sa Chonradh níos faide sa Tuaisceart, b'fhéidir gur mhair ar an ábhar gur léir nach raibh an cineál sin tacaíochta le fáil ón stát ansin—má bhí rud ar bith le déanamh ag an Chonradh sa tuaisceart, is ar a chonlán féin a dhéanfadh sé é.

Má tá an Conradh ar an dá thaobh den Teorainn ag teacht ar an tuiscint arís gur gá a sheasamh neamhspleách féin a bheith aige fiú amháin nuair atá dea-mhéin ag an stát i leith a chuspóirí, ní miste sin. I ndiaidh an iomláin is cuid de thoradh na tógála ón taobh istigh duine a bheith ábalta seasamh ar a bhonnaí féin.

---

[5] Is díol suntais éagsúlacht na ballraíochta seo ó thaobh cúlra sóisialta agus taithí saoil de—ó Rose Maud Young (Róis Ní Ógáin), aontachtaí Protastúnach de shliocht mhionuaisle Ghlinntí Aontroma (Ó Doibhlin, 1996, 12) go Tomás Bán Ó Concheanainn, mac Árannaigh a chaith a óige ar imirce i gCalifornia, agus ón drámadóir Seán O'Casey, a tógadh ina Phrotastúnach i bplódteach i mBaile Átha Cliath (Fallon, 1965) go dtí an scríbhneoir George Moore, ar mac le tiarna talún rachmasach Caitliceach as Contae Mhaigh Eo é. Fágann an meascán seo nach radacachas amháin a bhí mar inneall gluaiseachta sa Chonradh san am seo; is léir gur dúil san ársaíocht, tréith sách coimeádach, a mheall go leor eile isteach sa Chonradh. Mar sin féin, is cinnte go raibh flosc chun athraithe ón bhun ina chomhartha láidir sóirt ar obair an Chonartha sna laethanta tosaigh seo.

TAGAIRTÍ

De Blaghd, Earnán 1970. *Slán le hUltaibh*, Baile Átha Cliath: Sáirséal agus Dill

De h-Íde, Dubhghlas 1971. *Mise agus an Conradh*, Baile Átha Cliath: An Gúm

Daly, Dominick 1974. *The Young Douglas Hyde*, Baile Átha Cliath: Irish University Press

Dowling, Patrick J. 1935. *The Hedge Schools of Ireland*, Baile Átha Cliath: Talbot Press

Fallon, Gabriel 1965. *Seán O'Casey: the Man I Knew*, Londain: Routledge and Kegan Paul

Hamilton, Edwin 1992. *Adult Education for Community Development*, Nua-Eabhrac: Greenwood Press

Kelly, Thomas 1970. *A History of Adult Education in Great Britain*, Learpholl: University Press

Mac Aodha, Breandán 1972. 'Was this a Social Revolution?', in *The Gaelic League Idea*, in eagar ag Seán Ó Tuama, Corcaigh: Mercier Press, 20–30

Mac Néill, Eoin 1893. 'Toghairm agus Gleus Oibre', *Irisleabhar na Gaedhilge*, Márta

Ó Ceallaigh, Seán 1968. *Eoghan Ó Gramhnaigh*, Baile Átha Cliath: An Gúm

Ó Doibhlín, Diarmaid 1996. *Womenfolk of the Glens of Antrim and the Irish Language*, Béal Feirste: Iontaobhas Ultach

Ó Glaisne, Risteárd 1991. *Dúbhghlas de h-Íde: Ceannródaí Cultúrtha*, Baile Átha Cliath: Conradh na Gaeilge

Peers, R. 1958. *Adult Education: a Comparative Study*, Londain: Routledge and Kegan Paul

Plunkett, Horace 1904. *Ireland in the New Century*, Londain: Kenniket Press

Ryan, John 1945. 'Eoin Mac Néill (1867–1945)', *Studies*, 34, 433–448

Thaning, Kaj 1972. *N.F.S. Grundtvig*, Cópanhágan: Det Danske Selskab

A Lexical Trek through some Early Irish 'Valleys'

LIAM MAC MATHÚNA

St. Patrick's College, Drumcondra, Dublin

INTRODUCTION

THE TRULY luxurious wealth of Irish words for HEIGHT stands in marked contrast to the paucity of designations for VALLEY. P.W. Joyce remarked on the lexical abundance of terms for eminences contained in the inherited place-names of Irelandand proceeded to discuss them at considerable length, whereas Modern Irish *gleann* 'valley' and a handful of derivatives exhaust his treatment of topographical depressions.[1] This toponymic contrast can be seen to reflect the situation in the general vocabulary of the earlier language, which yields much material of interest in relation to mountains, hills and hillocks.[2] But, when one turns to the semantic field of valleys, only a handful, namely *glenn, fán, fánaid* and *srath*, together with a small number of compounds based on the first two, can be held to have had wide currency in the Old and Middle Irish periods. These early words for VALLEY form the focus of this paper, which considers the import of their occurrence in just three source types, viz. glosses, saga and hagiography. The first of these is composite, being represented by the three major Old Irish collections of glosses, preserved at Würzburg, Milan and St Gall,[3] the second is the first recension of Táin Bó Cúailnge,[4] the third *Bethu Phátraic*.[5] The Royal Irish Academy's *(Contributions to a) Dictionary of the Irish Language*[6] provides the controlling lexical context.

---

[1] *The Origin and History of Irish Names of Places*, I (Dublin, 1875; reprint, Dublin, Edmund Burke Publisher, 1995), pp. 378–440.

[2] See the author's 'Old Irish Heights and Word-Field Potential', *Studia Hibernica*, 24 (1984–88), pp. 29–50, and 'The Topographical Vocabulary of Irish: Patterns and Implications', *Ainm. Bulletin of the Ulster Place-Name Society*, 4 (1989–90), pp. 144–64.

[3] 'The Würzburg Glosses and Scholia on the Pauline Epistles', 'The Milan Glosses and Scholia on the Psalms', 'Glosses on Priscian (St Gall)', in *Thesaurus Palaeohibernicus. A Collection of Old-Irish Glosses Scholia Prose and Verse*, I–II, edited by Whitley Stokes and John Strachan (Cambridge: University Press, 1901, 1903; reprint, Dublin: Institute for Advanced Studies, 1975).

[4] *Táin Bó Cúailnge. Recension I*, edited by Cecile O'Rahilly (Dublin: Institute for Advanced Studies, 1976), abbreviated *TBC-I*.

[5] *Bethu Phátraic. The Tripartite Life of Patrick. I. Text and Sources*, edited by Kathleen Mulchrone (Dublin: Royal Irish Academy, 1939).

[6] Published Dublin 1913–1976. Abbreviated *DIL*. Unless otherwise stated the abbreviations used in this paper are those of *DIL*.

GLENN

As *DIL* informs us, in Old Irish *glenn* was a neuter s-stem, gs. *glinne*, ds. *glinn*, in Middle Irish, a masculine heteroclite: gs. *glinne* and *glenna*; ds. *glinn, glenn, glionn*; np. *glenna, glennta, IGT* Decl. § 66. *glinne* as gs. is condemned as 'lochdach', 1496.

GLENN, COMGLENN: THE GLOSSES

The Glosses provide just two examples of *glenn*, including one illustrating the fundamental contrast between it and *slíab* 'a mountain, a mountain-range': (1) *.i.* dialuid d*uai*d forlongais triglenn . iosofád dambidc *. semei .* dichlochaib ocatecht ⁊ dob*er*t maldachta foir da*n*o dimulluch int slebe *rl.* 'i.e. when David went into exile through the valley of Jehoshaphat, Shimei pelted him with stones as he went, and cursed him moreover from the top of the mountain etc.' (*Ml.* 58 c 4), where *glenn* has the added sense of a way, of affording a passage, and where the physical distinction is sharpened by reference to *mullach* 'the topmost part, top, crown, generally of a convex surface' of the mountain. The second occurrence is rather more stark: (2) *.i.* glenn *.i. quamuis* inu*eni*tur *caus magnu*m gl. *caus* 'i.e. a glen' (*Sg.* 138 a 12). The editors of *Thes.* point out in a footnote that as this is 'a corrupt text, caus is taken as "hollow"'.

   Although interpreted by the editors in another footnote as 'a word coined to express conualles', the occurrence of *comglenn* may be assumed to confirm implicitly the underlying contrast of *glenn* and *slíab*: (3) *.i.* innaslebe ⁊ inna comglinne 'i.e. the mountains and the convalleys'. (*Ml.* 81 c 16, with the editors' English translation extending the chain of coinings into yet another language). This phrase occurs after a succession of glosses which point out that 'a flood is customary in rivers after great rains' (*Ml.* 81 c 3), and that as a consequence 'there flows from the mountains on the firm lands that rich earth, i.e. which causes fertility to them' (*Ml.* 81 c 14). Citation (3) is actually a clarification of the gloss preceding it, which contains (4) [...] *.i.* innaísli ⁊ innacobsaidi. 'i.e. the low and the firm'. (*Ml.* 81 c 15). But, interestingly, Middle Irish has in fact also yielded an instance of this compound, again in the plural: (5) i comhglendaibh sleibhi 'in mountain glens' (*CCath.* 5632). Although these are the only two examples recorded in *DIL*, it will be readily appreciated that the prefixing of the exceedingly productive element *com-* to a noun such as *glenn* would have been regular in the language, even if prompted in both instances by perceived parallelism with the Latin *con-*. The ready availability of *com-* was enhanced by its weak semantic load. *DIL* summarises the situation: 'In all late compds. *com* may function as a mere intensive prefix "greatly, very, completely, great, complete etc." Frequently the prefix serves merely to provide an alliterating word.' (*C* 331.82–5). This is all the more probable in the light of the compounding of *com-* and *fán* to give *cobfán*, for which see below.

GLENN IN TÁIN BÓ CÚAILNGE

Glenn occurs in both narrative and place-name contexts in Táin Bó Cúailnge. Several of the examples of *glenn* are unexceptional in that they shed no light on the physical form of the valley to which they refer. In one case *glenn* is simply the landscape feature necessary to explain the name of the place to which the Donn Cúailnge has retreated with sixty heifers, that is Dubchaire Glinne Gaitt: (6) 'Ind adaig,' or sé, 'dochótár Ulaid ina nóendin, dolluid ⁊ trí fichit samaisce imbi conid fil i nDubc[h]airiu Glinne Gatt.' 'Ergid,' or Medb, '⁊ berid gatt eter cach ndís úaib.' Dogníat ón íarom. Is de attá Glend nGat forsin glind sein. '"The night that the Ulstermen fell into their debility he went away with sixty heifers about him and he is in Dubchaire in Glenn Gat." "Go," said Medb, "and take a withe between each pair of you." They do so then, and hence the glen is called Glenn Gat.' (*TBC-I* 985–9).

In another passage, *glenn* is merely the physical location of the encounter between Cú Chulainn and Fer Báeth, which is said to have motivated the naming of Glenn F.r Baíth[7]: (7) Fornessa sleig culind isin glind hi coiss Con Culaind co túargab ocá glún súas a cend. Dasrenga ass [...]. Focheird Cú Chulaind in sleig n-íarom i ndegaid Fir Baíth co n-érrmadair áth a dá chúlad co ndeochaid fora béolo sair co torchair tara aiss issa nglend [...]. Atbail fo chétóir Fer Báeth isinn glind. Is de atá Glend Fir Baíth. 'Cú Chulainn tramples a sharp shoot of holly in the glen into his foot and it came up to his knee and appeared there. He pulled it out [...]. Then Cú Chulainn threw the holly shoot after Fer Báeth and it struck the depression at the back of his neck and went out through his mouth, and he fell on his back in the glen[...]. Fer Báeth died at once in the glen. Whence the place-name Glend Fir Baíth.' (*TBC-I* 1776–89).

Alternatively, the same events are employed to explain the place-name Focherd Muirthemne, now Faughart, Co. Louth. Fer Báeth compliments Cú Chulainn's cast: (8) 'Focherd sin ém!' or Fer Báeth. Is de atá Focherd Murthemne. '"That is indeed a throw," said Fer Báeth. From this comes the place-name Focherd Muirthemne.' (*TBC-I* 1783–4). (9) Glenn Fir Baíth occurs later as a place-name as well (*TBC-I* 1829).

---

[7] Situated at Focherd Muirthemne, according to *Hog. Onom.*, p. 443, s.v. *g. firbáith.*

Furthermore, *glenn* occurs twice in the genitive singular in the phrase *geniti glinne*, explained by *DIL* s.v. *genit* as 'demoniac spectral women of the glen: a kind of other-world Amazons who with like supernatural beings appear with shrill cries on the battle-field': (10) bánánaig ┐ boccánaig ┐ geniti glinni ┐ demna aeóir 'the goblins and sprites and spectres of the glen and demons of the air' (*TBC-I* 2083, similarly at 2240–1).

However, there are a few instances in this first recension of Táin Bó Cúailnge, which provide more tangible semantic substance. In one, *glenn* and *túaithebair* 'hill, eminence, raised ground', essentially a rather literary onomastic term, are juxtaposed: (11) 'Anaid fris beós,' ol Conc[h]obar 'co taurcba grían co mmaith hi nglennaib ┐ hi tuaigebra*ch*aib na hÉrend.' '"Wait on a while," said Conchobar, "until the sun has risen well above the glens and mounds of Ireland."' (*TBC-I* 3924–5).

Another is provided by Mac Roth's elaborate description of the sight he saw when fog fell as he was reconnoitring and Fergus mac Róich's explanation of the scene: (12) 'doréccacha úaim in mag co n-acca in tromchiaich ro lín na glendu ┐ na fántu co nderna na tilcha eturru amail indsi i llochaib [...]. An tromcheó atchonnarcais ro lín na fántu, anála na trénfer sein ro lín na glenntu co nderna na tulcha amail indsi i llochaib eturru'. '"I looked out over the plain and I saw that a dense mist had filled the glens and valleys, so that the hills between them rose up like islands in lakes [...]. The dense mist you saw which filled the valleys was the breath of those champions which filled the glens and made the hills to rise among them like islands in lakes."' (*TBC-I* 3558-60, 3569–71).

Of particular relevance to the present study is the synonymous treatment of *glenn* and *fán* 'a slope, declivity, depression, hollow', for which see further below.

Finally, the following place-names containing *Glenn*, and not cited already, are to be found in this text: (13) hi nGlind Dáil Imda hi Cúalngi 'in Glenn Dáil Imda in Cúailnge' (*TBC-I* 1016), dar Glend nGatlaig 'through Glenn Gatlaig' (1023-4), i nImślige Glendamnach 'in Imślige Glendamnach' (1728, cf. 2314, 3363), i nGlenn Domain 'in Glenn Domain' (3358), i n-Imśligi Glindi Domain 'in the battle of Glenn Domain (3362, and as Imśligi Glinne Domain, by way of variant for Imśligi Glenndomnach at 3363). Despite their differing genitive singular forms, the compound Glenndomain and the uncompounded Glenn Domain, both originally meaning 'Deep Glen', may be taken as variants of the same name, as may Glenn Gatt and Glenn Gatlaig.[8] The simple (14) coa Glend

---

[8] See Thomas Kinsella, *Ireland of the Welcomes*, 24–6, Nov.–Dec. 1975, p. 24, s.v. *Glenn Gatlaig*.

(= co Geimen coa Glend in the LL version) 'to [Geimen in] his valley' (3460) seems to be a common noun rather than an established place-name.[9]

GLENN IN BETHU PHÁTRAIC

In *Bethu Phátraic*, as in the language in general, *glenn* is specifically and regularly contrasted with *slíab* 'a mountain, a mountain-range'. King Lóegaire macc Néill's elder daughter queries Patrick and his entourage: (15) 'Cía far nDia-si ⁊ cía airm hitá? In i nim no i talam? In fú talam no for talam no hi muirib nó i srothaib? In hi sleibib nó i nglennaib?' '"Who is your God and where does he dwell? Is it in the sky or on the earth? Is it under the ground or on the ground or in seas or in streams? Is it in mountains or in valleys?"' (*Trip.*[2] 1117–19). Patrick replies in Latin that their God is God of all things, 'Deus montium sublimium et conuallium humilium,' '"the God of high mountains and of low valleys,"' (1127–8). The same manuscript, Egerton 93, has an Irish version of Patrick's response by way of suprascript: dia na sleibti roard ⁊ na nglennta isil 'the God of the very high mountains and of the low valleys'.

Contextual juxtaposition of *glenn* and *slíab* is to be seen also when Patrick is promised by an angel:

(16)   'Bid latt cech ní imrega,
         cech tír cit réidi reba,
         etir sleibe is cella,
         etir glenda is ʼfeda;
         'Everything around which you shall go shall be yours, every land although they are level […], both mountains and churches, both valleys and woods.' (*Trip.*[2] 1277–80).

Similarly, other words for heights are contrasted with *glenn*, when the saint blesses the men of Munster:

(17)   Bennacht fora mbénna,
         fora lecca lomma,
         bendacht fora nglénna,
         bennacht fora ndromma.

         Ganim lir fo longaib
         ropat lir a tellaig,

---

[9] For this expression see Liam Mac Mathúna, 'The Topographical Components of the Place-Names in Táin Bó Cúailnge and Other Selected Early Irish Texts' in *Studien zur Táin Bó Cuailnge*, edited by Hildegard L. C. Tristram (Tübingen: Gunter Narr Verlag, 1993), pp. 100–13.

hi fánaib, i rédib,

i sléibib, hi mbénnaib.'

'A blessing on their peaks, on their bare, flat slabs, a blessing on their valleys, a blessing on their ridges. May their hearths be as many as the (grains of) sand of the sea under ships, on slopes, on level places, on mountains, on peaks.' (*Trip.*[2] 2566–73).

In the first stanza *benn* 'mountain, crag, peak, point; crest, summit' and *druim(m)* 'ridge, usually of elevated ground; hill' represent HEIGHT, while in the second, *slíab* joins *benn*, VALLEY or HOLLOW being represented by *fán*.

Nonetheless, the pre-eminence of the complementary contrast *glenn* : *slíab* is underlined by the attribution of *sléibide* io, iā 'mountainous', an adjective transparently derived from *slíab*, to *glenn* in (18) ⁊ fóbhúaratar isnaib glénnaib sléibidib iar soethur, 'and after exertion they found him in the mountainy glens' (*Trip.*[2] 1082-3), which forms part of an account of how Assicus was found by his monks. However, this is *DIL*'s only example of the use of *sléibide*, and it seems to have been an ad hoc coining to convey the sense of the Latin text *in conuallibus montanis*.

Bethu Phátraic contains just two place-names with *Glenn* as a component: (19) Glenn Indechta (in the accusative) in Island Magee, Co. Antrim (*Trip.*[2] 1914) and Taraill leis is[n]aib Glinnib sair 'He came eastwards into the Glens', of north Co. Leitrim (1683).

COMPLEMENTARY EVIDENCE FROM *DIL*

The only further major area of application of *glenn* 'valley' to be found in *DIL*, and not attested in the excerpted texts, is its metaphorical use in reference to two of the three worlds of Christianity, viz. 'this world', (20) hi nglind in t-shaegail 'in the valley of the world' (*PH*, 4906) and hell (21) i. ngliund na pian 'in the valley of pains' (*Ériu*, 2, 134 § 112). The same text stresses the depth of hell: (22) do mheit in glinde ⁊ dia fhudhomnai 'because of the size of the valley and because of its depth' (*Ériu*, 2, 132 § 109). Another religious text skilfully employs the inversion of the *glenn* : *slíab* contrast in a powerful metaphor of the old pagan order being turned on its head by the advent of Christianity. The preceding stanza has just asserted: 'The famous kings have been stifled: the Domnalls have been plagued, the Ciaráns have been crowned: the Crónáns have been magnified.' The argument continues:

(23)   Na mórslébe andaig
         ro tesctha co rinnib,
         dorónta col-léce

slébe donaib glinnib.

'The great mountains of evil have been cut down with spear-points:
forthwith have mountains been made of the valleys.' (*Fél. Prol.* 237–
40).

Borg Emna ro tetha,
acht mairte a clocha:
is rúam iarthair betha
Glenn dálach dá locha.

'Emain's fort it has vanished, save that its stones remain: the Rome of
the west of the world is thronged Glendalough.'
(*Fél. Prol.* 193–6)

FÁN

We may now turn our attention to *fán*, o, m., *IGT*, Decl. § 96, 'a slope,
declivity, depression, hollow' (*DIL*). Although *fán* is not widely attested in
our excerpted sources in the relevant senses, the Milan Glosses do in fact
provide us with a fine introductory example, where it is contrasted to the
substantivated *ard* o, 'high place, height': (24) .*i.* etir réid ⅂ amreid ⅂ etir
fán ⅂ ardd 'i.e. both level and unlevel, both valley and height.' gl. p*er*
tractús terrae (*Ml.* 140 a 2). Reference may also be made to citation (17)
above from *Bethu Phátraic*, where the contextual deployment of *glenn* is
mirrored by that of *fán* in succeeding stanzas.

The only other example quotable from these sources is:

(25)   Cros Chríst fri cach ndoraid
        eitir fán is telaig.
        'Christ's cross to meet every difficulty both on hollow and hill.' (*EIL*
        14.5c-d; 10th century).

The physical contrasting of *fán* and *tulach* 'hill(ock), mound' is to be
expected, but here it forms part of a prayer for protection and may well be
intended metaphorically (cf. current English references to the ups and
downs of life), just as *doraid* itself represents the substantival use in its
transferred sense of the adjective *doraid* 'difficult, uneven, rough', derived
from the negative prefix *do-* and *réid* 'level, smooth; in its figurative sense
easy'.

However, the trawling of other sources yields this fine detail from an
account of the end of the world:

(26)   Bid comard a sliab fri fán,
       [...]
       bid clár cosmail in domun
       conid ressid oenubull.
       'The mountain will be as high as the hollow; [...] the world will be a
       level expanse so that a single apple might roll across it.' (*Blathm.* 949–
       52).

That *slíab* and *fán* are opposites is the very premise on which this quotation
of Doomsday levelling down and levelling up is based.

COMPLEMENTARY EVIDENCE FROM *DIL*

A gloss quoted in *DIL* may be noted: (27) fan [...] i vallis (*O'Mulc.* 489).
Otherwise, *DIL* provides some further references to parts of the human
body: (28) Folt [...] co fán a chulad leis. 'A head of hair to the nape of his
neck.' (*LL* 34961–2 = MU^2 532) and (29) ar fán na bathaisi 'on the occiput'
(23 K 42, 417.20). Again, in the primary, physical sense one has (30) fo fán
'down a slope' (*Hy* v 55). This passes into the more or less metaphorical *i
fán* 'laid low, prostrated': (31) Dindgnai Her*end* [...] a mbith i fás ㄱ i fán
'The strongholds of Ireland, their being deserted and prostrate' (*LL* 19275–
7), which became common in later Irish with a variety of prepositions: *ar*
[=*for*], *i*, *le*, *re fán* 'astray, wandering (as a vagrant or exile), cast away,
desolate', e.g. (32) ar fán ㄱ ar fiarlaoid 'cast away and astray' (*TSh.* 2522).

FÁNGLENN

The tautological compound, *fánglenn* 'a hollow, dale', is quite well
attested, *DIL* recording six instances in all, including (33) etir feda is
fánglenna 'both woods and dales' (*Met. Dinds.*, III 426) and (34) Andar
leiss bátar indsi ás lochaib atchondaic ás 'fánglentaib na cíach. 'He seemed
to see islands in lakes above the slopes of the mists' (*TBC-LL*[10] 4184–5, the
compound being repeated at line 4201 = ós fántaibh, *St.*, and cf. *TBC-I*,
citation (12), and under *fánaid* below). The other four occurrences are
Dinds. 103, *Buile S.* 62.7, *CCath.* 3071 and *FM*, VI 2342. This latter 17th-
century example echoes citation (33): (35) hi ffedhaibh ㄱ hi
ffáinghlenntoibh 'in woods and in dales' (*FM*, VI 2342). In other words,
fánglenn was a Middle Irish compound, which continued into the Late
Modern period. Linking, as it does, the two most common words for

---

[10] *Táin Bó Cúalnge from the Book of Leinster*, edited by Cecile O'Rahilly (Dublin: Institute for
Advanced Studies, 1967, reprint 1970).

'hollow, valley' without imparting any consequent refining semantic nuance, *fánglenn* was at home in the verbose and rhetorical literary style which flourished in the Middle and Early Modern periods.

FÁNAID

Fánaid f. *fánuidh* f., (gs. *-adh*; pl. *fánta,* gp. *fántadh*) *IGT*, Decl. § 4. 'A declivity, descent, depression' (*DIL*).

In citation (12) we have already encountered a passage from the first recension of Táin Bó Cúailnge where there is quite unambiguous synonymity between *glenn* and *fánaid*. In this, the plain containing glens, valleys and hills donned the appearance of islands in a lake when enveloped in what seemed to be a heavy fog, but was explained as being the breath of champions. The first reference, *na glendu ⁊ na fántu*, simply links the accusative plural forms of *glenn* and *fánaid* by means of the conjunction ⁊ but when mentioned a second time these lexemes are employed, again in the accusative plural, in succeeding, parallel clauses, *na fántu [...] na glenntu*. The reversal of the order in which the two terms are cited underlines their interchangeability, at least in this particular section of *TBC-I*. In fact, these are the only excerpted occurrences of *fánaid*.

COMPLEMENTARY EVIDENCE FROM *DIL*

Turning to *DIL*, one notes (36) goro lína grían glenta ⁊ fánta ⁊ tulcha ⁊ tuaidibrecha na Hérend 'until the sun fills the glens and slopes, the hills and mounds of Ireland' (*TBC-LL* 4653–4, echoed with slight variation at 4655), where *fánaid* again seems to fulfil the role of synonymous lexical substitute for the more usual *glenn*. The same text yields (37) Barrallsam a tilcha dá n-éis co failet ina fántaib comtís comarda síat. 'We have levelled their hills behind them into lowlands, so that they might be of equal height.' (*TBC-LL* 4158–9). This overturning of the natural order of the landscape, already met with in citation (26), motivates (38) cuiridh na tulcha isna fantaib corop tir 'cast the hills into the hollows that they may be (level) land' (*RC*, 9, 16.11).

Modern Irish brought opposition to the substantivated *ard* o, 'high place, height': (39) i n-ard ná i bhfánaidh 'on hill or vale' (*A. Ó Dálaigh* liv 1) and the frequent use of the phrase *re (le) fánaid* 'downwards', e.g. (40) go dteilgthear ré fánaid i n-ifreann iad 'that they are cast downwards into hell' (*TSh.* 4304–5).

As to the overall frequency of *Fán*, *Fánglenn* and *Fánaid* in place-names, *Hog. Onom.* shows that while *Fán* was the first element in quite a number of these, *Fánglenn* occurs only once as toponym initial, and *Fánaid* not at all.

COBFÁN

With regard to *cobfán*, *DIL* summarises: o (*com* + *fán*) 'slope, hollow'. In nn. loc. see *Hog. Onom.* (*cabán*). Note also 'understood in Down and Fermanagh to mean a round, dry bare hill', *O'Don. Suppl.*

This compound of *fán* is altogether wanting from the excerpted corpus. However, a selection of *DIL*'s citations will set out its range and application: (41) 'cobhan .i. comhfhán' (*O'Cl.*), (42) tech [...] fil hi cobfan na tilchae 'a house which is on the slope of the hill' (*RC*, 21, 318 § 46), (43) rolín etrigeda ⁊ cobána ind ármaige 'which filled the furrows and hollows of the battlefield' (*TTr.² 941*) and (44) do ronadh cabhan ⁊ toll isin cloich 'a hollow and a hole was made in the stone' (*ITS* XVI 8.17). As *DIL* suggests, the following instance seems to have arisen from confusion with *cobás* o, n. 'juncture, connexion; void' (45) a cobán fil eter nem ⁊ talmain 'the slope/hollow which exists between heaven and earth' (*TTr.² 859* (*in n-etaruaill*, *LL* 32203 = *TTr.* 1392)), particularly in view of (46) Confacca ní in nglaschéo mór ra ercc in comás eter nem ⁊ talmain 'He saw a great grey mist which filled the void between heaven and earth.' (*LL* 11674–5 = *TBC-LL* 4183–4), which it cites s.v. *cobás*. Interestingly, this is the Dictionary's only example of *etaruall* 'interval, intervening space'. The citation is actually from the *LL* version of Mac Roth's surveying of the plain, and is followed immediately by the sentence already quoted under *fánglenn*, citation (34).

The derived adjective, *cabánach* 'hollow, hollowed out', is late and rare. *DIL* calls attention also to *cabhánach* 'full of little hills', *O'Don. Suppl.*

The paucity of these early examples of *cobfán* stands in rather stark contrast to its later manifestation as *cabhán*, which P. W. Joyce (1995, pp. 401–2) treats quite extensively, pointing out that this latter means 'a hollow or cavity, a hollow place, a hollow field'. On etymological grounds he holds: 'this is undoubtedly its primary meaning, for it is evidently cognate with Lat. *cavea*, Fr. *cabane*, Welsh *caban*, and Eng. *cabin*. Yet in some parts of Ulster it is understood to mean the very reverse, viz., a round dry hill; and this is the meaning given to it by O'Donnell in his Life of St. Columba, who translates it *collis* (Reeves, Colt. Vis. 133). This curious discrepancy is probably owing to a gradual change of meaning, similar to the change in the words *lug*, *mullan*, &c.' (op. cit., p. 401).

Whether, then, one is dealing with a single word for which there are diachronically two orthographic representations, an earlier *cobfán* and a later *cabán*, or an unusual case of twin homonyms and synonyms, belonging to different periods of the language, is a matter which may be resolved on consideration of the etymological possibilities.

SRATH

DIL says of *srath*: [orig. o, m.? But ds. *sraith*, Alex. 873]. Later also *sraith*. *srath (na habhann)* m. (gs. *sraith, sratha*), *IGT* Decl. § 38 (87.11). '(a) grass, sward; (b) valley, bottom, meadow or grassy place near a river, etc.' [...] Common in nn. loc. See *Hog. Onom.*

We may compare P.W. Joyce's definition, 'a holm or inch—the lowland along a river' (1995, p. 60).

As a regular element of the lexicon *srath* is absent from our excerpted sources. It does occur several times, however, as a place-name element in *Bethu Phátraic*: (47) Srath Pátraic ainmnig*ther* indíu. Domnoch Sratha [a] ainm o céin. Ro foí Pátraic fó domnach and, 'It is called Srath Pátraic today. Domnach Sratha was its name long ago. Patrick spent the night there on a Sunday' (*Trip.²* 1685-7), drem di Bretn*aib* Sratha Clúathe 'a group of the Britons of Strathclyde' (*Trip.²* 191), and Ard Sratha, in the genitive, now Ardstraw, Co. Tyrone (*Trip.²* 1090).

Despite the arrangement of examples in *DIL*, it is hard to be persuaded of the semantic primacy of '(a) grass, sward' as against '(b) valley, bottom, meadow or grassy place near a river, etc.', although it must be conceded that the chronologically earliest examples of the word, grouped under (a) do fit this definition rather better than that of (b), e.g. (48) israth gl. ingramine (*Thes.*, II 46.21), (49) graig óir budi and fri srath 'a herd of golden, yellow horses there on the sward' (*Im. Brain* 15) and (50) Moscing srathu 'He careers across grasslands (of a horse) (*LU* 8669 = *FB* 50). Sense (b) is to be seen in (51) dus in fagba sliab no srath / no iath forsa tarrasad 'to see if he would find mountainous land or a valley or land on which he might stay' (*SR* 2551–2). *DIL* takes the sense of *srath* as having already passed into 'brink' in (52) for s*rai*th na tiopraidi (*Buile S.* 28.16) and (53) for s*rai*th an topuir (*Buile S.* 82.17), where it combines with 'spring' and 'well', respectively. At any rate, *DIL*'s evidence for explicit use in connection with particular rivers is definitely Modern Irish, cf. (54) tar sraith Banna 'across the meadow of the Bann' (*L. Cl. A. Buidhe* 158.149) and (55) ar srathaib na Múaidhe 'on the meadow-lands of the Moy' (*IGT* Decl. ex. 1009). Finally, we may note (56) gach srath gach áth gac[h] abhann 'every river-valley, every ford, every river' (*Dán Dé* xxv 22).

CONCLUSION

This study has served to underline the dominance of *glenn*, later *gleann*, in the lexical field VALLEY throughout the history of the Irish language. Relatively unmarked semantically, *glenn* was complemented by the other members of the field discussed here, but it never yielded its primacy. The relative exclusivity of VALLEY as a lexical field and the long-term success of *glenn* within it contrast intriguingly with the more diverse challenge posed to the pre-eminence of *slíab* 'mountain, mountainous land' in the lexical field HEIGHT.

James Joyce's *Ulysses* in Icelandic

RORY McTURK

University of Leeds

IN THE introduction to *Ódysseifur*, his two-volume Icelandic translation of James Joyce's *Ulysses*, Sigurður A. Magnússon (I, vi) describes his original as 'one of the most difficult texts imaginable' for the translator, not only because Joyce was 'a magically gifted master of language', using English highly individually, but also because he did not hesitate to use 'words and phrases that were current in Hiberno-English at the turn of the century and are not normally found in English dictionaries, not even the biggest and the best ones'.[1] Linked with this is the fact that the work deals with political, religious and social issues of specifically Irish interest, often indirectly. There is also the author's weakness for puns, which are 'hard to translate satisfactorily'. The main difficulty, though, is the narrative technique of stream of consciousness, whereby 'an attempt is made to capture the unconnected thoughts and associations that occur when the mind is not directed towards a particular topic but is allowed to wander at will'. In a generous tribute to both editions (1974 and 1988) of *Ulysses Annotated* by Don Gifford (with Robert J. Seidman),[2] the translator states that if his translation is 'more accurate' (his inverted commas) than, for example, the Danish and Swedish ones and the two German ones, it is very largely due to this work. The translation is based on the 1988 reprint of the 'Corrected Text' reading edition of *Ulysses*, published in 1986; references here are by page number to the 1993 reprint of that same edition,[3] and by volume and page number to the translation.

In attempting to show what the translator does, it may be helpful to begin by indicating certain things that he does not do. With a few exceptions, such as his use of the form *Dyflinni* for 'Dublin' and his not altogether satisfactory translation of 'the liberties' (in 'Proteus', p. 31) as *Suðurbærinn* (I, 38) (meaning 'the south side of town'), he does not

---

[1] James Joyce, *Ódysseifur*, Sigurður A. Magnússon þýddi, 2 vols (Reykjavík: Mál og menning, 1992–93). As indicated in the text, references to this translation are by volume and page number. The English translations of passages from the translator's introduction, and the explanatory translations of Icelandic words and phrases used in his translation, are my own. The present article is an extended version of my review of the translation in *James Joyce Broadsheet*, no. 44 (June 1996), 2.

[2] Don Gifford with Robert J. Seidman, *Ulysses Annotated: Notes for James Joyce's Ulysses*, 2nd edn, revised and enlarged by Don Gifford (Berkeley, CA: University of California Press, 1988; repr. 1989). References to this work in the text specify the date (1988) of the second edition, and are by page number.

[3] James Joyce, *Ulysses*, ed. by Hans Walter Gabler with Wolfhard Steppe and Claus Melchior, Afterword by Michael Groden (London: The Bodley Head, 1986; repr. 1993). As indicated in the text, references to this edition are by page number.

attempt to adapt proper names to Icelandic forms, even in cases where one feels it might have been tempting for him to do so. For example, it might at first sight seem obvious to use the Icelandic word *blóm*, meaning 'flower', for the surname *Bloom*; if this had been done, the pun on 'Bloo ... Me?' and 'Blood' at the beginning of 'Lestrygonians' (p. 124) would have gone better into Icelandic than it actually does in the translation (it comes out as *Blo ... Ég* and *Blóð*, I, 151; since the M of 'Me?' has been lost here, the pun would have been helped by an accent mark on the first *o*). In fact, however, this policy of the translator's is a wise one, for several reasons. For one thing, patronymics are infinitely more common in Icelandic than surnames, which Icelanders consequently recognise as a foreign pheno-menon anyway; an attempt to adapt surnames to Icelandic spelling would seem highly unnatural to Icelandic readers. For another, if the translator had chosen the word meaning 'flower' in Icelandic for the surname *Bloom*, he would have been faced with the problem of how to render Bloom's chosen pseudonym *Flower*, first introduced in 'Lotus-Eaters' on p. 59 (I, 72); the translator in fact keeps to the English forms *Henry Flower* wherever the pseudonym occurs. Thirdly, if the translator had adapted personal names to Icelandic forms, he might well have made still more difficult for himself a task which must have been difficult enough already, but in which he succeeds brilliantly: that of producing an Icelandic version of the acrostic in 'Ithaca' (p. 555; II, 272) in which each line begins with a letter of the shortened form of Leopold Bloom's first name: *Poldy*; the translator succeeds not only in beginning the lines with the appropriate letters and making them rhyme, but also in making them approximate to the rules of alliteration characteristic of traditional Icelandic poetry.

While he does tend to translate Hiberno-English expressions, as will be indicated below, another thing that the translator does not do, in my view wisely, is translate in his text the many words and phrases in languages other than English that occur in his original. At the end of each volume he lists the words and phrases in question—along with various other more or less obscure references in the text—by page number, providing translations and, where necessary, brief explanations; in introducing each list he refers the reader to the second edition (1988) of *Ulysses Annotated*, from which many of his explanations appear to be derived, and emphasises that he has listed only those words and expressions which are particularly important for understanding the text. In the text itself, no indication is given that the explanations are there for those who need them; the experience of reading it in Icelandic is thus very comparable, at least as far as the relevant expressions are concerned, to that of reading it in the original.

A third and perhaps rather more surprising negative aspect of the translator's approach (though one which also, in my view, ultimately redounds to his credit) is that he does not make any particular attempt to convert the background of *Ulysses* in Classical legend into one in which the themes of his own mythological heritage might become prominent. The text does, after all, allude not infrequently to Old Norse myth and legend, with its references to the 'bloodbeaked prows' of the Lochlann galleys in 'Proteus' (p. 37; I, 45); to 'a Norse saga' in 'Scylla and Charybdis' (p. 174; I, 212); and to 'the hammerhurler' Thor, thundering 'in anger awful', in 'Oxen of the Sun' (p. 323; II, 15). It is worth noting also that the name *Allfather*, explained in *Ulysses Annotated* (1988, p. 196) as an appellation for Christ in esoteric Christianity, is also one of the many appellations of the god Óðinn in Old Norse mythology, and occurs more than once in the text of *Ulysses*, notably in 'Scylla and Charybdis' (p. 152; I, 186) and in 'Oxen of the Sun' (p. 345; II, 41). The translator certainly does not ignore these references in his own text; he reproduces the alliteration of 'Thor' and 'thundered' (though not of 'anger awful') and uses the Icelandic term applicable to Óðinn, *Alfaðir* ('Allfather'), in both the cases referred to. He does not make any more of them than the original warrants, however; nor does he make explicit, as one can imagine an Icelandic translator being tempted to do, any parallel between the one-eyed figure of Nelson, who presides over Dublin from the top of his pillar in O'Connell Street as a symbol of perfidious Britain (*'Perfide Albion!'*) (see 'Cyclops', pp. 266–67; I, 323), and Óðinn, who also has only one eye, who surveys all the worlds from his throne Hliðskjálf, and who, arguably at least, is a treacherous god, responsible for the deaths of some of his favourites.[4] Nor indeed does he invoke in this connection the god Týr, who like 'one-handled Nelson' (see 'Sirens', p. 227; I, 276) has only one hand, and who arguably also (but by no means certainly) is a god of justice.[5]

In all these respects the translator shows a humility in the face of the text with which he is dealing, and a sense that it can speak for itself without being brought more than is strictly necessary within the compass of the linguistic and cultural tradition of the readership for which it is intended.

The case is perhaps rather different with the translator's treatment of Hiberno-English expressions, a few examples of which may be given: 'ollav', occurring in 'Scylla and Charybdis' (p. 151; I, 186) and also (as

---

[4] For the idea of Nelson presiding in this way, see Harry Blamires, *The New Bloomsday Book. A Guide through Ulysses: Revised Edition Keyed to the Corrected Text* (London: Routledge, 1988; repr. 1995), p. 113. On the god Óðinn as a slayer of his favourites, see E.O.G. Turville-Petre, *Myth and Religion of the North: the Religion of Ancient Scandinavia* (London: Weidenfeld and Nicolson, 1964), pp. 118–19.

[5] This indeed is how Carolyne Larrington describes the god Týr in the Introduction to her recently published translation of the Poetic Edda, see *The Poetic Edda*, translated with an Introduction and Notes by Carolyne Larrington (Oxford: University Press, 1996), p. xv. For a much more cautious view see, however, R.I. Page, 'Dumézil Revisited', *Saga-Book*, 20, parts 1–2 (1978–79), 49–69.

'ollave') in 'Circe' (p. 416; II, 119), is rendered in both cases by the word *seiðmaður*, meaning 'sorcerer', 'wizard'; 'caubeen' in 'Scylla and Charybdis' (p. 158; I, 193) is rendered by *hattkúfur*, meaning 'worn out old hat'; 'gombeenwoman', also in 'Scylla and Charybdis' (p. 165; I, 202), and 'gombeen man' in 'Wandering Rocks' (p. 200; I, 243) are rendered respectively by the words *okurkerling* ('female usurer'), and *okrari* ('usurer') respectively; 'crubeens' in 'Circe' (p. 359; II, 57) is rendered by *grísalappir*, meaning 'pigs' feet'; and 'shebeenkeeper', also in 'Circe' (p. 368; II, 67), and 'shebeen proprietor' in 'Eumaeus' (p. 531; II, 245) are rendered by the words *sprúttsali* ('bootlegger') and *gestgjafi* ('innkeeper') respectively. As will be evident from what has been written so far, these renderings amount to unsignalled explanations of what the original terms mean; unsignalled, because the original terms themselves appear neither in the text of the translation nor in the explanatory lists at the end of each volume. The distinctively Irish character of the original terms is thus, regrettably, largely lost in the translation, as is also, for better or for worse, the effect of strangeness or difficulty that these terms are likely to have on the many English-speaking readers of *Ulysses* who are not readily familiar with Hiberno-English.

There is indeed a sense in which *Ulysses* is easier to read in this translation than in the original. The translator frequently, and indeed inevitably (it is hard to see what else he could have done), plumps for one interpretation where, at least for the reader without immediate access to commentaries, several are possible. What is such a reader to make, for example, of the adverb 'lourdily' in 'Proteus' (p. 31)? Something to do with French *lourd* ('heavy', 'clumsy'), perhaps, or with pilgrimages to Lourdes? Apparently following *Ulysses Annotated* (1988, p. 46), the translator goes for the former interpretation, rendering it as *klunnalega* ('clumsily') (I, 38); here the reader is relieved of speculation on possible alternative explanations and simply reads on. And how about the expression 'auric egg', used to describe the head (presumably) of George Russell in 'Scylla and Charybdis' (p. 153; I, 188)? Is 'egg' intended to suggest baldness, or thinness on top? And does 'auric' have anything to do with gold? (A bald head might, after all, shine like gold in a certain light.) Or with golden hair? Or with ears (which might be especially prominent on a bald or balding head)? Or with auras (as the adverb 'occultly', used at the end of the sentence, and the general theosophical context of the expression as used here might suggest)? The translator goes for this last possibility, rendering it *áruegg*, which certainly leaves room for continued speculation, but tends to exclude gold and ears, if not baldness, as likely associations. Here again the translator is following *Ulysses Annotated* (1988, p. 200), which, it emerges as one checks these points, has its own tendency to give only one interpretation where more than one are possible—a tendency for which an annotator of *Ulysses* would seem to have rather less excuse than a translator.

Another factor contributing to the greater ease with which *Ulysses* is likely to be read in this translation by Icelanders than in the original by native English speakers is the fact that Icelandic, as a 'native-resource oriented' language,[6] forms many of its words by the compounding of native elements. Thus *skækjuástir*, the first element in which means 'prostitute' and the second 'amorous relations', will not present for an Icelandic reader the problems of comprehension that 'scortatory love' might for an English-speaking reader (in 'Scylla and Charybdis', p. 165; I, 202); similarly, an Icelandic reader will have no difficulty with the term *ófyrirsjáanleiki* ('unforeseeability'), used to translate 'imprevidibility' in 'Ithaca' (p. 571; II, 291), whereas the latter term might well not be immediately comprehensible to a reader whose first language is English.

A healthy measure of difficulty is nevertheless retained in the translation, not least in its handling of some of the puns. Certain of these, it is true, appear to have defeated the translator, for very understandable reasons. If there is indeed a pun involving finger-nails and other kinds of nail in 'Hades' (p. 76; I, 93), as Blamires (p. 32)[7] suggests, this is not conveyed in the translation, and it is hard to see how it could be, since Icelandic has different words for the different kinds of nail; the nouns *nögl* ('finger-nail') and *nagli* ('nail' as in 'hit the nail on the head') are identical in sound and spelling only in certain of their oblique cases, which the translator cannot use in the relevant context without departing to an unnatural extent from the original.[8] The explicit pun with 'coffin' on the surname 'Coffey', also in 'Hades' (p. 85; I, 104), cannot be conveyed either; here the translator is compelled to place the English word *coffin* alongside the Icelandic word for 'coffin', *líkkista*, in order to indicate that a pun is involved. The pun of 'sun' with 'son' that seems intended, as Blamires (p. 63) also suggests, in 'Lestrygonians' (p. 135; I, 165; cf. also 'Eumaeus', p. 521; II, 232; and p. 532; II, 246) does not come across either in the translation; the Icelandic words *sól* ('sun') and *sonur* ('son') are simply too remote from one another in spelling and pronunciation to make

---

[6] The expression is borrowed from Robert Lord, *Teach Yourself Comparative Linguistics* (London: The English Universities Press Ltd, 1966; repr. 1967), p. 222.

[7] References to Blamires are by page number to Harry Blamires, *The New Bloomsday Book*, as referred to in note 4, above.

[8] The main cases in question are the dative and genitive plural, for which both nouns have the forms *nöglum* and *nagla* respectively. It may also be noted that *naglar*, the genitive singular of the strong feminine noun *nögl*, meaning 'finger-nail', is identical in spelling and pronunciation with *naglar*, the nominative plural of the weak masculine noun *nagli*, meaning 'nail' in the sense of a fastening device.

it viable. The ambiguity at the end of 'Scylla and Charybdis' of the description of Toby Tostoff as 'a ruined Pole' (p. 178; I, 217) is hardly conveyed by the phrase *gjaldþrota Pólverji*, which means neither more nor less than 'a bankrupt native of Poland' (the name 'Tostoff', incidentally, is conveyed by the noun *sprauta*, meaning 'syringe' or 'squirter'); 'cod's eye' in 'Cyclops' (p. 244; I, 297) becomes *þorskaugu* ('cod-eyes'), with no possibility of conveying the original's likely pun on 'God's eye' (cf. Blamires, p. 114); and it is unlikely that Icelandic readers of the translation will pick up as readily as English-speaking readers of the original the idea of a papal bull from the reference in 'Oxen of the Sun' to a bull being sent to Ireland by 'farmer Nicholas' (p. 327; II, 20; cf. Blamires, p. 144), since the Icelandic word for 'papal bull', *páfabréf*, cannot, as far as I can see, be easily punned with any of the Icelandic words for the animal 'bull', including the one mainly used in this context (*tuddi*). That said, it seems to me that the translator is being unduly modest in what he says in his introduction (I, vii) about his treatment of the pun of 'Lawn Tennyson' on 'Lord Tennyson' at the end of 'Proteus' (p. 42; I, 50). In Icelandic, the word for 'Lord', *lávarður*, would follow rather than precede the proper name; 'Lord Tennyson' would thus be *Tennyson lávarður*. Here the translator substitutes for *lávarður* the archaic word *lágarður*, which is close in sound, and (as will be evident) identical apart from one letter in spelling, to the word it is replacing. What it means, however, is 'surf' or 'surf-line'. Here the Icelandic reader will make associations with the idea of 'Lord' (conveyed by *lávarður*, of which *lágarður* , following the name *Tennyson*, will remind him), and, if he knows the word *lágarður*, with the sea, but not with 'lawn' or 'tennis'. As I have hinted, the translator's tone is apologetic in the account he gives of his treatment of this pun, but he might take comfort from the thought that whereas Joyce may here be challenging his readers to think of the lawns often mentioned in Tennyson's poetry (four times, notably, in Tennyson's *In Memoriam*),[9] the translation may here remind the Icelandic reader of the wave rolling shoreward in Tennyson's poem 'The Lotos[*sic*]-Eaters' (not to be confused with the fifth episode of *Ulysses*), the relevant part of which appeared in an Icelandic translation (by Magnús Ásgeirsson) in 1928.[10] The fact that this pun of Joyce's virtually

---

[9] As far as I can work out from the text of *In Memoriam A.H.H. Obiit MDCCCXXXIII* as printed in *The Works of Alfred Lord Tennyson, Poet Laureate* (London: Macmillan, 1884; repr. with many additions 1892; editor not named), pp. 247–86, the word 'lawn' occurs four times in that poem, in the sections numbered in that edition lxxxix (twice) (see p. 271), xcv and cxv (once each; see pp. 273 and 280 respectively); i.e. four times in all.

[10] This verse translation, entitled 'Lótófagar', renders into Icelandic the five stanzas of Tennyson's poem 'The Lotos-Eaters', but does not include the eight-stanza sequel to it known as 'Choric Song'. It was first published in Magnús Ásgeirsson's *Þýdd ljóð* I ('Translated poems', I) (Reykjavík, 1928), and is

compels his translator to use the relatively uncommon Icelandic word *lágarður* reinforces in the translation the element of challenge for the reader that is of course present, here and in so many other places, in the original. In at least one case the translator carries the punning process further than the original, when he adds an extra letter (printed, as in the original, with a line through it) to the Icelandic word for 'sympathy', i.e. *samúð*, in translating Molly Bloom's 'symphathy' (*sic*), in 'Penelope' (p. 624; II, 351); in Icelandic the extra letter, *b*, makes the word mean 'cohabitation' (*sambúð*).

Among other puns that the translator handles more or less successfully may be mentioned '*The Rose of Castile*' and 'Rows of cast steel' in 'Aeolus' (p. 111; I, 135), where the former expression comes out as *Ást í meinum*, meaning 'illicit love', and the latter as *Á stím einum*, apparently meaning 'on steam alone', or possibly 'full steam ahead' (it should be noted that the translator is here compelled to adapt the English word *steam* to Icelandic spelling and morphology in order to sustain the pun);[11] the pun in 'Lestrygonians' (p. 126; I, 154) of 'base barreltone voice' (on 'bass baritone voice'), which emerges as *bassabartunnurödd*, in which the elements *bassa-* and *-rödd* mean 'bass' and 'voice' respectively, but in which the elements *-bar-* and *-tunnu-* convey respectively the ideas of 'bar' (as a place for drinking) and 'barrel' (or 'tun'); the pun in 'Sirens' (pp. 221 and 234; I, 268, 284) of 'Met him pike hoses' (on 'metempsychosis'), which comes out as *Met him píkhosa*, where the first two words appear to be the English words *met* and *him*, but where the third is evidently a compound formed from the Icelandic words *píka* and *hosa*, meaning 'girl' (or 'woman's genitals') and 'hose' (in the sense of 'leggings') respectively (a native Icelandic speaker has pointed out to me that this compound, which appears to be a coinage of the translator's, might well suggest the meaning 'condom' to an Icelandic reader);[12] and the pun in 'Cyclops' of 'allegations' and 'alligator' (p. 276; I, 335), where the question 'Who made those allegations?' is conveyed by *hver fullyrðir það?* ('who's claiming

---

reprinted in Magnús Ásgeirsson, *Ljóðasafn* ('Collected poems'), ný útgafa aukin ('New edition, augmented'), 2 vols (Reykjavík: Helgafell, 1975), II, pp. 68–69. It has to be said that, although the translation graphically conveys the shoreward movement of 'the mounting wave', it does not in fact make use of the word *lágarður*.

[11] The dative singular masculine form (*einum*) of the adjective *einn* (meaning 'alone' here suggests that *stím* is the dative singular of a masculine noun of which the expected nominative form would be *stímur*. As far as I have been able to discover, no such noun is attested in Icelandic. The neuter noun *stím*, on the other hand, is attested, in the meaning 'speed', 'headway', with particular reference to the speed of a ship, and no doubt derives from the English word *steam*; the expression *á stíminu*, is, I am told, used by sailors to mean 'fully on course'. I am grateful to Örnólfur Thorsson, cand. mag., Visiting Fellow in Icelandic Studies at the University of Leeds, for help with this and other aspects of this article.

[12] The common words for 'condom' in Icelandic are *smokkur* and *verja*.

that?') and the reply 'I'm the alligator' comes out as *ég er fullorðinn* ('I'm grown up'); the verb *fullyrða* ('to affirm') and the adjective *fullorðinn* ('adult') are close enough in sound and spelling to make the pun effective.

Although the translator does not produce actual palindromes in place of 'Madam, I'm Adam. And Able was I ere I saw Elba' (in 'Aeolus', p. 113; I, 138), he translates the first of these as *Madame, ég er Adam*, which has the same meaning as in the original and in which the two nouns rhyme in Icelandic, as in English; and the second as *Og ég var Abel áður en ég sá Babel* (meaning 'And I was Abel before I saw Babel'), in which the nouns also rhyme and where the translator departs from the original in continuing the Old Testament associations introduced by the mention of Adam. Sometimes he is able to convey rhyme in the original with rhyme in Icelandic, as in the case of 'Rats: vats', translated as 'Rottur: pottur' (meaning 'rats: pot' [with 'pot' in the sense of 'container']; 'Lestrygonians', p. 125; I, 152); and in that of 'Old Mother Hubbard went to the cupboard', rendered by *Feitlagna Beta fékk ekki að éta* (meaning 'Big fat Betty got nothing to eat'), in 'Cyclops' (p. 267; I, 324). In the case of 'tomb: womb' in 'Aeolus' (p. 114; I, 139), where he is apparently unable to match the end-rhyme of the original, he produces two compound words in Icelandic: *leggöng: legstaður* (meaning 'vagina' and 'burial-place' respectively), in which the first elements are formally identical, so that an effect of alliteration is achieved as well as of first-syllable rhyme. In one case where the original itself combines alliteration and rhyme: 'Hughes and hews and hues' (in 'Scylla and Charybdis', p. 163; I, 199), the translator does so as well, adding perforce a touch of assonance: *Hughes og hús og hjú* (meaning 'Hughes and house and servant[s]'). In a case where the original combines alliteration and assonance: 'Hunter with a horn. Haw. Have you the?' (in 'Sirens', p. 237; I, 289), his virtually literal translation, which reproduces everything apart from the definite article, combines alliteration with rhyme: *Veiðimaður með horn. Húúú. Hefur þú?* In at least two cases where it is mainly alliteration that is prominent in the original, the translator makes it so in Icelandic. These are: 'Peter Piper pecked a peck of pick of peck of pickled pepper' (*sic*) in 'Scylla and Charybdis', p. 157; I, 192), which becomes in the translation: *Peter Piper pikkaði pipurlega og pent í pakka af pipar og peðraði pallinn* (meaning something like: 'Peter Piper prodded perkily and prettily at a packet of pepper and pockmarked the platform'), which shows indeed rather more inventiveness than the original; and 'Tipping her tepping her tapping her topping her', in 'Sirens' (p. 226; I, 274), which becomes *Hvakkar henni, hvískrar að henni, hvolfist yfir hana, hvarflar inní hana* (meaning 'gets her going, whispers to her, collapses on top of her, wanders into her'). Although the ptarmigan is very much an Icelandic phenomenon (as indeed is alliteration), the translator can I think be forgiven for not reproducing the alliteration of 'Do ptake [*sic*] some ptarmigan' in 'Lestrygonians' (p. 144; I, 176); it comes out simply as *Fáið yður rjúpubita* ('Do have some ptarmigan'), the politeness of the 'do' being conveyed in the Icelandic by the use of the honorific plural.

The Icelandic language has close equivalents for many of the English idioms that occur in *Ulysses*, and the translator takes full advantage of this. 'Out of the frying pan into the fire' goes neatly into Icelandic with *úr öskunni í eldinn* ('out of the ashes into the fire'), as the translator shows in rendering 'Out of the fryingpan of life into the fire of purgatory' in 'Hades' (p. 91; I, 112) as *Úr ösku lífs í eld hreinsunar* ('Out of the ashes of life into the fire of purgation'). 'On tenterhooks' in 'Eumaeus' (p. 517; II, 228) similarly finds its Icelandic counterpart readily enough, becoming in the translation *á nálum*, meaning literally 'on needles'. 'Walls have ears', which occurs in 'Lotus-eaters' (p. 68; I, 83) and in 'Circe' (p. 362; II, 60), is provided in each case with a more or less literal translation (*veggirnir hafa eyru*; *veggirnir eru með eyru*) which is consistent with present-day Icelandic usage as far as the meaning of the English expression is concerned, and which the translator, dealing as he is in both cases with an urban setting, seems to have found preferable here to the more traditional Icelandic idiom which expresses the same idea: *Oft er í holti heyrandi nær* ('In a forest a listener is often close by'). On the other hand, he has not hesitated to use the traditional Icelandic idiom: *Grípa gæsina meðan hún gefst* (meaning literally 'to grab the goose while it's available') as an equivalent of 'Make hay while the sun shines' in the context of Bloom following his next-door neighbour's servant-girl back from the butcher's in 'Calypso' (p. 49; I, 60); it seems indeed more appropriate in that context than the idiom used in the original.

One aspect of the narrative technique of stream of consciousness, the translator's understanding of which has been indicated above, is the tendency to leave sentences unfinished. Some of these are quotations, as in the case of 'Stopped short never to go again when the old', in 'Oxen of the Sun' (p. 346; II, 43). As *Ulysses Annotated* (1988, p. 443) makes clear, this is a quotation from the song 'My grandfather's clock'; what 'stopped short' was the clock, and the words of the clause introduced by 'when', which in fact constitutes the last line of each verse of the song, are, in the latter, as follows: 'when the old man died'. The last two words of this clause, as will be evident, have been omitted from the quotation in *Ulysses*. It is interesting to note that the translator has rendered this quotation as follows: *Stoppaði og gekk ekki framar þegar sú gamla*. This is an accurate translation, meaning 'stopped and did not go again when the old', except possibly for the fact that the forms *sú gamla*, meaning 'the old', clearly indicate feminine gender; since it is an old man that the song is referring to here (even though this does not emerge from the unfinished quotation) one might have expected the masculine forms *sá gamli*. Why has the translator given the feminine forms? He does, after all, acknowledge the help of *Ulysses Annotated* and was presumably in a position to check that it was a man that the quotation is referring to. Is he thinking of the word *manneskja*, meaning 'human being', which has feminine gender? Or has his attentiveness to *Ulysses Annotated* slipped for a moment, and does he think that *sú gamla* refers to the clock, the word for which in Icelandic (*klukka*) is also of feminine gender? Or does he think that *sú gamla* refers to an old woman? The best way to answer these questions, in my view, is to say 'yes' to all of them, and to acknowledge that while the translator may in one sense have made a slight mistake here, in another he has been creative, in continuing, opening up, redirecting and indeed increasing the possibilities of interpretation suggested by the original.

The translation thus shows a healthy balance of diffidence and audacity, of caution and inventiveness. The diffidence and caution show themselves in the translator's response to the mythological background of *Ulysses*, in his treatment of Hiberno-English expressions, and in his tendency to reduce in some cases the original's multiplicity and difficulty of interpretation. The audacity and inventiveness show themselves in his handling of many of the puns, in his treatment of passages involving rhyme, assonance and alliteration, and in his creative response (illustrated here by only one example) to the narrative technique of stream of consciousness. All in all, this is a magnificent translation, which with its high standard of accuracy and fruitfully provocative character will bring home to Icelandic readers much of the infinite richness and variety of Joyce's *Ulysses,* and will no doubt make its contribution to what is still an emergent literary genre: the Icelandic urban novel.

From Latin to French: Approaches to Alphabetization in Medieval Lexicography

BRIAN MERRILEES & JEAN SHAW
University of Toronto

JOHANNES Balbus introduces the fifth section, the lexicon, of his *Catholicon* which he completed in 1285, with the following statement about his methodology:

> In hac autem quinta parte procedam ubique secundum ordinem alphabeti. ita quod ex tali ordine de facili haberi poterit ortographya cuiuslibet hic posite dictionis. ut verbi gratia. Intendo tractare de amo et bibo. primo tractabo de amo quam de bibo quia .a. est prima littera in amo et .b. est prima littera in bibo et .a. est ante .b. in alphabeto¶ Item tractare volo de abeo et adeo. primo tractabo de abeo bis quam adeo adis quia .b. est secunda littera in abeo et .d. est secunda littera in adeo et .b. est ante .d. ¶ Item determinare intendo de amatus et amor. prius determinabo de amatus quam de amor quia .a. est tercia littera in amatus et .o. est tercia littera in amor et .a. est ante .o. [...]. Hunc autem ordinem cum magno labore et ardenti studio adinveni non tamen ego sed gracia dei mecum.[1]

The principles and practice of alphabetization, full and partial, go back to antiquity and two centuries before Balbus the first major lexicographer of the Middle Ages, Papias, author of the *Elementarium doctrinae erudimentum*, had already made a clear statement of his own organizational intention:

> Notare quoque cuilibet aliquid citius invenire volenti oportebit quoniam totus hic liber per alfabetum non solum in primis partium litteris verum etiam in secundis et tertiis et ulterius interdum ordinabili litterarum dispositione compositus erit. Prima igitur divisionis notatio per .a.b.c. et ceteras sequentes fiet litteras, que secundo quidem distinctionis ordine per easdem .a.b.c. ceteras maiores litteras ante quaslibet commutatas subdividetur [...][2]

If neither lexicographer was perfect in his application of the concepts outlined, both produced eminently consultable dictionaries, while retaining

---

[1] Cited from the Mainz edition, 1460.

[2] Cited from the Milan edition of 1476, cited with translation by Lloyd W. Daly and B.A. Daly, 'Some techniques in medieval Latin lexicography', *Speculum*, 39 (1964), 231, 233.

other principles of arrangement. Balbus in particular combines alphabetization with derivation and composition, the latter inherited from his own main source, the *Magnae Derivationes* of Hugutio and it was this combination which was passed on to bilingual dictionaries, including those glossing Latin by French that appear from the fourteenth century on. Nonetheless full alphabetization remained the first goal of organization in these Latin-French texts.[3]

When however compilers first attempted to set French words as lemmata to be glossed by Latin, the inversion process did not lead immediately to the level of alphabetization described or practiced by Papias or Balbus. There are three early manuscript dictionary texts, dating from the fourteenth and fifteenth centuries, in which French is given priority as the language to be defined by Latin, and each of these lexicons has a different approach to the ordering of French words and of their Latin definitions.

The earliest attempt is in Montpellier, Faculté de Médecine, H236, a fourteenth-century version of Guillaume Brito's *Expositiones vocabulorum Biblie*. A first scribe has copied what the work's editor, Anne Grondeux, calls a *Brito 2*, essentially Latin but with some French glossing as part of the text.[4] However, it is the work of a second scribe that is of particular interest. This second scribe has attempted to construct in the margin a French-Latin glossary of the Brito by giving for each French word a reference number that corresponds to a section of the Latin text. These numbers represent each half page of each letter of the Latin. The French words in the margin are listed according to their first letter but after that the ordering principle is the order of the *Brito 2* text. The examples given by the first describer of this system, B. Hauréau, are: II 'Aloine', II 'Amertume', V 'Aguille', V 'Aguillier', V 'Aguillons' [...].[5] Thus in section AII, the bottom of the first page, we have 'Hoc absincium. -cii, est quedam herba amarissimi suci, gallice 'Aloine', et accipitur pro amaritudine 'Amertume' and in AV, first half of the third page: Hec acus [...] gallice 'Aguille' and so on. 'Aigle' is followed by AXVIII and at the

[3] In Paris, BN. lat. 7692, the *Abavus* begins: Abbavus, abbas, abbatissa, abbassia, abreviare, abreviatio, abdicare, abdere [...]; the *Aalma* in Paris, BN. lat. 13032 has: Aalma, Aaron, ab, abactus, abamita, abavus, abbas, abbacia, abbatissa, Abdias, abdicativus, abdico, abditus, abdo [...]. Both were edited by Mario Roques, *Recueil général des lexiques français du moyen âge* (Paris: Champion, I, 1936, II, 1938). The *Dictionarius* of Firmin Le Ver has a more complex macro-entry structure involving a headword in fully alphabetized position followed by one to several sub-headwords in derivational order, see Brian Merrilees et William Edwards, eds, *Firmini Verris Dictionarius : Dictionnaire latin-français de Firmin Le Ver*, Corpus Christianorum : Continuatio mediaevalis: Lexica Latina Medii Aevii: Nouveau Recueil des lexiques latins-français du moyen âge, 1 (Turnhout: Brepols, 1994), pp. xxv–545.

[4]   Anne Grondeux-Troque, *Glossaires français du moyen âge : le manuscrit H236 de la Bibliothèque de la Faculté de Médecine: Etude critique et édition*, thesis. (Paris: Ecole Nationale des Chartes, 1990).

[5] *Histoire littéraire de France*, 29 (1885), 594.

bottom of page 9 (f.5 recto) we indeed find 'aquila'. The bases of this approach are first-letter or A-ordering combined with a numerical reference system.

A related approach is found in two consecutive manuscript volumes of the Bibliothèque Municipale of Angers, MSS 497 and 498, dating from the fifteenth century according to the catalogue, which contain what seems to be a unique compendium of assorted texts with a French-Latin glossary.[6] This abbreviated lexicon, which lacks the letters A through F presumably in a missing volume, begins each letter with an alphabetical listing of French words, each word followed by a folio number in Roman. The number refers to a folio of the letter in question where the French head-word is again found, this time followed by a substantial Latin definition. Within the body of the glossary the order of the French words follows no pattern that we are able to distinguish, though there are groups of entries where the principal Latin glosses, but not the French headwords, follow alphabetical order. Again numerical ordering is part of the system used, this time with a fully alphabetical index given before the dictionary itself. The indexes appear thus on folio 1r of Angers 497 (the list is repeated with a slightly different ordering on f. 19r):

gaber	ix
gager	xxi
galaces	xxvi
galice	
galilee	
gannir	xxvii
gant	viii
garczon	x
gargate	xiiii
gargane	xxvii
garder	xxvii
garir	
garriz	xxvii
gaude	xvii
gaigner	xxxiiii

This means that to find *gaber* one goes to folio 9 of the letter G, to find *gaigner* to folio 34. Folio G9 (= MS f.32v) does not in this case provide the meaning for *gaber* but a cross-reference: 'quere escharnir' which would fall under the letter E in the missing volume (A-F). Folio G34 should be

---

[6] *Catalogue général des manuscrits*, 31 (1898), 354.

MS f.57 but a gap is left on the verso page and *gaigner* appears as a headword at the top of f.58r glossed by 'lucror' and followed by derivatives and compounds of that verb. The lists of French words indexed and subsequently defined in this Anger dictionary are not lengthy, though many of the entries are substantial even encyclopedic.

The basis of the third dictionary, the fifteenth-century *Glossarium gallico-latinum* contained in Paris, Bibl. Nat., MS lat. 7684, is text-ordering. In this work French headwords organized by first letter only are glossed by Latin following the order of a source text. On the manuscript page the layout is simple and one might easily take the arrangement of the French lemmata as alphabetical, but as an 18th-century hand on the fly-leaf warns us it is 'non accurato litterarum ordine scriptum'.[7] Closer examination reveals what has happened. The compiler has clearly intended to set all French words beginning with the same letter together, but to achieve this he has gone through his Latin-French source as follows: from the Latin A he took all French words beginning in A in the order of their occurrence in the source text; then he went through the Latin B and again took all the French words in A and added them to the end of his first group; then through C, through D and so on. French words in B were next, again beginning with Latin A, then Latin B, following the same method. The result is a form of French-Latin dictionary but the determination of the order is only in part the first letter of the French headword and very much the order of the Latin glosses. To find a French word one must run through an entire letter or have an idea of the Latin word first to locate the French word it defines. Further examination reveals that the Latin glosses of the *Glossarium gallico-latinum* (henceforth *GGL*) generally follow an alphabetical order but the organization is partly derivational and many terms are clustered in families. Occasionally Latin derivatives will be placed as sub-headwords:

Abbé	abbas .tis	m
Abbasse	abatissa .sse	f
Abbeye	abbacia .cie	f
Ayole	abamitta .tte	f
Arriere chacer	abigo .gis, abegi,	
	abigere, abactum	a
<A>bominer	abominor .aris	
	.atus sum vel fui .ari	d
Abominacion	abominacio	f

---

[7] It is this same hand which provides the title. The full wording is: 'Glossarium Gallico-Latinum studiose licet non acurato litterarum ordine scriptum xv. Saeculo'.

Abominable	abominabilis .le	o
Abominablement	abominabiliter	
Avorté	abortus .ta .tum, abort-	
	ivus—idem	o
Acourcer	abbrevio .as .atum	n
Aurone?	herba, abrotanum .ni	n
Absent	absens .tis	o
Absencia	*absence*	f
Absenté	absentatus .ta .tum	o

ALPHABETIZATION AND TEXT-ORDERING

Although the manuscript layout of BN lat.7684 is by no means as polished as many medieval lexicographical manuscripts and one might be tempted to see it as a first draft on the way to a French-Latin lexicon, there are few signs of it not being a final product as it stands. Whether or not it is in final intended form, its organization raises some important methodological questions and it should not be dismissed too readily as a simplistic effort at alphabetization. There are ample precedents in the medieval Latin tradition for text-ordering as a principle and some of these continued to be used long after full alphabetization had been established. The *GGL* compiler indeed was resorting to a method that has a long history with a development that takes on a number of forms.[8]

In her very stimulating *Book of Memory* Mary Carruthers draws our attention to St Jerome's index and gloss of Hebrew names in the Bible:

> In its written form, Jerome's index is first catalogued by a particular book of the Bible, beginning with Genesis and proceeding in canonical order. The Hebrew words occurring within each book are then grouped alphabetically. But they are not 'fully' alphabetized, that is,

---

[8] There are a number of studies on the organization of indexes and other apparatus in medieval manuscripts. See, for example: M.B. Parkes, 'The Influence of the Concepts of *ordinatio* and *compilatio* on the Development of the Book', in *Medieval Learning and Literature: Essays Presented to Richard William Hunt*, ed. by J.J. Alexander and M.T. Gibson (Oxford: Clarendon, 1976), pp. 115–141; Richard H. Rouse and Mary A. Rouse, 'Statim Invenire: Schools and Preachers and New Attitudes to the Page', in *Renaissance and Renewal in the Twelfth Century*, ed. by Robert L. Benson and Giles Constable (Cambridge, Mass.: Harvard University Press, 1982), pp. 201–225; Lloyd W. Daly and B.A. Daly, 'Some Techniques in Mediaeval Latin Lexicography', *Speculum*, 39, (1964), 229–239; Olga Weijers, 'Lexicography in the Middle Ages', *Viator*, 20 (1989), 139–153; 'Les index au moyen âge sont-ils un genre littéraire?' in *Fabula in Tabula*, ed. by C. Leonardi, M. Morelli and F. Santi (Spoleto: Centro Italiano di Studi sull'Alto Medioevo, 1995), pp. 11–22.

not beyond the initial letter. Instead they are given in the order in which they occur in the actual text[9]

For example, words beginning in A in Genesis are listed thus:

Aethiopiam [...]	(Gen.2,13).
Assyriorum [...]	(Gen.2,14)
Adam [...]	(Gen.2,19)
Abel [...]	(Gen.4,2)
Ada [...]	(Gen.4,19)
Ararat [...]	(cf. Gen. 8,4)
Aschenes	(Gen.10,3)

The listing continues with words in B, C etc. Carruthers notes that Jerome claimed his index which followed each book in order was especially useful, 'particularly user-friendly', she says, in contrast to the work of his predecessors. It was a method of compilation that responded to the principle of mental concording and the mnemonic principles which he assumed that its users would also have. Absolute ordering, she suggests, is better adapted to the needs of readers working from a written codex physically open in front of them (p. 116). Carruthers goes on to discuss a 13th cty French Bible (Huntington Library, ms 1073) that has a fully alphabetical index of Hebrew words at its end but which also has a text-ordered listing as well, the latter more selective and keyed to familiar texts, proof that full alphabetization did not dislodge other methods of organization based on the alphabet.

The text-ordered method used by Jerome is developed and refined in a number of the manuscripts of Hugutio of Pisa's *Magnae Derivationes* which are based, as their name implies, on the principle of derivation. In this work, one headword can initiate several columns of derived words and there is no simple way of locating a desired word within a single article let alone knowing in which article one might look for it. For example, if one might readily seek *accentus* 'accent' under cano 'I sing', one might not necessarily guess that *sanguis* 'blood' is to be found under *sueo* 'to be agreeable'. Indeed, to overcome this difficulty most copies of Hugutio are accompanied by tables intended to guide the reader towards the right headword for the appropriate subheadword. It is within these tables that we find similarities to St Jerome's indexes and to *the Glossarium gallico-latinum*, but there are variations on the theme. The following examples of

---

[9] Mary J. Carruthers, *The Book of Memory : A Study of Memory in Medieval Culture* (Cambridge: University Press, 1990), p. 115.

Hugutio tables are by no means exhaustive, but the variety of types of organization they represent suggest much greater complexity of development than might at first be presumed:

EXAMPLE I

The first type has the following characteristics: a single column of words in A-order is set down, for the most part reproducing headwords from the lexicon but also some subheadwords, following the order of the text, but with no headword reference to locate subheadwords. The example here is from Paris, BN lat.16217 (f.166r):

augeo
auris
aula
audeo
aveo
ausculto
aer
aelyon
acuo
accidia
acone

Only three words of this sample (aelyon, accidia, acone) are subheadwords but their headwords are not given. Furthermore, as a register of headwords, this list is incomplete and might have included in their alphabetical position 'avernus, autumno, abba, abax, abissus, absida, abacuc'. It seems that all tables are selective in some way. However we can note that head- and subheadwords which are listed follow the *text order*.

EXAMPLE II

A second type of table has words grouped by first letter in one column with a second column of reference headwords. This second column represents the order of the text (it is also mostly alphabetical because of the nature of the text) and thus illustrates an overall organizing principle which we shall call *second-column ordering*. Divisions are made in the list of words of the first column, letter by letter, alphabetically, with a title 'Incipit capitulum dictionum incipientum a .a.' and so on.

The list of words extracted in our example, Paris, BN lat. 7625 (f.195r), is selective, even incomplete. The A words, for example, begin at M, though B words begin with B. The scribe in 7625 has also used wavy lines to join the words of column 1 to the reference headword of column 2. Often more than one word will refer to the same headword:

Incipit capitulum dictionum incipientum a .a.

aerimantia
armomantia ———→ man quod est videre
amurca   mergo .gis
amussis   mugio .gis
anicos .i. invictus
anicius ——————— nice vel nico
anomalus
astronomia ————→ noma vel norma

This type then is close to the *GGL* though that dictionary has no explicatory introduction nor any section titles. New letters in the *GGL* do, however, begin on a new page and often a blank page or more follows each letter.

EXAMPLE III

Here again we have two columns and each section of the first column is introduced by a formula reflecting the nature of its contents: 'capitula a. in b.' or 'a. in b. capitula', (that is headwords in A found under B). The ordering is to the first letter only (A-ordering) and the order is determined by the reference headwords and subheadwords in the second column, again following the order of the Hugutio text, and incidentally a more fully alphabetical order, though some words are not in sequence. Again we have 'second-column ordering', but the sectioning is more refined. Strangely there is no list of A words under A. Our examples are from Paris, BN lat. 7622 (f.1r), and the same type is found in BN lat.7623 and BN lat.16218 (ex-Sorbonne). Section headings and reference words in the second column are in red.

capitula a. in b.

affrosiades	balin
ambubaia	balinon
abatis	bata
acaron	belus
antibiblium	bibo .bis
acteus	bis
amphibologia	bole
etc.	

capitula a. in c.

accentus	cano
accendo	candeo .es
anomiani	canomia
anceps	capio
acaris	caris
anascena	catascena
etc.	

In two mss. at least (7622, 7623) the compiler, or perhaps we should say designer, of the tables is named, Petrus de Alingio Gebonensis, a native of thirteenth-century Genoa, mentioned by Aristide Marigo[10] and Lloyd W. and B.A. Daly, 1964. Petrus de Alingio explains his purpose thus in BN lat.7623, f.143r:

> Quoniam difficile et laboriosum erat invenire quasdam diciones tam simplices quam compositas in dirivationabus ugutionis contentas extra ordinem alphabeti petrus de alingio gebonensis incola ianuensis contra difficultatem illam et laborem hanc tabulam composuit in qua dicte dictiones per alphabetum et capitula in quibus ipse inveniuntur [...]:

EXAMPLE IV

There is an important change in this type. The first column is in AB-order and there is no apparent ordering of the reference headwords. This seems to be an important step towards *first-column ordering*, or sublemmata ordering. Our sample manuscripts here are Paris, BN lat. 16217 (f.168v), which has two kinds of tables, and Oxford, Bodleian, Laud 626 with one only:

> aaron in arbitrum.
> abrotonium in affros
> abiges in ago et abiges et alia et abactor
> abies in eo .is abicio
> abdomen in hostio
> aborigo in orior

Paris, BN lat. 7623 (f.147a) a third table gives a more extensive view of this type, with several subheadwords shown as joined to a reference headword, this time in what can be called a column:

---

[10] *I codici manoscritti delle Derivationes di Uggucione Pisano: saggio d'inventario bibliografico* [...] (Rome: Istituto di Studi Romani), 1936, p. x.

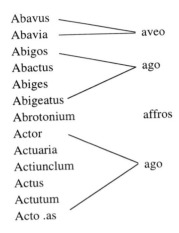

EXAMPLE V

Daly (1964) also mentions one example he found of ABC-ordering, that is to the third letter, in Rouen Bibl. mun. 1025, and we have noted Paris, BN lat. 7625C which sometimes goes beyond ABC-ordering and closer to a fully alphabetical table. Here the first column is strongly alphabetical and the second column mostly follows a text-alphabetical order. Our sample is from f.1r:

Abavia .vie		ubi	aveo .es 2b
Abba			
Abbas .tis			
Abbatissa .e			
Abatia .tie	ubi		autumno 2c
Abbax .cis			
[...]			
Abactus	ubi		ago .is 3c
Abalieno	ubi		alius 4b
Abamita	ubi		amo 4c
Abarcus .a .um	ubi		arbitror 8b
Abadis	ubi		bassis 10d
Abanus .ni		ubi	gigno 45d

What is to be noted here, besides the greater degree of alphabetization, is the presence of page and column indicators as well as the reference headword, though this system is abandoned after the first column. The use of numbers leads to other types that will combine headwords and various numbering systems, and brings us back to the first two French-Latin dictionaries we described where a combination of text- or alphabetically ordered words and of folio or other numbers expanded the referencing system. Indeed there is a full field of reference study here that we have just touched upon.

IMPLICATIONS

If the tables were actually used and not just a textual phenomenon, they must have satisfied some level of retrievability. Full alphabetization was already known, but in our lexicons there seems to be no real intention to try and implement it, although with a text as long as the *Glossarium gallico-latinum* with its 132 folios there is more of a chance that another step might have been planned. Mary Carruthers has shown that full alphabetization did not dislodge other methods of organization, but her explanation is that these were used particularly for familiar texts known orally and that they corresponded to mnemonic techniques. But texts like Hugutio's *Magnae Derivationes* and Brito's *Expositiones* were not such texts, nor was such a new creation as the *GGL* we began with. Were these tables and orderings simply transmission of method without much thought to usefulness or can we postulate such a concept as 'retrieval adequacy'? Petrus de Alingio's statement of intention cited above indicates they were indeed to be used. Further, there is evidence from one copy of the Latin-French *Aalma* BN lat. 14748 that bi-directionality was understood and used:

> Afin que plus tost et plus prestement les escoliers et autres puissent mettre le latin en françois et le françois en latin des moz de gramaire et par especial du livre nommé Catholicon. En ce livret nommé le Mirouer des nouveaux escoliers est mis le latin et aprés le françois des moz plus necessaires et acoustumez contenus ou dit Catholicon et d'aucuns autres moz.

This supposes that the user is sufficiently bilingual to find words by using both columns bi-directionally. In a unilingual framework Hugutio tables also imply bi-directionality.

Our recent analyses show that the GGL was a rather mechanical reversal of a Latin–French dictionary that may itself have had a more complex structure. It shares with the *Dictionarius* of Le Ver and another work close to Le Ver, the *Vocabularius familiaris et compendiosus*, printed by Guillaume Le Talleur in Rouen around 1490, an ordering of Latin terms and a substantial number of French terms not found elsewhere, similarities sufficient to point to a common source for part of their material. What is important for the *GGL* is that here and in other compilations we can note that dictionary users were not limited to a single alphabetical entry point and that approaches to alphabetization were indeed open and varied.

A Note on the Internalist/Externalist Debate.

FEARGAL MURPHY
University College, Dublin

FOR A LONG TIME, the study of the philosophy of language has seen exponents of externalist and internalist approaches to language argue their respective corners, but without any sign of either side throwing in the towel. The reasons for the prolongation of the debate in recent times would seem to be (i) both sides mean different things by the term 'language' and—as a result of this—(ii) use different methodologies to investigate the properties of language. On the one hand is the cultural, semantics based externalist view and on the other, the cognitive and syntax based internalist view. In this paper I will outline these different understandings of language and why they have continued up to the present. I will also show why I feel the internalist approach seems the most reasonable starting point. To make matters easier, only the writings of Hilary Putnam and Noam Chomsky will be used to epitomise each side of the debate.

Chomsky constantly asserts that the study of language should be approached as part of a naturalist/scientific inquiry, proceeding in the same way as any scientific inquiry and starting from the wealth of empirical data that Language makes available; while Putnam says that there are other ways to develop a 'deep understanding' of language alongside the scientific method and that Chomsky displays a 'prejudice' and 'adamant internalism' (Putnam 1993).

The difference can be even further refined; Chomsky says (Chomsky 1993, 212) that whatever is in the brains of any individual language users 'is about as interesting for naturalistic inquiry as the course of a feather on a windy day. The basic explanation must lie in the properties of the language faculty of the brain.' In other words, inquiry into anything other than the properties of the language faculty in the brain that allows the acquisition of language will not provide the answers to any serious questions about language as a natural phenomenon. Putnam is quite happy to deal with language as a cultural artefact. He says that 'cultural studies (history, anthropology, sociology and parts of philosophy, for example) [...] teach us vital facts about the world we live in and they can be *deep*, although with a different kind of depth than the kind Chomsky is talking about. *Languages and meanings are cultural realities.*' (Putnam 1993, 385. The italics are Putnam's).

So Putnam is content to take an approach quite different to Chomsky's but without actually asserting that it is a better style of analysis. Chomsky on the other hand is claiming that his approach actually is better. Chomsky does not regard cultural artefacts as analysable profitably within naturalistic inquiry. The basic difference seems to be that Putnam wants to look at how language is used and Chomsky wants to study what language is.

When we look at language as we use it, we feel that there must be some way that we successfully communicate and seem to hold the same meanings in common. The externalist position addresses the issues by proposing that there are meanings 'in the world', external to the language user, that the language user has access to; a shared language and set of meanings that are external to us; a shared and public enterprise (see Putnam 1975). It fits in most easily with the motions of 'folk psychology'; it seems only common sense that there are shared languages and shared meanings. But Chomsky points out (Chomsky 1995) that science has progressed by abandoning 'common sense foundations'. This seems to be in tune with Lewis Wolpert's analysis that scientific thought is quite different to common sense (Wolpert 1993).

While there is no agreement as to the exact nature of science, it can be characterised as being (and the following list is not exhaustive) data-driven, objective, empirical, and involving testability and idealisation. These are not necessarily features of philosophical or cultural inquiry. Because Chomsky wants to position linguistics firmly as a science, for him linguistics must demonstrate the features of a scientific endeavour; Putnam on the other has no such desire. Chomsky's wish to treat linguistics as a science has more to do with ensuring naturalistic inquiry rather than elevating the status of linguistics. By forcing the linguistics to conform to the properties of scientific inquiry, greater insight into language can be attained. This has been the case with all other inquiry into natural phenomena. Linguistics has been modelled on science before: the neo-grammarians revolutionised linguistics by demanding that linguistics be like the sciences of their day. It is the notion of language as a natural rather than cultural phenomenon that exercises Chomsky: 'We focus attention on aspects of the world that fall under this informal rubric [linguistic], and try to understand them better. In the course of doing so we may—and apparently do—develop a concept that more or less resembles the informal notion of 'language' and postulate that such objects are among the things in the world, alongside of complex molecules, electrical fields, the human visual system, and so on' (Chomsky 1995, 1). As long as we remember that 'whatever may be learned about folk science will have no relevance to the pursuit of naturalistic inquiry into the topics that folk science addresses in its own way', (Chomsky 1995, 14). A cultural/philosophical inquiry will have no qualms about using common sense notions as bulwarks of an investigation and so we can see straight away that the debate is not really about where meaning is located, but how to approach the study of language. The externalist view seems to stick to a 'folk psychology' approach (see Stich 1983), seeking to confirm its hypotheses rather than to re-evaluate them in the light of evidence. This is one of the classic features of the non-scientific, common sense approach according to Wolpert.

Meaning is a crucial element in Putnam's analysis (hence the title of the 1975 article 'The Meaning of "Meaning"'). It is the nature of meaning in language that interests him, but meaning holds no such pride of place in Chomsky's view of language. The reason can be seen in the quote from Chomsky given above. Chomsky wants to investigate all things that fall under the rubric 'linguistic'. Meaning would just be one of many things that would fall under this rubric, whereas for Putnam, meaning occupies centre stage, especially the meaning of lexical items as opposed to phrases up to and including sentences. Putnam seems convinced that language is primarily a semantic exercise, with everything else secondary to that. However, he seems to misunderstand Chomsky when Chomsky does address problems of meaning and reference, especially when Chomsky talks about the innate semantic properties that are available to us as language users. In both Chomsky 1992 and Chomsky 1993, examples are cited as to the facts about container nouns and their properties (colours refer to exteriors etc.). These points are not responded to by Putnam. The reason may be that Putnam does not see the point because they are not particularly relevant in his conception of language. The point Chomsky is making is that there are **innate** properties of meaning that are not external but are rather internal and are therefore not covered in an externalist analysis of language. The same kind of argument is offered based on the Binding Principles of Chomskyan theory. Putnam does not allow for innate linguistic properties however and instead argues for the role of Generalised/Multi-purpose Learning Mechanisms in language acquisition.

Putnam claims that there is no reason to assume any language specific innate properties and seeks to show that language can be learned via generalised learning mechanisms or general intelligence. However, this argument seems weak. It does not explain the fact that language is acquired in the same way by infants, passing through the same linguistic milestones in the same order. It also fails to explain the fact that certain types of mistakes are never made (the language acquirer shows sensitivity to phrase structure from the start) and it also fails to explain why, as Jean Aitchison puts it, 'even though intelligent animals seem capable of coping with some of the rudimentary characteristics of human language, they do not seem predisposed to cope with them (Aitchison 1989, 46). We would expect different facts if generalised learning mechanism were used to acquire language. There is no doubt that, as James McCawley said (quoted in

Harris 1994, 192) 'general purpose learning mechanisms clearly exist [...]
and it is absurd to suppose that they are shut off while language is being
acquired'. But these mechanisms, as McCawley's quote suggests, interact
with the language acquisition device rather than do its job.

Putnam and Chomsky have debated this issue in print (Piatelli-Palmerini
1980). If language is acquired through some innate language specific
faculty as Chomsky argues, then it seems only logical that this faculty
should be the focus of inquiry. If Putnam is correct in arguing that
language may be acquired in some other way, then Chomsky's argument
seems weaker. But Putnam offers no concrete explanation for how
language is acquired. His notions of how general intelligence or learning
strategies are used solely to acquire language are not developed to a point
where they may be seriously examined. Putnam also contradicts himself by
allowing for a 'speech centre' in the human brain while maintaining that
grammar is a property of language not in the brain of the language user.
This leaves it unclear as to what exactly the 'speech centre' in the human
mind is. Chomsky, in his response to Putnam, assumes that this speech
centre is in fact the neurally represented, internalised language. Perhaps
Putnam intended the speech centre to merely be the area that converts
language into speech in some way that allows language still to be a cultural
entity rather than a mental entity but it still leaves unexplained how the
cultural entity is accessed by the brain, specifically the speech centre. The
admission of the role of the speech centre looks very much like Putnam
adopting an internalist approach in spite of himself. It is also flawed in that
this 'speech centre' must also deal with more than just speakers of
language. It must also enable users of sign language or users of the Tadoma
method (see Carol Chomsky 1994) to use language.

Whatever about their debate about acquisition, the available facts seem
to suggest that language develops in a more or less regular way whatever
one's ability to learn anything else is like. This can be seen in cases of
savants like Christopher (Smith and Tsimpli 1995) or hyperlinguistic
children like Laura (Yamada 1990). Children with impaired cognitive
functions seem quite capable of acquiring language despite their cognitive
deficits. Of course, philosophers may argue that Christopher and Laura
have not in fact acquired language. They can make this statement by
defining language not as the ability to produce and recognise grammatical
sentences but rather as the ability to produce **meaningful** sentences. This
seems to be the basic distinction between Chomsky's and Putnam's views
of language. For Putnam it is not enough that we can distinguish
grammatical from ungrammatical sentences, regardless of their content, but
that we use language as, to quote from a reader on the philosophy of
language and mind, 'a code to expresses our inner thoughts' (Geirsson and

Losonsky 1996, 201). The crucial element being that it expresses our inner thoughts. If we are interested in the expression of thoughts rather than the code, then the hyperlinguistic Laura does not have language as she happily generates sentences that are false or meaningless (although well-formed). However if we are interested in how anyone (including Laura) can come to use the code, and where this code may be in order to be accessed, then we have to adopt an internalist approach. The nature of the use and acquisition of the code is not going to be explained if we only examine its successful use in expressing out inner thoughts. This leaves too many of the facts of language unexamined. There is way of explaining the phonological and morphological facts of language through semantics. In his analysis of language acquisition Putnam states that:

> The child is not trying to learn a bunch of syntactic rules as a kind of crazy end-in-itself. He is learning and wants to learn semantic rules [...].

and that

> [...] the learning of grammar is dependent on the learning of semantics.

From this we can see that Putnam places semantics to the fore in the study of language. For Chomsky syntax seems to be the main area of investigation. Why they could differ in their main area of investigation would seem to follow from and also lead to their divergent assumptions as to how the 'problem' of language should be tackled. Putnam is quite clearly stating that language should be seen as primarily semantic endeavour and he states that the syntax is dependent on semantics. This view is not supported by any of the evidence. The evidence of Laura shows that the semantic component of language can be very weak without any effect on the phonology, morphology or syntax. If language were based on a semantic task, her syntax, morphology and phonology should be impaired because of her semantic weaknesses. Laura's main problem seems to be in the area of semantics and conceptualisation but her syntax etc. seem well developed. If language were something that was acquired using general intelligence or multi-purpose learning mechanisms, Laura should show an inability to acquire syntax etc. because of her cognitive deficiencies. Putnam is shown to be wrong by the actual evidence.

This does not mean that Chomsky is necessarily correct but because his approach is more in line with the current evidence, it will lead to a greater insight into language. It also has the advantage that it demands an inquiry that is driven by the evidence rather than an approach that has already determined that language is not amenable to a naturalistic analysis. A naturalistic inquiry into language would be able to evolve and alter hypotheses about the nature of language as new evidence comes to light without being committed to preconceptions about how language must be.

As it stands, the externalist approach seems set to remain the dominant paradigm in the philosophy of language. It is a pity that this is the case as the externalist approach seems to run counter to the evidence that linguistics is uncovering. The externalist emphasis on semantics (especially lexical semantics) and reluctance to change assumptions in response to fresh evidence, means that deeper insight into language is prevented. There is a great need for philosophers and linguists to communicate with each other about language, but so far, it seems that language is not providing a good enough medium for this communication.

BIBLIOGRAPHY

Aitchison, Jean 1989. *The Articulate Mammal*, London: Routledge

Chomsky, Carol 1994. 'Analytic Study of the Tadoma Method: Language Abilities of Three Deaf-Blind Subjects, in *Noam Chomsky, Critical Assessments*, IV, ed. by Carlos Otero, London: Routledge, 548–581

Chomsky, Noam et al. 1993. *Language and Thought*, Rhode Island: Moyer Bell

Chomsky, Noam. 1986. *Knowledge of Language*, New York: Praeger

—1992. 'Explaining Language Use', *Philosophical Topics*, 20, 205–231

—1993. 'Naturalism and Dualism in the Study of Language', *International Journal of Philosophical Studies*, 2 (2), 181–209

—1995. 'Language and Nature', *Mind*, 104· 413, 1–61

Curtiss, Susan 1988. 'Abnormal Language Acquisition and the Modularity of Language', in *Linguistics: The Cambridge Survey*, II, ed. by F. Newmeyer, Cambridge: University Press, 90–116

Fodor, Jerry 1988. *Psychosemantics*, Cambridge, Mass.: MIT Press

—1994. *The Elm and the Expert*, Cambridge Mass: MIT Press

Fodor, J. and Lepore, E. 1992. *Holism: A Shoppe's Guide*, Oxford: Blackwell

Geirsson, H. and Losonsky, M., eds. 1996. *Readings in Language and Mind*, Oxford: Blackwell

Grayling, A. 1982. *An Introduction to Philosophical Logic*, Brighton: Harvester Press

Harris, Randy Allen 1993. *The Linguistics Wars*, London: Oxford University Press

Lewontin, Richard 1990. 'The Evolution of Cognition' in *An Invitation to Cognitive Science*, III, ed. by D. Osherson and E. Smith, Cambridge, Mass.: MIT Press, 229–239

Piatelli-Palmerini, M., ed. 1980. *Language and Learning: The Debate between Jean Piaget and Noam Chomsky*, Cambridge, Mass.: Harvard University Press

Pinker, Steve 1994. *The Language Instinct*, London: Penguin

Putnam, Hilary 1975. 'The Meaning of "Meaning"', in *Language Mind and Knowledge, Minnesota Studies in the Philosophy of Science*, VII, ed. by Keith Gunderson, Minneapolis: University of Minnesota Press, 131–193

—1978. *Meaning and the Moral Sciences*, London: Routledge

—1989. *Representation and Reality*, Cambridge, Mass.: MIT Press

—1992. 'Replies', *Philosophical Topics*, 20, 347–408

Russell, Bertrand 1946. *History of Western Philosophy*, London: George Allen and Unwin

Smith, Neil and Tsimpli, Ianthi-Maria 1995. *The Mind of a Savant: Language Learning and Modularity*, Oxford: Blackwell

Stich, Stephen 1983. *From Folk Psychology to Cognitive Science*, Cambridge, Mass.: MIT Press

Wolpert, Lewis 1992. *The Unnatural Nature of Science*, London: Faber and Faber

Yamada, Jeni 1990. *Laura: A Case Study for the Modularity of Language*, Cambridge, Mass.: MIT Press

Patterns of Epenthesis in Irish

MÁIRE NÍ CHIOSÁIN
University College, Dublin

1. INTRODUCTION

THE DEVELOPMENT of an epenthetic vowel in certain consonant clusters in Irish is noted in dialect descriptions (e.g. Breatnach 1947, de Bhaldraithe 1945, de Búrca 1970, Mhac an Fhailligh 1980, Ó Cuív 1975) and has been the focus of a number of theoretical works (e.g. Ó Baoill 1979, 1980, Ní Chiosáin 1991, Cyran 1994). The relevant clusters can be characterised in terms of their sonority profile: for example, a sequence of a liquid and a nonhomorganic voiced stop, e.g. [rg], is disfavoured in comparison to a sequence of a liquid and a nonhomorganic voiceless stop, e.g. [rk]; the latter sequence involves a greater difference in the sonority values of the consonants than the former which is traditionally regarded as subsequently undergoing epenthesis, compare d´arəg *dearg* 'red' and k´ark *cearc* 'hen'. An extension of the empirical base reveals additionally that prosodic structure plays a role in the conditioning of epenthesis. The clusters that are disfavoured in shorter words emerge in prosodically more complex words, e.g. l´e:rgəs *léargas* 'insight', purgədo:r´ *purgadóir* 'purgatory'. Epenthesis thus occurs only if it is consistent with requirements on prosodic structure. This paper seeks to explicate the relationship between epenthesis and higher prosodic structure in Irish. It is argued that although cluster constraints compel epenthesis, prosodic constraints, which are ranked higher in the hierarchy of constraints that characterise the phonology of Irish, constrain it. An initial set of data are presented in § 2.1 and an account that refers to a universal ranking of consonant clusters in terms of 'minimal sonority distance' is proposed in § 2.2. § 2.3 considers forms which require an account involving constraints on prosodic structure. The interaction of the two sets of constraints is then shown to account for the range of facts under consideration.

2. Epenthesis patterns in Irish

2.1 *The data*

Certain consonant clusters are disfavoured in monomorphemes in Irish. The clusters can generally be characterised as comprising a sonorant followed by a nonhomorganic voiced stop or a nonhomorganic fricative or glide.[1] Pairs of forms are given in (1) which are traditionally regarded as having undergone epenthesis, and in which the (input) clusters occur both word-finally and word-internally.[2] The nature of the cluster is indicated in the leftmost column abstracting away from whether the cluster is palatalised (indicated by C´) or nonpalatalised. This distinction, a phonemic one in Irish, is not relevant for present purposes. The epenthetic vowel is /ə/ in a nonpalatalised environment, /i/ in a palatalised environment.

(1)   Nonhomorganic clusters which undergo epenthesis:

a.	-rb	borəb	*borb*	'abrupt'
		bar´ibr´i	*Bairbre*	(name)
	-rm	gorəm	*gorm*	'blue'
		d´arəməd	*dearmad*	'mistake'
	-rf	d´arəfə	*dearfa*	'certain'
	-rv	tarəv	*tarbh*	'bull'
		s´er´iv´i:s´	*seirbhís*	'service'
	-rw	karəwat	*carbhat*	'tie'
	-rg	d´arəg	*dearg*	'red'
		ar´ig´əd	*airgead*	'money'
	-rf	fir´if´i	*foirfe*	'perfect'
	-rx	dorəxə	*dorcha*	'dark'
b.	-lb	al´ib´	*ailb*	'alb'

---

[1] For accounts of comparable data in Scottish Gaelic, see, e.g. Clements 1986, Sagey 1988, Bosch 1991, 1995.

[2] Since there are no vowel-zero alternations involving forms like those in (1), referring to an input cluster requires comment. Spreading of [back] in Irish (which represents the phonemic palatalised/non-palatalised contrast in consonants) is strictly local, within clusters or within certain consonant-short vowel sequences, see e.g. Ní Chiosáin 1994. The CONSONANTS in a CVC sequence do not affect each other. An exception to this generalisation involves examples like those in (1), where (morphological) final palatalisation affects the relevant non-adjacent consonants, e.g. final palatalisation of borəb *borb* 'abrupt' yields bir´ib´, *borib´ *boirb*, i.e.both the ultimate and the penultimate consonants are palatalised. Compare with (i) true clusters, e.g. alt/al´t´ *alt/ailt* 'article' (nom/gen) where both consonants are affected by final palatalisation and (ii) non-clusters, e.g. b´olər/b´olir´ *biolar/biolair* 'watercress' (nom/gen), where the penultimate consonant is not affected by final palatalisation. Since the consonants in the 'epenthetic' forms pattern with true clusters, it seems reasonable to posit clusters in the input forms.

	aləbə	*Alba*	'Scotland'
-lm	koləm	*colm*	'dove'
	s´el´im´id´i	*seilmide*	'snail'
-lv	s´aləv	*sealbh*	'possession'
	sil´iv´ir	*soilbhir*	'pleasant'
-lw	g´aləwən	*gealbhan*	'sparrow'
-lg	s´el´ig´	*seilg*	'hunt'
	aləgə	*alga*	'algae'
-lf	gal´if´ən	*gailfean*	'driving rain'
-lx	tuləxəx	*tulchach*	'hilly'

c. -nb	b´in´ib´	*binb*	'venom'
	banəbə	*Banba*	(a name for Ireland)
-nm	an´im´	*ainm*	'name'
	m´anəmə	*meanma*	'mind'
-nv	banəv	*banbh*	'piglet'
	an´iv´i:	*ainmhí*	'animal'
-nf	anəfə	*anfa*	'storm, terror'
-nx	donəxə	*Donnchadh*	(name)

In contrast, epenthesis does not occur into clusters consisting of a sonorant consonant followed by a voiceless stop:

(2)   Sonorant-voiceless stop clusters: no epenthesis

a. -rp	korp	*corp*	'body'
	ki´r´p´əx	*coirpeach*	'criminal'
-rt	gort	*gort*	'field'
	gortə	*gorta*	'famine'
-rk	k´ark	*cearc*	'hen'
	kir´k´i	*coirce*	'oats'

b. -lp	alp	*alp*	'swallow whole'
-lt	alt	*alt*	'joint'
	altu:	*altú*	'thanksgiving'
-lk	kal´k´	*cailc*	'chalk'
	kil´k´i	*cuilce*	'quilt'

c. -nt	kan´t´	*caint*	'talk'
	kantəl	*cantal*	'irritation'

Nor does epenthesis generally occur in homorganic clusters (with the exception of word-final -rn preceded by a short vowel).

2.2 *Intrinsic ranking of consonant clusters*

In order to account for the permissible and impermissible clusters in Irish, the notion of 'minimal sonority distance' (e.g. Greenberg 1978, Steriade 1982, Harris 1983, Selkirk 1984) is adopted, which requires that linearly adjacent segments be a certain distance from each other along a defined sonority hierarchy. While it is beyond the scope of this paper to develop a theory of sonority distance, the idea is implemented here with intrinsically ranked (violable) constraints mnemonically called *RG and *RK, disallowinging all sonorant-voiced stop/fricative and all sonorant-voiceless stop clusters, respectively. Since in Irish, clusters of the RK type are, in all prosodic circumstances, permissible, they are more harmonic than clusters of the RG type which, in examples like those in (1), are impermissible. The idea of relative harmony of phonological structure is implemented (as illustrated in (3) and (4) below) in Optimality Theory (Prince & Smolensky 1993) in terms of ranked constraints: *RG >> *RK, that is, *RG is ranked higher than *RK . Since epenthesis occurs into RG-type clusters, *RG must be ranked higher than a constraint that requires faithfulness to the input form and thus disfavours epenthesis (DEP); the constraint ranking is thus *RG >> DEP.[3] Candidate forms for d´arəg *dearg* 'red' and ar´ig´əd *airgead* 'money' are given in (3). Note: (i) *RG is not a constraint on complex codas, as illustrated by forms like ar´ig´əd below, where an intact cluster would be heterosyllabic; (ii) *RG is used to refer to both RG and R´G´ clusters, that is, both the nonpalatalised and the palatalised clusters, respectively. This convention is adopted throughout the paper.

			*RG	DEP
(3)				
Input = /d´arg/	a. ☞ d´arəg			*
	b. d´arg		* !	
Input = /ar´g´əd/	c. ☞ ar´i´gəd			*
	d. ar´g´əd		* !	

Assuming the input form contains the cluster rg, the optimal candidate in (3)a. (indicated by means of the pointing hand ☞) which contains an epenthetic vowel obeys *RG but violates DEP. The faithful candidate in (3)b. however violates the higher ranking constraint *RG.[4] The forms in (4)

---

[3] A high-ranking faithfulness constraint MAX is explicitly assumed which requires that all input material be parsed: *RG cannot be satisfied by underparsing one or other constituent consonant.

[4] That FtBin a constraint requiring binary feet (in this case bimoraic feet) is not what drives epenthesis in Irish is apparent from parallel forms containing the cluster rk, see (4), where epenthesis does not occur. Furthermore, there are numerous examples of monomoraic lexical (non-closed class) forms in Irish which

should be compared with similar forms containing the cluster rk, e.g. k´ark *cearc* 'hen' and kir‾k´i *coirce* 'oats', which do not undergo epenthesis. The cluster constraint *RK, representing the family of sonorant-voiceless stop cluster constraints, is therefore ranked below DEP. The optimal forms are the input forms which contain the cluster rk. (4)b and d both fatally violate the higher ranked faithfulness constraint.

(4)	Input = /k´ark/	*rg	DEP	*rk
a. ☞	k´ark			*
b.	k´arək		* !	
	Input = /kir´k´i/			*
c. ☞	kir‾k´i			*
d.	kir´ik´i		* !	

The input forms discussed so far are short forms, comprising one or two moras. However once longer input forms comprising three or more moras are considered, the role of prosodic constraints in determining epenthesis patterns in Irish becomes apparent.

2.3 *Prosodic constraints on epenthesis*

The prosodic factors that constrain epenthesis are (i) syllable weight and (ii) word-length. As to the first of these, epenthesis occurs in the relevant clusters word-internally following a short vowel but not following a long vowel. Examples of forms containing a pre-cluster long vowel are given in (5).

(5)   Forms containing a long vowel or diphthong preceding the cluster: no epenthesis

-rm	t´e:rmə	*téarma*	'term'
-rg	l´e:rgəs	*léargas*	'insight'
-lg	duəlgəs	*dualgas*	'duty'

The forms in (5) should be compared with those in (6) (repeated from (1)) in which short vowels precede the (same) clusters and which undergo epenthesis.

(6)   -rm   gorəm   *gorm*   'blue'

---

do not undergo any form of augmentation, e.g. t´ax *teach* 'house', kat *cat* 'ca'', lag *lag* 'weak', k´axt *ceacht* 'lesson', ab *ab* 'abbot', pu *puth* 'breeze'', b‾i *bith* 'existence'.

	d´arəməd	*dearmad*	'mistake'
-rg	d´arəg	*dearg*	'red'
	ar´ig´əd	*airgead*	'money'
-lg	s´el´ig´	*seilg*	'hunt'
	aləgə	*alga*	'algae'

Turning to word-length, epenthesis does not occur in trisyllabic or longer monomorphemic words of a certain shape, e.g. words containing three light syllables in which the cluster occurs between the first and second syllables.

(7)   Trisyllabic words containing the relevant clusters

-rm	s´armənəs	*searmanas*	'ceremony'
-r´m´	f´ir´m´imin´t´	*firmimint*	'firmament'
-rb	barbərəx	*barbarach*	'barbarian'
-lg	skolgərnəx	*scolgarnach*	'cackle'

The prosodic structure of monomorphemic words is clearly at issue. Note that epenthetic vowels are normally retained in derived forms regardless of prosodic structure; for example, in the related forms ar´i´g´əd *airgead* 'money' ar´i´g´ədəs *airgeadas* 'finance'. Examples of monomorphemic forms containing the relevant clusters are given in (8). These examples involve only those clusters where epenthesis can be compelled, e.g. rm, rb, lg etc. They do not involve words containing clusters that appear intact in all prosodic environments, e.g. rk, lp etc.[5] The prosodic structure is represented in the leftmost column, L = light syllable, H = heavy syllable and the location of the relevant cluster is indicated by a subscripted CC.

(8)   a. $L_{CC}LL$:rm   s´armənəs   *searmanas*   'ceremony'
         r´m´   f´ir´m´imin´t´ *firmimint*   'firmament'
         lg   skolgərnəx   *scolgarnach*   'cackle'
         rb   barbərəx   *barbarach*   'barbarian'

      b. $L_{CC}LH$ rm   t´er´m´in´a:l *teirmineál*   'terminal'
         lg   sm´olgəda:n   *smiolgadán*   'throat'
         rg   purgədo:r´   *purgadóir*   'purgatory'

      c. $LL_{CC}H$:rw/v   kas´ərwa:n   *caisearbhán*   'dandelion'

---

[5] It is useful, however, to be aware of parallel examples containing these clusters, e.g. examples in (2) above, korp *corp* 'body' (L), kir´p´əx *coirpeach* 'criminal' (LL) , as well as forms like kar´p´e:d *cairpéad* 'carpet' (LH).

d. L$_{cc}$LHL rm   kar´m´il´i:t´əx *cairmilíteach*   'carmelite'

    r´m´   d´er´m´it´i:t´əs *deirmitíteas*   'dermatitis'

The forms in (8) are all forms in which the optimal foot—a non-final initial bimoraic foot (see below)—can be constructed, as illustrated in (9).

(9)   H$_{cc}$L   (μ μ) μ   (8)

        L$_{cc}$LL   (μ μ) μ   (9)a

        L$_{cc}$LH   (μ μ) μ μ   (9)b

        LL$_{cc}$H   (μ μ) μ μ   (9)c

        L$_{cc}$LHL   (μ μ) μ μ μ   (9)d

Furthermore, [(μ μ) μ..] is also the structure obtained by epenthesis in the shorter forms given in (1), as illustrated in (10)a and b, along with the longer form in (10)c.

(10)   Note: Epenthesised syllable indicated by L̲

        INPUT   OUTPUT

        a. L$_{cc}$L   (L L̲) L   karəbəd   *carbad*   'chariot'

                              tar´if´ə   *tairbhe*   'benefit'

                              ar´i´g´əd   *airgead*   'money'

        b. L$_{cc}$H   (L L̲) H   purəgo:d´   *purgóid*   'purgative'

                              an´iv´i: *ainmhí*   'animal'

                              karəwa:n   *carbhán*   'caravan'

        c. L$_{cc}$HL (L L̲) H L   s´arəwo:ntə/   *searbhónta*   'servant'

                              s´arəvo:ntə

In the following account, constraints on foot structure in Irish are argued to constrain the emergence of the epenthetic vowel in Irish. The prosodic contraints at issue are Align-L, PARSE-SYLL and NONFINALITY as defined in (11) (e.g. McCarthy & Prince 1993a, Prince & Smolensky 1993).

(11)   (i) Align-L (Foot, Word): Align the left edge of each foot to the left edge of a word;

        (ii) PARSESYLL: Syllables are parsed into higher prosodic structure;

        (iii) NONFINALITY: Feet should not occur in word-final position.

With regard to the first of these constraints, Align-L, it may be noted that stress in the western and northern dialects of Irish falls on the initial syllable—thus left-alignment of prosodic feet is justified in this account. Southern Irish dialects, on the other hand, have a more complex stress system where in certain cases stress is attracted by a heavy syllable (see, e.g. Ó Siadhail & Wigger 1975, Ó Siadhail 1989, Ó Sé 1989, Doherty 1991, Gussmann 1995). Arguably, a constraint such as Weight-to-Stress (Prince 1990) compels additional foot-structure in these dialects. As regards the third constraint in (11), NONFINALITY, it is clear from the generalisation that epenthesis does not occur, for example, in words of the structure [(μ μ) μ], that Irish favours left-aligned non-final feet. As will be illustrated in the following sections, an epenthetic syllable in such forms, if footed, would result in a foot that is not left-aligned, and if unfooted, would result in an additional violation of PARSESYLL which requires that syllables be incorporated into higher prosodic structure, namely prosodic feet.

2.3.1 Non-epenthesising forms

Consider candidate output forms for *léargas* (5), *scolgarnach* (8)a. The optimal forms are those in which epenthesis does not apply and which best satisfy the prosodic constraints. As illustrated in the tableau below, once the prosodic constraints are ranked higher than the cluster constraints, violations of the lower-ranked constraints are not relevant. Thus although (12)a, the optimal form for *léargas*, contains the disfavoured cluster -rg-, it satisfies the prosodic constraints better than (12)b which contains an additional (unfooted) syllable as a result of epenthesis. (12)c avoids violations of PARSESYLL by footing the additional syllable, but as a result violates both NONFIN (by virtue of having prosodic structure at the right edge) and Align-L (since the second foot is not left-aligned).

(12)		Align-L	NONFIN	PARSESYLL	*RG	DEP	*RK
a. ☞	(l′e:r) . gəs			*	*		
b.	(l′e:) rə . gəs			* * !		*	
c.	(l′e:) (rə . gəs)	* !	*			*	
d. ☞	(skol . gər) nəx			*	*		
e.	(sko . lə) gər . nəx			* * !		*	
f.	(sko . lə) (gər . nəx)	* !	*			*	

In order to complete the account of non-epenthesising forms, one further, longer, prosodic form should be considered. Two candidate forms for kar′m′il′i:t′əx *cairmilíteach* 'carmelite' are considered in (13). The penultimate heavy syllable is footed in both candidates considered although this does not directly bear on the discussion. As in the case of the forms in (12), the additional syllable that results from epenthesis in (13)b yields a fatal violation of PARSESYLL.

(13)

	Align-L	NonFin	ParseSyll	*RG	Dep	*RK
a. ☞ (kar´m´i) (l´i:) t´əx	*		*	*		
b. (kar´i) m´i (l´i:) t´əx	*		**!		*	

2.3.2 *Epenthesising forms*

Assuming the ranking adopted above, i.e. Align-L >> NonFin, PARSESYLL >> *RG >> DEP >> *RG, we can compare the forms considered in (12) which do not undergo epenthesis with a form that does and that contains the same cluster, namely ar´ig´əd *airgead* . As is seen in (14), the optimal (non-final initial bimoraic) foot can be constructed only with the additional vowel supplied by epenthesis. Note, however, that both candidates considered below violate one prosodic constraint. Since the optimal form is clearly determined in this case by the lower-ranked cluster constraints, it must be concluded that the two prosodic constraints in question are unranked. In this way the candidates tie when evaluated with respect to the prosodic constraints, and the choice is determined by the lower ranked constraints.

(14)

	ALIGN-L	NONFIN	PARSESYLL	*RG	DEP	*RK
a. ☞ (a . r´i) . g´əd			*		*	
b. (a´r . g´əd)	*			*!		

As can be seen from the tableaux below, the cluster constraints, along with the faithfulness constraint that disfavours adding material to input forms, determine the optimal forms of all shorter words, that is, input mono- and bimoraic forms. The relevant input forms for *dearg*, *cearc* and *coirce* in (14) are /d´arg/, /k´ark / and /kir´k´i /. (15) c and f, which contain two epenthetic vowels (one (word-internally) to avoid the relevant cluster, another (word-finally) to facilitate the assignment of the optimal foot), are included to broaden the candidate set considered.

(15)

	Align-L	NONFIN	PARSESYLL	*RG	DEP	*RK
a. ☞ (d´a . rəg)		*			*	
b. (d´arg)		*		*!		
c. (d´a . rə) gə			*		**!	
d. ☞ (k´ark)		*				*
e. (k´ar . ək)		*			*!	
f. (k´a . rə) kə			*		*! *	
g. ☞ (kir´ . k´i)		*				*
h. ☞ (kir´i .) k´i			*		*!	

3. CONCLUSION

The pattern of epenthesis in Irish discussed reveals an interesting inter-action between prosodic and segmental constraints. The former outrank the latter as evidenced by the behaviour of words containing disfavoured consonant clusters. In these relatively longer words, satisfaction of the higher-ranked prosodic constraints determines the optimal form regardless of whether they contain disfavoured clusters. The same prosodic con-straints, however, do not determine the optimal candidate for shorter (mono- or bimoraic) inputs. Rather in these cases, the effect of the lower-ranked cluster constraints (which must ultimately be stated in terms of sonority distance) emerges.

REFERENCES

De Bhaldraithe, Tomás 1945. *The Irish of Cois Fhairrge, Co. Galway*, Dublin: Institute for Advanced Studies

Bosch, Anna 1991. 'Phonotactics at the Level of the Phonological Word', PhD dissert-ation, University of Chicago

—1995. 'A Gestural Analysis of Epenthesis in Scottish Gaelic', paper presented at the Celtic Linguistics Conference, University College Dublin, June 1995

Breatnach, Risteard B. 1947. *The Irish of Ring, Co. Waterford*, Dublin: Institute for Advanced Studies

De Búrca, Seán 1970. *The Irish of Tourmakeady, Co. Mayo*. Dublin: Institute for Advanced Studies

Clements, George N. 1986. 'Syllabification and Epenthesis in the Barra Dialect of Gaelic', in *The Phonological Representation of Supra-segmentals*, ed. by K. Bogers, H. van der Hulst, and M. Mous, Dordrecht: Foris, 317–336

Cyran, Eugeniusz 1993. 'Interonset Government Licensing and Epenthesis in Irish', MS, Lublin: Catholic University

—1994. 'Vocalic Elements in Phonology: a Study in Munster Irish', PhD dissertation, Lublin: Katolicki Uniwersytet Lubelski

Doherty, Cathal 1991. 'Munster Irish Stress', in *Proceedings of the Tenth West Coast Conference on Formal Lingusitics*, ed. by D. Bates, Stanford: CLSI, 115–26

Greenberg, Joseph H. 1978. 'Some Generalisations concerning Initial and Final Consonant Clusters', in *Universals of Human Languages,* II: *Phonology*, ed. by Joseph H. Greenberg, Stanford: University Press

Gussmann, Edmund 1995. 'Putting your Best Foot Forward', MS, Lublin: Catholic University, paper presented at the Celtic Linguistics Conference, University College Dublin, June 1995

Harris, James W. 1983. *Syllable Structure and Stress in Spanish: a Non-Linear Analysis, Linguistic Inquiry Monographs*, VIII, Cambridge, Mass.: MIT Press

McCarthy, John and Prince, Alan 1993. *Prosodic Morphology I: Constraint Interaction and Satisfaction*, Technical Report #3, Rutgers University: Center for Cognitive Science

Mhac an Fhailligh, Éamonn 1980. *The Irish of Erris, Co. Mayo*, Dublin: Institute for Advanced Studies

Ní Chiosáin, Máire 1991. 'Topics in the Phonology of Irish', PhD dissertation, Amherst: University of Massachusetts

—1994. 'Vowel Features and Underspecification: Evidence from Irish', in *Phonologica 1992, Proceedings of the 7th International Phonology Meeting, Krems, Austria*, ed. by Wolfgang U. Dressler, M. Prinzhorn, and J.R. Rennison, Turin: Rosenberg & Sellier, 157–164

Ó Baoill, Dónall P. 1979. 'Vowel Lengthening before Certain Non-Obstruents in Q-Celtic', *Coleraine Occasional Papers in Linguistics and Language Learning*, 6, 79–107

—1980. 'Preaspiration, Epenthesis and Vowel Lengthening—Interrelated and of Similar Origin?', *Celtica*, 13, 79–108

Ó Cuív, Brian 1975. *The Irish of West Muskerry, Co. Cork*, Dublin: Institute for Advanced Studies

Ó Sé, Diarmuid 1989. 'Contributions to the Study of Word Stress in Irish, *Ériu*, 40, 147–78

Ó Siadhail, Mícheál 1989. *Modern Irish: Grammatical Structure and Dialect Variation*, Cambridge: University Press

Ó Siadhail, Mícheál & Wigger, Arndt 1975. *Córas Fuaimeanna na Gaeilge*, Dublin: Institute for Advanced Studies

Prince, Alan 1990. 'Quantitative Consequences of Rhythmic Organization', in *CLS*, 26.2, *Papers from the Parasession on the Syllable in Phonetics and Phonology*, ed. by Karen Deaton, Manuela Noske and Michael Ziolkowski, Chicago: Linguistics Society, 355–398

Prince, Alan & Smolensky, Paul 1993. *Optimality Theory: Constraint Interaction in Generative Grammar*, Technical Report #2, Rutgers University: Center for Cognitive Science

Sagey, Elizabeth 1988. 'Non-Constituent Spreading in Barra Gaelic', MS, Irvine: University of California

Selkirk, Elisabeth O. 1984. 'On the Major Class Features and Syllable Theory', in *Language Sound Structure: Studies in Phonology Dedicated to Morris Halle by his Teacher and Students*, ed. by Mark Aronoff & R.T. Oehrle, Cambridge, Mass: MIT Press

Steriade, Donca 1982. 'Greek Prosodies and the Nature of Syllabification', PhD dissertation, MIT

Scéal na Teangeolaíochta Feidhmí in Éirinn

ÍOSOLD NÍ DHEIRG

Institiúid Teangeolaíochta Éireann

TÁ SIAD ann a déarfadh go bhfuil an Teangeolaíocht Fheidhmeach ann leis na céadta bliain, ainneoin nár tháinig an coincheap féin chun cinn go dtí lár na fichiú haoise. Léiríonn stair na Gaeilge ón tús go bhfuil dealramh leis an tuairim sin. Níl aon amhras nach féidir tús na Teangeolaíochta Feidhmí (TF) in Éirinn a rianadh siar go dtí tréimhse na Sean-Ghaeilge, mar a fheicfear ar ball.

Is é a chuir mé romham san aiste seo spléachadh a thabhairt ar na buaicphointí is sainiúla in éabhlóid na TF in Éirinn mar a fheictear domsa iad. Is cuid suntais gurbh ar an Ghaeilge féin a bhí taighde an lucht léinn dírithe riamh anall.

Féachaimis ar dtús ar shainmhínithe atá ar fáil ar an TF i bhfoinsí iontaofa, aitheanta mar iad seo a leanas:

> Term covering several linguistic subdisciplines as well as certain interdisciplinary areas that use linguistic methods: language pedagogy, psycholinguistics, language acquisition, second language acquisition, translation, contrastive analysis, language planning, lexicography, computational linguistics, ethnolinguistics, sociolinguistics, and others (Bussman 1996).

> A branch of linguistics where the primary concern is the application of linguistic theories, methods and findings to the elucidation of language problems which have arisen in other areas of experience (Crystal 1991).

Ar ndóigh, ní raibh fáil ag lucht léinn na hÉireann sa séú nó sa seachtú haois ar na teoiricí a luann Crystal. Ní hin le rá nach raibh siad ag saothrú i réimsí áirithe teanga a aithnítear mar chuid dhílis den TF an lá atá inniu ann. Orthu sin is ceart na réimsí seo a leanas a áireamh: foghlaim agus teagasc na teanga dúchais (Gaeilge) agus teangacha iasachta (Laidin), soláthar áiseanna teagaisc, .i. graiméir agus tráchtais ghramadaí, léamh agus scríobh agus pleanáil teanga (foclóireacht, téarmaíocht agus caighdeánú na teanga liteartha). I gcás teagasc teanga, is cosúil go raibh dhá chuspóir i gceist, mar atá teagasc na teanga liteartha mar chuid dhlisteanach de theagasc na teanga dúchais agus teagasc na Gaeilge agus na Laidine chun críche gairmiúla. Ní rabhthas dall ar fad ach oiread ar chúrsaí teoirice, óir bhí miondealú agus staidéar córasach ar siúl ní hamháin ar an

Laidin ach ar an teanga dhúchais féin, ní ab annamh i dtíortha eile an tráth sin (Ahlqvist 1980).

AN TÚS

Ba é cumadh aibítir an Oghaim an chéad chéim i stair na teangeolaíochta in Éirinn. Is cosúil gur sa dara nó sa tríú céad a cumadh an córas scríbh-neoireachta seo (Ahlqvist 1983, 10). Ar aibítir na Laidine a bunaíodh aibítir an Oghaim. Is féidir go raibh leagan amach na litreacha bunaithe ar chóras aicmithe litreacha na Laidine. Tugann na scríbhinní Oghaim atá ar fáil le fios go ndearnadh anailís ar chóras fuaimnithe na teanga, agus go raibh sí seo mar bhun leis an gcóras litrithe ar baineadh leas as (Ó Cuív 1966, Ahlqvist 1984). Léirítí na gutaí le pointí agus na consain le scríoba, agus ghearrtaí ar ghalláin iad. Bhíodh líne dhíreach ó bhun go barr na ngallán, agus ghearrtaí na pointí ar an líne nó an 'droim' mar a thugtaí air (McManus 1991). Ghearrtaí na scríoba trasna na líne nó ar dheis nó ar clé di. 'Flesc' an t-ainm a bhí ar an scríob (McManus 1991) agus is uaidh a shíolraigh an focal 'fleiscín' atá beo sa Ghaeilge i gcónaí.

Nuair a glacadh leis an gcreideamh Críostaí in Éirinn, tháinig lucht léinn faoi anáil na Laidine. Bhí an creideamh úr bunaithe ar theagasc an Bhíobla, agus b'éigean an Laidin a fhoghlaim leis an mBíobla a léamh. Níorbh ionann agus scoláirí i dtíortha eile, spreag an Laidin scoláirí na hÉireann chun staidéar a dhéanamh ar a dteanga féin chomh maith. Tosaíodh ar aibítir na Laidine a úsáid i scríobh na Gaeilge ag tús na seachtú haoise. Meabhraíonn scoláire ár linne féin dúinn an abairt *at-gaill grammataig greic* (rinne sé staidéar ar ghramadach na Gréigise) in *Amra Choluim Chille*, saothar de chuid an séú céad a chuirtear i leith an fhile thuata, Dallán Forguill. Seo an chéad sampla atá ar fáil d'úsáid an fhocail 'gramadach', iasacht ón Laidin atá in úsáid i gcónaí (Ó Cuív 1966, 1973). Is cruthú é seo, dar le Ó Cuív, go raibh cur amach ag an bhfile ar an mbunús Gréagach a bhí le teoiric na gramadaí an t-am sin, agus go raibh na filí tuata i mbun staidéir fhoirmiúil ar ghramadach agus ar mheadaracht na Gaeilge.

CÚRSAÍ TÉARMAÍOCHTA

Saothar cáiliúil a scríobhadh chun críche oiliúna ba ea *Auraicept na nÉces* ina bhfuil téacs Sean-Ghaeilge a scríobhadh sa dara leath den seachtú haois (Ahlqvist 1980, 1983). Ar na hábhair atá faoi chaibidil ann tá mar a tháinig ann don Ghaeilge, litreacha na Gaeilge agus na Laidine, inscne, rím agus ceisteanna caolchúiseacha eile. Is léir mar sin go raibh anailís theangeolaíoch ar siúl ar an teanga. Is díol spéise an *Auraicept* de bharr gur ann atá na tagairtí is sine do théarmaí áirithe a mbaintear leas astu sna tráchtais ghramadaí a scríobhadh ní ba dhéanaí. Ní miste a lua chomh maith go bhfuil idir théarmaí Laidine agus théarmaí Gaeilge sa téacs. Is é barúil Uí Chuív go bhfuil na téarmaí Gaeilge an-sean, agus go raibh tionchar ag an gcóras Oghmach ar na téarmaí teangeolaíochta a tháinig chun cinn ina dhiaidh sin (Ó Cuív 1966).

Sampla eile de shaothar téarmaíochta na ngramadóirí luatha is ea na gluaiseanna Sean-Ghaeilge sna lámhscríbhinní a grafadh sna mainistreacha. Is éard a bhí iontu ná nótaí as Gaeilge nó as Laidin ar imill na leathanach nó idir línte an téacs Laidine. Manaigh as Éirinn a bhunaigh na mainistreacha ina raibh cuid de na lámhscríbhinní seo á ngrafadh, leithéidí Würzburg (Litreacha Naomh Pól), Milano (tráchtas ar na Sailm) agus St. Gall na hEilbhéise (*Institutio Grammatica* Phriscian) (McCone 1994). Sa lámhscríbhinn cháiliúil úd atá na samplaí is líonmhaire le fáil. 244 leathanach atá i saothar Phriscian. Tá gluaiseanna scríofa ar gach leathanach acu sin, gluaiseanna ina bhfuil neart téarmaí teanga agus gramadaí. Mar seo a leanas a aicmíonn Ó Cuív iad:

1. téarmaí Laidine gan athrú;
2. téarmaí Laidine a Gaelaíodh .i. *abbgitir, carac(h)tar, conson, litir,* ⁊rl.;
3. téarmaí dúchasacha á n-úsáid mar théarmaí teicniúla chun brí na dtéarmaí Laidine a chur in iúl, .i. *aimser, fogur, briathar, lethed.*

Meabhraíonn an t-aicmiú seo dúinn a laghad athruithe a tharla sa chur chuige ag lucht téarmaíochta na Gaeilge ó shin i leith, ach amháin go bhfuil an Béarla in áit na Laidine le fada fada an lá.

Tráchtais na Meánaoise agus Caighdeánú na Teanga Liteartha

Rinneadh staidéar ar *Auraicept na nÉces* anuas go dtí an tríú haois déag ar a laghad agus b'as a d'eascair tráchtais ghramadaí na mBard sa mheánaois. Ba sa dara haois déag a lig na filí lena n-ais na hathruithe a bhí tagtha ar fhuaimeanna, ghramadach agus fhoclóir na teanga labhartha. Ní hiontas mar sin go raibh athruithe le sonrú i saothar na bhfilí chomh maith. I réimse na teanga féin agus i réimse na meadarachta a tharla an claochlú. I gcás na meadarachta, idirdhealaíodh an dán díreach (an fhilíocht shiollach) agus cineálacha eile meadarachta, mar shampla an t-óglachas agus an bhrúilingeacht (Ó Cuív 1973). Tugadh faoi scrúdú a dhéanamh ar an gcomhréir agus ar an deilbhíocht a bhí in úsáid sa teanga labhartha agus sin uile a chur i gcomórtas le gnás na teanga liteartha. B'as an taighde sin a d'eascair caighdeán úr liteartha bunaithe ar an teanga labhartha. Mhair an teanga liteartha chaighdeánach seo ceithre chéad bliain in Éirinn, agus níos faide fós in Albain, áit ar mhair an seanreacht go dtí lár na hochtú aoise déag. Is díol spéise go léiríonn an caighdeánú a rinneadh ar an teanga liteartha tuiscint ar leith teangeolaíochta a bheith acu siúd a chum é, dar leis an údar céanna (Ó Cuív 1973, 4).

Oiliúint Ábhar Filí agus na Tráchtais Ghramadaí

Chun críche oiliúna a tiomsíodh na Tráchtais Ghramadaí. Meabhraimis go raibh iliomad eolais i réimsí éagsúla le foghlaim ag an ábhar file: stair, dinnseanchas, ginealas, litríocht, agus i gcás na teanga féin, bhíodh foghraíocht agus fóneolaíocht, moirfeolaíocht, comhréir, meadaracht, léamh agus scríobh ar an gclár oibre (nó an siollabas mar thabharfaí air anois).

Is díol suntais gur aithin na gramadóirí an difear idir an teanga scríofa agus an teanga labhartha: ba nós leo tagairt do shamplaí de chaint neamhchaighdeánach agus do leaganacha canúnacha nuair ba ghá, go mór mór nuair a bhí siad le seachaint. Bhí tionchar áirithe, is léir, ag an teanga labhartha ar shaothar na ngramadóirí, agus tá roinnt mhaith plé sna tráchtais ghramadaí ar chúrsaí foghraíochta agus fóneolaíochta chomh maith (Ó Cuív 1980).

Téarmaíocht agus Úsáid Teanga chun Críche Gairmiúla

Saothar tábhachtach ó thaobh na TF ba ea na scríbhinní leighis. Bhí teaghlaigh áirithe a raibh cáil an léinn orthu sa réimse seo ag saothrú leo idir an tríú haois déag agus an seachtú haois déag. Scríobhaithe agus aistritheoirí ba ea iad arbh é a gcuspóir eolas ar chúrsaí leighis a bhailiú, a chaomhnú agus a bhreacadh síos nó a aistriú go Gaeilge dá mba ghá sin. Chomh maith leis an leigheas, ba nós leo ceisteanna fealsúnachta agus meitifisice a phlé. Chuige sin, níor mhór dóibh go leor saintéarmaí a sholáthar. Ní léir go raibh aon ródheacracht téarmaíochta acu agus saibhríodh an teanga go mór dá bharr (Williams ⁊ Ní Mhuiríosa 1979). Go deimhin, ar na scríbhinní is cáiliúla a aistríodh go Gaeilge tá *Regimen na Sláinte* (in eagar ag James Carney 1942–44).

Tionchar an Reifirméisin ar an TF

Cé go raibh coigistíocht, cogadh agus sléacht ar siúl in Éirinn sa seachtú haois déag, b'iontach an rath a bhí ar scríbhneoireacht na Gaeilge sa tréimhse chéanna. Ba mhór an tionchar a bhí ag an Reifirméisean agus ag an bhFrith-Reifirméisean araon ar shaothrú an phróis. Bhí na Protastúnaigh chun tosaigh ar na Caitlicigh i soláthar ábhar clóite. In Albain sa bhliain 1567 a foilsíodh aistriúchán a rinne Seon Carsuel ar leabhar liotúirge John Knox, *Foirm na n-Urrnuidheadh agus Freasdal na Sacramuinteadh*. Ba é *Aibidil Gaoidheilge agus Caiticiosma* (1571) an chéad leabhar a cuireadh i gcló in Éirinn féin. An Bhanríon Eilís a chuir an fhoireann cló ar fáil i 1571 le súil go n-aistreofaí an Bíobla go Gaeilge, ach níor tharla sé sin go dtí tús na seachtú haoise déag.

Má bhíothas le Protastúnaigh a dhéanamh de mhuintir na hÉireann, níor mhór an Bíobla a chur ar fáil dóibh ina dteanga féin ar dtús. Faoi 1632 bhí an obair sin ar siúl faoi threoir an tSasanaigh, William Bedell, Easpag na Cille Móire (Ó Madagáin 1988). Faoi 1637 bhí an Sean-Tiomna aistrithe, agus bheartaigh Bedell cló a chur air ina theach féin. Chuir Éirí Amach 1641 deireadh leis an tionscnamh sin. Níor foilsíodh é go dtí 1685.

Is fearr a d'éirigh leis an Tiomna Nua: sa bhliain 1602 nó 1603 a foilsíodh é faoi ainm Uilliam Uí Dhomhnaill. Foilsíodh an dá Thiomna in aon leabhar amháin i Londain i 1690, beagnach caoga bliain tar éis bhás Bhedell féin. Tugtar 'Bedell's Bible' ar an saothar seo ó shin i leith. Ní háibhéil a rá gur éacht a bhí ann nuair a mheabhraítear a laghad tacaíochta a thug na húdaráis eaglasta do dhearcadh Bhedell ar thábhacht na Gaeilge i gcúrsaí creidimh. Is fiú a lua go mba nós le cuid den chléir Chaitliceach leas a bhaint as Bíobla Bhedell cheal leagan Gaeilge de chuid a n-eaglaise féin a bheith acu—go deimhin, bhí Aodh Mac Aingil féin ar dhuine acu (Williams 1986).

Sula gcuirtear deireadh le scéal an Bhíobla, is ceart a rá cé gur aistrigh an tAthair Peadar Ua Laoghaire, an Canónach Pádraig Mac Giolla Cheara, An Canónach Coslett Ó Cuinn agus daoine eile na Ceithre Soiscéil agus codanna eile den Tiomna Nua, níor chuir na hEaspaig Chaitliceacha rompu an Bíobla ar fad a aistriú go dtí 1945, nuair a bhunaigh siad coimisiún chun na críche sin. B'éigean dlús a chur leis an obair nuair a chinn Dara Comhairle na Vatacáine ar na teangacha dúchais a úsáid sa liotúirge. Chuir na hEaspaig coiste stiúrtha ar bun i 1966 ar a raibh an cúigear sagart seo a leanas ag feidhmiú: Seán Ó Floinn, Donnchadha Ó Floinn, Tomás Ó Fiaich, Pádraig Ó Fiannachta (Coláiste Phádraig, Maigh Nuad), agus an tAthair Colmán Ó Huallacháin, O.F.M. Ar an Athair Ó Fiannachta a thit cuid mhaith den obair mar gurbh eisean rúnaí an Choiste agus gurbh air a leagadh cúram an Bíobla a fhoilsiú. Ina theannta sin uile ba é an t-eagarthóir é (An Bíobla Naofa 1981, Ó Madagáin 1988, Ó Glaisne 1996).

Níor mhiste a mheabhrú gur beart éacúiméineach ar deireadh thiar a bhí in aistriú seo an Bhíobla go Gaeilge: baineann idir Chaitlicigh agus Phrotastúnaigh leas as. Is é go fírinneach Bíobla lucht labhartha na Gaeilge uile é.

Scoláirí Gaeilge Lobháin

Faoi dheireadh na séú haoise déag bhí ord na bProinsiasach á ruaigeadh as a gcuid mainistreacha in Éirinn i gcaoi nach raibh aon áit acu ina bhféadfaidís oiliúint a chur ar a gcuid nóibhíseach ná ar a gcuid misinéirí. Socraíodh áit a fháil ar Mhór-Roinn na hEorpa chun na críche sin. Tharla go raibh aithne mhaith ar an Athair Flaithrí Ó Maolchonaire i gcúirt na Spáinne. Scoláire, aistritheoir agus Ardeaspag Thuama ó 1609 ba ea an Prionsiasach seo. Chuaigh aige tabhairt ar Rí na Spáinne, Pilib III, láthair a bhronnadh ar an ord i Lobháin mar aon le míle coróin de dheontas bliantúil. Coláiste San Antaine de Padua a baisteadh ar an bhforas nua. Ar an gcéad lá de mhí na Samhna 1607 a glacadh leis an gcéad bhuíon scoláirí.

Ba í Ollscoil Lobháin croílár intleachtach an chreidimh Chaitlicigh aimsir an Fhrith-Reifirméisin, agus ba é Coláiste San Antaine croílár intleachtach Chaitliceachas na hÉireann (Ó Buachalla 1982/83). Bhí cur amach ag scoláirí an oird ar an léargas úr a bhí tagtha chun cinn i measc lucht léinn, léargas a d'eascair as an Athbheochan agus as an Reifirméisean, go mór mór i gcúrsaí staire, idir stair náisiúnta agus an stair i gcoitinne. B'fhearr an tuiscint a fuair lucht léinn ar an tábhacht a bhain le foinsí bunaidh a cheadú agus le fianaise a aimsiú agus ar an bhfónamh a thiocfadh leo a bhaint astu mar thacaíocht lena raibh á áiteamh acu ina gcuid scríbhinní.

Bhí saothar na bProinsiasach fréamhaithe sa tuiscint úr seo. Chinn siad ar fhoinse eolais údarásach i dtaobh a dtír dhúchais a thiomsú. Ba é an Bráthair Mícheál Ó Cléirigh, croiniceoir agus staraí a roghnaíodh don obair seo. Ba é an treoir a tugadh dó 'lorg na seanleabhar do leanmhain', rud a rinne sé, agus ba é *Annála Ríoghachta Éireann* an toradh. Os rud é gur ar na 'seanleabhair' a bunaíodh na h*Annála*, ba ghá graiméar a sholáthar don té a d'fhéachfadh le meabhair a bhaint astu. Ba é Giolla Bríde Ó hEodhasa, 'an tAthair diadha foghlamtha Bonaventura Ó hEodhusa' mar a thug Aodh Mac Aingil air, a scríobh an graiméar Gaeilge úd as Laidin, *Rudimenta Grammaticae Hibernicae*. Ba dhoiligh duine ní ba fheiliúnaí a fháil chuige. File a fuair oiliúint sna bardscoileanna a bhí ann. Ghnóthaigh sé céim mháistreachta in Douai, agus bhí sé ar an gcéad bhuíon ar glacadh leo i gcoláiste na bPrionsiasach i Lobháin (Ó Cléirigh 1985). Saothar ceannródaíochta a bhí ann a raibh an-tionchar aige ar na graiméir Ghaeilge a thiomsaigh Flaithrí Ó Maolchonaire, agus daoine eile ina dhiaidh sin (Ó Maonaigh 1962, Williams & Ní Mhuiríosa 1979).

FOCLÓIREACHT

Ní dhearna na Proinsiasaigh faillí san fhoclóireacht ach oiread. I Lobháin sa bhliain 1643 a foilsíodh an t-aon saothar de chuid Mhichíl Uí Chléirigh a clóbhuaileadh agus é fós beo (de Bhaldraithe 1980), ba in *Foclóir nó sanasán nua ina mínighthear cáil éigin d'fhoclaibh cruaidhe na Gaoidheilge*. Is éard a bhí ann míniú i nGaeilge na linne ar fhocail ársa sa teanga. Thuairimeoinn gurbh é an fáth ar cuireadh cló air ná gur ghéar a theastaigh sé ó léitheoirí na 'seanleabhar'!

I measc na bhfoclóirithe eile a bhí san ord an t-am seo bhí Baothghalach Mac Aodhagáin, Muiris Ó Maolchonaire agus Seán Ó Cuirnín. Ar an drochuair, is beag dá saothar a mhaireann. Tháinig saothar eile slán, saothar cáiliúil a thiomsaigh Proinsiasach eile, Risteard Pluincéad, in Éirinn féin, i mainistir Átha Troim i 1662, *Vocabularium Latinum et Hibernum: Foclóir Lainne agus Gaoidheilge*. Tuairim is 34,000 ceannfhocal atá san fhoclóir, agus is i Leabharlann Marsh i mBaile Átha Cliath atá sé á choimeád. Is é an chéad fhoclóir dátheangach a tiomsaíodh in Éirinn é. Bhain foclóirithe eile a tháinig i ndiaidh an Phluincéadaigh earraíocht, agus go deimhin mí-léamh ar uairibh, as an bhfoclóir, leithéidí Edward Lhuyd, John O'Brien, Edward O'Reilly, Tadhg Ó Neachtain (de Bhaldraithe 1987).

Foinse an-tábhachtach maidir le stair na teanga agus saol sóisialta na linne is ea an saothar seo, a tiomsaíodh nuair a bhí an Ghaeilge i mbarr a nirt. Is dea-scéal do chách go bhfuil eagar á chur air faoi láthair i Scoil an Léinn Cheiltigh.

Ní mórán a bhí ar siúl sa TF in Éirinn i gcaitheamh na hochtú haoise déag, cés moite den fhoclóireacht. I dtús na naoú haoise déag a foilsíodh gramadéar William Neilson (Neilson 1808). Is díol spéise an leabhar seo i gcónaí ar an ábhar go bhfuil neart samplaí de Ghaeilge Chontae an Dúin ann, canúint a raibh an bás i ndán di ní b'fhaide anonn sa chéad sin.

LOGAINMNEACHA

Sa naoú haois déag freisin a cuireadh tús le taighde a dhéanamh ar logainmneacha na tíre nuair a fuair Seán Ó Donnabháin post sa tSuirbhéireacht Ordanáis i 1829. Ní raibh paróiste sa tír nár thug sé cuairt air agus é i mbun obair allamuigh. Bhreac sé an toradh i sraith litreacha, nó *Letters* (ar chuir an tAthair Mícheál Ó Flannagáin eagar orthu idir 1924 agus 1932. Caoga imleabhar ar fad a bhí iontu) (Boylan 1988). Ar ndóigh, ba é an t-eagrán de *Annála Ríoghachta Éireann* a d'fhoilsigh sé mar aon le haistriú 1848–1851, a mhórshaothar. Scríobh sé gramadéar Gaeilge chomh maith (O'Donovan 1845). Ar nós Uí Chomhraí, ba dhuine de mhórscoláirí dúchais na linne é Seán Ó Donnabháin.

Tá taighde ar logainmneacha na hÉireann ar siúl i gcónaí in Oifig na Suirbhéireachta Ordanáis faoi stiúir Choimisiún na Logainmneacha, agus tá saothar na mblianta á bhfoilsiú diaidh ar ndiaidh (Brainse Logainmneacha na Suirbhéireachta Ordanáis 1989, 1991).

An Teangeolaíocht Fheidhmeach agus Conradh na Gaeilge

Cé gur foilsíodh roinnt graiméar sa naoú haois déag, is beag athrú a tháinig ar an tslí ina mhúintí an dara teanga nó teanga iasachta. Nós na ngraiméar Laidine a leantaí agus ba bheag an cúram a rinneadh den teanga labhartha. Tar éis bhunú Chonradh na Gaeilge in 1893 a tosaíodh ar spéis a chur i múineadh na Gaeilge mar theanga labhartha, go mór mór de bhrí go raibh glactha le caint na ndaoine mar eiseamláir don fhoghlaimeoir. Pléadh modhanna teagaisc chomh maith, modhanna a d'fheilfeadh do dhaoine fásta. Ba é an tAthair Eoghan Ó Gramhnaigh a scríobh an chéad chúrsa Gaeilge, *Simple Lessons in Irish* (O'Growney 1897) ar mholadh Ardeaspag Bhaile Átha Cliath, an Dr Breathnach. Bhí an-tóir ar na *Ceachtanna* ach ní raibh siad gan locht. Dar leis an gCraoibhín go raibh siad róshimplí i gcaoi go gceapfadh na foghlaimeoirí go raibh sé éasca Gaeilge a fhoghlaim. Ar ndóigh, ní raibh aon ghléas eile ann an t-am sin ach iad (Mac Mathúna ⁊ Mac Gabhann 1981).

Faoin mbliain 1896 chuir an Conradh roimhe leas a bhaint as modh François Gouin, Beilgeach agus údar *Art d'enseigner et d'étudier des langues* (1880). Bhunaigh Peadar Mac Fhionnlaoich (Cú Uladh) a leabhar teagaisc, a ghnóthaigh duais Oireachtais, ar mhodh Gouin (Mac Ginley 1903). Tharraing an leabhar idir chaint agus chonspóid. Foilsíodh leabhar teagaisc eile an bhliain chéanna, *An Modh Réidh* (Mac an Fhailghe). Ba é an Modh Díreach a bhí in úsáid ann, agus gléas maith teagaisc do dhaoine fásta a bhí ann. Léiríonn na téacsleabhair seo an síorphlé a bhíodh ar siúl sa Chonradh faoin dóigh ab fhearr le Gaeilge a theagasc, go raibh meon oscailte ag lucht na gluaiseachta agus fáilte roimh smaointe agus modhanna nua ón iasacht (Mac Mathúna ⁊ Mac Gabhann 1981). Is léir freisin nach mar theanga mharbh ná mar theanga scríofa amháin ba mhian leis an gConradh go múinfí an Ghaeilge ach mar theanga bheo labhartha. Bhí an dearcadh seo chun tosaigh ar ghnáthchleachtas an chórais oideachais in Éirinn san am.

Gníomhaíocht Teanga an Stáit

Cuireadh tús le seirbhís aistriúcháin na Dála nuair a ceapadh Mícheál Ó Loinsigh as Baile Bhuirne mar aistritheoir ar fhoireann rúnaíochta na Chéad Dála i mí Mheithimh 1919. Nuair a bunaíodh an Saorstát, socraíodh i mí Mheán Fómhair 1922, go gcuirfeadh Cléireach na Dála aistriú oifigiúil Béarla go Gaeilge agus—dá mba ghá sin—Gaeilge go Béarla den reachtaíocht ar fáil. D'fhág sé sin go raibh ar Rannóg an Aistriúcháin téarmaí agus leaganacha Gaeilge de na dlíthe a d'achtaigh an Dáil a sholáthar, dualgas atá uirthi i gcónaí. Is fiú a lua freisin gurb í atá freagrach chomh maith as Conarthaí na gComhphobal Eorpach—nó an Aontais Eorpaigh anois—a aistriú go Gaeilge (Daltún 1983, 1965).

Ba léir do lucht na Rannóige ón tús nár mhór an Ghaeilge a chur in oiriúint do réimsí nua úsáide agus don saol nua a bhí roimpi. Tosaíodh dá bhrí sin ar chóras nua litrithe a leagan amach a d'fheilfeadh don chló Rómhánach (a bhí á úsáid sa Rannóg riamh anall). Ar an drochuair tharla athrú polasaí maidir le cúrsaí cló de thoradh ar an athrú rialtais i 1932. Tharla sé sin de bharr thionchar Chonradh na Gaeilge a bhí in éadan an chló Rómhánaigh. Ba sa bhliain 1945 a tugadh aghaidh ar an bhfadhb arís nuair a leag an Taoiseach, Éamon de Valera cúram ar an Rannóg 'coras litrithe gairid a mholadh a bheadh feiliúnach lena ghlacadh mar chaighdeán chomh-choitian sa chló Gaelach agus sa chló Rómhánach' (Daltún 1983, Ó Baoill, 1988). Foilsíodh an toradh sa bhliain chéanna sa leabhrán *Litriú na Gaeilge: Lámhleabhar an Chaighdeáin Oifigiúil*, mar eolas don phobal agus mar ghléas le litriú na teanga a chaighdeánú. Ní mór tagairt freisin do leabhar a raibh an-tionchar aige ar dhearcadh phobail na Gaeilge ar chaighdeánú na teanga: *Forbairt na Gaeilge*, a scríobh Niall Ó Dónaill, foclóirí, scoláire agus scríbhneoir Gaeltachta (Ó Domhnaill 1951). Rinneadh dul chun cinn arís i 1957 nuair a d'iarr an Taoiseach ar an bPríomhaistritheoir treoirleabhrán a scríobh a bheadh mar chaighdeán ag lucht scríofa cáipéisí oifigiúla, ag lucht oideachais agus mar eolas don phobal. Cuireadh an leabhrán, *Gramadach na Gaeilge agus Litriú na Gaeilge*, ar díol i 1958, agus bhí an-tóir ag an bpobal air. Bhí fáil faoi dheireadh ar chaighdeán oifigiúil litrithe agus gramadaí a bheadh in úsáid feasta i ndoiciméid oifigiúla, i bhfoclóirí, in áiseanna teagaisc agus le himeacht aimsire sa litríocht chruthaitheach.

Mar fhocal scoir, is fiú barúil an Ollaimh Cathal Ó Háinle a thabhairt ar fhorálacha an Chaighdeáin Oifigiúil (CO):

> Is iad na haidhmeanna a bhí leis na socruithe sin in CO [...] ná 'an comhaontas a bhunú in áit an easaontais' i dtaca leis na foirmeacha a nglacfaí leo, 'deimhniú a thabhairt ar nithe a raibh éideimhne ann ina

dtaobh' agus 'cruinneas agus slacht a chur in ionad an neamhchruinnis agus an neamhshlachta a thagann den easaontas agus den éideimhne' (CO, vii). Ainneoin go bhfuil sé áitithe ag scoláirí éagsúla nach bhfuil an caighdeán seo gan locht [...] ní féidir a shéanadh ná go bhfuil sé tar éis dul i gcion go mór ar scríobh na Gaeilge le glúin anuas agus go bhfuil sé tar éis na haidhmeanna úd a chur i gcrích cuid mhór. Is é atá mar dhúshraith faoi G[raiméar]G[aeilge na m]B[ráithre]C[ríostaí], ina bhfuil an cuntas is iomláine dá bhfuil ar fáil ar dheilbhíocht is ar chomhréir Ghaeilge na linne seo, agus faoin dá fhoclóir nua aimseartha, E[nglish] I[rish]D[ictionary] (1959) agus F[oclóir]G[aeilge]B[éarla](1977) (Ó Háinle 1994).

Saothar Foclóireachta

Foilsíodh méid áirithe foclóirí i gcaitheamh na fichiú haoise. Ar na cinn is mó tábhacht a thráchtfar anseo, is é sin, na cinn a cheadaítear i gcónaí agus a cheadófar sa chéad seo romhainn gan dé dearfa ar bith.

Ba é foclóir an Duinnínigh an chéad mhórfhoclóir Gaeilge–Béarla a cuireadh ar fáil. Ba éard a bhí ann eagrán nua leasaithe den chéad eagrán a thiomsaigh an Duinníneach i 1904, ar díothaíodh na plátaí a bhain leis in Éirí Amach 1916 (Dinneen 1927). Cur chuige ar leith a bhí ag an eagarthóir. Mar seo a leanas a chuireann sé síos air sa Réamhrá:

> In this dictionary the aim has been to select for quotation illustrative phrases and passages endowed with something of this deep and vital character of speech, the imaginative flow, the associative colour, that alone can reveal to the student the genius of the language.
>
> The folk-lore, the habits and beliefs, the songs and tales, the arts and crafts of the people as well as the history, topography and antiquities of the country have been pressed into service to throw light on the meanings of words or to supply words or expressions not previously recorded (Dinneen 1927, viii).

Maidir le ceist chasta na hortagrafaíochta, bhí caighdeánú áirithe déanta aige ar an litriú traidisiúnta sa chéad eagrán, agus lean sé leis an múnla céanna san eagrán nua 'with certain accepted modifications'.

Thiocfadh le duine an-chuid samplaí barrúla, tíriúla a aimsiú i measc ceannfhocal an tsaothair seo a dhealaíonn ó na mórfhoclóirí eile é (de Bhaldraithe 1983). Is deacair a shamhlú nach mbeidh leas á bhaint as mar fhoclóir agus mar leabhar adhairte chomh fada is a bheidh Gaeilge á léamh agus á scríobh in Éirinn.

Ba é an tAire Airgeadais, Earnán de Blaghd, a chuir an *Foclóir Béarla–Gaedhilge* á thiomsú sa chló Rómhánach. Ba é an tAthair L. Mac

Cionnaith, S.J., an t-eagarthóir, agus bhí Niall Ó Dónaill ina eagarthóir cúnta. Bhí faoi córas litrithe ní ba shimplí a cheapadh a thabharfadh aitheantas do na canúintí uile agus a réiteodh an fhadhb a bhain le mórchuid h-anna a bheith sáite isteach sna focail. Fuarthas amach go mbainfeadh deacrachtaí go leor le córas den chineál sin a cheapadh. Nuair a thug an Rialtas a tháinig i gcumhacht i 1932 treoir do lucht an fhoclóra cloí leis an gcló Gaelach, cinneadh ar chóras litrithe an Duinnínigh a úsáid, cés moite de líon beag focal a liostaíodh san fhoclóir (Mac Cionnaith 1935, xi). Tasc ar leith ab ea caighdeánú an litrithe nach raibh a uain tagtha go fóill.

Faoi scáth na Roinne Oideachais a cuireadh an dá mhórfhoclóir eile ar fáil. Bhí an t-am tráthúil, anois go raibh an CO ann, rud a chinntigh gurbh í an teanga chaighdeánach a bheadh sna foclóirí. Bhí glactha freisin leis an gcló Rómhánach. I 1945 a cuireadh tús le foclóir Béarla–Gaeilge faoi stiúir Thomáis de Bhaldraithe (Ó Floinn 1981). Foilsíodh an *English–Irish Dictionary* i 1959. Dearbhaítear sa Réamhrá gur cuspóir praiticiúil a bhí mar bhun leis an bhfoclóir:

> The aim of this dictionary is the practical one of providing Irish equivalents for English words and phrases in common use. It is not then to be regarded as an exhaustive word-store of modern literary Irish or of the current spoken language. Only a selection of the Irish material collected by the Dictionary Staff from printed and manuscript sources, appears in this dictionary [...] the dictionary is however primarily based on current usage, and draws on the older literary language or on neologisms only where the living speech of the Gaeltacht is found wanting.

Mínítear freisin i gcás na bhfocal teicniúil go mb'éigean leagan amháin a roghnú as i measc na leaganacha iomadúla Gaeilge a bhí cumtha ag údaráis éagsúla agus gur iarradh comhairle saineolaithe chun na críche sin (de Bhaldraithe, eag. 1959).

Ba é Niall Ó Dónaill eagarthóir an *Foclóir Gaeilge–Béarla* (1977), an ceathrú mórfhoclóir a foilsíodh sa chéad seo. Ba é aidhm an fhoclóra de réir an réamhrá 'an chuid is coitianta de stór focal na Nua-Ghaeilge a thabhairt le chéile agus a mhíniú i mBéarla. Cuireadh isteach na focail a raibh fianaise le fáil go bhfuil siad i ngnáthúsáid i dteanga an lae inniu. Lena chois sin cuireadh isteach focail áirithe as seanlitríocht na Nua-Ghaeilge nach n-úsáidtear go coitianta anois, ach a mbeadh a mbrí ag teastáil ó lucht léite na litríochta sin [...]. Cuireadh isteach, freisin, a lán téarmaí teicniúla nua-aoiseacha nach mbeadh súil leo i ngnáthfhoclóir, toisc nach bhfuil foclóir mór téarmaíochta curtha le chéile fós sa teanga' (Ó Dónaill 1977, vii).

Is iad na foirmeacha caighdeánacha atá ar na ceannfhocail a ngabhann míniú leo, ach cuireadh isteach foirmeacha malartacha atá coitianta sa teanga freisin, mar aon le seanlitriú aon fhocail a bhfuil athrú meánach air sa litriú caighdeánach (Ó Dónaill 1977, vii–viii). Tá córas crostagairtí i bhfeidhm a threoraíonn an t-úsáidire chuig an leagan caighdeánaithe i ngach cás.

Tasc breise a mb'éigean tabhairt faoi ba ea caighdeánú litriú na bhfocal nach raibh ar fáil i leabhrán an CO. De réir na rialacha a bhí leagtha síos ann a rinneadh an caighdeánú i gcomhar le Rannóg an Aistriúcháin, agus le Coiste Téarmaíochta na Roinne Oideachais i gcás nuathéarmaí teicniúla. Is díol spéise chomh maith go bhfuil roinnt leasuithe déanta san fhoclóir ar rialacha an CO, agus nach mór don úsáidire, dá bhrí sin, an foclóir a cheadú chomh maith le leabhrán an CO le teacht ar leaganacha caighdeánacha áirithe.

Cé nach foclóir mór é, ní bheadh aon chur síos ar fhoclóireacht na fichiú haoise iomlán gan tagairt a dhéanamh don *Foclóir Póca* (Roinn Oideachais 1986). Bunaíodh ar Fhoclóir Uí Dhónaill é, agus is é an chéad fhoclóir Gaeilge é ina bhfuil treoir tugtha faoin bhfuaimniú a ghabhann le gach ceannfhocal (Roinn Oideachais 1986, xi). Nuaíocht ar fad a bhí sa bheart a rinneadh agus ba chéim mhór ar aghaidh é ar an ábhar gur tugadh aghaidh ar fhadhb na gcanúintí san am céanna. Tuigeadh go gcaithfí cloí le fuaimniú amháin dá mb'fhéidir é i gcás gach ceannfhocail. Fuaimniú neodrach a lorgaíodh agus ba in rud a d'éiligh comhghéilleadh ar gach ceann de na canúintí. Bunaíodh fochoiste chun réiteach na faidhbe a aimsiú. Ba iad an Dr Dónall Ó Baoill (Cathaoirleach), Éamonn Ó Tuathail agus Pádraig Ua Maoileoin baill an fhochoiste. Leag siad siúd a gcuid moltaí faoi bhráid choiste comhairligh. Glacadh leo tar éis roinnt leasuithe a dhéanamh orthu. Dónall Ó Baoill (ITÉ) agus Seán Ó Briain (An Gúm) a scríobh an treoir foghraíochta agus a mhínigh an córas a cuireadh i bhfeidhm san fhoclóir (Roinn Oideachais 1986). Tá fáil ar thuarascáil agus ar chaiséad léirithe mar áis don úsáidire ar mhian leis breis eolais a fháil ar an gcóras foghraíochta atá san *Foclóir Póca*. Foilsíodh eagrán leasaithe faoin teideal *Foclóir Scoile* (Roinn Oideachais 1994). Ina theannta sin d'fhoilsigh an Gúm *An Foclóir Beag*, an chéad fhoclóir Gaeilge-Gaeilge don ghnáthléitheoir ina liostaítear 'na focail is simplí ar fad [...] fiú amháin tá, aici, agus, nó'.(Roinn Oideachais,1991). Is díol spéise freisin an stíl éasca, nádúrtha próis a úsáidtear sna hiontrálacha mínithe.

Mórshaothar eile ar cuireadh tús leis in Acadamh Ríoga na hÉireann i 1976–77 is ea Foclóir na Nua-Ghaeilge, foclóir Gaeilge–Gaeilge ina mbeidh fáil ar stór focal na Gaeilge ón seachtú haois déag go deireadh an chéid seo. Obair riachtanach í seo a chuirfeas an Ghaeilge ar chomhchéim le teangacha náisiúnta eile i ngnóthaí foclóireachta.

AN NUATHÉARMAÍOCHT

Aithníodh ó bhlianta tosaigh na hathbheochana teanga an tábhacht a bhí le soláthar téarmaí má bhíothas le meán cumarsáide nua-aimseartha a dhéanamh den Ghaeilge. D'eagraítí comórtais téarmaíochta faoi scáth Oireachtas na Gaeilge agus foilsíodh gluaiseanna in irisí éagsúla. Níor cuireadh bonn ceart faoin obair seo go dtí tar éis bhunú an tSaorstáit, nuair a aithníodh go mbeadh géarghá le téarmaíocht theicniúil a sholáthar sa chóras oideachais i gcomhair na scoileanna a bhí ag múineadh trí mheán na Gaeilge. Sa bhliain 1927, mhol cruinniú de chigirí an Bhrainse Cheard-Oideachais go dtosófaí ar théarmaíocht eolaíochta a thiomsú, rud a rinneadh le cúnamh Thórna (Tadhg Ó Donnchadha) agus Réamoinn Uí Chinnéide, léachtóir le ceimic i gColáiste Ollscoile Chorcaí. Leagadh an toradh faoi bhráid Sheoirse Mhic Niocaill, Príomhchigire Meánscoileanna. Mhol seisean don Roinn coiste téarmaíochta a bhunú chun téarmaí a chur ar fáil don Stair, don Tíreolaíocht agus ábhair eile (Ó Floinn 1981).

Glacadh le moladh an Phríomhchigire, agus tionóladh an chéad chruinniú den Choiste Téarmaíochta 8–12 Samhain 1928. Tá an obair ar siúl ó shin, agus is iomaí sin saintéarma a soláthraíodh i ngach gné den oideachas i gcaitheamh na mblianta, chomh maith le go leor réimsí eile den saol comhaimseartha (Nic Mhaoláin 1989, 1994, An Gúm 1993). Ainneoin gur teanga neamhfhorleathan an Ghaeilge, ní chiallaíonn sé sin go bhfuil thiar uirthi i gcomórtas le teangacha eile de chuid na hEorpa ó thaobh téarmaíochta de (Ó Deirg 1988). Mar a dúradh thuas, is é an cur chuige céanna nach mór a bhí in úsáid ag na gramadóirí luatha atá in úsáid ag lucht téarmaíochta an lae inniu (Ní Dheirg 1992). Is ceart a lua freisin go bhfuil rialacha cinnte leagtha síos chun focail iasachta a thraslitriú i gcaoi, ní hamháin go mbeidh cuma Ghaelach orthu, ach go mbeidh siad in oiriúint do chóras gramadaí na Gaeilge chomh maith (Ó hÓgáin 1983, Breathnach 1993).

TAIGHDE SOCHTHEANGEOLAÍOCHTA AN STÁIT

Ní miste tagairt a dhéanamh anseo don taighde a d'eascair as cinneadh an Rialtais sna seascaidí go mbunófaí coiste le scrúdú a dhéanamh ar dhearcadh an phobail ar cheist na Gaeilge. Tharla sna seascaidí gur nochtadh imní faoin easpa dul chun cinn a bhí le sonrú ar staid na Gaeilge agus faoin údar a bhí leis. Lena chois sin, bhí taighde John Macnamara ar an dátheangachas sa chóras bunscoile tar éis amhras a chaitheamh ar úsáid na

Gaeilge mar mheán teagaisc (Macnamara 1966). Bunaíodh Comhairle na Gaeilge i 1969 leis an scéal a fhiosrú. D'aithin an Chomhairle ansin a laghad eolas beacht is a bhí ar fáil faoi thionchar na bpolasaithe a bhí i bhfeidhm agus faoi dhearcadh an phobail ina dtaobh. D'iarr an Chomhairle ar an Rialtas coiste a bhunú chun scrúdú a dhéanamh ar na gnéithe bunúsacha seo den scéal.

I mí Mheán Fómhair 1970, bhunaigh an tAire Airgeadais, Seoirse Ó Colla, T.D., an Coiste um Thaighde ar Dhearcadh an Phobail i dtaobh na Gaeilge (CLAR) chun tuairisc a ullmhú faoi:

1. dhearcadh an phobail ar an nGaeilge agus ar na hiarrachtaí a bhí á ndéanamh len í a athbheochan mar ghnáthmheán cumarsáide;

2. thacaíocht an phobail do pholasaithe ar dócha gur fearr a d'éireodh leo an teanga a chur in úsáid mar ghnáthmheán cumarsáide i líon suntasach de réimsí teanga.

Ba é seo an chéad taighde sochtheangeolaíochta a rinneadh sa tír seo agus ba léir go raibh súil ag an Rialtas go bhfaighfí treoir sna torthaí i dtaobh na bpolasaithe ba cheart dó a chur i bhfeidhm. Ní hamháin sin, taighde ceannródaíochta a bhí ann nár tugadh faoina leithéid in aon tír eile roimhe sin.

Ba é an Dr Tadhg Ó Tuama, Iarstiúrthóir Taighde agus Forbartha Chomhlucht Siúicre Éireann, Cathaoirleach an Choiste. Bhí an bhallraíocht comhdhéanta d'ionadaithe ón Roinn Oideachais, an Foras Talúntais, Scoil an Léinn Cheiltigh, an Foras Bainistíochta, agus ar ndóigh, na hollscoileanna. Ina measc siúd bhí an tOllamh le Gaeilge i gColáiste na Tríonóide, Máirtín Ó Murchú, údar *Urlabhra agus Pobal*, an chéad leabhar sochtheangeolaíochta a scríobhadh as Gaeilge (Ó Murchú 1971). Bhí triúr speisialtóirí ón iasacht ann, na hOllúna J.A. Fishman, Ollscoil Yeshiva, Nua Eabhrach, W.F. Mackey, an tIonad Taighde Idirnáisiúnta ar an Dátheangachas, Quebec, agus J.L. Williams, Déan an Oideachais, Ollscoil na Breataine Bige in Aberystwyth.

Chuathas chun oibre le fonn: rinneadh suirbhéanna le heolas a bhailiú ar dhearcadh an phobail, ar chumas agus ar úsáid na teanga ina measc agus ar ábhair ghaolmhara. Cuireadh an Tuarascáil (An Coiste um Thaighde ar Dhearcadh an Phobail i dtaobh na Gaeilge 1975) faoi bhráid Aire na Gaeltachta i mí Dheireadh Fómhair 1975.

Taighde uileghabhálach sochtheangeolaíochta a bhí sa tionscadal. Leag sé bunchloch faoin taighde sochtheangeolaíochta sa tír seo a bhféadfaí tógáil uirthi. Rud eile, ar éigean is féidir tagairt don Ghaeilge san fhichiú haois gan an fhoinse luachmhar seo a cheadú. Ar ITÉ a leagadh cúram caomhnaithe na sonraí a ghin an tionscadal.

NUASHONRÚ NA TEANGEOLAÍOCHTA FEIDHMÍ AGUS BUNÚ ITÉ

Tar éis an dara cogadh domhanda tháinig cor i gcinniúint na TF agus borradh dá réir. Ba sna Stáit Aontaithe a tharla an t-athrú seo a bhéimnigh múineadh agus foghlaim teanga agus a d'aithin an TF den chéad uair riamh mar dhisciplín agus mar ábhar dlisteanach taighde inti féin. Ní hamháin sin, d'fhás réimsí úra taighde ar nós na sochtheangeolaíochta agus na síctheangeolaíochta a raibh sé i ndán dóibh gnéithe úra de chúrsaí teanga a thabhairt chun solais.

Ní gá cuntas a thabhairt anseo ar céard ba bhun leis an gcor nua seo sa TF sna Stáit Aontaithe, eolas atá ag lucht teanga le fada. Is leor chun críche an ailt seo tionchar na gluaiseachta sin in Éirinn a rianú.

Is díol suime gur Phroinsiasach a thug coincheap úr seo na TF go hÉirinn. Ba é sin an tAthair Colmán Ó Huallacháin, O.F.M., fealsúnaí, foclóirí, aistritheoir agus múinteoir teangacha a raibh seal caite aige sa Lobháin, sa Róimh, i gColáiste Phádraig, Maigh Nuad agus in áiteanna eile. Bhí iarchéim bainte amach aige i modheolaíocht theagasc teangacha in Ollscoil Georgetown, Washington D.C. Tar éis dó filleadh ar Éirinn, d'fhoilsigh sé alt san iris *Teachers' Work* (Ó Huallacháin 1962). An gá a bhí le taighde teangeolaíochta a dhéanamh ar an nGaeilge labhartha mar bhunús le soláthar cúrsaí feiliúnacha do dhaltaí bunscoile éirim an ailt. Ar mholadh Thomáis Uí Chuilleanáin, Cathaoirleach Chumann na gCigirí sa Roinn Oideachais, tugadh cuireadh don Athair Colmán labhairt leis na cigirí faoi théama an ailt. Ghlac an tAthair Colmán leis an gcuireadh. Mar thoradh ar an léacht a thug sé, ceapadh mar chomhairleoir teangeolaíoch sa Roinn Oideachais ar bhonn sealadach é chun an taighde riachtanach sin a dhéanamh. Sin mar a cuireadh tús i 1962-3 le *Buntús Gaeilge*, 'an tionscnamh ba mhó agus ba leithne scóip dá short ar tugadh faoi sa Roinn Oideachais ó bunaíodh í' (Ó Domhnalláin 1981, 1997).

Ba é cuspóir an taighde na heilimintí den teanga Ghaeilge idir fhoclóir is chomhréir ba mhinice a úsáidtí i ngnáthchaint na Gaeltachta a shainaithint, mórán mar a bhí déanta ag Roinn Oideachais na Fraince i gcás *Le Français Fondamental*. Ba í an teoiric a bhí i réim an t-am sin, dá dtiocfadh na heilimintí réamhráite a mhúineadh do thosaitheoirí, go mbeadh ar a gcumas caint shimplí sa sprioctheanga a ghiniúint agus cainteoirí dúchais a thuiscint.

Chuathas chun oibre sa Ghaeltacht (agus sa Ghalltacht áit a raibh an taighde céanna ar siúl i gcás an Bhéarla). Cuireadh na sonraí a bailíodh ar an ríomhaire chun críche anailíse. Foilsíodh na torthaí sa tuarascáil *Buntús Gaeilge* (Roinn Oideachais 1966). Ar an taighde seo a bunaíodh *Nuachúrsaí Comhrá na Roinne*, cúrsaí closamhairc a scríobhadh don bhunscoil agus don iar-bhunscoil ina dhiaidh sin.

Saothar ceannródaíochta a bhí sa tionscadal úd *Buntús Gaeilge*. Ba é go fírinneach an chéad taighde gairmiúil, eolaíoch, nua-aimseartha ar theagasc teanga ar tugadh faoi i réimse na TF in Éirinn.

Is mithid anois tagairt a dhéanamh do nuatheangacha na hEorpa, go háirithe an Fhraincis, an Ghearmáinis, an Spáinnis agus an Iodáilis, a bhí á dteagasc sa chóras iar-bhunscolaíochta. Tharla go raibh tóir ar théacsleabhair áirithe a d'fhoilsigh Holt, Rinehart & Winston i Stáit Aontaithe Mheirceá i 1962. Chuir an tAthair Colmán eagar ar aistriú Gaeilge de na leabhair seo (Côté 1964, LaGrone 1970, Rehder 1965). Chomh maith leis sin, eagraíodh cúrsaí inseirbhíse faoina stiúir do mhúinteoirí nuatheangacha sa Teanglann a chuir an Roinn ar fáil dó i mBaile Mhic Gormáin, Contae na Mí. Tosaíodh ar shaotharlanna teanga a chur isteach sna scoileanna, óir ba iad an gléas teagaisc teanga ba nua-aimseartha dá raibh ar fáil an t-am sin ag múinteoirí agus ag foghlaimeoirí teanga.

B'as an Teanglann a d'eascair Institiúid Teangeolaíochta Éireann (ITÉ), a bunaíodh i 1967, agus ceapadh an tAthair Colmán mar stiúrthóir uirthi. I dtús na bliana acadúla 1969, aistríodh an fhoireann go dtí uimhir 31 Plás Mhic Liam, Baile Átha Cliath, teach a chuir Aire Airgeadais na linne, Cathal Ó hEochaidh, ar fáil. Ba dhóigh le duine go raibh an rath i ndán don Institiúid agus dá stiúrthóir as sin amach; ar an drochuair ní mar sin a tharla. D'éirigh idir é agus an Roinn Oideachais agus cuireadh deireadh lena chonradh i 1971. Fuair sé post mar Ollamh le Gaeilge i 1973 in Ollscoil Nua Uladh igCúil Raithin, áit a raibh sé ag obair go dtí gur cailleadh é i 1979. Fágadh faoi Thomás Ó Domhnalláin, cigire bunscoile a bhí ag saothrú leis an Athair Colmán ó 1963 i leith, an Institiúid a chur ar a boinn arís. Ceapadh ina Stiúrthóir Gníomhach é agus atheagraíodh an Institiúid ina cuideachta i 1972. Fostaíodh tuilleadh foirne. Faoi 1976 bhí na ranna seo a leanas ag feidhmiú: Teangeolaíocht Struchtúrtha, Socheolaíocht Teanga, Síceolaíocht Teanga, Nuatheangacha agus an Leabharlann (Ó Deirg 1979).

Ba sa bhliain 1972 freisin a d'ainmnigh an tAire Oideachais Conn R. Ó Cléirigh, Ollamh le Teangeolaíocht i gColáiste na hOllscoile, Baile Átha Cliath, ina Chathaoirleach ar an Institiúid. Ón am sin go dtí gur cailleadh i 1995 é, thug sé cúnamh agus tacaíocht d' obair ITÉ agus do bhunú Chumann na Teangeolaíochta Feidhmí mar a fheicfear ar ball.

Ar na cúraimí a leagadh ar an Institiúid bhí leanúint ar aghaidh leis an taighde a chuir lucht CLAR i gcrích i réimse na suirbhéireachta teanga, rud a rinneadh (Ó Riagáin ┐ Ó Gliasáin 1984, 1994, Ó Riagáin 1986). Ar na tionscadail eile a cuireadh i gcrích, tá taighde ar athrú teanga i nGaeltacht Chorca Dhuibhne (Ó Riagáin 1992). Rinneadh anailís ar dháileadh na ndeontas £10.00 ar pháistí na Gaeltachta (Ó Gliasáin 1990), agus staidéar socheolaíoch ar Ghaelscoileanna i gceantar Bhaile Átha Cliath (Ó Riagáin ⁊ Ó Gliasáin 1979). Cuireadh eagar are Uimhir 70 den *International Journal of the Sociology of Language* inar pléadh ceisteanna a bhain le pleanáil teanga i gcás na Gaeilge (Ó Riagáin, eag. 1988).

Bhí Roinn na Teangeolaíochta Struchtúrtha gafa cuid mhaith le háiseanna teagaisc, ina measc *Cleachtaí Foghraíochta*, a céadfhoilsíodh i 1975 agus a bhfuil éileamh air i gcónaí (Ó Baoill 1975). Is éard atá sa leabhrán iliomad samplaí a léiríonn na difríochtaí idir fuaimeanna an Bhéarla agus fuaimeanna na Gaeilge, go háirithe i gcás na ndéfhoghar *ua* agus *ia* agus na gconsan *l* agus *n*. Gabhann caiséid leis an leabhar a fhreastalaíonn ar Ghaeilge Uladh, Chonnacht agus na Mumhan faoi seach.

Foilsíodh an dara heagrán de *Úrchúrsa Gaeilge* (Ó Baoill ⁊ Ó Tuathail 1992b, 1993). Cúrsa i scríobh na Gaeilge do mhic léinn tríú leibhéil atá ann. Baineadh leas ins an *Úrchúrsa* as torthaí an taighde a rinneadh ar earráidí scríofa Gaeilge a rinne sampla ionadaíoch de na hiarrthóirí ar scrúdú Gaeilge na hArdteistiméireachta (Ó Domhnalláin ⁊ Ó Baoill 1978 1979, Ó Baoill 1981). Saothar cúntach eile is ea *Réamhfhocail le Briathra na Gaeilge* (Ó Domhnalláin ⁊ Ó Baoill 1975) ina léirítear na réamhfhocail a ghabhann le briathra na Gaeilge, eolas a bhíonn de dhíth ar fhoghlaimeoirí agus, leis an fhírinne a dhéanamh, ar scríbhneoirí Gaeilge chomh maith.

Cé go bhfuil gramadach agus litriú caighdeánach ar fáil le fada, ní dhearnadh aon chaighdeánú ar fhuaimniú na teanga labhartha. Ba é a dhéanadh an foghlaimeoir ceann de na mórchanúintí a roghnú agus tamall a chaitheamh sa cheantar ina raibh sí á labhairt. Nós é seo a d'oir do mhuintir na hÉireann a raibh cur amach acu—má ba bheag féin é—ar na ceantair Ghaeltachta. Ach is iondúil nach mbíonn aon eolas ar Ghaeltacht ar bith ag an bhfoghlaimeoir iasachta. Cén chaoi a roghnódh a leithéid canúint Ghaeilge nó cén chomhairle is ceart a chur air?

Ó tharla ról lárnach a bheith ag an Roinn i leagan amach agus soláthar an chórais fhuaimnithe sa *Foclóir Póca*, tuigeadh go raibh an chéad chéim tugtha i dtreo chanúint lárnaigh. Scríobhadh tuarascáil (Ó Baoill 1986a ⁊ b) agus tionóladh cruinniú leis an gceist a phlé (Ó Baoill 1990).

Cé go mbeidh tóir i gcónaí ar Ghaeilge na Gaeltachta fad is a bheas sí ann, ní hin le rá nach mbeidh tóir ag foghlaimeoirí ón iasacht, ag foghlaimeoirí uirbeacha agus ag craoltóirí ar chanúint neodrach—is é sin, lárchanúint.

Réimse sách nua sa TF a bhfuil borradh faoi is ea teagasc teanga chun críche gairmiúla. Níl ceird ná gairm ann nach ngineann a dteanga sainiúil féin ina mbíonn focail agus leaganacha cainte a eascraíonn as an ngnó atá ar siúl acu, pé acu leigheas, talmhaíocht, eolaíocht, ealaíon, baincéireacht, nó eile atá i gceist. Is i gcomhar le dreamanna eile a thugann an Roinn faoi áiseanna teagaisc a chur ar fáil sa réimse seo, mar shampla an Comhchoiste Réamhscolaíochta i gcás an lámhleabhair a scríobhadh do thuismitheoirí ar mhian leo Gaeilge a labhairt sa bhaile lena gclann óg réamhscoile (Comhchoiste Réamhscolaíochta ┐ Institiúid Teangeolaíochta Éireann 1985), agus Coláiste an Gharda agus Gael-Linn i gcás an chúrsa ghairmiúil do ghardaí faoi oiliúint (*Ar Aghaidh* 1 ┐ 2, 1995). Ba iad an *Walsh Report* ar oiliúint an Gharda agus *Threshold Level* 1990 Chomhairle na hEorpa a spreag an comhthionscadal seo.

Ní mór tagairt freisin do na tuairiscí achoimre a bheartaigh baill na Roinne le déanaí ar na mórchanúintí. Tá fáil anois ar *Corca Dhuibhne* (Ó Sé 1995) agus *Gaeilge Uladh* (Ó Baoill 1996).

Ceann de mhórthionscadail na Rannóige ba ea Tionscadal na mBodhar, a mhaoinigh an tAontas Eorpach i 1993 ar chuspóir dó teanga na mbodhar in Éirinn a chódú agus eolas i dtaobh na mbodhar féin a chruinniú le cabhair suirbhé. Ba é seo an chéad uair riamh a ndearnadh a leithéid. Tá fáil ar na torthaí i dtuarascáil ina bhfuil dhá imleabhar: in Imleabhar 1 gheofar eolas ar chúrsaí daonáirimh agus ar stair, oideachas agus dearcadh na mbodhar ar a ndálaí saoil. Baineann Imleabhar 2 le staidéar teangeolaíochta agus anailís ar struchtúr teanga comharthaíochta na mbodhar (Matthews 1996). Eolas fíorthábhachtach agus fíorspéisiúil is ea an t-eolas a chuir an tionscadal seo ar fáil. Tá dóchas acu siúd a bhí ag obair air go gcuirfidh an t-eolas ar a súile don ghnáthphobal gur mionlach teanga sa tír seo is ea na bodhair agus go ngabhann a dtréithe agus a dtuairimí féin leo seo a úsáideann an teanga chomharthaíochta (Matthews 1996, Ó Baoill ┐ Matthews, le foilsiú).

I 1977 a bunaíodh Roinn na Síctheangeolaíochta. Cuireadh tús le hobair na Roinne in am a raibh cuid mhaith den phobal míshásta leis an gcaighdeán Gaeilge a bhí á ghnóthú ag a gclann ar scoil. Braitheadh go raibh laghdú tagtha ar chumas Gaeilge na n-ardranganna sa bhunscoil (Harris 1982). Lena chois sin, léirigh suirbhé náisiúnta a rinneadh i 1983 nach bhfaigheadh aon ghníomh oifigiúil ar son na Gaeilge an tacaíocht chéanna a gheobhadh gníomh ar chuspóir dó teagasc na Gaeilge a fheabhsú (Ó Riagáin ┐ Ó Gliasáin 1984). Ach mar a tharlaíonn go minic, ní raibh aon eolas cruinn ar fáil faoin scéal. Socraíodh nár mhór an fhadhb sin a réiteach. Ba in an fáth ar tugadh faoi staidéar oibiachtúil náisiúnta a dhéanamh ar chaighdeán na Gaeilge labhartha sa bhunscoil. Cumadh trialacha i gcomhar leis an Roinn Oideachais a chuir ar chumas na dtaighdeoirí caighdeán labhartha na teanga go mór mór a mheas (Harris 1984a ┐ b). Táthar ag tógáil ar an mbonn seo ó shin (féach mar shampla Harris ┐ Murtagh 1987, 1988), agus tá na bealaí tástála á bhfeabhsú agus á bhforbairt i gcónaí.

Is díol suime go bhfuil staidéar dírbhreathnaithe déanta sa seomra ranga féachaint céard é díreach a tharlaíonn ann, cé na modhanna agus na straitéisí a mbaineann na múinteoirí leas astu, dearcadh agus spéis na ndaltaí agus a dtuismitheoirí maidir le teagasc na Gaeilge agus mar sin de (Harris ⁊ Murtagh 1996a ⁊ b).

Céim eile chun tosaigh is ea foilsiú na tuarascála *Cúrsaí Nua Gaeilge na Bunscoile: Moltaí agus Ábhar Samplach* 1 ⁊ 2 (Harris, Ó Néill, Uí Dhufaigh, Ó Súilleabháin 1996c ⁊ d). Is éard atá ann moltaí mar aon le neart samplaí praiticiúla a d'ullmhaigh Grúpa Oibre de chuid ITÉ don Chomhairle Náisiúnta Curaclaim agus Measúnachta (CNCM). Léiríonn an Tuarascáil na bealaí éagsúla inar féidir an cur chuige cumarsáideach a fheidhmiú sa seomra ranga. Ní call a rá gur mór an cúnamh an saothar seo do mhúinteoirí bunscoile agus d'fhoilsitheoirí téacsleabhar araon.

Taighde spéisiúil eile atá ar na bacáin is ea Tionscadal na Naíonraí ar cuspóir dó measúnú a dhéanamh ar thaithí na naíonraí. Tá sé i gceist freisin eolas a bhailiú faoi chumas teanga na dtuismitheoirí agus a ndearcadh ar na naíonraí, faoi mhodheolaíocht na stiúrthóirí agus thorthaí na tástála a rinneadh ar bhreis is dhá chéad leanbh (Hickey, le foilsiú).

NUATHEANGACHA

Sa bhliain 1976 a ceapadh an chéad chomhairleoir nuatheangacha, Delma Uí Cheallacháin, iarchigire a raibh obair cheannródaíochta déanta aici i réimse na nuatheangacha. Bhí léargas nua ag teacht chun cinn arbh é a chuspóir an cur chuige cumarsáideach a fheidhmiú i múineadh teangacha. Chuige sin ba ghá siollabas nua a shainmhíniú agus a leagan amach. Rinneadh teagmháil le lucht oiliúna múinteoirí nuatheangacha agus leis na múinteoirí féin. Tugadh le chéile iad ag dhá sheimineár a tionóladh faoi scáth ITÉ i 1977 agus arís i 1979 (Institiúid Teangeolaíochta Éireann 1977, 1979). Lean Nóra French, comharba Dhelma, agus ansin Joe Shiels, leis an obair seo, ar ndóigh.

Tharla go raibh méid áirithe taighde déanta ag Comhairle na hEorpa a bhain leis an gcur chuige cumarsáideach. Cé gurbh ar theagasc teanga d'aosaigh a bhí obair na Comhairle dírithe idir 1971 agus 1978, bhíothas den tuairim nár mhiste an Leibhéal Tairsí, mar a tugadh ar an tionscadal, a chur in oiriúint do na scoileanna (van Ek 1976, Porcher, Huart, Mariet 1980). Tosaíodh ar thurgnaimh phíolótacha sna ballstáit, agus chinn an Chomhairle ar ionadaithe agus saineolaithe ó na tíortha sin a thabhairt le chéile chun eolas agus taithí a mhalartú. Is ceart a lua freisin gurbh é tuairim mheáite na saineolaithe nach bhféadfaí an cur chuige nua a chur i bhfeidhm go dtí go mbeadh fáil ar na háiseanna teagaisc a bhí riachtanach chuige sin.

I dtús na bliana 1980, thug buíon speisialtóirí cuairt ar Bhaile Átha Cliath thar ceann na Comhairle (Council of Europe, Council for Cultural Co-operation 1980). Mar thoradh ar an gcuairt agus ar mholtaí na speisialtóirí, thacaigh an Chomhairle leis an obair a bhí ar siúl in Éirinn, agus naisceadh Tionscadal Nuatheangacha ITÉ le Tionscadal Nuatheangacha na Comhairle.

Thionóil lucht an Tionscadail seimineár in ITÉ ar 7 Meitheamh 1980. Pléadh agus aontaíodh scáilsiollabas inar tugadh le fios nár mhór siollabas tagartha leasaithe a chur ar fáil do na teangacha uile a thabharfadh treoir faoi soláthar áiseanna teagaisc le haghaidh scéim phíolótach an Tionscadail a bhí le tosú i bhfómhar na bliana 1981 (Little, Singleton, French, Sheils 1980). Leanadh ar aghaidh le sainmhíniú agus le dearadh siollabais, bunaithe ar an gcur chuige cumarsáideach (Ruane ┐ Singleton 1982, Sheils 1982a ┐ b, 1986). Tugadh tús áite don Fhraincis (arbh í an mhórtheanga iasachta ba mhó a bhí—agus atá—á teagasc in Éirinn). Tugadh grúpa múinteoirí le chéile a scaoileadh saor le cead na Roinne Oideachais chun a bheith rannpháirteach sa Tionscadal. Obair dheonach ar fad a rinne siad, faoi stiúir Joe Sheils agus Seán McDermott. D'fhoilsigh Comhlucht Oideachais na hÉireann an tsraith Salut! 1–3 (1983–5). D'fhoilsigh an Gúm eagráin Ghaeilge i gcomhar le Comhlucht Oideachais na hÉireann agus ITÉ. Ar na háiseanna teagaisc eile a ghin an Tionscadal bhí Wie geht's 1 ┐ 2 (1988 ┐ 1990) a sholáthair Siobhán Supple, Ciao, Anne Clark (ITÉ 1986–88) agus ¡A la Escucha!, ¡Qué suerte entender! agus ¡De Charla ..! Natuca Cordón (ITÉ 1990, 1989, 1982).

Ní miste a mheabhrú gur i gcomhar le dreamanna éagsúla a cuireadh obair an Tionscadail i gcrích. Le cois ITÉ bhí baill den CLCS lárnach inti mar aon le lucht tríú leibhéil agus na múinteoirí féin. Is fiú a lua freisin gur fhoilsigh Comhairle na hEorpa leabhar ó pheann Joe Sheils ina bhfuil cur síos ar mhodhanna agus ar bhealaí éagsúla leis an gcur chuige cumarsáideach a fheidhmiú sa seomra ranga (Sheils 1988).

Is iondúil go gcuireann foras taighde torthaí a chuid oibre ar fáil ina chuid foilseachán agus ní taise don Institiúid é. Bunaíodh an iris Teangeolas i 1975, mar ghléas eolais rialta faoina cuid oibre. Na baill foirne is mó a sholáthraíonn an t-ábhar, ach bíonn fáilte freisin roimh scríbhneoirí seachtracha ar mhaith leo cuntas a fhoilsiú faoina gcuid taighde ar ghnéithe den TF agus ar oideolaíocht na mbeotheangacha. I 1988 a tháinig an chéad uimhir de Language, Culture and Curriculum ar an bhfód. Iris idirnáisiúnta taighde í seo ina bpléitear ilteangachas, dátheangachas, cultúr agus teagasc teangacha, cúrsaí curaclaim agus ábhair ghaolmhara. Cuireadh tús chomh maith le Plean Taighde trí bliana a sholáthar ina bhfuil cuntas ar na tionscadail taighde atá ar siúl nó atá beartaithe (Institiúid Teangeolaíochta Éireann 1987, 1993).

Mar fhocal scoir, is mór is fiú an sliocht seo thíos le Mary Ruane a athléamh i bhfianaise a bhfuil ráite faoi bhláthú na TF i réimse na nuatheangacha in Éirinn:

> Co-operation between practitioners, the state and applied linguistics has also had a long and fruitful history in Ireland and I will end [...] by providing some encouraging examples of this co-operation. The first is the important role played by linguists and applied linguists in the debate on the teaching of foreign languages in the primary school at a time when there was extensive public pressure to have it introduced into that sector of the educational system (Harris 1991). Another example was the debate on the establishment of an interdisciplinary language awareness programme at school level in the Irish education system (Singleton 1992). Finally, Irish applied linguists in a variety of institutions have collaborated on an ongoing basis with the state and with language teachers to play a significant role in the renewal of foreign language syllabuses at all levels of the educational system (Ruane 1996).

MAR A THÁINIG ANN DO CHUMANN NA TEANGEOLAÍOCHTA FEIDHMÍ

Cuntas mion go leor a thugtar anseo thíos ar an gCumann de bharr an tacaíocht a thug an tOllamh Ó Cléirigh dó ó thús le linn dó a bheith ag feidhmiú mar Chathaoirleach ITÉ (Cumann na Teangeolaíochta Feidhmí 1975, 1976).

Tharla gur eagraigh an t-eagras teanga idirnáisiúnta, Association de Linguistique Appliquée (AILA) tionól i gCópanhávan i 1972. Bhí Kathleen Tierney ag plé le nuatheangacha i gColáiste Teicneolaíochta Shráid Chaoimhín, a bhí á riar ag Coiste Gairmoideachais Chathair Átha Cliath, ó 1964 i leith. Bhí sí i gceannas ar Roinn na dTeangacha sa Choláiste. D'fhreastail sí ar an tionól; ba í an t-aon ionadaí as Éirinn a bhí i láthair. Casadh teangeolaithe cáiliúla uirthi ar nós S.P. Corder, M.A.K. Halliday agus an Sualannach, Dr Max Gorosch, rúnaí feidhmitheach AILA. Ba léir go mb'fhiú comhcheangal a bhunú idir lucht teanga in Éirinn agus AILA. Mhol Gorosch mar chéad chéim go mbunófaí craobh den eagras idirnáisiúnta in Éirinn agus go lorgfaí comhcheangal. Luadh Institiúid Teangeolaíochta Éireann (ITÉ) mar eagras feiliúnach chuige sin.

Nuair a d'fhill Kathleen Tierney abhaile, phlé sí an scéal le cúpla duine, ina measc Tomás Ó Domhnalláin, Stiúrthóir Gníomhach ITÉ, Seán Mac Íomhair, ball de Choiste Feidhmiúcháin ITÉ, agus Delma Uí Cheallacháin, iarchigire nuatheangacha sa Roinn Oideachais a bhí ag múineadh i Sráid Chaoimhín. Ní feasach go díreach cé a leag an scéal faoi bhráid Choiste

ITÉ. Is léir gur pléadh an scéal roimh ré leis an gCathaoirleach, Conn R. Ó Cléirigh, Ollamh le Teangeolaíocht Theoiriciúil i gColáiste na hOllscoile, Baile Átha Cliath, a thug lántacaíocht don tionscnamh. Thagair sé don ghnó ag cruinniú an Choiste Feidhmiúcháin a tionóladh ar 22 Márta 1973. Dúirt sé go mba mhaith le hAILA craobh a bhunú i mBaile Átha Cliath, '[...] and approaches had been made to him to have ITÉ sponsor the setting up of this branch'. Socraíodh go rachadh an Cathaoirleach i gcomhar le daoine eile chun an chraobh a bhunú. Thagair sé arís don ghnó ag an 10ú cruinniú den Choiste Feidhmiúcháin ar 15 Márta 1974. Thairg Seán Mac Íomhair liosta daoine a bhí ag saothrú cheana féin i réimse na dteangacha a chur ar fáil, rud a rinne sé. Bhain siad den chuid is mó le forais tríú leibhéil ar fud na tíre mar aon le forais eile ar nós an Choláiste Teiripe Teanga, Roinn na Seirbhíse Poiblí, an Roinn Oideachais, *A.V.Teaching Centre*,agus, ar ndóigh, ITÉ féin.

Ar 10 Feabhra 1975 sheol Rúnaí ITÉ, Carmel Ní Mhuircheartaigh, cuireadh chuig daoine a raibh baint acu le cúrsaí teanga teacht chuig cruinniú chun bunú craobh d'AILA a phlé. Is éard a dúradh sa litir:

> Tá roinnt daoine ar spéis leo brainse den AILA (Association Internationale de Linguistique Appliquée) a bhunú sa tír seo tar éis a iarraidh ar an Institiúid saoráidí a chur ar fáil chun cruinniú a thionól d'fhonn go bhféadfaí socruithe a phlé maidir le brainse Éireannach den Chumann a bhunú agus é a chomhcheangal leis an gcumann idirnáisiúnta. Séard a bheadh i gceist sa chruinniú tosaigh seo ná scata beag daoine a bhfuil spéis acu sa ghnó a thabhairt le chéile chun cibé socruithe ar cheart a dhéanamh maidir lena leithéid de bhrainse a chur ar siúl anseo a phlé. Má bhunaítear brainse den chumann dá réir sin, ba ghnó dó ansin a chuid imeachtaí féin a riaradh agus a reáchtáil faoi mar ba thoil leis na baill féin.
>
> Tá áthas orm mar sin cuireadh a thabhairt duit teacht chun cruinnithe a bheas ar siúl in oifigí na hInstitiúide, 31 Plás Mhic Liam, ar an Aoine, 21 Feabhra 1975, ar 3.00 p.m.

Tionóladh an cruinniú agus bhí na daoine seo a leanas i láthair: an tOllamh Ó Cléirigh (Cathaoirleach), Seán Mac Íomhair, Stiúrthóir na Teanglainne, Coláiste na hOllscoile, Gaillimh, Clíona Mhic Mhathúna (Roinn na Gearmáinise, Coláiste na hOllscoile, Baile Átha Cliath), an Dr Dónall Ó Baoill (ITÉ), Tomás Ó Domhnalláin (Stiúrthóir ITÉ), an tOllamh Máirtín Ó Murchú (Coláiste na Trionóide), Gearóid Ó Súilleabháin (Príomhchigire sa Roinn Oideachais) agus an Dr Barbara Wright (Ollamh le Litríocht na Fraincise, Coláiste na Tríonóide). Fuarthas leithscéal uathu seo a leanas: an tOllamh Tomás de Bhaldraithe, Muiris Bodhlaeir, an tOllamh F.M. Higman

(Coláiste na Tríonóide), an tAthair Fidélis Mac Éinrí (An Coláiste Teiripe Teanga) agus Kathleen Tierney. Carmel Ní Mhuircheartaigh a ghníomhaigh mar rúnaí.

D'eascair na pointí seo a leanas as an bplé:

Buntáiste a bhain le craobh den AILA a bhunú in Éirinn go mbeadh rochtain ag na baill ar imeachtaí AILA agus go mbeifí páirteach i malartú eolais le craobhacha eile de chuid an eagrais.

Bhain fadhb leis an sainmhíniú a thabharfaí ar an Teangeolaíocht Fheidhmeach. Dá mbeadh sé róchúng, ní bheadh ach líon beag daoine páirteach in imeachtaí na craoibhe, agus thiocfadh narbh fhiú craobh a bhunú in aon chor. Dá mbeadh sé leathan go leor le cúram a dhéanamh de riachtanais lucht teagaisc teanga, b'fhiú cinnte craobh a bhunú.

Feidhm amháin a luadh leis an gcraobh ná pátrúnacht a dhéanamh ar thionóil a thabharfadh fóram dóibh siúd a bhí ag saothrú i réimse na TF. Léireodh tionóil dá leithéid líon na ndaoine ar spéis leo an t-ábhar agus a bhí gafa leis.

Cinneadh ar chraobh d' AILA a bhunú. Tuigeadh nár bhain a raibh i láthair le gach gné den TF, agus nár mhór dá bhrí sin teagmháil a dhéanamh le gach dream a bhí gníomhach i gcúrsaí teanga. Níor mhór chuige sin liosta uileghabhálach a thiomsú. Thabharfaí cuireadh do na daoine a bhí liostaithe bheith i láthair ag cruinniú tionscnaimh Chumann na Teangeolaíochta Feidhmí (Irish Association for Applied Linguistics) nó IRAAL mar a thugtar air go hiondúil. Ar Sheán Mac Íomhair agus ar Chlíona Mhic Mhathúna a leagadh cúram an liosta a ullmhú agus ina theannta sin, iarradh orthu dréachtbhunreacht nó bróisiúr eolais faoin chraobh a scríobh agus cóipeanna díobh a sheoladh chuig a raibh i láthair ag cruinniú an lae sin.

Ar 20 Meitheamh 1975 sheol Carmel Ní Mhuircheartaigh an litir seo a leanas chuig na daoine a liostaigh Seán Mac Íomhair agus Clíona Mhic Mhathúna. Leis na hollscoileanna agus na coláistí oideachais is mó a bhain na daoine seo, ach bhí ionadaithe ón Roinn Oideachais, Roinn na Seirbhíse Poiblí, Coláiste Shráid Chaoimhín, An Coláiste Teiripe Teanga agus ITÉ féin ina measc. Chuir an litir aidhm an chuiridh in iúl go hachomair:

AILA—Craobh Éireannach a bhunú

A Chara,

D'iarr roinnt daoine ar spéis leo craobh d'AILA (Association Internationale de Linguistique Appliquée) a bhunú sa tír seo, d'iarr siad ar an Institiúid seo saoráidí a chur ar fáil do réamhchruinniú beag chun go bhféadfaí an cheist a phlé.

Cuireadh cruinniú dá réir sin ar siúl i mí Feabhra seo caite agus aontaíodh i bprionsabal go mba cheart craobh d'AILA a chur ar bun sa tír seo. Socraíodh go n-ullmhódh cuid de na daoine a bhí i láthair dréacht bhunreachta (sic) don chraobh agus go gcuirfidís liosta ar fáil, chomh fada agus ab' fhéidir, de na daoine atá ag obair sa réimse seo, ionas go bhféadfaí scéala a chur chucu faoin ghnó. D'aontaigh an Institiúid seo a bheith freagrach as an obair rúnaíochta agus as cóiríocht/saoráidí a chur ar fáil don chraobh.

Tá dréacht bhunreachta (sic) curtha ar fáil agus tá cóip istigh leis seo mar eolas. Istigh leis seo freisin tá doiciméad eolais mar gheall ar an gCumann Idirnáisiúnta.

Moladh go dtionólfaí cruinniú bunaidh chomh luath agus is féidir chun Cumann na Teangeolaíochta Feidhmí a chur ar bun go foirmiúil. Is áthas liom, mar sin, cuireadh a thabhairt duit teacht go dtí an cruinniú sin a thionólfar in áras na hInstitiúide seo, 31 Plás Mhic Liam, Dé Luain, 7 Iúil 1975 ar 7.30 p.m.

Tionóladh an cruinniú tionscnaimh ar 7 Iúil in ITÉ. I láthair bhí Kathleen Tierney, Dearbhal Ní Chárthaigh (NCPE An Coláiste Náisiúnta Corpoideachais), an Dr Barbara Wright, Seán Mac Íomhair, Clíona Mhic Mhathúna, Terence J. Moran, An Foras um Ardoideachas, Luimneach, an Dr Dónall Ó Baoill, Tomás Ó Domhnalláin, Donncha Ó Laoire (Roinn Oideachais), Adèle Mac Avock (Ionad Oiliúna na Seirbhíse Poiblí), an tOllamh Ó Cléirigh, agus Peadar Mac an Iomaire, Coláiste na hOllscoile, Gaillimh.

Cinneadh ar iarratas ar chomhcheangal le hAILA a sheoladh chuig Rúnaí Ginearálta an eagrais sin, an tOllamh Bertil Malmberg, maille le cóip den dréachtbhunreacht agus ainmneacha bhall choiste na Craoibhe nua.

Ar an 15 Iúil a seoladh an t-iarratas agus é sínithe ag Seán Mac Íomhair ina cháilíocht mar Chathaoirleach na Craoibhe. Seo thíos an litir:

At a meeting on 7 July 1975, the Irish Association for Applied Linguistics agreed to seek affiliation with full active membership to l'Association Internationale de Linguistique Appliquée.

The Linguistic Institute of Ireland has agreed to provide secretarial services and facilities for the Association at its headquarters, 31 Fitzwilliam Place, Dublin 2.

I enclose a list of names of the members of the Committee and a copy of the constitution of this recently formed Association and request that the application for affiliation to AILA be considered.

Ba iad baill an Choiste:

An tUachtarán: Seán Mac Íomhair, Stiúrthóir na Teanglainne, Coláiste na hOllscoile, Gaillimh;

Rúnaí Feidhmeach: Kathleen Tierney, Roinn na dTeangacha, An Coláiste Teicneolaíochta, Sráid Chaoimhín, Baile Átha Cliath

Rúnaí Comhfhreagrais: Carmel Ní Mhuircheartaigh, Rúnaí ITÉ

Cisteoir: Terence J. Moran, Ceann Roinn na Rúise, An Foras Náisiúnta um Ardoideachas, Luimneach

Gnáthbhaill: Clíona Mhic Mhathúna, Roinn na Gearmáinise, Coláiste na hOllscoile, Baile Átha Cliath, An Dr Dónall Ó Baoill, Oifigeach Taighde, ITÉ, An Dr Barbara Wright, Ollamh le Litríocht na Fraincise, Coláiste na Tríonóide, Baile Átha Cliath

Mhol Coiste IRAAL d'aon ghuth go gcomhthoghfaí an tOllamh Máirtín Ó Murchú, Ollamh le Gaeilge i gColáiste na Tríonóide, mar bhall den Choiste. Seoladh litir chuige faoi dháta 10 Meán Fómhair ag fiafraí de an mbeadh sé toilteanach a bheith mar bhall comhthofa. Freagra dearfa a fuarthas uaidh agus comhthoghadh d'aon ghuth é.

Tairgeadh ballraíocht institiúideach do ITÉ ar 1 Nollaig 1975. D'fhág sé sin go raibh 27 gnáthbhall, ball amháin comhthofa agus ball institiúideach amháin sa Chumann faoi dheireadh na bliana 1975. Tionóladh an chéad chruinniú bliantúil in Ionad na Múinteoirí, Droim Conrach, ar 28 Meán Fómhair 1976.

Leagadh iarratas IRAAL ar chomhcheangal le hAILA faoi bhráid chruinniú de choiste idirnáisiúnta an eagrais sin in Pisa, in Eanáir 1976. Fuair Seán Mac Íomhair scéala i litir faoi dháta 30 Eanáir ón Ollamh G. Nickel, Rúnaí Feidhmeach AILA, gur glacadh le hiarratas IRAAL (Cumann na Teangeolaíochta Feidhmí 1975–). Chinntigh an gníomh úd go raibh aitheantas idirnáisiúnta gnóthaithe ag an gCumann úr.

IMEACHTAÍ IRAAL

Ní raibh moill ar an gCumann imeachtaí a reáchtáil dá chuid ball. An chéad léacht a eagraíodh ná caint a thug an Dr Carl James, Roinn na Teangeolaíochta, Coláiste Ollscoile Thuaisceart na Breataine Bige, ar anailís earráidí, ábhar a raibh saineolas aige air. Ar 2 Deireadh Fómhair 1975 a tugadh an léacht, 'The Conduct of Error Analysis' faoi choimirce ITÉ agus IRAAL. Chuir an tOllamh Ó Cléirigh Seomra an Bhoird i gColáiste na hOllscoile, Ardán Phort an Iarla, ar fáil don ócáid. D'fhreastail trí scór nó mar sin ar an léacht.

Socraíodh seimineár ar an fhoghraíocht feabhais i dteagasc an dara teanga a reáchtáil faoi Cháisc 1976. Léacht ghinearálta a chuirfeadh tús leis na himeachtaí. Ansin roinnfí an lucht éisteachta i ngrúpaí oibre de réir teanga. Beartaíodh go dtabharfadh gach grúpa tuairisc ar na torthaí ag deireadh an lae ag seisiún ginearálta. Roghnaíodh na topaicí seo a leanas i gcás na nuatheangacha:

1. teoiric, teicnící agus teagasc an aistriúcháin sna cúrsaí Fraincise tríú leibhéil, agus leagfaí béim ar leith ar chúrsaí stílíochta;
2. teagasc na Gaeilge mar dhara teanga agus fadhbanna an dátheangachais;
3. anailís chontrárach an Bhéarla agus na Gearmáinise;
4. teanga sainchuspóirí: teicneoirí agus eolaithe i mbun foghlaim an dara teanga;
5. anailís earráidí foghlaimeoirí ardleibhéil sa bhFraincis.

D'éirigh thar barr leis an seimineár. Ba é R.B. Walsh (Risteárd B. Breatnach), Coláiste na hOllscoile, Baile Átha Cliath a thug an léacht tionscnaimh, 'Difficulties encountered by Hiberno- English speakers in using the sound systems of Irish and French', ar 24 Aibreán 1976 sa Choláiste (Cumann na Teangeolaíochta Feidhmí 1975 ar aghaidh).

Tionóladh an chéad seimineár bliantúil i gColáiste na Tríonóide i mí an Mhárta 1978 (Mac Íomhair 1978). Trí chuid a bhí ar an gclár:

1. Príomhléachtaí,
2. Múineadh agus foghlaim teangacha,
3. Teangeolaíocht feabhais

Is díol spéise gur ar an ócáid seo a pléadh sealbhú na Gaeilge mar chéad teanga don chéad uair riamh i gcomhluadar léannta (Mac Mathúna 1979). Ba mhór ab fhiú freisin an t-aitheantas a tugadh don teangeolaíocht feabhais, réimse fíorthábhachtach ó thaobh oideachais agus leighis.

Ón am seo i leith feictear patrún úr ag teacht chun cinn in imeachtaí IRAAL, is é sin, eagrú seimineár dhá uair sa bhliain agus na léachtaí á bhfoilsiú in iris an Chumainn, *Teanga*. Cuireadh an chéad imleabhar ar fáil i 1979 inar foilsíodh léachtaí an chéad seimineáir. Foilsíodh tuilleadh léachtaí de chuid an tseimineáir chéanna agus seimineár 1980 agus 1981 sa dara agus sa tríú himleabhar (1981). Ar na téamaí a bhí faoi chaibidil sna seimineáir seo i gcaitheamh na mblianta bhí teangeolaíocht fheidhmeach, oideachas sa mháthairtheanga, foclóireacht agus téarmaíocht, Gaeilge mar chéad teanga.

Cé gur ábhar bunaithe ar na seimineáir a bhí in *Teanga* sna blianta tosaigh, leathnaíodh scóip na hirise de réir a chéile. Tosaíodh ar ailt a fhoilsiú ar ghnéithe éagsúla den TF, gnéithe a d'eascair as spéis na mball aonair. Foilsíodh imeachtaí comhdhálacha i bhfoirm monagraf ar leith chomh maith (Ó Baoill, eag. 1992a). Ní dhearnadh faillí i mBéarla na hÉireann ach oiread (Ó Baoill, eag. 1985). Beart eile fós a rinne an Cumann ná seimineáir do lucht iarchéime a reáchtáil faoi stiúir saineolaithe aitheanta. Orthu sin bhí an Dr J. McCloskey (Séimeantaic, 18–19 Aibreán 1986), Dr Rose Maclaren (Pragmataic, 4 Aibreán 1987), Dr J.L. Kallen (Comhréir, 5 Samhain 1988). Ina theannta sin tugtar cuireadh do theangeolaithe aitheanta léacht a thabhairt do bhaill an Chumainn. Orthu sin áirítear Rod Ellis, Annette Karmiloff-Smith, Máire Ní Chiosáin, Miriam Broderick, Dónall Ó Baoill, Joe Sheils agus daoine eile nach iad.

I 1985 a tháinig *Teanglitir* ar an bhfód, nuachtlitir an Chumainn a sholáthraíonn eolas 'ar imeachtaí an chumainn féin agus ar aon imeachtaí eile a bhaineann le cúrsaí na Teangeolaíochta Feidhmí in Éirinn agus in áiteanna eile'.

Mórócáid i stair IRAAL ba ea an mhórchomhdháil idirnáisiúnta 'Language, Education and Society in a Changing World' a tionóladh le linn do Tina Hickey (ITÉ) a bheith ina huachtarán. I gColáiste Oideachais Marino a tionóladh an Chomhdháil 23–25 Meitheamh 1994. D'fhreastail taighdeoirí as gach cearn den domhan uirthi. Bhí neart ann as Éirinn freisin (féach liosta na bpáirtithe in *Teanglitir*, 20, 1994). D'éirigh thar barr leis an gcomhdháil agus ní háibhéil a rá gur chuir an ócáid le cáil IRAAL thar lear. Foilsíodh cuid de na léachtaí in *Teanga* 15 1995, agus tá leabhar bunaithe ar imeachtaí na comhdhála ar fáil (Hickey ⁊ Williams 1996).

Níl aon amhras ná go ndeachaigh bunú IRAAL go mór chun tairbhe d' fhorbairt na TF sa tír seo. Tugadh fóram do lucht teanga agus do theangeolaithe araon ina dtiocfadh leo gach gné den TF a phlé agus torthaí a gcuid taighde a chur i gcló. Tá 'fiche bliain ag fás' curtha de ag an gCumann faoin am seo, agus tá gach cosúlacht air go bhfuil saol fada bisiúil i ndán dó sna blianta romhainn amach.

COLÁISTE NA TRÍONÓIDE: CENTRE FOR LANGUAGE AND COMMUNICATION STUDIES

Tharla rud nó dhó i gcaitheamh na seachtóidí a chabhraigh go mór le cur chun cinn na TF i mBaile Átha Cliath. Ba é an chéad rud gur bheartaigh údaráis Choláiste na Tríonóide foirgneamh nua a thógáil do Dhámh na nEalaíon. Socraíodh agus an foirgneamh á leagan amach go gcuirfí foras nua isteach ann a dhéanfadh freastal ar an TF. Ba é D.G. Little, Roinn na Gearmáinise, a chéadsmaoinigh ar a leithéid. Chomh maith leis sin, bhí ITÉ agus IRAAL ar an bhfód cheana féin agus bhí go leor daoine ag cur spéise i réimse nua seo na TF. Tharla ag an am céanna go raibh moltaí maidir le forbairtí nua a d'fhéadfaí a thionscnamh á lorg ag an Údarás um Ard-Oideachas ó na hollscoileanna. Theastaigh ón Údarás teicneolaíocht agus forbairt acadúil a mhaoiniú. Ba éard a bhí ó Little ionad a bhunú ina mbeadh rudaí eile chomh maith le teicneolaíocht, .i. taighde sa teangeolaíocht fheidhmeach mar bhun leis an teicneolaíocht. Osclaíodh Foirgneamh na nEalaíon i 1978, agus bhí an t-ionad nua mar chuid de. Tugadh *Centre for Language and Communication Studies* (CLCS) air, ainm a thug le fios gur ábhair nua agus dearcadh nua a bheadh in uachtar ann. D'fheidhmigh Little mar Stiúrthóir Gníomhach go dtí gur ceapadh ina Stiúrthóir i 1979 é. Tugadh ansin faoi thaighde a dhéanamh sular tosaíodh ar theagasc. Ar an gcaoi sin téann an taighde chun fónaimh do theagasc teangacha mar a bhí beartaithe ón tús.

Seo a leanas feidhmeanna an CLCS :

1. cúnamh teicniúil a chur ar fáil do theagasc agus d' fhoghlaim teanga;
2. taighde a dhéanamh sa teangeolaíocht theoiriciúil agus sa teangeolaíocht fheidhmeach;
3. ról múinteoireachta a fhorbairt (University of Dublin, Trinity College, 1995).

Eagraíodh na cúrsaí acadúla seo a leanas:

Dioplóma Iarchéime sa Teangeolaíocht Fheidhmeach agus i dTeagasc Teanga (1982);
Dioplóma Iarchéime sa Teangeolaíocht (1983).

Sa bhliain 1986 cuireadh M.Phil. sa Teangeolaíocht Fheidhmeach agus M.Phil. sa Teangeolaíocht in áit an dá chúrsa dioplóma.

Fadhb amháin nár mhór a réiteach ba ea gan fáil a bheith ar dheiseanna foilsithe in Éirinn ag teangeolaithe. Cinneadh dá bhrí sin ar an gcúram a chur ar an CLCS . Foilsíodh an chéad pháipéar sa tsraith *CLCS Occasional Papers* i 1981: *Language Transfer: a Review of Some Recent Research* (Singleton). Cuireadh breis is dhá scór ar fáil go dtí seo, éacht nach beag. Ghnóthaigh an tsraith seo cáil idirnáisiúnta don CLCS .

Foilsíodh dhá thuarascáil ar chúrsaí siollabais a bhain leis an nGaeilge. Taighde ar shiollabas a d'fheilfeadh don fhoghlaimeoir fásta a bhí sa chéad cheann (Little, Ó Murchú, Singleton 1985). Siollabas le haghaidh chúrsa chun críche cumarsáide a bhí ann agus é bunaithe ar a raibh déanta cheana féin ar shainmhíniú siollabais ag Tionscadal Nuatheangacha Chomhairle na hEorpa agus agus ar thaithí na n-údar a bhí páirteach i dTionscadal Nuatheangacha ITÉ. Bhain an dara tuarascáil le hobair a bhí ar siúl ar phleanáil struchtúir ar a mbunófaí cúrsaí agus modhanna nua teagaisc a mbeadh an cur chuige cumarsáideach mar chuid dhílis díobh. Dhá chuid atá sa tuarascáil: tugtar eolas faoin gcur chuige cumarsáideach i gCuid 1, agus soláthraítear siollabas cumarsáideach samplach i gcuid 2 (Little, Ó Murchú, Singleton 1986) atá bunaithe ar an taighde a rinneadh ar shiollabas an fhoghlaimeora fásta.

Maidir le mic léinn iarchéime, is iondúil go mbíonn trí dhosaen nó thart air i mbun staidéir agus seisear díobh sin ón iasacht. Bíonn scór eile i mbun dochtúireachta, agus ceathrar nó cúigear díobh ó thíortha thar lear.

FORAIS EILE

Nuair a bunaíodh an dá Fhoras Náisiúnta um Ard-Oideachas i Luimneach i 1972 agus i mBaile Átha Cliath i 1975, tógadh céim eile chun cinn i bhfoghlaim agus i dteagasc nuatheangacha. Cur chuige feidhmeach a bhí in uachtar sna forais nua ón tús. Ní hiontas mar sin gur béimníodh an úsáid a bhainfí as na teangacha féin seachas staidéar ar an litríocht, arbh é gnáthnós na Ranna Teanga sa chuid ba mhó de na forais tríú leibhéil. Rud eile, thiocfadh leis na mic léinn staidéar ar nuatheangacha a nascadh le staidéar ar ábhar praiticiúil—gnó nó margaíocht nó a leithéidí. Tá stádas ollscoile ag an dá fhoras ó 1989, agus fás agus forbairt dá réir tagtha ar an obair atá ar siúl acu i réimse na nuatheangacha. Ní mór a lua freisin go bhfuil cúrsa MA sa Teangeolaíocht Fheidhmeach ar chlár acadúil Choláiste na hOll-scoile, Corcaigh, le tamall anuas.

Ní dhearna Acadamh Ríoga na hÉireann faillí i ngnó na nuatheangacha ach an oiread. Bunaíodh an *National Committee for Modern Language Studies* sa bhliain 1968. Tionóladh an chéad chruinniú i dtús 1969. Ceisteanna a bhaineann leis na nuatheangacha sna forais tríú leibhéil is cúram don choiste. Thionól an Coiste an chéad siompóisiam taighde dá chuid (Research Symposium) in Eanáir 1975. D'éirigh chomh maith sin leis gur socraíodh go n-eagrófaí a leithéid gach uile bhliain. Bunaíodh fochoiste, *National Commission for the Teaching of Modern Languages* i 1970 chun déileáil le nuatheangacha sna forais dara leibhéil agus chun gléas cumarsáide a bhunú idir múinteoirí nuatheangacha agus an Coiste Náisiúnta.

Ar an taighde a d'fhoilsigh an tAcadamh, níor mhiste tagairt go speisialta don dá shuirbhé a rinneadh 1) ar scéim mhalartaithe scoileanna dara leibhéil sa tír seo le scoileanna thar lear (Ruane 1987), agus 2) ar an soláthar a dhéantar do theangacha iasachta san iar-bhunscolaíocht in Éirinn (Ruane 1990), ina scrúdaítear an míchothrom atá le sonrú sa réimse seo ó thaobh soláthair, éilimh agus rochtana. Léirítear freisin na himpleachtaí a eascraíonn as an bhfianaise seo do lucht polasaí agus pleanála san oideachas. Foilsíodh tuairisc freisin ar theagasc agus ar fhoghlaim teangacha chun críche gairmiúla, réimse tábhachtach don fhoghlaimeoir fásta (Broderick 1994).

Foras taighde reachtúil is ea Institiúid Ardléinn Bhaile Átha Cliath a bhunaigh an Taoiseach, Éamon de Valera, i 1940 (Ó Murchú 1990). Ba chuid den Institiúid Scoil an Léinn Cheiltigh, agus ba é an príomhchúram a leagadh uirthi an Léann Ceilteach a chur chun cinn, go háirithe léann na Gaeilge agus oiliúint lucht taighde chuige sin. Cé nach TF sa ghnáthchiall a bhí agus atá ar bun sa Scoil, ní hin le rá nach bhfuil obair fhónta déanta aici a chuaigh chun tairbhe don TF. Is leor na tuairiscí a scríobhadh ar chanúintí na Gaeilge idir 1944 agus 1975 a lua, arbh é an mórshaothar *Linguistic Atlas and Survey of Irish Dialects* (Wagner 1958, 1964, 1966, 1969) a mbuaic. Réimsí eile den TF a d'fhreastail an Scoil orthu is ea áiseanna teagaisc (Ó Siadhail 1980) agus téarmaíocht/foclóireacht (Ó Siadhail 1978).

An Teangeolaíocht Fheidhmeach i dTuaisceart Éireann

Taighde ar chanúintí Béarla oirthear Uladh is mó a bhí ar siúl ón tréimhse iarchogaidh i leith, agus é sin faoi thionchar G. B. Adams (1948, 1962, 1980, 1986). D'eagraigh sé suirbhé canúnach an *Belfast Naturalists' Club* agus bhí eolas ar na canúintí á bhailiú aige chomh fada siar le 1951. Nuair a bunaíodh an *Ulster Folk Museum* aistríodh an t-ábhar uile isteach ann. Sin mar a bunaíodh Cartlann Chanúna Chúige Uladh.

Cés moite de Bertz (1975), is beag a bhfuil déanta ar chanúintí uirbeacha sna Sé Chontae Fichead. Ní hamhlaidh atá sna Sé Chontae. Cuireadh tús le staidéar ar chanúintí Bhéal Feirste i 1975 le cabhair dheontais ón *Social Science Research Council* le haghaidh an tionscadail 'Speech Community and Language Variation in Belfast'. Ba iad James agus Lesley Milroy mar aon le Rose Maclaren, a bhí ina bhun. Foilsíodh an toradh san *Belfast Working Papers in Language ⁊ Linguistics*. Idir 1976 agus 1982 foilsíodh go leor alt spéisiúil ar Bhéarla Uladh. Cuireadh le téamaí na hirise ó 1985 i leith agus pléitear gnéithe eile den TF inti anois chomh maith le cúrsaí canúna.

Bhí taighde teangeolaíochta ar siúl in Ollscoil Nua Uladh (Ollscoil Uladh anois) sna seachtóidí chomh maith. Ba é *Occasional Papers in Linguistics & Language Learning* gléas foilsithe na dtaighdeoirí ó 1976 go dtí 1986. Is trua nár foilsíodh aon uimhir eile ó shin go bhfios dúinn.

Nuair a chuaigh an tAthair Ó Huallacháin chun oibre in Ollscoil Nua Uladh, Cúil Raithin, leagadh cúram theagasc na Gaeilge air. Béarlóirí ar fad a bhí á dteagasc aige. Spreag an taithí a fuair sé sa seomra ranga é chun leabhar tagartha a thiomsú a chabhródh le mic léinn a raibh bunGhaeilge sealbhaithe acu a gcuid earráidí a cheartú nó a sheachaint. Bailíodh corpas mór earráidí de chuid na mac léinn agus rinneadh anailís orthu. Bunaíodh an graiméar ar thorthaí na hanailíse. Seo a leanas sainmhíniú na n-údar féin i mbrollach an tríú eagráin dá saothar 'Is é earra atá ann córas deachúil ceartaitheach ar earráidí foghlaimeoirí faoina ndéanann an teagascóir Gaeilge an foghlaimeoir le Béarla a threorú ó earráidí ina chuid aistí, le go ndéanfaidh sé sin a cheartú é féin ón lámhleabhar.' (Ó Huallacháin ┐ Ó Murchú 1981).

Buíon eile a bhí ina sea sa tréimhse chéanna ba ea an *Northern Ireland Speech Language Forum*. Gnéithe de theiripe teanga is mó a bhíodh faoi chaibidil san Fhóram. Cnuasach páipéar a léadh ag cruinniú a tionóladh ar 30 Aibreán 1975 san *Belfast Hospital for Sick Children* a bhí sa chéad uimhir den iris *Northern Ireland Speech Language Forum Journal*. Is iomaí sin gné den TF a pléadh inti sna blianta ina dhiaidh sin, ina measc teagasc teanga, canúintí Béarla Uladh agus dearcadh an phobail orthu. Cuireadh deireadh leis an bhFóram in Aibreán 1987.

Maidir le scéal na nuatheangacha (an Ghaeilge san áireamh) sa chóras oideachais, tá taighde déanta agus eolas curtha ar fáil faoi phleanáil agus fheidhmiú polasaí teanga an Stáit (Pritchard 1990, 1991, Andrews 1991, 1993) agus faoin nGaeilge i bpolasaí an BBC (Mac Póilín ┐ Andrews 1993). Chomh maith leis sin, bunaíodh an *Modern Language Association of Northern Ireland* i 1977. Foilsíodh an chéaduimhir dá n-iris, *NIMLA*, i 1978, ar chuspóir di feidhmiú mar 'forum for everyone concerned with the teaching and the study of modern languages—Irish, French, German, Spanish, Italian and Russian, in the province'.

FOCAL SCOIR

Chuir mé romham sa chuntas seo scéal na TF ó thús go dtí anois a ríomh. Is oth liom go bhfuil codanna den scéal a mb'éigean a fhágáil ar lár cheal spáis. Tugadh faoi deara, tá súil agam, gur faoi bhrat na TF seachas faoi bhrat stair na Gaeilge *per se* a tugadh faoi chuid na Gaeilge den scéal a insint. Ní háibhéil a rá gurbh í stair na Gaeilge stair na TF leis na céadta bliain. Ní hamhlaidh atá an lá atá inniu ann; i dteannta na Gaeilge ní mór ar a laghad an teangeolaíocht feabhais, teanga chomharthaíochta na mbodhar, na nuatheangacha atá á múineadh sa chóras oideachais agus, ar ndóigh, gnéithe de Bhéarla na hÉireann a chur san áireamh chomh maith.

Maidir leis an dá theanga atá in úsáid in Éirinn, b'fhiú breis taighde a dhéanamh ar an gcaoi a bhfuil siad á labhairt ag aicmí éagsúla i dtimpeallacht uirbeach agus i dtimpeallacht tuaithe. Tá sé thar am lorg Shéamais Moylan (1996) agus P.L. Henry (1957, 1958) a leanúint, agus caitheamh mar an gcéanna leis na canúintí uirbeacha.

Tuilleann teagasc an Bhéarla mar theanga iasachta méid áirithe airgid do mhuintir na tíre seo. Ach cén saghas Béarla a mhúintear—Béarla Bhaile Átha Cliath? Cé acu leagan? Nach bhfuil sé in am dearcadh an phobail ar na canúintí Béarla atá á labhairt in Éirinn a fhiosrú go heolaíoch?

I gcás na Gaeilge is fíor a rá go bhfuil taighde nach beag déanta ar chanúintí na Gaeltachta. Níor mhiste mar sin féin staidéar a dhéanamh ar chaint na Gaeltachta mar atá sí anois, mar atá déanta go sonrach ag Stenson ┐ Ó Ciardha (1986, 1987). Níor cheart faillí a dhéanamh i nGaeilge na cathrach ach oiread mar is iomaí cainteoir maith Gaeilge a bhfuil cónaí air/uirthi i gceantar uirbeach. Gabhann tábhacht faoi leith le taighde den chineál seo ar an ábhar go mbeadh tairbhe le baint as dá ndéanfaí athbhreith ar an gCaighdeán Oifigiúil   féachaint ar ghá é a leasú i bhfianaise na n-athruithe a tháinig ar an teanga bheo le tríocha éigin bliain anuas.[1]

TAGAIRTÍ

Adams, G.B. 1948. 'An Introduction to the Study of Ulster Dialects', *Proceedings of the Roya*l Irish *Adademy*, 52 C, 1–26

—1962. 'Cartlann Chanúna Chúige Uladh', *An tUltach*, 399, 6–7

—1980. 'Common Features in Ulster Irish and Ulster English', *Occasional Papers in Linguistics and Language Learning, New University of Ulster*, 7, 85–103

—1986. *The English Dialects of Ulster: an Anthology of Articles on Ulster Speech*, in eagar ag M. Barry ┐ P. Tilling, Holywood: Ulster Folk & Transport Museum

Ahlqvist, Anders 1980. 'Les Débuts de l'étude du langage en Irlande', in *Progress in Linguistic Historiography*, in eagar ag Konrad Koerner, Amsterdam: John Benjamins, 35–43

—1983.*The Early Irish Linguist: an Edition of the Canonical Part of the* Auraicept na nÉces, *with Introduction, Commentary and Indices*, Heilsincí: Societas Scientiarum Fennica (Commentationes Humanarum Litterarum, LXXIII)

—1984. 'Téarmaíocht Ghramadaí na Gaeilge', *Studia Hibernica*, 24, 89–96

—1994. 'Litriú na Gaeilge', caib. 1 in McCone et al. 1994

[1] Ba mhaith liom buíochas a ghabháil leo seo a leanas as a gcúnamh: Tomás Ó Domhnalláin, Iarstiúrthóir ITÉ, an tOllamh Tomás de Bhaldraithe nach maireann, An tOllamh Máirtín Ó Murchú, Dr D.G. Little, an Dr Éamonn Ó hÓgáin, Máire Ní Ící, an tSr Carmel Ní Mhuircheartaigh, Máire Seoighthe, Anne Smyth, Miriam Carolan, Caoimhín Ó Marcaigh, Antain Mag Shamhráin, Seán Mac Íomhair, an Dr Liam Mac Mathúna, John Trim, Joe Shiels agus le mo chomhleacaithe, an Dr Pádraig Ó Riagáin, an Dr John Harris agus an Dr T. Hickey.

Tá mé buíoch chomh maith den Dr Eoghan Mac Aogáin, Stiúrthóir ITÉ, agus den Dr Dónall Ó Baoill as a gcuid moltaí. Tá buíochas ar leith tuillte ag Kathleen Tierney a roinn a cuid eolais liom go fial faoi bhunú Chumann na Teangeolaíochta Feidhmí. Chabhraigh foirne na leabharlann seo a leanas liom chomh maith: An Leabharlann Náisiúnta, Acadamh Ríoga na hÉireann agus Scoil an Léinn Cheiltigh.

Tá mé faoi chomaoin mhór ag Órla Ní Chanainn a chuir cló agus cruth ar an iomlán. Liom féin aon mhíchruinneas nó easnamh atá sa saothar seo.

Andrews, Liam S. 1993. *The Irish Language in Northern Ireland: the Training of Primary and Post-Primary Teachers*, Ljouwert/Leeuwarden: Fryske Akademy

Ar Aghaidh Linn 1 ┐ 2: Gardaí i mbun Oibre 1995. Baile Átha Cliath: ITÉ ┐ Coláiste an Gharda

Bertz, Siegfried 1975. *Der Dubliner Stadtdialekt—eine synchronische Beschreibung der Struktur und Variabilität des heutigen Dubliner Englischen, Teil I, Phonologie*, Freiburg im Breisgau: Inaugural-Dissertation zur Erlangung der Doktorwürde der Philosophischen Fakultäten der Albert Ludwigs-Universität

An Bíobla Naofa, arna Aistriú ón mBuntéacs faoi threoir ó Easpaig na hÉireann maille le Réamhrá agus Brollaigh 1981. Maigh Nuad: An Sagart

Boylan, Henry 1988. *A Dictionary of Irish Biography*, 2 heagrán, Baile Átha Cliath: Gill ┐ Macmillan

Brainse Logainmneacha na Suirbhéireachta Ordanáis 1989. *Gasaitéar na hÉireann: Ainmneacha: Ionad Daonra agus Gnéithe Aiceanta*, Baile Átha Cliath: Oifig an tSoláthair

—1991. *Liostaí Logainmneacha*, Baile Átha Cliath: Oifig an tSoláthair

Breathnach, Colm 1993. 'Spléachadh ar Obair na Téarmaíochta', *Teangeolas*, 32, 17–24

Broderick, Miriam 1994. *Languages for Special Purposes*, Baile Átha Cliath: Royal Irish Academy

Bussmann, Hadumod 1996. *Routledge Dictionary of Language and Linguistics*, Londain: Routledge

Carney, James, eag. 1942–44. *Regimen na Sláinte*, Baile Átha Cliath: Oifig an tSoláthair

Coiste um Thaighde ar Dhearcadh an Phobail i dtaobh na Gaeilge/Committee on Language Attitudes Research 1975. *Tuarascáil arna Chur faoi Bhráid Aire na Gaeltachta/Report as Submitted to the Minister for the Gaeltacht*, [Baile Átha Cliath:] Oifig an tSoláthair

Comhchoiste Réamhscolaíochta ┐ Institiúid Teangeolaíochta Éireann 1985. *Basic Irish for Parents: a first Handbook in Irish for Parents with Children in Naíonraí or in Primary School. BunGhaeilge do Thuismitheoirí: an Chéad Lámhleabhar Teanga do Thuismitheoirí a bhfuil Páistí i Naíonraí nó sa Bhunscoil acu*, Baile Átha Cliath: ITÉ ┐ An Comhchoiste Réamhscolaíochta

Côté, Dominique et al. 1964. *Le Français: Écouter et Parler*, Baile Átha Cliath: Oifig an tSoláthair

Council of Europe Council for Cultural Co-operation 1980. *Modern Languages Project, School Sector. Intensive Visit organised by the Irish Authorities within the Framework of the Interaction Network in the School Sector of the Modern Language Project Dublin/Ireland, 31 January–2 February 1980*, Report by R. Bergentoff (CC-GPA), 8, Strasbourg

Crystal, David 1991. *A Dictionary of Linguistics and Phonetics*, 3ú eagrán, Oxford: Blackwell

Cumann na Teangeolaíochta Feidhmí 1975 ar aghaidh. *Miontuairiscí*

Daltún, Séamus 1965. 'Traduttore, Traditore', *An tUltach*, 423, 3–5

—1983. 'Scéal Rannóg an Aistriúcháin', *Teangeolas*, 17, 12–26

De Bhaldraithe, Tomás, eag. 1959. *English-Irish Dictionary*, Baile Átha Cliath: Oifig an tSoláthair

—1980. 'Foclóirí agus Foclóireacht na Gaeilge', *Maynooth Review*, 6.1, 3–15

—1983. 'Aisling an Duinnínigh', *Comhar*, 424, 16–25
—1987. 'An Pluincéadach—Ceannródaí Foclóireachta', *Teangeolas*, 22, 19–25
Dinneen, Patrick S. eag. *1927. Foclóir Gaedhilge agus Béarla: an Irish-English Dictionary, New Edition, Revised and Greatly Enlarged*, Baile Átha Cliath: Comhlucht Oideachais na Éireann do Chumann na Sgríbheann nGaedhilge
Van Ek, Jan A. 1976. *The Threshold Level for Modern Language Learning in Schools*, Strasbourg: Council of Europe; Londain: Longman, 1977
Gramadach na Gaeilge agus Litriú na Gaeilge: an Caighdeán Oifigiúil 1958. Baile Átha Cliath: Oifig an tSoláthair
An Gúm [1993]. *Catalóg Foclóirí/A Catalogue of Dictionaries*, Baile Átha Cliath
Harris, John 1982. 'Achievement in Spoken Irish at end of Primary School', *Irish Journal of Education*, 16, 85–116
—1984a. *An Ghaeilge Labhartha sna Bunscoileanna: Gearrthuairisc ar Thorthaí Taighde*, Baile Átha Cliath: ITÉ
—1984b. *Spoken Irish in Primary Schools: an Analysis of Achievement*, Baile Átha Cliath: ITÉ
—1991. 'Second and Foreign Languages in Primary Education: Issues and Research', cuid 1 in *Foreign Language Teaching in Primary Schools*, Baile Átha Cliath: I(rish) N(ational) T(eachers') O(rganisation)
Harris, John ⁊ Murtagh, Lelia 1987. 'Irish and English in Gaeltacht Primary Schools', caib. 7 in *Third International Conference on Minority Languages: Celtic Papers*, in eagar ag Gearóid Mac Eoin, Anders Ahlqvist, Donncha Ó hAodha, Clevedon: Multilingual Matters
—1988. 'National Assessment of Irish Language Speaking and Listening Skills in Primary School Children: Research Issues in the Evaluation of School-based Heritage Language Programmes', *Language, Culture & Curriculum*, 12, 85–130
—1996a. 'Topic and Language Activity in Teaching Irish at 6th Grade in Primary School: a Classroom Observation Study', caib. 22 in Hickey ⁊ Williams 1996
—1996b. *An In-Depth Study of the Teaching and Learning of Irish at Sixth Grade in Twenty Schools Nationally*, Baile Átha Cliath: ITÉ
Harris, John, Ó Néill, Pádraic, Uí Dhufaigh, Máire, Ó Súilleabháin, Eoghan 1996a. *Cúrsaí Nua Gaeilge na Bunscoile: Moltaí agus ábhar samplach, iml. 1: Naíonáin shóisearacha—Rang 2, Tuarascáil Ghrúpa Oibre ITÉ don Chomhairle Náisiúnta Curaclaim agus Measúnachta*, Baile Átha Cliath: ITÉ
—1996b. *Cúrsaí Nua Gaeilge na Bunscoile: Moltaí agus Ábhar Samplach, iml. 2, Rang 3–6* [...] Baile Átha Cliath: ITÉ
Henry, Patrick L. 1957. *An Anglo-Irish Dialect of North Roscommon*, Baile Átha Cliath: University College, Dublin
—1958. 'A Linguistic Survey of Ireland: Preliminary Report', *Lochlann*, 1, 49–208
Hickey, Tina ⁊ Williams, Jenny, eag. 1996. *Language, Education and Society in a Changing World*, Baile Átha Cliath ⁊ Clevedon: IRAAL ⁊ Multilingual Matters
Hickey, Tina le foilsiú. *Early Immersion in Ireland: the Naíonraí*, Baile Átha Cliath: ITÉ
Institiúid Teangeolaíochta Éireann 1977. *Seminar on Modern Language Syllabus Definition, 23–24 September 1977*, St. Patrick's College, Drumcondra, Baile Átha Cliath: ITÉ
—1979. *Seminar on Syllabus Definition 1979*, Baile Átha Cliath: ITÉ
—1986–1988. *Ciao!*, Baile Átha Cliath: ITÉ

—1987. *Plean Forbartha* 1988–92/Development Plan 1988-92, Baile Átha Cliath: ITÉ

—1989. *¡Que Suerte Entender!*, Baile Átha Cliath: ITÉ

—1990. *¡A la Escucha!*, Baile Átha Cliath: ITÉ

—1991. *Foilseacháin/Publications*, Baile Átha Cliath: ITÉ

—1992. *De Charla* [...], Baile Átha Cliath: ITÉ

—1993. *Plean Forbartha 1993–1997/Development Plan 1993–97*, Baile Átha Cliath: ITÉ

LaGrone, Gregory et al. 1968. *Español: Entender y Hablar*, Baile Átha Cliath: Oifig an tSoláthair; Nua-Eabhrac: Holt, Rinehart & Winston, 1961

Little, David, Singleton, David, French, Nóra, Sheils, Joe, eag. 1980. *Modern Languages Syllabus Project for Post-Primary Schools: Skeleton Syllabus Principles and Guidelines, eagrán leasaithe*, Baile Átha Cliath: ITÉ

Little, David, Ó Murchú, Helen, Singleton, David 1985. *A Functional-Notional Syllabus for Adult Learners of Irish*, Baile Átha Cliath: Trinity College CLCS

—1985. *Towards a Communicative Curriculum for Irish*, Baile Átha Cliath: Trinity College: CLCS

Little, David, Ó Meadhra, Bébhinn, Singleton, David, eag. 1986. *New Approaches in the Language Classroom: Coping with Change. Proceedings of the Second Natonal Modern Languages Convention held at Trinity College, Dublin, 31 January and 1 February 1986*, Baile Átha Cliath: Trinity College CLCS

Mac an Fhailghe, Pádraig 1903. *An Modh Réidh leis an nGaedhilge do Mhúineadh*, Baile Átha Cliath: An Cló-Chumann

[Mac Aogáin, Eoghan] 1996. 'ITÉ—The Linguistics Institute of Ireland', *ALTE News*, 42, 4–5

Mac Aogáin, Parthalán 1980. 'Gramadóirí Gaeilge ar fán san Eoraip', *An tUltach*, 57(7), 25–6

Mac Cionnaith, Láimhbheartach 1935. *Foclóir Béarla agus Gaedhilge: English-Irish Dictionary*, Baile Átha Cliath: Foilseacháin an Rialtais

McCone, Kim 1994. 'An tSean-Ghaeilge agus a Réamhstair', caib. 2 in *Stair na Gaeilge*, in McCone et al. 1994

McCone, Kim, McManus, Damian, Ó hÁinle, Cathal, Williams, Nicholas, Breatnach, Liam, eag. 1994. *Stair na Gaeilge in ómós do Phádraig Ó Fiannachta*, Maigh Nuad: Roinn na Sean-Ghaeilge, Coláiste Phádraig

Mac Ginley, Peter T. 1903. *Handbook of Irish Teaching*, Baile Átha Cliath: Connradh na Gaedhilge

Mac Íomhair, Seán 1978. 'IRAAL—Irish Association for Applied Linguistics', *AILA Bulletin*, 324, 44

McManus, Damian 1991. *A Guide to Ogam*, Maigh Nuad: An Sagart

Mac Mathúna, Seán ┐ Mac Gabhann, Risteard 1981. *Conradh na Gaeilge agus an tOideachas Aosach: Staidéar ar Theagasc na Gaeilge don Phobal Aosach i Ranganna Chonradh na Gaeilge i dtosach a Ré*, Indreabhán: Cló Chois Fharraige

Macnamara, John 1966. *Bilingualism and Primary Education: a Study of Irish Experience*, Dún Éidean: Edinburgh University Press

Mac Póilín, Aodán ┐ Andrews, Liam 1993. *BBC agus an Ghaeilge/BBC and the Irish Language*, Béal Feirste: An tIontaobhas Ultach/Ultach Trust

Matthews, Patrick A. 1996. *The Irish Deaf Community Survey Report: History of Education, Language and Culture*, Baile Átha Cliath: ITÉ

Moylan, Séamas 1996. *The Language of Kilkenny: Lexicon, Semantics, Structure*, Baile Átha Cliath: Geography Publications

Neilson, William 1808. *An Introduction to the Irish Language*, Baile Átha Cliath

Ní Dheirg, Íosold 1992. 'Glór gan Chabhair Choigcríche'? Smaointe ar Théarmaíocht na Gaeilge agus ar Ról na Nua-Iasachtaí', *Teangeolas*, 30/31, 12–15

Nic Mhaoláin, Máire 1985. 'Tuilleadh faoin gCaighdeán', *Teangeolas*, 20, 5–7

—1989. 'Téarmaí idir Mhín is Gharbh', *An tUltach*, 63, 11–14

—1994. 'Filíocht na Foclóireachta nó an Teanga Bhithnua', *An tUltach*, 71.11, 4–11

Northern Ireland. *Department of Health and Social Services/Registrar General, Northern Ireland 1993. The Northern Ireland Census 1991: Irish Language Report, Prepared Pursuant to Section 4(1) of the Census Act Northern Ireland*, Béal Feirste: HMSO

Ó Baoill, Dónall P. 1975. *Cleachtaí Foghraíochta*, Baile Átha Cliath: ITÉ

—1981. *Earráidí Scríofa Gaeilge: cuid 3, Réamhfhocail agus Comhréir: Earráidí a tharla in aistí Gaeilge na hArdteistiméireachta 1975*, Baile Átha Cliath: ITÉ

—1983. 'Is Beannaithe Lucht an Chaighdeáin óir is leo ...', *Teangeolas*, 17, 40–46

—eag. 1985. *Papers on Irish English*, Baile Átha Cliath: IRAAL

—1986a. *Lárchanúint don Ghaeilge*, Baile Átha Cliath: ITÉ

—eag. 1986b. *Lámhleabhar Téipe* [ag gabháil le Ó Baoill 1986a]

—1988. 'Language Planning in Ireland: the Standardization of Irish', *International Journal of the Sociology of Language*, 70, 109–26

—eag. 1990. *Úsáid agus Forbairt na Lárchanúna*, Baile Átha Cliath: Bord na Gaeilge

—eag. 1992a. *Insealbhú na Gaeilge mar Chéad Teanga/Acquisition of Irish as a First Language*, Baile Átha Cliath: IRAAL

—1995. 'IRAAL 20 Bliain ag Fás/IRAAL's 20th Anniversary', *Teanglitir*, 22, 1–3

—1996. *An Teanga Bheo: Gaeilge Uladh*, Baile Átha Cliath: ITÉ

Ó Baoill, Dónall P. ┐ Ó Tuathail, Éamonn 1992b. *Úrchúrsa Gaeilge*, eagrán leasaithe, Baile Átha Cliath: ITÉ

—1993. *Úrchúrsa Gaeilge: Freagraí ar na Cleachtaí*, eagrán leasaithe, Baile Átha Cliath: ITÉ

Ó Baoill, Dónall P. ┐ Matthews, Patrick A., le foilsiú. *The Structure of Irish Sign Language*, Baile Átha Cliath: ITÉ

Ó Buachalla, Breandán 1982/83. '"Annála Ríoghachta Éireann" is "Foras Feasa ar Éirinn": an Comhthéacs Comhaimseartha', *Studia Hibernica*, 22/23, 59–105

Ó Cléirigh, Tomás 1985. *Aodh Mac Aingil agus an Scoil Nua-Ghaeilge sa Lobháin*, an dara heagrán a d'ullmhaigh Tomás de Bhaldraithe, Baile Átha Cliath: An Gúm

Ó Cuív, Brian 1966. 'Linguistic Terminology in the Mediaeval Irish Bardic Tracts', *Transactions of the Philological Society*, 1965, 141–64

—1973. *The Linguistic Training of the Mediaeval Irish Poet*, Baile Átha Cliath: Scoil an Léinn Cheiltigh

—1980. 'A Medieval Exercise in Language Planning: Classical Early Modern Irish', in *Progress in Linguistic Historiography*, in eagar ag Konrad Koerner, Amsterdam: John Benjamins, 23–34

Ó Deirg, Íosold 1979. 'The Linguistics Institute of Ireland: a Profile', *Linguistic Reporter*, 22.1, 5

—1988. 'The Open Door: Terminology in a Lesser-Used Language', *Teanga*, 8, 43–57; *Termnet News*, 20, 15–20

Ó Domhnaill, Niall 1951. *Forbairt na Gaeilge*, Baile Átha Cliath: Sáirséal ┐ Dill

Ó Domhnalláin, Tomás 1981. 'Buntús Gaeilge—Cúlra, Cur le Chéile, Cur i bhFeidhm', *Teangeolas*, 13, 24–32

—1997. 'Buntús Gaeilge agus Bunú ITÉ', sa leabhar seo

Ó Domhnalláin, Tomás ⅂ Ó Baoill, Dónall P. 1978. *Earráidí Scríofa Gaeilge, cuid 1: Earráidí Briathra* [...], Baile Átha Cliath: ITÉ

—1979. *Earráidí Scríofa Gaeilge, Cuid 2: Ainmfhocail, Cáilitheoirí', Forainmneacha, Cónaisc agus Míreanna* [...], Baile Atha Cliath, ITÉ

—1975. *Réamhfhocail le Briathra na Gaeilge*, Baile Átha Cliath: ITÉ

Ó Dónaill, Niall 1977. *Foclóir Gaeilge-Béarla*, Baile Átha Cliath: Oifig an tSoláthair

O'Donovan, John 1845. *Grammar of the Irish Language*, Baile Átha Cliath: Hodges ⅂ Figgis

Ó Floinn, Tomás 1981. 'Scéal na Téarmaíochta sa Chóras Oideachais', *Teangeolas*, 12, 17–15

Ó Glaisne, Risteárd 1988. 'Léann agus Diagacht Protastúnach in Éirinn 1500-1700', caib. 11 in *An Léann Eaglasta in Éirinn 1200–1900*, in eagar ag Máirtín Mac Conmara, Baile Átha Cliath: An Clóchomhar

—1996. 'Bíobla ó Mhaigh Nuad', caib. 52 in Ó Glaisne, *Pádraig Ó Fiannachta*, Baile Átha Cliath: Coiscéim

Ó Gliasáin, Mícheál 1990. *Language Shift among Schoolchildren ir Gaeltacht Areas 1974–84: an Analysis of the Distribution of £10 Grant Qualifiers*, Baile Átha Cliath: ITÉ

Ó Háinle, Cathal 1994. 'Ó Chaint na nDaoine go dtí an Caighdeán Oifigiúil', caib. 11 in McCone et al. 1994

O'Growney, Eugene 1897. *Simple Lessons in Irish*, I–IV, Baile Átha Cliath: Connradh na Gaedhilge

Ó hÓgáin, Éamonn 1983. 'Téarmaí Teicniúla sa Ghaeilge: Caighdeánú agus Ceapadh le Céad Bliain anuas', *Teangeolas*, 17, 27–33

Ó Huallacháin, Colmán L. 1962. 'How Modern Language Teaching Methods Could Help Irish Teachers Quickly', *The Teacher's Work*, 21.2, 81–4

—1980. 'Towards a Bibliography of Irish Gaelic Language Teaching Materials from the Seventeenth Century until Today', *Occasional Papers in Linguistics and Language Learning, The New University of Ulster*, 7, 153–77

Ó Huallacháin, Colmán L. ⅂ Ó Murchú, Máirtín 1981. *Irish Grammar, Revised and Enlarged: OIDEAS* [3ú eagrán]. Cúil Raithin: An Léann Éireannach, Ollscoil Nua Uladh; Irish Decimalized Error Advice System

Ó Madagáin, Breandán 1988. 'An Bíobla i nGaeilge 1600–1981' in *An Léann Eaglasta in Éirinn 1200–1900*, in eagar ag Máirtín Mac Conmara, Baile Átha Cliath: An Clóchomhar, 176–86

Ó Maonaigh, Cainneach 1962. 'Scríbhneoirí Gaeilge an Seachtú hAois Déag', *Studia Hibernica*, 2, 182–208

Ó Murchú, Máirtín 1971. *Urlabhra agus Pobal/Language and Community*, Baile Átha Cliath: Oifig an tSoláthair

[Ó Murchú, Máirtín] 1990. *School of Celtic Studies: Fiftieth Anniversary Report 1940–1990*, Baile Átha Cliath: Scoil an Léinn Cheiltigh

Ó Riagáin, Pádraig 1986. *Public and Teachers' Attitudes towards Irish in the Schools: a Review of Recent Surveys*, Baile Átha Cliath: ITÉ

—eag. 1988. *Language planning in Ireland: International Journal of the Sociology of Language*, 70

—1992. *Language Maintenance and Language Shift as Strategies of Social Repro-duction: Irish in the Corca Dhuibhne Gaeltacht 1926–1986*, Baile Átha Cliath: ITÉ

Ó Riagáin, Pádraig ⁊ Ó Gliasáin, Mícheál 1979. *All-Irish Primary Scools in the Dublin Area: Report of a Sociological and Spatial Study of All-Irish Medium Schools in the Greater Dublin Area, with Special Reference to their Impact on Home and Social Network Use of Irish*, Baile Átha Cliath: ITÉ

—1984. *The Irish Language in the Republic of Ireland 1983*, Baile Átha Cliath: ITÉ

—1994. *National Survey on Languages 1993*, Baile Átha Cliath: ITÉ

Ó Sé, Diarmuid 1995. *An Teanga Bheo: Corca Dhuibhne*, Baile Átha Cliath: ITÉ

Ó Siadhail, Mícheál 1978. *Téarmaí Tógála agus Tís as Inis Meáin*, Baile Átha Cliath: Institiúid Ardléinn Bhaile Átha Cliath

—1980. *Learning Irish: an Introductory Tutor*, leabhar agus caiséid. Baile Átha Cliath: Institiúid Ardléinn Bhaile Átha Cliath

Porcher, Louis, Huart, Michelle, Mariet, François 1980. *Adaptation de 'un niveau-seuil' pour des contextes scolaires*, Strasbourg: Conseil de l'Europe

Pritchard, Rosalind M. O. 1990. 'Language Policy in Northern Ireland', *Teangeolas*, 27, 26–35

—eag. 1991. *Motivating the Majority: Modern Languages in Northern Ireland*, Londain: Centre for Information on Language Teaching and Research in association with the University of Ulster

Rehder, Helmut et al. 1965. *Deutsch: Verstehen und Sprechen*, Baile Átha Cliath: Oifig an tSoláthair

Roinn Oideachais 1966. *Buntús Gaeilge: Réamhthuarascáil ar Thaighde Teangeo-laíochta a Rinneadh sa Teanglann*, Rinn Mhic Gormáin [Baile Átha Cliath: Oifig an tSoláthair]

Roinn Oideachais 1986. *Foclóir Póca: English-Irish/Irish-English Dictionary*, Baile Átha Cliath: An Gúm

—1991. *An Foclóir Beag: Gaeilge/Gaeilge*, Baile Átha Cliath: An Gúm

—1994. *Foclóir Scoile: English-Irish/Irish-English Dictionary*, Baile Átha Cliath: An Gúm

Ruane, Mary ⁊ Singleton, David, eag. 1982. *Innovations in Curriculum and Exami-nations at Second Level: Proceedings of the National Modern Languages Convention held at Trinity College, Dublin on 29 and 30 January 1982*. Baile Átha Cliath: Trinity College Centre for Language and Communication Studies

Ruane, Mary 1987. *Expanding Horizons: a Report on Visits and Exchanges in Second-Level Schools*, Baile Átha Cliath: Royal Irish Academy

—1990. *Access to Foreign Languages*, Baile Átha Cliath: Royal Irish Academy

—1996. 'Language, Education and Applied Linguistics in a Changing World: Response to Mitchell', caib. 2 in Hickey ⁊ Williams, eag. 1996

Scoil an Léinn Cheiltigh 1990. *Foilseacháin sa Léann Ceilteach: Catalóg 1990*, Baile Átha Cliath: Institiúid Ard-Léinn Bhaile Átha Cliath

Sheils, Joe 1982a. 'An Example of Curriculum Development: the ITÉ Modern Languages Project in the Classroom', in Ruane ⁊ Singleton, eag. 1982

—1982b. 'The ITÉ Modern Languages Project: an Experiment in a Communicative Approach to Second Language Learning', *Compass*, 11.2, 11–22

—1986. 'Implications of the Communicative Approach for the Role of the Teacher', in Little, Ó Meadhra ⁊ Singleton 1986, 52–5

—1988. *Communication in the Modern Languages Classroom*, Strasbourg: Council of Europe

Singleton, David 1992. 'Education towards Language Awareness in Ireland', *Language Awareness*, 1.1, 47–57

Stenson, Nancy ⅂ Ó Ciardha, Pádraic 1986. 'The Irish of Ráth Cairn : a Supplement to "Linguistic Atlas and Survey of Irish Dialects"', *Zeitschrift für celtische Philologie*, 41, 66–115

—1987. 'The Irish of Ráth Cairn, Pt 2', *Zeitschrift für celtische Philologie*, 42, 116–37

University of Dublin, Trinity College 1995. *Report of the ESF-Funded Project to Consolidate and Develop Modules for Students of other Disciplines implemented by the Centre for Language and Communication Studies 1 October 1993–30 September 1994*, [Baile Átha Cliath]

Wagner, Heinrich 1958, 1964, 1966, 1969. *Linguistic Atlas and Survey of Irish Dialects*, I–IV, Baile Átha Cliath: Scoil an Léinn Cheiltigh

Williams, J.E. Caerwyn ⅂ Ní Mhuiríosa, Máirín 1979. *Traidisiún Liteartha na nGael*, Baile Átha Cliath: An Clóchomhar

Williams, Nicholas 1986. *I bPrionta i Leabhar*, Baile Átha Cliath: An Clóchomhar

IRISÍ A BHAINEANN LEIS AN TEANGEOLAÍOCHT FHEIDHMEACH IN ÉIRINN[2]

Belfast Working Papers in Language and Linguistics, Baile Shiúrdáin: University of Ulster, 1, 1976–

Foilseachán/Publication, Baile Átha Cliath: Institiúid Teangeolaíochta Éireann, 1, 1974–19, 1981

FTA Bulletin [comharba 'FTA Newsletter'], Baile Átha Cliath: French Teachers' Association, Bealtaine 1976–

FTA Newsletter, Baile Átha Cliath: French Teachers' Association, Márta 1973–Márta 1975

Language, Culture and Curriculum, Clevedon: ITÉ/Multilingual Matters, 1, 1988–

The Language Teacher/An Múinteoir Teanga, Baile Átha Cliath: Institiúid Teangeolaíochta Éireann, 1, 1988–3, 1990

Newsletter of the School of Celtic Studies, Baile Átha Cliath: Scoil an Léinn Cheiltigh, 1, 1987

NIMLA Journal of the Modern Language Association of Northern Ireland, Cúil Raithin: University of Ulster, 1, 1978–

Northern Ireland Speech Language Forum Journal, Béal Feirste: The Forum, 1, 1975–10, 1984

Nuacht ITÉ/ITÉ News, Baile Átha Cliath: Institiúid Teangeolaíochta Éireann, 1, 1992–

Occasional Papers in Linguistics and Language Learning, Cúil Raithin: New University of Ulster, 1, 1976–11, 1986

Páipéar Ócáide/Occasional Paper, Baile Átha Cliath: Institiúid Teangeolaíochta Éireann, 1, 1977–

Ráiteas Eolais, Baile Átha Cliath: Institiúid Teangeolaíochta Éireann, 1, 1974

Teagasc na Gaeilge, Baile Átha Cliath: Comhar na Múinteoirí Gaeilge, 1, 1980–6, 1989

[2] Comharthaíonn fleiscín (–) ag deireadh iontrála go bhfuil an iris á foilsiú i gcónaí.

Teanga: Bliainiris na Teangeolaíochta Feidhmí in Éirinn/The Irish Yearbook of Applied Linguistics, Baile Átha Cliath: Cumann na Teangeolaíochta Feidhmí/Irish Association for Applied Linguistics, 1, 1979–

Teangeolas [comharba *Ráiteas Eolais*], Baile Átha Cliath: Institúid Teangeolaíochta Éireann, 2, 1975–

Teanglitir, Baile Átha Cliath: Cumann na Teangeolaíochta Feidhmí, 1985–

Tuarascáil Bhliana, Baile Átha Cliath: Institúid Teangeolaíochta Éireann, 1975–

Tuarascáil Taighde/Research Report, Baile Átha Cliath: Institiúid Teangeolaíochta Éireann, 12, 1985–

The Poetic Version of the Voyage of Snédgus and Mac Ríagla[*]

DONNCHA Ó hAODHA

University College, Galway

I OFFER below an annotated translation into English of the poetic version of this voyage-tale. The poetic version was first edited, with a German translation, by Rudolf Thurneysen.[1]

There is only one complete MS copy of the poem: YBL, 11b–13b. (There is a second copy of the final ten stanzas, also in YBL.) Although this poetic version of the tale is regarded by all scholars who have examined the question as the earliest surviving account, it does not occur in the MS as a unit on its own. It is in fact integrated within a prose version which seems to derive from the poem.

This prose version was first edited by Whitley Stokes, omitting the poetry.[2] Thurneysen in 1904 edited the poetry without its accompanying prose; see above. Van Hamel finally edited both poetry and prose, although separately; see again above. In Van Hamel's book the prose is to be found on pp. 82–85, and the poetry (as already stated) on pp. 86–92. The actual sequence in the MS is as follows, using the line-numbers of Van Hamel's edition of the prose:

Prose ll. 1–48, followed by stanzas 1–8 of the poem;
Prose ll. 51–55, followed by stanzas 9–12 of the poem;
Prose ll. 56–63, followed by stanzas 13–21 of the poem;
Prose ll. 64–79, followed by stanzas 22–33 of the poem;
Prose ll. 80–84, followed by stanzas 34–37 of the poem;
Prose ll. 85–87, followed by stanzas 38–39 of the poem;
Prose ll. 88–114, followed by stanzas 40–66 of the poem;
Prose ll. 115–132, followed by stanzas 67–76 of the poem.

The first of these sections contains an introduction to the tale (stanzas 1–3 of the poem) and an account of the first incident of the voyage (stanzas 4–8). This is followed by a narrative of seven further adventures, almost

---

[*] Abbreviations in the following are as found in the *Dictionary of the Irish Language* (including *Contributions to a Dictionary*[...]) (Dublin: Royal Irish Academy, 1913–76), itself cited as *RIA Dict.*

[1] *Zwei Versionen der mittelirischen Legende von Snédgus und Mac Riagla* (Halle, 1904), pp. 9–26. (For corrections to his edition see the same author in *ZCPh*, 5 (1905), 418 ff. See also Thurneysen, *ZCPh*, 6 (1908), 234–5 for a further note.) The poem was subsequently edited, without translation, by A.G. van Hamel: *Immrama* (Dublin: Stationery Office, 1941), pp. 86–92.

[2] *RC*, 9 (1888), 14–25.

always involving a visit to an island. I follow Van Hamel below in using Roman numerals to signal the beginning of each of the eight adventures from stanza four on.

Although these 76 stanzas are thus found integrated within a prose *cum* verse text in the only complete copy, the evidence—including the metrical evidence—is that they constitute a poetic unit on their own, and that in fact they represent the earliest surviving version of this voyage-tale, dating perhaps from the tenth century. As already stated, the accompanying prose seems to derive from the poem. There are later prose versions of the tale also, one of which (again in YBL) concludes with the closing stanzas 67–76 of our poem (with their account of the eighth adventure of the voyage by the two clerics).[3]

The metre of the poem is almost exclusively *dechnad cummaisc,* most often of the pattern 8, 4, 4, 8. The pattern of the first stanza however seems to be 7, 7, 4, 8. I have noted also below that stanzas 62 and 66 seem to have the pattern 7, 5, 7, 5. I intend to return to the question of the metre of the poem elsewhere.

In the Notes below references to 'Thurneysen' or to 'Van Hamel' are of course to their editions of the poem, as cited above. Since the only complete copy of the poem is late, it does require emending. I have not adverted in the Notes to those cases where there is general agreement about the emendation required. I have however noted the matter where e.g. I prefer the interpretation or suggestion of one editor over the other.

I am aware of course that the ideal would be a fresh edition of the poem. Nevertheless I venture to offer the present contribution in tribute to the memory of one of my first teachers of Old Irish.

TRANSLATION

1. Snédgus and Mac Ríagla of the *familia* of Colm Cille—such was their virtue: they loved the king of heaven's kingdom.

2. They entered on to[4] the angry sea (which requires a total effort) at the beginning of the reign of Donnchad after the ruin of Domnall.

---

[3] Cf. W. Stokes, *RC,* 26 (1905), 166.

[4] Thurneysen read the MS here as *Arroldatar* and translated 'Als sie [...] gegangen waren'. Van Hamel read *Irroldatar* and emended to *Inróldatar.* Although the reading is unclear, van Hamel's is more likely to be the correct one. Moreover the latter reading, as emended slightly by van Hamel, results in the stanza consisting—not of a subordinate—but of a principal clause, which is the norm in the poem.

3.   They happened upon a great amount of mysteries[5]—no short protection—on the islands of the fearsome ocean above the sea.

I

4.   After the fatigue of rowing at the end of three days (a pure tale)—well was it endured, a burning thirst seized them due to it.

5.   Christ son of Mary, who is greater than any faith, had compassion on them; he placed them—in the form made of hide—upon a stream pleasing to taste and sweet.

6.   The victorious brothers[6] were satisfied—a power which is not crazy generosity—with tasty liquid, and it was bestowed like new milk.

7.   'Let us desist from it, the rowing of our coracle—a journey of[7] strength—[to see] if it be Christ's will whether we may still be underneath or upon it.[8]

8.   Let our oars rest on the floor of our boat, if the larder is empty; keen-sighted bright-pure king—let our voyage lie in the hands of the son of Mary!'

II

9.   They voyaged afterwards to an island—a course without complaint—a fence of silver of very great contrivance [lay] across its centre.

10.   Wainscoting of bright pure silver at the end of it—fragments of beauty[9]—it was the fishing-weir of the island.[10]

11.   There used to leap up to that waterfall[11]—music of the land—heavy strong[12] salmon as big as a male yearling.

---

[5] The MS reads here *Dosrala for mor di ruinib de* 'They happened upon a great amount of mysteries of God'. Since the line is hypermetrical by one syllable Thurneysen suggested omitting the prep. *for*. I prefer to follow van Hamel in omitting the final *de* 'of God'.

[6] MS *ín brathair buada*. It is scarcely necessary, following van Hamel, to emend to *buadaig*.

[7] Lit. 'with'.

[8] i.e. upon the sea.

[9] I take MS *caíme* to be a preposed gen.; it is scarcely necessary with van Hamel to emend to *caíni*.

[10] The imperfect final rhyme in this stanza is noteworthy, between *cindse* (containing the dat. sg. of *cenn*) and *hinnse* (gen. sg. of *inis*). Cp. e.g. the imperfect final rhyme in the following stanza 11 here: between *(n)írend* and *(colpthaigh) firind*.

[11] i.e. the weir. I accept here the emendation by van Hamel of MS *eassam* to *e(a)s-sain*.

12.   It (both the silver, and the large smooth salmon) supplied the household of God, whom they serve—the cry of every host.[13]

III

13.   It was the Son of God who led[14] their voyage, according to laws of purity; a flood brought them afterwards to another island.

14.   [There were] youths in front of them above the stronghold of the island who had no nobility; over the surface of the land they had cats' heads and a human body.

15.   A warrior came out of the island—of Irish speech[15]—without spear, without loathsomeness to the beach to meet the clerics.

16.   He welcomed the clerics—renowned group—his appearance was beautiful; he was a true brother of the men of Ireland.

17.   He recounted to them the manner of their voyage upon which had gone from the land of Ireland—it was a journey which helped[16]—the crew of a coracle.

18.   'We came, a band, on a voyage—a journey on the fair shore—in the power of life;[17] none of them [now] lives except only me.

19.   They suffered martyrdom at the hands of foreigners without faith; it is they[18] who dwell without any conscience on the island'.

---

[12] Again I accept van Hamel's emendation of MS *tolgaidh* to *tholgdai.*

[13] Following the suggestion originally made by Thurneysen, stanzas 11 and 12 here have been transposed from their order in the MS—especially for reasons of sense.

[14] The MS reads *condo ruid* here. There is a dot under the line between the *con*-symbol and the preceding letter. Van Hamel interprets this dot as a *punctum delens* in respect of the following *con*-symbol. Although such an interpretation of the MS evidence is very questionable, nevertheless I agree with van Hamel that one should read *doruid* (trisyllabic) here. The same verbal form occurs in stanza 24 below.

[15] I follow Thurneysen here in taking MS *arusc fenech* not as a cheville, but as gen. pl. governed by the preceding *oclach.*

[16] I take MS *foraid* here to be = *fo-ráith.*

[17] MS *uas bethaig brig.* Lit. '*over* the power of life'. I follow Thurneysen's original suggestion here in understanding the MS form *bethaig* (instead of gen. sg. *bethad*) as being due to the influence of the preceding preposition *uas.* I prefer this interpretation as against emending to *betha,* gen. sg. of *bith* 'world'.

[18] I read here with Van Hamel (and the MS) cons. pres. *bit e,* rather than (as suggested by Thurneysen, following Strachan) emending to *it e.* The reference presumably is to the 'youths' of stanza 14 above.

20.   That man gave tasty food—renowned fate—to the clerics in the little coracle in which they were.

21.   Each party of them blessed the other—renown which you seek—here he remains until we may [all] meet in the land of another world.[19]

IV

22.   A blast of wind blew them—who belonged to a congregation[20] of great dignity—to a high island in which stood a tree with beautiful birds.

23.   On the top of the tree the praiseworthy birds of the plain of heaven sang chants—a joy to the heart—it was a vigorous strain.

24.   Holy was the bird who led the choirs—without any jealousy; he had a golden form, a fitting head and wings of silver.[21]

25.   The just bird with noble mystery preached to them about what God performed of good before the creation of creatures.

26.   He preached the birth of Christ from the illustrious maiden—perpetual melody—including baptism and resurrection and his passion.

27.   When he preached tidings of doom to the feast-day congregations, they used then[22] beat their wings against themselves until they were exhausted.

28.   Noble blood flowed[23] from their sides—with the roar of a sea-storm— on [hearing of] Christ's crucifixion and of the final judgement.

29.   There flowed from them the shower of blood[24]—a difficult course—it was [as] kings' oil, it was [as] wine, it was [as] communion, it was [as] a relic.

[19] The poet seems to intrude himself into the poem at this point, but the relevant clause at the end of the stanza here may have been based on a commonly used expression.

[20] I understand (with Thurneysen) MS *samgha* as = *sámtha*, gen. sg. of *sámud*, lit. 'of a congregation (of great dignity)'.

[21] I read here, with Thurneysen, *con[a] deilb óir, / co cend chóir, co n-eitib argait.*

[22] I take *diu* here to be a form of *didiu.*

[23] I would read with Thurneysen here: *Silis fuil sla(i)n*, understanding the verb to be intrans. and so emending the adj.

[24] I follow the MS here: *Braín na fola ferais uadhaib* (taking *Braín* to be asg. of the *o*-stem), rather than emending with van Hamel to *Bráenu.*

30.   A leaf was thrown over the clerics—the Lord loved them—not secretly, [it was] as broad as the hide of a great team-ox.[25]

31.   'Take it with you', said the bright bird—fair fame—radiant [was] the stout prize; it was [afterwards] on the altar of Colm Cille.

32.   Beautiful the tree, the trunk of which does not wither,[26] nor the colour of [its] leaves; under the top of the ancient tree there would be room for [all] the men[27] of great Ireland.

33.   Noble the prayer of those birds—with words of promise—bright pure psalms and victorious sweet canticles.[28]

V

34.   They bestowed a blessing at the melodious tree—a visit with every piety; by a peaceful sailing they went to another land.

35.   They saw numerous people—of mad[29] appearance—possessing blemished extremities:[30] with dogs' heads and equine mane.

36.   The same one—faithful Christ—took pity on them: a cleric of great conscience[31] came out of the island.

37.   The cleric of great learning—bright the venerable law—gave to the King's household fish and wine and wheat.

VI

38.   What could be more strange? There was revealed [to them] on their travels a working-party in a field with heads of tall pigs upon them.

---

[25] For the second half of this stanza I (along with van Hamel) follow the interpretation and emendations proposed by E.J. Gwynn in *Hermathena*, 44 (1926), 67–68.

[26] I read *na creadba [a] c[h]orp*, a reading which provides the required eight syllables in the line. The following (second) line of the stanza reads: *na dath nduille*.

[27] Thurneysen (and van Hamel) emended MS *tallsat (firo)* to *tallfad* here; I translate accordingly.

[28] The second half of this stanza reads: *salm ghil glandai / canntoic buadaigh bindi*. It is clear that one needs to emend the nouns to pl. forms: *sailm* and *canntoici*.

[29] For MS *(n)dreachdhai* here—a rare adj. of uncertain meaning—cf. *RIA Dict.*, s.v. *drechda*, which follows Thurneysen.

[30] The MS reads *la himle on*. My translation is tentative here; cf. *RIA Dict.* s.v. ? *imdel* 'border, edge'?, and s.v. *immellach*, adj., 'bordering'. On the other hand Thurneysen suggested emending *himle to himbed*: 'nebst einer Menge von Schandflecken'.

[31] With *co mét cubais* here cp. in stanza 19 *cen cuid cubais* 'without any conscience'.

39.   In the best of the weather of very fair summer—which causes bodies to glow—it was then they reaped[32] their fields, the strong, robust[33] men.

VII

40.   They sang psalms—more radiant than speech:[34] renowned the journey[35] to a land in which there was a company of the men of the Gaels.

41.   The sweet cry of the troop of women of the island; harmonious melody; beloved, fitting music: it was performed for them by the side of the coracle.

42.   'Sing also', said the cleric—radiant his learning—'May the Son of God lead us':[36] it is the sweet melody[37] of the women of Ireland'.

43.   'Let us all go', said the women with beautiful hair, 'you will have shelter[38] in the house of the king of the virgin island'.

44.   When they rested in the house of the king with the law of the Féni,[39] the festive, cheerful lord said: 'Welcome, clerics!'

45.   From where is your race?' 'From the land of Ireland—a sure course— I do not conceal a secret: we are of the *familia* of Colm Cille'

46.   'How is the host of the land of Tara—with[40] tumult of battles? Do you know how many of Domnall's sons are [still] alive?'

---

[32] I follow here the emendation *bobgatar*, proposed by Thurneysen originally, for MS *tocbatar*.

[33] The MS reads here *fir triuin talcu*. The (MI) use of acc. *talcu* for the nom. form is, as Thurneysen pointed out, highly exceptional; it is occasioned here at the end of the third line by the provision of consonance with the rhyming end-words of the second and fourth lines: *curpu, ngurtu* (MS *ngurto*).

[34] I emend MS *celebraidh* at the end of the first line here to *labrad*, since the line as it stands has a syllable too many. Thurneysen noted that such an emendation breaks the (linking) alliteration with *clothach* at the beginning of line two, but such alliteration is not universal in the poem.

[35] The word used here, *roíden* (MS *roidhen*), rhyming with *Goídel* (MS *gaidhel*) at the end of line four, was derived by Thurneysen from *ro-fedan*. It does not seem to occur elsewhere; cf. *RIA Dict.*, s.v.

[36] We seem to have here (*Mac de don fe*) a variant version of the opening line of the hymn ascribed to Colmán moccu Clúasaig, *Sén Dé do-n-fé* 'May the blessing of God lead us'. Cf. *Thes. Pal.*, II, 298 ff.

[37] For the word (*longaire*) here translated 'sweet melody', literally apparently 'blackbird's cry', cf. *RIA Dict.*, s.v.

[38] I accept here the emendation suggested by van Hamel of MS *dib* to *dín* 'shelter', which also rhymes with gen. *ríg* in the interior of the following (fourth) line of the stanza.

[39] I read here with van Hamel *i tig [ind] ríg recht[a] fénich.*

[40] Lit. 'of'.

47. The cleric declared knowledgeably—[his] dignity was confirmed: 'Over the house-post of the fortress[41] there are three sons of the king of Tara alive.

48. Fiacha son of Domnall fell—certain [are] the accounts—at the hands of the Fir Roiss; he has come to rest[42] in the clay of his abode.

49. Here is[43] the pair by whom he fell—stronger than a host—[it was] a victory rich in casts: Diarmait rich in oil, and Ailill.

50. There were banished[44] upon the sea for that deed (without any delay) sixty couples of no ferocity.'

51. 'It is true for you, O clerics of the Lord—a penalty which was attested—it is a true testimony; it is I who killed the son of the king of Tara.

52. We left our country for ever—long journey of a band of guests[45]—for us it is profitable until we go forth to judgement.

53. Good is our dwelling-place beside the King of just and fine lordship: without crude sin, without wickedness, without suffering, without stain.[46]

[41] I read here with van Hamel os *cath*rach *cli,* rather than (with Thurneysen) os *cath*air *cli* 'auf dem linken Stuhl'.

[42] i.e. he has been buried. I construe this stanza with van Hamel, rather than with Thurneysen: 'Fiacha [...] ist gefallen [...]; durch die Männer von Ross fand er Ruhe; im Boden ist seine Wohnung'.

[43] MS *Assa.* This word, meaning 'here is, behold' is hardly to be taken literally here. The cleric, whether Snédgus or Mac Ríagla, names for the king of the island the two who took the life of Fiacha. In stanza 51 below the king says that he himself killed the son of Domnall. By implication therefore the king of this island is either Diarmait or Ailill, more likely the former perhaps. In the case of the third line of this stanza which is a syllable short in the MS: *coib corach,* I follow Thurneysen's suggested emendation to *[ba] coib corach.* The adj. *corach* here rhymes with the epithet *(olach)* of Diarmait in the interior of the fourth line. One could alternatively perhaps understand the rhyme to be between *córach* and *ólach,* in which case the relevant phrases would translate 'a just victory' and 'festive Diarmait'. Of course *olach/ólach* may have been a sobriquet of Diarmait.

[44] The MS reads here *Esrócartha.* It seems reasonable with van Hamel to emend the preverb to A*s-.* The meaning is clear: Thurneysen translated 'Ausgewiesen wurden'. The corresponding prose text reads *ro chuirit.* It would seem that beside *fúacair (fo-úacair, fócair)* in the sense 'declares outlaw, banishes'— cf. *RIA Dict.* s.v. *fúacair*—there was a further derivative—*as-fócair*—of which we have here what appears to be the only attested example.

[45] The MS reads *sirset con gresso* here and has a syllable too many in the line. I follow Thurneysen's proposed emendation rather than that of van Hamel.

[46] The final rhyme here is between *caíne* and *gaile,* which latter is to be read as *gaíle.* See *RIA Dict.,* s.v. *gaíle.*

54. Beautiful is the island upon which we came[47]—a pious saying—a holy land in which are Enoch and Elijah.

55. Noble is the house with swan's colour—a swift cry—in which Elijah is meditating upon the blazing Judgement'.[48]

56. It is he[49] who extended a beneficent welcome—swift speech—to the two belonging to the *familia* of Colm Cille the cleric.

57. The *summa* of the sages was set in place by him (a growing festival): a beautiful, fitting book of the four gospels[50] with fringes of gold and silver.

58. Elijah said to the assembly[51] of bright prophets: 'The preaching which I will do in regard to the promptness of the Judgement[52] will be prudent and strong.

59. The Antichrist will declare an eloquent sermon—bitter is that cry—woe to the one who is not on guard during that hour in that gathering:

60. The gathering of the men of heaven—heart's strength, a vast 'plunder'; the gathering of the men of hell—a terrifying 'triumph'; the gathering of the men of earth.

61. Christ will come to them along with hosts from blessed heaven; the son of the Virgin [and] God the Father will strike down death'.[53]

[47] I follow Van Hamel, rather than Thurneysen, in construing this line and in emending MS *diano rala* to *diandon rala*. Cp. in the corresponding prose: *Maith ind inis i tám.*

[48] I follow van Hamel here also in taking it as certain that stanzas 54 and 55 form (the concluding) part of the speech by the king of the island which begins in stanza 51. The house (*tegdais*) referred to here—of Elijah—is presumably distinct from the house of the king of the island referred to in stanza 44: *i tig* [*ind*] *ríg*; cf. note 39 above.

[49] i.e. Elijah.

[50] For the word *cotur* (from Lat. *quattuor*) used here, cf. Thurneysen, *ZCPh*, 6, 234.

[51] As Thurneysen pointed out, the 'assembly' (*senadh*) here mentioned must refer to the two clerics on the voyage. Cf. note 54 below.

[52] MS *fri heim mbratha*. I take it (tentatively) that we have here a substantival use of the adj. *éim* 'prompt, ready, timely'.

[53] Thurneysen read the MS here as *silis in cel*. Van Hamel understood the second element to be the negative particle (*ni*) rather than the article, and he read *ní chél* 'I will not conceal it'. I think that van Hamel is correct in reading *ni* rather than *in*, especially since the scribe, in this text at least, most often writes the article as *an*. On the other hand from reading *ní chél* Van Hamel is in effect led to rewrite the last line of the stanza. Thus his suggested text reads: *silis, ní chél, / mac in námait ngér dia athair* 'the son will slay—I will not conceal it—the bitter enemy for his father'. It makes much more sense to merely emend *ni* to *in*, and to otherwise read with the MS: *silis in cel /mac na hingini dia athair*, which I have translated above. It is true that the concluding phrase could be taken to mean 'für seinen Vater', as

62.   Noble was the messenger who came, with generosity of heart, to supply the three of them with food from heaven.[54]

63.   'A great thing: two lakes—their clear gaping course was foretold—a lake of water which will give forth no produce, a strong lake of fire.[55]

64.   They would have reached Ireland a long time ago, by means of God's flood, were it not for Martin and Patrick interceding with him'.[56]

65.   'Why do we not see noble Enoch of the swift sayings? That would be a meeting which would make us happy', said the cleric.

66.   'He is at the secret place, it is[57] a secret honourable place, until we all go into the battle to meet our martyrdom'.

VIII

67.   The son of God looked upon their journeyings—the following of a congregation—without rough danger, until another tall island was reached.[58]

68.   Noble the house to which they came—most noble of dwellings—in which lives the blessed king with men and with possessions.

Thurneysen did originally. It is much more likely however to mean 'God the Father' and Thurneysen reached this conclusion himself on Strachan's suggestion; cf. ZCPh, 6, 234.

[54] I read this stanza as follows: *Huasal teachtaire doluidh, / ba coible cridhi, / co[a] timtireacht a triur / do biudh (muntere) nime.* It would seem that the syllabic pattern of this stanza is 7,5,7,5, which of course is a departure from the norm in the poem. Cf. also stanza 66 below. I follow above the emendations proposed by Thurneysen. I would however assume that the poss. adj. *a* required by the sense after *co* at the beginning of the third line and which was restored by Thurneysen, would in practice have been elided metrically and that the words *triur* and *biudh* (which rhyme with each other) should be read as disyllabic. The reference to 'the three of them' (*a triur*) must be to Elijah and the two voyagers.

[55] I take this and the following stanza 64, with van Hamel, to be a resumption of Elijah's speech above. This stanza (63) begins with the rare form *Nuallsa*, which I have translated 'a great thing'. Thurneysen pointed out that the same form occurs at the beginning of line 54 of the prologue to the Martyrology of Óengus, where it is glossed *oll indso .i. mor indso*. In the case of the second line, translated here 'their clear, gaping course was foretold', I follow van Hamel's interpretation; I also follow his metrical division of the first and second lines: *Nuallsa, dá loch, / tairchét a rréimm n-ecnach ngenech.*

[56] I accept van Hamel's emendation here; he reads *oca guidi* for MS *ica nguidhe.*

[57] I accept van Hamel's insertion of the copula form *is* at the beginning of the second line here. We seem to have here also a stanza with the syllabic pattern 7, 5, 7, 5 as in stanza 62 above.

[58] I follow van Hamel here, in emending MS *co rosat* to *co rosacht*. One should note that the final rhyme in this stanza is imperfect: between *tuile* and *aile.*

69.   A hundred doors out of its sides—a bringing about of lights!—a beautiful proper[59] altar and a priest before each door.

70.   Wine was distributed among them—with the glories of good deeds—among both men and women; they went to Communion at Mass.

71.   'Say to the host of the island of Ireland after your travels that the punishment of the Lord is at hand for them because of their deeds.[60]

72.   Men in ships, warriors with spears, without any faith whatsoever; the 'plague' will be great, they will inhabit[61] the land of the island up to a half.

73.   Neglect of the precept of the king of heaven—the worst of deeds—blame for it[62] is not swift—that is what will bring the punishment upon them.

74.   Thirteen months upon your travels—congregation of a vigorous one[63]—since the storm of the joyous sea abounding in animals sent you forth.

75.   We will prefer that what you relate with lively words, with white palms, with swift feet should be of our tidings.

76.   I beseech Patrick and Enoch and Elijah that I may possess heaven with no sorrow and with swift brightness.[64]

[59] The MS form c(h)air at the end of the third line here—making internal rhyme with gráid in line four—is to be read cháir. See RIA Dict., s.v. cóir for the later variant cáir.

[60] I read here with van Hamel assa ngnímaib. The speech which begins here is uttered presumably by 'the blessed king' of stanza 68.

[61] It is clear from the context that the reference is to the future here. The actual MS variants are: trebait (pres.) and trebsat (pret.).

[62] I follow at the end of the third line the MS variant a tair (=táir) here—rhyming with variant daib (=dáib) in the interior of the fourth line.

[63] i.e. congregation of Colm Cille presumably. Forms of the word translated 'congregation' here (in reference to the two monks on the voyage)—samad (=sámud)—occur also in stanzas 22 and 67 above, as Thurneysen has pointed out (ZCPh, 6, 235).

[64] The last stanza here in the 1 sg. is to be attributed to the narrator of the poem. The speech of 'the blessed king' seems to have ceased in the previous (second-last) stanza, viz. stanza 75.

Knowledge and Power in *Aislinge Óenguso*

TOMÁS Ó CATHASAIGH
Harvard University

ISLINGE ÓENGUSO[1] is one of the most engaging of the early Irish sagas. It tells how Óengus, son of a god and goddess, the Dagdae and the Boann, falls in love with a beautiful woman whom he has seen in his dreams; he loses his appetite and becomes emaciated. When his 'disease' has been diagnosed, the gods traverse Ireland in search of the woman. She is at length identified as Cáer Iborméith, daughter of Ethal Anbúail, who is king of Síd Úaman, an Otherworld habitation in Connacht; she lives in a lake in Munster, spending one year as a swan and the next in human form. When Óengus is taken to the lake, Cáer is in human form; Óengus recognizes her, but he cannot make contact with her. Óengus returns to the lake when Cáer is in the form of a swan. He summons her to him, and they make love; they sleep in the form of two swans and then circle the lake three times and fly to Óengus's home at Bruig na Bóinne, where Cáer remains with him as his wife.

The linguistic evidence suggests that *Aislinge Óenguso* was composed in the eighth century.[2] It survives in a single vellum manuscript, London, British Library MS Egerton 1782, written, for the most part in 1517, by members of the Ó Maoilchonaire family; in all probability, it was written for Art buidhe Mac Murchadha Caomhánach, who died while it was in progress.[3] Egerton 1782 contains a large number of early Irish tales, including *Táin Bó Cúailnge* and a group of tales which are connected in one way or another with the *Táin*, and which are described in some sources as *remscéla* (prefatory tales). *Aislinge Óengusso* is one of this group in Egerton 1782. In the course of the *Aislinge*, Ailill, king of Connaught, and his wife, Medb, help Óengus in the arduous task of winning his beloved

---

[1] Francis Shaw, *The Dream of Óengus: Aislinge Óenguso* (Dublin: Browne and Nolan Limited, 1934). The text was edited, with a translation, by Edward Müller, 'Two Irish Tales. I. Aislinge Oengusso: The Dream of Oengus', *Revue Celtique*, 3 (1877), 342–50. Corrigenda to Müller's readings were given by R. Thurneysen, 'Zu irischen Texten', *Zeitschrift für Celtische Philologie*, 12 (1918), 400, and by Shaw, pp. 31–32. There is a translation by Kenneth Hurlstone Jackson, *A Celtic Miscellany: Translations from the Celtic Literatures* (London: Routledge and Kegan Paul, 1951), pp. 99–103; 2nd edn (Harmondsworth: Penguin Books, 1971), pp. 93–97. In the present article, references to the Irish text are to the numbered paragraphs of Shaw's edition; references to Jackson are to the Penguin edition. Translations in the present article are Jackson's, unless otherwise indicated.

[2] Shaw, p. 37.

[3] Robin Flower, *Catalogue of Irish Manuscripts in the British Museum* (London: British Museum, 1926; repr. as *Catalogue of Irish Manuscripts in the British Library [formerly British Museum]* (Dublin: Institute for Advanced Studies, 1992)) II, 262.

Cáer, and at the end of the tale it is explained that this is why Óengus had an alliance with Ailill and Medb, on foot of which Óengus accompanied them on the cattle-raid which is the subject of the *Táin*. Now none of the surviving recensions of the *Táin* refer to Óengus, and it has therefore been suggested that the link which is made at the end of *Aislinge Óenguso* with the events of TBC 'is probably an artificial one'.[4] Shaw discussed the matter at some length and claimed that 'we may conclude with certainty that the text had originally no connection with the great epic, that the last paragraph is a later addition and a forgery, added to the text about two centuries after the date of the original composition'.[5] On the other hand, Carney contended that five tales, *Táin Bó Fraích*, *Táin Bó Dartada*, *Táin Bó Regamain*, *Táin Bó Flidais*, and *Aislinge Óenguso*, show a common relationship to the events of *Táin Bó Cúailnge*: 'Ailill and Medb are about to embark upon the great military expedition celebrated in TBC. But it is first necessary for them to gain allies, and cattle to feed the army on the march'.[6] He points out that all of the tales 'are necessarily prior in time of action to TBC',[7] and adds that 'the general pattern is (a) a love interest involving someone closely associated with Ailill by blood or by alliance, (b) the securing for Ailill, as a result of the particular romantic situation, of either cattle or allies, or both'.[8]

It is possible that in a version of the *Táin* which has not survived, Óengus came to the assistance of Ailill and Medb. In any case, we probably owe the survival of *Aislinge Óenguso* to the fact that the compilers of Egerton 1782 classified it as a prefatory tale to the *Táin*, and hence included it in the set of these tales which they transcribed. Thanks to the enlightened patronage of Art buidhe Mac Murchadh Caomhánach, and to the scholarship and industry of the Ó Maoilchonaire family, we have a sixteenth-century transcription of an eighth-century tale. The text has inevitably undergone some changes in the course of transmission, so that, in Shaw's words, 'the language of the text as preserved in the manuscript may be said to be Old Irish with a very strong leaven of early and late Middle Irish forms'.[9] In his edition, Shaw has normalized the text to an Old Irish standard; quotations in the present paper are from the normalized text,

---

[4] Flower, p. 286.

[5] Shaw, pp. 28–29.

[6] James Carney, *Studies in Irish Literature and History* (Dublin: Institute for Advanced Studies, 1955), p. 62.

[7] Carney, p. 62.

[8] Carney, p. 62.

[9] Shaw, p. 32.

except where a different form is imposed by what has become known about Old Irish since 1934.

The tale opens with the dream which gives it its title. Here is Jackson's translation:[10]

> Oenghus was asleep one night,[11] when he saw a girl coming towards him as he lay on his bed. She was the loveliest that had ever been in Ireland. Oenghus went to take her hand, to bring him to her in his bed. As he looked, she sprang suddenly away from him; he could not tell where she had gone. He stayed there till morning, and he was sick at heart. The apparition which he had seen, and had not talked with, made him fall ill. No food passed his lips. She was there again the next night. He saw a lute in her hand, the sweetest that ever was; she played a tune to him, and he fell asleep at it. He remained there till morning, and that day he was unable to eat.
>
> He passed a whole year while she visited him in this way, so that he fell into a wasting sickness.

What follows in the body of the tale is an account of the wooing and, ultimately, the winning of Óengus's teasing visitant. But it is, for much of the time, a vicarious wooing and winning, since Óengus is in no condition to act on his own behalf. The woman who appears to him engages his interest but he is unable to detain her, and he does not know where she disappears to: he lacks the power and the knowledge which would enable him to cope with the situation into which he has been thrust. Indeed, having failed to make contact with the woman, Óengus 'was sick at heart' (*nipo slán laiss a menmae*, § 1); 'he fell ill' (*do-génai galar ndó*, § 1); and 'no food passed his lips' (*nícon luid biad inna béolu*, § 1). On the day after the woman's second appearance 'he was unable to eat' (*nícon ro-proind*, sic leg, § 1). At the year's end he has become afflicted with a wasting sickness (*serg*, § 2). Later on in the tale, his father the Dagdae says to Óengus, *Ní ségdae dúnn ná cumcem do socht* (§ 9). Jackson translates, 'We feel it to be discourteous that we cannot content you',[12] but this fails to convey the sense of the Irish text, and in particular of the word *socht*. Shaw in the

---

[10] Jackson, p. 93.

[11] Literally 'another night'; Shaw's suggestion that *in n-aidchi n-aili* (MS *hind aidqi n-aile*) means 'one night' is not correct. The reference here is to *Fís Conchobuir* 'Conchobor's Vision', which precedes the *Aislinge* in the manuscript, and which opens with the words: [B]*uí Conchopur macc Neusa aidqi n-ann ina chotlud con facco ní ind oiccbein chuicci* 'Concobor mac Nessa was asleep one night, when he saw a young woman coming towards him' (Flower, p. 286). This is almost identical with the opening of the *Aislinge*; *aidchi n-and* and *in n-aidchi n-aili* are correlative.

[12] Jackson, p. 95.

glossary to his edition (s.v.) says that the meaning of *socht* is obscure, but in the meantime the word has been elucidated by Calvert Watkins,[13] who points out that in the Old Irish period its basic meaning is 'stupor', and observes that 'this "stupor" is [...] a pathological state imposed impersonally from outside on one'.[14] In the light of this, the Dagdae's words may be translated, 'It is unfortunate for us that we cannot deal with your stupor'.

Óengus's love for Cáer is visited upon him; he has neither hand nor part in bringing it about. (It is interesting in this respect to recall Shaw's observation that 'the most striking characteristic of the style of *Aislinge Óenguso* is the writer's strongly marked predilection for passive and impersonal constructions.)[15] Deprived though he is of his appetite and his strength, Óengus nevertheless ultimately succeeds in consummating his love for Cáer. What I propose to do in this paper is to analyse the successive stages in the process whereby this consummation is achieved. The key to the success of Óengus's amorous enterprise is the acceptance, by him and by others, of the deferral of his goal. Over a period of four years, the plot advances through a sequence of delegated functions. The emphasis, both in the language and in the action, is on various kinds and degrees of knowledge and of power, and these are orchestrated in such a way as to lead, step by step, to the union of Óengus and Cáer.

The first step that must be taken in relation to Óengus's illness is diagnosis. The reader knows the cause of Óengus's illness, but the members of his household do not, and he does not tell them (*nícon epert fri nech*, § 2), because, as we later learn (§ 4), he did not dare to do so. In this early part of the tale, the emphasis is on knowledge, and on the lack of it. Óengus 'could not tell where she had gone' (*nícon fitir cia arluid húad*, § 1), and 'no one knew what was wrong with him' (*ni fitir nech cid ro mboí*, § 2). When the physicians of Ireland were brought together, even they did not know what was wrong with him in the end' (*nícon fetatar-som cid ro mboí asendud*, 2). Fergne, physician to Conchobor king of Ulster, is then sent for. Fergne, who in other texts is invariably called Fíngen,[16] has magical diagnostic powers: he can tell from a man's face what his illness is, and he can tell from the smoke which comes from a house how many people are ill in it. He recognizes that Óengus has fallen in love with someone who is absent from him. The diagnosis is confirmed by Óengus,

---

[13] Calvert Watkins, 'Sick-maintenance in Indo-European', *Ériu* 27 (1976), 21–25.

[14] Watkins, p. 24.

[15] Shaw, p. 33.

[16] Shaw, pp. 20–23. Shaw substitutes *Fingen* in his normalized text; Jackson used *Fínghin.*

who tells Fergne how he has been seeing the woman every night in his dreams. Óengus has now been liberated from the dread of speaking about the cause of his illness, and he can seek help, which Fergne advises him to do. In response to Óengus's confirmation of his diagnosis, Fergne says, 'It does not matter. It has been destined for you to make love to her. And send a request to your mother the Boann that she come to speak to you' ('Ní báe,' ol Fíngen, 'ro-tocad (sic leg.)[17] duit cairdes frie; ocus foítter úait cossin mBoinn, cot máthair, co tuidich dot accaldaim, § 3).

Fergne's words here help us to understand what happens in this tale. The use of the phrase ní báe ('it does not matter') may seem odd, in view of the seriousness of Óengus's condition, but its significance derives from what immediately follows it, which is the re-assurance that Óengus is destined to achieve union with the woman. The phrase ní báe recurs, as we shall see, at a number of points in the tale, always as an expression of refusal to be daunted by difficulties which might seem to threaten the achievement of the consummation of Óengus's love. It is followed on each occasion by words or actions which take the hero forward towards his ultimate goal. Fergne, for his part, does not suggest that Óengus should passively await the fulfillment of his destiny; his advice is rather that the Boann should be asked to help.

The Boann is summoned to Óengus's side, she is told of his condition, and asked by Fergne to have the whole of Ireland scoured to see if she could find a young woman to answer the description of the one whom Óengus has seen. The Boann spends the second year of Óengus's illness doing this, but she has no success. (We discover later in the tale that the young woman was in the form a swan for the whole of that year.) Fergne is summoned again, and he recommends that they seek help of the Dagdae. This the Boann does, but the Dagdae says that he knows no more than she does (Ní móo mo éolas in-dáthe-si, § 5). Fergne says that the Dagdae does indeed know more, for he is the king of the síde of Ireland. He goes on, however, to suggest that they send to Bodb, king of the síde of Munster, for his knowledge is much spoken of throughout Ireland (is deilm a éolas la hÉirinn n-uili, § 5).

The Dagdae's emissaries say to Bodb: 'We do not know (nícon fetammar) where in Ireland is the woman whom he has seen and loved' (§ 6), and they tell him that he is bidden by the Dagdae to seek the woman throughout Ireland. Bodb agrees to do so, asking for a year's delay 'to find out the facts of the case' (co fessur fis scél, § 6.) By the end of the year, which is the third one of Óengus's illness, Bodb has found the woman at

[17] See J. Vendryes, Review of Shaw, Études Celtiques, 1 (1936), 159–62, p. 162.

Loch Bél Dracon (Lough Muskry) in Crotta Cliach (the Galtee Mountains), and he asks that Óengus come to Bodb so that they may find out whether Óengus recognizes the young woman when he sees her. When Óengus comes to Bodb's *síd*, and has been duly welcomed, Bodb asks him to come with him to see if he would recognize the girl, and he adds, 'even if you do recognize her, I have no power to give her to you (*ní-s-cumcaim-si*), and you may only see her (§ 7)'. They went to the lake, and 'they saw three times fifty grown girls, and the young woman herself among them. The girls did not reach above her shoulder. There was a chain of silver between each couple; and a necklet of silver round her own throat, and a chain of refined gold' (§ 8). When Óengus tells Bodb that he recognizes the young woman, Bodb says, 'I can do no more for you' (*ní-m thá-sa cumacc deit*[...] *bas móo*, § 8). Óengus is not disturbed by this: 'That does not matter then, since I have seen her; I cannot take her this time' ('*Ní báe són ém* [...] *óre as sí ad-condarc; ní cumcub a breith in fecht so*', § 8). Óengus has made an important advance: the young woman whom he loves, but whom he has known only from his dreams, has been located, and he has seen her in the flesh. He accepts that Bodb does not have the power to bestow the young woman upon him. But he has one further demand to make on Bodb's knowledge, which is the name and identity of the woman. 'I know it truly ('*Fetar* (sic leg) *écin*'),' says Bodb, 'she is Cáer Iborméith, daughter of Ethal Anbúail from Síd Úaman in the land of Connaught' (§ 8).

All of this is duly related to the Dagdae, who responds by expressing regret that he has no power to help Óengus (*Ní ségdae dúnn* [...] *ná cumcem do socht*, § 9). Bodb advises the Dagdae to go to Ailill and Medb as the young woman is in their province.

The Dagdae goes to Connacht and receives a lavish welcome. The Dagdae tells Ailill that he has come to see whether they would bestow the daughter of Ethal Anbuail upon Óengus. Ailill says that they have no power over her (*ní linni a cumacc*, § 10), but that if they had such power (*dia cuimmsimmis*, § 10) she would be given to him. The Dagdae then proposes that Ailill summon Ethal to him, but when Ethal is sent for he divines Ailill's intentions, and declines to go, saying that he will not give his daughter to the Dagdae's son. Ailill is told that Ethal 'cannot be made to come, (for) he knows why he is summoned' ('*Ní étar fair a thuidecht; ro-fitir aní dia congarar*, § 11.) 'No matter (*Ní báe*)', says Ailill, 'he shall come, and the heads of his warriors shall be brought with him'

(§ 11). There follows the harrowing of Síd Úaman by the combined forces of the Dagdae and Ailill: they brought out three score heads and Ethal was taken in captivity to Crúachu.

Ailill demands that Ethal give his daughter to Óengus, but Ethal says, 'I cannot (*ní cumcaim*); her magic power (*cumachtae*) is greater than mine (§

12).' When asked by Ailill what great *cumachtae* she has, Ethal says that she spends every other year in the shape of a bird, and the other years in human shape. Ailill next tries to find out what year she is in the shape of a bird; Ethal declines to answer, but under threat of beheading he finally does so, announcing that at the next Samain she will be at Loch Bél Dracon in the shape of a bird with thrice fifty swans. He adds that he has prepared a feast for them. The Dagdae intervenes at this stage and says, *Ní báe lemm-sa íarum, óre ro-fetar a haicned do-s-uc-so* (§ 12). The first part of this is clear: it means 'it does not matter to me, then', or, as Jackson has it, 'I do not care, then', but what is the meaning of the second part? Shaw says that 'the meaning of this sentence is not quite clear'; he proposes that *do-s-uc-so* be taken as subj. pres. sg. 2 with infixed pron. sg. 3 fem., and he translates, 'since you know her nature, let you bring her';[18] compare Jackson's 'since you know her nature, do you bring her'.[19] This interpretation is formally possible, provided we take *do-uc* as imperative rather than subjunctive. But it does not seem to me to be at all compatible with the context. I suggest rather that we translate, 'since I know her nature, do you take her'. On this reading, the Dagdae is saying that he is satisfied with the knowledge which he has now acquired of the woman's nature, and that he is happy that Ethal proceed with his Samain feast for her and her companions. In other words, he is not demanding that the woman be handed over to him at this time.

Then a treaty is made between them, between Ailill and Ethal and the Dagdae, and Ethal is released. The Dagdae goes home and fills Óengus in on what has happened, and he tells him to go at the next Samain to Loch Bél Dracon, and to call Cáer to him from the lake. And so we come to the final scene, in which the consummation of Óengus's love for Cáer is preceded by what is essentially a contract between the two. Óengus calls Cáer to him, and she says, 'I will go, if you will undertake on your honour that I may come back to the lake again'. He pledges his honour.

> She goes to him then, and he embraces her. They fall asleep in the form of two swans, and go round the lake three times, so that there should be no loss of honour for him. They go away in the form of two white birds till they come to Bruig Maic ind Óaic, and sing a choral song so that they put the people to sleep for three days and three nights. The young woman stays with him after that.[20]

---

[18] Shaw, p. 61.

[19] Jackson, p. 96.

[20] My translation.

In this transaction, Óengus guarantees to maintain the integrity of what we now know to be the woman's nature and magic power, her *aicned* and *cumachtae*, and he redeems his promise by joining her in assuming the form of a swan. And he is duly awarded when the young woman stays with him.

Fergne, as we have seen, had prophesied that Óengus would be united with Cáer, his words being *ro-tocad* (sic leg.) *duit cairdes frie* (§ 3). *Cairdes* in this context doubtless means 'sexual union', but the word can also denote a treaty of friendship; it is used of the treaty between the Dagdae and Ailill and Ethal (§ 13), and of the alliance between Óengus and Ailill and Medb which, according to our tale (§ 15), led to Óengus's participation in the cattle-raid which is the subject of *Táin Bó Cúailnge*. The crucial role of allies in the achievement of ends is clear in *Aislinge Óenguso*. Having availed himself of the knowledge and power of a number of personages, Óengus is able to approach his beloved, and, having accepted and abided by the terms laid down by her, he is united with her and takes her to Bruig na Bóinne as his wife.

A Manner and Temper Peculiar to Himself: An Enquiry into Samuel Johnson's Political/Literary Relations

TIARNÁN Ó CLÉIRIGH
University of Cambridge

IN THE SUMMER of 1762 Samuel Johnson was awarded his pension from George III; the public outcry, at least from that portion of the public as were represented in the journals, periodical essays and pamphlets of the day, was noisy and temperamental. Briefly, it seemed as if Johnson had moved from his tactically opportune sideline stance of professional 'opposition', to a more benign, conciliatory, establishment pose; and that the former hard-line, Jacobite, non-juror had been successfully bribed by an establishment of which he had previously been vehemently critical.

> POMPOSO; *Fame* around should tell
> How he a slave to int'rest fell [...]
> How to all Principles untrue,
> Not fix'd to *old* Friends nor to *New*,
> He damns the *Pension* which he takes
> And loves the STUART he forsakes[1]

Johnson's acceptance of Lord Bute's/George III's offer of a state pension precipitated a torrent of abuse which with his customary commitment and lack of equivocation, Johnson had invited by his forthright definition of 'pension' in the *Dictionary* as 'pay given to a state hireling for treason to his country'. John Wilkes and Charles Churchill launched the first of many attacks in the scathingly anti-Government *North Briton*:

> No man, who has read only one poem of his, *London*, but must congratulate the good sense and discerning spirit of the minister, who bestows such a part of the public treasure on this distinguished friend of the public, of his master's family, and of the constitution of this country.

Boswell later recorded Johnson's reaction to others' perceptions of his altered political allegiances:

> 'Why, sir, (said he, with a hearty laugh), 'it is mightily foolish noise that they make. [...] I am the same man in every respect that I have ever been; I retain the same principles. It is true, that I cannot now

---

[1] Churchill, *The Ghost*, III, pp. 797–8, 817–20.

> curse (smiling) the House of Hanover; nor would it be decent for me
> to drink King James' health in wine that King George gives me money
> to pay for. But, Sir, I think that the pleasure of cursing the house of
> Hanover, and drinking King James' health, are amply overbalanced by
> three hundred pounds a year.[2]

bringing out beautifully, and as he implies Johnson intends, Johnson's, perhaps playful, avaricious conviviality: that loyalty to either King is easily weighed in the balance of £ 300.

Johnson's letter to Lord Bute indicating his acceptance of the pension is in essence as neat a formula of political disinterestedness as any political commentator could endorse; and whilst being warmly grateful is couched in Johnson's characteristic impersonally authoritative, generalising mode as to be an unimpeachable statement of independence:

> Bounty always receives part of its value from the manner in which it is
> bestowed; your Lordship's kindness includes every circumstance that
> can gratify delicacy, or enforce obligation. You have conferred your
> favours on a man who has neither alliance nor interest, who has not
> merited them by services, nor courted them by officiousness; you have
> spared the shame of solicitation, and the anxiety of suspense.[3]

Here Johnson's recognition of Lord Bute's instinctive courtesy in the matching courtesy of his reply, whilst self-consciously asserting the independence of the recipient and of the *bestowal*, is an expression of independent, self-assertion located within a scheme of patronage and non-partisan journalism. Johnson later wrote dispassionately of Lord Bute that although a very honourable man and one who meant well, he 'had his blood full of prerogative, was a theoretical statesman, a book-minister, and thought this country could be governed by the influence of the Crown alone'.[4]

Hawkins in his habitually cool, thorough-going lawyerly way, weighs up the pros and cons of Johnson's action of accepting the pension and arrives at an almost Johnsonian conclusion:

> It is yet difficult, if not impossible, to justify Johnson, both in the
> interpretation given by him of the word *pension*, and in his becoming a

---

[2] James Boswell, *The Life of Samuel Johnson, LL.D.* (1791), ed. by G.B. Hill (Oxford 1887), rev. by L.F. Powell, 6 vols (Oxford, 1934-50), I, pp. 429.

[3] *The Letters of Samuel Johnson*, ed. R.W. Chapman, 3 vols (Oxford, 1952); rev. by B. Redford, 5 vols (Oxford, 1992–4). Letter, 20 July 1762.

[4] *Life*, II, p. 353.

pensioner: in one instance or the other he was wrong, and either his discretion or integrity must be given up: in the former, he seems, in some of his actions, to have been wanting, in the latter never: not only charity, but reason, therefore, directs us in the opinion we are to form of an act which has drawn censure on his conduct, and proves nothing more than that he was not equally wise at all times.[5]

Thirteen years after the pension award, on 8th March 1775 when Johnson published what was his last political pamphlet *Taxation No Tyranny*, the reaction which it unleashed was, if anything, more vehement than that provoked by the pension acceptance. There were four editions of the pamphlet within that month.

Perhaps the single most decisive act in the series of incidents that led to the breaking away of the thirteen American colonies from Britain was the formation in the Autumn of 1774 of the American Continental Congress. The impact of the publication of the Congress's 'Declaration of Rights' was such that Johnson was engaged to publish what the Government clearly intended as pro-establishment propaganda. However, by 1775 the movement for American autonomy was sufficiently advanced that, as such, *Taxation No Tyranny* would have been almost entirely ineffective. Johnson, unlike North, seems to have been well aware of this, and he wrote *Taxation No Tyranny* as a counter-blast manifesto on behalf of the British subject (and tax-payer) against the American position. The invective is rich with Johnsonian vehemence, distinguished by a close legal and constitutional argument, and Johnson is utterly disparaging of the self-aggrandizement and self-enrichment which he perceives to be the true motives behind the flimsy legalistic and patriotic arguments advanced by the Americans. He reduces the colonists arguments to two principle points of issue: whether or not the central government at Westminster has the constitutional right to enforce fiscal legislation in the outlying parts of the British dominions, and whether or not 'taxation without representation' is legal and equitable? Johnson advances a convincing legal case in support of both issues, and more recent analysis seems not merely to have upheld his judgment, but to have endorsed it:[6]

---

[5] Sir John Hawkins, *The Life of Samuel Johnson, LL.D.* (1792), abbr. and ed. by B.H. Davis (London, 1962).

[6] R.L. Schuyler, in *Parliament and the British Empire: Some Constitutional Controversies Concerning Imperial Legislative Jurisdiction* (1929) vigorously affirmed the first proposition, later upheld by Richard Pares in *George III and the Politicians*, 1953, p. 32, n. 2. L.H. Gibson in *The Coming of the Revolution, 1763–1775*, (1954), (pp. 233–34) fully endorses the second.

> In sovereignty there are no gradations. There may be limited royalty, there may be limited consulship; but there can be no limited government. There must in every society be some power or other from which there is no appeal. [...] It is not infallible, for it may do wrong; but it is irresistible, for it can be resisted only by rebellion, by an act which makes it questionable what shall be thenceforward the supreme power.

Congress's contention that George III's ministerial policies were bound to lead to the 'enslavement' of the British people as well as the Americans, Johnson dismisses as fantastic cant: 'The present generation [of British who are paying the cost of the Seven Years' War] seems to think itself in more danger of wanting money than of losing liberty', but he reserves most of his contempt, not for the Americans, but for their British allies and abettors:

> To love their country has been considered as virtue in men, whose love could not be otherwise than blind, because their preference was made without a comparison; but it has never been my fortune to find, either in ancient or modern writers, any honourable mention of those who have with equal blindness hated their country. These anti-patriotic prejudices are the abortions of Folly impregnated by Faction, which being produced against the standing order of nature, have not strength sufficient for long life.

But Johnson's most telling, and strikingly modern, thrust against the spurious claims of the Americans comes at the close of the pamphlet:

> We are told that the subjection of Americans may tend to the diminution of our own liberties: an event, which none but very perspicacious politicians are able to foresee. If slavery be thus fatally contagious, how is it that we hear the loudest yelps for liberty among the drivers of negroes?

Which, reflecting Johnson's earlier response to Lord Bute, encapsulates both Johnson's swingeing disdain of the ideological posturing of the American politicians, but also neatly demarcates the moral/political boundaries between subordination and subjugation.

Johnson was now perceived as a reactionary political turncoat who had been bankrolled by the North Government. The newspapers claimed that Johnson's pension was the bribe, and the recent award of an honourary degree from Oxford, where Lord North was Chancellor, the reward for Johnson's apparent betrayal of his earlier opposition stance. These reports were followed by publication of a string of critical pamphlets: *Resistance No Rebellion*, *Taxation Tyranny*, and *Tyranny Unmasked*; even the *Gentleman's Magazine* whose initial success Johnson had ensured through his earlier political writings was firmly dismissive:

If these positions are admitted, we have profited little by the boasted Revolution; and the British nation has shifted sovereigns to very little purpose if only to change their names.

Which stands out, even if in a somewhat wistful, nostalgically abusive way, from the mainstream of knee-jerk responses to Johnson's carefully researched propositions.[7]

A month later the reaction had not abated: 'The patriots pelt me with answers' Johnson wrote delightedly to John Taylor[8]; but perhaps the most heartening reaction, for as deeply involved a political journalist as Johnson, was the publication of one of his first pieces of sustained political writing, *Marmor Norfolciense*, which he had originally published in the *Gentleman's Magazine* in May 1739, but this time with a sarcastic preface by 'Tribunus'[9] purporting to illustrate the supposedly apparent shift in Johnson's political allegiances and the toning down of his 'opposition' standpoint.

John Hawkins' opinion—as ever, based on a more than usually critical, legal reading (bearing in mind his was the opinion of an experienced lawyer and magistrate)—dissented vigorously from the chorus of disapproval:

> *Taxation No Tyranny* has not only never received an answer, but the converse of the proposition has never yet been so proved, by arguments founded on legal principles, as to make a vindication of Johnson's reasoning necessary, for any other purpose than that of preventing the ignorant from being misled.[10]

Coleridge's is another notably positive response to the pamphlet, and his reaction to *Taxation* is very appealing in the alacrity with which he picks up on Johnson's method:

> I like Dr. Johnson's political pamphlets better than any other parts of his works—particularly his *Taxation No Tyranny* is very clever and spirited.[11]

Coleridge's attention is caught immediately by Johnson's characteristic wit and vigour, and his response is certainly worthy of Johnson's expectations. He does not react to Johnson either by adopting a political stance in order

---

[7] Helen Louise McGuffie, *Samuel Johnson in the British Press, 1749-1784: A Chronological Checklist*, (London 1976).

[8] *Letters*, ed. Redford, II, 197-8.

[9] Francis Webb (*DNB*).

[10] Hawkins, *Life*, p. 222.

[11] *Table Talk*, 16 August 1833.

to 'read' Johnson, nor does he insist on pronouncing upon Johnson's political stance before commenting on Johnson's literary endeavour.

As with his earlier, boozier, comment to Boswell on his post-pension altered perception of Kings, Johnson clearly emphasises in the piece that he has no time whatsoever for what he perceives to be merely a variety of political posturing: what really matters to him is the *general* stability in society whereby a happier more peaceful existence for every man, black or white, is assured, and justice has a firmly *legal* basis.

Recently there has been some lively controversy debating interpretations of Johnson's political identity[12]. The debate hinges on the divergence between evidence based on close documentary reading and the necessary more general historical interpretation—never an easy task—but in Johnson's case the process is bedevilled both by Johnson's love of dialectic, and the sheer mass of biographical evidence. The 'fiction' of Boswell's *Life* and his suitability as an interpreter through whom the complexity of Johnson's politics can be assessed with any confidence, has become a focal point in the discussion. *Taxation* made Boswell very unhappy:

> The extreme violence which it breathed appeared to me so unsuitable to the mildness of a Christian philosopher, and so directly opposite to the principles of peace which he had so beautifully recommended in his pamphlet respecting Falkland's Islands that I was sorry to see him appear in so unfavourable a light.[13]

More than simply picking up Boswell's ideological disagreement with Johnson, Donald Greene has also examined Boswell's competence to act as a barometer to the climacterics of Johnson's politics:

Again, in May 1769, Boswell learned that Johnson was staying with the Thrales in Brighton and notes, 'During this visit he seldom or never dined out. He appeared to be deeply engaged in some literary work.' But about what that literary work was, Boswell again displayed no curiosity. For Boswell, Johnson is primarily the amusing table companion and conversationalist, not the dedicated professional writer who locks himself up from distracting acquaintances and does not dine out when he has serious work to do and a deadline to meet.[14]

---

[12] H. Erskine-Hill, 'The Political Character of Samuel Johnson', in *Samuel Johnson: New Critical Essays*, ed. by Isobel Grundy (London, 1984), pp. 107–36.; D.J. Greene, *The Politics of Samuel Johnson*, 2nd edn, (London 1990); J.C.D Clark, *English Society 1688–1832*, (Cambridge, 1985), and J.C.D Clark, *Samuel Johnson*, (Cambridge 1994).

[13] *Life*, II, p. 312.

[14] Donald J. Greene, *The Politics of Samuel Johnson*, 2nd edn (London, 1990), pp. xvi-xvii.

Which is perhaps a little harsh on Boswell, but one cannot help sympathising with the gist of Greene's concern that Boswell, certainly by comparison with Hawkins, Chambers or Reynolds, while being an excellent thumbnail-sketch artist and social diarist, is perhaps not the best person to look to for an accurate or detailed perspective on the earnestness of Johnson's attention to politics.

> That I am a Tory, a lover of power in monarchy, and a discourager of much liberty in the people, I avow. But it is not clear to me that our colonies are compleatly our subjects (*Life*, II, 312.)

Ultimately, what seems to separate the parties in the debate on Johnson in *Taxation* is an inability to perceive, or, for that matter, to match Johnson's preferred discursive, dialectical ability; both in his argumentative method and in his attempt at a realistic appraisal and depiction of a systematically pragmatic political process. For Johnson, a paradoxical stance was not an inherently contradictory one; the fact that one could contain in an argument—often with equal vehemence—disparate and opposing points of view, was for him a testament of dialectic sophistication, and not, some sort of occasionally, usefully applied, sporadic inability on his part to arrive at or to maintain a consistent standpoint.

The high point amidst the thundering denunciations was the re-issue of *Marmor Norfolciense*[15], a very timely reminder, though this can hardly have been what the publishers intended, of Johnson's complex and multi-faceted political, journalistic skills.

Johnson had published *Marmor Norfolciense*, a piece of very lively, ironic and vigorously Scriblerian anti-Government/Walpole invective in the Spring of 1739. As with *Taxation*, *Marmor* has been variously used to pronounce on Johnson's political allegiances. Howard Erskine-Hill[16] uses a detailed and very scholarly account of the evidence in *Marmor* to identify the political thrust of the poem, and he then attributes this more generally to Johnson's broader political outlook; thereby rubbing out the complexity and variety in Johnson's politics, without observing that Johnson clearly revelled in adopting an 'opposition' pose (c.f. *The Patriot—False Alarm*) as he does here, gleefully maintaining a pitch of satirical invective in this daringly polemical pamphlet.

---

[15] *Marmor Norfolciense; or, An Essay on an Ancient Prophetical Inscription in Monkish Rhyme Lately Discovered near Lynn*; By Probus Britanicus. *Works*, XIV, 1–36.

[16] Howard Erskine-Hill, *The Political Character of Samuel Johnson*, in *Samuel Johnson: New Critical Essays*, ed. by Isobel Grundy (London, 1984).

The piece purports to be an account of the deciphering of an ancient inscription on a stone dug up in a field in King's Lynn, the town for which Robert Walpole was member of Parliament. Written in the tradition of Swift's *Memoirs of Martin Scriblerius* and *A Tale of a Tub* and Pope's *Dunciad*, the force of the satire is due both the extraordinary way in which Johnson keeps comedy and sedition going at the same time, and the hilarious psychological portrait of the commentator, a smug, scholarly hypocrite whose veneration for his own work is boundless:

That sobriety and modesty with which it becomes every learned man to treat a subject of such importance [...] with what laborious struggles against prejudice and inclination, with what efforts of reasoning, and pertinacity of self-denial, I have prevailed upon myself to sacrifice the honour of this monument to the love of truth.

Professor Erskine-Hill maintains that the piece is direct Jacobite sedition. Of the lines:

Kings change their laws, and kingdoms change their kings [...]
Nor shall the lyon, wont of old to reign
Despotic o'er the desolated plain,
Henceforth th'inviolable bloom invade,
Or dare to murmur in the flow'ry glade;
His tortur'd sons shall die before his face,
While he lies melting in a lewd embrace;
And, yet more strange: his veins a horse shall drain,
Nor shall the passive coward once complain.

he says: 'in making the common charge that government and court sacrificed the interests of England to those of Hanover, Johnson handles it in such a way that he not only reflects on George II specifically, and on kings generally, but, much more dangerous, on the Hanoverian succession precisely: the horse.' But, as with his later coverage of the *Political Debates*, the difficulty lies in ascertaining the extent of Johnson's seditious posturing, in this case for the sake of an hilariously ribald commentary on George II's sex-life.

It is perhaps not surprising, given Johnson's penchant for opposition and Robert Walpole's uniquely powerful and equivocal domination of English politics from 1727 to 1742, that Walpole became Johnson's principal target in his three political satires of this period[17]. However, the opportunity that Edward Cave offered Johnson in reporting on debates in the three sessions

---

[17] *London, Marmor Norfolciense*, and *A Compleat Vindication of the Licensers of the Stage*, in *Yale Edition of the Works of Samuel Johnson* (New Haven, Conn., 1977), pp. vi, x.

of Parliament between 1740 to 1743 resulted in a startling reversal in Johnson's treatment of Walpole, and added considerably to the complexity of Johnson's on-going political commentary.[18]

On February 13, 1741, Carteret in the House of Lords, and Sandys in the House of Commons, introduced the motion to request the King to dismiss Walpole. This was the climax of many unsuccessful attempts to bring down Walpole - the war in Spain was going badly, and with Frederick of Prussia's aggression against the Silesian territories of Maria Theresa, the prospect of England's becoming involved on the losing side of a great continental war was ominous; to Walpole's opponents in Parliament this must have seemed an opportune moment.

Johnson's account of the debate is a wonderfully, dramatically organised piece of rhetoric. There are only eleven speeches reported on the main motion and each is infused with a theatrical sense of moment that, to my mind, contains far more of the ingredients of real dramatic tension than Johnson had managed to generate in *Irene*. Cartaret's speech, proposing the Address, moves with superbly weighty concern:

> Such is the present unhappy state of this nation, and such is the general discontent of the people, that tranquillity, adherence to the government, and submission to the laws cannot reasonably be hoped, unless the motion I shall now make clear to make you Lordships be complied with: And I move, Than an humble address be presented to his Majesty, most humbly to advise and beseech his Majesty, that he will be most graciously pleased to remove the Right Honourable Sir Robert Walpole, Knight of the most noble Order to the Garter, First Commissioner of his Majesty's Treasury, and Chancellor of the Exchequer, and one of his Majesty's most honourable Privy Council, from his Majesty's presence and councils for ever.[July 1741, p.350]

and Hervey's reply for the defence is couched in unimpeachably statesman-like wisdom:

> To condemn a man unheard is an open and flagrant violation of the first law of justice, but it is still a wider deviation from it to punish a man unaccused; no crime has been charged upon this gentleman proportioned to the penalty proposed by the motion, and the charge that has been produced is destitute of proof.

[18] *Parliamentary Debates*, ed. by John Stockdale, 2 vols (London, 1787); repr. in Works of Samuel Johnson, ed. by Arthur Murphy (London, 1811).

> Let us therefore, my Lords, reverence the great laws of reason and
> justice, let us preserve our high character and prerogative of judges,
> without descending to the low province of accusers and executioners,
> let us so far regard our reputation, our liberty, and our posterity, as to
> reject the motion [August 1741, p.124]

The temperature of the Debate rises as the superbly violent invective is
deployed against Walpole, and Sandys paints a vividly shocking picture of
Westminster:

> When the cries of the exasperated people shall be too loud to be
> repressed, and vengeance shall impend over those heads which have
> so long been lifted up with confidence. [...] Then will the corrupter
> and his associates, the lacqueys of his train, the slaves of his
> levee....who have sold their country for opportunities of debauchery,
> and wasted the rewards of perfidy in the pleasures of the stews of
> court, implore the protection of their military friends.

The weight of Johnson's disapprobation is behind the opposition until,
finally, Walpole, who has not uttered a word during the course of the
lengthy, noisy debate, stands and asks simply: 'That I may know the whole
accusation against me before I offer my defence'. The opposition leap at
the opportunity and Walpole is again forcefully and noisily denounced. He
stands for the last time and with the sort of deferential, wounded *sang froid*,
after the preceding tumult, that one can almost imagine the quiet, troubled
gratitude and careful deliberation as he speaks, acknowledging first his
supporters:

> The gentlemen who have already spoken in my favour have indeed
> freed me from the necessity of wearying the House with a long
> defence [...] their zeal and their friendship so ardent, that I shall speak
> with less warmth in my own cause.
>
> As to myself, I now not how I have given occasion to any charge of
> rapacity or avarice, or why I should be suspected of making exorbitant
> demands upon his Majesty's liberality, since, except the places which
> I am known to possess, I have obtained no grant from the Crown, or
> fewer at least than perhaps any man who has been supposed to have
> enjoyed the confidence of his sovereign.
>
> This little ornament upon my shoulder [Order of the Garter] though
> it may be looked on with envy and indignation in another place, can it
> be supposed to raise any resentment in this House, where many must
> be pleased to see those honours which their ancestors have worn
> restored again to the Commons.

> For my part, that innocence which has supported me against the clamour of the opposition will establish my happiness in obscurity, nor shall I lose by the censure which is now threatened any other pleasure than that of serving my country.
>
> *When he had done speaking, the question was put and carry'd in the negative 290 to 106* [April 1743, pp. 180-3]

Clearly, in his casting of Walpole as tragic hero, Johnson was unable to resist the urge to write a vividly, fictional piece of drama; but, as it was a faction within his own party which was ultimately responsible for toppling Walpole, perhaps also Johnson's sense of fairness and his aversion to party politics played a part in the shaping of the drama.

Each of the writers commenting on Johnson's dramatic abilities as a political speech writer sum up Hawkins as endorsing Johnson as to the accurate representation of each speaker;[19] but this does not seem to me to be *quite* what Hawkins means. Surely this is Johnson the role-player, or the novelist, who is operating within a system. In his candid appraisal of the debates of the day, he is easily capable of construction a fiction that is so lifelike and persuasive that contemporary commentators and subsequent writers are persuaded both by the verisimilitude of Johnson's writing and the political disinterestedness of his abilities in presenting the various arguments in debate, to mistake them for the real thing.

Hawkins, a careful, contemporary student of the events reported, gives a delightful account of Johnson's speech writing in the *Debates*:

> It was curious to observe how the deceit operated. [...] Johnson had the art to give different colours to the several speeches, so that some appear to be declamatory and energetic, resembling the orations of Demosthenes; others like those of Cicero, calm, persuasive; [...] others bear the characteristic of plainness, bluntness, and an affected honesty as opposed to the plausibility of such as were understood or suspected to be courtiers [...]. Voltaire was betrayed by it into a declaration, that the eloquence of ancient Greece and Rome was revived in the British senate.[20]

The *Debates* are impressive examples of the political journalist's art at a very early stage of its development, rebutting any simplistic claims of Johnson's supposed political allegiances; and they reflect provocatively on

---

[19] John Wain, *Samuel Johnson* (London, 1974); Robert Giddings, *The Fall of Orgilio*, in *Samuel Johnson: New Critical Essays*, ed. by Isobel Grundy (London, 1984), pp. 86–106; John Cannon, *Samuel Johnson and the Politics of Hanoverian England* (Oxford, 1994).

[20] Hawkins' *Life*, p. 58.

one of Johnson's more familiar utterances on politics, written at the time he was engaged on the *Debates*:

> Political Truth is undoubtedly of very great Importance, and they who honestly endeavour after it, are doubtless engaged in a laudable Pursuit. Nor do the Writers on this Subject ever more deserve the Thanks of their Country, than when they enter upon Examination of the Conduct of their Governors, whether Kings Senates, or Ministers.[21]

Which illustrates the complexity of Johnson's own sense of involvement in writing the fiction of his life and times. Johnson was too self-conscious, too keenly aware of the function of the writer within society, and of the historical political pressure to which contemporary politics was subject, simply to adopt a single political identity allying him with the narrow ideology of those whose intellects and abilities he not only doubted, but whose blinkered outlook he could never espouse in a simplistic way that would have branded him an 'either/or':

> Of political evil, if we suppose the origin of moral evil discovered, the account is by no means difficult, polity being only the conduct of immoral men in public affairs.[22]

In essence, the argument over whether Johnson was a Tory, or indeed an arch-Tory, is unsuitable. Presuming to stamp Johnson, a most variable thinker, with a reductive, party label which in itself fails to recognise the complexities of the variations in the party system during the eighteenth century, begs too many questions, as Johnson himself noted epigraphically: 'Men willingly believe what they wish to be true.'[23]

Examples of Johnson's complexity and generosity of argument occur in almost every area of his output. The three major pieces which I have cited illustrate Johnson's method of consciously evading a single, easily-discerned position, inimical both to his wide-ranging liveliness of approach to debate and his mistrust of partisan politics. But this general recommendation to an order of greatness in complexity is almost self-denyingly, contradictorily, turned back on itself in a sort of mimetic movement to enact and then amplify Johnson's idea:

As a question becomes more complicated and involved, and extends to a greater number of relations, disagreement of opinion will always be

---

[21] Johnson in *The Gentleman's Magazine*, January 1739, p. 3.

[22] 'Review of Soame Jenyns' in *Samuel Johnson*, ed. by Greene (Oxford Authors, 1980) p. 541.

[23] *The Adventurer* No. 69: Caesar's Gallic War (III, 18).

multiplied, not because we are irrational, but because we are finite beings, furnished with different kinds of knowledge, exerting different degrees of attention, one discovering consequences which escape another, none taking in the whole concatenation of causes and effects, and most comprehending but a very small part; each comparing what he observes with a different criterion, and each referring it to a different purpose:

> We have less reason to be surprised or offended when we find others differ from us in opinion, because we very often differ from ourselves. (*The Adventurer*, 107)

Johnson's perception is ultimately explosive: ideology becomes cant, loyalty becomes partisan. The outward-bound trajectory of his increasingly complex thought process is contained within a general matrix of understanding; but this authority is tempered by its generality, insisting on the inherent potential of divergence that characteristically 'complicated and involved' questions demand.

I have proposed an examination of Johnson's political writing as reflecting his native discursiveness, which is, ideally, how I would end: I would not risk a disservice to the subject by straining to arrive at a conclusion that is anything less than inconclusive, but what I would propose is that when a writer of Johnson's skill and complexity comments on political events, it is necessary to use the inherently suggestive complexity of the thought as the basis for an analysis, as literary as it might be historical, and to interpret Johnson's position accordingly; and not, despite the characteristic firmness of expression, as being necessarily definitive.

Nullius addictus in verba magistri jurare.[24]

---

[24] 'Committed to the ideology of no ideologue' the motto with which Johnson prefaced his writings for the *Rambler*, and also that of the Royal Society.

Srónaíl Mhírialta i Lámhscríbhinn ón Séú Céad Déag

TOMÁS Ó CONCHEANAINN
Deilgne, Co. Chill Mhantáin

TÁ tuairisc tugtha ag Robin Flower ar an lámhscríbhinn atá againn anseo, Harley 5280 (gearrthagairt mar Hl. as seo síos).[1] Giolla Riabhach Ó Cléirigh a bhí ar an scríobhaí, agus ba sa gcéad leath den séú céad déag a bhí sé i réim. Luann Giolla Riabhach log scríofa a leabhair, mar atá, Corr Leasa Conaill (*a Cuirr Lessa Conaill dam*), áit is eol dúinn a bheith in aice le Cora Droma Rúisc (Carrick-on-Shannon), ach ar thaobh Ros Comáin den tSionainn.[2]

Is córas aduain mírialta litrithe atá in úsáid sa lámhscríbhinn seo cuid mhaith, litriú a bhfuil tuairisc tugtha ag Séamus Mac Mathúna air as *Immram Brain*.[3] Tá cúpla córas aduain litrithe mar seo le feiceáil i lámhscríbhinní atá againn ón gcúigiú agus ón séú céad déag, as Connachta go háirithe. Aisteach go leor, meastar go coitianta (ar lorg Thurneysen) gur i gcuid acu seo atá na leaganacha is dílse ar na téacsanna a tháinig ó Chín Droma Sneachta.[4]

Is gné an-suntasach den litriú i dtéacs cáiliúil eile atá in Hl., *Tochmarc Emire*, an tsrónaíl mhírialta atá luaite thuas. Tá sí sin le fáil go háirithe mar urú ar an gconsan sna forainmneacha atá bunaithe ar na réamhfhocail *do* agus *di* (*de*); agus mar *n*, gan cheangal soiléir comhréire, roimh ghuta tús focail. Tá beagán eile aduaine i gceist freisin agus pléifear sin i bhfo-ranna (iii) agus (iv) thíos.

Maidir leis an tuiscint a bhí ag scríobhaithe na seanteanga ar fheidhm an uraithe, go háirithe an ghné fhorleathnaithe de nach mbíonn faoi réir sheanrialacha na comhréire, tá an trácht beag seo ag Lewis agus Pedersen air i bparagraf faoin teideal 'The psychological value of sandhi-*n* in Ir':

> Apparently sandhi-*n* came to be regarded in OIr. and MIIr. as a separate morphological element to denote some grammatical relationship, and so was used even after an intervening non-eclipsing

---

[1] *Catalogue of Irish Manuscripts in the British Library* [*formerly British Museum*], 3 iml. (Londain, 1926-53), II (le Robin Flower; 1926, athchló 1992), 298–323.

[2] Corlis, i bparáiste Eachdhroma (Aughrim), Co. Ros Comáin. Bhí scoil ag Clann Uí Mhaoil Chonaire ann; féach *Irish Men of Learning*, le Paul Walsh (BÁC, 1947) 48.

[3] *Immram Brain: Bran's Journey to the Land of the Women*, in eagar ag Séamus Mac Mathúna (Tübingen, 1985), 482–4.

[4] Is eol anois cuid de na téacsanna a bhí sa lámhscríbhinn Ultach sin (a cuireadh le chéile san ochtú céad, b'fhéidir); tá tuairisc tugtha orthu in *Die irische Helden- und Königsage*, le Rudolf Thurneysen (Halle, 1921), 15–18; féach freisin Mac Mathúna, *Immram Brain*, 454–69.

word: MlIr. *bunsaig* ṁ-*báisi* (g. sg.) ṁ-*bunloisthi* 'his toy-javelin with
its fire-hardened butt-end' (lit. 'his rod of play bottom-burnt') LL. 62a
48; *delg* n-*argit* (g. sg.) n-*and* 'a silver brooch therein' LU. 5205f.;
déde didiu n-*and* 'two things, then, are therein' Wb. 1a 5 (*didiu* 'then'
from *di ṡudiu*).[5]

Tá an ghné neamhchaighdeánach srónaíola sin le fáil go tréan sa téacs seo
Tochmarc Emire in Hl.; agus bheadh roinnt de na samplaí ar dheacair
tabhairt faoi iad a mhíniú ach mar chuid den fhiontar dána litrithe seo ag an
scríobhaí, nó b'fhéidir mar fhoirmeacha bréagársa. Tá na samplaí sin ar fad
as an téacs seo in Hl. curtha i gcló trom agam.

Is as an eagrán a rinne Kuno Meyer de leagan Hl. na chéad tagairtí atá
curtha síos.[6] Ina ndiaidh sin tugaim na foirmeacha as an téacs atá le fáil i
dhá lámhscríbhinn eile, RIA D iv 2 (luaite feasta mar S)[7] agus RIA 23 N 10
(feasta mar N).[8] Go coitianta níl an síneadh fada le fáil sa téacs seo sa trí
lámhscríbhinn sin, ach tá sé curtha isteach ag van Hamel san eagrán tacair
sin a bhunaigh sé ar S.

Tá tugtha agam anseo freisin, mar fhianaise an-tábhachtach ar theanga
an téacs, na sleachta comhfhreagracha atá le fáil sna bloghanna de atá
tagtha slán i Leabhar na hUidhre (LU).[9] Tá fós roinnt foirmeacha luaite
agam as *Immram Brain*, go háirithe mar atá siad in Hl. agus sna bloghanna
den téacs sin atá tagtha slán in LU. Is as eagrán Shéamuis Mhic Mhathúna
de *Immram Brain* atá na samplaí sin curtha síos anseo.[10]

---

[5] *A Concise Comparative Celtic Grammar*, le Henry Lewis agus Holger Pedersen (Göttingen, 1937), 115 (§ 191).

[6] Kuno Meyer, 'Tochmarc Emire la Coinculaind', *Zeitschrift für celtische Philologie*, 3 (1910), 229–63.

[7] Seasann S anseo do 'Stowe (Collection)', teideal cnuasaigh a raibh an lámhscríbhinn seo ann tráth i Sasana. Is i gCill Chormaic, in Uíbh Fhailí, a cuireadh an lámhscríbhinn le chéile (sa dara leath den chúigiú céad déag, is cinnte) ach baineann sí le traidisiún liteartha Chonnacht. Seán Mac Aodhagáin ab ainm do dhuine de na scríobhaithe, an té a scríobh isteach *Tochmarc Emire*; féach *Catalogue of Irish Manuscripts in the Royal Irish Academy*, lgh 3297–307 (uimh. 1223). Is dóigh gurbh é an Seán mac Conchobhair Mhic Aodhagáin a bhí ina ollamh ag Clann Riocaird, agus a fuair bás sa mbliain 1487, an scríobhaí seo.

[8] Cuireadh an lámhscríbhinn seo le chéile tigh Sheáin Uí Mhaoil Chonaire, *Bailein Chuimine*, ar Loch Bó Deirge ar an tSionainn (Ballycummin, paráiste na Cille Móire (Kilmore), Ros Comáin) sa bhliain 1575; féach *Facsimiles in Collotype of Irish Manuscripts VI: MS. 23 N 10 (formerly Betham 145)*, le R.I. Best (BÁC, 1954). Is do leathanaigh na macasamhla sin atá tagairt sna samplaí as N.

[9] Is san Acadamh freisin atá an lámhscríbhinn stairiúil seo (23 E 25); féach *Lebor na hUidre: The Book of the Dun Cow*, in eagar ag R.I. Best agus Osborn Bergin (BÁC, 1929; an 3ú hathchló 1992). Tá ceist an ghaoil idir na leaganacha den téacs *Tochmarc Emire* atá (i) in LU agus (ii) in Hl. 5280, RIA D iv 2 agus RIA 23 N 10 pléite agam in 'Textual and Historical Associations of Leabhar na hUidhre', *Éigse*, 29 (1996), 65–120 (lgh 91-120).

[10] Féach thuas, n. 3. Tá na samplaí as an téacs sin luaite thíos i bhfo-roinn (v).

Seo iad na samplaí den tsrónaíl mhírialta atá le fáil in *Tochmarc Emire* in Hl.:

(I) SRÓNAÍL AR *DÓ, DE, DÍ, DÍB* AGUS AN RÉAMHFHOCAL *DO*[11]

§ 6   Ar batar secht mec imblesan ina rigroscoib .i. a cethair isan dalai suil, a tri isan tsuil n-ali **ndo** Hl.; Ar batar secht meic imlesain ina rigroscaib .i. a chethair isin dara suil do ⁊ a tri isin tsuil eile S; Ar batur secht mic imlesain ina rigroscaip .i. a ceathair isin dara suil do ⁊ a tri isin suil aile N 22.4–5

     Ar bátár /^(sect meic imlesain ina rígrosc .i. a cethair) (*i láimh eile*) / isindala súil ⁊ a tri hisin tsuil aile do LU 10150–2

§ 7   setig ba togai la Coin Culaind de tochmarc **ndo** Hl. ('céile ar mhaith le Cú Chulainn a dhul á tochmharc dó féin'); setig bud toga la Coin Culainn do thochmarc do S; setcid bud toga la .c.c. do tochmarc do N 22.14

     sétig bad toga la Coin Culaind do thochmarc dó LU 10161–2

§ 8   dús in faigepdis [...] ingen rig no roflathav [...] bud ail do togai ⁊ de tocmarc **ndou** Hl.[12] ('féachaint an bhfaighidís iníon rí nó ró-fhlatha dob áil a thoghadh nó a iarraidh le tochmarc dó'); dús in fuigebdais [...] *ingin* rig *nó* roflatha [...] ɔ neoch bud ail do Choin Chulainn do thogu ⁊ do tochmarc S; dus fuighbetais [...] ingen rig *nó* roflatha [...] bud ail do c.c. do thoga ⁊ do tochmarc N 22.21–3

     dús in faigébtais [...] ingen ríg nó roflatha [...] do neoch bad áil do Choin Culaind do thoga ⁊ do tochmarc LU 10171–2

ni fuarotar ingen [*in áit* 'ingin'] bud togai la Coin Culaind de tocmarc **ndo** Hl. ('ní bhfuaradar bean óg ba rogha le Cú Chulainn a dhul á tochmarc'); ni fuarutar *ingin* bu togu la Coin Culainn do tochmarc S; ni fuaradur ingen bu togha la .c.c. do tochmarc N 22.24

---

[11] Ní le litriú Hl. amháin a bhaineann an ghnéith seo, urú a chur ar fhorainm réamhfhoclach a thosaíonn le *d-* (agus *n* a bheith roimh ghuta tosaigh forainme, e.g. *n-and*). Tá srónaíl mar seo le fáil i lámhscríbhinní eile as Connachta, e.g. *gaphus eulcaire fer ndib*, RIA 23 N 10, lch 61.16 (sa scéal *Immram Brain*; cf. fo-roinn (v) thíos; Leabharlann Náis. na hÉir., MS G 7, col. 5.24 *Dopreth Geur ma[c] oi Neuch i rraith ndo* 'Tugadh Gér, mac Uí Necae, mar urra (i.e. i mbarántas) dó' (sa scéal *Orgain Brudne Uí Dergae*); féach freisin thíos, n. 28.

[12] Deir Meyer linn an fhoirm áinsíoch *ingin* a léamh anseo, agus forlíonann van Hamel foirm ghiorraithe na lámhscríbhinne mar 'ingin'. Tá pointe spéisiúil comhréire anseo, áfach, i.e. go bhfuil oibriú an bhriathair caillte ag an gcuspóir ó tharla an dá rann inscne sin a bheith dealaithe chomh mór sin óna chéile san abairt. Tá freisin foirm an ainmnigh *ingen* scríofa amach gan giorrú in N agus in LU. Maidir le gaol leaganacha an téacsa seo féach an t-alt in *Éigse* atá luaite thuas, n. 9.

ní fúaratar ingin ba toga la Coin Culaind do tochmarc LU 10173–4

§ 10   acht ingen pad comad*uis* **ndo** Hl. ('ach bean óg a d'oirfeadh dó'); acht ingen bud comadais do S; acht ingen bud comadais do N 23.4
acht ingen bad chomadais dó LU 10186–7

⁊ na bad coimdich **ndou** do bancelib Erenn mona beth samlaid Hl. ('agus nár chuibhe (chuí) dó í mar bhanchéile mura mbeadh sí amhlaidh');[13] ⁊ nad bud coimde do do bancelib muna b*eith* samlaid S; ⁊ na bud choimde do do phanceilip muna beth samlaid N 23.5–6
⁊ nábad chomdi dó do banchéli mani beth samlaid LU 10188–9

[*bearna in LU as seo síos go dtí § 78*]

§ 28   imcomaircid a arai, edon Loeg,˙ **ndou** [...] Hl. ('d'fhiafraigh a charbadóir, is é sin Laogh, de') [...]; imcomaircid a ara do .i. Laeg [...] S; imcomairccid a ara do .i. Laogh N 115.26

§ 29   boie occa miniougud **ndo** Hl. ('bhí sé á míniú dó');[14] bai oca miniugad do S; bai oca | |[15] miniugad do N

is dei imoru as-perour Eomon Machou **ndii** Hl. ('is é an chúis atá le Eamhain Mhacha a thabhairt uirthi'); Is de im*morro* as-bert Emain M*acha* S; Is de is-bert .imm. Emain M*acha* N 118.3

§ 47   do dignad **ndou** ('mar shólás dó') ier cath Moicchi Tuiriud Hl.; do didnad do iar cath Muigi Tuired S; do dignad do iar cath Muige Tuiredh N 120.27–8

do-rigne cnoc **nde** Hl. ('rinne(adh) cnoc de'); do-rigni cnoc mor de S; do-rigne cnoc mor de N 120.30

§ 63   ni ro genair nach ercoid **ndou** Hl. ('ní dhearna sí [an ollphéist] aon urchóid dó'); ni forgenair nach n-ercoit do S; ni forgenar nach n-erchoid dó N 123.33-4

---

[13] Is in LU atá an leagan ceart san uatha, *bancéli*; agus is mar mhacalla ar thagairt atá roimhe sin sa téacs (§10), i.e. cén duine 'de ingenaib Érenn' a b'fhiú le Cú Chulainn 'do acallaim ⁊ do thochmarc', atá an uimhir iolra in Hl. (*do bancelib Erenn*), in S (*do bancelib*) agus in N (*do phanceilip*).

[14] Bhí Cú Chulainn anois ag míniú 'na himacallma' a tharla idir é féin agus Eimhear roimhe sin do Laogh.

[15] Léimeann an téacs ó lch 115 *ad fin.* go dtí lch 118 *ad init.*, de bharr botúin a rinne an scríobhaí; tá nóta tugtha aige faoi sin.

§ 64 Do-beurt and ingeun dicc ⁊ mir **ndo** Hl. ('thug an bhean óg deoch agus greim bia dó'); Do-bert ind ingen dig ⁊ mir do S; Do-bert in ingen di[g] ⁊ mir do N 124.13

§ 65 Incoisscid an t-oclaech eulus **ndo** tar an maug ndobail Hl.[16] ('tugann [*go lit.* teagascann] an t-óglach eolas (an bhealaigh) dó tar an machaire mí-ádhúil'); Incoiscid int oclaech eolas tarsa mag ndobail S; Inchoisced in t-oclach eolus tarsan mag ndobiul [*sic*] N 124.16

A leth in moigi no seichtis doine **ndei** Hl. ('an leath den mhachaire a ngreamaíodh [cosa] daoine de agus iad seactha'); A leth an maige no sectais daini de S; A leth an maighe no sechtais daine de N 124.16–7

To-beurt an t-oclaech ruoth **ndo** Hl.; Do-bert int oclaech roth do S; Do-bert in t-oclach roth do N 124.18–9

Don-beurt div uball **ndo** Hl. ('Thug sé úll do'); Do-bert dano uball do S; Do-bert dano uball do N 124.19–20

§ 66 Ro tairngir 'diu in t-oclaech cetno **ndo** Hl. ('Rinne an t-óglach céanna tairngreacht dó'); Ro tairrngir dano in t-oclaech cetna do S; Ro thairngir dano in t-oclach cetna do N 124.28

§ 67 amal ro forchan ind oclaech **ndo** Hl. ('mar a theagaisc an t-óglach dó'); amal do forcan int oclaech do S; amal do forchan in t-oclach do N 124.32

§ 68 condo cor **nde** Hl.; conda cor de ('so that he left it behind him, passed it', van Hamel) S; conda cor de N 11.11

co faco ar an gildie dia hóidh a toil **ndii** Hl.; co n-accai foran ngilla a toil di S; con n-acaigh forin ngiolla a toil di N 11.15-6[17]

§ 69 nus frithail Cu Culaind amail pid foglaim **ndou** ho aeis iead Hl. ('d'fhreastail Cú Chulainn iad [cleasa laoich eile] amhail is dá mbeadh sé á bhfoghlaim ar feadh a shaoil'); nos frithail Cu Chulainn amal bud foglaim o ais do iat S; nus frithail .c.c. amal bu foglaim o ais do iat N 11.25

§ 70 Do-mbeurt iarum ind ingen comairli **ndov** Co[i]n Culaind Hl.[18] ('Thug an bhean óg ansin comhairle do Chú Chulainn'); Do-bert iarom in

---

[16] Níl an forainm réamhfhoclach ach sa gcéad sampla díobh seo.

[17] Idir an trí leagan tá comhréir agus brí an chlásail seo doiléir.

ingen comairli do Choin Chulainn S; Do-bert iaram in ingen comairle do .c.c. N 11.29

arin cuorud ich n-errid **nde** Hl. ('go gcuirfeadh sé "léim bradáin an ghaiscidh" de'); arin corad ich n-erred de S; arin corad ich n-err*ed* de N 11.31[19]

co tartath a tri drinnroisc **ndo** Hl. ('nó go dtugadh sí a thrí mhian dó'); co tartad a thri hindrosc dó S; co tartat a tri drinnroiscc do N 11.32–3

§ 74   de-breuth deug suain **ndo** riam Hl. ('tugadh deoch suain dó roimh ré'); do-breth deog suain do riam S; do-bretha deog shuain d<o> N 12.24

ba hoenúar **ndo-ssom** innsin Hl. ('ba haon uair amháin dó-san sin'); ba oenuair do-som indsin S; ba aenuair do-sum indsin N 12.28[20]

§ 75   immacomarnic **ndo-ssom** friu i triur Hl. ('thug seisean aghaidh orthu triúr'); imcomarnic do-som friu a triur S; imchomarnic do-som friu a triur N 25.3

§ 76   Facbaiss Cv Chulaind dornnaisc n-oir **ndo** Hl. ('d'fhág Cú Chulainn ordnasc dó [i.e. lena aghaidh]'); Facbaid Cú Chulainn dornaisc oir do S; Facbaid .c.c. dornasc oir do N 25.19

¬ is-pert co mbad é a ainm do-bretha [?*do-bérthae*] **ndov** Conlui Hl. ('agus dúirt go mba Conla a thabharfaí mar ainm air'); ¬ is-bert mad é ainm do-bretha do Conla S; ¬ is-bert coma he ainm do-bretha do Conla N 25.20-1

§ 77   Aidchisi fris an conair do legivd **ndii** Hl. ('D'iarr sí air an casán a fhágáil aici'); Atchisi fris in conair do lecen di S; Atchisi frisin conair do lecan di N 25.26

---

[18] Seo an t-aon sampla atá sa téacs de shrónaíl ar réamhfhocal. Faightear urú uaireanta sa tSean-Ghaeilge ar réimíreanna neamhaiceanta, e.g. réamhfhocal: 'Only in later Glosses are proclitics occasionally nasalized; e.g. *bec n-di ulc* 'a little of evil' Ml. 46a1 (R. Thurneysen, *A Grammar of Old Irish* (BÁC, 1946), §237).

[19] Tá bearna anseo sa leagan cainte mar go bhfuil an focal *cor*, atá gaolmhar leis an mbriathar, fágtha ar lár trí mhíthuiscint ar an gcomhréir, a bhfuil *figura etymologica* i bhfeidhm inti sa leagan bunúsach: *fo-ceird* (nó *do-cuirethar*) *cor n-iach n-erred de*.

[20] Chuirfeadh an deoch suain codladh tréimhse 'cetheora n-úar fichet' ar dhuine eile, ach 'ba óenúar' do Chú Chulainn é sin.

fo-cerd ich n-errid **nde** svass doridesse Hl. ('cuireann sé "léim bradáin an ghaiscidh" de suas arís'); fo-ceird ich n-err*ed* de suas doridisi S; fo-ceird ich n-err*ed* de suas doridhisi N 25.28-9

§ 78   ro cachain **ndo** tria himus forhossnai, conad ann is-pert na priathru sai **ndou** Hl. ('chan sí dó trí mheán *imbas forosnai*, gur dhúirt sí na briathra seo dó'); ro cachain do tria imas forosnad, conid and as-bert na briathra so do S; ro cachain tria imhus forosnai, conad and as-bert na briathra so do N 26.5-6

     arcáchain dó tria imbas forosnai conid and as-bert na bríathra sa dó LU 10348-9

§ 80   Iss iatt robo lucht oenlongai **ndov** .i. Lvgaid [...] Hl. ('Is iad an lucht a bhí in aon long leis'); Is iat dobo lucht oenlunga do.i. Lugaid [...] S; Is iat dobo lucht aenlunga do .i. Lugaid [...] N 125.8-9

     Is iat robo lucht oenlunga dó .i. Lugaid [...] LU 10431-2

§ 81   Atfet an ingen do leri **ndou** Hl. ('d'eachtraigh an bhean óg ar fad dó'); Adfet do an ingen coleir S; Atfet do an ingen co leir N 125.16

     Adfét dó ind ingen du léir LU 10441-2

§ 82   mad ail **ndi** Hl. ('más áil léi'); ina dail S (van Hamel); mad ail di N 125.28-9

     mad ail di LU 10454

     [*Níl téacs aon tsleachta as* §§ *83–6 thíos ar fáil in* LU *anois*]

§ 83   O ro cuir a scis **nde** Hl. ('nuair a chuir sé a thuirse de'); O ro chuir a scis de S; O ro chuir a scis de N 125.29

Bliadain lan **ndo** oice-ssin Hl. ('Bliain iomlán aige leis [i.e. ina bhun] sin'); Bliadain lan do aci-sin S; bliadain lan do aici-ssin N 126.1

§ 86   co torchair ochtar cecha beme **ndib** Hl. ('gur thit ochtar le gach buille díobh'); co torcair ochtur cach beime dib S; co torcair ochtur cach beime dip N 126.20-1

Focerd Forcoll bedc **nde** tar dua na rátha imach Hl. ('Chuir Forghall léim de tar mhúr na rátha amach'); Foceird Forgall bedg de S; Foceart Forgall bedg de N 126.22

Marbais Cv Chulaind cet fer **ndib** ann Hl.[21] ('Mharaigh Cú Chulainn
céad fear díobh ann'); Marbais Cu Chulainn cet fer dib and S; Marbuis
.c.c. cet fer dip ann N 126.28

(II) *N* ROIMH GHUTA TOSAIGH

[*Níl téacs aon tsleachta sa roinn seo ar fáil in LU anois*]

I bhForainmneacha Réamhfhoclacha:

§ 46   ⁊ do-cuirset in mac **n-uaduib** assa noi issan port a mbatar ol suide Hl.
('chuireadar an mac uathu as a mbád sa bport a raibh siad dá bharr
sin'); ⁊ do-cuirsidar in mac uadaib ol suidiu S; do-cuirsitur in mac
uadhaib asi[n] noi i t*í*r a mbatur ol suidiu N 120.21–2

§ 77   Ataninntai Cv Cvlaind coa muindtir **n-iarum** fessne Hl.[22] ('Ansin
d'iompaigh Cú Chulainn ar ais chuig a mhuintir féin'); Atonintai iar
sin Cú Chulainn aitherruch coa muintir fesin S; Atonintai iar sin Cú
Chulainn aitherrach coa muintir feisin N 25.22–3

In Ainmfhocail:

§ 43   An ri **nAnond** is-rubart ⁊ a gniæ Hl. ('An Rí Anann adúirt mé [i.e. atá
ráite agam], agus a ghiolla'); In ri Anann as-rubart ⁊ a gnia S; In ri
nAnann as-rubart ⁊ a gnia N 119.18

§ 72   den di err*ig* **n.x.** Hl. ('don dá air-rí dhéag');[23] don da airrig dec S; don
da airrigh .x. N 12.16[24]

§ 75   co mbatar in da **n-idhnæ** drech ria dreich Hl. ('go raibh an dá bhuíon
chatha aghaidh ar aghaidh'); co mbatar in da idna drech fri dreich S;
co mbatur in da idnai dreach fri dreich N 12.32

---

[21] Urú anseo, b'fhéidir, faoi anáil an fhocail roimhe atá sa ghinideach iolra; ach níl dóthain ceangail
comhréire i gceist le go bhféadfaí a rá gur urú caighdeánach atá ann. Níl fhios againn, dar ndóigh, an
mbeadh urú dá shórt á shamhlú ag an scríobhaí seo le focail a thosaíos le *c*, *p* nó *t*.

[22] Tá *iarum* anseo in áit an dá mhír *iar sin* agus *aitherrach* sa dá leagan eile, agus tá fós an focal curtha
as a ord ceart sa chlásal.

[23] B'fhéidir go síleadh léitheoir éigin ar an gcéad amharc gurbh í an uimhir dhéach den ainmfhocal
eirr ('gaiscíoch carbaid'), i.e. *eirrid*(*h*), atá in 'err*ig*', ach níl anseo ach ceist litrithe, *e*- in áit *ai*-, rud atá le
feiceáil go coitianta. Scríobhtaí *airrí* ('fo-rí') mar *uirrí* freisin.

[24] Is *déc* ('déag') atá i gceist le .*x*. anseo.

In Aidiacht:

§ 68   co na tarnaic den droched a ceunn **n-aili** de tocbail Hl. ('sa gcaoi nár
        éirigh leis an droichead a cheann eile a ardú'); co na tarnic don drochet
        an cenn aile do tocbail S; co na tarnic don droiched an cenn aile do
        togbail N 11.10–11²⁵

(III) URÚ AR AITHRIS AN ÁINSÍGH

§ 81   Iss airiu 'fuil **an mbron-sa** issan dunadh Hl. ('Is é an fáth leis an
        mbrón seo a bheith sa dún'); is airi fil an bron-sa san dun S; Is aire fil
        in mbron-sa isan dunsa N 125.14
          is airi fil in bron sa sin dún LU 10439

Ní féidir a shamhlú gur aithris atá ansin thuas ar nós na Sean-Ghaeilge, i.é.
an t-áinsíodh i ndiaidh *fil* i gcásanna áirithe. D'fhéadfadh sé gur macalla atá
sa sampla sin thuas as an abairt seo atá díreach roimpi seo san alt céanna
mar seo:

§ 81   Atchluin Cú Chulainn iarom an mbrón fora cind i ndún in rig S
        ('Cloiseann Cú Chulainn an t-olagón roimhe amach i ndún an rí');
        Atcluin c.c. iaram an mbron fora cinn in *n*dun in rig N 125.12–3.
          Atchluin Cu Chulaind íarom in mbrón fora chind oc dún ind ríg LU
        10436–7.

Cé gur tharraing scríobhaí Hl. foirm chéasta an bhriathair chuige anseo
choinnigh sé fós an fhoirm áinsíoch san ainmfhocal:

        Atcloss do Co[i]n Culaind an mbron ar a cind i ndun ind ricch.

Is cosúil freisin gurb í foirm an ainmfhocail san uimhir dhéach, *dá*
baindeilb, atá ar aon déanamh lena 'réim' (foirm áinsíoch), *an mbaindeilb*,
a tharraing an t-urú isteach in Hl. sa leagan seo leanas:

§ 84   iss ed botar ann, da **mbandeilb** is cóimhe boi forsan mbith Hl. ('is
        éard a bhí ann an dá phearsa mná is caoimhe (maisiúla) a bhí ar an
        domhan'); is ed batar and da bandeilb is caime bai forsin mbith S; is

---

²⁵ Níl aon difríocht brí idir *den, de* sa gcéad sampla agus *don, do* sa dá chás eile, mar nach bhfuil i
gceist ag an scríobhaí anseo ach -*e*- mar ghuta doiléir in áit -*o*-. Seasann *den* sa gcéad sampla anseo don
réamhfhocal *do* leis an alt, i.e. *don*, mar atá sa dá shampla as S agus N; cf. na samplaí in §72 thuas. Go
coitianta sa Meán-Ghaeilge ruaigeadh an litriú *do* an *di* (*de*); ach is go mírialta a dhéantaí an t-athrú *do* →
de / *di* i scríbhinn, mar atá anseo, agus mar atá inniu in *de réir* (i.e. *do réir* go stairiúil; féach *DIL* s.v.
riar).

ed batur ann an da banndeilph is caoeime[26] bui forsan mbith N 126.7–8

(IV) SRÓNAÍL INMHEÁNACH I MBRIATHRA COMHSHUITE

B'fhéidir go raibh tuiscint éigin ag scríobhaí an téacsa in Hl. ar úsáid an tseanfhorainm láir *a*[n-] go réamhthagrach agus gur mheas sé go mba cheart ar chuma éigin leas a bhaint as sna cásanna seo:

§ 30 ⁊ **den-berad** biad dii ocon tened Hl.[27] ('agus tugann siad bia di ag an tine'); do-berait biad di icon teinid S; do-beraid biad di icin tene N 116.1–2

§ 37 **Don-bert** an Daghda din Mhoirrigain an ferond sen Hl. ('Thug an Daghdha an fearann sin don Mhór-Ríon'); Do-bert in Dagdai don Morrigain an ferann sin S; Do-uert in Da2 [='Dadha' = 'Dagha'] don Morrigain an ferann sin N 117.15–16

§ 65 **Don-beurt** div uball ndo ⁊ **is-mbeurt** friss ara liad di laur amal no liad ind ublau [*léigh* 'uball'] Hl. ('thug sé úll dó [lena threorú] agus dúirt leis leanacht den talamh mar a leanadh an t-úll [de]'); Do-bert dano uball do ⁊ atbert fris ara liadh de lar [...] S; Do-bert dano uball do ⁊ is-bert fris ara liad do lar [...] N 124.19-20.

Is cosúil gur mheas an scríobhaí sin gur chóir an -*n*- choibhneasta a úsáid sa sampla seo leanas i ndiaidh an fhrása ainmfhocail (*A nDorcell*), mar a bheadh ann i ndiaidh frásaí áirithe (e.g. *in tan* 'nuair') sa tseanteanga:

§ 33 A nDorcell .i. in coill fil etarro, didiu ron-bammaur Hl. ('Is i *nDorcell / nOircel, i.e. an choill atá eatorru, a bhíomar'); I nOircel do badmar etorro .i. an caill etarro S; In Orcel do bamar eturru .i. in chaill fil eturru N 116.24

Níor chóir urú a bheith ar thús-chonsan an bhriathair sa gcás seo leanas, mar nach raibh srónaíl choibhneasta ná réamhthagairt i gceist ina leithéid sin ó cheart:

§ 77 As-pert som **nad mbvie** occo conar diroisevd acht fon ald mor [*recte* mora] ro boi foi Hl. ('Dúirt sise nach raibh conair aige ar a ngabhfadh sé acht thart faoin aill *mhór [*recte* mhara] a bhí faoi'); at-bertsi nach

---

[26] Tá *punctum delens* faoin -*a*- sa bhfocal seo.
[27] '*Lies* tenid' adeir Meyer linn.

boi ocai leth do choised acht isind alt mara boi foi S; at-bertsom nach
boi occai leth do coised acht isind alt mara boi fai N 25.25–6

(V) SAMPLAÍ AS *IMMRAM BRAIN*

Tugann Mac Mathúna in *Immram Brain*, sa gcaibidil ar 'Linguistic
Analysis' (lgh 321–418), tuairisc ghearr (lch 336) ar an tsrónaíl ar
fhoraimneacha réamhfhoclacha ('Nas. of prepositional pronouns'), agus
deir sé faoi shampla atá in § 63 den téacs: 'One ex. may have been
contained in the archetype: *gabais éolchaire fer ndib*'.

Mar adeir Mac Mathúna tá an sampla seo (= *ndíb*) den tsrónaíl le fáil in
Immram Brain i dtrí lámhscríbhinn, Rawlinson B 512 (15ú céad), 23 N 10
agus Stockholm Vitterhet Engelsk II (16ú céad); ach níl an tsrónaíl le fáil
anseo sa leagan atá in Egerton 88 (16ú céad), in Hl. ná in LU.

Is dóigh gur *gabais éolchaire fer diib* a bhí curtha síos in *Immram Brain*
ar dtús, abair i gCín Droma Sneachta, mar atá i Leabhar na hUidhre,
lámhscríbhinn atá saor ón mírialtacht seo.[28]

---

[28] Tá freisin, mar atá tugtha ag Mac Mathúna, *Immram Brain*, lch 336, sa bparagraf 'Nas. of
prepositional pronouns', samplaí de shrónaíl ar an bhforainm réamhfhoclach *dó* le fáil sa téacs sin i gcuid
de na lámhscríbhinní, mar seo: *ndo* 29.124; 32.137; 32.142; agus na samplaí seo den *n* roimh ghuta
tosaigh, *nand* [i.e. 'n-and'] 62.275, *noad* [i.e. 'n-uad'] 61.255.

Metre and Phonology in *Cúirt An Mheán-Oíche*

BRIAN Ó CUÍV
Dublin Institute for Advanced Studies

IN 1977 I discussed some aspects of the *Cúirt* in a paper on 'Metrics and Phonology' read at a conference in The New University of Coleraine.[1] I dealt with the matter again in a seminar I gave in the Institute during the Michaelmas term in 1987 when I added some new topics to the discussion. In the meantime in 1982 had come Liam P. Ó Murchú's *Cúirt an Mheón-Oíche* in which serious attention was paid to phonological and metrical aspects of the poem. Under the heading 'modh eagarthóireachta' (pp. 14–15) Ó Murchú described some systematic changes from *caighdeán* spelling which he made 'Chun go mbeadh ar chumas an léitheora an struchtúr meadarachta a thabhairt leis ón leathanach', and in his introductory remarks (p. 67) to the section on 'Nótaí Teanga' he referred to the poet's use of 'rialacha agus foirmeacha malartacha [...] chun freastal ar riachtanais mheadarachta an tsaothair', and he went on to say 'isí an mheadaracht féin a socróidh dúinn, ar uairibh, cén fhoirm a bhí i gceist ag an bhfile'.

Readers seeking guidance on metrical matters in Ó Murchú's edition will find relevant observations not only in the sections on 'Fóneolaíocht' (67–70), 'Deilbhíocht' (70–8), and 'An Mheadaracht' (79–86), but also at places in the textual notes (49–66) where, for instance, attention is called to (i) several phrases in which elision is required by the metre, such as *snó uirthi* 165, *bheith ag súil* ['v′e 'su:l′] 290, *sódh aige* 321, *dlí againn* 367, *bó aici* 437, *hóighe uirthi is só* ['ho:r′ hə'so:] 491, etc., (ii) word-accent falling on *iairmbéarlaí* or historically unstressed syllables, as in *féna cionta* ['f′e:nə 'k′u:ntə] 458, *le gach beirt* ['l′e gax 'b′er′t′] 521, *tré gach tíortha* 635, etc., (iii) pronunciation of individual words as required in certain contexts, e.g *craobhacha* [kri:xə] 203, *daora* [di:rə] 268, *in aghaidh* [ə'nu:] 295, *leamhais* [l′û:s′] 527, etc., (iv) syllable reduction in *tar éis* > *t'réis* 25, 457, *do réir* > *d'réir* 633, *piléar* > *pléar* 664, *aráin* > *'ráin* 666, *foláir* > *fláir* 928, these being in addition to *coróin* 649, and *dearóil* 361, mentioned on p. 70, to which we might add *phriacail* 133 for which an earlier spelling is *peiriacail*. In all such instances readers not familiar with the metrical conventions of assonantal verse will need to turn from the textual spelling to the later parts of the book for guidance.[2] The main purpose of the present article is to consider once more some matters

---

[1] See *Occasional Papers in Linguistic and Language Learning*, 6 (Coleraine, 1979), 108–23.

[2] For an interesting discussion of the problems confronting editors of modern Irish accentual verse see Tomás de Bhaldraithe, 'An Litriú i bhFilíocht Aiceanta na NuaGhaeilge', *Ériu*, 23 (1972). 214–26.

relating to the metrical structure of the poem. It is not intended to be a comprehensive treatment of the subject.

Since modern Irish verse, such as in the *Cúirt*, is accentual and asson-antal, basic to its metrical structure are elements in the phonology, and especially the vocalic system. In a footnote (n. 7) on p. 81 Ó Murchú has listed sixteen vowels and diphthongs which he recognised in the poem: i(:), e(:), a(:), o(:), u(:), iə, uə, au, əu, əi, ia. He said of them 'Leo féin a dheineann na fóinéimeanna seo comhfhuaim ach deineann [i], [o], [a] comhfhuaim lena chéile go minic.' Unfortunately he did not illustrate the latter part of that statement with examples, either in the section on 'Fóneolaíocht' or that on 'Meadaracht'. As regards [au] and [əu] as separate phonemes he said 'Is de réir Í Chuív (op. cit. 119) a dhealaím [au] agus [əu] óna chéile.' He did not discuss at all the setting-up of [iə] and [ia] as separate phonemes which I had dealt with in my Coleraine paper (p. 120), and in fact in the 'Fóneolaíocht' section he cited no example of the diphthong [ia] or of its orthographic representation. It is only in the textual notes (on 271–2, 705–6, 763–4, 913–4, and 933–4) that he called the attention of the reader to the use of the [ia] diphthong, and even then he omitted to do so in the case of the first example in the *Cúirt*, that is, in 53–4 where *miar, fiain, éadan,* and *créachtach* assonate in the medial feet. Commenting on lines 705–6

> *Ó scéal go scéal ag bréagadh a smaointe*
> *Béal ar bhéal 's ag méaracht síos air,*

Ó Murchú said 'is é an défhoghar "Muimhneach" úd [ia] atá sna chéad samplaí de *scéal* agus *béal* agus é sna samplaí eile', but I see no evidence to support this assertion.

Assonance of stressed short vowels merits special attention, for in many instances the textual spelling, whether historical, scribal or *caighdeán*, is not a clear guide. In his 'Fóneolaíocht' Ó Murchú has indicated a few of the relevant developments, namely *e > i* in *seinm* 644, *deineann* 102, *teinne* 605, *i > e* in *milleadh* 630, *mhilleas* 881, *filleadh* 551, 784, *ea > e* in *beag* 520, 890, *o > a* in *folach* 273, *orthanna* 334. Having considered the poem as a whole I have come to the conclusion that for the most part Merriman assonated the short vowels on a system of three levels: high (V^1), mid (V^2), and low (V^3), with fairly wide phonetic parameters at each level. At the level of V^1 I would see the phonemes [i] and [u], including their allophones. At the level of V^2 I would see the phonemes [e] and [o], with their allophones. And at the level of V^3 I would see the phoneme [a]. I list here the letters or groups of letters which I have noted as representing each of the levels set out above: V^1: *i, io, iu, u, ui, ei, oi, o, ai*; V^2: *ei, ea, o, oi, ai, u*; V³: *a, ai, ea*. Here are some examples of assonances at each level to illustrate the diversity of orthographic forms.

V¹: *foilithe : chuile : d'fhuiling : cuilithe* 37–8, *uimhir : d'imigh* 75–6, *rithe : imigh : deineann : tuilleadh* 101–2, *iomad : siorraigh³ : muirear : muir* 103–4, *fuinneamh : fiuchadh* 155–6, *doineantach : chruinnigh* 205–6, *giodamach : Sisile* 327–8, *iongantas : bhruinneall* 347–8, *iongantas : laigeacht : tubaist : imigh* 365–6, *soineanta : srimile : duine : chuige* 433–4, *cuideachta : siolla* 557–8, *cruinnithe : ingní : uilleanna : chroibh* 577–8, *cuirfidh : tiocfaidh* 637–8, *fir : seinm* 643–4, *d'imigh : deineadh* 721–2, *phiocfaidh : fiorthann* 729–30, *laigede : fiche* 735–6, *cumasach : iomadach : (a)gainne : fuil* 777–8, *droinge : deimhin : loinge : duine* 787–8, *chonairc : uimhir* 801–2, *urchar : tiocfaidh* 841–2, *chuirimse : foirfeach* 891–2, *siolla : cuireadh : baineannach : iomadach* 903–4, *chuid : foireann* 927–8, *gile : cuma* 973–4, *foilitheach : uireaspach : doirfeach : foirfe* 979–80, *foirinne : fuineadh : fhurus : urraimse* 985–6, *cloistear* (MS *cluistear*) : *critheadh* 1013–4.

V²: *bholgach : tholgach : cholgach : dhoirrgeach* 47–8, *ullamh : focal : mogall : molaimse* 111–2, *leibide : mheidir* 377–8, *feiceann : ceileann* 397–8, *mheilt : teist : chreid : bheag* 519–20, *fheicim : doille : leithre : hoileadh* 603–4, *mheilleas : feitheamh* 881–2, *bheirim : beag* 889–90, *eile : hoileadh : ndeirim : feicim* 915–6, *coir : deich* 993–4, *adeirim : beirig : goirim : faigh* 999–1000.

V³: *searbh : sealbh : tamall : bharra* 11–2, *bhain : chaith* 175–6, *aithnid : bean* 181–2, *falach : ceannasach* 273–4, *maille : arthanna* 333–4, *deacair : gairid* 421–2, *marach (< mara mbeadh) : scannal* 443–4, *snamanadh : ceangladh* 499–500, *ghlanas : bhaineas* 501–2, *ca bhfuil : calcadh* 815–6, *ceangail : as sin* 853–4, *bainigí : feannaigí* 875–6.

In assessing the three levels set out above I have taken into account (i) phonological developments with which many readers will be familiar, such as vowel-raising in certain contexts whereby *ai, ei, oi*, and *o* may give *oi* or *ui, i, ui*, and *u*, respectively, and (ii) the existence at both literary and dialectal level of variant forms, such as *ollamh* as well as *ullamh*. In including *mheilleas : feitheamh* 881–2 under V² I have accepted Ó Murchú's judgement that vowel-lowering of *i > e* in *mhilleas*, as indicated by the spelling *mheillios* in the Cambridge manuscript, was in accordance with the poet's speech, but since *fitheamh* is a common Munster variant of *feitheamh* there is an element of doubt. Not so, however, in the case of *Leis*

---

³ Cf. *galair : searraigh* 780; the inflected form with stressed *io* (pronounced /u/), which is found elsewhere in Munster dialects, may be a back-formation from a nominative form with forward accent, [sˊəˈrax]. However, I see no evidence of forward stress in words in *-ach* in the *Cúirt*; note, for instance, initial stress in *gealach* 272, *cailleacha* 286, *baileach* 543, *fheasach* 675, *chuideachta* 911.

sin : *meilleadh* (MS *meille*) 629–30. I have noted a number of instances where the assonance seems to be outside the normal parameters, such as 255–6 where assonance would seem to be between *gofa* and *gculaithe*, 343–4 (*mealla* : *cumainín*), 395–6 (*canbhás*: *cá bhfios*; we might read *ca* instead of *cá*; cf. *ca bhfuil* in 614, 733, etc.), 459–60 (*bheirim* : *leagaithe*), 747–8 (*gcaitheadh* : *tuilleadh*), as well as questionable assonances in medial feet in 301–2 and 707–8.

In his section on 'Meadaracht' Ó Murchú, adopting a word used by Seán Ó Tuama in 1964[4] with reference to the *Cúirt*, spoke (p. 79) of 'na "mórthulchaí" líofachta úd a chuireann chomh mór sin le healaíontacht an tsaothair tríd síos'. He went on to demonstrate that, in addition to the basic pattern of the assonantal couplet with four feet to a line which is fundamental to the poem, there are passages, ranging from two couplets to six, where assonantal correspondences of various kinds established internal relationships which were presumably intentional and which demonstrated the sophistication of Merriman's use of his metre. Some examples of the assonantal patterns may be useful at this point, starting with the single couplet and proceeding up the scale through the fully-assonating four-line unit to the looser combinations of couplets and quatrains to which Ó Murchú called special attention.

> *Ba gnáth me ag siúl le ciumhais na habhann*
> *ar bháinseach úr 's an drúcht go trom* (lines 1–2)
> - á - ú - ú - əu

> *Bhíodh éanla i gcrainn go meidhreach mómhar*
> *Is léimreach eilte i gcoillte im chóngar,*
> *Géimreach adharc is radharc ar shlóite,*
> *Tréanrith gadhar is Reynard rompu.* (lines 19–22)
> (-) é - əi - əi - ó -

Ó Murchú cited lines 3–14 in illustration of his analysis of the linked units.

> *In aice na gcoillte i gcoim an tsléibhe*
> *Gan mhairg gan mhoill ar shoilse an lae.*
> *Do ghealadh mo chroí an uair chínn Loch Gréine,*
> *An talamh 's an tír is íor na spéire,*
> *Taitneamhach aoibhinn suíomh na sléibhte*
> *Ag bagairt a gcinn thar dhroim a chéile.*
> *Do ghealfadh an croí bheadh críon le cianta*

---

[4] *Studia Hibernica*, 4 (1964), 7–27, p. 21; see also Dáithí Ó hUaithne, *Cúirt an Mheán Oíche*, p. 12.

Caite gan bhrí nó líonta 'o phianta,
An séithleach searbh gan sealbh gan saidhbhreas
D'fhéachfadh tamall thar bharra na gcoillte
Ar lachain 'na scuainte ar chuan gan ceo
Is an eala ar a bhfuaid 's í ag gluaiseacht leo.

He showed the linking assonances in this diagram:

3–4	- a - - əi - əi - é
5–8	(-) a - - í - í - é -
9–10	(-) a - - í - í - iə -
11–12	(-) é - a - - a - - əi -
13–14	(-) a - - uə - uə - ó

In all Ó Murchú listed 104 assonating couplets, 20 assonating four-line units, and 116 linked units, of which 43 are four-line units, 32 six-line, 23 eight-line, 13 ten-line and 5 twelve-line, the lines quoted above being one of the last group. Lines 33–6 illustrate the four-line linked unit—as distinct from the four-line assonating unit.

In aice na gcrann i dteannta trínse,
Taca lem cheann 's mo hanlaibh sínte.
Ar cheangal mo shúl go dlúth le chéile,
Greamaithe dúnta i ndúghlas néalta.

Here the vowel /a/ is the linking feature:

(-) a - - au - au - í -
(-) a - - ú - ú - é -

There is another feature in the poem which in a very different way provides a link between couplets or groups of couplets. It has to do with the structure of each line of an assonating couplet in terms of the number of syllables in each of the four feet of which it is comprised. In discussing the metrical feet (pp. 81–2) Ó Murchú followed the analysis given by me in 1977: monosyllabic /v:/; disyllabic /v: -/, /v -/, /v: v:/, /v v:/; trisyllabic /v: - -/, /v - -/, /v v: -/, /v - v:/.[5] I might have added that monosyllabic feet are found only at the end of a line, whereas disyllabic and trisyllabic feet may be in any position. Examples are: monosyllabic /v:/ *trom* 2; disyllabic /v: -/ *bháinseach* 2, /v -/ *Dath an* 17, /v: v:/ *bpálás* 72, /v v:/ *calaois* 90; trisyllabic /v: - -/ *Shoilsigh an* 856, /v - -/ *Taithneamhacht* 7, /v v: -/ *gcillín*

---

[5] See *op. cit.*, p. 119. Here I use v to indicate a short vowel and v: to indicate a long vowel.

na 301, /v - v:/ *aprún* (pron. *aparún*) 264. Although Ó Murchú mentioned the types of feet, he seems to have been overlooked the structural aspect of their occurence. The line-structure of the examples quoted above, as based on the number of syllables in each metrical foot or unit, is as follows:

(-) 2 2 2 1

(-) 2 2 2 2

(-) 3 2 2 2   (3–10)
(-) 2 3 3 2   (11–12)
(-) 3 2 2 1   (13–14)

(-) 3 2 2 2

Neither the *caighdeán* spelling nor the semi-historical spelling which was in vogue up to fairly recent times is adequate to convey to readers the spoken forms required by assonantal metres. Accordingly there are several matters which must be taken into account in assessing the line-structures of the *Cúirt*, many of which have been mentioned by Ó Murchú at one place or another in his editorial comments, and some of which I consider together here.

(1) In a number of couplets an unstressed syllable at the beginning of the second line is to be counted as part of the last foot of the first line, e.g

> *Scriosadh an tír is níl 'na ndiaidh*
> *In ionad na luibheanna acht flíoch is fiaile* (79–80)

Similarly in lines 157–8, 187–8, 307–8, 597–8, 627–8, 749–50, 873–4, 1007–8.

(2) The phonetic realisation of syllables in which a lenited consonant features in the spelling, which may result either in the loss of a syllable, e.g. *luibheanna*, pronounced [li:nə], in line 80 above, or the retention of the historical structure, e.g. *duilleabhar* in lines 27–8

> *Bhí duilleabhar craobh ar ghéaga im thimpeall,*
> *Fiorthann is féar 'na shlaodach taoibh liom.*[6]

Similar retention of lenited consonants is seen in the words *tsléibhe* (71), *cnámha* (237), *amharc* (280, 555), *deimhin* (787), *bhfábhar* (828), *labhair* (905). On the other hand the loss of the lenited consonant is more in accord

---

[6] Ó hUaithne's spelling *duilliúr* is quite misleading.

with the normal dialectal development and is accordingly more common. The spelling used by Ó Murchú in his text frequently obscures this development although in such instances it does have the advantage of indicating the relevant syllable structure, e.g. *chroí* (5), *suíomh* (7), *shamhlaíos* (45), *fiain* (53), *dúirt* (61), and so on. In his section on 'Fóneolaíocht' Ó Murchú has indicated the phonetic values to be given to syllables in which lenited consonants have been lost, including, in some cases, alternative pronunciations as determined by the context, e.g. *comhar* [kô:r] 887, [kû:r] 409, *aghaidh* [ai] 37, [u:] 295, *rogha* [rəu] 159, [ro:] 321.

(3) Lengthening or diphthongisation of short vowels before long liquids which is general in Southern Irish dialects is another important factor in the determination of assonantal patterns. In his 'Fóneolaíocht' Ó Murchú has noted some of the relevant developments, viz. *i* + *nn*, *m* > [i:], *ei*, *oi* + *ll*, *nn*, *m* > [əi], *o* + *nn*, *ll*, *m* > [əu], *a* + *rr* > [a:], *o* + *rr* > [o:], *a* + *nn*, *ll*, *m* > [au]; and he has listed as exceptional forms *caoimse* 169 (for *coimse*), *glónradh* 551, *lómmrach* 141, and *táirnthe* 146. More extensive treatment of the subject would have been helpful. For instance lengthening or diphthongisation takes place not only before *ll*, *nn*, and *rr*, but also before some consonant groups beginning with *l*, *n*, or *r*, e.g. *ls*, *nc*, *nd*, *nl*, *nr*, *ns*, *nt*, *rd*, *rl* and *rn*. Furthermore the development with vowels other than those listed above is very relevant, viz. *ai*, *ea*, *io*, *ui*, and *u*, and as well as that in the case of *i*, *ei*, *oi*, *o*, and *a*, there are additional developments that Ó Murchú did not discuss. These include *i* > [əi] in *fillte* 257, *mhillfeadh* 556, *milseacht* 776, *rinn* 1012; *ei* > [e:] in *réimpi* 26; *oi* > [i:] in *poimp* 436, *droim* 8, and possibly in *soilseach* 490 (: *trilseach*, MS *troílseach*); *o* > [o:] in *sómpla* 1010, > [u:] in *lonrach* 234, 490, *consaigh* 105 (MS *cúbhansaig*), *fonsaí* 268, *cúnamh* 306 (MS *cúmhna* < *congnamh*), *a* > [u:] in *anlann* 378.

I set out here in summary form developments with *ai*, *ea*, *oi*, *io*, *ui*, and *u*, which I have noted:

ai + *rr*, *rd*, *rn*, *rng* > [a:], *airde* 15, *chairde* 317, *tairne* 878, *tairngthe* 146; + *rd* > [e:], *haeirde* 49; + *ll*, *nn* > [əi], *bhaill* 359, *gcrainn* 19; + *nt* > [i:], *caint* 157, *cainte* 164; either [əi] or [i:] in *bainse* : *sainte* 593–4.

ea + *ll*, *m*, *nn*, *nd*, *ns*, *nt*, *ng* > [au], *geall* 121, *feam* 756, *dteannta* 33, *seandaigh* 198, *ceansa* 124, *ceantair* 55 *seang* 465.

oi + *rn*, *rs* > [o:], *doirne* 547, *toirneach* 319, *toirse* 507.

io + *m*, *nn*, *nl*, *ns*, *nt* > [u:], *liom* 403, *mionn* 152, *ionladh* 401, *tionscailt* 883, *fionsaigh* 456, *cionta* 180.

ui + *ll* > [əi], *thuill* 420; + *m*, *nn*, *nch*, *ng* > [i:], *suim* 483, *cruinn* 549, *Chuinche* 454, *chuing* 474; + *rn* > [u:], *muirne* 998.

u + *m*, *ns*, *nt*, *rd*, *rl* > [u:], *cumtha* 234, *bunsaigh* 106, *puntaibh* 661, *durdam* 527, *urla* 231.

(4) Epenthesis is a feature whose use by Merriman is frequent and accordingly must be taken into account in relation to syllable count. The epenthetic vowel is present in the spelling of many words in the Cambridge manuscript to which Ó Murchú attaches great importance, e.g. *mairig* 4, *tologach* 18, *glasara* 29, *anafadh* 43, *doirrigeach* 48, *focalaibh* 61, *toramach* 110, *seasamhach* 131, *doilibhir* 187, *aithfirion* 279, *macanas* 325. For the most part Ó Murchú has used the historic or *caighdeán* spelling for these words, and he has not noted the scribal spelling in pp. 47–8 nor has he discussed the phenomenon in detail. In general Merriman's use of the epenthetic vowel is in line with developments seen in many modern Irish dialects, as the spellings quoted above show. Occasionally he varies his usage. Thus *aithne* has an epenthetic vowel in 375 but not in 431, and *aithnid* is disyllabic in 727. The word *easnamh* has no epenthetic vowel in 650 and 678, but assonance with *cheannasach* in 171–2 points to a variant usage. Noteworthy is the fact that the word spelt *bachallach* assonates as a disyllable in 232.

(5) Elision resulting in syllable reduction occurs in over half the lines in the *Cúirt*. In the following discussion the round brackets have been supplied to indicate the elision. Among the contexts I have noted are:

(i) Junction of final vowel and following unstressed initial vowel, e.g. *me (a)g* 1, *chroí (a)n* 5; in this context I include phrases with v.n. ending in *-adh* or with other words ending in *-adh*, e.g. *luasc(adh) im thimpeall* 42, *bréag(adh) a smaointe* 705, *cog(adh) is an bás* 100, *tuill(eadh) ina n-áit* 102.

(ii) Elision of final unstressed short vowel before following stressed vowel, e.g. *fachnaoid(e) airdnirt* 89, *len(a) fhuílleach* 384, *dá gcual(a) é* 521, *bréig(e) é* 527, *duin(e) eile* 915.

(iii) Elision (or omission) of vocative particle, e.g. *'Aoibheall, 'fháidhbhean* 168.

(iv) Reduction of *agus* to *'gus*, *is*, or *'s*, notwithstanding the frequent retention in the text of the *a* of *agus* or *i* of *is*, e.g. *úr 's an drúcht* 2, *cortha (i)s an codladh*, 31, *an dlí (a)gus* 91.

(v) Elision of *i* of *ina*, e.g. *lachain 'na scuainte*, 13, *cúirt 'na suí* 64, *mná (i)na muirear* 104.

(vi) Omission of *do* (preverbal particle), e.g. *croí bheadh críon* 9, *inné bhí (a)n spéir* 23, *ghluais* 67; but retention of *do* is not uncommon, e.g. *do ghoill sé* 73.

(vii) Omission of *do* (preposition), (a) before v.n., e.g. *céile (a) phósadh* 195, *é scríobh* 1016; but it may be retained, e.g. *dlí do chloí* 122; note both usages in *An pósadh dhiúltadh acht drúis do shéanadh* 818; (b) in other contexts, e.g. *líonta ('o) phianta* 10, *an dlí seo ('o) ghnáth* 129, *tollairí ('o)n tsórt so* 109, *sa méid seo ('o)m shiúlta* 181.

(viii) Elision (or omission) of initial *i* of *inneosad*, e.g. *nó (in)neosad* 399, *mar neosad* 166.

(ix) Elision of initial vowel of pronominal forms of *ag* and *ar*, e.g. *snó (ui)rthi* 165, *baile (a)gam* 432, *só (ai)ge* 321, *bó (ai)ci* 437, *dlí (a)gainn* 367, *laoigh (a)cu* 368.

(x) Elision of unstressed final syllable of stressed word, e.g. *shíolr(aigh) an dúchas* 549, *suíf(idh) an chuideachta* 911, *d'ord(aigh) an tsíbhean* 1005, *an teaghl(aigh) i bhfeighil* 557, *mórchuid mag(aidh) orth(u) ag* 326, *m'agh(aidh a)gam foilithe* 37, *m'agh(aidh a)gus m'éadan* 274, *cún(amh) an Deamhain* 306, *cún(amh) a g dúbailt* 339 (MS *cúmhna* in both instances).

(xi) Elision of initial vowel of *idir*, e.g. *ór (i)dir lámha* 438, *lá (i)dir lámha* 569.

It is noteworthy that in several instances the reading of the Cambridge MS supports the interpretations set out above.

(6) Forward word-stress, a common feature in modern Munster dialects, e.g. *éadóchas*, with stress on the second syllable, in lines 249–50

> *Gan radhairc gan gliocas in imirt mo chóra,*
> *Mo threighid! cár mhiste me rith in éadóchas?*

There are many instances of the historical word-stress, e.g. *fásáil* 261, *cheárdán* 262, *luaithghrís* 298, *clóicín* 387, but exceptions are not infrequent. I have noted forward word-stress in (a) simple words (including names), and (b) compound words or words with a prefix, and (c) in pronominal form of the preposition *ag*. Examples are (a) *neosad* (editorial for *inneosad* which is the spelling in 399) 166, 659, *imíos* 177, *féasóige* 200, *doilíosach* 205, *ribíní* 259, *rufaí* 260, *gabáiste* 304, *ghalánta* 335, *anáile* 359, *bhotháin* 409, *Sileáin* 410, *Breacáin* 451, 454, *aráin* 451, 666, *'Calláin* 452, *pholláirí* 579, *biotáille* 594, *nádúra* 633, *socúil* 667, *milliún* 736; (b) *dea-dhoirseach* 142, *míbhéasach* 223, *drochdhuine* 393, *ró-bhaoch* 506, *truamhéileach* 585, *dath-aoibhinn* 590, *athlíonadh* 591, *mhíchuíosach* 701, *treasaosta* 804, and, with double stress, the first stress being in a different foot, *shíorthaispeánadh ǐ -/ā -/* 275, *fíoriomána* 276, *an-mhíchumtha /a - -/ū -/* 971, *cromshlinneánach /ou -/ ā -/* 976; (c) *againne* 778.[7]

There is another aspect of word-stress which is worth considering at this point. In his discussion of metrical feet Ó Murchú called attention to a

---

[7] There is further evidence of forward word-stress in pronominal forms of *ag*, a feature normal in Munster dialects, in the *Cúirt*, although in the other instances the second syllable has not the full metrical accent. For examples see above in the discussion of elision.

metrical feature which I discussed in my Coleraine paper, namely, the
occurrence of assonantally significant long vowels other than at the
beginning of a metrical foot, in other words feet with double stress or
secondary stress (*op. cit.*, 119–23). Ó Murchú cited one example, the feet
ainigí and *bean an tí* in lines 533–4, and he listed four other couplets in
which he noted the feature. In fact the feature is more common, if my
interpretationm of it is correct. However, I think that the example in lines
533–4 cited by Ó Murchú is to be discounted. I would take lines 533–6 as
an assonantal unit, with the medial feet having assonantal pattern
/a - -/a - -/

> *anfach ainigí*
> *ceangailte is bean an tí*
> *leagaithe ar smeachaidí*
> *bhainne dhá greadadh le.*

Since the medial feet must assonate fully it is clear that the long vowels in
ainigí, *bean an tí*, and *smeachaidí* are non-significant. For the same reason
the long vowels in *fásáil* and *cheárdán* are non-significant in the medial
feet *brách gan fásáil* and *bhreá lem cheárdán* in 261–2, as are those in
farairí and *sladairí* in the medial feet *feasach me farairí* and *greamaithe ag
sladairí* in lines 429–30.

On the other hand I have noted what I consider to be valid examples of
this assonantal ornament (a) in the beginning of the line, (b) in medial
position, and (c) in the final foot. Examples are (a) *Dhá lá : bpálás* / ā ā /
71–2, *an-iomdha : aprún* /a - ū/ 263–4, *Magairlín : Taithigín* /a - ī/ 341–2,
Collóid : Bunóc : Posóid : Cuinneog /u ō/ 533–6, *Teallaí : Ballaí* /a ī/ 671–
2, *Bainigí : feannaigí* / a - ī/ 875–6, with further examples in 885–6, 989–
90, and 1011–12;

(b)　　*Falsacht fear dlí is fachnaoide airdnirt,*
　　　Cam is calaois, faillí is fábhar (lines 89–90)
　　　/au -/ a ī/a ī/ ā -/

　　　Insan uair a ghoil sí folcaí fíochmhar
　　　Is d'fhuascail osnaí gothaí a cainte (lines 163–4)
　　　-/ua -/o ī/o ī/ī -/

　　　Dochar is díobháil is síorchrá cléibh ort
　　　A thoice le místáid 'o shíol gá is déirce (lines 363–4)
　　　(-)/o - -/ī ā /ī ā / ē -/

> *Ag consaigh ainmhí Thradaí an phónra*
> *Is fionsaigh fhalchaí Chreatlaí an chorda* (lines 455–6)
> -/ū -/a ī/a ī/ ō -/[8]

There is a further example in lines 301–2, but the assonances present a difficulty, as does the lack of a syllable in the second medial foot.[9]

(c) *saoithiúil : gnaíúil* /ī ū/ 213–4, *scálaí : cártaí* / ā ī/ 285–6, *magúil : ladús* /a ū/ 441–2. In addition I have noted an example with double stress in both initial and medial feet in lines 267–8:

> *Búclaí is fáinní is lámhainní síoda*
> *Is fonsaí, práslaí is lásaí daora*
> (-)/ū ī/ ā ī/ ā ī/ī -/

In a slightly different category is the double stress in the verbal form, *achtaimíd* in line 871, where the long vowel in the third syllable is given full stress at the beginning of the first of the medial feet:

> *Achtaimíd mar dhlí do bhéithe*
> *An seacht fó thrí gan cuibhreach céile*
> (-)/a -/ī -/ī -/ ē -/

According to my examination of the occurrence of metrical feet within the lines, having taken into account the features set out above, I have found nine varieties of line-structure in the poem: (1) 2221, (2) 2222, (3) 3221, (4) 3222, (5) 2331, (6) 2332, (7) 3332, (8) 2223, (9) 3223. The distribution of these on the basis of couplets is as follows: (1) 5, (2) 120, (3) 36, (4) 251, (5) 2, (6) 95, (7) 2, (8) 1, (9) 1, the first occurrence of each variety being in the lines set out here: (1) 1–2, (2) 15–16, (3) 3–4, (4) 25–6, (5) 17–18, (6) 31–2, (7) 111–12, (8) 277–8, (9) 375–6. It is obvious that, with the occurrences of varieties (2), (4) and (6) being so numerous, there would be many sections of the poem where line-structure, rather than assonantal features, would act as a linking or unifying agent. I indicate here those in which three or more couplets are linked, starting with the variety whose occurrence is most frequent and citing the lines and the number of couplets.

(4) 3222: Lines 25–30 (3), 39–44 (3), 113–20 (4), 123–8 (3), 143–50 (4), 179–84 (3), 269–76 (4), 327–34 (4), 337–48 (6), 353–8 (3), 379–84 (3),

---

[8] My metrical analysis is based on Ó Murchú's text as printed here. However, if we read the expected form *Thrarda í* in the first line we can postulate epenthesis with the medial feet having a structure /a—ī/.

[9] See my comments in *Éigse*, 13 (1969–70), 80, and Ó Murchú's note in pp. 52–3 of his edition. His entry 'cillín na hátha, the kiln near the ford' in the 'Foclóir' is clearly an error. Apart from the fact that the word *áth* 'a ford' is masculine, both context and grammar point to the word *áith* 'a drying-kiln', which goes back to the Old Irish period and which is feminine.

395–408 (7), 413–26 (7), 435–50 (8), 457–66 (5), 473–510 (19), 545–58 (7), 583–602 (10), 607–16 (5), 639–44 (3), 673–8 (3), 729–36 (4), 753–60 (4), 793–808 (8), 839–44 (3), 873–82 (5), 885–92 (4), 895–902 (4), 905–10 (3), 919–28 (5), 947–70 (12), 973–8 (3), 1002–6 (3).

(2) 2222: Lines 49–54 (3), 67–72 (3), 173–8 (3), 227–32 (3), 467–72 (3), 527–32 (3), 679–84 (3), 691–706 (4), 761–72 (6), 823–34 (6), 857–72 (8), 993–8 (3), 1005–10 (3), 1015–20 (3).

(6) 2332: Lines 101–10 (5), 211–22 (6), 245–50 (3), 291–6 (3), 427–34 (4), 539–44 (3), 559–64 (3), 573–8 (3), 645–52 (3), 655–60 (3), 693–8 (3), 777–82 (3), 911–18 (4).

(3) 3221: Lines 3–10 (4), 73–8 (3), 719–30 (6).

The most sustained passage structurally is in lines 473–510 where in nineteen couplets the *seanduine* bemoans his plight. Within the same passage there are four sections where there is assonantal linking: lines 473–8, 481–90, 491–8, and 503–6, that is, fourteen couplets in all.

Notwithstanding the regularity in assonances and structure in *Cúirt an Mheán Oíche*, there are noteworthy assonantal irregularities in the initial foot in a number of lines, as Ó Murchú has pointed out on pp. 82–3. I do not propose to discuss these here as there is no obvious emendation for most of them. In a few lines where a syllable is lacking reasonable emendations, indicated here by the use of square brackets, come to mind: *Le teacht [na] ré ná tar éis bheith lán di* 288, *Nách taitneamh ná téamh [ná] aon phioc grá dho* 676. Ó Murchú did not comment on 676, but in a note on 288 he mentioned the fact that some manuscripts have *na ré*. Writing in *Gadelica*, 1 (1912–13), 198, T.F. O'Rahilly pointed out that while the insertion of *na* makes the line metrically regular 'it is against all good MS. authority'. He also commented on an irregularity in 890: *Is beag liom bás gan barrghoin pian dóibh*, where metrical regularity, as Ó Murchú pointed out in a textual note, would require a second unstressed syllable between *beag* and *bás*. Although O'Rahilly was able to cite manuscript authority for *an bás*, he was not willing to accept that reading. Another possibility, although I have no manuscript authority for it, would be to read *Is beag orm* (pronounced [orəm]) *bás*. I am quite sure that many editors of classical Irish bardic verse have been far less reluctant to emend texts against all the manuscript evidence, even when they had autograph copies before them. Whether they were correct in doing so is another matter.[10]

---

[10] Pádraig Ó Macháin has touched on such editorial problems in 'The Early Modern Irish Prosodic Tracts and the Editing of "Bardic Verse"', in *Metrik und Medienwechsel/Metrics and Media*, ed. by Hildegard L.C. Tristram, (Tübingen: Gunter Narr Verlag, 1991) pp. 273–87.

Buntús Gaeilge agus Bunú ITÉ

TOMÁS Ó DOMHNALLÁIN
Baile Átha Cliath

RÉAMHRÁ

THART ar seachtó cúig bliain ó shin a tosaíodh ar an nGaeilge a mhúineadh mar ábhar éigeantach i scoileanna náisiúnta na hÉireann. Trí sheachtain a bhí rialtas neamhspleách Shaorstát Éireann i gcumhacht faoi Art Ó Gríofa nuair a fógraíodh, le *Fógra Poiblí Uimhir a 4*, nár mhór, ó Lá Fhéile Pádraig, 1922 amach:

(i)   uair an chloig sa ló a thabhairt do theagasc na Gaeilge, nó do theagasc ábhar léinn i nGaeilge, i ngach scoil náisiúnta;

(ii)   gan an Béarla a úsáid i rang naíonán ar bith dá mbeadh go leor den Ghaeilge chuige sin ag múinteoir an ranga.

Is féidir an tréimhse sin a roinnt ina dhá chuid agus a rá go raibh cumas Gaeilge na múinteoirí agus caighdeán Gaeilge na mac léinn sna scoileanna náisiúnta ag dul i bhfeabhas de réir a chéile ar feadh an chéad chuid den tréimhse, ach gur mheath a bhí ag teacht ar an dá ghné sin sa dara cuid di. Is é sin le rá gurb é mo thuairim gur tharla barr feabhais maidir le staid na Gaeilge sna scoileanna náisiúnta tamall roimh an mbliain 1950. Tá léiriú agus cosaint ar an tuairim sin le léamh in áit eile uaim[1] agus níl mé chun an tuairim sin a phlé sa pháipéar seo. Is leor a rá go raibh an-bhrú ar an nGaeilge sa chóras oideachais idir 1922 agus 1950 agus gur caitheadh an-dúthracht ar fad léi i rith na tréimhse sin. Bhí laghdú ag teacht ar an mbrú, áfach—agus ar an dúthracht—ón mbliain 1946, nó mar sin, ar aghaidh.

AN CÚLRA

Níorbh fhada i ndiaidh na bliana 1922 gur thosaigh na múinteoirí ag iarraidh maolú ar an mbrú a bhí ar an nGaeilge agus ba iad sin, trí Chumann na Múinteoirí Náisiúnta, a d'iarr na leasuithe ar chlár na Gaeilge a cuireadh i bhfeidhm sa bhliain 1926. Ina dhiaidh sin féin lean siad leo ag gearán faoi airde an chaighdeáin Ghaeilge a bhí á lorg sna scoileanna. I lár na dtríochaidí nó mar sin thosaigh daoine eile, líon beag d'ollúna ollscoile

---

[1] Tomás Ó Domhnalláin, 'An Ghaeilge sa Chóras Oideachais', *An Sagart*, 23.2 (1980), 5–12.

agus de pholaiteoirí agus, níos faide anonn, grúpaí tuismitheoirí anseo agus ansiúd, ag taobhú leo.

CLÁR GAEILGE NA BUNSCOILE: 1934

An clár nua Gaeilge a cuireadh i bhfeidhm sa bhliain 1934, níor ghéill sé puinn d'éileamh seo na múinteoirí: ardú ar an gcaighdeán a bhí á lorg ag an Roinn Oideachais a tharla dá bharr. De réir a chéile mhéadaigh ar mhí-shástacht na múinteoirí. Sa bhliain 1941 d'fhoilsigh siad tuarascáil thábhachtach i dtaobh teagaisc na Gaeilge agus i dtaobh teagaisc ábhar eile trí mheán na Gaeilge, tuarascáil a léirigh mí-shástacht múinteoirí le scéal na Gaeilge sna scoileanna.[2] Bhí siad buartha go mór mór faoi dheachracht na dtéacsleabhar léitheoireachta a bhíodh le léamh ag na daltaí scoile, go háirithe sna hardranganna, agus ba mhinic a thóg siad an cheist sin leis an Roinn Oideachais. Bhí sé de ghearán acu go mbíodh an foclóir ró-dheacair sna téacsleabhair sin agus go mbíodh an iomarca focal nua ag teacht isteach iontu.

Ar deireadh thiar thóg an Roinn ceann dá gcuid gearán: thart ar lár na gcaogaidí cuireadh coiste Roinne ar bun chun clár na Gaeilge sna scoileanna náisiúnta a iniúchadh, féachaint ar ghá leasuithe a dhéanamh air. Seán Ó Conchubhair, a bhí ina rúnaí ar an Roinn Oideachais níos faide anonn, a bhí ina chathaoirleach ar an gcoiste sin.

An clár Gaeilge a bhí i bhfeidhm ag an am sin, clár na bliana 1934, bhí treoir iomlán faoi, agus faoi mhodhanna a mhúinte, leagtha síos i leabhrán arbh teideal dó *Notes for Teachers—Irish*.[3] An modh oibre a bhí leagtha síos sa leabhrán sin bhí sé go mór chun tosaigh ar mhodhanna múinte teangacha na linne agus b'fhiú go mór do mhúinteoirí an lae inniu staidéar a dhéanamh ar an gcur chuige atá léirithe ann. Ní mór a rá go raibh múinteoirí na linne, go mór mór iad sin a oileadh ó thús na dtríochaidí ar aghaidh, an-oilte sa chur chuige a bhí i gceist, mar ba chuid dá gcúrsa oiliúna, agus cuid dá scrúdú cheannchúrsa é, eolas ar na modhanna múinte a bhí leagtha síos sna *Notes for Teachers*.

Bíodh sé sin mar atá, d'aontaigh coiste úd na Roinne go raibh gá le hathruithe áirithe ar chlár teagaisc na Gaeilge ar mhaithe lena shimpliú, agus thagair siad go sonrach don ghá a bhí le heolas oibiachtúil a chur ar fáil ar an méid den Ghaeilge—foclóir, comhréir agus deilbhíocht—a bheadh riachtanach ag na céimeanna éagsúla foghlama. Thug siad féin faoi shainmhíniú a thabhairt ar an méid de na nithe sin ar cheart a theagasc i

---

[2] *Report of the Committee of Inquiry into the Use of Irish as a Teaching Medium to Children whose Home Language is English* (Baile Átha Cliath: I.N.T.O., 1941).

[3] *Notes for Teachers—Irish* (Baile Átha Cliath: Oifig an tSoláthair, 1933).

ranganna Naíonán–I, ach chuir siad in iúl ina dtuarascáil dheiridh go mbeadh gá le taighde eolaíoch teanga ar an nGaeilge sula bhféadfaí dul thairis sin leis an ngnó. Taighde ar na focail, ar an gcomhréir, agus ar an deilbhíocht is minice a úsáidtear sa chaint a bhí i gceist acu.

Ba ag an gcéim sin a iarradh orm féin a bheith páirteach san obair. Glaodh orm chun na hoifige agus fiafraíodh díom an mbeinn sásta leagan nua de na *Notes for Teachers—Irish* a ullmhú de réir torthaí mhachnamh an Choiste Roinne a bhí tar éis a chuid oibre a chríochnú. Thoilíos tabhairt faoin obair agus fuaireas cóipeanna de mhiontuairiscí cruinnithe an Choiste le dul ag obair orthu.

AN TATHAIR COLMÁN

Tharla ag an am sin go raibh mé féin i mo Rúnaí ar Chumann na gCigirí agus Tomás Ó Cuilleanáin ina Chathaoirleach air. Cuireadh de dhualgas orainn beirt clár a leagan amach le haghaidh seimineáir a bhí le bheith ar siúl le haghaidh na gcigirí go léir. Is cuimhin liom go maith gurbh é Tomás Ó Cuilleanáin a thagair d'alt a bhí sa *Teachers' Work*,[4] alt a scríobh an tAthair Colmán Ó Huallacháin, a bhí ag an am sin tar éis bliain a chaitheamh in Ollscoil Georgetown, Washington, D.C., ag déanamh staidéir ar mhodhanna múinte teangacha. Dúirt Tomás go mba mhór an ní é údar an ailt a fháil le léacht a thabhairt ag seimineár na gcigirí. Ba é an t-ábhar a bhí san alt an gá a bhí le taighde teangeolaíoch a dhéanamh ar an nGaeilge labhartha le go bhféadfaí cúrsaí oiriúnacha a ullmhú le haghaidh leanaí bunscoile. Bhí sé sin ag teacht go hiomlán le torthaí mhachnamh Choiste na Roinne a ndearna mé tagairt dó thuas. Ba é bun agus barr an scéil gur tugadh cuireadh d'údar an ailt, an tAthair Colmán, léacht a thabhairt do na cigirí ar an ábhar a bhí i gceist san alt, rud a rinne sé ar ball. Bhí Rúnaí Cúnta na Roinne, Seán Mac Gearailt, ina Chathaoirleach le linn na léachta agus nuair a thuig sé gurbh ionann an rud a bhí i gceist sa léacht agus an rud a bhí molta ag coiste na Roinne, shocraigh sé go gceapfaí an tAthair Colmán go sealadach mar Chomhairleoir Teangeolaíochta sa Roinn Oideachais chun an taighde riachtanach a bhí i gceist a dhéanamh. Cuireadh in iúl dom féin ag an am chéanna go raibh an Roinn tagtha ar mhalairt aigne faoi na *Notes for Teachers—Irish* a athfhoilsiú agus dúradh liom leanúint le mo ghnáthobair chigireachta go fóill.

---

[4] Colmán Ó Huallacháin, 'How Modern Language Teaching Methods Could Help Irish Teachers Quickly', *The Teachers' Work*, 21.2 (1962), 82–84.

AN TEANGLANN, RINN MHIC GORMÁIN

Thosaigh an tAthair Colmán Ó Huallacháin ag obair mar Chomhlairleoir Teangeolaíochta don Roinn Oideachais um dheireadh na bliana 1962, ach níorbh fhada go bhfuair sé amach nach bhféadfadh sé dul chun cinn sásúil a dhéanamh dá leanfadh sé ag obair leis ar a chonlán féin. D'iarr sé cúnamh ar an Roinn Oideachais agus glaodh orm féin chun na hoifige arís agus iarradh orm dul ag cabhrú leis. Bhíos sásta é sin a dhéanamh agus thosaíos ag obair leis an Athair Colmán i bhfómhar na bliana 1963. Leanas liom ag obair ar an taighde Gaeilge a bhí idir lámha againn beirt go dtí gur foilsíodh *Buntús Gaeilge*[5] sa bhliain 1966.

Is i gColáiste na bProinsiasach i Rinn Mhic Gormáin a bhí an tAthair Colmán lonnaithe ag an am sin agus is ansin a bhí a lárionad oibre aige. I dtús ama ba é an taighde teangeolaíoch, ar eascair buntús Gaeilge as, an cúram ba mhó a bhí air, mar ní raibh de chabhair aige ach clóscríobhaí. Mar sin féin níorbh fhada gur ghlac sé cúraimí eile air féin, cúrsaí le haghaidh múinteoirí ar mhodhanna múinte teangacha agus mar sin de. Thug sé faoi ionad a thógáil dó féin ar thalamh an choláiste i Rinn Mhic Gormáin. Ba é a bhí san ionad sin trí nó cheithre sheomra mar oifigí, leabharlann agus saotharlann teanga, an dara saotharlann teanga sa tír, de réir mo chuimhne. (Bhí an chéad cheann tógtha cheana ag an Ollamh Tomás de Bhaldraithe i gColáiste na hOllscoile, Baile Átha Cliath). Tamall ina dhiaidh sin chuir an tAthair Colmán an dara saotharlann leis an ionad, mar go raibh sé ag teastáil, dar leis, chun tréanáil i dteangacha iasachta a chur ar shagairt agus ar dhaoine eile a bheadh ag dul thar lear mar mhisinéirí. Tiomnaíodh an foirgneamh go léir don Spiorad Naomh agus thug an tAthair Colmán *An Teanglann* ar an ionad. D'oscail an tAire Oideachais, An Dr. Pádraig Ó hIrighile, T.D., *An Teanglann* go h-oifigiúil ar an 7ú Márta, 1965. Ina dhiaidh sin bheannaigh a Shoilse Liam Cairdinéal Mac Conmhidhe an foirgneamh nua, tar éis dó Aifreann a léamh i nGaeilge i láthair Uachtaráin na hÉireann, Éamon de Valera, i séipeal an Choláiste. As sin go dtí 1967 is as *An Teanglann* a thagadh litreacha agus foilseacháin an Athar Cholmáin.

Ba é an Dr. Ó hIrighile a bhí ina Aire Oideachais nuair a ceapadh an tAthair Colmán ina Chomhairleoir Teangeolaíochta sa bhliain 1962 agus chuir sé spéis i gcónaí sa taighde a bhí ar siúl againn. Thug sé níos mó ná cuairt amháin orainn i Rinn Mhic Gormáin chun an dul chun cinn a bhí á dhéanamh againn a bhreathnú agus a phlé linn. Ba é Seoirse Ó Colla, T.D. a tháinig ina dhiaidh mar Aire Oideachais agus léirigh seisean chomh maith spéis ar leith san obair. Is cuimhin liom é a theacht chugam i mo sheomra

---

[5] *Buntús Gaeilge* (Baile Átha Cliath: Oifig an tSoláthair, 1966).

sa Roinn Oideachais féachaint cé mar a bhí an obair ag dul ar aghaidh agus cén uair a mbeadh toradh ar fáil. Ba é Donnchadh Ó Máille, T.D. a bhí ina Aire Oideachais i ndiaidh Sheoirse Ó Colla agus chífimíd ar ball cé mar a léirigh seisean spéis in obair na Gaeilge freisin.

Ba le cabhair deontais ón Roinn Oideachais a tógadh *An Teanglann* agus ba ionann stádas dó mar fhoirgneamh ó thaobh na Roinne de agus an stádas a bheadh ag aon scoil náisiúnta sa tír: é dílsithe in iontaobhaithe le húsáid mar ionad oibre do lucht taighde agus mar ionad staidéir agus mar ionad oiliúna le haghaidh múinteoirí Gaeilge agus nua-theangacha eile. Bhí sé áisiúil mar ionad comhdhálacha agus cúrsaí do mhúinteoirí agus mar ionad tréanála dóibh, mar bhíodh áiseanna eile choláiste Rinn Mhic Gormáin—ionaid chodlata, bialann agus seomraí ranga, gan trácht ar linn snámha agus áiseanna eile caithimh aimsire—ar fáil i rith laethe saoire macléinn an choláiste.

Nuair a thosaíos féin ag obair leis an Athair Colmán i bhfómhar na bliana 1963 bhíodh orm taisteal ó mo ionad cónaithe i mBaile Átha Cliath gach lá. Leanas den nós sin ar feadh tamaill go dtí gur bhraitheas nár ghá dom an t-aistear sin a chur díom gach uile lá. Uaidh sin amach is i mo theach féin in mBaile Átha Cliath a bhínn ag obair de ghnáth agus ní théinn go dtí An Teanglann ach de réir mar a bhíodh sé riachtanach chun go mbeadh comhdháil agam leis an Athair Colmán nó chun go mbuailfimís beirt le duine nó le daoine eile. Le fírinne, bhíodh sé níos áisiúla dom go minic a bheith i mBaile Átha Cliath i rith an lae chun a bheith ag plé le lucht códála nó le lucht áiritheoirí IBM nó eile.

BUNTÚS GAEILGE: AN TAIGHDE

Ba iad na modhanna teangeolaíocha ('linguistic methods') na modhanna múinte a bhí faiseanta maidir le teangacha a mhúineadh ag an am sin, go mór mór i Meiriceá agus sa Fhrainc, agus ba iad sin na modhanna a raibh an tAthair Colmán tar éis eolas a chur orthu thall. Ba bhunphrionsabal de na modhanna sin é go mbunófaí an teagasc i dtús foghlama ar na heilimintí den sprioctheanga—focail, deilbhíocht, comhréir—is minice a tharlaíonn sa ghnáthchaint. Measadh dá múinfí na heilimintí sin den sprioctheanga don fhoghlaimeoir i dtús foghlama go mbeadh ar a chumas caint an ghnáthchainteora ó dhúchas a thuiscint gan mhoill, agus go mbeadh ar a chumas chomh maith é féin a chur in iúl i gcaint shimplí go luath agus go saoráideach. Ba é an cuspóir a bhí leis an taighde a bhí le déanamh ar an nGaeilge, mar sin, ná eolas cruinn a chur ar na heilimintí den Ghaeilge is minice a tharlaíonn sa ghnáthchaint.

Chuireamar romhainn, mar sin, eolas a chur ar thrí ghné den teanga mar a labhraíonn gnáthmhuintir na Gaeltachta í:

(i) foclóir,

(ii) deilbhíocht,

(iii) comhréir nó structúr.

FOCLÓIR

Maidir le foclóir, bhí sé faighte amach ag lucht teangeolaíochta roimhe sin go raibh trí shaghas foclóra ann:

(a) feidhmfhocail,

(b) focail ghinearálta,

(c) sainfhocail.

Is iad na feidhmfhocail nó na focail ghramadúla na focail bheaga nach féidir abairtí a chur le chéile gan iad: *is, ag, agus, ea, mé, sé,* etc. Áirítear forainmneacha, réamhfhocail, míreanna, etc. chomh maith le corrainmfhocal agus corrbhriathar in aicme na bhfeidhmfhocal. Ainmfhocail, aidiachtaí, dobhriathra agus briathra a thagann faoin dá aicme eile: focail ghinearálta agus sainfhocail. Is é an difríocht atá eatarthu nach n-úsáidtear na sainfhocail ach nuair a bhítear ag caint ar ábhair ar leith, mar shampla, an t-ainmfhocal *sneachta* nó an briathar *reoidh* nuair a bhímid ag caint ar an aimsir, na focail *ceacht, foghlaim* ag baint le scolaíocht, na focail *slaghdán, leigheas, ar fónamh,* ag baint le cúrsaí sláinte etc., ach úsáidtear na focail ghinearálta i gcaint ar ábhair ilghnéitheacha, mar shampla, na briathra *téigh, déan;* na hainmfhocail *duine, baile;* na focail cháilithe *mór, maith, deas;* agus mar sin de.

Chuir an tAthair Colmán roimhe leathmhilliún focal de ghnáthchaint reatha na Gaeltachta a chur ar théip, caint ó gach Gaeltacht sa tír, caint a chloisfí ar ghnáthócáidí i dtithe, i siopaí, ar leac an teallaigh agus ar cholbha na sráide; caint sheandaoine agus caint daoine óga agus mar sin de. Is trí anailís a dhéanamh ar an gcaint sin a thiocfaí ar an bhfoclóir (feidhmfhocail agus focail ghinearálta), ar an deilbhíocht agus ar an gcomhréir is minice a úsáideann cainteoirí Gaeilge. Ní thabharfadh an anailís sin dúinn, áfach, na sainfhocail riachtanacha a bhainfeadh le hábhair speisialta: aimsir, sláinte, bia agus deoch, etc. Rinneadh aithris sa chuid sin den obair ar thaighde a bhí déanta sa Fhrainc, taighde a raibh *Le Français Fondamental* mar thoradh air. Cuireadh ceistiúcháin amach chuig 260 cainteoir dúchais sa Ghaeltacht agus iarradh orthu an fiche focal ba riachtanaí, dar leo, a bhain le gach ceann d'fhiche ábhar a bhreacadh síos. Ba é an toradh a bheadh air sin cnuasach de 104,000 focal; roghnófaí mar fhocail riachtanacha (sainfhocail) na focail ba mhinice a tharlódh san iomlán sin. Toisc gur le haghaidh Béarlóirí na Galltachta a bheadh na cúrsaí Gaeilge á n-ullmhú, déanadh bailiúchán den saghas céanna d'fhocail

Bhéarla ó 260 cainteoir Béarla sa Ghalltacht, rud a thabharfadh 104,000 focal Béarla ar na hábhair cheannann chéanna. Déanadh anailís ríomhaire ar an iomlán sin de 208,000 focal chun teacht ar na sainfhocail ba riachtanaí dar leis an lucht faisnéise. Bhí an chéim sin den obair beagnach críochnaithe nuair a thosaíos féin ag glacadh páirte sa taighde.

Idir an dá linn bhí na téipeanna á líonadh de ghnáthchomhrá na Gaeltachta, bhí siad á mbailiú agus an t-ábhar orthu á scríobh i gcóipleabhair i ngach Gaeltacht sa tír. Ansin clóscríobhadh an t-iomlán san oifig a bhí againn. Bhí sé ar intinn leathmhilliún focal reatha cainte a bhailiú mar sin agus a iniúchadh, mar a dúirt mé thuas. Shocraíomar, áfach, an leathmhilliún focal a roinnt ina chúig chuid, 100,000 focal i ngach cuid, agus gach 100,000 focal díobh sin a scrúdú mar aonad ann féin. Bhí gach aonad de 100,000 focal déanta suas de 100 sliocht, agus míle focal i ngach sliocht. Agus na sleachta á roghnú againn thugamar cothrom na féinne do gach Gaeltacht, de réir líon na gcainteoirí Gaeilge i ngach Gaeltacht acu. Chuamar ag obair ar an gcéad 100,000 focal. Cheapamar cóid agus modh oibre chun áireamh ríomhaire a dhéanamh ar thitim gach uile fhocal den 100,000 sin, gach focal ar leith agus gach foirm ar leith de gach focal san áireamh. Chuireamar oiliúint ansin ar fhoireann códaitheoirí a chuirfeadh na cóid i bhfeidhm ar na 100,000 focal clóscríofa. Bhí gach focal le cur ar chárta ríomhaire ansin sula bhféadfaí na focail a chur tríd an ríomhaire le próiseáil.

Nuair a bhí an anailís ríomhaire ar siúl ar an gcéad 100,000 focal de na comhráite Gaeilge ón nGaeltacht bhíomar den tuairim go mbeadh obair den saghas céanna le déanamh againn ar cheithre mheall eile comhrá, 100,000 focal i ngach meall acu. Ní mar sin a tharla, áfach, mar a chífimid ar ball.

Ag an am seo ní raibh i gceist ag an Athair Colmán aon anailís a dhéanamh ar na comhráite ach anailís foclóra: bhí aithris á dhéanamh aige ar na scoláirí sa Fhrainc a chuir Le Français Fondamental le chéile. Ba bheag a rinneadar sin leis na comhráite a bhí bailithe acu ach áireamh a dhéanamh ar na focail a tharla sna comhráite agus anailís a dhéanamh orthu maidir le tuiseal, le huimhir agus mar sin de. Thairis sin níor dhéan siad anailís ach ar líon beag foirmeacha comhréire, mar shampla na slite éagsúla chun ceist a chur ar dhuine agus mar sin de. Ní mór cuimhneamh air nach raibh áiritheoirí leictreonacha ag na scoláirí sin, ach go rabhadar ag brath ar chomhaireamh láimhe amháin.

Chuireas in iúl don Athair Colmán gur mheasas nárbh fhiú dúinn an méid sin oibre a tharraingt orainn féin muna mbeadh de thoradh dá bharr againn ach liostaí focal, mar go mba thábhachtaí i bhfad eolas a chur ar chomhréir na teanga .i. eolas a chur ar na struchtúir agus ar mhinicíocht a dtitime sa chaint. Bheadh an t-eolas sin ag teastáil chun cúrsaí céimithe a ullmhú le haghaidh na ranganna éagsúla sna scoileanna.

Ar deireadh ghlac an tAthair Colmán leis an moladh sin uaim ach d'fhág sé fúm féin ar fad ceapadh modha oibre chun teacht ar an eolas sin. Chomh fada agus ab eol dúinn ag an am ní raibh taighde den saghas sin déanta ar aon teanga in aon tír ar domhan. Ghlac mé orm féin, mar sin, córas a cheapadh chun struchtúir theanga den saghas céanna a thabhairt le chéile ionas go mbeadh ar ár gcumas titim gach struchtúir ar leith a bhreathnú agus minicíocht a thitime a áireamh.

STRUCHTÚR NA TEANGA

Fad a bhí códáil agus próiseáil á dhéanamh ar an chéad 100,000 focal den ábhar, mar sin, chuaigh mé féin ag obair ar an dara 100,000 de chaint na Gaeltachta. Chuireamar romhainn an uair seo dhá staidéar ar leith a dhéanamh den aon iarracht amháin:

(i)   staidéar domhain iomlán a dhéanamh ar gach briathar a tharlódh: a mhinice a tharlódh gach briathar ar leith agus *gach foirm* de gach briathar, an saghas úsáide a tharlódh i ngach cás, úsáid na modhanna, na n-aimsirí, na bpearsan, agus mar sin de;

(ii)   an chaint go léir sa 100,000 focal sin a roinnt ina struchtúir, nó in a haonaid chomhréire (abairtí, fo-abairtí, clásail, frásaí), le go bhféadfaí aonaid den saghas céanna a thabhairt le chéile, a áireamh agus a iniúchadh.

Ar ndóigh bheadh briathar mar lárfhocal i ngach aonad díobh sin de ghnáth, ach chuir sé ionadh orainn ar ball a liacht aonad cainte nó aonad comhréire a bhí gan briathar ar bith iontu.

Ba é ceapadh an chóid le haghaidh áirimh na struchtúr an chuid ab achrannaí ar fad den obair, agus is é mo chuimhne anois gur chaitheas ráithe nó níos mó ag triail agus ag feabhsú, ag atriail agus ag athfheabhsú. Ar deireadh thiar, áfach, b'éigean glacadh le leagan áirithe den chód, b'éigean foireann nua códála a oiliúint agus na cóid nua a chur i bhfeidhm ar an dara 100,000 focal chun go bhféadfaí iad a chur tríd an ríomhaire.

AN TORADH

Nuair a bhí torthaí ar fáil ón chéad 100,000 focal agus ón dara 100,000 focal tharla rud a thug an-uchtach dúinn, rud a chuir ina luí orainn go rabhamar ar an mbealach ceart: nuair a cuireadh cuntas na mbriathra ón chéad rith i gcomparáid le cuntas na mbriathra ón dara rith tugadh faoi deara gurbh iad na briathra céanna a tháinig as an dá rith; ní amháin sin, ach bhí an-chosúlacht idir minicíocht agus ord a dtitime, go mór mór i gcás na mbriathra ba mhinice a tharla. Mar shampla, ba mhar a chéile an chéad 14 bhriathar i ngach liosta agus tharla siad san ord céanna. Neartaigh sé sin an tuairim a bhí againn gurbh iad na feidhmfhocail chéanna agus na focail ghinearálta chéanna a thiocfadh as gach grúpa 100,000 focal comhrá. Tar éis dúinn an dá liosta briathar a scrúdú go géar, thángamar ar an tuairim ná beimís ach ag cur ama amú le hanailís *den saghas céanna* a dhéanamh ar a thuilleadh den chaint a bhí ar téip againn, mar go mba é an toradh céanna a thiocfadh as.

De thoradh na hoibre a bhí déanta bhí eolas curtha againn ar na feidhmfhocail agus ar na focail ghinearálta—na hilfhocail go léir—a tharla i 100,000 focal de ghnáthchomhrá na Gaeltachta, ar mhinicíocht úsáide gach foirme ar leith de gach ceann de na focail sin agus ar a ndeilbhíocht. Bhí eolas curtha againn freisin ar gach aonad comhréire a tharla i 100,000 focal reatha cainte agus ar a mhinice a tharla gach aonad. Chomh maith leis sin bhí na liostaí sainfhocal riachtanacha againn roimhe sin ó Ghaeilgeoirí agus ó Bhéarlóirí. As an iomlán sin roghnaíodh na haonaid chomhréire ba mhinice a tharla—144 aonad ar fad; roghnaíodh an 500 feidhmfhocal agus focal ginearálta ba riachtanaí agus cuireadh leo 1,000 de na sainfhocail ba mhinice a tharla; cuireadh leosan liosta de na foirmeacha briathartha ba mhinice a úsáideadh sa 200,000 focal reatha comhrá ar déanadh anailís orthu. Is ar an iomlán sin le chéile a tugadh *Buntús Gaeilge* agus is é a bhí ar intinn againn cúrsaí tosaigh Gaeilge sna bunscoileanna a bhunú ar an ábhar sin. Ní mór dom a rá go ndeachthas i gcomhairle le saineolaithe canúna, duine as gach Gaeltacht, i dtaobh focal nó foirmeacha áirithe a roghnú thar focail nó foirmeacha eile; mar shampla, ba iad na saineolaithe sin a roghnaigh *fearthainn* thar *báisteach, carr* thar *gluaisteán, leictreachas* thar *aibhléis* agus mar sin de. Cuireadh na liostaí comhréire, foirmeacha briathartha agus focail i gcló i gCuid II de *Bhuntús Gaeilge*. Tá eolas níos iomláine faoi dheilbhíocht agus faoi thorthaí an taighde go léir le léamh i gCuid I den leabhar céanna. (Ní miste a rá gurbh fhocal nuachumtha é an focal *buntús,* agus gurbh é an tAthair Colmán féin a cheap é. Bhí leagan Gaeilge den teideal *Le Français Fondamental* á lorg againn agus phléamar roinnt leaganacha eile sular aontaíomar ar an bhfocal *buntús*).

BUNTÚS GAEILGE: CUR I BHFEIDHM

Bhíos féin agus an tAthair Colmán ag obair le chéile fós ar cheapadh modhanna chun feidhm a bhaint as an ábhar a bhí i mBuntús Gaeilge chun an teanga a mhúineadh sna scoileanna. Ó bhí an taighde a bhí déanta againn bunaithe ar riachtanais na modhanna teangeolaíocha a bhí i bhfaisean i Stáit Aontaithe Mheiriceá ag an am, chinneamar ar mhodhanna múinte a bheadh gaolmhar leosan a cheapadh. Theastaigh uainn modh a bheadh bunaithe ar phictiúir a chur i bhfeidhm agus thug an tAthair Colmán cuairt ar Mharocó chun modhanna múinte na Fraincíse ansin a bhreathnú. Ba as an turas sin a eascair úsáid deilbhíní chun teagasc na Gaeilge a léiriú.

NA CÚRSAÍ GAEILGE

Fágadh fúm féin ina dhiaidh sin cúrsa trialach Gaeilge a cheapadh. Ba bheag baint a bhí ag an Athair Colmán le hullmhú na gcúrsaí ná lena gcur i bhfeidhm i scoileanna ina dhiaidh sin. Bhí sé tógtha suas lena ghnó féin mar chomhairleoir teangeolaíochta don Roinn Oideachais, ach, ar ndóigh, bhí sé ina bhall de choistí éagsúla sa Roinn a bhí ag plé leis na cúrsaí éagsúla. Ba é an gnó ba mhó a bhí idir lámha aige um an am sin, áfach, oiliúint mhúinteoirí nuatheangacha agus leaganacha Gaeilge de leabhair Mheiriceánacha a fhoilsiú le húsáid i meánscoileanna in Éirinn chun nuatheangacha Eorpacha a mhúineadh de réir na modhanna nua. Ba iad na leabhair a bhí i gceist: *Ecouter et Parler* (Fraincis), *Verstehen und Sprechen* (Gearmáinis), agus *Entendir y Hablar* (Spáinnis). Téacsleabhair ab ea iad sin a fhoilsigh Holt, Rinehart and Winston (Nua-Eabhrac) le húsáid sna Stáit Aontaithe agus bhí cead faighte ag an Athair Colmán leaganacha Gaeilge díobh a chur ar fáil in Éirinn. Le fírinne, ba iad cigirí Bhrainse an Mheánoideachais anseo a rinne an t-aistriúchán ar na leabhair sin agus a chaith dúthracht mhór leis an saothar. Mar sin féin nuair a foilsíodh na leabhair níor tugadh aitheantas ar bith do na haistritheoirí ná ní raibh a n-ainmneacha leis na leabhair: ní raibh ach ainm an Athar Cholmáin leo mar Eagarthóir Gaeilge. Foilsíodh an chéad leabhar díobh, *Ecouter et Parler*, sa bhliain 1964 agus na cinn eile ina dhiaidh sin.

Maidir leis an eolas a bhí i *mBuntús Gaeilge* a chur i bhfeidhm ar chúrsaí Gaeilge sna scoileanna, bhí sé i gceist ó thús leas a bhaint as na modhanna teangeolaíocha sna cúrsaí a d'eascródh as torthaí an taighde. Tar éis staidéar a dhéanamh ar na modhanna sin agus ar a n-úsáid thar lear, agus tar éis don Athair Colmán cuairteanna a thabhairt ar thíortha iasachta a raibh siad á n-úsáid iontu, chinneamar ar fheidhm a bhaint as an modh closamhairc .i. modh a mbeadh pictiúir mar lár sa teagasc ann. Bhí seift le ceapadh ansin leis na pictiúir sin a chur os comhair na leanaí. Chinneamar beirt ar deireadh ar phictiúir ghearrtha—*deilbhíní* a thugamar orthu—a úsáid, agus iad a bheith inghreamaithe inghluaiste ar chlár dubh de shaghas éigin.

Mé féin a bhí freagrach as an leagan Éireannach den mhodh teangeolaíoch a oibriú amach. Bhí níos mó ná tríocha bliain de thaithí agam ag an am ar úsáid an mhodha A, B, C sna scoileanna, agus thuig mé go maith a éifeachtaí is a bhí an modh sin ag na múinteoirí a leanadh na treoracha a bhí sna *Notes for Teachers—Irish*. D'fhéachas chuige, mar sin, nach gcaillfí an chuid ab fhearr den seanmhodh i gcur i bhfeidhm an mhodha nua. Ba iad na cúig chéim a bhí i gceacht de réir an mhodha nua ná:

Céim I	:	Cloisteáil agus Aithint;
Céim II	:	Aithris;
Céim III	:	Athrá ó Spreagthaigh;
Céim IV	:	Cleachtadh Múnlaí agus Foclóra;
Céim V	:	Saorchomhrá Cruthaitheach.

Ba sna trí chéim thosaigh ba mhó a bhí tionchar an mhodha nua le sonrú, go mór mór in úsáid agus i láimhseáil na ndeilbhíní mar ghléas mínithe agus mar spreagthaigh chainte, ach bhí tionchar an mhodha A, B, C le feiceáil go soiléir i gcéimeanna IV/V. Bhí Cúrsa A agus Cúrsa B ag teacht isteach i gCéim IV agus ba ionann ar fad, nach mór, Céim V agus Cúrsa C den seanmhodh .i. na leanaí féin ag caint ar a gconlán féin agus iad ag baint feidhme as an gcuid nua den teanga a bhí foghlamtha acu i gceangal leis an méid den teanga a bhí acu roimhe sin.

Scríobhas sraith thrialach cheachtanna de réir an mhodha nua agus roghnaíos líon áirithe de mhúinteoirí a bheadh sásta na ceachtanna a thriail ar feadh tréimhse áirithe. Tugadh i a ceachtanna agus cláir adhmainteacha mhiotail do leath na múinteoirí le haghaidh na ndeilbhíní agus tugadh na ceachtanna agus cláir níolóin scuabtha don leath eile. Nuair a bhí leath na gceachtanna trialte, malartaíodh na cláir, ionas go raibh caoi ag gach múinteoir ar an dá shaghas cláir a thriail. Líon gach múinteoir a bhí páirteach sa triail ceistiúchán faoin modh nua agus thug siad a gcuid tuairimí agus a gcuid moltaí. Ní gá a rá gur cuireadh an-spéis sa triail agus gur thug cuairteoirí céimiúla—an Rúnaí Parlaiminte Pádraig Ó Fachtna, T.D., a bhí níos deireanaí ina Aire Oideachais, ar dhuine acu—cuairteanna ar na ranganna a bhí páirteach sa triail. Bhí gach uile dhuine, idir mhúinteoirí agus oifigigh na Roinne Oideachais, thar a bheith sásta leis an mhodh nua agus leis an gcur chuige a bhí léirithe sna ceachtanna trialacha. Ba iad na cláir níolóin scuabtha ba rogha leis na múinteoirí chun na deilbhíní a chur á láimhseáil orthu.

Ba é an buntáiste ba mhó a chonaic na múinteoirí sa chur chuige nua ná go mbeadh cúrsa réamhdhéanta á thabhairt dóibh: bheadh leabhar ina lámha acu a mbeadh gach ceacht ullmhaithe leagtha amach dóibh ann, bheadh pictiúir (deilbhíní) acu chun gach céim de gach ceacht a léiriú agus thabharfaí clár dubh faoi leith dóibh leis na ceachtanna Gaeilge a léiriú. Roimhe sin, ar ndóigh, bhíodh orthu a scéimeanna bliana agus a gceachtanna laethúla féin a ullmhú, idir ábhar agus chur chuige, idir mhodh agus phictiúir (dá mbeadh pictiúir acu, rud nach mbíodh de ghnáth). Níorbh aon ionadh é, mar sin, gur thosaigh múinteoirí seachas iad sin a bhí sa chéim thrialach, gur thosaigh siad ag iarraidh go dtabharfaí na ceachtanna nua agus an fearas nua dóibh. Cuireadh brú dá réir ar an Roinn Oideachais agus ghéill an Roinn don bhrú, gan fanacht le toradh comparáide meáite idir an seanmhodh agus an modh nua. Chuir an Roinn coiste treorach, faoi Ghearóid A. Ó Súilleabháin, Roinnchigire, ar bun chun an obair a stiúrú. Ceapadh dhá fhoireann saothair: foireann le cúrsaí a ullmhú le haghaidh ranganna na scoileanna náisiúnta agus foireann le brúchúrsa le haghaidh scoileanna iarbhunoideachais a ullmhú.

NUACHÚRSAÍ COMHRÁ

Mé féin a bhí i mbun ullmhú na gcúrsaí nua bunscoile agus thoghamar Proinsias Mac Suibhne, a bhí ina mhúinteoir náisiúnta ag an am, le bheith ina chúntóir agam. Bhí ealaíontóirí páirtaimseartha ar fáil againn leis na pictiúir (deilbhíní) a ullmhú. Thosaíomar ag obair linn ag ullmhú ceachtanna le haghaidh ranganna I-II agus á dtriail ar fud na tíre. Triail bhliana a bhí i gceist an uair seo agus le linn na trialach ghlacamar le comhairle ó mhúinteoirí agus ó chigirí sular leasaíomar na ceachtanna agus sular leathnaíomar amach iad ina gcúrsaí dhá bhliain faoi na teidil *Hóra, a Pháid!* agus *Dúisigh, a Bhríd!* (1967). Ag an am chéanna bhíomar ag obair ar chúrsa le haghaidh ranganna III–IV agus cuireadh an cúrsa sin freisin faoi thriail i scoileanna ar fud na tíre. Thógadh sé cúpla bliain nó níos mó chun cúrsa dhá bhliain a ullmhú, a thriail agus a fhorbairt mar sin.

Ba ag an gcéim sin den obair a tugadh ardú céime dom féin agus cuireadh cúram eile ar fad orm sa Roinn nuair a ceapadh mé i m'Oifigeach Closamhairc chun post nuachruthaithe faoin teideal sin a líonadh. Ba é Seán de Búrca, Cigire, a ceapadh i m'áit i mbun na gcúrsaí nua Gaeilge agus lean seisean den obair, ag forbairt cúrsaí ranganna III/IV, ag ullmhú cúrsa le haghaidh ranganna V/VI agus á thriail agus mar sin de. Lean Seán den obair sin: ag cruthú, ag forbairt agus ag feabhsú, ag cur deilbhíní agus téipeanna agus áiseanna eile ar fáil, agus ag oiliúint na múinteoirí sna modhanna nua, go dtí lá a bháis roinnt blianta ina dhiaidh sin, go ndéana Dia trócaire ar a anam.

Ba é an coiste stiúrtha, a raibh teachtaithe ó chumainn na múinteoirí ina mbaill de, a roghnaigh as *Buntús Gaeilge* an méid den teanga a bheadh le múineadh do gach rang ar leith. Ní mór dom a admháil anois gur chuir sé ionadh orm féin i ndeireadh na dála gur measadh go nglacfadh sé an tréimhse bhunoideachais ar fad—breis agus ocht mbliana—chun freastal sna cúrsaí comhrá ar an méid den Ghaeilge a bhí i *mBuntús Gaeilge,* ach sin mar a tharla de bharr machnaimh an choiste stiúrtha. Chuir sé díomá orm, chomh maith, mar ba é a thuig mé de bharr an staidéir a bhí déanta agam ar na modhanna teangeolaíocha gurbh *i dtús foghlama* amháin a bhainfí feidhm as na modhanna sin. Bhí mé sásta i m'aigne go dtí sin nach mbeadh gá leo i ranganna ab airde ná rang III nó rang IV, ach de réir mar a tharla leanadh dá n-úsáid ar feadh na tréimhse bunscoile ar fad, agus fiú i dtús na tréimhse meánscoile!

Cibé ar bith, de thoradh na hoibre go léir chuireamar sé leabhrán ar fáil le haghaidh na múinteoirí—lámhleabhar le haghaidh gach ranga sna scoileanna náisiúnta, deilbhíní agus téipeanna ag dul le gach leabhrán díobh. Rinneadh socruithe faoi leith le haghaidh scoileanna a mbeadh dhá rang nó níos mó á dteagasc le chéile iontu. Chomh maith leis sin ullmhaíodh réamhchúrsa le haghaidh ranganna naíonán, ionas gur cuireadh seacht gcúrsa ar fad ar fáil le haghaidh scoileanna náisiúnta. Chomh luath agus a bhí na cúrsaí ar fad le fáil, mar aon leis na deilbhíní agus na téipeanna, tosaíodh ar stiallscannáin a chur ar fáil le haghaidh múinteoirí ar mhaith leo stiallscannáin a úsáid in ionad deilbhíní. Tuigfear an dua a bhain le hullmhú na stiallscannán nuair a deirim gur ullmhaíodh stiallscannán amháin le haghaidh gach ceachta i ngach leabhar, thart ar fiche pictiúr i ngach stiall .i. thart ar 600 pictiúr ar fad le haghaidh gach leabhráin. Cuireadh ar fáil freisin amhráin a bheadh oiriúnach le haghaidh gach cúrsa comhrá agus cuireadh na hamhráin ar théipeanna mar chabhair do mhúinteoirí ar theastaigh sé sin uathu. Níos déanaí, nuair a bhí cúrsaí agus fearas curtha ar fáil le haghaidh gach ranga, tosaíodh as an nua ag forbairt agus ag leasú gach cúrsa acu, agus cuireadh eagrán leasaithe de gach cúrsa ar fáil, maille le deilbhíní agus le stiallscannáin nua.

ÁBHAR LÉITHEOIREACHTA

Ní raibh ansin ach taobh an chomhrá. Níor mhór freastal ar an léamh agus ar an scríobh freisin. Is prionsabal de na modhanna teangeolaíocha é go dtugtar tús áite do labhairt na teanga agus gur ina dhiaidh sin a mhúintear an léamh agus an scríobh. Chuathas i gcomhairle leis na foilsitheoirí téacsleabhar bunscoile agus míníodh an scéal dóibh. Tionóladh cruinnithe ar fhreastail idir fhoilsitheoirí agus oifigigh na Roinne Oideachais orthu agus ba é an toradh a bhí ar na cruinnithe sin gur fhoilsigh trí chomhlacht sraitheanna leabhar—téacsleabhair léitheoireachta, leabhair bhreise léitheoireachta agus leabhair shaothair—le haghaidh gach ranga bunscoile. Ba é an prionsabal a cuireadh i bhfeidhm i gcás gach leabhair acu sin nach n-úsáidfí focal ar bith in aon leabhar acu nach mbeadh ar eolas ag na leanaí de bharr na gceachtanna comhrá a mhúinfí dóibh roimh ré. I dtosach, le fírinne, féachadh chuige go mbeadh an t-ábhar léitheoireachta sé mhí chun deiridh ar ábhar na gceachtanna comhrá. Ba sna leabhair shaothair a dhéanfadh na leanaí a n-iarrachtaí tosaigh ar na nGaeilge a scríobh agus níor ceadaíodh focal ar bith iontu sin ach oiread ach focail a bhí cloiste léite ag na leanaí roimh ré. Ar an gcaoi sin a deimhníodh go gcomhlíonfaí prionsabal na modhanna teangeolaíocha: labhairt na teanga roimh a léamh agus a scríobh. Ba é Gearóid A. Ó Súilleabháin, Cigire, a rinne na socruithe go léir leis na foilsitheoirí i leith na nithe sin.

Nuair a bhí an obair sin go léir ar siúl ar mhaithe le Gaeilge na mbunscoileanna, bhí coiste agus foireann oibre na meánscoileanna ag obair leo chomh maith. Chuir siad dhá chúrsa ar fáil .i. *Bunsraith Gaeilge* le haghaidh daltaí na chéad bhliana meánscoile a bheadh ar bheagán Gaeilge, agus *Téanam Ort* le haghaidh ghnáthdhaltaí meánscoile. Thoiligh na foilsitheoirí leabhair léitheoireachta agus leabhair shaothair bunaithe ar an dá chúrsa sin a chur ar fáil, mar a rinne siad i gcás na scoileanna náisiúnta roimhe sin.

Meabhrán

Ba ghnáth le múinteoirí agus le lucht foghlama na Gaeilge 'cúrsaí buntúis' agus 'modhanna buntúis' a thabhairt ar na cúrsaí Gaeilge go léir atá luaite thuas agus ar na modhanna múinte a bhain leo. Le fírinne, ní bhaineann an focal *buntús* le cúrsaí ná le modh: is é atá i gceist san fhocal *buntús* ná an méid is lú den Ghaeilge a bheadh ag teastáil ó dhuine chun é féin a chur in iúl go simplí sa Ghaeilge agus chun caint shimplí a thuiscint. Ba iad na *modhanna closamhairc* na modhanna a cuireadh i bhfeidhm sna cúrsaí go léir atá luaite thuas agus na *cúrsaí closamhairc* ba cheart a thabhairt orthu. Is féidir go mbeidh an t-ábhar atá i *mBuntús Gaeilge* á úsáid amach anseo nuair a bheidh na cúrsaí thuasluaite agus na modhanna closamhairc imithe as faisean agus iad dearmadtha ag múinteoirí agus ag mic léinn na linne sin. Is dócha gurbh é tionscamh *Bhuntús Gaeilge* an tionscnamh ba mhó agus ba leithne scóip dá shórt ar tugadh faoi sa Roinn Oideachais ó bunaíodh í.

Ó Rinn Mhic Gormáin go Baile Átha Cliath

Sa Teanglann i Rinn Mhic Gormáin a bhí an tAthair Colmán lonnaithe ar feadh an ama go léir a raibh *Buntús Gaeilge* á ullmhú, ó 1962 go dtí cur amach an leabhair sa bhliain 1966 agus ina dhiaidh sin. Sa Teanglann a bhínn féin ag obair gach lá freisin i dtús an taighde.

Nuair a bhí céim áirithe den obair thaighde sroichte againn ba éigin dúinn cabhair bhreise a lorg agus ceapadh Gearóid A. Ó Crualaoich, M.A. mar chúntóir taighde. Déanadh socrú sealadach le Gearóid go gcuirfí lóistín ar fáil dó sa Teanglann féin agus go bhfaigheadh sé béilí sa choláiste. Leanadh de sin go ceann tamaill. De réir a chéile, áfach, thánas féin agus Gearóid den tuairim gurbh fhearr a oirfeadh ionad oibre i mBaile Átha Cliath dúinn beirt ná a bheith ag brath ar sheomraí sa Teanglann. Rinneas socrú go mbeadh seomra ar fáil againn i bhfoirgnimh na Roinne Oideachais i Sráid Mhaoilbhríde i mBaile Átha Cliath agus ba ansin a bhínn féin agus Gearóid ag obair as sin amach. Bhí sé sin sásúil go maith dúinn, mar bhí seirbhísí na Roinne Oideachais—clóscríobh, cóipeáil agus araile ar fáil againn ansin. Is san oifig sin a chuireamar críoch leis an obair ar an taighde a bhain le Buntús Gaeilge, is ann a chuireamar an leabhrán sin le chéile sa bhliain 1966 agus is ón oifig sin a scaipeadh an leabhar. Mar sin féin bhí an tAthair Colmán fós lonnaithe sa Teanglann i Rinn Mhic Gormáin agus théinnse síos ansin de réir mar ba ghá le haghaidh cruinnithe agus comhdhálacha leis.

Bhí an tAthair Colmán ag teacht ar mhalairt aigne um an dtaca seo i dtaobh an tsuímh ab oiriúnaí dá lárionad saothair féin. Tuigeadh dó anois go mba dheacair foireann saothair a mhealladh go dtí Rinn Mhic Gormáin agus a choimeád ann. Bhí sé den tuairim chomh maith go n-oirfeadh dó gan a bheith chomh mór is a bhí sé faoi smacht oifigeach na Roinne Oideachais. Ba é an cuspóir a chuir sé roimhe anois foras a chur ar bun a mbeadh gach gnó a bhainfeadh le leathnú na Gaeilge faoina chúram. Chuir sé roimhe chomh maith lárionad saothair i mBaile Átha Cliath a bhaint amach dó féin. Shroich meamram oifig an Aire Oideachais, Donnchadh Ó Máille, T.D., thart ar an am seo ag moladh dó Foras Gaeilge a chur ar bun a mbeadh lámh aige i ngach rud a bhain le leathnú na Gaeilge i measc phobal na tíre. Tháinig an meamram sin ó Chomhlacht Comhairleach na Gaeilge, Coiste a cheap an tAire Airgeadais roinnt blianta roimhe sin agus a raibh an tAthair Tomás Ó Fiaich (a bhí ina Chairdinéal níos faide anonn) ina Chathaoirleach air. Moladh sa mheamram sin go mbeadh coiste ceannais de thimpeall seisear nó seachtar i mbun an fhorais nua, go mbeadh stiúrthóir lánaimsireach ina bhun, go mbeadh buanfhoireann ag an bhforas chomh maith le áitreabh sásúil agus leorsholáthair áiseanna agus airgid a bheith aige.

INSTITIÚID TEANGEOLAÍOCHTA NA HÉIREANN (1967)

Is cosúil gur de thoradh an mheamraim sin, agus b'fhéidir de thoradh brú a bhí ar an Aire ó airdeanna eile, a bhunaigh Donnchadh Ó Máille T.D., Aire Oideachais, Institiúid Teangeolaíochta na hÉireann sa bhliain 1967. Ceapadh An tAthair Colmán mar Stiúrthóir ar an Institiúid sin ó lá a bhunaithe agus ainmníodh Coiste Comhairleach 'chun cabhair a thabhairt i stiúrú na hInstitiúide'. Bhí Tomás Ó Floinn, M.A., Rúnaí Cúnta na Roinne

Oideachais, ina chathaoirleach ar an gCoiste sin agus bhí dáréag eile ainmnithe mar bhaill den choiste, mé féin ina measc. Ní miste sleachta as an bpreas-ráiteas a cuireadh amach ag an am a thabhairt:

> Great progress has been made in the science of linguistics generally in recent times and it is a source of much satisfaction that this country has been to the forefront in this field mainly through the work of the Gormanston Language Centre which was set up in 1964 through the cooperation of the Franciscan Order and the Department of Education. The work of the Centre in the training of teachers in audio-lingual methods of teaching modern continental languages is well known. One of the most significant products of this collaboration between the Order and the Department has been *Buntús Gaeilge* published last year, the result of scientific research which is now accepted internationally as a major breakthrough in the linguistic field.
>
> In order to consolidate the progress already made and to ensure that further research—in Irish, English and other modern languages—be carried out on an orderly and scientific basis, Mr. O'Malley has, with the approval of the Government decided to accord to the Language Centre the status of an Institute under State patronage and to broaden the scope of its activities. The Institute will deal with research in connection with methods of teaching modern languages, with the in-service training of teachers, and with research concerning the psychological and sociological problems of language learning and aspects of applied linguistics generally. The Institute will provide a valuable service in all matters relating to language teaching and its establishment, it is believed, will be welcomed by educationalists in general.

Ba iad seo an dáréag a ainmnigh an tAire don Choiste Comhairleach:

> Proinsias Mac Cana, Ph.D,;
> Tomás Ó Canainn, B.Sc., Ph.D., A.M.I.E.S.;
> Gearóid Mac Eoin, M.A., D.Phil. (Bonn);
> Dáithí Ó hUaithne, M.A.;
> An tAthair Breanndán Ó Doibhlinn, M.A. D.D.;
> Eoghan Ó hAnnluain, M.A., A.T.O.;
> An tAthair Solanus Ó Laoghaire, B.A., A.T.O., O.F.M.;
> Tomás Ó Domhnalláin, B.A., A.T.O.;
> Treasa Ní Ghiolláin, B.A.;
> Brian Mac Mathúna, O.S.;

An Cornal Eoghan Ó Néill, Stiúrthóir, Comhdháil Náisiúnta na Gaeilge;
Máirtín Ó Murchú, M.A.

Níor ainmnigh an tAire aon Rúnaí ar an gCoiste Chomhairleach, ach níorbh fhada gur líon an Roinn Oideachais an bhearna sin dúinn. Cheap an Roinn Carmel Ní Mhuircheartaigh, B.A., a bhí ina hOifigeach Feidhmiúcháin ag an am, chun dul i mbun cúraimí rúnaíochta an Choiste. Lean Carmel i mbun na ndualgas sin go ceann ceathrú céid, nach mór, go dtí gur éirigh sí as a post chun dul isteach in ord rialta sa bhliain 1990. Le fírinne, ní raibh ach beirt a raibh baint acu le gnó I.T.É. go leanúnach tríd síos ó 1967 go dtí gur fhág mé an Institiúid sa bhliain 1979 .i. mé féin agus Carmel. Ní mór a rá gurbh uirthi sin a thit an chuid ba throime den obair riaracháin nuair a bunaíodh Institiúid nua mar chomhlacht stáit sa bhliain 1972. Fad a bhíos féin i mbun Stiúrthóireachta na hInstitiúide bhí Carmel mar ghiolla gualainne agam agus, mar a dúirt mé leis an gCathaoirleach níos minice ná uair amháin, murach go raibh Carmel ann chun ualach an riaracháin a thabhairt uirthi féin ní leanfainn i mbun na Stiúrthóireachta chomh fada agus a fhan.

Thagadh Coiste Comhairleach na hInstitiúide nua le chéile ó am go ham de réir mar a cheapthas gá a bheith le cruinniú: tionóladh 17 gcruinniú ó bhunú na hInstitiúide i ndeireadh na bliana 1967 go dtí deireadh na bliana 1969. Is léir ó mhiontuairiscí na gcruinnithe sin gur beag dul chun cinn a déanadh i rith an ama sin chun cuspóirí na hInstitiúide a chur chun cinn. Bhí easaontas i measc an choiste ó thús faoi na cuspóirí sin, ach bhí easaontas ina measc chomh maith faoi dháiliú airgead don Institiúid, faoi cheapadh foirne na hInstitiúide agus faoin modh ina gceapfaí iad, faoin teagmháil ar cheart a bheith idir an Roinn Oideachais agus an Institiúid agus a Stiúrthóir, faoi áitreabh nó foirgnimh a chur ar fáil, faoin gcríoch a bhí i ndán don Institiúid agus faoi nithe eile. Is beag cruinniú a bhíodh ann nach dtagadh ceist nó dhó díobh sin faoi chaibidil agus bhítí ag iarraidh ó am go ham agallamh leis an Aire Oideachais nó meamram a chur chuige mar gheall orthu.

I rith an ama bhí an Stiúrthóir ag iarraidh obair na hInstitiúide a choimeád ar siúl. Oiliúint mhúinteoirí Gaeilge agus múinteoirí nua-theangacha Eorpacha an obair ba mhó a bhí ar siúl aige. Níl aon amhras ná go raibh tionchar ag an obair sin ar mhúinteoirí teangacha na tíre agus gur scaipeadh eolas ar na modhanna nua, na modhanna closlabhartha, ina measc.

Ba i rith an ama seo leis a tosaíodh ar chomhaltachtaí a chur ar fáil chun mic léinn oiriúnacha a chur chuig ranna teangeolaíochta in Ollscoileanna thar lear, mar ba léir don Stiúrthóir agus don Choiste nach mbeadh foireann éifeachtach ar fáil ag an Institiúid go deo muna gcuirfí tréanáil ar mhic léinn a mbeadh an Ghaeilge ar a dtoil acu agus spéis acu sa teanga agus i gcultúr na hÉireann. Ba é Alan Hudson an chéad macléinn ar tugadh comhaltacht dó agus chuaigh seisean go hOllscoil Yeshiva i bhfómhar na bliana 1968. An bhliain ina dhiaidh sin bronnadh comhaltacht ar Dhónall Ó Baoill, fear a bhain dochtúireacht amach san am ba lú ab fhéidir agus a bhí ar ais ag obair san Institiúid laistigh de thrí bhliain. In Ollscoil Michigan sna Stáit Aontaithe a bhain Dónall amach a chéim dhochtúireachta.

I dtús na bliana 1969 a thosaigh an Dr Joshua A. Fishman ó Ollscoil Yeshiva ag cur spéise i gcúrsaí na hInstitiúide agus chuir sé sraith mholtaí ar fáil maidir léi agus maidir le cur chun cinn na Gaeilge i gcoitinne in Éirinn. Tharla díospóireachtaí ag cruinnithe den Choiste Comhairleach faoi na moltaí sin agus chuir an tAire Airgeadais, Cathal Ó hEochaidh ag an am, spéis iontu chomh maith. Chuir seisean in iúl go mbeadh sé sásta déanamh de réir na moltaí sin. Fear eile ar iarradh comhairle air ab ea E. Glyn Lewis ó Ollscoil Swansea, a bhí tráth ina Chigire Ceannais i mbun Oifige an Oideachais sa Bhreatain Bheag. Chuir seisean meamram fada ar fáil i dtaobh an ghnó ar cheart a bheith ar siúl ag an Institiúid agus i dtaobh an eagair a ba cheart a bheith uirthi. I bhfómhar na bliana 1969 (ar an 28ú Lúnasa) tháinig Joshua Fishman, Glyn Lewis, Máirtín Ó Murchú, an tAthair Colmán agus mé féin le chéile chun moltaí a sholáthair faoi thodhchaí na hInstitiúide, faoin obair ar cheart di tabhairt fúithi, faoi chúrsaí foirne agus uile. De thoradh an chruinnithe sin chuireamar meamram ar fáil, agus chuir Glyn Lewis meamram eile ar fáil i dtaobh taighde ar cheart a dhéanamh agus i dtaobh fhorbairt na hInstitiúide. Chuir an Stiúrthóir a thuarascáil féin ar fáil chomh maith agus léirigh sé ann a mhíshástacht leis an dul chun cinn a bhí déanta i rith an dá bhliain a bhí caite ó cuireadh an Institiúid ar bun. Pléadh na doiciméid sin go léir ag cruinniú den Choiste Comhairleach ar an 17 Deireadh Fómhair, 1969 agus ba é an toradh a bhí ar an ngnó gur fágadh faoi fhóchoiste pleanála moltaí deimhnitheacha a sholáthar, rud a rinne siad i meamram eile a seoladh chun na baill ar an 12 Samhain, 1969. Tar éis plé fada a dhéanamh ar an meamram sin agus ar an ngnó i gcoitinne, ba léir nach raibh an coiste sásta leis an Institiúid mar a bhí sí agus gur mheas siad go raibh athruithe bunúsacha ag teastáil. Tharla sé sin ag an gcruinniú deireanach den Choiste Comhairleach a tionóladh ar an 5 Nollaig, 1969. Ag deireadh an chruinnithe sin léirigh an Stiúrthóir a bhuairt faoi chúrsaí ama, sa mhéid is go raibh a chonradh féin leis an Roinn Oideachais leathchaite. Ag cur críche leis an gcruinniú sin dó dúirt an Cathaoirleach Tomás Ó Floinn, Rúnaí Cúnta na Roinne Oideachais, go raibh sé den tuairim go raibh dhá rogha ann:

(i)   Institiúid neamhspleách a bheith ann le bunús reachtúil fúithí,

nó

(ii)   Insititiúid ag gníomhú mar chuid d'ollscoil a bheith ann. ,

Dúirt sé go bpléifeadh sé an dá rogha sin leis an Roinn Oideachais agus leis an Aire Oideachais. Socraíodh ansin go mbeadh cruinniú speisialta den Choiste Comhairleach ann ar an 16 Eanáir, 1970 chun stádas na hInstitiúide a phlé. Níor tharla an cruinniú sin riamh, áfach. Cuireadh ar athló é cúpla uair agus ar deireadh thiar seoladh litir chuig gach ball den choiste ar an 6 Feabhra, 1970 ag cur in iúl go raibh 'ceist todhchaí na hInstitiúide á breathnú faoi láthair ag an Aire Oideachais, agus, dá bhrí sin ní féidir san eadarlinn cruinniú den choiste a thabhairt le chéile'. Ba é Pádraig Ó Fachtna, T.D. a bhí ina Aire Oideachais ag an am sin, post a líon sé ó mhí Iúil, 1969 go dtí mí Mhárta, 1973.

B'shin deireadh, de réir dealraimh, leis an Institiúid a chuir an tAire Donnchadh Ó Máille ar bun. Is cosúil gur ligeadh an Institiúid in éag agus go raibh deireadh mar sin le post an Stiúrthóra, an Athar Cholmán Ó Huallacháin, O.F.M. Pé scéal é, fuair an tAthair Colmán litir ón Roinn Oideachais um thús mhí Bhealtaine, 1971 ag cur in iúl dó nach raibh a sheirbhísí mar Stiúrthóir ag teastáil ón Roinn a thuille. Bhí sé sin ina scéal mór ag na nuachtáin agus ag na hirisí Gaeilge ar feadh tamaill, ach ina dhiaidh sin níor chualathas aon scéal oifigiúil faoi Institiúid Teangeolaíochta go dtí fómhar na bliana 1972. Idir an dá linn ghlac an tAthair Colmán le post mar Ollamh le Gaeilge in Ollscoil Nua Chúige Uladh i gCúl Raithne.

Ag féachaint siar dom ar chúrsaí Institiúide 1967 measaim anois go raibh roinnt chúiseanna gur theip uirthi. Ar an gcéad dul síos creidim gur cuireadh an Institiúid sin ar bun ar ordú an Aire, Donnchadh Ó Máille, T.D., gan dóthain réamhmhachnaimh, gan dóthain réamhullmhúcháin, a bheith déanta chuige. Ansin nuair a tháinig an t-am chun cúrsaí nua Gaeilge a cheapadh le haghaidh na scoileanna de bharr thaighde Bhuntús Gaeilge ní raibh d'achmhainn ná de mhisneach ná de ábaltacht ag an Institiúid tabhairt faoin obair sin. Níos tábhachtaí fós, nuair a bhunaigh an tAire Airgeadais Comhairle na Gaeilge i mí Mheithimh na bliana 1969 is cosúil nár mheas an Chomhairle sin go mbeadh ar chumas na hInstitiúide taighde a dhéanamh de réir mar a bhí ag teastáil ón gComhairle. Cibé ar bith, cheap siad a gcóras féin chun an taighde a chur i gcrích, an taighde i leith na Gaeilge ba thábhachtaí a déanadh sa tír seo go dtí an t-am sin. Agus an buille ba mheasa ar fad, bhí aonad taighde an Choiste um Thaighde ar Dhearcadh an Phobail i dtaobh na Gaeilge lonnaithe san fhoirgneamh a ceannaíodh le haghaidh Institiúide Teangeolaíochta na Éireann.

INSTITIÚID TEANGEOLAÍOCHTA ÉIREANN 1972–80

Chaith an Roinn Oideachais beagnach trí bhliain ag déanamh ullmhúcháin le haghaidh bhunú na hInstitiúide nua: Institiúid Teangeolaíochta Éireann. Cuideachta faoi Theorainn Rathaíochta gan Scairchaipiteal a bhí le bheith inti faoi Acht na gCuideachtaí, 1963. Ar an ábhar sin bhí ar an Roinn Oideachais comhairle a ghlacadh le go leor ranna eile stáit sula bhféadfaidís an smaoineamh a chur i ngníomh: an Roinn Airgeadais, Oifig an Phríomh-Aturnae Stáit, Rannóg Aistriúcháin na Dála agus an tOireachtas féin. Ar deireadh thiar áfach bhí gach rud réidh agus cláraíodh an Institiúid nua ar an 27ú Deireadh Fómhair, 1972. Tionóladh an chéad chruinniú de na comhaltaí ar an 17 Samhain, 1972. Ceapadh an Coiste Feidhmiúcháin ag an gcruinniú sin agus tháinig siadsan le chéile ar an 20 Samhain, 1972 in oifig na hInstitiúide ag 31, Plás Mhic Liam. Bhí Oifig na nOibreacha Poiblí tar éis an oifig sin a chur ar fáil tamall roimhe sin ar ordú an Aire Airgeadais. Thug an tAire an t-ordú sin de bharr bhrú a chuir an tAthair Colmán Ó Huallacháin air sna blianta deireanacha a raibh sé ina Stiúrthóir ar Institiúid Teangeolaíochta na hÉireann.

AN INSTITIÚID AGUS NA COMHALTAÍ

Fiche comhalta a cheap an tAire Oideachais don Institiúid nua an chéad lá ariamh, ach tá cead ag na comhaltaí cur leis an líon sin le cead ón Aire agus tig leo comhaltaí nua a cheapadh de réir mar is gá. Ceaptar comhaltaí le haghaidh tréimhse chúig bhliain ach is féidir iad a athcheapadh ina dhiaidh sin. Is iad na comhaltaí atá freagrach as an Institiúid agus as gach rud a bhaineann léi, ach gur ghá dóibh gníomhaíochtaí áirithe dá gcuid a chur i gcead an Aire. Tá de chumhacht ag na comhaltaí Coiste Feidhmiúcháin a cheapadh a mbeidh ón a chúig go dtí a naoi de bhaill air agus is fúthu sin a fhágtar gnáthriaradh na hInstitiúide. Is fúthu leis a bhíonn an Stiúrthóir ag obair.

Is é an tAire Oideachais a cheap an chéad Chathaoirleach den Institiúid, An tOllamh Conn R. Ó Cléirigh, Ollamh le Teangeolaíocht i gColáiste na hOllscoile, Baile Átha Cliath agus is é chomh maith a cheapfaidh gach Cathaoirleach feasta, as painéal chúig ainm a chuirfidh an Institiúid faoina bhráid. Ghníomhaigh Conn mar Chathaoirleach ó 1972 go dtí gur cailleadh in Aibreán 1995 é . Go ndéana Dia trócaire air.

Is iad seo na comhaltaí a ainmnigh an tAire le gníomhú le Conn R. Ó Cléirigh mar Chathaoirleach:-

Muiris Bodhlaeir, Coláiste Oiliúna Dhún Chéirigh, An Charraig Dhubh, Co. Átha Cliath, Ollamh le Gaeilge;

Séamus Ó Ciosáin, An Roinn Airgeadais, Státseirbhíseach;

Pádraig Ó Coimín, An Foras Talúntais, Baile Átha Cliath 4, Socheolaí Taighde;

Gearóid Ó Crualaoich, Coláiste na hOllscoile, Corcaigh, Antraipeolaí Taighde;

Tomás Ó Domhnalláin, An Roinn Oideachais, Státseirbhíseach;

Seán Ó hÉigeartaigh, Roinn an Oideachais, U.C.D., Léachtóir le hOideachas;

Risteárd Ó Foghlú, An Roinn Oideachais, Príomh-Chigire Meánscoileanna;

Risteárd Mac Gabhann, Roinn an Léinn Ghaelaigh, Ollscoil Nua Uladh, Léachtóir le Gaeilge & Teangeolaíocht;

Seán Mac Íomhair, An Teanglann, Coláiste na hIolscoile, Gaillimh, Stiúrthóir Teanglainne agus Oide Iolscoile;

Carl James, Dept. of Linguistics, University College of N. Wales, Bangor, Lecturer in Linguistics;

Thomas Kellaghan, Educational Research Centre, St. Patrick's College, Dublin 9, Director of Research;

John Lyons, Dept. of Linguistics, University of Edinburgh, Professor of General Linguistics;

Mícheál B. Ó Míodhacháin, An Roinn Oideachais, Státseirbhíseach;

Tomás Ó Nualláin, Coláiste Mhuire, Marino, Uachtarán Choláiste;

Mícheál Mac Shiúrtáin, Coláiste Phádraig, Dromconnrach, Léachtóir in Oideachas;

Gearóid A. Ó Súilleabháin, An Roinn Oideachais, Státseirbhíseach;

Séamas V. Ó Súilleabháin, Coláiste Phádraig, Má Nuat, Ollamh le hOideachas;

Tadhg Ó Tuama, Comhlacht Siúicre Éireann, Ceatharlach, Stiúrthóir Taighde;

Jac L. Williams, Department of Education, University College of Wales, Aberystwyth, Dean of Faculty of Education.

Ag an gcéad chruinniú a bhí acu thogh na comhaltaí an Coiste Feidhmiúcháin mar a leanas:

M. Bodhlaeir;
P. Ó Coimín;
G. Ó Crualaoich;
T. Ó Domhnalláin;
Dr. T. Kellaghan;
Br. S. Ó Súilleabháin.

Ní miste a rá ag an bpointe seo gur chuir sé ionadh ar Chonn R. Ó Cléirigh gurbh eisean a toghadh le bheith ina Chathaoirleach ar an Institiúid nua. Ar ndóigh níor cheart go mbeadh aon ionadh air, mar gurbh eisean an t-aon ollamh ollscoile sa tír ag an am arbh ollamh le teangeolaíocht é. Ach b'shin é an saghas duine é Conn: ní chuirfeadh sé é féin chun tosaigh ar dhaoine eile! Ach ba é cúis a ionaidh, a dúirt sé liom, go roghnódh rialtas Fhianna Fáil nó aire Fhianna Fáil riamh duine mar eisean ná raibh aon bhá léirithe aige le Fianna Fáil riamh, ach a léirigh i gcónaí ina shaol gur leis an Lucht Oibre a thaobhaigh sé. Ar an ábhar sin, a dúirt sé liom, bhí sé mórálach as gurbh eisean a toghadh thar aon duine eile agus lean sé de bheith mórálach as sin a fhad a mhair sé. Ba cheart a rá, chomh maith, nárbh fhada gur thaispeáin Conn go raibh an Cathaoirleach ceart ceaptha ag an Aire: chuir sé chun saothair go dúthrachtach agus lean an dúthracht sin go dtí an lá ar cailleadh é sa bhliain 1995. Má chuir Conn chun saothair go dúthrachtach féin, bhí sé séimh cneasta i gcónaí ag plé le gach éinne, idir chomhaltaí na hInstitiúide agus an fhoireann oibre, mé féin san áireamh. Níor tharla easaontas dá laghad eadrainn ar feadh na mblianta a rabhas ag obair faoina threoir, ná níor tharla achrann ná easaontas ag cruinniú ar bith den Institiúid a fhad is a bhí Conn ina Chathaoirleach.

LAETHANTA TOSAIGH NA hINSTITIÚIDE.

Bhí go leor deacrachtaí le sárú orthu ag Conn agus ag baill na hInstitiúide nua nuair a chuadar i mbun a gcuid dualgas i mí na Samhna, 1972.

Ar an gcéad dul síos ba léir dóibh go mba dheacair teacht ar Stiúrthóir a mbeadh na cáilíochtaí inmhianaithe agus an taithí riachtanach aige, mar ná raibh morán scoláirí teangeolaíochta sa tír ag an am. Ní móide ach oiread go mbeadh fáil ar iarrthóir cáilithe a mbeadh lánchumas ar an nGaeilge aige nó aici. Chomh maith leis sin bhí doicheall curtha ar chuid mhaith scoláirí sa tír ag eachtra na chéad Institiúide Teangeolaíochta agus ag an tslí ar cuireadh críoch léi agus le post an Athar Cholmán Ó Huallacháin mar Stiúrthóir. Thuig an Cathaoirleach nua agus comhaltaí na hInstitiúide mar sin go mba dheacair dóibh Stiúrthóir agus foireann oibre a chur ar fáil.

Ag an gcéad chruinniú den Institiúid nua mar sin ar an 20 Samhain, 1972 moladh go saorfaí mé féin ó mo chuid dualgas oibre sa Roinn Oideachais ionas go raghainn ag obair san Institiúid mar Stiúrthóir Sealadach. Chuireas in iúl go mbeinn sásta glacadh le socrú mar sin dá gcomhlíonfaí coinníollacha áirithe maidir le mo stádas pearsanta sa Roinn Oideachais agus san Institiúid. Bhí an cheist seo ina ábhar díospóireachta idir an gCoiste, an Roinn Oideachais agus Roinn na Seirbhíse Poiblí beagnach go dtí deireadh na bliana 1973. Ar deireadh thiar, áfach, fuaireas litir ón Roinn Oideachais ar an 28 Nollaig, 1973 ag tairscint ardú réime dom i bpost mar Chomhairleoir Teangeolaíochta sa Roinn ón dáta sin ar choinníoll go mbeinn sásta dul ag obair in I.T.É. mar Ollamh Taighde agus Stiúrthóir Gníomhach. Ghlacas leis an tairscint agus leis na coiníollacha tuarastail agus eile a bhí luaite leis. B'shin mar a tharla gur thosaíos ag obair san Institiúid ar an 31 Nollaig, 1973.

Maidir leis an deacracht a bhí ann faoi theacht ar theangeolaithe cáilithe chun dul ag obair san Institiúid, déanadh gníomh ag an gcéad chruinniú céanna sin ar mhaithe leis an deacracht a réiteach : bronnadh comhaltacht ar Gerald P. Delahunty M.A. chun staidéar a dhéanamh in Ollscoil California sna Stáit Aontaithe agus comhaltacht eile ar John W. Harris M.A. chun staidéar a dhéanamh in Ollscoil Siceago. Chomh maith leis sin ceapadh an Dr Dónall Ó Baoill, a bhí tar éis dochtúireacht a bhaint amach sa teangeolaíocht in Ollscoil Mhichigan, ina Oifigeach Taighde san Insititiúid. Bhí comhaltacht ag an Dr. Ó Baoill ón sean-Institiúid ón mbliain 1969. Ainmníodh dlíodóir chomh maith chun comhairle dlí maidir le pointí áirithe a thabhairt agus cuntasóir chun córas cuntasaíochta a bhunú a bheadh ionghlactha ag Ard-Reachtaire Cuntais agus Ciste an Rialtais.

Nuair a chuas i mbun oibre ar an 31 Nollaig, 1973 bhí seilbh ag Comhairle Náisiunta na gCáilíochtaí Oideachais i 31 Plás Mhic Liam agus bhí cuid de na seomraí a bhí fágtha i seilbh an Choiste um Thaighde ar Dhearcadh an Phobail i leith na Gaeilge a bhí ag obair de bharr moltaí Chomhairle na Gaeilge. Tar éis dúinn seomraí a chur in eagar agus troscán agus fearas a sholáthair bhí earrach na bliana 1974 ann sula rabhamar in n-ann tabhairt faoin obair i gceart. Rud eile a chuir bac le dul chun cinn na hInstitiúide i rith na bliana 1974 ab ea ganntanas airgid. Cé gur ullmhaíomar éileamh ar dheontas-i-gcabhair de £65,000 i rith na bliana 1973, bhí an t-éileamh sin ró-mhall agus ní fhuaireamar mar dheontas-i-gcabhair le haghaidh 1974 ach £ 30,000, de réir mar a bhí iarrta ar ár son ag an Roinn Oideachais roimh ré. Ar an ábhar sin, cé go raibh ceapadh Leabharlannaí/Oifigigh Eolais in a phríomhriachtanas ag an gCoiste Feidhmiúcháin, b'éigean an ceapachán sin a chur siar go dtí an chéad bhliain eile. Mar sin féin cuireadh tús leis an leabharlann agus tosaíodh ar leabhair agus ar irisí a chur ar fáil. Chomh maith leis sin bunaíodh comhoibriú le C.I.L.T. (An Coiste um Eolas ar Mhúineadh Teangacha) i Londain.

Socraíodh gan mhoill go gceapfaí Oifigeach Taighde nua mar Leabharlannaí/Oifigeach Eolais. Socraíodh chomh maith go gceapfaí comhairleoir i leith mhúineadh nua-theangacha. Líonadh an dá phost sin i rith na bliana. Íosold Ní Dheirg, M.A. a ceapadh mar leabharlannaí/oifigeach eolais agus Delma Ó Ceallacháin go sealadach mar chomhairleoir nua-theangacha. Ceapadh Mícheál Ó Gliasáin mar oifigeach taighde go sealadach chun obair a dhéanamh i dtaca le suirbhé a bhí ar siúl ar thionchar na gcúrsaí nua Gaeilge sna scoileanna. Chomh maith leosan tugadh cead post nua mar chúntóir leabharlainne a bhunú.

Is léir mar sin go raibh an fhoireann oibre ag dul i líonmhaire i rith na bliana 1975, ach má bhí, bhí scóip na hoibre ag leathnú chomh maith. Mar sin cuireadh meitheal oibre ar bun roimh dheireadh na bliana sin chun pleanáil a dhéanamh maidir le hobair na hInstitiúide agus chun plean oibre a sholáthair. Chaitheas féin cuid mhór ama ag obair ar an bplean sin faoi threoir an Choiste Phleanála idir 1975 agus 1977, tráth a raibh an plean ullamh againn.

Leanadh de chomhaltachtaí a chur ar fáil chun céimithe oiriúnacha a chur thar lear ar chúrsaí staidéir a bhain le teangacha nó le teangeolaíocht. Ghlac Ailbhe Ní Chasaide le comhaltacht chun staidéar a dhéanamh in ollscoil Bangor. Ghlac Nóra French le comhaltacht chun staidéar a dhéanamh in Ollscoil Essex. D'éirigh go han-mhaith leis an mbeirt sin agus chaitheadar araon tréimhsí ag obair in I.T.É. níos deireanaí nuair a bhí a gcúrsaí críochnaithe acu.

Tosaíodh um an am sin ar ráiteas eolais faoin teideal *Teangeolas* a chur amach cúpla uair sa bhliain chun eolas a scaipeadh ar an Institiúid agus ar an obair a bhí ar siúl inti. Tá an iris sin beo fós sa lá atá inniu ann agus í ag teacht amach cúpla uair in aghaidh na bliana. Íosold Ní Dheirg atá ina hEagarthóir ar *Theangeolas* anois. Agus tharla ócáid thábhachtach i rith na bliana 1976 nuair a thug an tAire Oideachais Risteárd de Búrca, T.D., cuairt ar an Institiúid ar an 28ú Bealtaine chun leabharlann na hInstitiúide a oscailt go hoifigiúil.

CLABHSÚR

Ní féidir críoch a chur leis an gcuntas seo gan tagairt do bhás léanmhar agus bás obann an Athar Cholmán Ó Huallacháin a tharla i Rinn Mhic Gormáin ar an 20ú Deireadh Fómhair, 1979. Bhí sé imithe ón Institiúid le roinnt blianta ag an am, ach má bhí féin chuir sé spéis in obair na hInstitiúide i gcónaí. Tar éis an tsaoil, murach an t-alt úd uaidh sa *Teacher's Work* sa bhliain1962 agus murach an obair a rinne sé ar ullmhú *Bhuntús Gaeilge*, ní dócha go gcuirfí Institiúid Teangeolaíochta na hÉireann ar bun sa bhliain 1967, agus murach an Institiúid sin ní móide go mbunófaí Institiúid na bliana 1972 ariamh. Chaitheas a sé nó a seacht de bhlianta ag obair leis an Athair Colmán agus bhíomar cairdiúil le chéile i gcónaí, fiú nuair a bhí an garbhshíon timpeall orainn. Go dtugaí Dia suaimhneas síoraí dá anam uasal.

B'éigean dom féin éirí as obair sa Roinn Oideachais de bharr aoise ar an 30ú Márta, 1978. Bheadh cead agam leanúint ar aghaidh ag obair mar Stiúrthóir san Institiúid go ceann roinnt blianta eile. Mheasas áfach, go raibh mo chion déanta agam. Níor chuireas romham ó thús ach an Institiúid a chur ar a bonnaibh agus í a stiúrú tríd na blianta achrannacha tosaigh go dtí go mbeadh glachta léi ag lucht léinn agus ag lucht oideachais ár dtíre féin. Mheasas go raibh an sprioc sin bainte amach um an dtaca sin agus chuir mé in iúl don Chathaoirleach agus do na comhaltaí nach fada eile a leanfainn i bpost an Stiúrthóra. Níor éirigh liom scaradh leis an oifig, áfách, go dtí an 4ú Samhain, 1979 nuair a thoiligh mo chara agus mo chomhghleacaí, Tomás Ó Cuilleanáin, glacadh leis an bpost ar bhonn sealadach.

Language Use Surveys in Western Europe: Towards a Comparative Analysis

PÁDRAIG Ó RIAGÁIN
Institiúid Teangeolaíochta Éireann

BACKGROUND

PRIOR to the 1960s, most language surveys were conducted in Third World countries e.g. in Africa, India and the Philippines. In practically every case, the motive for undertaking the survey was to inform some aspect of the policy of national or imperial governments. Grierson's monumental 11-volume survey of languages in India was carried out at the turn of the century, although the final volume was not published until 1929. It was initially conceived as part of a wide-ranging programme by the British administration in India to built up a detailed data-base on all matters relating to public policy.

In Africa, the West Africa Languages Survey was begun in 1960 under the direction of Joseph Greenberg, but this survey took a narrowly linguistic approach. It was financed by the Ford Foundation and most of the senior staff on the survey teams were of American origin. In 1968–71 the same foundation established the five-nation Survey of Language Use and Language Teaching in Eastern Africa (Ethiopia, Kenya, Tanzania, Uganda and Zambia). As the change in title might suggest, these surveys took a more sociological approach. (See Fishman 1974, and Ohannessian, Ferguson, Polomé 1975 for more detailed discussions). The underlying motive here was the belief that an informed language policy was essential to a country's economic and social development.

As far as I could establish, the first specifically policy-related language surveys in the developed world were conducted in Canada in 1965 for the Royal Commission on Bilingualism and Biculturalism. Two national sample surveys were conducted among adults (N=4071) and teenagers (N=1365). The surveys were primarily designed to collect information about opinions on a wide range of language policy issues, but the surveys also collected considerable additional information about the language background of the respondents, their competencies, behaviours and attitudes.

There are over fifty minority autochthonous language groups in the member states of the European Union at present, and this number will increase as new member-states join the Union. In a mere handful of member-states (Finland, Great Britain, Ireland and Spain are examples that come to mind), the national five or ten-yearly Census of Population includes one or more questions about minority languages. Where such data was available, some preliminary estimates of the spatial, temporal and social distribution of speakers of the minority language(s) were possible in earlier decades (See, for example, Price 1969, Petrella 1978). Nonetheless, it is worth making a distinction between these earlier studies and more recent research which utilised social survey methodology.

One of the first such surveys was undertaken by Pietersen in Friesland in 1967. This was followed in 1973 by the national language attitudes survey conducted in Ireland and, later in the 1970s, by a number of surveys conducted in Finland (Allardt et al. 1979). In the 1980s, the Minority Languages Survey Project was undertaken in the UK among immigrant groups and further surveys were conducted in Friesland and Ireland. The 1990s saw the geographical spread of language use surveys become yet wider with surveys in The Basque Country, Ireland, Friesland, Wales and in a number of other regions such as Galicia, Languedoc-Roussillon and Sorbia. (Further details of the Basque, Frisian, Welsh and Irish surveys can be found below).

Although the history of population censuses dates back into the last century, and there are some examples of earlier surveys, practically all the examples of social survey research cited above were conducted after 1960. This suggests a relationship between the conduct of this type of survey and other policy and technical developments which occurred in the same period. On the one hand, technical developments in the computer industry made it possible to process large volumes of data quickly and cheaply. Secondly, the emergence of language issues on to the policy agenda of many states, and a simultaneous shift to the operational procedures of planning in governmental decision-making, all created a demand for reliable, up-to-date data. Language surveys were seen to meet this need in the process of formulating and implementing language policy.

THE ROLE OF LANGUAGE SURVEYS IN POLICY RESEARCH

By using appropriate statistical procedures and techniques, it is possible to reliably estimate the main social and demographic characteristics of language groups by interviewing relatively small samples of respondents. Furthermore, with a questionnaire that has been specifically designed to examine language use patterns, it is possible to collect a very wide battery of data about many aspects of language competence, language acquisition, language use and language attitudes. The descriptive and analytical possibilities of survey data, therefore, far exceeds that of the typical census and their value in policy formulation and evaluation is accordingly much greater.

However, there is considerable variation in the indicators used to measure and describe language situations in the surveys conducted to date. Measures, for example, of language proficiency and language use are different in almost every data-base. This diversity in methodological approaches is not altogether disadvantageous to the overall research endeavour. One of the benefits is that a much wider range of concepts and indicators have been developed and tested in the field than any individual survey could, in practical terms, accomplish. Nonetheless, these advances have to be set against the very considerable problems which arise when the need occurs to compare the responses *between different survey samples.*

These inconsistencies in language survey research, together with the relatively limited availability of data from other sources, combine to impair the development of studies of the impact of European policies and socio-economic processes on language groups. The sometimes contradictory trends apparent across language groups cannot be explained except by reference to the way larger scale, global economic, political and social processes are advantaging some social groupings and cultures while simultaneously disadvantaging others. This critical interaction between the global and the local/regional can only be examined through well designed and co-ordinated European-wide studies which, in turn, require a bank of comparable data for each language community. The problematic consequences of methodological differences between surveys do not, therefore, need to be emphasised. They are the same, albeit within the specific field of language, as those which arise in attempts to integrate and harmonise national and regional data-bases in all areas of European social and economic policy.

THE EUROPEAN LANGUAGE SURVEY RESEARCH NETWORK

In 1994, with financial support and encouragement from DG XXII of the European Commission, a research network was established between four institutions, all of whom were engaged in long-term language-related survey research, to address these issues in a systematic way. The participating institutions are (a) Hizkuntza Politikarako Sailordetzal Deputy Ministry for Language Policy (Vitoria-Gastiez, Basque Country, Spain); (b) The Fryske Akademy (Ljouwert/Leeuwarden, Netherlands); (c) Institiúid Teangeolaíochta Éireann/The Linguistics Institute of Ireland (Baile Átha Cliath/Dublin, Ireland), and (d) Research Centre Wales (University of North Wales, Bangor, United Kingdom).

At the time (1994), all of the participating institutions had just conducted, or were about to conduct, large-scale surveys in their language communities. Because this substantial data-base was already established, and having regard to the problems noted in the preceding paragraphs, the network members felt that it was very appropriate time to initiate the comparative process, at least as far as minority language communities in Europe are concerned.

In conducting a comparative appraisal all relevant aspects of survey research method have to be considered. Differences between surveys can arise from the different social, cultural and policy contexts within which they are conducted. These contexts determine the overall shape and purpose of each survey. Secondly, different theoretical orientations lead, among other things, to different conceptualisations of basic indicators (e.g. competence). Finally, operational considerations (e.g. research budget, sample size and design, size and structure of questionnaires, etc.) can lead to differences. A full discussion of these topics is not possible here, but some of the more important issues are summarised in the sections which follow.

DIFFERENCES IN CONTEXT

Even a superficial examination of the evidence will make it clear that there are differences in the size, social structure and policy environment of the four language communities (see attached bibliography for references to the main published surveys in each case). For example, recent surveys would suggest the proportion who use Irish as their first or main language to be something around 5% (176,000 in actual figures). A further 10% or so of the population use Irish regularly but less intensively (350,000). In Wales, a 1991 survey found that about 17% of the population (460,000) were fluent or 'fairly' fluent in Welsh. However, and this points up the problem I have already mentioned, there is no language use survey in Wales statistically comparable with the Irish surveys. In the Basque Country, about 20% (600,000) were returned as Basque speakers in the 1991 census, but only about half of Basque speakers actually use the language, i.e. about 10% overall. Finally, in Friesland, 74% of the population (440,000) claimed to be able to speak Frisian, and most of these (60% overall) used the language in their homes.

The four case studies manifest a considerable degree on variance on demographic and linguistic criteria. Other criteria would support this conclusion. For example, the four cases clearly encompass a wide range of sociolinguistic circumstances, ranging from situations where the linguistic distance between languages is great, e.g. Basque/Spanish, Welsh/English and Irish/English, to situations where there is a much closer affinity, e.g. Frisian/Dutch. Yet it is also possible to exaggerate differences. Placed in the context of European minority languages, most commentators rank these cases as broadly representative of minority language situations in Europe.

One of the first studies to attempt a comprehensive overview of the European situation was that undertaken by Petrella in 1978. His approach was mainly demographic, in which language communities were ranked according to the known population of speakers. Within his four categories, the present case-studies occupy positions in the middle two categories. That is to say, none of the cases rank alongside the largest of the minority language groups, (Catalan), but neither are they ranked among the rather large group of communities whose speakers number less than 100,000

Allardt's study in 1979 attempted a more complex scheme of classification which was not just about language. He cross-classified a measure of 'resources' (in fact, a measure made up of linguistic, economic and political factors) against a measure of what he termed 'ethnic mobilisation'. This yielded a 9-cell matrix. Again, however, the four cases in this comparison are again ranked in the middle on one or both of these measures. In the five-category classification scheme formulated by the European Bureau for Lesser Used Languages, the four cases are located in three of the five, i.e. small independent nation-states (Ireland), small nations without a state (Wales, Friesland) and small nations without a state with members in more than one state (Basque).

Finally, the Euromosaic study (1996) formed a classification system with five categories. The classification is based on a large number of variables. Nonetheless, the position of the four cases remains middle-ranking, i.e. outside of the very largest and the very smallest language groups.

DIFFERENCES IN THEORETICAL ORIENTATION

The four surveys involve quite different theoretical positions, even though some are closer than others. This is partly because survey research in some regions (e.g. Ireland and Friesland) is long-established, and there is, therefore, a need to maintain continuity with earlier surveys. It is also partly a reflection of the manner in which different needs are perceived by the different researchers and how this perception feeds into the research design. A state language planning agency will be likely to develop the theoretical orientation in quite different ways from those operating with a university environment, even if only because the goals and expectations of the entire survey exercise is conceived of in different ways. It should also be recognised that whatever the guiding insights of theory, there are always the local conditions which determine how theoretical issues are structured, leading to particular orientations within different settings. Indeed, there is an increasing belief that it is possible to go even further, treating what has been regarded as objective positions as mere theoretical discourses.

As already noted, both the Frisian and the Irish studies have a history of research pertaining to the minority languages that dates back to the 1960s and early 1970s. This is partly a consequence of the expansion of the relevant social sciences in Europe during the 1960s, and the associated increase in the willingness to base policy upon the results of such research. It also relates to the increase in political activity around minority issues at this time and the manner in which it led to an increased demand for associated information. It is no coincidence that the Welsh study, influenced to a great extent by the Irish study, sought to obtain funds for the work as early as 1975. On the other hand it is also significant that the Welsh Language Board, the main body responsible for implementing state policy by reference to the Welsh language group has not undertaken a language use survey but rather has commissioned an attitudinal survey not dissimilar to the initial Irish language survey of attitudes undertaken in 1973. Political circumstances precluded the development of survey research on the Basque language group until the Basque country achieved autonomous status within the Spanish state in 1982. As a consequence the Basque and Welsh surveys, which were undertaken for the first time in the 1990s, have rather more in common with each other than they do with the other two surveys.

The Welsh study was not undertaken with any specific policy objectives in mind. It begins from the position that a language group is a social group, but it also maintains that social groups overlap by reference to membership. In pursuing its theoretical arguments it deploys orthodox sociological principles to study language groups as one of many coterminous and overlapping social groups. The emphasis upon the language group as a social group allows the authors to conceive of language group production, reproduction and non-reproduction in such a way that inter-generational language transmission or non-transmission is conceptualised simultaneously with the process of new intra-generational entry into the language group. This obliges a consideration of the factors responsible for these three processes:

- the influence of migration upon language group endogamy;
- the relevance of the three primary agencies of language reproduction—the family, the community and formal education;
- the relevance of community and formal education for the production process.

Thus, the independent variable that explains the change in the context of the language group is the general process of economic restructuring and the way it affects such elements as in and out migration via variations in the circulation of capital, or in the manner in which it influences policy formation.

The Basque study was designed as part of an attempt to investigate the most appropriate means of developing an explicit language policy which would promote the use of the Basque language. As such, it was building upon the limited amount of available information, primarily the 1986 census data. It therefore sought to validate existing information, to bench mark the existing situation, and to extend the existing information. Given the need to establish ability levels and to obtain information about the variable use of language within the population and across situations, these elements had to be related within an overall schema. To this should be added the inevitable need to establish the attitude of the general population that exists among those whose ultimate goal is the implementation of policy objectives. Perhaps the most evident input into the Basque work derives from the ethnolinguistic vitality perspective. This draws in a range of structural variables including demographic, institutional and status elements. The interplay between these three sets of variables are seen to determine the degree of ethnolinguistic vitality that conditions intra-group interaction, an interaction that draws language into play. Therefore, unlike the Welsh study, it does not seek to explain variation in these factors by reference to processes of economic restructuring and its effect upon labour markets.

In common with the Frisian study, the 1993 survey in Ireland has inherited the methodological and, to a certain extent, the theoretical input of a previous study (CLAR 1975). The earlier study adopted an approach which was heavily influenced by the psychological and anthropological orientation that prevailed in North America during the 1960s. Its focus is very much upon how attitudes determine language choice, with attitudes being regarded as the independent variable and rational choice being influenced by intermediate variables which ultimately result in choice of language as the dependent variable. While other data was collected and indeed utilised through cross tabulation it does not appear to have involved a systematic theoretical approach. However, in the 1993 survey, the focus shifts to those attitudes that have relevance to the analysis of social reproduction. Considerable emphasis is placed upon the primary socialisation agencies—the home and the school and upon language prestige as a motivational factor. On the basis of an earlier study Ó Riagáin (1992) has sought to focus the Irish research on Hechter's influential work on internal colonialism and the concept of the cultural division of labour and Bourdieu's work on social and cultural reproduction. These concepts have the advantage of extending the differentiation based upon social class and the relations of production to social groups that are marked and constituted by reference to cultural attributes. This approach allows the analyst to recognise the manner in which culturally marked social group relate to the economic order, leading to an emphasis upon local and regional labour markets, labour market segmentation and associated issues.

As already noted, the Frisian study shares with the Irish study the need to develop a framework that accommodates earlier work undertaken in 1967 and 1980. The current study seeks to follow the same objective as these earlier surveys in establishing an overview of language use, ability and attitudes. These objectives are encapsulated in the need to ascertain 'who speaks what, to whom, how and why?' The current study does not purport to rely heavily upon an explicit theoretical input. However, it is important to note that a study which does not purport to proceed from a deductive position is, nonetheless, able to generate meaning full statements about the relationship between what are regarded as key variables and even to proceed to what are regarded as theoretical statements. Yet it is also clear that the work is essentially descriptive in the sense that the bulk of the work involves establishing relationships between variables rather than explaining such relationships.

It should be evident that the four surveys deploy quite different theoretical orientations, some of which are more explicit than others. This must be seen within the context of the history of survey research within the different language groups and also in relation to the perceived goal of the survey itself.

OPERATIONALISING THE RESEARCH

The aspects to be discussed under this heading include questionnaire design, sampling procedures, the recruitment and training of interviewers, fieldwork procedures, and data processing. Only two of these factors will be examined here—questionnaire design and sampling procedures.

The questionnaire is, for most people, is the most visible aspect of survey methodology. It is also the point in the survey process where the contextual, policy and theoretical considerations which I have been discussing will become most apparent. I can demonstrate this by looking at the distribution between the four surveys of two classes of question which are common to all four: attitudes and language use.

As can be seen from Table 1, there are marked differences between the surveys as regards the proportion of questions dealing with language attitudes. In the Irish survey about half of the questions concerned language attitudes; in the Frisian survey about one third, but in the Basque and Welsh surveys far less attention was given to this topic.

Table 1: Number and Percentage of Attitudinal Questions

Survey	Total No. of Qs.	No. of Attitude Qs	Attitude Qs as% of Total
Ireland	267	123	46
Friesland	233	73	31
Basque Country	246	36	14
Wales	317	23	7

Notes: For the purposes of this table all discrete questionnaire items were counted.

Not only do the number of questions differ but so also do the type of language attitudes examined. Ireland and Friesland, for example, place considerable emphasis on 'policy preference' type questions, while in the Basque Country and Wales questions on perceptions of public and institutional support and vitality receive most attention. On the other hand, if the surveys are ranked by the proportion of questions dealing with aspects of language use, the order is the exact reverse. Here we find that the Welsh survey, which contained the smallest number of attitudinal questions, has the largest proportion of questions about language use.

Table 2: Number and Percentage of Language Use Questions

Region	Total No of Qs	No of Language Use Qs	Language use as % of Total
Wales	317	134	42
Basque Country	246	62	25
Friesland	233	43	18
Ireland	267	34	13

These differences cannot, of course, be assessed against any ideal standard. They simply reflect the diversity of backgrounds and approaches. But they also lessen the possibility of establishing a common data-base. In total, the four questionnaires contain over one thousand discrete questionnaire items. If the criterion for a 'common' questionnaire item in all four surveys is exact concordance in the wording and structure of a question, there were very few such questions.

Sampling. In contrast to a census of the whole population, these surveys only interview a small fraction of those 'populations'. Nonetheless, these language surveys seek to generalise of from their findings to the population of the Basque Country, Friesland, Republic of Ireland and Wales. In order to sustain this generalisability, the size of the sample and the sampling principle are of great importance. Quite apart from the problems with questionnaires which have already been discussed, differences in the sampling methods among surveys inhibit a full comparative use of the data. First of all, there are differences in minimum age of respondents. These range from 12 years in the Frisian sample to 18 years in the Irish survey. Second, but far more importantly, the Basque, Frisian and Irish cases are samples drawn from the total population of the relevant administrative area, whereas the Welsh sample was stratified according to 'Welsh speaking', and thus limited to the Welsh language group.

TOWARDS A EUROPEAN MINORITY LANGUAGE SURVEY QUESTIONNAIRE

However, the fact that many questions in the surveys, while not exactly the same, address similar issues and often show similarities in wording and structure, suggested that there is substantial degree of agreement about key concepts, notwithstanding the contextual and theoretical differences which have just been acknowledged. Similarly, if the inclusion of questions that are similar in less than four, but more than one, of the surveys is allowed, the list of such concepts becomes quite considerable. They include questions in all of the key domains of bilingual analysis—language ability, language use, language attitudes and, of course, basic socio-demographic items.

The evidence of these common, if not identical, elements led the research network to two conclusions. First, it was felt that with some adjustments to accommodate differences in sampling procedures and questionnaire formats, that a modest beginning could be made in the task of assembling a European data-base on minority languages (see the network's report for a discussion and practical development of this proposal). Secondly, and perhaps more urgently, it was felt essential that survey directors should pay more attention to the need to include comparable questions. To this end, the report of the network recommends that all surveys should include a short module of common questions.

It is not anticipated, nor would it be practical or desirable, that minority language use surveys be identical in all respects, but it is argued that the inclusion of a module of common questions will still allow for adequate coverage of items specific to particular communities and situations. The fact that substantial differences exist even in the four 'parent' surveys will, it is hoped, reassure those who may feel that the inclusion of a common module in minority language surveys will prevent other surveys attending to the particularities of their own language situations. Both objectives, participating in a European-wide exercise to collect comparable data about minority language situations and meeting local requirements, are compatible.

ACKNOWLEDGEMENTS

This paper is based upon, and includes extracts from, the report of the European Language Survey Research Network which was submitted to the European Commission in June 1996. The author of this paper was also one of the authors, and a co-ordinating editor, of that report, but he would wish to warmly acknowledge the extent to which the ideas and empirical data presented here draw on the work of the other partners and, in particular the contribution of the principals from each participating agency, Glyn Williams, Durk Gorter and Xabier Aixpurua. (Copies of the report can be obtained from Institiúid Teangeolaíochta Éireann, 31 Fitzwilliam Place, Dublin 2).

REFERENCES

(a) THE BASQUE COUNTRY

Eusko Jaurlaritza Hezkuntza 1995. *Euskararen Jarraipena/La Continuité de la Langue Basque*, Gasteiz: Eusko Jaurlaritzaren Argitalpen Zerbitzu Nagusia

Eusko Jaurlaritza 1994. *Euskara 81–91*, Gasteiz: Euskal Estatistika Erakundea

(b) FRIESLAND

Gorter, Durk and others 1984. *Taal yn Fryslân*, Ljouwert: Fryske Akademy

Gorter Durk and Jonkman, R.J. 1995. *Taal yn Frylân op'e nij besjoen* ['Language in Friesland revisited'], Ljouwert: Fryske Akademy

Pietersen, L. 1969. *De Friezen en hun tual*, Drachten: Laverman

(c) IRELAND

Committee on Irish Language Attitudes Research 1975. *Final Report*, Dublin: The Government Stationery Office

Ó Riagáin, Pádraig 1992. *Language Maintenance and Language Shift as Strategies of Social Reproduction: Irish in the Corca Dhuibhne Gaeltacht 1926-86*, Dublin: ITÉ

—1997. *Language Policy and Social Reproduction in Ireland*, Oxford: Clarendon Press

Ó Riagáin, Pádraig and Ó Gliasáin, Mícheál 1994. *National Survey on Languages 1993: Preliminary Report, Research Report*, 18, Dublin: ITÉ

(d) WALES

Carter, Harold and Aitchison, Jean 1994. A *Geography of the Welsh Language 1961–1991*, Cardiff: University of Wales Press

Welsh Office 1993. *Welsh Social Survey*, Cardiff: Statistical Section of the Welsh Office

Williams Glyn, ed. 1987. *The Sociology of Welsh, International Journal of the Sociology of Language*, 66 [special issue]

GENERAL REFERENCES

Allardt, Erik 1979. *Implications of the Ethnic Revival in Modern Industrialised Society: A Comparative Study of the Linguistic Minorities in Europe*, Helsinki: Societas Scientiarum Fennica

Allardt, Erik and others 1979. *Multiple and Varying Criteria for Memberships in a Linguistic Minority: The Case of the Swedish Speaking Minority in Metropolitan Helsinki*, Helsinki: University of Helsinki Research Group for Comparative Sociology

European Bureau for Lesser Used Languages 1993. *Unity in Diversity*, Dublin: EBLUL

European Commission 1996. *Euromosaic Report*, Brussels: European Union

Ohannessian, Sirarpi, Ferguson, Charles A. and Polomé, Edgar C. 1975. *Language Surveys in Developing Nations*, Arlington: Center for Applied Linguistics

Petrella, Riccardo 1978. *La Renaissance des Cultures Régionales en Europe*, Paris: Editions Entente

Price, Glanville 1969. *The Present Position of Minority Languages in Western Europe*, Cardiff: University of Wales Press

Cnuasach Focal ó Iarthar Luimnigh

PÁDRAIG Ó SNODAIGH ┐ SEÁN UA SÚILLEABHÁIN
Baile Átha Cliath *Coláiste na hOllscoile, Corcaigh*

BROLLACH

A TURNAE ina bhaile dúchais, An Caisleán Nua Thiar, Co. Luimnigh, ba ea an Dr. Robert Cussen a raibh de theist bhreise air gur staraí áitiúil den scoth é, ársaitheoir den seandéanamh, bailitheoir leabhar (leabharlann chlúitiúil curtha le chéile aige atá an-láidir maidir le stair áitiúil agus le filíocht na hÉireann), é críochnúil agus cúramach ag bailiú eolais, cuiditheach leis an eolas sin, cúirtéiseach, sochaideartha.

Am éigin sa bhliain 1969 chas sé ar fheirmeoir ó áit siar an bothar uaidh a bhí ag maíomh as líon na bhfocal Gaeilge a bhí aige. Scríobh an Dr. Cussen, a bhí bodhar go hiomlán beagnach ar Ghaeilge é féin, scríobh sé giotaí síos uaidh, agus ar ball d'fhiafraigh sé díom an mbeadh spéis agam dul níos sia leis mar scéal. Gan amhras bhí.

Mac feirmeora an fhoinse nua-aimsithe seo aige, Maurice Barrett (Muiris Baróid) a saolaíodh sa bhliain 1899 agus a tógadh ar fheirm a mhuintire sa bhaile fearainn Baile Uí Eidhnigh (Ballyyne), gar don seanmhuileann faoi scáth Chnoc an Rúscaí breis agus ceithre chiliméadar siar ó thuaidh ón gCaisleán Nua Thiar i dtreo Charraig Chiarraí. Tá Carraig Chiarraí 40 ciliméadar soir ón mBaile Dubh i mbarúntacht Chlainne Muiris i dtuaisceart Chiarraí, áit atá ar imeall iartharach Chois Sionna ar an taobh theas di. Ó fheictear an abhainn ón dúthaigh áirítear ceantar Mhuiris i gCois Sionna freisin.

Chaith Muiris a shaol ar fad, beagnach, de dhealramh, ar fheirm sin a mhuintire go dtí gur cailleadh é in aois a 73 sa bhliain 1972. Fear a raibh spéis aige riamh sa Ghaeilge, deirtear, agus i seanchas a thimpeallachta féin: é ar a rothar go minic ar turas go láthair inspéise amháin nó eile. Bhí a rothar fairis a chéadóir dom bualadh leis i dtigh an Dra. Cussen, áit ar scríobhas síos dornán focal Gaeilge uaidh, tráth a d'iarras air a thuilleadh a bhreacadh ar phár, rud a dhein, agus ócáid ar fhiafraíos de an mbeadh sé sásta blúirí éigin dá chuid Gaeilge a chur ar téip dom—mé ag glacadh leis gur díol suime a chanúint agus a chuid foghraíochta chomh maith leis an stór focal a bhí aige.

Thoiligh sé a leithéid a dhéanamh, agus, ar mo chéad turas eile siar, chuireas ar taifead téipe comhrá trír idir an Dr. Cussen, Muiris agus mé féin—mise ag iarraidh Muiris a threorú i dtreo na bhfocal Gaeilge, fad is ab fhéidir dom, le linn na hatha gairide sin. An t-eolas scríofa sin agus an téip is ábhar do phríomhroinn an ailt seo—an scagadh atá déanta orthu ag an Dr. Seán Ua Súilleabháin.

Mhothaíos agus mhothaigh an Dr. Cussen nach raibh deireadh déanta: go raibh tuilleadh fós ann, ach b'in tuilleadh nár tarlaíodh; nó ar shlí éigin shíl Muiris go rabhas ag déanamh airgid as a chuid Gaeilge, agus ar an ábhar sin dhiúltaigh sé aon bhreis a thabhairt gan táillí cuí a fháil—táillí nár cuireadh aon fhigiúr riamh orthu. Cidh trácht, níor cheannaíos, cheal foinn sa chomhthéacs, agus cheal acmhainne pé'r bith. Níor éirigh liom ná le Dr. Cussen teacht thar an gconstaic. Ar an dara lá de Bhealtaine 1970 scríobh Muiris litir chuig an Dr. Cussen á rá nach raibh fonn air a thuilleadh oibre a dhéanamh ar an ábhar. Ní rófhada ina dhiaidh sin gur cailleadh é. Níor phós sé riamh.

Aon duine amháin i gCo. Luimnigh a bhí taobh le Gaeilge amháin de réir dhaonáireamh 1911. Ní raibh Gaeilge ag tuismitheoirí Mhuiris de réir na foinse céanna, ach bhí an dá theanga aige féin (12 bhliain), ag a bheirt dearthár (14 agus 18) agus ag a dheirfiúr (19). Más ea is ar scoil ó mhúinteoirí taistil an Chonartha a d'fhoghlaim na leanaí pé Gaeilge a bhí acu. I dteach ceann tuí (nó adhmaid) agus ballaí fód (nó adhmaid), nach raibh ann ach dhá sheomra, a bhíodar ina gcónaí. De réir *Tuarascáil Choimisiúin na Gaedhealtachta* (1926) bhí 124 (13% den daonra) in Ardach (toghcheantar) a mhaígh détheangachas sa bhliain 1911, agus 6% faoi 1925. Pé Gaeilge a bhí i mBaile Uí Eidhnigh, de réir dhaonáireamh 1911, is ag na leanaí a bhí, ní ag na tuismitheoirí. Níor chainteoir dúchais, ná mac cainteora dúchais é Muiris más ea, rud a fhágann, is baolach, nach bhfuil againn ach a bhfuil againn.

* * *

'Gaolainn' ba rogha canúint ag Conn Ó Cléirigh, agus fiú más ar éigean atá a rian ar an gcnuasach seo is feiliúnach ar roinnt slite go bhfoilseofaí anseo é in ómós dó, nó phléas leis é ó thráth go chéile, ach b'in ribín a d'fhan ar an méar fhada go nuige seo. Bhí caidreamh leanúnach agam le Conn le breis agus tríocha bliain anuas. An-chara leis freisin mo chara, compánach, comhairleoir, cuspa, col seisir, comh-Cheatharlaíoch, an tOllamh *Emeritus* Donal McCartney, comhbhall le Conn i bPairtí an Lucht Saothair, comrádaí dá chuid i bpolaitíocht Choláiste na hOllscoile, Baile Átha Cliath, agus comhchreidmheach san nuafhocal nach saoi go spraoi.

Ach ceangal is dlúithe fós an ceangal clainne. B'as an gCaisleán Nua Thiar i gCo. Luimnigh, mar a deirim, do Robert Cussen a chuaigh gan baol buille bachaille go Coláiste na Tríonóide mar ar ghnóthaigh sé dochtúireacht le dlí agus áit inar chas sé le Kitsy McCartan ón gCaisleán Nua, Co. an Dúin, bean a phós sé ar ball. Iníon leis an mbeirt í mo chéile

Clíodhna, bean ar bhuail mé léi agus muid araon inár dteagascóirí sinsearacha le Roinn na Staire i gCOBÁC.

Agus mise ag déanamh na céime istoíche i gCOBÁC bhí Ann McCabe mar theagascóir staire agam bliain amháin—ba chomhtheagascóirí muid ar ball. Iníon le hEileen McCartan, deirfiúr Khitsy (máthar mo chéile) is ea Ann, col ceathrair le Clíodhna, agus ar ndóigh céile ionmhain Choinn.[1]

PÁDRAIG Ó SNODAIGH

RÉAMHRÁ[2]

D'fhoilsigh Nioclás Breathnach trí liosta d'fhocail Ghaeilge ó iarthar Luimnigh,[3] ach is fairsinge go mór an t-ábhar ón mBaróideach anseo síos.

Níorbh aon chainteoir dúchais Gaeilge Muiris Baróid (Maurice Barrett): mar a mhínigh sé féin, focail Ghaeilge is ea iad seo a chuala sé i mBéarla a cheantair dhúchais. Dá réir sin tá pointí áirithe foghraíochta trí chéile aige: caoile agus leithne roinnt consan, go háirithe *r* agus *n*; [k] agus [x] in áit a chéile go minic; [aː] mar a bheimís ag súil le [ɑː]; guta soiléir thar ceann [ə] nó [ɪ]. Bhí liosta déanta de na focail seo ag an mBaróideach, agus is amhlaidh a bhí sé á léamh amach don taifeadán: níl amhras orm ná go gcuireann an leagan scríofa amú é fo-uair, agus is dóigh liom go bhfuil rian an mhodha oibre seo le brath go háirithe ar ghutaí neamhaiceanta.

CANÚINT

[oː] a deir an Baróideach le *ó* in aice consain shrónaigh, agus ba é an dálta céanna ag cainteoirí Nioclláis Bhreathnaigh é. Fágann sin gur le himeallacha thoir, thuaidh agus thiarthuaidh na Mumhan a bhaineann [uː] a dhéanamh de *ó* nó *omh* sa suíomh seo: siné an nós in oirthear Chorcaí (pointe 7 ag Wagner),[4] Déise Phort Láirge agus Thiobraid Árann, Contae an Chláir agus fíoriarthar Ghaeltacht Chorca Dhuibhne. Is é Dún Chaoin

---

[1] Chuidigh Clíodhna agus John Cussen, Aedeen Ireland, Pádraig Ó Cearbhaill, Alan Mac an Bhaird, Donagh Warke, Máire Nic Mhaoláin, agus Cormac Ó Gráda liom ar bhealaí éagsúla an nóta seo a chur le chéile. Mo bhuíochas leo.—P.Ó S.

[2] Tá buíochas nach beag ag dul do Bhrian Ó Cúrnáin a chabhraigh liom a lán máchailí a ruagairt as an obair seo. Ba mhinic nárbh fhéidir linn an ní céanna a aireachtaint ón téip, agus b'é a dheininn sna cásanna sin mo chomhairle féin a leanúint, rud a fhágann gur mise amháin faoi deara a bhfuil fanta de lochtaí ar an saothar. Táim buíoch, leis, de Thaisce Cheol Dúchais Éireann a thug cúnamh teicniúil dom chun an téip a ionramháil.—S.Ua S.

[3] 'Focail Ghaedhilge atá le Clos sa Bhéarla a Labhartar sa Chaisleán Nua, Co. Luimnigh', *Éigse*, 5 (1946), 203–08, *Éigse*, 6, (1950), 169–79; *Éigse*, 7 (1953), 47–51.

[4] H. Wagner, *Linguistic Atlas and Survey of Irish Dialects*, 4 iml. (Baile Átha Cliath: Institiúid an Ard-Léinn, 1958–69), I (1958), II (1964).

(pointe 20 ag Wagner) i gCorca Dhuibhne, agus as sin tamaillín soir an bóthar, an t-aon áit amháin in iarthar Dheasmhumhan a bhfuil an t-athrú seo le brath.

Tá gaol le Gaeilge na nDéise le brath sna focail PRIAMPÍN (PROIMPÍN), PROUMPALÁN (PRIOMPALLÁN), agus SÍABHRA (SÍOFRA). Is é is dóichí go léiríonn HÍNTAR gur [ki:n´t´] a deirtí in iarthar Luimnigh, dála Cho. an Chláir, le caint, ach níl an focal áirithe sin againn ar an téip.

Is gnáthaí [n´] mar fhuaimniú ar -nn- caol idir chonsain aige. [ŋ´] a deir an Baróideach sna focail ainnis (aingise), ainniseoir (aingiseór) agus tá an dá ní aige sa bhfocal buinneach. D'fhuaimnítí na focail ainnis agus ainniseoir ar an dá chuma ar an mBaile Dubh i gCo. Chiarraí chomh maith,[5] agus fuarthas cheana i gCo. Luimnigh é.[6] Tugann Pádraig de Brún samplaí ó lámhscríbhinní de chuid na haoise seo caite agus na haoise seo inar scríobhadh -ng- nó ngh thar ceann -nn- i dtuaisceart Chiarraí.[7] [ŋ´] a deirtear le -nn- caol i Múscraí agus sna Déise; [ŋ´] ba ghnáthaí a fuair Wagner i gCill Orglann (pointe 17) agus i gClaeideach (pointe 16), ach d'aimsigh sé foshampla de [n´] sa dá áit sin,[8] ionas gur gearr a chuaigh an t-athrú fuaime -nn- > [ŋ´] siar ó theorainn Chorcaí agus Chiarraí.

Tagann fianaise an Bharóidigh leis na foinsí eile a thugann le fios go raibh an fhuaim [ŋ´] le fáil mar mhalairt ar [n´] ag freagairt do -nn- caol stairiúil idir ghutaí nó i ndeireadh focail i gCo. Luimnigh, i dtuaisceart Chiarraí agus, b'fhéidir, fiú amháin i ndeisceart an Chláir.

MODH OIBRE

Ón téip an fhoghraíocht atá tugtha anso do réir mar a bhí sí ann agus le tuiscint. Baintear tarrac as na siombail chéanna atá in B. Ó Cuív, *The Irish of West Muskerry* (Baile Átha Cliath: Dublin Institute for Advanced Studies, 1944) ach amháin sna pointí seo a leanas: scríobhtar [əi] ag freagairt do [ai] agus [əi] an leabhair sin, agus [əu] mar a bhfuil [au] agus [ou] ansin, agus baineadh feidhm as roinnt comharthaí breise: [n] chun an

---

[5] Stiofán Ó hAnnracháin, *Caint an Bhaile Dhuibh* (Baile Átha Cliath: An Clóchomhar, 1964), lch 34.

[6] Breathnach, *Éigse*, 5, 203. Litrítear an focal *ainniseoir* mar *angishore*, in Michael Hewson, 'A Word-List from South-West Clare', *North Munster Antiquarian Journal*, 9, (1962–63), 182–8; ach d'airigh Wagner [n´] agus [N´] ag malartú le chéile idir gutaí ag freagairt do -nn- stairiúil i gCill Bheathach (pointe 22), agus níor aimsigh Nils M. Holmer, *The Dialects of Co. Clare*, 2 iml. (Baile Átha Cliath: Acadamh Ríoga na hÉireann, 1962), ach [n´] amháin sa suíomh so i ndeisceart an Chláir, ar an gcuma gur deacair na tuairimí éagsúla a thabhairt dá chéile; i ndeisceart an Chláir níor ghabh Holmer chomh fada soir le Baile na Caillí, láthair taighde Hewson.

[7] 'Scéal Gaeilge ón Tóchar', *Journal of the Kerry Archaeological and Historical Society*, 8 (1975), lgh 136–74 (lch 139).

[8] Wagner, II, pointe 16, 120; pointe 17, 244.

scaoileadh srónach a bhíonn ag an mBaróideach sa chnuasach *rn* a chur in úil, [ɩ] in áit [i] mar a mbíonn *i* doiléir, [k^h] ar [k] a bhfuil análú trom ina dhiaidh a bhíonn aige in ionad [x] uaireanta, [w] sa bhfocal *cuileann* (*cwihlin*) chun consan débheolach a dhéantar le beola cruinnithe a chomharthú, agus [·] mar chomhartha ar leathfhaid; [L´], ach é bheith beagán lag i gcomparáid le [L´] Chonamara, a dúirt sé sa bhfocal BAILETHÓIR (BAILITHEOIR), agus aon uair amháin in LEATH-HABHAILE (LEATH AN BHAILE); cuireann [ˌ] consan siollach in úil. Cuirtear sleamhnóga láidre i gcéill sa bhfogharscríobh. Consain charballacha is ea *l* agus *n* ag an mBaróideach, dar liom. Bíonn iarraichtín caoile le brath ar *n*, ach airítear *n* níos leithne aige ar uairibh, go háirithe le hais [ɑ]. Cuirtear comhartha na caoile leis an *n* is minice aige, cé gur lag an chaoile í, chun idirdhealú idir an dá shaghas, agus airítear go minic aige é mar a mbeadh *n* leathan ag cainteoir dúchais Gaeilge; tuigtear gur caoile an *n* a bhfuil comhartha na caoile leis in aice guta chaoil ná in aice guta leathain, go háirithe más fada do na gutaí. Maidir le *r*, consan cuimilteach is ea é ag an mBaróideach, agus bíonn buille beag le mothú ina thosach uaireanta. Mar a bhfuil [r´] sa chló foghraíochta is amhlaidh atá an *r* seo ardaithe ag an gcainteoir. Níl cáilíocht na téipe le moladh, rud a fhágann nárbh fhéidir caoile agus leithne consan áirithe a aithint le haon chruinneas i gcónaí, agus go bhfuil fuaimeanna cuimilteacha báite ag siosarnach uair umá seach. B'éigean comhartha na caoile a chur idir lúibíní ar uairibh, agus tarrac a bhaint as na lúibíní < > chun fuaimeanna doiléire eile a chur in úil. Ní raibh le déanamh ach pé fuaimniú a chuir sé leis an bhfocal a chur síos agus aird an léitheora a dhíriú ar mháchailí an ábhair ar an gcuma seo.

Ciallaíonn (t) gur ón téip a luaigh Pádraig Ó Snodaigh an sampla nó an míniú atá roimhe; cuireann (DC) in úil gur i láimh an Dra. Cussen atá an chuid sin scríofa; i bpeannaireacht an Bharóidigh féin atá corp an eolais. Má aithnítear an focal cuirtear leagan éigin atá mar cheannfhocal nó mar chrostagairt sa bh*Foclóir Gaeilge-Béarla* le Niall Ó Dónaill (Baile Átha Cliath: Oifig an tSoláthair, 1977), nó leagan ó P.S. Dinneen, *Foclóir Gaedhilge agus Béarla : An Irish-English Dictionary* (Baile Átha Cliath: The Educational Company of Ireland, Ltd., thar ceann The Irish Texts Society, 1927) idir lúibíní ina dhiaidh, fiú amháin más ionann litriú dóibh; cuireadh *UaD* i ndiaidh ceannfhocail ó fhoclóir an Duinnínigh, agus * roimh fhocal nach bhfuil le fáil in aon cheann den dá fhoclóir sin, ach atá á mholadh ar a shon sin mar 'cheartleagan' d'fhocal de chuid an Bharóidigh.

AN CNUASACH

a b[h]íle-cac-a bhíladór (*a mhíle cac a <...>), *like you'd say, "Oh dear!" if things were going against you, a declaration of some class, of a person, say, around the cows—things going against them, not working out right.* (DC) [vˊíːlˊə kɑk a viːlˊədoːr(ˊ)]

a bhoucailín × 2, (a bhuachaillín), *little boy* (t) [ɑ vuːkʊlˊíːnˊ]

a circín (a chircín)

a croid[h]e geal (*a chroí geal) [a xriː gˊal]

a croid[h]e na nainghil, a croidhe na ainghil (a chroí na n-aingeal)

a dhratár, a dhrátar (? a dheartháir)

a ghrád[h], a grádh (a ghrá) [a ɣraː]

a ghrágal × 2, (a ghrá geal) [a ɣraː gˊilˊ]

a glégal, a gléigil (*a ghléigeal, *a ghléigil)

a leanbh (a leanbh)

a mbhínach, a mbínach (a bhuíonach, a mhaoineach) [a viːnˊək]

a mhic ó × 2

a stór (a stór) [a sdoːr]

a stór mo steach × 2

aerach (aerach) = *rakish* (t); Q: *"What way are that family doing—have they much to put in the news at all?".* A. *"Whisha! I think* aerac!" = *at the two ends of the bean—not doing well.* (DC) [eːrək]

aingise × 2 (ainnis) = *indifferent* (?); *"Wisha! I visited poor so-and-so!" "What kind are they after the death?" "Wisha!* aingise, *God help us!"* [aŋˊ ɪsˊe](DC)

aingiseór (ainniseoir) = *an unfortunate person* (t); *"I was in with Dinny Davis!" "Did he offer you any cup of tay?" "No." "Wisha the hungry* aingiseor, *he wouldn't give you the itch."* (DC) [aŋˊ ɪ'sˊoːr(ˊ)]

amadán (amadán)—*a fool* (t) [amə'dɑːnˊ]

amalóg (amlóg), *"a poor amalóg"* = *a harmless kind of person, soft, easy to dupe, like wax* (DC); = *a person that was misfortunate* (t) [amə'loːg]

anam, M'ainm o'n díollis a croide! (? M'anam 'on diabhal is a chroí)

anam, tanam an riacar, tanam anríacar (*t'anam 'on riachair (?) < t'anam 'on riabhach + t'anam 'on diachair)

árnan, arnán (airneán), *"Those young people are out all hours of the night, when you go to get them out of bed in the morning they're* arnaning *and falling asunder—no energy!"* (DC); = *drowsy, dozing off* (t) [ɑːrⁿ'n(ˊ)ɑːn, ɑːr'nɑːnˊɪŋˊ]

artnanes,[9] = *a nickname for a person you didn't like—some kind of a*
    <reflection>. (DC)

bacach, bocach (bacach); *a hungry old* bacach *(a rough sound)* (DC); *a* bacac =
    a person without any principles (t); cf. BOCACH-NA-FEITISHE
    [bə'kɑk]

bacachán (bacachán) = *a person staggering along—very lame* (t)
    [bakə'xɑːn(´)]

bacadór, bacadór *then would be a person sponging* (t); *I'd be going to go to the*
    next house, I'd travel here, and I'd go down a couple of miles along
    I'd be bacadóring *around—filling the stomach* (t) **[bakə'doːr,**
    bakə'doːrɩŋ´]

bacal (bachall) = *a walking-stick* (t); *I gave such a one a stroke of the* bachal
    (t); *(a soft sound, down in the skull) = a stick—applied to an old man*
    carrying a stick, tripped by a smart-alec. "*If I had that* dratarhín, *I'd*
    give him the bacal. (DC) **[bakəl, ba<x>əl]**

bacaram (? bachram), bacharam —*of rain; We may thank the big* metheul
    (mehul) *that the last wynd was finished, just before the* bacaram
    (sudden rainfall). **[baxərɩm]**

bailethóir (bailitheoir); *I'd come into Mr. Cusson here, and I'd say 'Is there any*
    chance you'd have so many books?'; and I'd go to a farmer, and I'd
    say 'Is there any chance you'd have the loan of a slán *to go cutting*
    turf tomorrow?': I was a great bailitheor. *No! I'm making a mistake—*
    'tis a person pursuing or hunting from house to house, a home pursuit,
    pursuing home[10] (t) **[baL´ɩ'hoːr]**

baitín × 2 (baitín) = *a crop or wattle. Landlord or politician, etc., had no*
    respectalbe followers—just a crowd of baitín *boys; I gave him the*
    baitín *across the shoulders* (t); **[ba'<t´>iːn´]**

balbh (balbh) *then was supposed to be the tongue someway defective, with a*
    lump or a swelling in it (t); "Taidhg balbh" (t) **[baləv]**

balbhání (*balbhánaí), *a stuttering person then was a* balbhánaí (t)
    [balə'vɑːn(´)ɩ̈]

bán (bán), *Man setting* bán *(baan) potatoes, had the name of a good spade-*
    worker—"great for turning scoltaí(s)" *(skull theaz) (thees)*

banbh (banbh) = *young pig* (t) **[banɩv]**

bártnach × 2 (bairneach) *some kind of a fish* (t); bártnach *a person that hadn't*
    shape or make—an old jelly-fish—sluggish—some sort of shell fish
    that hadn't shape nor make. Feud between the leggy Kennedys and the
    butty Barretts—one day Paddy Barrett (5'5") was walking home with

---

[9] Scaoileadh srónach sa chnuasach *rn*, ní foláir, a chuireann *t* in úil.

[10] Chuimhnigh sé ar an bhfocal *baile* agus tháinig mearbhall air!

his carpet bag of tools touching almost the ground. He passed Kate
Mulcahy's pub and outside the door sunning himself stood John
Kennedy ('Long Johnny' the arch enemy who hadn't shape nor size).
With him was Tom Barrett, who said 'What are you travelling in, little
maneen?'' Paddy: 'I'm travelling in "bartnacks"' (hitting at John's
leggy and sluggish appearance). (DC) [bɑːr⟨n⟩hnək]

básán (?) = básdán

básdán (básadán, básachán), *What can you expect from that oul' dying* básdán; *the poor man, he isn't able to work.* (t) [bɑːs'dɑːn]

béachacán (béiceachán) = *a person with a kind of a crabbity little face on him—that oul'* béachachán (t) [bˈeːə<kx>ɑːnˈ]

béal-gárrtha (béal gearrtha) *I was digging potatoes now today, and somone asks me where I left the spade. —"Up at the* béil geárrtha.*" That means 'the mouth of the cutting' where I gave off cutting before.* (t) [bˈeːl gˈaːrhə, bˈeːlˈ gˈaːrhə]

beart (beart), *A* beart *of hay;* bart *—of hay* [bˈart]

béim (béim) = *a 'bame' of a man, ready to give a blow; a* béim *of a woman—the Amazonian type; a strong bame of a man; having ability to give a strong blow;* béim *of a woman—an 'Amazon'*

bioránach (bioránach), *her* bioránac *of a daughter* (t) [bˈi'rɑːnˈək]

bláms, *a* bláms *of a fool* (t) [bˈlˈaːmz, bˈlˈaːms]

bleáthach, *a* bleá<c>ach *of a fool* (t) [bˈlˈaːhəx]

blú-blá [bə'luː bˈᵊlɑː]

bocach-na-feitishe (*bacach na feitise); *I can't say what it is, I just heard it around there.* [bə'kɑk na fˈetˈisˈɪ, bə'kɑk nɑ fˈetˈɪsˈɪ]

bodach (bodach) —*of a farmer*

bodalach (? bodalach) = *the bladder of the pig. They'd never say 'the bladder of the pig; we used to take out the* bodalac *of the pig, and massage it and so forth, and dry it a bit and put it into an oul' cover of a football, and make a football—a bladder of it.* (t) [bodələk, bodəlˈək]

bodóg (bodóg) = *cow—from shape of udder; someone was seen going down to the cow-house—"I think now 'tis time to brag th'oul* bodóg" (t) [bə'doːg]

bogán (bogán), *A soft egg was called a* bogán.

bolgadán × 2 (bolgadán) = *the small, very paunchy person; a person with a big pot-belly on him* (t) [boləgəd ɑːn]

bónéis, *Such a fellow has a great let out in him—his chest stuck out […] " By God, he's a great* bóinéas.*" Whatever it meant I don't know now. You could hear it. But I knew who it was referring to, and I knew it had something got to do with that character—a kind of 'out-of-my-way' class of a fellow.* (t) [boː'nˈeːs] bóneó-breach (bainne bó bleacht), *Would they be the daffodils? ...—speckled something. Would they be cowslips?* (t) [**boːn´iː oː brax, boːn´iː oː b´rax, boːn´iː oː b´rak**]

bórán [**boːr'haːn´**]

bóric, bóraic (? buairc UaD), *then, was a short bit of timber cut to make a hurling ball of it*[11] [**boːrɪk´**]

boricín (barraicín),[12] *finishing up to a horse-rail of turf would be a* barraicín (t) [**barə'k´ɪːn´**]

bórseó; *there was some kind of a shindy some place or another—a kind of an argument, and I heard always: "there was great* bórseó *down the road that night"—some argument over politics, or over something* (t) [**(')boːr's´oː**]

bostún (bastún) = *a person without any character* (t) [**bas'duːn**]

bothán (bothán) = *like a* scailp—*a small house* (t); [**bo'haːn´**]

bouraní (bodhránaí); *A person would be a bit on the deaf side, then—"that oul' bouránaí wouldn't understand a word you'd be saying"* (t); [**bəu'raːniː, bə'r ɑːniː**]

bousín (boghaisín); *'tis likely we'll get rain—I saw a* bousín *around the moon last night.* (t) [**bəu's´iːn´**]

braddí (*braddy) (< bradach) *"I have a* braddí *cow there, and where did she break out only over five or six feet of a wall?"* [**brad´iː**]

brag (? bligh) [= *to milk*]: BODÓG [**brag´**]

bramaire (bramaire); *"that woman—she working and killing herself' and her* bramaire *of a daughter doing nothing, only fattening up."* (t) [**bramərə**]

brat (brat) *of hay; laying down a layer of hay, then, was a* brat *of hay* [**brat**]

brathamán, *Plenty work would take some of the* tisbí, tiospach, *or* brathamán *out of mischievous young fellows; 'We're jaded and torn and dragged all day working, and there wouldn't be half the* brathamán *in ye if ye were doing something all day the same as we were.'* [**brɑːhə'maːn´, brahə'maːn´**]

brelic (breillice); *a* breilic, *then, would be a* breilic *of a fool* (t); [**brel´ɪk´**]

broch (broc) = *badger*

brónach (brónach); *I went into such a one, she was after burying the husband, and she was very* brónach (t) [**bᵊroːn(´)əx, broːon´əx**]

brouchán (broghchán) = *a badger tendency in a person* (t); = *a badger, aplied to a stubborn, over-edgy, surly kind of a person—'Yera! that ould*

---

[11] Cf. Breathnach, *Éigse*, 6, 170.

[12] = '*caipín ar ualach móna*', Breathnach, *Éigse*, 5, 203.

broucan, *you could ask no questions from that fellow!"* (DC)
[brəu'kɑːn´, broːu'kɑːn´, brəu'xɑːn´]

brouli (< breall), *A* brouli *(browly), a muttering and scowling person.*

brus (brus) **[bᵊrus]**

brúscar (brúscar), *Such a person now, he did* brúscar: *that he came in and upset everything s<l>ashed some things around, he was in a bit of a temper; he made* brúscar *of everything—giblets* (t) **[bᵊruːsgər, bᵊruːsgər´, bruːsgər]**

búa (bua) **[buːᵘ]**

búacailín (buachaillín) **[buːkɪl´iːn´]**

búailim-scía (buailim sciath) = *a kind of a challenger, kind of high and mighty, like the old soldiers, a [...], <tree-lopper>—looking for all coming to take them on* (t) **[buːl´ɪm´s´g´iː]**

buailtán × 2 (buailteán), *a* búltán *of a stick* (t); *So-and-so gave X the* buailtán *on the head, and he—X—fell down in a dead* sodar." **[buːl´tɑːn´]**

búailteór (buailteoir) = (?) *I think that's a person that would be striking terror, that they'd frighten all before them* **[buːl'tɑr, buːl´'toːr]**

búcalán (buachallán) = *ragweed, ragwort* (t) **[buːxʊlɑːn, buːkəlɑːn]**

bud-a-glugar (bodach gliogair) = *a kind of a herb: you'd get it in gardens [...] and so forth—greenish with kind of hairy stalks on it, and at intervals along it you'd meet—like you'd see <in> seaweed—bladders, and of course they'd collapse under the least pressure—glugars, like the soft egg, you see.* (t) **[bod a glugər]**

budahín (*bodaichín); *If I was thatching a house I'd have a little circular bit or straw or rushes, wound around kind of like a jar, and I'd put* scalaps *down on it. Will you bring me out a* budahín *of* scalaps. *A* budahín = *what contained the* scallaps. (t); **[bud´ɪ'hiːn´]**[13]

budógs (< buttocks an Bhéarla), *Child for some misdemeanour was smacked on* tón *or* budóg(s)

builig (boilg) **[bil´ɪg´]**

buineach (buinneach) = *purge; a calf that would be a bit deranged in the flow of their system* (t); *such a person—pale and washy: 'they had the colour of the* buineach' (t) **[bi'n´akʰ, bɪ'ŋ´ak]**

bun-na-rú = *yellow <pencilly land>, or reddish kind of ground* (t) **[bun´ n´ə hᵊruː, bun na hruː]**

búrhán (? buaithreán, buarán) **[buːr'hɑːn´]**

c<wi>nhlin (? cuileann)

---

[13] [bodə'hiːn´], Breathnach, *Éigse*, 5, 203.

cabara, cobra, cobara (cabaire) = *having a mouth on one for giving gab; I wonder if the title of* cobara *given to an irritating individual, had its roots in* cabra—*poor quality land (poor quality person)?* [**kabərə**]

cábóg (cábóg) = *an idiot* [**kɑːˈboːg**]

cabra (? cabrach) *I wonder if the title of* cobara *given to an irritating individual, had its roots in* cabra —*poor quality land (poor quality person)?*

cabún × 2 (cábún) = *An effeminate type of man.* [**kɑːˈbuːn(ʹ)**]

cadéi (ceaidé) [**kʹaˈdʹeː**]

cafarín (caifirín), Cafarín *covered woman's head.*

cam-reilge (cam reilige) [**kəum relʹɪgʹe**]

cant (ceant) = *auction*

carabóg × 2, *A hollow, or depression, in a field was often brought to a level with a load of* carabóg(s) *and* scráu(s) [**karəˈboːg**]

caracán (carracán) [**karəˈkɑːnʹ**]

casóg (casóg) [**kaˈsoːg**]

castór (castóir) [**kasˈdoːr**]

ceannobalach [**kʹəunʹ obələk**]

ceannrán [**kʹəunᵊʹrɑːnʹ**]

ceannrání

ceartig! (ceartaigh) = *order to cow when milking* [**kʹartɪgʹ**]

ceócarail (DC)

ceócharán (? ceochrán) [**kʹoːxər<ɑ>ːnʹ**]

Ceólán × 2 (ceolán), *was a lightheaded person (perhaps), whistling and humming, with head in air.* [**kʹoːˈlɑːn**]

ceóltóir (ceoltóir) [**kʹoːlʹtoːr**]

Chlash [(?) bhlash], *Yank of over 40 years absence said* <C>hlash.

cíaróg, ciarog (ciaróg), *Wondering why some fine-looking girl married a* drousóg *or* ciaróg *of a man, people often concluded that 'I suppose she had the* nádúr *for him.'* [**kʹiːˈroːg**]

cillín (cillín) (DC)

cinnáibhre × 2 (cneámhaire), *Did* cinnáibhre *mean a knave?* [**kʹɪˈnʹaːvʹɩrə**]

cinnster (cinstear UaD), *Person or animal who had damaged something beyond repair point, was said to have made* cinnster *or* práuc *of it.*

cippadaríol (cipidiríl) [**kʹipʹəðəˈriːlʹ**]

ciseach (ciseach) [**kʹɩˈsʹak**]

cish —*turf* (ceis); *kish = a basket of turf; 30 kishes to the hundred of turf* [**kʹisʹ**]

cístín [**kʹiːsʹˈdʹiːnʹ**]

ciotóg (ciotóg) = *left-handed* [**kʹiˈtoːg**]

cláfseání (cnáimhseálaí) [**kʹlʹɑːfʹʹsʹaˈnʹiː**]

cláirín = *hearty meal* [**klɑːˈriːnʹ**]

clashín(s) [**kʹlʹaˈsʹiːnz**]

cleas-a-cúile (cleas an chuaille) [**kʹlʹas a kuːlʹe**]

cleithre (cleithire) [kʼlʼehəre]

clíabhán (cliabhán) [kʼlʼiːʼv(ˊ)ɑːnˊ]

clíanistig (cliamhain isteach) [kʼlʼiənˊ ɩ'sʼˊdˊigˊ]

clíochán [k<l>(ˊ)iːʼxɑːnˊ]

clob (? clab)

clout (clabhta) = clout *of a wattle.*

cloutín(s) (*clabhtín) = *nappies*

cluisí [kluːziː]

clúisín(s) (cluaisín) [kluːʼsˊiːnˊz]

clústar [k<lˊ>uːstɩrˊ]

cnap (cnap) × 2 *Rowdy threw a* cnap *of a stone through a window.* [kn(ˊ)ɑp]

cocal (cochall) —*of a hat on top of a womans head;* cocal, a cocal *of a hat;* cocal = *bunch of a bonnet, or hat*

coínlín (coinlín) [kiːnˊ'hlʼiːnˊ]

cóir(*ing*) (comhar) [koːrʊŋˊ]

comar (cumar) = *gulch* [kumər]

córach [koːrək]

córíac (comhairíoch), *He is a great* córíac *for going to funerals.*

cosamacodí (ar chos bhacóide)

costerwans (caisearbhán), *Young boys and girls collected* costerwans = (Cas tsaramán(s)—w—) *cutting them with an unpointed knife. The herb somewhat resemblied dandelion, and was used for fowl-feeding— meal, etc. added.*

crabanta (crabanta) [krabən(ˊ)tə]

cracalí (craiceálaí) [kra'kɑːliː][14]

cráidte (cráite) [kraːtˊɩ]

cráidtecán, craidtecán (cráiteachán), *Probably descriptive of a malcontent—a* craidtecán. [krɑːtˊək ɑːn(ˊ)]

crinlins = *long straight hay with seeds on it.* (DC)

croc (? croch) [krok]

cromadí (cromada) [krɑmədˊiː]

crounán (? crónán) [krəu'nˊɑːnˊ]

crounc, *Person had a* crounc *on him over the fire (i.e. hunched).*

crouncán (? cancrán) [krəuŋ'kɑːnˊ]

crour (creabhar) [krəur]

crú mhúthar é, *Sounding like* 'mo crú mhúthar é!' *when applauding a good rendering of song.*

crúbh(s) [kruːb]

---

[14] *sic.*

crúbóg (crúbóg) = *a bitter person, not much to look at, very ready to 'pinch'* *people*; crúbóg = *crabfish, said of certain kind of person.*

crustóg × 2, *A few* crustóg(s), *with bacon and cabbage, made a nice dinner.* [kros'doːg][15]

crut × 2 (cruit), *I think I read somewhere or another, that the reference to an old person hanging over the fire, with a* crut *on him, or her, originated from the rough resemblance such a person bore to a* crut *(harp); this would mean, of course in profile.* [kr<u>t]

cuc (coc); *Person who had been abused outside a church on Sunday, for instance, would say, later, to others: "Only for where it happened I'd straighten the* cuc *on him (to rhyme with 'duck').*

cúg, cúag, *A* slíbhín *of a relative* cúg(d) *(= came by) a sum of money,—see* *na Bhán *with 'Is tú cúg go duit idir mé gus Día.'*[16] [kuːg]

Cúil é!, cúail e!, *Not so many years ago hurlers and footballers always said* c<ú>il é *when the ball went aside behind goal posts:*
| cúil é (*a point*) | G O A L M O U T H | cúil é (*a point*) | ['kuːl´,eː]

cúile (cuaille), *A long and lightly built man or youth was termed a* cúile *(pole).*

cur-cuis (cor coise) [kor kis´]

cúrlún × 2 (cuirliún), Cúrlún *was a giddy, half-simpleton.* [kuːr'hᵊl´uːn´]

curra-grifín (codladh grifín) [korə gᵊri'f´iːn´]

curraig [korɪg´]

cus(*ing*) (< cos) = *single leg hop step & leap* [kosʊŋ´][17]

cwinhlin (? cuileann) [kwil´ɪn´]

dailc, dhailc (dailc) *A strong* dailc *of a man.* [dɑl´k´]

dailtín [dal´'t´iːn´]

dálc (*pron. dawk*) [Béarla < 'dealg' na Gaeilge], *Farmer was said to have got a 'dawk' by selling cattle at pounds under value; purchaser probably having got five pounds per head profit within an hour.*

dara-dhéal (daradaol) [darə'deːl]

Dartán, dhartán (dartán) *of a young woman—degenerated into 'heifer' later on.* [dɑr'tɑːn]

dathúil (? dathúil) [dɑː'huːl´][18]

dé maith le shúil orm

dei<r>c(s) = *sourish*

deis [d´es´]

[15] Amhras air; cf. CRÚSTÓG, CRÚSTÓISC, Breathnach, *Éigse*, 7, 48.

[16] 'Is tú a chuaigh go dlúth idir mé 'gus Dia', M.F. Ó Conchúir, *Úna Bhán*, (Indreabhán, Conamara: Cló Iar-Chonnachta, 1994), lch 222.

[17] Nó b'fhéidir [kos´ʊŋ´]; siosarnach ar an téip.

[18] *sic.*

deoc-a-dorash (deoch an dorais) [dok^h₁₉ a dorʰs ́]

desh é! (*ordering a cow to get into correct position in her stall*)

dhoul (dall) [dəul]

dhúr-sé-dhars<í> (dúirse dáirse) [duːrsˈʻ dɑːrsˈe]

dhúricín (? diuiricín) [du<r>ʰk ́iːn ́]

díamas (díomas), *She has great dheemus on her 'allie-blaster' of a daughter.*
Woman picked great 'dímas' (*pride*) *out of her* 'péarla' *of a daughter.*

dol [dol]

dothul (doicheall) [dohəl]

dradara (dradaire) [dradəre]

dramhuíl (dramhaíl) [draːˈviːl ́]

dratarhín (dradairín), (*a soft sound, down in the skull*) = *a stick—applied to an*
old man carrying a stick, tripped by a smart-alec. If I had that
dratarhín, *I'd give him the* bacal. (DC)

dratháirín (deartháirín) [draˈhaːriːn ́]

drianán (driongán) = *a worn out old man*; drianán(s) = *old clothes* [dᵊriːˈn ́ɑːn ́,
dᵊriːˈn ́ɑːn ́z]

dríbh, dríb (dríb, draoib) *Man, very drunk, often had* dríbh, drídar, drídalac<h>
of porter on his clothes, of face. [dᵊriːb ́]

drídalach (? dríodarnach), *Man, very drunk, often had* dríbh, drídar,
drídalac<h> *of porter on his clothes, or face.* [dᵊriːdələk ^h]

drídar × 2 (dríodar), *Man, very drunk, often had* dríbh, drídar, drídalac<h> *of*
porter on his clothes, of face. [dəˈr(́)iːdər]

drín [dᵊriːn ́]

drólín × 2 (dreoilín), *'Winding' somebody up, making him or her, their slave,*
virtually—such a person was said to be making a drólín *or* mamalínac
of another. [droːˈl ́iːn ́]

dromach (dromach) [druˈmɑk ^h]

dross (dreas), *Arrival at bog and farmhouse offered to take a* dros (*pr.* dross) *at*
the slán, *or churning-barrel.*

drothacharac, drothacharach (drochacrach), *An irritable unsocial person, was*
said to be drothacharac. [droˈhɑkərək]

drousóg × 2, *Wondering why some fine-looking girl married a* drousóg *or*
ciaróg *of a man, of a man, people often concluded that 'I suppose she*
had the nádúr *for him.'* [drəuˈsoːg]

dúcas (dúchas) [duːxəs]

dúd [duːd ́]

---

¹⁹ *sic.*

dúderálí × 2 (? dúdaire, dúdálaí), A dúderálí *took an hour to tell what could be related in ten minutes.* [**duːdəˈr ɑːliː**]

dúg (diúg) [**d ⁻³uːg**]

dúidín (dúidín) = *clay pipe* [**duːˈd ʹiːn ʹ**]

dúiricín (diúiricín), A *fine* dúiricín *of a child.* [**duːrɪk ʹiːn ʹ**]

dúradán, (dúradán, dúramán) *Said of the 'Silent O Moyle' type of man:* "'Tis pure torment trying to drag a word out of th'oul dúradán'

durn (dorn), durn *of oats* [**dor ⁿn(ʹ)**]

durnín (doirnín) [**dor ⁿn ʹiːn ʹ**]

Eir'-in áirde (éirí in airde) [**ˈəɪrɪˈnɑːrd ʲe**]

éiric × 2 (éiric) *Someone stole an iron from a forge, or demolished a fort, or lios, and got an* éiric, *i.e. got 'queer' or became crippled.* [**eːrɪk ʹ**]

faille [**fɑl ʹ**][20]

failm (failm) *of an ash plant*

faire (faire) [**fɑre**]

faire go deó (faire go deo)

fáisht

fámaire (fámaire) [**fɑːmərə**]

fán-óir (fáinne óir), fán-óir *on you!*; *In praise of his (her) partner, having saved the situation at a game of cards:* 'Fán-óir *on you.'* [**fɑːn ʹ oːr**]

fastúch (fostúch) [**fɑsˈduːx**]

fathach (fathach) [**fɑhək ʰ**]

feilc × 2 (feirc) *Young man, seen in town, on a Church holiday, with a* feilc *in his hat was said to be on the lookout for a wife.* [**f ʹel ʹk ʹ**]

féirín (féirín), A *young man who had got a worthless wife, was said to have got a 'fairin' in her (sarcastically, of course).*

feóthadán (feochadán), *(?) Heard it in reference to persons with 'stinging' tongues.*

fia bán (? fia-bhán) = *whitish grass* (DC)

fiarcán (fadharcán) [**fəɪrˈk ɑːn**]

fíasta-fáiste (faoiste fáiste) [**f ʹiːs ʹdə fɑːs ʹdə**]

fíle-dhearg (? *fiaile dhearg) = *red shank—weed* [**f ʹiːl ʹ ɪ jarɪg ʹ**]

fiobán (fadhbán) [**fəɪˈbɑːn**]

fíonán (fionnán), Fíonán *from the bogs was good bedding for calves, pigs, etc.*

fisaracht, phiseracht (fiosracht) [**f ʹisərəkt**]

flathúil (flaithiúil) [**flɑˈhuːl ʹ**]

fleister [**f ʹl ʹestər**]

flíep (flíp), *Person got* fléic *or* flíep *of a fist from another.*

---

[20] *sic.*

flopsh × 2 [**flɑp´s´**]

folbó (? failbó, haileabó)[21] [**fɑlbo:**]

fósc (? fóisc), *Well-developed child, or adult was a fósc.* [**fo:s´k´**]

francach, *She hadn't the brains of a* francach—*a rat, evidently.*

fraochán, fréacán × 2, (fraochán), *A local labouring man, and a farmer, had a*
    bitter dispute one day. The farmer came from a mountainy area many
    years before, having bought a farm in the valley. The latter asked the
    labourer did he know to whom he was speaking. With feigned servility
    the enemy replied:—'To be sure I do, aren't you Lord Fréacán?'
    [**fre:'xɑ:n**]

fúairhé (fuarthé) [**fu:r(´)'he:**]

fústar (fústar) [**fu:sdər**]

fúta-fata [**fu:tə fɑtə**]

fútharnach × 2 (fuairnimh)[22] = *dull pain in face and jaws* [**fu:hərn´ək**]

gairbhín(s) (gairbhín), *The* gairbhín(s) = *rough*

gárcach (gearrcach) [**g´a:rxəx**]

garrán [**g´ə'rɑ:n´**]

garsún [**gɑr'su:n**]

gascíach (gaiscíoch) [**gɑs´'g´iəx**]

géig (? géag) [**g´e:g´**]

geócach, geóchac (geocach), *'If you saw the* góhec *of the* geóchac.' [**g´o:xəx**]

geosadán [**g´o:səd ɑ:n(´)**]

geounch (geanc), geounch —*of a nose* [**g´əuŋ´k**]

gíarhóc (? géaróg) [**g´i:r'ho:k**]

gibóg(s) (giobóg) [**g´i'bo:gz**]

gideracán × 2, *'There's a* gideracán *over there, since yesterday'*—*referring to a*
    birth. [**g´idərək ɑ:n**]

gidhán (gigeán UaD), *Neighbours' verdict on sober and easy young man, who*
    had just married a very energetic young woman:—After a week or
    two, she'll straighten—or soften, the gidhán *in him.*

gidim (giodam) [**g´id´ɩm´**]

giobal, gibal(s) (giobal), *Person with clothes in* giobal(s), *or in* sraimín(s), *was*
    often likened to rags on a bush near a blessed well. [**g´ibəlz**]

gléigal (gléigeal) [**g´l´e:g´ɩl´**]

gleótórín, gleóthórín (gleoiteoirín UaD), *Young man sometimes was said to be*
    in a gleótórín *with his 'young lady', and prospective in-laws.*
    [**g´l´o:'to:ri:n´**]

glib [**g´l´ib´**]

---

[21] Cf. *failbó .i. an idle person* — *usually big and fat*, Breathnach, *Éigse*, 6, 173.

[22] Cf. FUARTHNACH, Breathnach, *Éigse*, 6, 173.

glidera [g'l'idərə]

gligín (gligín) [g'l'i'g'i:n']

glírum *of light* [g'l'i:rəm]

glócach [glo:kəx]

glóracán (glórachán) = *name given to a person rather loud of voice.*

glórán (gleorán) [g'l'o:'rɑːn']²³

glúcac, glúcach (gliúcach) *'That blind* glúcac *wouldn't know a cow from a stack of hay.'* [gl'u:kəx]

glugar (glugar), *An infertile egg was a* glugar, *with its derivative,* gluggaire, *describing a 'scatter-brains'.*

glugara, gluggaire (gliogaire), *An infertile egg was a* glugar, *with its derivative,* gluggaire, *describing a 'scatter-brains'.*

góhec, *"If you saw the* góhec *of the* geóchac.*"*

golúcar (? gall-luachair) [gəlu:kər]

gorlóg [gɑr'hᵊlo:g]

grámhar × 2 (grámhar), *'You'd like to be talking to her, she's so* grámhar.*'* [gᵊra:vər]

granóg (gráinneog) = *hedgehog. Bitter selfish woman was sometimes referred to as 'a bitter little* granóg*'.* [gra'n(')o:g]

grig (griog) = *tantalize;* Child often purposely grig(ged) *comrades by sucking sweets with a great show of stisfaction—they having none.* [grig']

gríos (gríos) [gᵊriəs]

gríosach (gríosach) [gᵊri:sək]

griscin (? gríscín) [gris'g'ɪn']

gróg (gróg) *of turf* [gro:g]

grug [grog]

gubaire (gobaire) [gobəre]

gubbí (< gob) [gob'i:]

gwhál (gabhál) *of turf* [gvɑ:l]

híntar (? ag caint ar)²⁴—*Our ancestors had a few words to describe young men* indiscrimately ag híntar na mná *which are unprintable.*

íersmuire (*iarsmaire)²⁵ [i:r(')smʊre]

lá breág[h] paocas le Dia (lá breá buíochas le Dia)

lá hí, láithí [lɑ:hi:], *get kind of cross if you stared at him; a* lá hí *little boy: very* <washy> (DC)

labh (? leamh) [l'av']

---

²³ = *Heracleum sphondylium,* 'the hogweed or cowparsnip', Breathnach, *Éigse,* 6, 172.

²⁴ [ki:n't'] a deirtí le *'caint'* i bhformhór Cho. an Chláir, Holmer, *The Dialects of Clare,* I, § 90; Wagner I, mapa 110.

²⁵ Cf. Seoirse Mac Clúin, *Caint an Chláir,* 2 iml. (Baile Átha Cliath: Oifig an tSoláthair, 1940), II, s.v.

labhó [**l´a'vo:**][26]

lacéi [**l´a'k´e:**]

l'amadán (leathamadán) [**lamə'dɑ:n**]

langhaire (langaire) [**l´aŋ´ɩre**]

lapadóg (t) [**lapə'do:g**]; cf. SLAPADÓG

lártnach, lártnach *of an ape*, A lártnach *of an ape.* [**l´a:rhⁿnəx**]

láthar Dhé × 2 (i láthair Dé)

lathéisc, leathhéisc, *Person was sick of somebody's* lathéisc. [**l´a'he:s´k´**]

leath-habhaile, leathhabhaile (? leath an bhaile), *A woman visitor, demanding tea, commenting on private affairs of her hosts, etc., was said to have come in with her* leath-habhaile *(half at home).* [**l´ahə'vaL´ə, l´aha'val´ə**]

leath-hónsuch (leathóinseach) [**l´ah o:n´s´ək**]

leibide [**l´ebɩde**]

leirig *of hay* [**l´erɩk´**]

léit[h]e = *tea, mostly water;* A certain woman would have as much meaś *on her sup of* léithe *as if it were tea (probably derived from* leat[h]-huisce[27]— *half water.* [**l´e:hə**]

leithidín [**l´ehɩ'd´i:n´**]

lhiar (ladhar) *of potatoes* [**ləiər**]

liber (liobar), *Someone threw a* liber *of a cloth on top of a clean one—a dirty cloth—probable derived from* libernach.

libernach × 2 (liobarnach), *Someone threw a* liber *of a cloth on top of a clean one—a dirty cloth—probable derived from* libernach. [**l´ib´ərn´ək**]

lic (lic, leac) = *brink* [**l´ik´**]

líerna × 2 (liairne), *A slouching person, and, perhaps, with an unsocial disposition, was called an oul'* líerna. [**l´i:rn´ə**]

ligin [**l´ig´ɩn´**]

lopadóg

lopín (laipín) [**la'p´i:n´**]

losad (losaid)—*bread making* [**lasɩd´**][28]

lúbaire × 2 (lúbaire), *Man referred to as a long* lúbaire *was usually stooped, with a raking stride.* [**lu:bəre**]

lúbán × 2, *Person doubled up with pain from blow, or illness was in a* lúbán. [**lu:'bɑ:n**]

lug (log) [**log**]

lúidín (lúidín) [**lu:'d´i:n´**]

---

[26] Cf. LEABHÓ, Breathnach, *Éigse*, 6, 174.

[27] *recte = liathuisce, léithuisce.*

[28] Cf. [**losɩd´**], Breathnach, *Éigse*, 5, 206; (?) foghraíocht bunaithe ar an litriú anseo.

lurgadán (lorgadán) [**lorəgəd ɑːn**]

lusalín (? ros an lín) [**los ə'l´i:n´**]

madra-gaoithe (madra gaoithe) [**mɑdərə giːhι**]

maggara —*title for watch* [**mɑgəre**]

mahg (maig), mahg *in neck* [**mɑg´**]

máilín (máilín) [**mɑː'l´i:n´**]

M'ainm o'n díal (? *M'anam 'on diabhal)

maisge! (maisce, ambaiste) [**mɑs´g´e**]

maistín × 2 (maistín), *'Sure no decent girl would marry the likes of him—running in a* maistín *after women.'* [**mɑs´'d´i:n´**]

maith go leor × 2 (maith go leor), *He was* maith go leor *coming from town to his own place.* [**mɑgι'l´oːr**]

malabhóg (mealbhóg) [**mɑlə'voːg**]

mamalínac, mamalínach (mamailíneach), *'Winding' somebody up, making him or her, their slave, virtually—such a person was said to be making a* drólín *or* mamalínac *of another* [**mɑmə'l´i³n´ək**]

maneen na mhéos [**m´an´i:n´ nə meːs**]

maoil (maol) —*cow* [**meːl**]

mar a 'eadh *[pronounced]* yah (mar dhea) [**mɑrə'ja**]

marbhán (marbhán) [**mɑrə'vɑːn(´)**]

martínach × 2 (mairtíneach), *Nasty comment on young married man.* [**mɑr'tiən(´)ək**]

masa fein × 2 (*um basa féin), *Mhuise!* masa fein, *but he did it.*

mash[29] (? maise), —*parading one's best girl* [**mɑs´**]

meas (meas) [**m´as**]

méir (? maor) = *A leading man; we had the* méir *of Skerhoo (Shana Golden).*

méiscire (méiscre, méirscre) [**m´eːs´g´ιrə**]

metheul (meitheal), *We may thank the big* metheul (mehul) *that the last wynd was finished, just before the* bacaram *(sudden rainfall).*

mhastar [**vɑsd´ər´**]

mhéos (maos) [**meːs**]

mhuise (muise), *Mhuise!* masa fein, *but he did it;* 'Mhuise! nac maith hé!' *or* 'nhá mban' *in applauding a good performance by man or beast.*

mía (mí-ádh) [**m´i:'ɑː**]

míobh, miabh (maíomh), *Was said of a young man who got a useless wife: 'No one need* miabh *her on him';* míobh = *begrudge* [**mi:v**]

míarog (méaróg) [**m´i'roːg**]

miastar[30] (máistir) *'With mock gravity: I asked the young* miastar *(master).'*

---

[29] ma<o>sh.

[30] ?? .i. [**məis´d ιr´**]; cf. *lhiar* <*ladhar*.

mille-bota [mˈilˈιˈbɑtə]

míltóg (míoltóg), *I wouldn't care to have much to do with that little* míltóg.

mínac, mínach (mianach), *The* mínac *of the good workman was in son, from his father before him.* [mˈiːˈnˈɑkʰ]

mínsín (minnsín UaD, s.v. minnseach) [mˈiːnˈˈsˈɛnˈ]

míonánin *of hay* [mˈiːˈnˈɑːnˈɛnˈ]

míoróg (? méaróg), *'Put a* míoróg *(a* nádarnán*) on the suckie-calf.'*

misamín (mismín) = *wild thyme*

mo corp ó'n dial × 2

Mo lhoum is maghachar (Mo lom is (?) m'angar)

mo stórach × 2

móntán (móinteán) = —*hay* [moːnˈtɑːnˈ]

mothul (mothall); *Person with* mothul *of hair was said to be like 'Cotter na gruaige'.* [muhul]

mount (mant), Mick mount = *toothless*

múcacán (*múchachán) = *a person caught in the 'pipes' wheezing and ejecting mucus, and phlegm; An asthmatic person—very much caught in the 'pipes' (a* múcacán*);* múcacán—*caught in the 'pipes'*

muige

Muire

mups, *'There was a* mups (u *pron. as* u *in* utter) *on her; I suppose it was because I didn't invite her to my house the night of the party.'*

Murraca Mór (Murchadh Mór) *'She saw Murragha More with him' Said of a young woman who married a cruel, or worthless man*

músh [muːsˈ]

musht (? muist)[31] [musˈtˈ]

múta-máta (múta máta) [muːtə mɑːtə]

nactar [n̩aktər]

nádar [nˈaːdər]

nadarnán × 2, *"Put a* míoróg *(a* nádarnán*) on the suckie-calf."* [nˈaːdərnˈaːnˈ]

nádúireacht, nhádhúracht (nádúrthacht), *said in sarcasm of a woman who wept as much as or more than the bereaved, at a neighbour's funeral—She was crying with the* náduireacht. [nɑːˈduːrəkt]

nádúr (nádúr), *Wondering why some fine-looking girl married a* drousóg *or* ciaróg *of a man, people often concluded that 'I suppose the had the* nádúr *for him'.*

námhúntact, nhámhúntacht (? neamhmheontach, neamhiongantach UaD),[32] *Person trying to get into another's good graces, using words such as*

---

[31] Ach cf. MUISTIÚIL T. de Bhaldraithe, *Foirisiún Focal as Gaillimh* (BaileÁtha Cliath: Acadamh Ríoga Éireann, 1985), s.v.

[32] Fianaise is ea [uː] an Bharóidigh ar an gceart a bheith ag an nDuinníneach.

follow, was termed námhúntact. *'I always liked yere family. I'd care to go nowhere for a day to enjoy myself, but to ye. Ye're the talk of everywan, ye're so open-hearted. If I wanted the loan of a few pounds, I'd ask it of ye, before I'd go to my own brother or sister, honest!'* [nɑː'vuːntəkt]

nóinsín [n´oːn´s´iːn´]

nónín (nóinín) [n´oː'n´iːn´]

núdí-nádi (niúide neáide, niúdar neádar) [n´uːd´ɨ n´aː...]

ochón [oxoːn(´)]

ónsuch (óinseach) [oːn´s´əx]

pádál, pádál(*ing*) [pɑː'dɑːl, pɑː'dɑːlɪŋ´]

páistín (páistín) [pɑːs´'d´iːn´]

paunach (páinteach),[33] *A paunach of a rat was trapped.*

pauntán (? ponntán) [pəun'tɑːn]

péarla × 2 (péarla), *Woman picked great 'dímas' (pride) out of her 'péarla' of a daughter.* [p´eːrlə]

peata (peata) [p´atə]

píascin [p´iːs´g´ɪn(´)]

pilárdí [p´ɪ'l´aːrdiː]

pin-gaille(s), *Pompous 'high-steppers' were often said to be 'like the pin-gaille(s) long 'go'.*

píonán [p´iː'n´ɑːn´]

píopán = *jowl* [p´iː'pɑːn]

piosán (? peasán) [p´ɪ'sɑːn]

pisacán [p´isəkɑːn´]

pisóg (piseog) [p´ɪ's´oːg]

plámás (plámás) [plɑː'mɑːs]

plebiste [p´l´eb´ɪs´de]

pleisth (pleist) [p´l´es´t´]

plispín [p´l´is´'b´iːn´]

plounc (planc, plaic) *of bacon*

plugaiste [plogɪs´də]

poltóg (paltóg) [pal'toːg]

pountán [pəun'tɑːn]

prabaire (preabaire) [prabɪra]

práuc, práuch (? práca´bráca), *Person or animal who had damaged something beyond repair point, was said to have made* cinnster *or* práuc *of it.* [prɑːk]

priampín (proimpín), priampín *of fowl;* = *tail-base of fowl* (t) [prəim´'p´iːn´]

---

[33] Cf. *páintheach,* Donncha Ó Cróinín (eag.), *Seanachas Amhlaoibh Ó Luínse* (Baile Átha Cliath: Comhairle Bhéaloideas Éireann), lch 332.

priseach-bhuid[h]e (praiseach bhuí) **[prɪ's´ɑk viː]**

proumpalán (priompallán) **[prəumpəlɑːn]**

pruich = *worn spade* **[pruk]**

púicín (púicín) —*calf's* **[puː'k´iːn´]**

puitachán —*smallpox (?)*; puitacán, *In writer's early years, was mystified by reference to one old person, or another as 'my oul' puitacán; later I found out that it meant pits or holes in the face—the unpleasant aftermath of smallpox.* **[putəkɑːn´]**

púnsún (puinsiún) **[puːn´'s´uːn´]**

puscam (? pus cam) **[pus kəum]**

pusgarbh (? pus garbh) **[pus gɑrɪv´]**

pusíl (pusaíl, s.v. pusaireacht) **[pu'siːl´]**

rábaire (rábaire) **[raːbəre]**

racar, *The racar was name given to a quarrelsome person.*

ráini, rauní, *very* rauní *to get knuckles skinned in frosty weather.* **[rɑːn´ɪ]**

raméis (ráiméis) **[raː'm´eːs´]**

rathín (ráithín) —*hay* **[raː'hiːn´]**

ráuc (rác), ráuc-*ed* = *raided an orchard, or a cash desk; Shop till was* rauc(*d*), *also bird's nest*

rhétór (réiteoir) **[reː't´oːr]**

rí-rá **[riː rɑː]**

ríabal (ríobal) **[riːbəl]**

ríach (riabhach), ríach —*cow; Hannie* ríach **[riəx]**

ríanálí **[riː'nɑːliː]**

ríanan **[riː'n´ɑːn´]**

rille-ralle (? brille bhreaille) **[ril´ɪ ral´ɪ]**

rotha × 2, *Did such word apply to a* roué, *a sensualist? Occasionally heard: 'That low* rotha'. **[rohə]**

rúga-péiste (? *ruagadh péiste) **[ruːgə p´eːs´də]**

rúscalí **[ruːs'gɑliː]**

rútálí (*rútálaí), rútálí = *a blundering clumsy workman* **[ruː'tɑːlɪ]**

rútín (rúitín), *Stone in cow's* rútín *often lamed her.*

sabhí —*softie* **[sɑvhiː]**

saothar (saothar) = (?) *panting; Person panting and blowing was said to have a* séadán *or* saothar *on him.* **[seːhər]**

saramhán (? searbhán), *Sour, snappish man was termed a* saramhán (--w--).

scab (cab) = *mouth—in contempt*

scailp (scailp), *'The carry-on of her, and the* scailp *she came out of!!'*; bothán = *like a* scailp—*a small house* (t) **[sgal´p´]**

scalum (screalm UaD), scalum = *hard mud beneath surface* **[sgal´əm´]**

scaramhán ×2 (? scarbhán) *Did* scaramhán(s) *mean shallow chatterers?* **[sgɑrə'vɑːn´]**

scart × 2 (scairt), scart = *sudden burst of laughter* [sgɑrt´]

scathán (scáthán)—'*scahaun gazing all day*' = *admiring one's self in the mirror*; scathán —*addict, admiring oneself in the mirror* [sgɑ'hɑːn]

sceilimish (sceilmis) [s´g´el´ɪm´ɪs´]

sceilp (sceilp), *During a row, person was often said to have got a* sceilp *of a fist in the poll.*

schalnó (scéal nua) [s´g´al noː]

scía (sciath) [s´g´iːɪ]

sciolán × 2 (sceallán) = *potato seed* [s´g´ɪ'lɑːn]

scirtán (sceartán) [s´g´ər'tɑːn]

scobaire × 2 [sgabɪre]

scoltaí(s), *Man setting* bán *(baan) potatoes, had the name of a good spade-worker*—'*great for turning* scoltaí(s)' *(skull theaz) (thees)*; scoltí(s) = *turning 'skults'* [sgol'tiːz]

scounráuni (*scanránaí), *Did it refer to one who was a bit of a terrorist?*

scribe = *spade work, pron as in English*; scroibe[34] = *spadework* [s´g´rəib´]

scrottí —*hair* [sgrat´iː]

scúb, scúib (scuab) [sguːᵘb]

scudalach (scodalach) [sgodəlːkʰ]

sculóg (scológ) = *farmer with more airs and vanity than his few acres would entitle him to.*

séadán × 3 (séideán), *Person panting and blowing was said to have a* séadán *or* saothar *on him.* [s´eː'dɑːn]

seadh, "Seadh! *You paid for your own bad acts*"

sean-duine× 2 (seanduine) [s´an´ din´e]

seilimide × 2 (seilmide), *A* seilimide *(shell-snail) was name given to person who shunned company, a "solitary."* [s´e´lɪmɪde]

sgeacara (? sceachaire) [s´g´axərə]

sgeilp = *a slice. Took a shkelp of[f] finger or hand with the knife.*

shaughrán (seachrán) *An elderly couple, having no one to care them, were in*[35] *the* shaughrán.

shebanach (seibineach) [s´ebən´ək]

shourach (seamharach) [s´əurək]

shugatín, sugatín, *Person hated a particular* sugatín. [s´ugɪt´iːn´]

síabhra, shíabhra (síofra), '*That oul'* síabhra *nearly has second sight.*' [s´iːvəre][36]

---

[34] *síneadh fada bainte de* i *agus* o *curtha isteach.*

[35] *sic.*

[36] Cf. R.B. Breathnach, *Seana-chaint na nDéise*, II, (BaileÁtha Cliath: Scoil an Léinn Cheiltigh, 1961), s.v. SÍOBHARA.

síag (síog) [s´iːg]

siantúil ×2, sintúil, siontúil, (saintiúil), *Very tactful, sociable person was termed*
siantúil *(sine—) (sinethooil)*. [səin´´t´uːl´, səin´´t´uːl´]

síd[h]e-gaoithe (sí gaoithe) [s´iə'giːhʊ]

síle = *a betty, house-rabbit* [s´iːl´e]

siománach × 3 (síománach), *'The dirty* siománach! *'Tis just what he'd do.'*
[s´iː'mɑːnəx]

slacta (slacht) [slɑ<x>t<ə>]

slán (sleán), *Arrival at bog and farmhouse offered to take a* dros *(pr. dross) at*
the slán, *or churning-barrel*. [slɑːn]

slán leat

slapadóg × 2 [slɑpə'doːg]

slíabhín × 2, slíbhín (slíbhín), *The* slíbhín *was the 'smootheen', 'oily' one, who*
tried to gain his ends by peaceful penetration. [s(´)l´iː'v´iːn´]

sligín [s´l´i'g´iːn´]

slisóg × 2 [s´l´i's´oːg]

slitín

slog *of milk = a drink*

slounán (sleamhnán) [sləu'nɑːn]

slounaní (sleamhnánaí) [sləu'nɑːn´iː]

sluggara [slogərə]

smailc [smɑl´k´]

smiderín(s) (smidirín); *'Ducks' Down—and no* smiderín(s) *was a game played*
with small flagstones. Marks were lost if flags got smashed in pitching.
[sm´idəriːnz]

smíer *of hay* [sm´iːr, sm´iːr]

smíralí × 2 [sm´iːr'hɑːlɨ]

smíste (smíste) [sm´is´de]

smól (smól) [smoːl]

smusíl × 2, smúsíl(*ing*) (smúsaíl), *Speaking with a combination of tearfulness,*
snivelling, and pig-whispering, was called smúsíl(*ing*) [smu'siːl´]

smut, *'I sat a* smut *of praties'*

sná-bhuidhe (? snámhaí) [snɑː'vɨ]

snas (*sediment*) [snɑs]

snib, *So-and-so is a hungry* snib = *snipe*

sodar, *So-and-so gave X the* buailtán *on the head, and he—X—fell down in a*
dead sodar.

solcar-croidhe × 2 —*word used by late Mr. R. Cussen* [solkər kriː]

sonúcar (sonuachar), *Young men who had done some good service to elderly*
people, often got the wish 'sonúcar *to you.'* 'Mo léir! *but he met a*
sonúcar *in her'—admiring reference to man who had got a good wife,*
in every respect.

soumpalán (? *samplán) [səumpəlɑːn]

spadóg = *person having large-size unshapely feet*

spailpín × 2 (*in contempt*) [sbɑl̠ʹpʹiːnʹ]

spaul × 2 (spalla) = *stone* [sbɑːl]

sporán × 2 (sparán) [spərʹhɑːn]

spórtín (spóirtín) [sboːrʹtʹɛnʹ]

spradalac [spradələxʰ]

spridóg × 2 (? spideog),³⁷ *Child, light of body, and not too robust was called a* spridóg (spiridóg). [sprɪʹdoːg]

spruc (sprioc) [spruk]

sprusóg [spruʹsoːg]

srabh × 2, sramh (sreabh), *Person milking cow, with short jerky pulls, was advised by another to take a fine long* sramh. [sᵊrav]

sraimín, sramín(s) (sraimín), *Person with clothes in* giobal(s), *or in* sraimín(s), *was often likened to rags on a bush near a blessed well;* [sraʹmʹiːnz]

srounán (srannán UaD), (*srounaun*), *Woman said that after a good dinner, she took a* srounán (*doze*) *before the kitchen fire, for a few hours.*

sruthán × 2 [sruʹhɑːnʹ]

stailc, stailch (stailc) [sdɑlʹkʹ]

stán, *A person did* stán (*became very angry*).

sthag × 2 [sʹdɑgʹ]

stola-fata [sdoləʹfad̪ə]

stothal, stuthul (stothall), *Someone would say that he (she) caught an enemy by the* stuthul, *and gave that person a hard tugging.* [sdohəl]

stoul (steall), '*There was great* stoul(*ing*) *of porter at the wake.*' — '*stouling*' *to rhyme with '*fowling*'*

stouncán (steancán), shtouncán (streancán) *of a song* [staunʹkɑːnʹ]

stráic × 2, stráic (*of a woman*) [sdraːkʹ]

stramalach × 2 (*sraimleach), *Sheaves of corn, badly made, and bound were said to be* stramalac. [sdraməløx]

straparí × 2 [sdrapəʹriː]

strílóg × 2 [striːʹlʹoːg]

strónsa × 2 (stróinse), '*She's a great* strónsa *with all* teine-breach *on her shins.*' [stroːnʹsʹe]

struch-strach, struc-stroc [sdruk sdrɑk]

strus [sdᵊrus]

stucí(s) (stoca), *Stockings often playfully referred to as my* stucí(s) (*plu*).

³⁷ Cf. *sprideoigín*, C. Ó Duilearga agus D. Ó hÓgáin (eag.), *Leabhar Stiofáin Uí Ealaoire* (Baile Átha Cliath: Comhairle Bhéaloideas Éireann, 1981), lch 47.

studdara (stodaire, dodaire) *of a horse*, studdera —*horse* [**sdodǝre**]

stul (? stoll) = *to cuff*; *A youngster was said to have got a* stull(*ing*) *for some misdemeanour.* [**sdou^hl**]

stur, [']*Poor oul'* stur['] *was used with a mixture of compassion and love (rhyme with 'fur').*

sturc × 2 [**sdʹork**]

stúsí (stiúsaí), *reference was often made to 'that* shtúsí'. [**sʹdʹuːsiː**]

súdar [**suːdǝr**]

súgan (súgán) [**suːgņʹ**]

súil (súil) = *water outlet*; súil = *water outlet in fence* [**suːlʹ**]

súilín(s) × 2 (súilín) = *milk bubbles* [**suːʹlʹɪnz**]

súmadór × 2 (súmadóir) [**suːmǝdoːr**]

súrach × 2 (? suarach) [**suːrǝk**]

t'anam an díol (t'anam 'on diabhal)

taca (taca), (*Long before the Government started their above-named organisation, young people keeeping company, were said to be* taca*ing, with latter a deleted in favour of* k); *Long years ago, young people keeping company were said to be* tac(a)(k)*ing, '*tack^u*ing'. Last a in* taca *deleted in favour of* k. [**takʹe**]

tamal × 2 (tamall) = *time spent working with a person often a farmer* [**tɑmǝl**]

taobh-bhfód × 2 (taobhfhód)—*spade-work term* [**teːvʹhoːd**]

taobhán × 2 [**teːvʹhɑːnʹ**]

taoíbhín × 2 (taoibhín) [**teːvʹhiːnʹ**]³⁸

teine-breach (*tine bhreac), '*She's a great strónsa with all* teine-breach *on her shins*'

teórí, '*That oul'* teórí'

<thiarla>

thránín (tráithnín), *A crop of hay was said to be very poor, nothing in the bottom, only a handful of* thránín(s)

tíorlí × 2 [**tʹiːrǝʹlʹiː**]

tioscán × 2 (taoscán), '*I bought a* tioscán *of hay yesterday*' [**tǝisʹgɑːn**]

tiospach × 3, tisbí (teaspach), *Plenty work would take some of the* tisbí, tiospach, *or* brathamán *out of mischievous young fellows.* [**tʹɪsʹbɑk**]

tisbí, cf. TIOSPACH [**tʹizbʹiː**]

tóhar (? tóchar) [**toːhǝr**]

tóin-a-bhán, *bad white land, rock near surface.* (DC)

tóin-a-hub, *the dirty old scrub.* (DC)

tón (tóin), *Child for some misdemeanour was smacked on* tón *or* budóg(s).

tór × 2 (tóir) = *pursuit* [**toːr**]

---

³⁸ *sic.*

tradarí, tradari × 2 **[tradᵻriː]**

trálach × 2 (trálach, tálach) = *pain in wrist* **[trɑːlək^h]**

trépster(*ing*) × 2, traipstar **[treːpˊstərtˊ]**

trí-na-céile × 2 **[triː nˊᵻ kˊeːlˊe]**

tripal, tripul (triopall)—*rushes* **[tˊrˊipˊəl]**

trothar × 2 **[trohər]**

troudéis, troudais × 2, *'Twas hard to get a particular article out of a certain place:—Every oul'* troudéish *thrown in there.* **[trəu'dˊeːsˊ]**

túcalach × 3 (tuathallach), *Man had many good qualities in him, although he was a bit* túcalach **[=]** *(edgy).* **[tuːxələk]**

tuice (toice), *Cheeky young girl was called a* tuice *(pron. thuih-kih).*

tullera (tollaire), *A lazy old* tullera *of a fellow.*

túpalis (tuaiplis) **[tuːpəlᵻsˊ]**

tur (tor, toradh)—*slight regard for,* tur = *not thinking too highly of an article* **[tor]**

turc × 2 (*obstinate person*) **[tˊork]**

turumas × 2 (tormas) **[torəmᵻsˊ]**³⁹

Uíbh Ráthach, *Another saying was in referring people who were a little on the rough side as being like the* Uíbhráthach(s). *Not very flattering to the South-West Kerry folks! Unnecessary to add that the latter possessed a high degree of civilization.*

FOCAIL BHÉARLA:

allie-blaster, *She has great dheemus on her 'allie-blaster' of a daughter.*

brugage **[brugᵻtsˊ]**

bulling, *A word was often used to describe person in a violent mood as 'bulling'. No coarseness here. Such term seems to have been derived from the Irish words* ar buille *with the ar deleted, also the e of* buille.

caflir, *I wonder if* caflir *came from the word 'caviller'—one raising silly objections to others' statements, and so on.*

clatar of a fist on the jaw

clip of a fist

cnat, k'nat (< 'gnat' an Bhéarla) = *name given—as far as I can think—to 'dry', unsociable little man.* ('*My oul'* cnat')

cric **[krikˊ]**

fluster

gamódle **[gˊa'mˊoːdˊlˊ]**

hawking *up from the throat* (DC)

³⁹ *sic.*

mantamar(s) [**m´an´t´ɩmərz**]

potar(ing), *pottering around—persons going aound in circles (literally), not doing much for themselves, or anybody; bungling*

scrabb, *a* scrabb = *bit of a farm*

scrabbí —*farm* [**s(´)g(´)rab´iː**]

scráu (= 'scraw' an Bhéarla), *A hollow, or depression, in a field was often brought to a level with a load of* carabóg(s) *and* scráu(s)

smootheen, *The* slíbhín *was the 'smootheen', 'oily' one, who tried to gain his ends by peaceful penetration.*

sparable, *'an oul' sparable of a tooth kept me awake all last night'*

spotted bread, *Many people, almost unfailingly, described as 'spotted bread' the ordinary currant cake—somewhat similar to the meaning of Barm-breac.*

thá(s) = *marbles*

trimin(s) × 2 (*rosary*) [**trim´ɩnz**]

LOGAINMNEACHA:

Átha-tsligín

Branar, the

Clash

Clún, the

Cúil-'aithín-na-slat

Doirin ná-pláigh

Gáire-an-lin = *Garryanlin*

Gleann dubh

Gleann garbh

Gortín

Ínsín na sná

Lishín na binna.

Locán

Macha

Móintín na trap

Mother glas

Muinérín Beag

Páirc an aifrinn

Páirc-garbh

Páirc-na-seana-reilg *supposed to have been the graveyard of those who died in one of those 'long forgotten battles, fought on shore and plain'.*

Poul a báidte

Pucéidín

Réa

Rútach
Seana-mhacha
Tóhar, the

SEÁN UA SÚILLEABHÁIN

DAR LE

RUAIRÍ Ó hUIGINN
Coláiste Phádraig, Má Nuad

MAR BHRIATHAR uireasach agus réamhfhocal a rangaítear an leagan cainte seo i bhfoclóirí agus i ngraiméir na Nua-Ghaeilge.[1] Mar fhrása dobhriathartha atá sé ag *DIL*.[2] 'It seems, seemed, would seem (to), methinks' a thugann Ó Dónaill mar aistriú air, agus an bhrí chéanna, a bheag nó a mhór, atá ag an Duinníneach leis, mar atá ag *DIL*. Oibrítear go coitianta i nGaeilge an lae inniu é, m.sh.[3]

[1]   *Dar leis go bhfaca sé taibhse GRGI § 678*

[2]   *Dar léithe gur chualaidh sí mar a bheadh casachtaigh ann CÓir, 197*

[3]   *Bhí a cheann is a chosa buailte ar a chéile, dar leat MR, 25*

[4]   *Nach é an lá a bhí fada, dar liom Innism., 59*

[5]   *'Sílim' 'is dóigh liom' agus 'dar liom féin' sin trí fiadhnaisi a bhíos ag an mbréag Seanfh. Chonn., 625*

[6]   *Dar leis féin dá dtéadh sé ann ina chosa boinn [...] go mbeadh an turas déanta aige STLaighléis, 28*

[7]   *Dar liom gur cheart dom a bheith ag siolpaireacht ar na cíocha fós An tOileánach, 14*

[8]   *Ach dar leis go marbh a bhí sí OLD, 35*

Tá fianaise ar a úsáid freisin i nGaeilge na hAlban agus sa Manainnis.

II

Tá sinsearacht fhada ag *dar le* is féidir linn a rianadh siar go dtí aimsir na Sean-Ghaeilge, tráth a raibh riar maith foirmeacha aige. Ina measc sin tá

---

[1] Fch. *FGB*, Ó Duinnín, s.v. *dar*, *Graiméar Gaeilge na mBráithre Críostaí* (Baile Átha Cliath, Mac an Ghoill, 1960) §§ 347, 383.

[2] *DIL = Dictionary of the Irish Language* (Baile Átha Cliath: Acadamh Ríoga na hÉireann, 1913–76) s.v. *dar*. Mar dhobhriathar freisin atá sé ag Dieckhoff s.v. *ar leam*.

[3] Tá aistriúchán Béarla curtha agam leis na samplaí as téacsanna Gaeilge nár scríobhadh san aois seo.

inda(r) la, at(t)a(r) la, atá la, da la, ta la, anda(r) la, dar la, mar aon le mionmhalairtí eile ar cúrsaí litrithe is údar lena mbunáite,[4] m.sh.

[9]   *ata lat rabad assu a todiusgud ade* 'it seems to you their wakening would be easier' Wb. 25 b 17

[10]   *Atar lind is coll ro coillead ar tarbfeis* 'it appears to us that our bullfeast has   been violated' *BDD*, 160

[11]   *Adar lind issí siut inn ingen* 'it appears to us that that is the girl' *Acall.*, 5672

[12]   *noch da linn ba firinne* 'yet we supposed it were righteousness' Wb. 31 d 5

[13]   *ar itt e tri mer dligid insin 'domen'* ₇ *'talam'* [leg. da lem?] ₇ *'rochuala'* 'for those are the three rash things of law, 'I thought' and 'it appears to me' and 'I heard' *CIH*, 919.35

[14]   *inda leu som nisroissed imned na erchrae do grés a soinmigi* 'they fancied neither trouble nor decay could reach their prosperity forever' Ml. 39 c 34

[15]   *anda leis bid assu a dénum nach ráithi alaili* 'it seems to him that it will be more convenient to practise them at some other period' *Ap.Chráb.* § 19

[16]   *indar leo is nem dorochair for talmain* 'it seemed to them that the sky fell on the earth *Trip2*, 495

[17]   *andar lemsa [...] is tu Cailti mac Ronain* 'it appears to me that you are C.'*Acall.*, 4208

[18]   *dar liom ni ferr son la Romhanu* 'it seems to me that the Romans do not prefer it' *CCath*, 1054

Cuid suntais gur i dtéacsanna Sean-Ghaeilge is mó atá teacht ar fhoirmeacha nach bhfuil *-r* ina ndeireadh, i.e. *ata/da/ta/inda la,* ach tagann na foirmeacha seo leis an *-r* chun tosaigh go mór i dtréimhse na Meán-Ghaeilge. Ní hannamh taobh le taobh iad sa téacs céanna nó mar mhalairt ar a chéile i lámhscríbhinní éagsúla den téacs céanna, m.sh.

---

[4] *DIL* s.v. *dar*

Trip.[2]	**inda** 221, 238, 2299
	indar 495, 1440,
TBC-1	**indar** 34, 35, 337, 428, 429, 580, 878, 943, 975, 2574, 3141, 3164,
	inddar 3579
	dar 2977
TBC-LL	**indar** 1268, 2468, 3580, 3616.
	andar 1689, 3798, 4184, 4185, 4186, 4187,
	dar 1236, 1687, 3624
TBC-St	**indar** 1447
	dar 203, 1108, 1273, 2459, 3121, 3527, 4091, 4092, 4093, 4095, 4467
TTebe	**anddar** 1603
	adar 145, 3313, 3384, 4675,
	dar 1767,
CCath.	**indar** 341, 1841, 4803, 5690,
	atar 2151, 2951, 3059, 3310, 3695, 4418, 5295, 5961
	adar 405, 2180
	dar 1030, 1054, 1360, 1502, 1793 (v.ll. *atar, indar*), 5049
PH	**indar** 1951, 2059, 2418, 2668
	dar 2044, 2593, 2693, 2767
Acall.	**andar** 6202
	adar 4434, 5672
	dar 1277, 1755, 2495, 2501, 3294, 5195, 6837, 7008, 7177, 7274, 7653, 7867

Baintear leas as an malartú idir foirmeacha aonsiollacha agus foirmeacha déshiollacha ar mhaithe le cúrsaí meadarachta, nós a bhí freisin in aimsir na Sean-Ghaeilge:

[19a]   *Dalim rugénair iarsin/cen mathair cen athargein* 'methought he was born afterwards without mother without father' *Thes.*, II, 291 v.2

[19b]   *Indalim ba brathair dam/m'athirse a mathirsem* 'methought he was my brother, his mother my father' ibid., v.5

[20a]   *is cethrar acom breith ind/andar lind nímthucsat ass* 'and four men bringing me in, it seems to me they have not taken me out' *CCellaig* (leag. 1), 406

[20b]   [*is*] *ceathrar* [*a*]*com breith ind,/dar lind nocho tucsad as CCellaig*
        (leag. 2), 472

Chuaigh an fhoirm *adar/atar le* i léig go hiomlán tar éis aimsir na Meán-
Ghaeilge, agus ní chastar orainn ina dhiaidh sin ach an dá fhoirm atá in [20]
thuas, *andar* agus *dar*.

An fhoirm ghearr *dar liom* a úsáidtear sa bhfilíocht chlasaiceach, mar a
gcaitear leis mar iarbhéarla neamhaiceanta:[5]

[21]   *Dar leat is lór do mhíchéill* 'you would think it is sufficient folly'
        DDána, 6 v.25

[22]   *Dar liom ní adhbhar uabhair* 'it appears to me that it is no cause for
        pride' ibid., 1 v.4

[23]   *Dar leat as é Conn nó Cathaoir* 'you would think he is C. or C.'
        Butler Poems, 461

Dar is coitianta freisin i dtéacsanna próis de chuid na Nua-Ghaeilge
Moiche, ach feictear an leagan fada *andar* taobh leis.

[24]   *andar leo comad é in Spirat Náem tísad isin tegdais* 'they thought it
        was the Holy Spirit that would come into the abode' *Grail*, 252

[25]   *andar leo no tháirsitis i traite* 'they thought they would catch them
        instantly' *Hugh Roe*, 14.12[6]

Ón seachtú haois déag ar aghaidh, is foirmeacha aonsiollacha amháin a
chastar orainn.[7] *Dar le* an ceann is coitianta orthu seo ach tá teacht freisin
ar leagan a bhfuil *r* caol ina dheireadh, m.sh.

[26]   *Dob aite, dair liom, a gclú, a n-ainm, 's a gcáil* 'more pleasant to me
        was their name, fame, and reputation' *DBN*, I, 101.4

[27]   *'Dair leam féin' ar Conán 'do marbhadh mo chú'* 'it appears to me'
        said C. 'that my hound has been killed' *Trí Bruidne*, 58

---

[5] Cáit Ní Dhomhnaill, *Duanaireacht* (Baile Átha Cliath: Oifig an tSoláthair, 1975), lch 9.

[6] *Andar la* amháin atá sa téacs seo a bhfuil claonadh láidir chun ársaíochta ann. Fch freisin 16.16,
82.11, 114.12, 220.27, 230.23.

[7] Tá teacht ar an leagan *i ndar le* (*indar le*) i scríbhinní Mháirtín Uí Chadhain, m.sh. [...] *a bhain an
ghaimh as an aithis a tugadh dóibh i ndar leo fhéin* BBroghach lch. 29. De réir an údair féin (ibid. lch.
193) bhí an leagan seo in úsáid i gceantair éagsúla i nGaillimh, ach ní thugann sé a thuilleadh eolais
faoina úsáid ná faoina dháileadh. Ní léir an *í* an tseanfhoirm *indar/andar* atá i gceist leis seo, mar a
d'áitigh an Cadhnach, nó is forás deireanach é inar cuireadh an réamhfhocal *i* leis an leagan *dar le*. Níor
tháinig mé ar fhianaise eile ar an bhfoirm seo a bheith in úsáid sa gcaint.

[28]   *Tá tú binn, súgach [...] rathamhail, m[a]orga dair liom* 'to me you
         are cheerful, merry [...] successful and sedate' *Amh. Chear.*, I, 356

Oibriú sandhi nó tionchar an réamhfhocail *ar* is ciontaí leis an bhforás seo.
Tabharfar faoi deara go dtarlaíonn a leithéid chéanna i nGaeilge an lae
inniu i leaganacha ar nós *dar fia, dar príosta* srl., mar ar minic *r* caol i
ndeireadh an réamhfhocail *dar* (/der′/).[8]

Tá fianaise againn chomh maith ar fhoirmeacha gan an *d-* tosaigh. I
dtéacsanna próis agus filíochta a bhaineann leis an tréimhse iarchlasaiceach
is mó a chastar orainn iad seo, m.sh.

[29]   *Mar chubhthar air tuinn ..../Tá a píob, 'air liom, 's a bráighe* 'her
         throat and neck seem to me to be like foam on a wave' *Duan M.*, 42,
         l.3

[30]   *[...]an teagasc sa na fearan air leo fein acht air paistibh* 'the teaching
         which, in their opinion, is suitable only for children' *SCU*, 1429

[31]   *Do chí tú beannlomáin mhóra daruigh, 'ar leat féin* 'you see big
         branching logs of oak, as you may think' *E.Ó Cl.*, 2411

[32]   *ar leam go bhfeicim ar an gcroith é* 'it seems to me that I see him on
         the cross' *Searmóra*, 135

Is cosúil arís eile gurb é tionchar an réamhfhocail *ar*, agus an malartú idir
dar agus *ar* i leaganacha eile is bun leis seo.[9]

Tá roinnt samplaí den fhoirm *tar le* le fáil i Leabhar Chlainne Raghnaill
(17–18ú haois) ar de bhunadh Albanach é:

[33]   *Tar leó nach roibh do curuim ar marcshluagh na nGórdónach acht a
         bheith ag tesairgin na ccoisigedh o nuile chuntabhart* 'it seemed to
         them that the cavalry of the Gordons had no duty to perform but to
         defend the foot from every danger' *Rel. Celt.*, II, 186.27

Dar le [dar l′ə/l′e:] an ghnáthfhoirm atá ag an leagan seo i nGaeilge an lae
inniu. Ar an bhforainm réamhfhoclach a thiteann béim an ghutha agus
lagbhéim a bhíonn ar an bhfocal *dar*. Is minic a thagann laghdú dá bharr ar
ghuta *dar* i nGaeilge Chúige Uladh.

An fhoirm *aid le* a úsáidtear ina áit sna Déise, m.sh.

[34]   *aid leat ná beadh costas na dlighe aici* SD, I, 150

---

[8] Fch *GCF* §414 (lch 225).

[9] M.sh. *ar ndóigh/dar ndóigh, ar m'anam/dar m'anam* srl.

[35]   *aid liomsa ní bheadh an teach cluthar a dhaochain* CSS, 164

Más le *dar le* a bhaineann an fhoirm seo ó cheart, is cosúil gur ó na foirmeacha gan an *d-* tosaigh (fch. 29, 30 thuas) a shíolraíonn sí. Níor mhór glacadh leis, ina cheann sin, go ndearna /d´/ den /r´/ deiridh, forás atá le sonrú ar chanúintí eile Gaeilge ach nach bhfuil mórán fianaise air sa gceantar seo. Glacann Ó hAirt leis, áfach, gur ó *a fhaid le* a thagann foirm seo na nDéise.[10]

Tá an nath cainte le fáil i nGaeilge na hAlban agus sa Manainnis mar a nglacann sé na foirmeacha *ar leam,*[11] *er lhiam* faoi seach:

[37]   *ar leam gur h-ì a' ghrian* 'it seems to me that she is the sun' *Bàrdachd Ghàidhlig,* 246, l. 6509

[38]   *ar leam gu bheil e sin* 'I think that is it' *ZCPh,* 4, 261

[39]   *er lhiam dy re shen eh* 'I thought that was it' *HLSM,* II, 150

[40]   *er lesh y dooiney shoh nagh vel eh jeeragh* 'this man thinks it is not straight' ibid., 150

Is cosúil nach minic a bhaintear leas as sa gcaint i nGaeilge na hAlban agus gur mar leagan liteartha is mó a mhaireann sé.[12] San áit a ndeirtear é, áfach, ní hannamh /h/ ina thús, (i.e. /hor/, /har/).[13] Mar *thar le* a scríobhtar seo in amanna, m.sh.

[41]   *thar leis gun do ghabh an gruagach boch* 'he thought that the wizard was delighted' *WHT,* I, 13

Is féidir glacadh leis gur ón bhfoirm seo a thagann *ar* (/hor/, /har/) *le,* agus go síolraíonn siad araon ó fhoirm shéimhithe de *tar le* a pléadh thuas (fch. 33). Ní léir cé acu is díghlórú tánaisteach an *t-* tosaigh na foirme seo[14] nó is malartú canúnach eile a théann siar i bhfad sa teanga (fch. 13 thuas) é.

---

[10] D.Ó hAirt, eag., *Díolaim Déiseach* (Baile Átha Cliath: Acadamh Ríoga na hÉireann, 1988), s.v. *faid.*

[11] Fch. Dwelly s.v. *ar,* Dieckhoff s.v. *ar leam* 'adv. herli:um according to my opinion'

[12] '*Ar leam* does not appear to be widely attested in Scottish speech' Ó Baoill *Contributions* lch.111. Fch. freisin John MacInnes 'Some Gaelic Words and Usages' *Transactions of the Gaelic Society of Inverness,* 49 (1974–6), lch. 447.

[13] Fch Dieckhoff s.vv. *ar leam, thar leam,* agus McInnes loc.cit. Tá fianaise freisin ar /h/ tosaigh sa Manainnis; fch. *HLSM,* lch. 150.

[14] Faoi thionchar an réamhfhocail *t(h)ar?* Ar ndóigh tá fianaise mhaith freisin ar *ar leam* (gan an /h/ tosaigh) i nGaeilge na hAlban, ach is cosúil gur mar fhoirm liteartha a mhaireann sé; fch MacInnes, loc.cit.

III

Is féidir roinnt ranna a dhéanamh de fhoirmeacha an leagain cainte seo a chastar orainn sa tseanlitríocht, mar atá, (a) foirmeacha a bhfuil -r ina ndeireadh (atar, indar, dar) v. foirmeacha atá d'uireasa an -r (ata, inda, da). (b) foirmeacha déshiollacha (ata(r), inda(r)/anda(r)) v. foirmeacha aonsiollacha (da(r), ta).

Maidir le (a), as lsí na Meán-Ghaeilge atá sa samplaí is luaithe in *DIL* a bhfuil an -r ina ndeireadh (i.e. *indar la, dar la*) agus glacann Marstrander[15] leis dá réir gur forás tánaisteach é. Tá teacht, áfach, ar *dar/indar/atar* i roinnt téacsanna as tréimhse na Sean-Ghaeilge atá ar fáil i lsí deireanacha (m.sh. *Táin Bó Cuailnge, Táin Bó Fraích* srl.), agus tugann a leithéid seo ar Mheid a áitiú nár ghá gur sine na foirmeacha gan an -r ach gur dóichí gur 'alte Varianten' iad.[16] Ar a shon sin, ba dheacair dul thar fianaise na ngluaiseanna atá i lámhscríbhinní comhaimseartha, agus ó tharla go bhfuil na foirmeacha gan -r le fáil i dtéacsanna eile de chuid na Sean-Ghaeilge, is cosúla ná a mhalairt gur nuáil atá sna foirmeacha le -r.

Bhí Marstrander den bharúil gurbh é tionchar an réamhfhocail Mheán-Ghaeilge *ra/ri*, a shíolraigh ó mheascán de *la* agus *(f)ri*, ba chiontaí leis an -r, i.e. *(in)da ra > indar ra > indar la*. Cé go bhfuil samplaí de *ra/ri* in áit *la*, is minicí go mór *la* in áit *(f)ri/ra/re*, go dtí go mbaineann sé an talamh go hiomlán de agus go dtiteann *fri* i léig.

D'fhéadfaí cuimhniú freisin ar th'onchar na faí céasta den bhriathar. Ar -a(i)r a chríochnaíonn an-chuid foirmeacha den fhaí chéasta (aim.láith., fáist., modh fosh. láith., modh ord.) agus is minic a thugann an réamh-fhocal *la* gníomhaí an bhriathair i gceist, mar a tharlaíonn i gcás *dar la*. Thiocfadh dó gur faoina thionchar seo a cuireadh an -r deiridh le *inda*, i.e. *bera(i)r la X, cana(i)r la X: (in)da la X >(in)dar la X.*

Más forás tánaisteach é an -r deiridh, pé ar bith cén míniú a thabharfar ar a bhunús, ní furasta teacht ar mhíniú sásúil ar bhunús an leagain bhunaidh. Is cosúil gur foirm bhriathartha atá ann agus nach abairtín copaileach ar nós *(is) dóig la* srl. é. Tar éis a bhfuil d'fhoirmeacha ag an nath cainte seo sa tSean- agus sa Meán-Ghaeilge, is léir go bhfuil cailciú nach beag imithe air. Ní athraíonn sé de réir aimsire ná modha, agus cuireann sé suas de mhíreanna briathartha ar nós *ní, in, nach* srl.

Tá na foirmeacha déshiollacha agus na foirmeacha aonsiollacha bunaithe sna foinsí is sine. An mhír *da* (nó *ta*) atá i gcoitinne acu, ach tá neamhsheasmhacht ag baint leis an gcéad siolla, mar a mbíonn *in-/an-* nó

---

[15] *DIL*, s.v. *dar*

[16] Wolfgang Meid, *Die Romanze von Fraech und Findabair* (Innsbruck: Beiträge zur Kulturwissenschaft, 1970), lch. 197

a-, sin nó go gcailltear ar fad é. Tabharfar faoi deara nach ndéantar comhshamhlú idir *-n* deiridh na chéad mhíre agus *d-* tosaigh na dara coda, i.e. ní gnách go ndéantar *innar/annar* de. Is cosúil gur de bharr urú nó glórú ar *t-* atá an *d-* tosaigh ann.

Maidir leis an gcéad gcuid, ní léir an bhfuil réimíreanna éagsúla briathartha i gceist (m.sh. *ad-*, *in-*) nó míreanna de chineál eile iad. Meabhraíonn *DIL* dúinn gur cosúil an malartú seo leis an malartú a fheictear idir *in-* agus *a-* sna leaganacha comparáideacha *indaas*, *adaas* srl.[17] Ní théitear níos faide ná sin leis an gcomparáid, áfach. Glacann Pedersen leis gur foirmeacha den bhriathar substainteach atá i gceist[18] mar a ghlacann van Hamel,[19] Vendryes[20] agus MacBain[21] ach ní dhéantar mórán plé ar a dheilbhíocht, a chomhréir, ná ar a fhorás.

Ina dhiaidh sin, ní léir dom briathar ar bith eile a bheadh feiliúnach ó thaobh foirme de. Más é an tamhan *-tá* atá i gceist, ní mór glacadh leis gur foirm neamhaiceanta spleách den bhriathar atá ann, agus go bhfuil nasc idir é agus an réimír nó réamhfhocal a théann roimhe. A thionchar seo, is cosúil, is ciontaí leis an urú/glórú atá ar an *t-* tosaigh.

De bhrí gur foirmeacha cailcithe iad *inda/ata* ní léir an forás ar an mbriathar *-tá* sa gciall 'exists, is' atá in 'seems to, thinks' nó an forás ar bhrí eile den bhriathar é. Ná ní léir cén bhunfheidhm a bhí ag *la* sa nath cainte. D'fhéadfaí cuimhniú ar fhorás *-tá la* 'is with, has' > 'thinks', ach ní iondúil clásal a bheith mar chomhlánú ar *attá la*.

Is féidir leas a bhaint as an mbriathar *-tá* nó as an gcopail, áfach, le clásail a thabhairt i gceist i roinnt nathanna eile Is sna leaganacha *cia beith* 'though it be (a fact that)' agus *má beith* 'if it be (a fact that)' is mó a chastar an briathar substainteach orainn sa bhfeidhm seo, m.sh.

[42]   *ma beith ara ndena nech dinaib noibaib huaill* 'if it be that any of the saints be guilty of pride' Ml. 51 a 16

[43]   *cia beith ara rogba bóairechas* 'even though he were to attain to position of a *bóaire* (though it be that...)' *Críth Gabl.*, 67

---

[17] Maidir leis na foirmeacha seo fch. anois Pierre-Yves Lambert 'Le Complément du comparatif de supériorité en vieil-irlandais', *Études celtiques*, 31 (1995), 167–177, mar a n-áitítear gur ar *oldaas* srl. atá na foirmeacha seo bunaithe.

[18] Ped., II, 432–3.

[19] *Comp.C.C.* lch. 142 s.v. **atá** [...] **atá lium** *it seems to me* (also: *I have*). Is cosúil, áfach, nach ndéanann sé idirdhealú idir *attá* (le /t/) agus *ata* (le /d/).

[20] *Lexique*, s.v. *ata.*

[21] *An Etymological Dictionary of the Gaelic Language* (Inverness, 1911), s.v. *ar* 'seems [...] where *ta*, *tar* is the verb tha (thathar), is, with prep. or rel. in- before it'.

ach faightear taobh amuigh de na leaganacha seo freisin é, m.sh.

[44]   *ar ro-bí to-gaítha laxe i fail trócaire* 'for laxity can be deceptive
         beside clemency (i.e. it can be that...)' *Celtica*, 7, 64 l.51

I gcás *inda(r)/ata(r) la*, mar sin, d'fhéadfaí cuimhniú ar fhoirm laghdaithe
den bhriathar *-tá* sa gciall 'it is (a fact that)' agus an réamhfhocal *la* leis an
ngníomhaí a thabhairt i gceist, i.e. *(in/a)-ta limm* 'it is (a fact) in my
opinion' > 'it seems to me'.

IV

Maidir le comhréir *dar le*, is féidir leis seasamh roimh an gclásal atá faoi
réir aige nó teacht ina dhiaidh. Tig leis suíomh idiraisnéiseach i lár an
chlásail a ghlacadh chomh maith, m.sh.

[45]   *agus chualaidh se an t-ógánach díth-múinte, dar leis féin, a' botalaigh
         ag n-a dhoras MR*, 12

[46]   *agus do chrom sé ar a bheith a' cur síos do n-a chara féin, dar leis, ar
         an gcúilfhionn óig* [...] *OLD*, 49

Faoi mar a bhí sa tSean-Ghaeilge, is mar aonad neamhspleách as féin is mó
a sheasann *dar le* san abairt, agus ní gnách míreanna briathartha nó cónaisc
a nascadh leis. Tarlaíonn a leithéid, áfach, i nGaeilge Theilinn, m.sh.

[47]   *Dubhairt fear aca leis an fhear eile go ndar leis gur mhothuigh sé ceol
         CFT*, 80

[48]   *Nuair a dar liom é a bheith in am réasúnta* [...] *ibid.*

Tugann Lucas le fios gur san aimsir chaite amháin a bhaintear leas as *dar le*
i nGaeilge Ros Goill,[22] ach ní léir go bhfuil na teorainneacha chomh docht
céanna sna canúintí eile.

San áit ar roimh an gclásal a sheasann *dar le* sonraíonn *FGB* gur féidir
feidhm a bhaint as na cónaisc *go (gur)* nó *nach (nár)* (m.sh. 1, 2, 6–8
thuas), nó teacht gan cónasc ar bith agus an clásal a fhágáil neamhspleách
(m.sh. 35 thuas).

Comhréir *dar le* ba ábhar d'aiste a scríobh Tadhg Ó Donnchadha
('Torna') in *An Muimhneach* i dtríochaidí na haoise seo.[23] Ba é a

---

[22] *GRGI* § 578.
[23] Bealtaine 1933, lch 77.

bhreithiúnas sin ar an gceist nár cheart úsáid a bhaint as an bhfoirm spléach den bhriathar ar chor ar bith, i ngeall air gur leagan cainte é *dar le* a fhanann taobh amuigh den chomhréir agus nach ndéantar ceangal comhréire idir é agus an clásal a thagann ina dhiaidh. Luaigh sé freisin gurbh é an nós seo an gnás sa tseanlitríocht. Cuireadh go tréan in éadan a bhreithiúnais faoin Nua-Ghaeilge, ní nach ionadh, agus bhí scoláirí eile in ann samplaí as Gaeilge na haoise seo a chur ar fáil lena thuairim a bhréagnú.[24] Bhí aitheantas tugtha d'úsáid an chónaisc sna clásail seo fiú i bhfoclóir an Duinnínigh, cé gur luaigh sé gur ghnáthaí teacht gan cónasc. Mar sin féin, d'áitigh Ó Donnchadha gur truailliú ar shean-nós ba bhun le *go* nó *nach* a úsáid i ndiaidh *dar le* agus gur san 18ú haois a thosaigh an truailliú sin.

Sula dtabharfar aghaidh ar an gceist sin, níor mhiste aird a tharraingt ar fheidhm a bhaintear as *dar le* i nGaeilge Chúige Uladh nach luaitear sna foclóirí ná sna graiméir. Sa gcás seo is é an chaoi a dtugann *dar le* machnamh duine i gceist i bhfoirm ráitis dhírigh,[25] m.sh.

[49]   *Dar leis féin, má imrím na méir agus gan na máite a bheith gann,*
       glanfaidh mé a gcuid lámh agus liom féin an imirt go tóin CÓir, 41

[50]   *Dar léithe féin 'ba mhaith ariamh é go dtí seo' CÓir,* 79

[51]   *Dar le Seán, a Mhícheáil, bainfidh mé do mhí-apaidh asat os coinne*
       an tsagairt MR, 10

[52]   *Dar le Ceallaigh is fear domh breith isteach ort MR,* 15

Taobh amuigh den úsáid seo, is í an fhoirm spléach den bhriathar (i.e. le *go* nó *nach*) is coitianta go mór fada sna samplaí Nua-Ghaeilge atá feicthe agam as na canúintí éagsúla. Feadh m'eolais, is annamh anois a chastar an leagan eile dúinn (m.sh. 35 thuas),[26] cé gur cinnte go raibh sé ní ba choitianta roimhe seo. Ní hamháin é sin, ach is í an fhoirm spléach den bhriathar a úsáidtear freisin i nGaeilge na hAlban agus sa Manainnis (fch. 13–17 thuas), rud a thabharfadh le fios go dtéann an nós seo siar i bhfad.

Clásal neamhspleách, áfach, a leanadh *inda/ata la* sa tSean- agus sa Meán-Ghaeilge mar is léir ó shamplaí 17–29 thuas. Ní gné

---

[24] Fc. Donn Piatt *An Muimhneach*, Meitheamh 1933, lch.87 'An Doirnealach' [=Seán Mac Maoláin?] *An tUltach*, Meitheamh 1933, lch 4.

[25] Is léir go raibh éiginnteacht ag eagarthóirí agus ag scríbhneoirí ag baint úsáid dóibh as an dul seo. In amanna is idir uaschamóga a chuirtear an machnamh a leanann *dar le*. In amanna eile cuirtear idirstad ina dhiaidh, agus in amanna eile fós fágtar an ráiteas lom gan aon mharcáil.

[26] Samplaí eile in *GRGI* § 578, *BBroghach* 146.

neamhchoitianta den teanga fochlásal a fhágáil gan cónasc ná gan comhartha fo-ordaithe sa tSean-Ghaeilge, agus is deis comhréire í atá an-suntasach sna téacsanna is sine, m.sh.

[53]   *is derb lium attá latsu* 'I am certain that you have it' Wb. 29 d 14

[55]   *asbertside contra Ezechiam atbélad* 'He said to Hezekiah that he would die' Ml. 16 c 10

ach baintear leas freisin as deiseanna éagsúla fo-ordaithe (m.sh. an tsrónaíl choibhneasta nó cónaisc)[27] agus faoi dheireadh ré na Meán-Ghaeilge is gnáth feidhm a bhaint as *co/go* nó *nach/na* i bhfochlásail mar seo i mórán gach cás.

Bhí seasamh ar leith ag *dar le* sa gcóras seo sa méid is go gcuireadh sé suas go hiomlán de chónaisc agus den tsrónaíl choibhneasta ní hamháin i dtréimhse na Sean-Ghaeilge ach ar feadh cuid mhaith de thréimhse na Meán-Ghaeilge chomh maith. Ní hionann mar sin é agus briathra ar nós *as-beir, ro-fitir* srl. nó leaganacha ar nós *is dóig la, is derb la* srl. a dtagann athrú ar a gcomhréir le linn na tréimhse seo. Is é an chaoi a bhfuil mar a bheadh 'idirstad comhréire' idir *dar le* agus an chuid eile den chlásal, rud a thabharfadh le tuiscint nach amháin ar fhoirm an natha a bhí cailciú imithe ach ar a chomhréir freisin. An clásal neamhspleách gan marcáil a úsáidtear sna samplaí ar fad i ngluaiseanna Würzburg agus Mhilan agus i dtéacsanna ar nós *Táin Bó Cuailnge* (gach leagan), *Táin Bó Fraích, Togail na Tebe, Passions and Homilies from the Leabhar Breac, Acallam na Senórach* (leagan 1*)*, agus mórán eile.

Tá teacht ar shampla amháin a mbaintear feidhm as an tsrónaíl choibhneasta ann in *Bethu Phátraic*, i.e.

[56]   *is ed inda lemm rombu sí córus na creitme* 'it seemed to me that it was a rite of the faith' *Trip*[2], 2299

ach sa gcás seo is féidir a áitiú gur don fhorainm *ed* atá an clásal ag tagairt agus nach ionann é dá bharr agus na samplaí eile.

Deis eile comhréire a fheictear sa téacs seo go mbaintear feidhm as forá ainm bhriathartha i ndiaidh *inda la*, m.sh.

[57]   *inda lais Cothraige do thiachtain isteach i roibhe* 'he thought he saw Patrick coming into the place was' *Trip*[2], 221

Castar corrshampla eile den chomhréir seo orainn sa Meán-Ghaeilge, m.sh.

---

[27] Fch *GOI* §§ 503, 505.

[58] *adar leis in Roim do toidhecht i ndeilbh mná da innsaigid* 'it seemed
to him that Rome approached him in the guise of a woman' *CCath*,
405

agus mar is léir ó [48] thuas, maireann sé anuas go dtí Gaeilge an lae inniu,
más go himeallach féin é.

Is i ndeireadh ré na Meán-Ghaeilge, sa dara haois déag, a tosaíodh ar
úsáid a bhaint as cónaisc le *dar le*. Tá roinnt samplaí i dtéacsanna a
bhaineann leis an aois sin.

[59] *indar let co tuitfedh la fuasnadh na cétgaeithi doticfadh* 'you would
think that it would fall at the tumult of the first-coming wind' *CCath*,
341

[60] *atar la cach curbo seac[h]na na soilsi 7 curbo hecra greini rob ail
ann* 'it seemed to every one that avoidance of light and eclipse of sun
was desired there' ibid., 4418; féach freisin 5499, 5689

[61] *dar limsa na fail áth for abaind* [...] 'it seems to me that there is not a
ford on a river[...]' *LL*, 23043 (*Cath Ruis na Ríg*)

Ach fós féin sna téacsanna seo is gnách clásail a fhágáil gan mharcáil.

Baintear leas as an dá dheis comhréire i bhfilíocht na Nua-Ghaeilge
Clasaicí, m.sh.

[62] *dar leat gur thuit 'n-a tathamh* 'you would think she fainted' *DDána*,
27a v.25

[63] *dar lat nach máthair Moire* 'you think that M. is not (our) mother'
ibid., 24 v.8

[64] *dar liom is eagail duit-si* 'I think you are afraid' *LBranach*, 3397

[65] *dar liom féin ní doiligh di* 'It seems to me that it is not difficult for her'
ibid., 3207

ach arís is coitianta go mór fada, de réir mo chomhairimhse, an clásal a
fhágáil gan an cónasc.

Is é a fhearacht chéanna é i dtéacsanna próis na linne. Tá teacht ar an dá
nós le *dar le/andar le* i gcuid acu, m.sh.

[66a] *anndar leis go rabhadar dhá rón ghlasa ag deól a dhá chíoch* 'it
appeared to him that two grey seals were sucking his paps' *Acall.*, 2 ii
139.23

[66b]   *indar leam bádor dhá rón mhóra mhuirídhe ag deól mo chíogh* ibid.,
        139.28

ach is treise fós an sean-nós, agus is é amháin a fhaightear i roinnt
téacsanna fiú ag deireadh ré na Nua-Ghaeilge Moiche (m.sh. *Beatha Aodha
Ruaidh Uí Dhomhnaill, Trí Biorghaoithe an Bháis*).

Maireann an dá nós sa tréimhse iarchlasaiceach agus tá fianaise orthu
araon i dtéacsanna próis agus in amhráin de chuid na hochtú agus na naoú
haoise déag. Arís i dtéacsanna den chineál seo, is díol suntais a sheasmhaí
is atá an tseanchomhréir, agus go deimhin is í is treise go minic.

Munlaíodh an leagan cainte seo am éigin roimh na foinsí scríofa is
luaithe atá againn agus is mar fhoirm chailcithe cuid mhaith atá sé sna
foinsí sin. Is léir ón méid atá anseo nach ar a dheilbhíocht amháin a
chuaigh an cailciú ach ar a chomhréir freisin. Is féidir breathnú ar úsáid an
chlásail neamhspleáigh ina dhiaidh mar ársaíocht, agus fiú más féidir úsáid
an chónaisc leis a rianadh siar chomh fada le tréimhse na Meán-Ghaeilge,
is le fíordheireanas i stair na teanga a d'éirigh leis an dul comhréire seo é
féin a bhunú le *dar le*.[28]

NODA

Is de réir an Dictionary of the Irish language (*DIL*) atá bunáite na nod a úsáideadh san
alt seo. Tá na cinn seo a leanas de bhreis ar an méid sin:

Acall.2	Neasa Ní Shéaghdha, *Agallamh na Seanórach*, I-III (Baile Átha Cliath: Oifig an tSoláthair, 1942)
Amh.Chear.	Tomás Ó Máille, eag., *Amhráin Chearbhalláin* (Londain, Cumann na Sgríbheann nGaedhilge, 1915)
Ap.Chráb.	Vernam Hull, eag., 'Apgitir Chrábaid': The Alphabet of Piety' *Celtica*, 8 (1968), 44–89
Bbroghach	Máirtín Ó Cadhain, *An Braon Broghach* (Baile Átha Cliath: Oifig an tSoláthair, 1948)
CCS	T. Ó Muirithe, *Cúrsaí an tSean-Shaoghail*, Arland Usher do scríobh (Baile Átha Cliath: Oifig an tSoláthair, 1948)
CFT	Úna Uí Bheirn, *Cnuasach Focal as Teilinn* (Baile Átha Cliath: Acadamh Ríoga na hÉireann, 1989)
CIH	Daniel A. Binchy, eag., *Corpus Iuris Hibernici* (Baile Átha Cliath: Institiúid Ard-Léinn Bhaile Átha Cliath, 1978)

---

[28] Táim buíoch de Chiarán Ó Duibhín, Damian McManus, Liam Breatnach, Roibeard Ó Maolalaigh
agus Seosamh Watson as tagairtí agus samplaí a chur ar fáil dom agus mé i mbun an ailt seo. Mé féin
amháin atá freagrach as an tuiscint a baineadh as na samplaí sin agus, dá réir, as marach ar bith atá ar an
alt.

CÓir   Máire (Séamus Ó Grianna) *Caisleáin Óir* (Baile Átha Cliath: Faoi Chomhartha na dTrí gCoinneal, 1934)

DBN   Cuthbert Mac Craith, eag., *Dán na mBráthar Mionúr*, I (Baile Átha Cliath: Institiúid Ard-Léinn Bhaile Átha Cliath, 1967)

Dieckhoff   H.C. Dieckhoff, *A Pronouncing Dictionary of Scottish Gaelic*, athchló (Glaschu: Gairm, 1992)

Duan. M.   Séamus Laoide, *Duanaire na Midhe* (Baile Átha Cliath: Conradh na Gaeilge, 1914)

Dwelly   E. Dwelly, *Faclair Gaidhlig gu Beurla*, 9ú heagrán (Glaschu: Gairm, 1977)

FGB   Niall Ó Dónaill (eag.) *Foclóir Gaeilge–Béarla* (Baile Átha Cliath: Oifig an tSoláthair, 1977)

GCF   Tomás de Bhaldraithe, *Gaeilge Chois Fhairrge: an Deilbhíocht* (Baile Átha Cliath: Institiúid Ard-Léinn Bhaile Átha Cliath, 1953)

GRGI   Leslie W. Lucas, *Grammar of Ros Goil*l Irish.(Béal Feirste: Institute of Irish Studies, 1979)

HLSM   George Broderick, *A Handbook of Late Spoken Manx*, II (Tübingen: Max Niemeyer Verlag, 1984)

Innism.   P. Ua Concheanainn, *Innismeadhoin* (Baile Átha Cliath: Foilseacháin an Rialtais, 1931, eagrán nua, 1993)

MR   Séamus Ó Grianna, *Mícheál Ruadh* (Dún Dealgan: Preas Dhún Dealgan, 1925)

Ó Baoill *Contributions* Colm Ó Baoill, *Contributions to a Comparative Study of Ulster Irish and Scottish Gaelic* (Béal Feirste: Institute of Irish Studies, 1978)

OLD   Heinrich Wagner ⁊ Nollaig Mac Congáil, *Oral Literature from Dunquin, Co. Kerry* (Béal Feirste: Institute of Irish Studies, 1983)

SCU   Cainneach Ó Maonaigh, eag., *Searmónta Chúige Uladh* (Baile Átha Cliath: Institiúid Ard-Léinn Bhaile Átha Cliath, 1965)

Seanfh.Chon.   Tomás S. Ó Máille, eag., *Seanfhocla Chonnacht*, I (Baile Átha Cliath: Oifig an tSoláthair, 1948)

SD   Michael Sheehan, *Sean-Chaint na nDéise* (Baile Átha Cliath: Institiúid Ard-Léinn Bhaile Átha Cliath, 1944)

Searmóra   J. Richardson, *Seanmora ar na Príom Phoncib na Chreideamh* (Londain, 1711)

STLaighléis   Tomás de Bhaldraithe, eag., *Seanchas Thomáis Laighléis* (Baile Átha Cliath: An Clóchomhar, 1977)

TBC-1   Cecile O'Rahilly, eag., *Táin Bó Cuailnge. Recension* I (Baile Átha Cliath: Institiúid Ard-Léinn Bhaile Átha Cliath, 1976)

TBC-LL   Cecile O'Rahilly, eag., *Táin Bó Cuailnge from the Book of Leinster* (Baile Átha Cliath: Institiúid Ard-Léinn Bhaile Átha Cliath, 1967)

Trí Bruidhne   Neasa Ní Shéaghdha agus Máirín Ní Mhuirgheasa, eag., *Trí Bruidhne* (Baile Átha Cliath: Oifig an tSoláthair, 1941)

WHT   John F. Campbell *Popular Tales of the West Highlands*, I-III (London: Paisley, 1890–93)

Language Contact and the Development of Irish Directional Phrase Idioms

NANCY STENSON

University of Minnesota

P HRASAL idioms consisting of a verb plus adverb or intransitive preposition are well known in Germanic languages, where they have been referred to variously as verb-particle constructions, phrasal verbs, separable prefix verbs, and compounds.[1] In English, these constructions vary semantically, from those whose meaning is fairly transparent with respect to that of the component parts, like *throw out*, to some which are quite opaque, such as *turn up* 'arrive' or *stand up* 'fail to keep an appointment with'.[2] They differ syntactically from the simple locative and motion phrases which superficially resemble them (e.g., *run up the hill* vs. *look up the number*) in several respects, and have been discussed extensively in recent linguistic literature (Guéron 1985, Kayne 1985, 1994, Koopman 1991, den Dikken 1995).

Celtic languages, in contrast, are not particularly known for such constructions, and similar collocations in these languages have never been thoroughly examined (there is no mention of them in recent surveys like MacAulay 1993 and Ball 1993, for example, nor in language-specific works such as Ó Siadhail 1989). In contemporary colloquial Irish, however, phrasal constructions of similar form are found fairly commonly, many of them clearly borrowed from English. Either the particle, the verb, or both may be imported, as in (1)–(3), often with minimal assimilation beyond the verbal ending *-áil* which typically supports verbal loans.

(1)   a.***Tháinig** siad **back**. 'They came back'
        b. *Bhí creathnach ag Tom Saile, ach tá sé **tugtha away** aige.*
           'Tom Saile had seaweed, but he's given it away.'

(2)   a. *Nuair a **turnáil** sí suas [...].* 'When she turned up[...]'
        b. *Ná bí ag **hintáil thart**.* 'Don't be hinting around.'

---

[1] Earlier versions of this paper were presented to the Tenth International Congress of Celtic Studies in Edinburgh, and to the Linguistics Club Colloquium of the University of Minnesota. I am grateful to the members of both audiences for helpful feedback. Remaining flaws are my own responsibility. The fieldwork on which part of this study is based has been supported at various times by the American Council of Learned Societies, the Irish American Cultural Institute, and the University of Minnesota.

[2] The centrality of such forms is further illustrated by their enormous productivity, as attested in the many slang expressions formed on this pattern: *buzz off, space out, flake out, piss off, veg out,* etc.

(3)   a. [...] *mar bíonn Maidhc Phat Willie ag* **hangáil about** *leis.*
       [...] 'because MPW hangs about with him.'
       b. *Bheadh sé go maith le haghaidh cupla lá, you know, le* **switcháil off**.
       'It would be good for a couple of days, you know, to switch off.'

Similar phrases consisting wholly of native Irish lexical items are also found. Some, as in (4), have exact English analogues, on which they may well be calques, although independent development can't be ruled out a priori.[3] Others, as in (5), are not precise calques of their English equivalents, although they can often be translated by a similar idiom; these are less obviously borrowed.

(4).   a. *Ní* **oibríonn** *sé* **amach** *'chuile uair.* 'It doesn't work out every time.'
       b. *Tagann sé isteach fóinteach*[4] 'It comes in handy'

(5)   a. *Bíonn sé ag* **caitheamh anuas** *i gcónaí ar 'chuile dhuine.*
       'He's always putting everyone down.' (lit. 'throwing downward on')
       b. *Ba dhóbair dom tosú ag* **cur amach** *arís ar maidin inniu (DD)*[5]
       'I almost started throwing up again this morning.' (lit. 'putting out')[6]

This study will examine these idioms in the context of other phrasal predicates native to Irish. Although the constructions of (1)–(3) initially appear quite alien to Irish and a startling escalation of familiar borrowing processes (Sjoestedt 1928, de Bhaldraithe 1953, Hickey 1983, Stenson 1990, 1993), further examination reveals parallel constructions in the native lexicon, with syntactic behaviour that differs from their English counterparts. Consideration of the full range of phrasal verb constructions shows that the development of constructions like those in (4)–(5) fits patterns of idiom formation dating to the earliest stages of the language, the independent growth of which offered an existing framework for the introduction of the English loans.

---

[3] It is, however, worth noting, as pointed out by Steve Hewitt (pc), that while similar phrasal predicates are found in Welsh, another language in long-term contact with English, they are absent from Breton.

[4] This particular construction also occurs with an English adjective complement, in the forms shown in (i) *Tagann sé isteach handáilte* and (ii) *Tagann sé isteach handy.*

These are indeed more frequent than the version in (4b) which is attested only once from an older and fairly conservative speaker. It seems likely that (4b) is indeed of English origin, with the use of *fóinteach* as a calque representing an attempt to further gaelicize the common borrowed forms above.

[5] Sources of examples from texts or other sources than fieldwork are identified in parentheses. The key to the abbreviations for the sources is given at the end before the references.

[6] *Caitheamh amach* 'throwing out' is also used to express the meaning 'vomit'. *Suas,* the closest equivalent to English *up* is not used.

1. DIRECTIONAL ADVERBS

The Irish constructions most closely analogous to English phrasal verbs are prototypically composed of a verb plus one of the directional adverbs *isteach, amach, síos, suas, siar*, etc. Most verb+directional collocations are in fact semantically literal directionals, the canonical case being an intransitive motion verb combined with an adverb indicating direction of the movement.[7] The directional may be accompanied by further adverbial specification of the goal, as in (6), or it may appear alone, as in (7), with only the discourse context to identify the endpoint.[8]

(6)   a. ***Chuaigh** sé **isteach** sa bpub ar chuma ar bith.*
       'He went into the pub, anyway.
    b. *Bíonn siad ag **dul siar** go Conamara.*
       'They go west(ward) to Connemara.'

(7)   a. *Tá siad **imithe siar** a' d' iarraidh video.*
       'They've gone westward looking for a video.' (i.e., to the nearest shop)
    b. *Nach **ndeachaigh** Nan **suas**?*
       'Didn't Nan go up?'(i.e., in a fixed direction, to a particular house /shop)

Transitive verbs may also convey directionality with the addition of the same adverbials, but do so covertly. The verb itself does not necessarily denote motion (although it may, cf. 8a); it is the combined meaning of the verb+directional sequence that implies movement—usually of the direct object under agency of the subject.

(8)   a. ***Shín** sé **amach** a lámh.* (DD) 'He stretched out his hand.'
    b. *Anois an **ligfidh** tú **isteach** mé?* (H) 'Now will you let me in?
    c. [...] *é a **thabhairt suas** ag an áit a rabhdar ag **cur síos** an foundation.* (DD)
       '[...] to take it up to where they were laying the foundation.'

In other cases, as in (9), the movement implied is only figurative or metaphorical, as in the growth of a child, the utterance or writing of words, or the abstract motion along the line of vision or into an alliance or association.

---

[7] Similarly, many English verb-particle formations have literal locative or directional counterparts, e.g., *look up into the trees,* alongside *look it up in the dictionary*[...]

[8] Like their English particle counterparts, these directionals may also be used transitively: (i) *Chuaigh sé amach an doras* 'He went out the door'; (ii) *Cé hé sin ag tíocht aníos an bóthar?* 'Who's that coming up the road?'

(9)   a. *Nuair a bhí mo mháthair ag **fás suas** [...]*
          'When my mother was growing up [...]'
     b. *Is mó a **thaganns** an Ghaeilge **amach**.* 'Irish comes out most.'
     c. *D'fheicfeá 'chaon tsúil aige ag **breathnú amach** [...]. (H)*
          'You could see each eye looking out [from under his hat]'
     d. *[...] an dream a **vótáil isteach** sa gComhargadh sinn. (WPP)*
          '[...]the crowd who voted us into the Common Market[...]'

Still other combinations appear to have lost all semantic directionality; the resulting idioms are opaque to the movement interpretations of previous examples.

(10)   a. ***Chuir** sé **suas** do mo thairiscint [...]. (WPP)* 'He refused my offer.'
     b. *Mná sa tír seo—**cuireann** siad **suas** le go leor.*
          'Women in this country—they put up with a lot.'
     c. *Dúirt an dochtúr le Annie toitíní a **thabhairt suas**.*
          'The doctor told Annie to give up cigarettes.'

The examples in (6)–(10) represent a semantic continuum of idiomaticity in directional usage, ranging from the canonical adverbial use in (6)-(7) to the phrasal idioms of (10), which are semantically unanalysable. Borrowed constructions tend to fall near the opaque end of the scale, although more literal directionals are also found (cf. 1a).[9] Some verb+directional combinations may of course have both literal and idiomatic uses as illustrated by (8c) and (10c) and by the pairs in (11)–(13).

(11)   a. *Shílfeá go **leigfeadh** sé **síos** é. (F)*
          'You'd think that he'd let it down.'
     b. ***Lig** muintir na hÉireann **síos** é.*
          'The people of Ireland let him [= Pádraic Pearse] down.'

(12)   a. *Thóg sise coinneal agus **chroch** sí **suas** í [...](SmB)*
          'She took a candle and hung it up [...]'
     b. ***Chroch** sé **suas** port aerach. (SmB)*
          'He played a lively jig.'

(13)   a. ***Fuair** muid éadach cosanta **amach** as an stór. (DD)*
          'We got protective clothing out of the storage room.'
     b. ***Fuair** muid **amach** go raibh na buíonta uilig ag obair in éindí. (DD)*
          'We found out that all the groups were working together.'

---

[9] It is not always a clearcut matter which category a given phrase falls into, as the boundaries between degrees of idiomaticity may be somewhat blurred.

Finally, at the extreme of idiomaticity are constructions in which not only the verb+directional combination, but also other constituents (usually a direct object NP), constitute a fixed part of the idiom. Some fixed-VP idioms are shown in (14).

(14)   a. [...] *nach raibh **cur amach** an mhadadh aige i mBéarla.*(*H*)
            'who hadn't enough English to put the dog out (had no English at all)'
        b. *Nuair a **bhain** mé **amach** ceann cúrsa* [...] (*DD*)
            'When I reached my destination [...].'
        d. ***Sháigh** fear Luimnigh a ladar **isteach**.* (*DD*)
            'A Limerick man stuck in his two pence worth.'

2. SYNTAX OF THE VERB-PARTICLE CONTINUUM

Although the phrasal verbs in (6)–(10) form a semantic continuum as noted, true directionals are distinguished from the metaphoric and opaque groups by certain patterns in both the lexical composition process and their syntactic behaviour. First, the range of particles used idiomatically with a given verb is considerably more limited than for true directionals. Intransitive motion verbs occur with a full range of directional particles, apparently constrained only by the lexical semantics of the verb (e.g., *teacht* 'come' is limited to speaker-oriented directionals). To illustrate, (15) lists directionals found with each of several common motion predicates (including covert motion) in over a thousand pages of text examined. Gaps are most likely accidental.

(15)   a. ***dul*** *abhaile/isteach/amach/síos/suas/anonn/anall/anonn 'is anall/ thart/siar /soir/as/amú*
        b. ***teacht*** *suas/anuas/isteach/amach/aníos aniar/abhaile/anonn/anall/ thart*
        c. ***rith*** *isteach/amach/síos/suas/síos agus suas/ aníos*
        d. ***imeacht*** *siar/isteach/amach/thart/anonn/suas/abhaile*
        e. ***cur*** *amach/isteach/síos/anuas/suas/anall/abhaile*

Metaphorical and opaque verb+particle combinations are more limited; each verb which enters into such idioms is typically limited to two or three directionals (added prepositions may increase the range of idioms available, as with *cur* below).

(16)   a. *cur amach* 'vomit'
           suas 'build'
           suas le 'tolerate'
           síos 'record, assert'
           síos ar 'describe, discuss'
           isteach ar 'interrupt, disturb'
       b. *leagan amach* 'knock out, render unconscious'
           suas 'impregnate, knock up'
       c. *piocadh amach* 'pick out, select'
           suas 'pick up, acquire, learn'
       d. *tabhairt suas* 'raise, abandon'
           amach 'scold'

As is well known, literal directional adverbs all have locative counterparts,
(e.g., *isteach* 'inward/*istigh* 'inside', *soir* 'eastward'/*thoir* 'in the east').
Unlike their directional equivalents, however, locative adverbs do not seem
to enter into idiomatic constructions; only literal locative interpretations are
available for them in most cases. Moreover, English idioms based on
locative PPs and particles (*be into*, *be up for*) do not seem to be borrowed.[10]

The idiomaticity of the directional forms, however, extends to
occasional locative meaning, particularly in adjectival or predicational
constructions such as (17a-d) but also in the occasional phrasal verb, as
(17e-f).

(17)   a. *B'as an tír **isteach** é.* (*H*) 'He was from inland'
       b. [...] *stocaí fada gorma **suas** go glúiní* (*H*)
          '[...] long blue socks up to the knees'
       c. [...] *os cionn na mbuidéal is airde suas* [...](*SmB*)
          '[...] above the highest bottles [...]'
       d. *Bhí cail an cheoil **amach** ar Antaine Beag* (*SmB*)
          'Antaine Beag had a reputation as a musician.'
       e. *Tá siad a' d'iarraidh 'chuile dhuine a choinneáil **siar**.*
          'They are trying to hold everyone back.'
       f. [...] *na feitheacha ag seasamh **amach** ar nós rópaí* [...] (*DD*)
          '[...]the sinews standing out like ropes[...]'

---

[10] One exception to the lack of idiomaticity with locatives is: (i) *Tá mo bhrionglóidí istigh.* (*H*) 'My dreams have come true'. This is doubtless related to the idiom *teacht isteach* 'come to pass', which represents a case of a literal motion verb+directional used metaphorically ; as such, its idiomaticity falls at the more transparent end of the scale, which may account for the transference of idiomatic meaning to the locative construction.

Where true directionals are concerned, ellipsis of the associated motion verb is possible, movement being implicit in the particle:

(18)   *Cé a d'fheicfeadh sé chuige **anuas** an cosán ach an Bacach Buí.* (*H*)
        'Who should he see [coming] toward him down the path but the BB.'

Idioms, which lack the redundancy of the motion verb-directional combination, naturally do not permit ellipsis—forms like (19) with ellipsis of the verb *cur* (intended meaning 'I heard her interrupting you') are not found:

(19)   **Chuala mé í isteach oraibh.*

While true directionals can occasionally be clefted, as in (20), the directional component of lexically unitary verb-particle idioms cannot, as (21) shows.

(20)   a. **Abhaile** a chuaigh sé.* (*SmB*) 'He went **home**.'
        b. *[...] gur **anuas** ón Athair a **thuirling** an Mac.* (*KIC*)
           'that the Son came **down** from the Father.'
        c. *[...] **Isteach** sa seomra sin a chuirfeas mé iad.*
           'I'll put them into **that room**.'

(21)   a. ***Suas** a chroch sé port.*[11]
        b. ***Isteach** orm a bhíonns sé ag cur.*
        c. ***Suas** a ghlan sé an teach.*

The two groups also differ in the range of constituents which cooccur with the true directionals and the idiomatic verb particle constructions. Motion verbs may be accompanied by a prepositional phrase coreferential to the subject, which conveys a completive meaning, but idiomatic sequences cannot.

(22)   a. *Ghluaiseadar leo.* 'They took off.'
        b. *D'imigh sé leis.* 'He went away.'
        c. *Ghluais léi isteach.* 'She went on in.'
        d. *Glan leat amach.* (*H*) 'Clear out.'

---

[11] The situation is complicated by the fact that not all literal directionals can easily be clefted either; thus (i) *??Suas a chroch sé peictiúr* is not particularly felicitous either, possibly for independent semantic reasons. However bad such examples are, though, speakers consulted uniformly preferred them to the clefted idioms such as (21).

These may cooccur with true directional adverbs, as in (22c), and with non-motion verbs used metaphorically to convey motion as in (22d) but they are not attested with idiomatic uses of directionals, even where an original motion verb is part of the phrasal predicate (*tar isteach ar*, etc.).

As illustrated in (23), a variety of other syntactic material can intervene between the verb and the directional element of motion predicates, including subjects, direct objects, prepositional and adverbial elements with various semantic roles (source, goal, manner, time) or several of these in combination:

(23)   a. *Tá píosa le dul acu sin síos go dtí an Snaidhm i gCiarraí. (DD)*
         'They had some distance to go down to Sneem in Kerry.'
       b. *Caitheann muid eadrainn an ráille isteach ar an bhaigín mór fada.(DD)*
         'Between us, we throw the rail in onto the big long wagon.'
       c. *Shiúil muid ó cheann thuaidh an tolláin síos tríd. (DD)*
         'We walked from the north end of the tunnel down through it.'
       d. *Do chuatar iarom na Cristaighe isin cathair isteach. (CC)*
         'Then the Christians went in to the city.'

More idiomatic predicates in contrast tend to be more limited in verb+particle separability. In general, only the subject and some direct objects may intervene between verb and particle used in metaphoric and semantically opaque constructions. I will return to these word order restrictions later in comparing Irish and English idiom behaviour.

The greater flexibility of true motion predicates compared with idiomatic verb-particle predicates suggests a structural difference between examples like those in (6)–(7) and those in (9)–(10), wherein the particle of the idiomatic constructions is analyzed as a unit with the verb, whereas the true directional particle is an adverbial adjunct to the verb phrase.[12] Semantically, this also seems correct. When true directionals are accompanied by prepositional phrases or adverbs which further specify the direction of the motion, as in (6), the directional and the adverbial adjunct often form a semantic unit, governed by the verb. Where adverbial phrases occur with idiomatic verb-particle constructions, they are not governed semantically by the verb, but by the entire phrasal predicate consisting of verb plus directional particle.

---

[12] The position of covert motion predicates as in (8) is somewhat less certain. Tentatively they seem to pattern with the more semantically transparent predicates of (6)–(7), but further investigation of their behaviour is needed for a definitive determination.

3. Other Idiom Formation Patterns

The verb-particle constructions introduced above constitute part of an extensive system of phrasal idioms in Irish, in which verbs combine with a variety of elements to create distinct lexical forms. The creation of phrasal predicates from verbs of rather general semantic scope combined with nominal direct objects which determine the predicate meaning (*déan iarracht*, 'try'; *lig osna* 'sigh', etc.) is well known and will not be considered further here. Another lexical creation strategy more closely related to the directional constructions under investigation is the combination of verbs (often the same semantically vague verbs) with prepositions: *déan ar*, 'move toward', *déan as* 'get away, escape', *tabhair as* 'spirit away', *tar as* 'shrink, expand', *tóig de* 'give up, leave alone, *tóg ar* 'blame'. These may combine with directionals to create still other lexical items. Compare:

(24)   a. *tóg do* 'take to, against': *olc a thógáil do* 'to take a grudge against'
              'reveal to': *Thóg sé a aghaidh dóibh* 'he revealed himself to them'
          b. *tóg suas* 'lift, improve': *Tá an aimsir ag tógáil suas* 'the weather is improving'
          c. *tóg suas do* 'take up, adopt as a practice': *Féach an rud a thóg sé suas dó
              féin* 'see what he has taken it into his head to do'

A number of the most highly idiomatic of the opaque class of verb-particle constructions are of this Directional+Preposition type, e.g., *cuir isteach ar* 'interrupt, disturb', *cuir suas le* 'put up with, tolerate', *cuir suas do* 'reject, refuse', etc.

Verb+Preposition phrases, like Verb+Directional constructions, vary in idiomaticity and in their syntactic flexibility, ranging from those which freely combine with any semantically appropriate NP to those with a fixed phrase:

i. Simple PP: the argument of P may be any semantically appropriate NP. These are by far the most frequent; nearly every common verb combines with several prepositions. The meaning of the V-P combination may be fairly transparent (*tar ar* 'come upon, arrive at') or quite opaque (*éirigh as* 'give up, abandon').

ii. Fixed PP: a specific phrasal object with a given verb is associated with a specific meaning, analogous to examples like (14), but without the directional; e.g., *cur i gcrích* 'accomplish', *tabhairt faoi deara* 'notice'.

iii Reflexive PP: the PP object is a pronoun, coreferential with the subject of the sentence. Meanings of these phrases are often highly idiomatic, e.g., *lig sé air* 'he pretended', *chuir sé leis* 'he thrived', *chuir sé faoi* 'he settled'.

iv. Non-referential: the PP is a third person singular masculine pronoun form, but there is no entity to which it refers. Often the only potential antecedent does not match in gender or number, nor is there any obvious discourse referent:

(25)   a. *Chuaigh an ghrian faoi*. (**fúithi*) 'The sun set.'
        b. *Chuir mé an solas/na soilse/an tine as* (**astu/aisti*)
          'I put out the light(s)/fire.'
        c. *Cuir air na soilse*. (*orthu) 'Turn on the lights.'
        d. *Bhí ailse uirthi ach tháinig sí tríd/as*. (*tríthi/aisti)
        e. *Tugadh as é/í/iad*. 'He/she/they was/were spirited away (taken off).'

These resemble the directional constructions illustrated above in that the idiom is composed solely of a verb and a (synchronically) unanalyzed particle. They are also the rarest of the prepositional idioms. They seem to be limited to the few prepositions above, especially *as*.[13]

4. HISTORICAL DEVELOPMENT

A look at earlier stages of the language shows that none of the phenomena discussed above is in any way extraordinary or innovational in modern Irish. All the phrasal construction types can be found as far back in the language as the Bardic period, and some go back to Old Irish. As the following examples from the *RIA Dictionary* attest, Old and Middle Irish had their share of opaque directional idioms, reflexive prepositional idioms, non-referential prepositional idioms, as well as combinations of the above, along with the more transparent V-P idioms and literal directionals.

(26)   a. *do-beir immach* 'concede': *ni thiubar amach go bratha*. 'I'll never concede.'
          fo-ceird immach 'lose': *fon-rollassat immach alloeg*. 'They lost her calf.'
        b. *do chuirethar eatarru*. 'they quarrel.'
        c. *do-icc ass* 'run out, come to an end': *tanic in bliadain ass*. 'The year came to an end.'
        d. *téit istech ar* 'attacks': *do chuaidh isteach ar Thomás*. 'He attacked Thomas.'

Such idiomatic structures may have been rarer than they are in the modern language, but there is no doubt that they existed. Even if most of the specific idioms found today developed in modern times, the type was there from the beginning. Within modern Irish we can trace the development of

---

[13] In all cases that I am aware of, the prepositional form is in fact ambiguous between a 3sgm. interpretation and an uninflected preposition. I assume the former analysis here, because prepositions cannot otherwise be stranded in Irish; this assumption is supported by the case of *air*, where the ambiguity holds only in speech but the written language distinguishes the bare and inflected prepositions. In (25c), the inflected form is used.

idiomatic verb-particle forms alongside that of the canonical directional usage. A preliminary examination of various texts from the 16th–20th centuries shows a fairly consistent growth in use of both literal and idiomatic uses of directional adverbs, illustrated in Table 1.

TABLE 1: USE OF DIRECTIONAL AND VERB-PARTICLE IDIOMS IN TEXTS

Century/texts	Pages	Total # examples	Examples /page (approximate)	Literal:Idiomatic (approximate)
16th–18th	381	74	1/4-6	1:1
19th				
KIC	103	25	1/4	1:1
TFG	18	18	1/1	2:1
F	unavailable	15	unavailable	2:1
SG	88	60	1/1.5	2:1
Other misc.	145	102	1/2	2:1
DG	18	9	1/2	2:1
20th				
H	40	128	3/1	3:1
SmB	100	35	1/3	1.5:1
WPP	127	132	1/1	2:1
DD	177	533	3/1	4:1
A	20	132	6/1	2:1
IS	72	113	1.5/1	2:1

In the 16th–8th centuries, only 74 examples of directional adverbs were found in a total of over 300 pages, or approximately one every 4–6 pages. The ratio of literal (including covert) directional interpretations to idiomatic (metaphoric motion and opaque) was about equal. Beginning in the 19th century, we see the origins of the widespread contemporary pattern in a steady and dramatic growth in use of phrasal verb-particle constructions in texts of all kinds. The most conservative of these, a mid-century catechism, has a similar distribution to that of the earlier texts.

The remaining 19th and early 20th century texts show increased frequency of directional usage, but also an increase in the literal-to-figurative ratio. That is, while the number of idiomatic expressions with directionals increases noticeably over the earlier period, the increase in literal usage is even greater. The growth of the idiomatic verb-particle

constructions, then, appears to be correlated with a general growth in use of directional particles.[14]

TABLE 2: ATTESTED PHRASAL VERBS IN TEXTS

16th C	17th C	18th C	19th–20th C
teacht	*druidim*	*titim*	*siúl*
dul	*déanamh*	*dúnadh*	*suigh*
ligean	*cur*		*síneadh*
────	*tógáil*		*sgartadh*
tabhairt amach	*éirí*	*cur anuas*	*rith*
dul as	*gearradh*	*fáil amach*	*sileadh*
	────	*baint amach*	*sleamhnú*
	fostú amach	*déanamh suas*	*cromadh*
	cur síos	*cur amach*	*seideadh*
	cur suas de	*fiuchadh amach*	*tuirling*
	líonadh suas		*treorú*
			bualadh

Dialann Deoraí (selected examples)			
ruaig	*leagan*		*éalú*
seoladh	*tarraingt*		*gabháil*
léim	*brú*		*caitheamh*
tiomaint	*díbirt*		*iompar*
doirteadh	*mealladh*		*scaoileadh*
taoscadh	*sluaisteáil*		*iontú*
────	────		────
ithe X anuas de	*ligean síos*		*cur suas le*
cur isteach idir	*glaoch isteach ar*		*breathnú amach*
líonadh amach	*íoc amach*		*glanadh suas*
shoutáil isteach	*socrú síos*		*déanamh amach*
dul síos 'decline'	*bheith anuas air*		*dul siar ar*
fáisceadh isteach	*luchtaithe síos*		*éirí amach*
	etc.		*cur isteach ar*
			etc.

The dotted line separates predicates used productively with literal directionals from idiomatic forms.

An examination of the particular examples of the construction found in each text confirms a growth in the number of different phrasal idiom types in use as well. While directional compounds from the 16th–18th centuries are formed primarily on the motion verbs *dul*, *teacht*, and the transitive verbs *tabhairt*, *cur*, *baint*, the 19th–20th century texts show an explosion of new combinations. The list in Table 2 illustrates the increase, listing verbs

---

[14] A register effect may also be operating here. The twentieth century texts, particularly H and DD, are much more colloquial in tone than the earlier literary materials and even the folkloric texts of SG, for example. The more journalistic A and WPP, and the literary SmBEA, show a ratio similar to that of earlier materials. It is unlikely that register alone accounts for the increase in absolute numbers or in lexical variety of the forms, however, nor for the enormous increase of idiom tokens in DD over H. Similar register variety is harder to find in earlier texts, although ideally one would like comparable data. It would also be of interest to compare the development English phrasal verbs (and literal directional phrases) to see if comparable changes in frequency and distribution are found over time.

only in the century where they are first attested and only a selection of the many new 20th century combinations. Because of the explosion of new tokens in *DD*, it is listed separately.

This enormous growth in the last century, then, has helped pave the way for the introduction of English verb-particle idioms in the most recent generations.

5. ENGLISH AND IRISH VERB-PARTICLE SYNTAX

When we compare the Irish phrasal idioms with their English counterparts, we find a similar semantic range, but different syntactic behaviour. Although transitive verb-particle constructions in both Irishand English exhibit the alternative word orders V–P–NP and V–NP–P, (called by den Dikken (1995) the inner-particle and outer-particle orders, respectively), the variant orders are constrained by different rules in the two languages. With simple unmodified NP objects, both languages allow the two orders relatively freely, illustrated for English by such pairs as *He put out the cat/He put the cat out*, and for Irish by (27)–(28).

(27)   a. *Cen fáth nár chuir tú na bratacha dubha suas dom? (SG)*
         'Why didn't you put up the black flags for me?'
     b. *[…] go gcuirfidís suas bratacha dubha.(SG)*
         '[…] that they would put up black flags.'

(28)   a. *Chuirfeadh an Parliament seo riaghalacha diongbhála síos […].*
         (PmB) 'This Parliament will record firm rules […].'
     b. *[…] do chuirfeas síos gach ní ar a thiocfam do dhéanamh. (PmB)*
         '[...] that will record everything that we can do.'

This freedom holds in English, however, only for constructions where the meaning of the whole is fairly transparently derived from that of its components. In the most highly idiomatic constructions, the particle must follow the direct object, as seen in the following examples (from den Dikken 1995)[15].

(29)   a. *She stood the fellow up.* (**stood up the fellow.*)
     b. *He let the girl down.*   (**let down the girl.*)
     c. *The government will see the crisis through.* (**see through the crisis.*)

---

[15] Not all English speakers agree with these judgements; some find both orders acceptable at least in (a) and perhaps (b). However, even if the ordering is more flexible than den Dikken claims, English still contrasts with Irish, which seems to prefer the inner particle order in such cases, as noted below.

In Irish, subtly different patterns of preference emerge. There is a tendency in Irish texts for the outer particle form to be used most when further adverbial or prepositional adjuncts occur in the VP, as in (27a), although it also occurs without adjuncts, as in (28a)). Most cases of inner-particle order have a phrase final NP, with no adverbial material (27b, 28b), although again exceptions can be found.

Moreover, the ordering flexibility in Irish extends somewhat to the most semantically opaque idioms, although these seem to prefer the inner-particle order, in contrast to the English examples of (29). The opaque idioms in (30) were originally produced with the inner-particle order, as shown. Native speakers asked for judgements generally accepted the alternative order, although usually expressing a stylistic preference for the inner particle order.[16]

(30) a. ***Bhain sé amach*** *tigh Sheáin 'ac an Iomaire.* (*H*)
      'He reached Seán 'ac an Iomaire's house.'

   b. *Cén fáth ar* ***thug*** *tú* ***suas*** *an Pill?*"
      'Why did you give up the Pill?"

   c. ***Phioc sé suas*** *go leor sna tithe ósta.* (*WPP*)
      'He picked up a lot [i.e., of German] in the pubs.'

   d. ***Chroch an pobal*** *suas 'Hail Glorious St. Patrick'.* (*DD*)
      'The congregation began to sing HGSP.'

Outer-particle idioms are also attested, as in (31), and again, the alternative order seems permissible (although again, some speakers preferred the original).[17]

(31) a. ***Sháigh*** *fear Luimnigh a ladar* ***isteach***. (*DD*)
      'A Limerick man stuck in his two pence worth.'

   b. ***Bhain*** *muid Londain* ***amach***.
      'We reached London.'

The fixed-object idiom (31a) illustrates yet another difference from English, where fixed-object idioms are always of the inner-particle type (e.g., *bring up the rear, trump up a case, put in an appearance*).[18]

---

[16] One individual, the oldest and most conservative speaker consulted, rejected the outer particle order in (30d), but didn't like the attested original much either. He readily accepted both orders for all other examples, but was one of those who consistently expressed a preference for the inner-particle order.

[17] Whether this difference in preference is due to the difference in length of the NPs involved (see below) or simply to a tendency to prefer the first form heard is not clear at this point, but should certainly be tested.

[18] Even if the order of a particular such idiom is fixed, the class as a whole shows both orders (compare (31a) to (14b), for example).

In English, a pronominal direct object precludes NP final order; only (32c) with final particle but not a final pronoun is possible, a fact which has been accounted for various ways in the syntactic literature:

(32) a. *Ann **looked** the number **up***.
      b. *Ann **looked up** the number*.
      c. *Ann **looked** it **up**/***up** it*.

Conversely, just the opposite pattern applies in Irish, as part of a more general pattern moving pronouns to the right edge of a clause in Irish (cf. Stenson 1981).

(33) a. ***Phioc** Bríd na leabhartha **suas***. 'Bríd picked the books up.'
      b. ***Phioc** Bríd **suas** na leabhartha*. 'Bríd picked up the books.'
      c. ***Phioc** Bríd **suas** iad/*iad **suas***. 'Bríd picked them up.'

When the direct object NP of a phrasal verb is particularly long (e.g., by conjunction or the presence of a relative clause or other lengthy modifiers), English strongly prefers NP-final order (the phenomenon known as 'heavy NP shift').

(34) a. *Will **dropped off** the packages which he had bought*.
         *?*Will **dropped** the packages which he had bought **off***.
      b. *Pat **picked up** Spanish, French, Greek and Russian while living abroad*.
         *?*Pat **picked** Spanish, French, Greek and Russian **up** [...]*
      c. *Cathy **looked up** the number of her old college friend from Denver*.
         *?*Cathy **looked** the number of her old college friend from Denver **up***.

In Irish, however, both orders can be found, even with heavy NPs:

(35) a. *[...] do **bhuain** Bél Átha Senaigh agus Dhúin na nGall **amach***. (*TFG*)
         '[...] reached Bél Átha Senaigh and Donegal'.
      b. *[...] agus **do leig** urrthuinn dá ionathar tre mhullach a mheidhe agus a mhórbhuinne **amach***. (*PCT*)
         '[...] and he pulled out through the top of his trunk and his mighty breast a considerable amount of his intestines'.

Although separation of the verb and particle by lengthy NPs is relatively rare, some native speakers will accept the discontinuous order when presented with it. Speakers consulted on examples like those in (36) considered both orders to be acceptable (the order with verb and particle adjacent was the one actually attested).[19]

(36)   a. ***Chrochadar suas*** *a seolta móra bácóideacha chomhfhada comhdhíreacha go barraibh na gcrann.* (*SG*)

        b. ***Chrochadar*** *a seolta móra bácóideacha chomhfhada comh dhíreacha **suas** go barraibh na gcrann.*
        'They raised their large bellying, equally long straight sails up to the tops of the masts.'

When true directionals cooccur with a locative adverb or PP, English requires the order Directional +Locative:

(37)   a. *Jean **ran out** into the street.*
        b. **Jean **ran** into the street **out**.*

Although the same order is preferred in Irish, as well, the directional is also attested following the locative:

(38)   a. ***Thagbhatar*** *na diabhail in nech slan beo sin al-lar na sluagh amach an san fhirmament **suas**.* (*CC*)
        'It was not long after that until the devils lifted that sound man, alive, out of the midst of the hosts, up into the firmament.'
        b. ***Do chuatar*** *iarom na Cristaighe isin cathair **isteach**.* (*CC*)
        'Then the Christians went into the city.'
        c. ***Chuaigh*** *Ageolandus cona shluagh tar in cathraigh **amach**.* (*CC*)
        'A. went out with his host past the city.'
        d. [...] *siorrán Carraig an Ronaigh ag **briseadh** uirthi **isteach**.* (*H*)
        '[...] the mist of Carraig an Ronaigh breaking in on it.'

The directional-final order appears to have been more common in earlier periods. It still can be found to a limited degree in this century, although contemporary speakers are reluctant to accept such constructions, finding them rather stilted.

To return now to the borrowed verb-particle idioms with which we began, they can be seen to conform in all crucial respects to the Irish rather than the English verb-particle patterns. Pronouns obligatorily follow the particle (39), longer NPs may precede (40), and for simple NP objects, the

---

[19] Strength of speakers' preferences varied, but only one speaker of four consulted rejected (36b) altogether. Interestingly, the acceptability of sentences like (36b) correlated directly with speakers' facility with English, the reverse of what one might expect if English influence is taken to play a role in the development of the constraints on these constructions.

degree of ordering freedom is indistinguishable from that of the native phrasal idioms (41).

(39)   a. ***Thóg** mo dhuine **over** é.* 'Your man took it over.'
          Thóg mo dhuine é **over.*
       b. *Ar **hireáil** tú **amach** í?* 'Did you hire it out? (i.e., rent it)
          Ar **hireáil tú í **amach**?*

(40)   ***Thóg** sé pub in Áth Buí **over**.* 'He took over a pub in Athboy.'

(41)   a. *[...] nuair a bhíonns tú ag **handáil** fear **over** [...].*
          '[...] *when you're handing a man over* [...].'
       b. *Tá siad ag **handáil over** duine inniu.*
          'They're handing someone over today.'
       c. *Céard atá siad le déanamh–é a **handáil over**?*
          'What are they to do–hand him over?'

The number of borrowed phrasal idioms with transitive verbs is still relatively small, and often the constructions in which they appear do not allow for testing word order options (e.g., object-initial verbal noun phrases such as (41c), or relative clauses with the object extracted). Moreover, intuitions are slippery and difficult to elicit with the crucial idioms, due to sociolinguistic stigmatization of the forms. Further study, and much patience, will be needed to verify a consistent pattern and determine whether the ordering options of borrowed verb-particle idioms are indeed always identical to those of native constructions, but at present there is no reason to suspect otherwise.

6. CONCLUSION

On examination, the verb-particle idioms of (1)–(4) prove to be not quite as alien as they initially appear. Though clearly derived by borrowing or calquing English phrasal idioms, they fit a native pattern of idiom formation that can trace its pedigree back to the earliest attested stages of the language. Native combinations of V+Directional and V+PP, both literal and idiomatic, exist from earliest times. Idioms have increased alongside a more general growth in use of their literal directional counterparts throughout the modern period, and have paved the way for the increased modern borrowing of specific Verb+Particle idioms, through both calques and outright importation of English idioms. However, this borrowing is by no means random or unconstrained. Most borrowed particles fill lexical gaps or provide specialized meanings distinct from similar native particles in ways typical of languages in contact throughout the world. Moreover, the borrowed idioms are subject to the same syntactic rules that govern Irish phrasal idioms rather than those of English, and thus are firmly rooted in the Irish lexical and syntactic systems.

BIBLIOGRAPHY

A: *Anois*, selected issues, 1989–1995.
CC: Hyde, Douglas, *The Conquests of Charlemagne* (London:Irish Texts Society, 1917)
DD: MacAmhlaoibh, Dónall, *Dialann Deoraí* (Dublin: an Clóchomhar, 1952)
DG: Lloyd, J.H., 'Diarmuid and Gráinne as a Folktale', *Gadelica*, (1910), 83–100
F: University College, Dublin Folklore Archives, texts collected by Colm de Bhailis
H: Stenson, Nancy, *Scéal an Haicléara: the Irish of 19th Century Mid-Connacht* (in preparation)
IS: Ó Flatharta, Antoine, *Imeachtaí na Saoirse* (Béal an Daingin: Cló Iar-Chonnachta, 1986)
KIC: Mahon, William, ed., *Dr. Kirwan's Irish Catechism by Thomas Hughes* (Cambridge, Mass.: Pangur Publications, 1991)
PmB: Ó Cuív, Brian, ed., *Parliament na mBan* (Dublin: Institute for Advanced Studies, 1952)
PCT: Williams, N.J.A., ed., *Pairlement Chloinne Tomáis* (Dublin: Institute for Advanced Studies, 1981)
SmB: Ó Conaire, Pádraic 1918. *Seacht mBua an Éirí Amach*, 2nd edition ed. by Tomás de Bhaldraithe (Dublin: Sairséal agus Dill, 1967)
SG: Ó Fotharta, Domhnall, *Siamsa an Gheimhridh* (Dublin: Patrick O'Brien, 1892)
SML: *Sgéalta Mhuintir Luinigh* (1933)
TFG: Ó Lochlainn, Colm, ed. *Tobar Fíorghlan Gaeilge* (Dublin: The Three Candles, 1939)
WPP: Ó hEithir, Breandán, *Willie the Plain Pint agus an Pápa* (Dublin and Cork: Mercier, 1977)

REFERENCES

Ball, Martin, ed. 1993. *The Celtic Languages*, London and New York: Routledge
De Bhaldraithe, Tomás 1953. 'Nua-iasachtaí i nGaeilge Chois Fhairrge', *Éigse*, 7, 1–34
Den Dikken, Marcel 1995. *Particles*, Oxford: University Press
Dictionary of the Irish Language Based Mainly on Old and Middle Irish Materials 1913-1975. Dublin: Royal Irish Academy
Guéron, Jacqueline 1987. 'Clause union and the Verb-Particle Construction in English', paper presented at *17th North-East Linguistic Society* meeting
Hickey, Raymond 1982, 'The Phonology of English Loan-Words in Inis Meáin Irish', *Ériu*, 33, 137–156
Kayne, Richard 1985. 'Principles of Particle Constructions', in *Grammatical Represent-ation*, ed. by Jacqueline Guéron, Hans-G. Obenauer and Jean-Yves Pollock, Dordrecht: Foris, 101–140

—1994. *The Antisymmetry of Syntax*, Cambridge, Mass.: MIT Press

Koopman, Hilda 1991. 'The Verb Particle Construction and the Syntax of PPs', MS, UCLA

MacAulay, Donald, ed. 1993. *The Celtic Languages*, Cambridge: University Press

Ó Siadhail, Mícheál 1989. *Modern Irish: Grammatical Structure and Dialect Variation*, Cambridge: University Press

Sjoestedt, Marie-Louise 1928. 'L'Influence de la langue anglaise sur un parler local irlandais', in *Mélanges Benvéniste*, Macon: Protat Frères, 81-122

Stenson, Nancy 1981. *Studies in Irish Syntax*, Tübingen: Gunter Narr Verlag

—1990. 'Patterns of Initial Mutation in Irish Loanwords', Éigse, 24, 9–25

—1993. 'Patterns of Variation in Irish Loan Phonology', in *Principles and Predictions: the Analysis of Natural Language*, ed. by Gregory Iverson and Mushira Eid, Amsterdam: John Benjamins, 151–166

The *sef*[...]Realization of the Welsh Identificatory Copular Sentence

T. ARWYN WATKINS
Swansea

IN OLD WELSH the identificatory copular sentence can be realized as follows: Copula + Anticipatory Predicate + Subject + Postponed Nominal Predicate.[1] There are however restrictions on this type of realization. It is confined to simple/main clauses of positive declarative sentence types. Furthermore, sentences must have nominal (i.e. noun or noun phrase) subject and predicate. In the extremely limited amount of OW that has survived there are two certain examples of the structure:

> is em hi chet   tri   uceint torth (*LL*, xlv)
> it-is it her tribute three twenty loaf
> 'this is its tribute, thirty loaves'
> issem   ir e hinnuith issid   diguedham oll *in Pagina Regulari* (*Comp*)
> it-is it the e that-one which-is last   all   ...   ...

The second sentence is translated (*BBCS*, 3, 256–57) as 'that *e* is the last of all [...]'. The sentence explains which *e* it is that's noted in the previous sentence, and would be more accurately rendered as 'it's that *e*, that one which is last of all in the *Pagina Regulari*'.

In two further probable examples the Latin word glossed functions as postponed predicate:

> issem i anu (gl. *Genius*) (*MC*)
> 'that's his name, *Genius*'

> em ir cisemic (gl. *primus*) (*JG*)
> 'that's *ir cisemic, primus*'

The last example has deleted copula.

Three examples of the original structure were found in the MW texts read. Two are from the early poetry. In the first, *neud*, alternative 3 sg. pres. indic., is the copular form. The second has *yw*, the medial form of the

---

[1] A comprehensive discussion of the various types of descriptive and identificatory copular sentences in OW and MW will be found in T. Arwyn Watkins and Proinsias Mac Cana, 'Cystrawennau'r Cyplad mewn Hen Gymraeg', *BBCS*, 18 (1958–60), 1–25. An exhaustive collection of *sef* structures in selected MW prose texts is classified and discussed in Emrys Evans, 'Cystrawennau *sef* mewn Cymraeg Canol', *BBCS*, 18 (1958–60), 38–54.

copula (as well as initial *is*). It is a later accretion and supernumerary to the syllabic count:

> Neud ew hun bet Kintilan (*CLlH*, 49.xii.2)
> 'That's what this one is, Cynddylan's grave'

> Ysef (yw) y hefras [...] y gwaet (*CLlH*, 39.xi.52)
> 'That's what its custom is, [...] its blood'

The third is from *Kulhwch ac Olwen*, the oldest of the MW tales:

> ys   hwy yr rei   hynny nynhyaw a pheibyaw (*WM*, 480.39)
> it-is they the ones those   ...   and   ...
> 'That's who those are, Nyniaw and Peibiaw'

Three features of the original *sef* structure are exemplified in the last example. One is concord between anticipatory and postponed predicates, both *hwy* and *nynhyaw a pheibyaw* are plural. (cf. *ew* and *bet,* both singular masculine in *CLlH*, 49.xii.2). Another is concord between subject *(yr rei hynny)* and its referend *(deu ychen bannawc* 'two horned oxen') which occurs in a previous sentence. The third feature is the tense function of the copula, third singular present indicative. As it happens this is the only tense that occurs in original examples of the structure. The absence of others is solely due to the paucity of OW material; other tense forms do occur in the corresponding OI structure. In relation to the copula, it should be noted that though tense variants would have occurred, person variants would not. Only third singular forms could occur in this type of structure, since both subject and predicate were obligatorily nominal.

In respect of two of these features (concord of the two predicates and tense function of the copula) the *Kulhwch* example reflects an obsolete situation. By the time of MW *ys* and *ef* had coalesced and petrified in the form *(y)sef* (the earlier bisyllabic form had final stress). There was consequently no longer concord between the two predicates, except of course when the postponed predicate was singular masculine. In the first example below the postponed predicate is feminine singular, in the second plural. The form *sef* is unchanged:

> Sef yw honno gwreic doget urenhin (*WM*, 453.17)
> 'That's who she is, King Doged's wife'

> Sef oed y rei hynny. Seith cantref Dyuet [...] (*WM*, 81.23)
> 'That's what they were, the seven cantrefs of Dyfed [...]'

For the loss of tense for the copula, no uniform solution emerged. When the head-noun of the subject phrase was post-modified by a relative or copular clause, the tense of the initial copula would have been obligatorily in concord with the verb of that clause. Consequently, since, in an assumed original *Bu hwy kennadeu a aeth. Idic [...] ac eueyd [...] 'These were the messengers who went, Iddig [...] and Hefeydd [...]', the third singular preterite was denoted by aeth as well as bu, there was no loss of tense when the petrified form sef emerged (as in the extant Sef kennadeu a aeth. Idic [...] ac eueyd [...] WM, 42.18). But when the subject was a verbless phrase, a solution to the loss of tense from initial copula had to be found. It was effected by the insertion of a medial copula between sef and the subject. In the third singular present indicative the obligatory form was yw; in the case of the other tenses the shape of the copula remained the same as it would have been in initial position:

> Sef yu henne en Lladin: Saltus ferinus [...] (HGVK, 5.27)
> 'This is what that is in Latin, Saltus ferinus [...]'

> sef oed y rei hynny Gog a Magog [...] (DB, 29.11.12)
> 'That's what those were, Gog and Magog [...]'

This development is neatly encapsulated in the RM form of WM, 480.39 (above):

> Sef yw y rei hynny. nynnyaw. a pheibaw [...] (RM, 121.14)

The advent of medial copula gave rise to sentences where the subject is pronominal. Such a form was not permissible in the original sef structure, and even in MW examples are rare:

> Sef oedynt. Gwalchmei[...] A gweir[...] Ac owein[...] (WM, 118.19)
> 'That's who they were, Gwalchmei[...] and Gweir[...] and Owein [...]'

The corresponding version in the more circumspect RM avoids pronominal subject:

> Sef tri marchawc oedynt. Gwalchmei [...] a geneir [...] ac owein [...]
> RM 194.12
> 'That's who the three horsemen were, Gwalchmei [...] and Geneir [...] and Owein [...]'

It should be noted that tri marchawc and oedynt do not represent subject-copula concord; tri marchawc is the predicate of the subject phrase. Its (pronominal) subject is subsumed in oedynt, 3 pl. imperfect of the copula.

We do sometimes come across apparent copula-subject concord. The only examples found were in translation-based works, and the concord could be reflecting usage in the source material:

> sef ynt y rei hynny, y daeretwyr [...] (*LlB*, 70.4)
> 'That's who those are, the tax-collectors [...]'

Alternatively the demonstrative phrase could be in apposition to a pronominal subject subsumed in the copula form, thus yielding the translation 'That's who they are, those people, the tax-collectors'.

When the tense of a *sef* sentence is carried by the verb of a relative (or copular) clause, the head-noun may be its subject, object, adverbial or predicate. In the case of the first two, the relative particle is *a*, and for the third it is *y(d)*. There is no particle between fronted predicate and copula:

SUBJECT:

> Sef seithwyr a dienghis. Pryderi. Manawydan [...] (*WM*, 56.34)
> 'These were the seven men who escaped, Pryderi, Manawydan [...]'

OBJECT:

> Sef gwreic a uynnawd gwreic ieuank [...] (*YBH*, 6)
> 'That was the woman he took, a young woman [...]'

ADVERBIAL:

> Sef lle y doethont ygyt y bresseleu [...] (*WM*, 27.28[2])
> 'That was the place where they got together, in Preseleu [...]'

PREDICATE:

> Sef kyuryv wr oed Ueuryc, guas mavr, tec [...] (*BD*, 72.23)
> 'That's the sort of man Meurig was, a big handsome youth [...]'

---

[2] The form is *y bresseleu* in *RM*, 18.2 also. This is probably a misinterpretation on the part of both copyists. In their source the form would have been *i presseleu*. This would represent spoken [əm mhreseleü]. It should have been 'modernized' as *ym presseleu* 'in Preseleu'. *WM* made a somewhat similar error in copying a word that would have been written *ampren in* his source. He assumed that *p* represented [b] (as it often could), and so updated to *ambren WM*, 388.2. But in earlier orthography *mp* stood for [mh]. It should have been 'modernized' as *amhren* 'son of Pren'. This time *RM* got it right (*RM*, 246.19).

As noted already, *sef* sentences are always identificatory, i.e. both arms of the sentence must be 'determinate'.[3] Definite NPs are inherently so. Indefinite NPs may be determinate or indeterminate. In the following sentence both *blodeuwed* and *tylluan* are determinate:

> Sef yw blodeuwed tylluan or ieith yr awr honn (*WM*, 109.27)
> 'That's what a *blodeuwed* is, an owl in present-day parlance'

The head-noun in the following is definite (and therefore determinate) despite absence of definite article. In the MW *sef* sentence, a relative clause definitizes its head-noun. Consequently, the definite article is, in such cases, obligatorily omitted:

> Sef   kennadeu   a   aeth. Idic[...] ac eueyd [...] (*RM*, 29.16)
> it-is-it messengers who went ... and ...
> 'These were the messengers who went, Iddig [...] and Hefeydd [...]'

Copula + subject has the same definitizing effect on the head-noun of the subject phrase:

> Sef seithwyr oedynt. Cradawc [...] ac euehyd [...] (*WM*, 50.4)
> 'This is who the seven men were, Cradawg [...] and Hefeydd [...]'

Apparent exceptions to the 'omission' rule can usually be satisfactorily explained. One sentence quoted as an exception is this:

> Sef y niuer a aeth[...] Gwalchmei [...] a Riogoned [...] (*WM*, 411.27)
> 'This was the company that went[...], Gwalchmei[...] and Riogonedd [...]'

The *y* before *niuer* is in the Peniarth 4 MS, but it is not the definite article. It is the result of orthographic metanalysis. The word *yniuer,* with prosthetic-*y* before *n* is common in MW (see *GMW*, 12). In *RM* and Peniarth 6 the form which occurs is *niuer* without *y: Sef niuer* [...] (*RM*, 265.10, *WM*, p.206.17).

A commonly occurring variant of the head-noun/antecedent + relative clause structure is that in which head-noun is unexpressed:

---

[3] The terms 'determinate' (and 'indeterminate') are used in connection with Welsh syntactic rules involving predicative function. Determinate NPs cannot appear after predicative *yn.* Thus, *Y ferch bert yw Siân* 'Siân is the pretty girl' cannot be transformed as **Y mae Siân yn y ferch bert.* On the other hand indeterminate NPs can: *Merch bert yw Siân* 'Siân is a pretty girl' → *Y mae Siân yn ferch bert.* Conversely, indeterminate NPs cannot appear immediately after medial forms of the copula: **Siân yw merch bert* (ct *Siân yw'r ferch bert*). A third distinction has already been noted. An indeterminate NP cannot in MW appear in a *sef* sentence. **Sef yw Siân, merch bert / *Sef yw merch bert, Siân* would not have been possible in MW.

UNEXPRESSED SUBJECT:

> Sef a doeth dy nyeint [...] (*WM*, 89.35)
> 'That's who came, your nephews [...]'

UNEXPRESSED OBJECT:

> Sef a wystlwys.gwrgi [...] (*WM*, 88.5)
> 'That's whom he gave as hostage, Gwrgi[...]'

UNEXPRESSED ADVERBIAL:

> Sef y cudyawd y mywn llaw gist [...] (*WM*, 93.30)
> 'That's where he hid it, in a small chest [...]'
> (The *RM* version has the antecedent expressed in the latter: *Sef lle y cudyawd* [...] 'That's the place where he hid it[...]' *RM*, 68.13.)

Two structures in the *sef* + unexpressed antecedent type have become formulaic. The first is *sef* + particle *a* + inflected form of *cael* ' to have/to obtain' + its subject + *yn* + genitive pronoun + appropriate form of *kynghor* 'council'+ predicate (verb-noun clause):

> Sef a gausant yn eu kynghor duunaw ar eu llad (*WM*, 68.8)
> 'This is what they decided in their council, they agreed to kill them'

The other was *sef* + particle *a* + inflected form of *gwneuthur* 'to make/to do' + its subject + predicate (verb-noun clause):

> Sef a wnaeth y gwraged kyscu [...] (*WM*, 28.15)
> 'This is what the women did, they slept [...]'

We now come to the third feature associated with the original *sef* structure, the anaphora connected with the subject. The subject refers back to a previous (usually immediately preceding) sentence or sentence constituent. The anaphora can be effected by the subject head-noun:

[...] dy alw vyth *blodeuwed*. Sef yw *blodeuwed* tylluan [...] *RM*, 80.5[4]
'[...] to ever call you *Blodeuwedd*. That's what a *blodeuwedd* is, an owl[...]'

When the anaphora is effected by a demonstrative, it is the extended form of the demonstrative that occurs, i.e. *hwnnw* m.sg., *honno* f.sg., *hynny* neuter sg.[5] Masculine and feminine forms refer to 'concrete' items:

[...] *y maharen* [...], sef oed *hwnnw*, teyrnas Media [...] *YBY*, 48.20
'[...] *the ram* [...], this is what *that* was, the kingdom of Media[...]'

[...] *vn geluydyt*. Sef yu *honno* credu y'r gwir Duw[...] *ChO*, 10.15
'[...] *one skill*. That's what *it* is, believing in the true God [...]'

(The gender of the demonstratives proves that the reference in both the above examples is anaphoric.) The neuter form refers to an 'abstraction' (see *EWG*, 96). However redactors are not always in agreement as to what constitutes 'abstract' and what is 'concrete'—as the following versions of the same sentence show:

PENIARTH 4:

[...] y *geir* a erchyssit it. Sef oed *hwnnw* tewi (*WM*, 419.19)
'[...] the *order* that has been given to you. That's what *it* was, to hold your tongue'

PENIARTH 6:

[...] y *geir* a erchit itt. Sef oed *hynny* tewi (*WM*, p. 210.9)
'[...] the *order* that was given to you. That's what *it* was, to hold your tongue'

There is no plural substantival demonstrative, so the phrase *y rei hynny* (with plural adjectival demonstrative *hynny*) substitutes:

---

[4] *Blodeuwed* is a proper noun in the lead sentence and a common noun in the *sef* sentence. *RM* is quoted because the more careless *WM* copyist wrongly inserted predicative *yn* before *blodeuwed* in the lead sentence, thus turning a proper noun into a common noun: *dy alw uyth yn blodeuwed* 'to ever call you an owl' *WM*, 109.27. The editor of *PKM* followed *WM* in this error and made an additional one by giving the common noun in the *sef* sentence a capital: *Sef yw Blodeuwed, tylluan* 'That's what Blodeuwedd is, an owl' *PKM*, 91.15.

[5] The extended forms refer to a person or thing out of sight, or a word, statement or idea already expressed. They are therefore well suited to anaphoric reference. Earlier a rare example of simple demonstrative was quoted: *Neud ew hun bet Kintilan* 'That's what his one is, Cynddylan's grave' *CLlH*. 49.xii .2. But here the object being referred to is visible, and the poet is pointing at it.

> [...] *deu ychen* [...] ys hwy *y rei hynny* nynhyaw a pheibyaw (*WM*, 480.35)
> '[...] *two oxen* [...] That's who *they* are, Nyniaw and Peibiaw'

The anaphora can be effected by a modifier of the head-noun:

> [...] *deu uroder* [...], sef oed *eu* henweu, Bazin a Bazil (*YCM*, 113.11)
> '[...] *two brothers* [...]. These were *their* names, Bazin and Bazil'

This is always the case when the head-noun is unexpressed:

> [...] hyt pann uu abreid *im* ymdianc [...] Sef a wneuth*um inheu* [...] mynet [...]
> (*WM*, 492.3)
> '[...] until it was with difficulty that*I* fled [...]. What *I* did was this [...], I went [...]'

In this situation the anaphora has no deictic-explanatory force. This type of structure functions in effect as a continuation of the narrative. In fact there are examples where no anaphora whatsoever is involved. In the following example the subject *pawb* has no preceding point of reference:

> Sef a wnaeth pawb yna, moli Duw[...] (*WLSD*, 3.21)
> 'Everyone then did this, they praised God [...]'

Phonologically there is a pause, an open juncture, in the original form of the *sef* sentence between the subject and the postponed predicate. In some MSS the pause is marked (albeit not always consistently) by installing a 'point' between them:

> Sef kyfryw chware a wneynt. taraw a wnai pob un [...] (*WM*, 24.25)
> 'This is the game they played, each one would strike [...]'

> Sef kennadeu a aeth. Idic[...] ac eueyd [...] (*WM*, 42.18)
> 'These were the messengers who went, Iddig [...] and Hefeydd [...]'

In edited versions of the texts the pause is normally marked by a comma:

> Sef yw blodeuwed, tylluan [...] (*PKM*, 91.15)
> 'That's what a *blodeuwedd* is, an owl [...]'

The comma is included when the head-noun is unexpressed:

> Sef a wystlwys, Gwrgi [...] (*PKM*, 72.20)
> 'That's whom he gave as hostage, Gwrgi [...]'

There is however one group of *sef* sentences which is an exception to this practice. When the head-noun of the subject phrase is unexpressed adverbial, editors almost without exception do not mark a pause:[6]

> Sef y dyuu myn yd oed meichad yn cadw kenuein o uoch (*CO*, 1.7)
> '[...] it came in a place where a swineherd was keeping a herd of swine' (*Mab*, 95.8)

> Sef yd oed yn eisted[...] yn y ystauell[...] (*Owein*, 1)
> 'He was sitting [...] in his chamber [...]' (*Mab*, 155.1)

Both editors and translators regard sentences such as these as alternative realizations of the neutral positive declarative sentence and not as copula sentences with postponed predicates. The punctuation of the MSS shows that this situation had already developed in MW. There are in fact numerous *sef y(d)* sentences in MW where a postponed predicate interpretation is not possible:

> Sef y clywei arueu am ben hwnnw [...] (*WM*, 54.28)
> 'He could feel armour on that one's head [...]' (*Mab*, 36.13)

> Sef y kynhelleis inheu y gyuoeth [...] (*WM*, 394.42)
> 'I withheld his dominions [...]' (*Mab*, 236.3)

There is confirmation in the way that contemporary MW MSS select *sef y(d)* or other structures indifferently as realizations of the positive declarative sentence:

> *Peniarth 7*:   Sef yd oed gei yn seuyll ar lawr y neuad (*WM*, 606.24)
> *Peniarth 4*:   A chei oed yn sefyll ym perued llawr y neuad (*WM*, 122.22)
> 'And Cei was standing on the floor of/in the middle of the floor of the hall'

> *Peniarth 7*:   [...] ef a wyl gwreic [...] (*WM*, 613.15)
> *RM*:   Sef y gwelei wreic [...] (*RM*, 203.22)
> '[...] He can/could see a woman [...]'

> *Peniarth 4*:   Ac ef a doeth y goet [...] (*WM*, 129.2)
> *RM*:   Sef y deuth y goet [...] (*RM*, 200.23)
> 'And he came to a wood [...]'

---

[6] There is an example of the editor of *PKM* inserting a comma in a *sef y(d)* sentence: *Sef y cydyawd, y mywn llaw gist* 'That's where he hid it, in a small chest' *PKM*, 77.19. His decision may well have been influenced by the *RM* form where the head-noun is expressed: *Sef lle y cudyawd* [...] 'That's the place where he hid it [...]' *RM*, 68.13.

The development applies also to *sef a* constructions:

> *Peniarth 7:*   Sef a dwawt gwalchmei yna [...] (*WM*, 623.18)
> *RM:*   Ac yna y dywawt gwalchmei[...] (*RM*, 212.18)
>   'And then Gwalchmei said [...]'

Further attestation of this loss of 'postponed predicate' function is seen in one of the 'formulaic' structures, *sef* + *a* + *cael* [...]. In some texts *sef a* and *sef y(d)* seem to be in free variation:

BREUDWYT RONABWY:

> Sef a gawssant yn eu kyghor.ellwng [...] (*RM*, 144.10)
> Sef y kawssant yn eu kyghor gossot [...] (*RM*, 144.17)
> 'They decided to release/to place [...]'

BRUT DINGESTOW:

> Sef a gauas gvyr Ruuein yn eu kyghor [...] kyrchu allan[...] (*BD*, 38.26)
> Sef y cavssant yn eu kyghor kyrchu [...] (*BD*, 46.12)
> 'The Romans/They decided in their council [...] to set forth/to attack [...]'

The medieval texts from which most of our quotations have been selected are the story-telling texts—'fictional' compositions such as the native tales in *WM* and *RM*, and translated 'fictional' compositions such as those deriving from *Historia Regum Britanniae*, *La Geste de Boun de Hamtone*, and *Vita Davidis*. It is in these and comparable works that is found a high proportion of *sef a*, and *sef y(d)* structures—sentences deriving from the unexpressed head-noun group. It was argued above that such sentences had become nothing more than alternative realizations of the neutral positive declarative sentence. By contrast, they very rarely occur in 'non-fictional' texts such as the law texts or the 'factual' historical texts. We found none for instance in *Llyfr Blegywryd* (*LlB*) or *Llyfr Colan* (*LlC*) (edited law texts), nor in *Brut y Tywysogyon* (*BT*) or *Historia Gruffud Vab Kenan* (*HGVK*) (edited 'historical' texts), nor in the 'geographical' text *Delw y Byd* (*DB*). Only one occurs in the MW translation of the Promptuarium Bibliae (*YBY*).

The *sef a* and *sef y(d)* structures were essentially an item in the syntactical repertoire of the *cyfarwyddiaid*, the medieval story-tellers, and the end of the story-telling tradition resulted in the rapid disappearance of *sef a* and *sef y(d)* sentences from prose compositions. Examples in the compositions of the sixteenth century are very few and far between. There are none for instance in the collection of folk tales in British Museum MS Egerton 2586 (c.1588), see *RhG*, II, 78–85.

The parenthetic-explanatory *sef* + copula + anaphoric subject + predicate survived somewhat longer, and there are examples in MSS of the last half of the sixteenth century. The following is from a translation (c.1585) of The Voyage of the Wandering Knight:

> [...] vy mwriad [...], sef oedd hynny myned i gaisio kywrd [...] (*RhG*, I, 99.23)
> '[...] my intention[...], this is what it was, to go to try and meet [...]'

Already however *sef* had emerged as an independent appositive conjunct. The examples here are from William Salesbury's *Oll Synnwyr pen* [...] 1547 (repr. Bangor: Jarvis and Foster, 1902), [5.28] and [8.24]) respectively:

> Ac am hyn o weithred sef am gyffredino hyn o ddiarebion [...]
> 'And for this act, that is, for publishing these proverbs [...]'

> [...] or Ital sef o wlat Ruuein [...]
> '[...] from Italy, that's to say from the country of Rome [...]'

In the first version of the complete Bible (1588), this is *sef*'s sole function. The following is from 'Hanes Esther':

> [...] yn teyrnasu o India hyd Ethiopia, sef ar gant a saith ar hugain o
> dalaithau (RhG, II 85.16)
> '[...] ruling from India to Ethiopia, that is, on one hundred and twenty-
> seven provinces'

This development resulted in the disappearance of MW *nyt amgen* 'that is'. This appositive conjunct usage of *sef* is the only one which has sur–vived to the present day. However it is now found only in the most formal of registers, such as *Y Beibl Cymraeg Newydd*, Swindon, Cymdeithas y Beibl, 1988:

> [...] llyfr y cofiadur, sef y cronicl [...] (Esther 6.3)
> '[...] the book of the *cofiadur*, that's to say the chronicle [...]'

Even in these registers it has to all intents and purposes been displaced by *hynny yw*, a process which had begun as early as the following from Cardiff MS 7 (1564–65):

[...] amser i fwyd ag amser i lochwyd; hynny yw amser i weddio Duw
ag amser i lawenychrwydd (*RhG*, I, 68.4)
'[...] a time for food and a time for retreat, that is, a time to praise God
and a time for rejoicing'

BIBLIOGRAPHY

BBCS: *Bulletin of the Board of Celtic Studies* (Cardiff: University of Wales Press, 1921–)

BD: *Brut Dingestow*, ed. by Henry Lewis (Cardiff: University of Wales Press, 1942)

BT: *Brut y Tywysogyon* or *The Chronicle of the Princes, Red Book of Hergest Version*, ed. by Thomas Jones (Cardiff: University of Wales Press, 1955)

ChO: *Chwedlau Odo*, ed. by Ifor Williams (Wrexham: Hughes and Son, 1926)

CLlH: *Canu Llywarch Hen*, ed, by Ifor Williams (Cardiff: University of Wales Press, 1953)

CO: *Culhwch ac Olwen*, ed. by Rachel Bromwich and Daniel Simon Evans (Cardiff: University of Wales Press, 1988)

Comp: Ifor Williams, 'The Computus Fragment', *BBCS*, 3 (1926–27), 245-272 (p.257)

DB:Delw y Byd, ed. by Henry Lewis and Paul Diverres (Cardiff: University of Wales Press, 1928)

EWG: Sir John Morris-Jones, *An Elementary Welsh Grammar: Phonology and Accidence* (Oxford: Clarendon Press, 1921)

GMW: Daniel Simon Evans, *A Grammar of Middle Welsh* (Dublin: Institute of Advanced Studies, 1964)

HGVK: *Historia Gruffud Vab Kenan*, ed. by, Daniel Simon Evans (Cardiff: University of Wales Press, 1977)

JG: Whitley Stokes, 'The Welsh glosses [...] in the Codex of Juvencus', *Transactions of the Philological Society* (1860-61), 204-49

LL: *The Text of the Book of Llan Dâv*, ed. by John Gwenogvryn Evans and John Rhŷs (Oxford: Clarendon Press, 1893)

LlB: *Cyfreithiau Hywel Dda yn ôl Llyfr Blegywryd*, ed. by Stephen Joseph Williams and John Enoch Powell (Cardiff: University of Wales Press, 1942)

LlC: *Llyfr Colan*, ed. by Dafydd Jenkins (Cardiff: University of Wales Press, 1963)

Mab: *The Mabinogion*, trans. by Gwyn Jones and Thomas Jones (London: J. M. Dent and Sons Ltd, 1949)

MC: Whitley Stokes, 'The Old-Welsh glosses on Martianus Capella [...]' *Kuhns Beiträge*, 7 (1873), 385–410

Owein: *Owein or Chwedyl Iarlles y Ffynnawn*, ed. by R.L. Thomson (Dublin: Institute for Advanced Studies, 1975)

PKM: *Pedeir Keinc y Mabinogi*, ed. by Ifor Williams (Cardiff: University of Wales Press, 1930)

RM: *The Text of the Mabinogion [...] from the Red Book of Hergest*, ed. by John Rhŷs and John Gwenogvryn Evans (Oxford: Clarendon Press, 1887)

RhG, I: *Rhyddiaith Gymraeg: Y Gyfrol Gyntaf* [...] (Cardiff: University of Wales Press, 1954)

RhG, II: *Rhyddiaith Gymraeg: Yr Ail Gyfrol* [...] (Cardiff: University of Wales Press, 1956)

WLSD: *The WelshLife of St David*, ed. by Daniel Simon Evans (Cardiff: University of Wales Press, 1988)

WM: *Llyfr Gwyn Rhydderch: Y Chwedlau a'r Rhamantau*, ed. by John Gwenogvryn Evans (Cardiff: University of Wales Press, 1973)

YBH: *Ystorya Bown de Hamtwn*, ed. by Morgan Watkin (Cardiff: University of Wales Press, 1958)

YBY: *Y Bibl Ynghymraeg*, ed. by Thomas Jones (Cardiff: University of Wales Press, 1940)

YCM: *Ystorya de Carolo Magno*, ed. by Stephen Joseph Williams (Cardiff: University of Wales Press, 1930)

The Black and White *Adunaton*

CALVERT WATKINS
Harvard University

BLACK and white are doubtless the prototypical antithesis, the abstraction underlying dark and light, night and day, often contrasting earth and heaven, as well as symbolically evoking evil and good, or death and life. We may assume black and white as a perceptual and cognitive universal.

The *adunaton* (Greek ἀδύνατον 'impossible') is the term for a variety of rhetorical or thematic figures involving impossibilities, impossible tasks or actions, or daunting antitheses or paradoxes of the type 'make the long roads short, make the short roads long; make the high mountains low, make the low mountains high'.[1] This example is from the Hittite Ritual of ꝝZuwi (Laroche, *Catalogue des textes hittites*, 412).

Let us look at three examples of *adunata*, playing on the antithesis of black and white, taken from two earlier Indo-European cultures, Hittite and Roman, and one contemporary, namely Irish. That the languages are related is irrelevant. Any similarity of the figures reflects only the universals of human cognition and the creativity of the human imagination, as the third member of the comparison, which I offer here to Conn Ó Cléirigh's memory, shows well enough.

Hittite culture makes extensive use of the *adunaton* in verbal spells of sympathetic or homeopathic magic, which are spoken by the performer, typically the ᴹᵁᴺᵁˢŠU.GI or 'Old Woman', in the course of a ritual. A great many of these are displayed as similes,[2] and are responsible for much of the freshness and charm of these ancient texts, as for example,

> IGI-zi-an GIM-an ᴳᴵŠḫurkin EGIR-zi-iš an-da
> *Ú-UL* ú-e-mi-ya-zi i-da-lu-uš-ša UD.KAM-az
> EN SISKUR le-e KAR-zi (KBo 11.14 ii 22–24)

> As the back wheel does not catch up with the front wheel, so let
> the evil day not catch up with the celebrant.

---

[1] Cf. Heinrich Lausberg, *Elemente der literarischen Rhetorik*[8], §187,36. Munich: Max Hueber Verlag.

[2] See the extensive and very useful representative collection of Hittite similies by A. Ünal 'The role of magic in the ancient Anatolian religions' in *Essays on Anatolian Studies in the Second Millennium B.C.*, ed. by H.R.H. Takahito Mikasa, *Bulletin of the Middle Eastern Culture Center in Japan*, 3 (1988), pp. 52–82. Jaan Puhvel calls attention to the parallel use of similies in Hittite and Homeric Greek in his short monograph of 1991 *Homer and Hittite*, Innsbrucker Beiträge zur Sprachwissenschaft, Vorträge und Kleinere Schriften, XLVII.

We may take as typical the ritual implementation of a verbal *adunaton* in the private ritual against family dissension by Mastigga, the Old Woman of Kizzuwatna (Laroche, *Catalogue des textes hittites*, 404). The archetype of the text was probably composed around 1500 BC, in the Early Middle or Late Old Hittite period, as some features of orthography and grammar suggest; the main copies of the first version of the text were produced in the New Kingdom, those of versions two (a virtual duplicate of version one) and three (an abridged paraphrase) in Middle Hittite times, but later than the archetype. Version 2A (now published as KB0 39.8) is edited by L. Rost in MIO 1(1953) 345-379, version 1 (KBo 2.3+) is translated by A. Goetze in ANET 350ff.

I take the relevant passage from version 1B (KUB 12.34+) where it is most complete, with the more noteworthy variants from version 2A in appended notes. First comes the description of the actions of the Old Woman ('DEED'), followed by the spoken spell ('WORD').

---

ii   10 nu MUNUSŠU.GI IM-aš DUGišnūran[a] iēzzi
       nu=kan iššanan[b] tepu anda dāi
       12 kappani=ya=kan G[E₆] anda peššiyazi[c]
       n=at=kan *ANA* 2 EN SISKUR šer arḫa
       14 waḫnuzi nu kiššan memai[d]

---

       kāš=wa IM-aš maḫḫan[e] wappui[f] EGIR-pa *ŪL*
       16 paizzi kappani=ma=wa ḫarkēšzi[g] *ŪL*
       nu=war=at=za tamai NUMUN-an *ŪL* kišari[d]

---

       18 iššanaš=ma=wa=kan[h] kāš DINGIRMEŠ-aš NINDAḫarši *ŪL*
       paizzi kēdas=a=wa=kan *ANA* 2 EN SISKUR.SISKUR
       20 idāluš EME-aš[i] NÍ.TE-ši[j] *QATAMMA* lē paizzi

---

[a] 2A (ii 55) DUG]ḫupuwāi

[b] 2A išnan

[c] 2A šuḫ]ḫai

[d] 2A omits the paragraph line

[e] 2A māḫḫan māḫḫan, with older spelling; perhaps dittography since GIM-an GIM-an 'however, in whatever manner' seems inappropriate for the sense.

[f] 1A wappū i, 2B wappuwai

[g] 2A ḫarkīēšzi

[h] 2A išnaš=ma=wa=kan

The Old Woman makes a kneading-pan (*išn-ūra*) (var. a
  ḫupuwa-vessel) of clay
and she puts a little dough (*išna-*) in it
and throws (var. shakes) black cumin in it
and waves it over the two
celebrants, and she speaks as follows:

'Even as this clay does not go back to the riverbank,
and the (black) cumin does not turn white
nor become another seed,

---

and this dough does not go to the gods as bread,
so may the evil tongue likewise not go to the body of
these two celebrants.

A passage adduced by Rost (p. 373) shows that *kappāni* is a garden product which comes (presumably as seed) both black and white: KUB 7.1 i 19-20 *mān INA* UD 2 KAM *lukkatta nu ŠA* ᴳᴵˢŠAR.ŠAR.ᴴᴵ·ᴬ *ḫūman* BABBAR *kappāni* GE₆ *kappāni* [...] 'When it gets light on the second day, then everything from the gardens, white *kappāni*, black *kappāni* [...]'. In all likelihood GE₆ *kappāni* 'black *kappāni*' is the Hittite name for '*Nigella sativa* (Fennel-flower) from the Mediterranean region [...] the seeds, called black cumin, are used for seasoning in the Old World. Not the same as those of cumin (*Cuminum cyminum*), a plant of the Parsley family.'[3] As a garden flower (*N. damascena*) Nigella is known as Love-in-a-mist. Nigella seeds (black cumin) are familiar as a flavoring for Armenian string cheese, commercially available in the U.S. and surely elsewhere. The light-colored seed of the cumin, on the other hand, widely used in Indian and Latin-American cuisines, among others, and attested as a spice already in the Linear B tablets (*ku-mi-no* MY Ge 602, 605), is presumably what the Hittites called BABBAR *kappāni* 'white *kappāni*'. Both plants are annuals, and easily grown in gardens (Hittite ᴳᴵˢŠAR.ŠARᴴᴵ·ᴬ) from seed, as the same *Garden Encyclopedia* notes.

---

[i] 2A lālaš

[j] 2A tue]kki, omits QATAMMA

[3] E.L.D. Seymour, *The Garden Encyclopedia*, New York: Wm. H. Wise and Co., 1939, s.vv. Nigella, Cumin.

The 'logic' of the spell is clear. The evil tongue of quarrel and strife will be kept from reaching the celebrants by the power of the three objects being ritually manipulated. The clay of the (man-made) model kneading-pan will never return to its natural state and locus, the riverbank; the (man-made) dough will never reach its intended cultural state (that of bread); and the seed will never change into an antithetical natural state: black will not become white. The *adunaton* is thus both inherent (Nature) and controlled (Culture).

The Early Latin comic genius Plautus (ca. 254–184 BC) makes use of the same *adunaton*. In the (conventional) scene three of the *Mostellaria* or Little Ghost, the youth Philolaches is eavesdropping on a conversation between his mistress, the courtesan Philemation, and her maid Scapha. In an aside, he expresses his displeasure at Scapha, in a perfect *versus quadratus* [4](l. 257):

> Nunc adsentatrix scelesta est, dudum aduersatrix erat.

> A minute ago she was all negative, and now she's all positive, the bitch.

Then the conversation between the two women continues (258–260):

> Philemation: Cedo cerussam.
> Scapha: Quid cerussa opust nam?
> Philemation: Qui malas oblinam.
> Scapha: Vna opera, era, ebur atramento candefacere postules.
> Philolaches: Lepide dictum de atramento atque ebore. Eugae, plaudo Scaphae.

> Philemation: Give me the white.
> Scapha: What do you need white for?
> Philemation: To do my cheeks.
> Scapha: My lady, you're asking me to make ivory white with ink in one operation.
> Philolaches (aside): Nicely put about the ink and the ivory. Hey, bravo for Scapha!

The poet has called attention to the figure of *adunaton* with a nice touch of self-referentiality; the 'bravo!' is for Plautus, like the forms of *plaudo* in the last line of most comedies.

---

[4] The popular meter of Caesar's soldiers' ribald marching song: *Ecce Caesar nunc triumphat, qui subegit Galliam* [...]. It and the following verses cited are in Roman comedy termed the trochaic septenarius, a Roman development of the trochaic tetrameter catalectic. Pace Gerard Murphy in *Early Irish Metrics*, pp. 21ff., and before him Rudolf Thurneysen in *RC*, 6 (1885) pp. 29–47, this meter can hardly be the source of the Irish syllabic meters of *dán dírech*.

These, then, are two figures of *adunaton*, both playing on the antithesis of black and white, from two ancient cultures, of the mid-second and late first millennia BC. In each the abstract colors are presented symbolically and indexically by familiar substances in the two cultures, two black and white garden spice seeds in the one case, inherently white ivory and inherently black ink on the other. Latin *atramentum* 'ink' is literally 'blackening', from *ater* 'black'. In both figures the *adunaton* itself involves becoming or making white: Hittite *ḫarkēšzi*, Latin *candefacere*.

'Ancient ways of speech', and 'ancient modes of thought', as I have sometimes sententiously evoked them, turn out not to be very different from what we say and think ourselves, right now. This is one of the lessons of philology and historical linguistics. The *adunaton* as a figure of speech is still with us, and the antithesis of black and white is created afresh with every dawn. Any one of us could produce examples galore. Let me here offer only one, a visual image from twentieth-century Ireland, in fond memory of Conn Ó Cléirigh. It has the classic linguistic form of *adunaton*. The 'familiar substance in the culture' and its attendant message may be left to speak for themselves.[5]

GUINNESS

ní ḟēidir
an duḃ
a cur ina
ḃán air

---

[5] However, it may just be noted that this phrase is more regularly found in a slightly different shape in Modern Irish, i.e. *an dubh a chur ina gheal ar dhuine* 'to persuade someone that black is white, to bamboozle s.o.': see Niall Ó Dónaill, *Foclóir Gaeilge–Béarla* (Dublin: Stationery Office, 1976) p. 457; cf. also Patrick S. Dinneen, *Foclóir Gaedhilge agus Béarla: An Irish–English Dictionary* (Dublin: Irish Texts Society, 1927), p. 374. Also, we wish to acknowledge our gratitude to Guinness's for permission to publish the picture of one of their advertisements [Eds].

Indices

INDEX NOMINUM